16th Edition

The Criminal Law Handbook

Know Your Rights, Survive the System

Paul Bergman, J.D. & Sara J. Berman, J.D.

SIXTEENTH EDITION   JANUARY 2020

Editor   MICAH SCHWARTZBACH

Cover Design   SUSAN PUTNEY

Book Design   SUSAN PUTNEY

Proofreading   IRENE BARNARD

Index   UNGER INDEXING

Printing   BANG PRINTING

ISSN 1940-722X (print)

ISSN 2328-0573 (online)

ISBN: 978-4133-2719-9 (pbk)

ISBN: 978-4133-2720-5 (ebook)

This book covers only United States law, unless it specifically states otherwise.

Please note

We believe accurate, plain-English legal information should help you solve many of your own legal problems. But this text is not a substitute for personalized advice from a knowledgeable lawyer. If you want the help of a trained professional—and we'll always point out situations in which we think that's a good idea—consult an attorney licensed to practice in your jurisdiction.

Dedication

With love to Francesca and Nicholas; and to Julia and Daniel.

Acknowledgments

We gratefully acknowledge the following people, whose contributions are reflected over the many editions of this book:

Jake Warner and the late Steve Elias, whose hopes and expectations for the book we have done our best to fulfill.

Over the years, the book has greatly benefitted from the input of the dedicated and knowledgeable Nolo editors whose efforts on previous editions of the book are still reflected in this 16th edition. The editors include Janet Portman, Rich Stim, and Lisa Guerin. Thank you to Nolo editors Diana Fitzpatrick, Ilona Bray, John McCurley, and Amy Loftsgordon for help with this 16th edition. And finally, special gratitude to our editor Micah Schwartzbach, whose continued extraordinary care, creative insights, and dedication to a fair criminal justice process have helped us to make this 16th edition the best it can be.

The current edition also reflects the past contributions of law professors Laurie Levenson, David Sklansky, Peter Arenella, David Dolinko, Robert Goldstein, Michael Graham, John Ciroli, Beth Parker, and Chance Meyer, as well as the experiences of public defender Michael Roman, probation officer Ron Schlesman, Steve Harvey, Esq., and Randy Even, Esq. Thanks also to Heidi and Bob B., whether they want to be acknowledged or not.

For this 16th edition, special thanks to Prof. Steve Friedland, Senior Scholar and Professor of Law at Elon University School of Law; Prof. Heather Baxter, Professor of Law at Nova Southeastern Shepard Broad College of Law; and Prof. Nicole Noël, Professor of Practice at Nova Southeastern Shepard Broad College of Law, for sharing their expertise and perspectives regarding important criminal law, procedure, and justice issues.

Finally, a continuing shout-out to the many talented and resourceful employees of Nolo, who put their hearts and souls into producing books that make life better for people trying to cope with our complex legal system.

About the Authors

Paul Bergman is a Professor of Law Emeritus at the UCLA Law School and a recipient of two University Distinguished Teaching Awards. His books include *Criminal Law: A Desk Reference* (Nolo); *Nolo's Deposition Handbook* (with Moore, Nolo); *Reel Justice: The Courtroom Goes to the Movies* (with Asimow); *Trial Advocacy: Inferences, Arguments and Techniques* (with Moore and Binder); *Trial Advocacy in a Nutshell; Represent Yourself in Court: How to Prepare & Try a Winning Civil Case* (with Berman, Nolo); *Depositions in a Nutshell* (with Moore, Binder, and Light); *Lawyers as Counselors: A Client-Centered Approach* (with Binder, Tremblay, and Weinstein); *Evidence Law and Practice* (with Friedland and Benham); *Cracking the Case Method* (with Goodman and Holm); *Fact Investigation* (with Binder); and *You Matter: Ten Spiritual Commitments for a Richer and More Meaningful Life* (with Rabbi Mark Borovitz). He has also published numerous book chapters and articles in law journals.

Sara J. Berman is a graduate of the UCLA School of Law. Sara currently serves as the Director of Academic and Bar Success Programs for the AccessLex Center for Legal Education Excellence. She has served for decades in faculty and administrative leadership roles in law schools in California and Florida, and is the author of numerous articles and books, including *Pass the Bar Exam: A Practical Guide to Achieving Academic & Professional Goals,* and *Bar Exam MPT Preparation & Experiential Learning For Law Students: Interactive Performance Test Training*, both published by the American Bar Association. Sara is also the coauthor along with Paul Bergman of Nolo's *Represent Yourself in Court: How to Prepare & Try a Winning Civil Case.*

Table of Contents

Your Legal Companion

When can a police officer make an arrest? Is it a good idea to talk to the police? Who decides whether to charge someone with a crime, and what crime to charge? Is self-representation ever a good idea in criminal cases? Should defendants conceal their guilt from their attorneys? What factors might convince a judge to release a jailed person on low bail—or waive bail altogether? All of these questions can be perplexing, particularly if you're not familiar with the criminal justice system.

You may be asking these questions because you, a relative, or a friend have been arrested and charged with a crime. Or perhaps you've been the victim of one. Maybe you're a teacher, social worker, or counselor who needs clear answers to pressing questions so you can help others understand how the criminal justice system works. Perhaps you love television police and courtroom dramas and want to know more about what would happen if these were real cases.

This book is for all of you.

It is written in an easy-to-understand question-and-answer format to explain the criminal justice system, inside and outside the courtroom and offers the following:

- If you are facing criminal charges, this book will help you know enough about what's going on to intelligently participate in important decisions that are likely to affect the outcome.

- If someone close to you faces criminal charges, you'll want to know what is happening and how you can be of help —for example, does it matter whether you are there in the courtroom when your friend or relative is arraigned?

- If you are a victim of a crime, you, too, will want to understand how the process works and where in the process you can expect to have an effect on how the case is prosecuted.

Whatever prompts your interest, the criminal justice system belongs to you. You have a right to know how it works. The information in this book tells you what you never learned in high school civics.

In summary, our goal in this book is to cultivate educated clients, educated relatives and friends of defendants, educated victims, and educated citizens.

Our book is in no way intended as a detailed guide to self-representation. While the information in the book will no doubt assist those defendants who choose self-representation, the authors assume that those facing criminal charges for which jail or prison is a possibility are represented by an attorney, either privately retained or appointed at government expense. The book is, however, designed to empower criminal defendants by helping them understand every phase of the criminal justice process and what types of defenses and strategies are available to them.

If you are charged with a crime and seek to represent yourself, understand that criminal laws and procedures can be so complex that even judges can get them wrong. In one California case, for example, Garcia (a prison inmate) was charged with carrying a concealed weapon in prison. Garcia represented himself, and he asked the judge to order the sheriff to bring a few other prisoners to court so that they could testify on his behalf at the trial. The judge refused Garcia's request, on the ground that Garcia first had to serve subpoenas on the prisoners and Garcia hadn't done that. As the judge told Garcia during the trial, "That's your problem, Mr. Garcia, that's not the court's problem. We're not here to practice law or do your work for you … I will not give you suggestions. I will not give you advice. I have previously encouraged you to consult with counsel … you've declined that."

Despite this rather condescending lecture, the judge was wrong. Under California law, the judge could order the prisoners to be brought to Garcia's trial even if Garcia had not subpoenaed them. (*People v. Garcia,* Cal. Ct. of Appeal 2008.)

Throughout the book, we have included examples that illustrate specific questions, sample dialogues of court proceedings, and specific tips for the reader. Sample documents commonly used in the criminal justice process are located at the end of the chapter in which they are discussed. And, at the end of the book, you'll find a glossary that defines many criminal law terms that appear throughout the various chapters.

Note that the examples in this book are provided as illustrations only. They are not designed to predict exactly what will happen in a particular case.

This book describes the criminal justice system as it tends to operate throughout the country. But each state, as well as the federal government, has its own set of criminal laws and procedures. Thus, if you need to know the terms of a specific law, or the procedures your local court will follow, for example, you will need to consult the rules for your jurisdiction.

> **! CAUTION**
>
> **The law may differ.** Many of this book's legal principles are based on interpretations of the United States Constitution by the U.S. Supreme Court. In many instances, those principles apply throughout the country. But states have their own laws and constitutions, and state courts can interpret their constitutions in ways that afford defendants greater rights. It has been said that "the federal Constitution … represents the floor for basic freedoms; the state constitution, the ceiling." (*Traylor v. State,* 596 So. 2d 957, 962 (Fla. 1992).)

Get Updates, and More Online

If there are important changes to the information in this book, we'll post them at:
www.nolo.com/back-of-book/KYR.html

Introduction:
A Walk-Through of the Case of *State v. Andrea Davidson*, a Fictional Robbery Prosecution

This walk-through is intended to quickly familiarize you with what may happen as a case wends its way through the criminal justice system. While no two cases follow the identical procedural path, the example provides an overview of the process and serves as a guide to where you'll find answers to the questions posed in the walk-through, as well as loads of additional important information.

Andrea Davidson is walking along a public street when Officer Kevin Daniels walks up to her and says, "Excuse me, I'd like to ask you a few questions."

Can the officer legally do this?

Does Officer Daniels have to possess reliable information connecting Andrea to criminal activity before he can question her?

Does Andrea have to answer the officer's questions? Is it a good idea for her to talk to the officer even if she doesn't have to?

If Andrea believes that she has done nothing wrong, does she have anything to lose by talking to the officer?

See Chapter 1, *Talking to the Police*.

For many folks who are stopped and questioned, lawfully or otherwise, contact with the criminal justice system ends after the police finish "on the street" questioning. But as an example in our walk-through, Andrea has a long road ahead of her. Before questioning Andrea, Officer Daniels proceeds to "frisk" her (pat down her outer clothing).

What's the difference between a frisk and a search?

Can police officers search suspects as a matter of routine?

If, during the frisk, the officer feels what seems to be a suspicious object, can the officer remove it from Andrea's clothing?

See Chapter 2, *Search and Seizure*.

Officer Daniels removes a gun from Andrea's coat and arrests her for carrying a concealed weapon.

What constitutes an arrest?

Do police always take an arrested suspect to jail?

Was the officer required to get a warrant before arresting Andrea?

See Chapter 3, *Arrest: When It Happens, What It Means*.

Andrea is taken to jail by Officer Daniels.

What will happen to Andrea when she's booked into jail?

How soon will Andrea have a chance to bail out of jail?

What's the difference between posting cash bail and buying a bail bond?

See Chapter 5, *Booking and Bail: Checking In and Out of Jail.*

Feeling very alone and scared, Andrea considers contacting a lawyer.

Does Andrea have a right to an attorney? What if she can't afford to hire one?

If Andrea wants to represent herself, does she have a right to do so? Is self-representation generally a good idea?

How can Andrea find a lawyer if she's in jail?

What's the difference between private lawyers and public defenders?

If Andrea is represented by a lawyer, does the lawyer make all the decisions?

If Andrea talks to the lawyer while she's in jail, is their conversation confidential?

What does it mean for the government to have to provide Andrea with "due process of law"?

See Chapter 7, *Criminal Defense Lawyers*, Chapter 8, *Understanding the Attorney-Client Relationship in a Criminal Case*, and Chapter 17, *Fundamental Trial Rights of the Defense.*

Multiple Coverage of Some Subjects

As you read through the book, you may notice that the same topic may arise in more than one chapter. For example, we refer to "motions *in limine*" in Chapters 19 and 21. We do this to reduce cross-referencing and to help readers who want to read about a particular part of the criminal justice process before reading the book from beginning to end.

Suspecting that Andrea was the culprit who had robbed a convenience store a short time before her arrest, Officer Daniels and another police officer question Andrea about her whereabouts at the time of the robbery.

What are the "*Miranda* rights" that police officers often read to suspects?

If the police fail to warn Andrea of her *Miranda* rights, does the case have to be thrown out?

If Andrea starts talking to the police before they can warn her about her *Miranda* rights, can what she says be used against her in court?

See Chapter 1, *Talking to the Police.*

Officer Daniels asks Andrea to participate in a lineup to determine whether the store owner who was robbed at gunpoint, Hilary Julia, is able to identify Andrea as the robber.

What happens at a lineup?

Does Andrea have to participate in the lineup?

Instead of conducting a lineup, could the police have shown the store owner a picture of Andrea?

If Andrea has a lawyer, does she have the right to have her lawyer attend the lineup?

Can the police compel Andrea to speak during the lineup?

See Chapter 4, *Eyewitness Identification: Psychology and Procedures*, and Chapter 17, *Fundamental Trial Rights of the Defense.*

Andrea's answers to Officer Daniels's questions lead the officer to suspect that evidence linking Andrea to the robbery is inside her home (such as some of the loot and a cap that the robber wore during the robbery). Officer Daniels wants to get hold of this evidence.

Does the officer need to obtain a search warrant before entering Andrea's home?

If the officer legally enters Andrea's house looking for evidence connecting her to the robbery and finds illegal drugs, can the officer seize the drugs and charge Andrea with another crime?

If the officer enters Andrea's house illegally, does the case against her have to be dismissed?

See Chapter 2, *Search and Seizure.*

Andrea is formally charged with armed robbery.

Does Officer Daniels make the decision about whether to charge Andrea with a crime?

How long does the government have to decide whether to charge Andrea with a crime?

Does the prosecutor have to seek an indictment from a grand jury?

What does the prosecution have to prove to convict Andrea of armed robbery?

See Chapter 6, *From Suspect to Defendant,* and Chapter 12, *Criminal Laws and Their Language.*

Andrea is taken to court and "arraigned" on the armed robbery charge.

What will the courtroom be like?

If Andrea doesn't have a lawyer yet, what should she do? Can she represent herself?

What happens at an arraignment?

Is the arraignment judge authorized to release Andrea from jail?

See Chapter 9, *A Walk Through Criminal Court*, and Chapter 10, *Arraignment.*

Andrea tells the arraignment judge that she wants a lawyer but can't afford to hire one, so the judge appoints a lawyer to represent her.

Will the attorney ask Andrea to tell her side of the story?

Can the attorney do anything to help Andrea if she tells the attorney that she committed the robbery?

What kinds of legal challenges can a defense attorney make before a case goes to trial?

Does the lawyer have to keep everything Andrea says confidential?

What decisions about her case does Andrea have the right to make?

See Chapter 8, *Understanding the Attorney-Client Relationship in a Criminal Case*, Chapter 11, *Developing the Defense Strategy*, and Chapter 19, *Motions and Their Role in Criminal Cases*.

Andrea's lawyer talks to her about the possibility of entering into a plea bargain.

What rights would Andrea give up by pleading guilty?

Can her lawyer insist that Andrea enter into a plea bargain?

What does Andrea have to gain by pleading guilty?

What factors will influence any "deal" that Andrea is offered?

What is the judge's role in the plea bargaining process?

See Chapter 10, *Arraignment*, and Chapter 20, *Plea Bargains: How Most Criminal Cases End*.

Andrea pleads not guilty at the arraignment, and decides that even though she has a lawyer she should try to find out more about the crime she's charged with.

Andrea's lawyer tells her that robbery is a specific intent crime. What does "specific intent" mean, and how will the prosecutor try to prove it?

What are the possible defenses that Andrea can raise at trial?

See Chapter 11, *Developing the Defense Strategy*, Chapter 12, *Criminal Laws and Their Language*, and Chapter 13, *Common Defenses to Criminal Charges*.

At the conclusion of Andrea's arraignment, the judge schedules a date for a preliminary hearing.

What is the purpose of a preliminary hearing?

Do Andrea and her lawyer have a right to be present at the preliminary hearing?

How can a preliminary hearing benefit the defense?

See Chapter 16, *Preliminary Hearings*.

At the conclusion of Andrea's preliminary hearing, the judge finds there is probable cause to try her for robbery and sets her case for trial. Andrea's attorney tells her, "I'll continue gathering information in preparation for trial."

Does the prosecutor ever have to turn information over to the defense?

Does the defense ever have to turn over information to the prosecutor?

Does the defense have a right to interview prosecution witnesses?

What can Andrea do to help her attorney investigate the case?

See Chapter 14, *Discovery: Exchanging Information With the Prosecution*, and Chapter 15, *Investigating the Facts*.

Though most cases end with dismissals or guilty pleas before trial, Andrea's case does go to trial.

Why does the prosecution get to present its evidence first?

What is the hearsay rule?

If Andrea testifies, can the prosecutor offer evidence of her previous illegal conduct?

Is Andrea entitled to a jury trial?

Can the prosecution force Andrea to testify?

Does Andrea have to convince the judge or jury of her innocence?

See Chapter 17, *Fundamental Trial Rights of the Defense*, Chapter 18, *Basic Evidence Rules in Criminal Trials,* and Chapter 21, *The Trial Process.*

Andrea is found guilty of armed robbery and a date is set for sentencing.

What happens at a sentencing hearing?

How might Andrea be punished other than or in addition to going to jail?

What factors are likely to affect Andrea's sentence?

What can Andrea do to earn the lightest possible sentence?

If, after she's been found guilty, Andrea uncovers for the first time an important witness who supports her alibi defense, what can she do?

See Chapter 19, *Motions and Their Role in Criminal Cases,* and Chapter 22, *Sentencing.*

Andrea believes that her conviction was a mistake and wants to appeal it.

How do appellate court judges find out about what took place at Andrea's trial?

Will appellate court judges consider Andrea's argument that the jury shouldn't have believed the prosecutor's witnesses?

If the trial judge made an error of law, will the appellate court necessarily overturn Andrea's conviction?

See Chapter 23, *Appeals and Writs.*

The conviction is overturned because the judge mistakenly barred certain evidence from the trial. Andrea is retried and this time is found not guilty.

Can the prosecutor appeal the not guilty verdict to a higher court?

Can the prosecutor refile the armed robbery charge in the future if new evidence turns up?

Can the prosecutor ask the judge to order a new trial on the ground that the jurors afterwards said that they thought that Andrea was guilty but that she didn't deserve punishment?

See Chapter 13, *Common Defenses to Criminal Charges*, Chapter 17, *Fundamental Trial Rights of the Defense,* and Chapter 19, *Motions and Their Role in Criminal Cases.*

Andrea's conviction and five-year prison sentence are upheld on appeal, so Andrea has to serve time in state prison.

Can Andrea do anything to improve bad prison conditions?

If Andrea has a child, will she lose custody of her child?

Can Andrea vote while she is in prison or after she is released?

Can Andrea earn money while she is in prison?

Does Andrea have a chance to be released early on parole?

See Chapter 27, *Prison Rules.*

Comparison of Federal and State Systems

The vast majority of criminal prosecutions take place in state courts. The list below highlights some of the key differences between state and federal criminal systems:

- **Jurisdiction ("power" to decide cases).** A state has power over defendants who violate the laws of that state. The federal government has power over defendants who commit criminal acts on federal property (for example, an assault in a national park) or whose criminal acts cross state lines (for example, a kidnapper who transports a victim from Iowa to Missouri or a seller who deals in drugs that have crossed state lines). The federal government also has jurisdiction over a group of federally defined crimes, such as offenses related to immigration fraud, U.S. customs violations, and government violation of federal rights. It also has jurisdiction where, for example, someone tries to steal federally insured money. A state and the federal government can have "concurrent" power over a defendant when the same criminal activity violates both state and federal laws (for example, selling drugs or robbing banks). In those situations, state and federal prosecutors make case-by-case decisions as to whether a defendant will be prosecuted in state or federal court. In fact, sometimes *both* the state and the federal governments prosecute the same defendant.

- **Police Officers.** Typical state police officers are county sheriffs and city police officers. Typical federal police officers are agents of the FBI and DEA (Drug Enforcement Administration).

- **Prosecutors.** Federal criminal prosecutions are handled by U.S. attorneys, who are appointed by and are ultimately responsible to the U.S. attorney general. State prosecutors, many of whom are elected on a countywide basis, carry a variety of titles: Common ones are district attorney, state's attorney, and city attorney.

Comparison of Federal and State Systems (continued)

- **Defense Attorneys.** Most criminal defendants qualify for government-paid defense attorneys. Government-paid attorneys are usually employed either by an office of the Federal Public Defender or a county's public defender office.
- **Trial Courts.** Most federal criminal prosecutions occur in United States district courts. State courts carry such titles as "superior court," "municipal court," "police court," or "county court," depending on the state and the seriousness of criminal charges.
- **Judges.** Federal trial judges are known as district judges; they are appointed for life by the president, subject to confirmation by the U.S. Senate. State court judges are typically initially appointed by governors and then are subject to election every few years. State court trial judges carry such titles as superior court judge and municipal court judge. In both state and federal courts, magistrates may preside over pretrial hearings, such as bail hearings, as well as less serious criminal trials.
- **All-Purpose vs. Specialized Judges.** Federal courts use the "all-purpose judge" system. This means that the same judge almost always presides over a case from beginning to end—that is, from a defendant's first court appearance to final acquittal or sentencing. Some states also follow the all-purpose judge model. In many states, however, judges are specialized. For example, one judge may determine bail , another judge may hear pretrial motions, and a third judge may preside over a trial.

Talking to the Police

The overbearing police interrogation designed to wrench a confession from a quivering suspect is an enduring dramatic image. Though the image is largely a relic of the past, police officers do conduct potentially adversarial questioning in a variety of circumstances. This chapter discusses situations in which people risk incriminating themselves by responding to police officers' questions.

> **TIP**
>
> **Prosecutors can be counted on to use suspects' words against them.** Even a seemingly innocuous or innocent explanation may appear to link a suspect to a crime when the words are recounted by a police officer. People who have even a remote suspicion that they may be accused of a crime should *never* talk to a police officer without first talking to a lawyer. To make sure that a prosecutor can't claim that silence in response to a police officer's questions is evidence of guilt, a person may say something like, "I do not want to discuss this and I am exercising my right to remain silent."

Police Questioning of People Who Haven't Been Taken Into Custody

This section deals with police attempts to question people who are not in custody.

These situations commonly include:
- on-the-street questioning
- car stops for traffic violations
- investigatory visits to homes or offices
- email questions, and
- telephone conversations.

Do People Have to Report Crimes to the Police?

Generally, neither a crime victim nor a witness who sees a crime take place has a legal obligation to report the crime to the police. Though a crime is an offense against the public as a whole, reporting is usually a matter for people's individual consciences and circumstances. However, be aware that:
- Laws in many states require people in certain positions to report particular types of crimes. For example, teachers, social workers, and medical professionals may have to report suspected child abuse.
- Someone who takes active steps to conceal either a crime or its perpetrator may be charged with being an "accessory after the fact."
- A few states have enacted laws that make it a crime to see a felony occur yet fail to report it. Few prosecutions have taken place under such laws, however.

For background information about mandatory reporting laws, see Eugene Volokh, "Duties to Rescue and the Anti-Cooperative Effects of Law," 88 *Georgetown Law Journal* 105 (1999).

Can police officers detain and question people without justification?

No. In the absence of legal justification, police officers cannot detain people in order to question or search them. However, so long as an officer does not detain a person against the person's will without justification, the officer does nothing wrong by seeking information. (*U.S. v. Drayton*, U.S. Sup. Ct. 2002.)

People who are stopped by the police and do not want to answer questions or agree to a search should protect themselves by asking whether they are free to leave. If an officer refuses to allow a person to leave, a courtroom—rather than the street— is a safe place to argue about the legality of the officer's actions.

Is it a crime to refuse a police officer's request for identification?

Possibly. Many states have enacted "stop and identify" laws. Under these laws, if a police officer reasonably suspects that someone has engaged in criminal activity, the officer can detain that person and demand identification. Refusal to provide identification then becomes illegal resistance of an officer's lawful order. (*Hiibel v. Nevada*, U.S. Sup. Ct. 2004.)

Also, laws typically require drivers who are stopped for speeding and similar infractions to provide identification when an officer requests it.

> **EXAMPLE:** Jones is standing outside his parked truck. Noticing that Jones fits the description of a man who took clothing from a nearby store about a half hour earlier, Officer Juarez demands Jones's identification. Jones refuses to provide his ID. Because Officer Juarez reasonably suspected that Jones might have stolen the clothing, Jones's

refusal to provide identification would violate a "stop and identify" law.

Is it illegal to "flip off" a police officer?

Rude gestures and nasty comments to police officers are forms of free speech that under ordinary circumstances are not illegal. But hostile reactions to a police officer in the presence of others can constitute disturbing the peace or even attempting to incite a riot. And behaving rudely toward the police can motivate them to find something illegal you might have done—for example, jaywalking.

Can someone who starts to answer a police officer's questions decide to stop the interview?

Yes. People have the right to halt police questioning at any time simply by indicating a desire not to talk further.

Does refusal to answer a police officer's questions constitute loitering?

In some sense and some circumstances, yes. Laws in many states define loitering along the lines of "wandering about from place to place without apparent business, such that the person poses a threat to public safety." Under these laws, if a police officer observes suspected loitering, the officer can demand identification and an explanation of the person's activities. If the person fails to comply, the officer can arrest the person for loitering. Therefore, the refusal to answer questions is only a problem if the officer has also observed the person loitering.

The Questionable Legality of Loitering Laws

Many people argue that police officers use loitering laws to clear neighborhoods of "undesirables." Some courts have held loitering laws to be unconstitutional on the grounds that they are enforced discriminatorily against poor people and members of ethnic minority groups and that they unduly restrict people's rights to travel on public streets. However, the safest place to challenge the validity of a loitering law is in the courts, not on the streets to a police officer's face.

EXAMPLE: Officer Icia Yu is dispatched to Upscale Meadows after a resident calls the police to complain that a woman has been walking back and forth along the streets for over an hour, with no apparent purpose. From a distance, the officer observes the woman for a few minutes, and sees her stopping occasionally to peer into residents' backyards. Believing that she may be planning a burglary, Officer Yu confronts the woman and asks her to provide identification and explain what she is doing in the neighborhood. The woman refuses to respond. Under the loitering laws of many states, Officer Yu can arrest the woman for loitering. The officer had a reasonable basis to believe that the woman posed a danger to the community. Because she didn't identify herself or explain why she was in the neighborhood, the officer could arrest her.

Had the woman responded to Officer Yu, the officer might not have arrested her for loitering. However, depending on exactly what she did, she might be subject to arrest for a different offense, such as trespass (unlawful entry on someone else's property).

Can people who have done nothing wrong sue and recover money "damages" from police officers who seek to question them?

No. Even in the complete absence of probable cause to arrest or suspicion to detain, police officers have the same right as anyone else to approach people and try to talk to them. Thus, in general, police officers do not interfere with people's civil rights merely by seeking to question them. But in the absence of a legitimate reason, police officers cannot detain people who want to move on in order to continue to question them.

EXAMPLE: Officer Stan Doff knocks on the front door of Dee Fensive's home. When Dee answers the door, the officer says, "I'd like to ask you a few questions about a robbery that took place across the street a few minutes ago. Have you noticed any suspicious people hanging around the neighborhood lately?" Dee indicates that she does not want to talk and closes the door. Officer Doff then leaves. The officer has not violated Dee's rights. The officer has a right to try to question Dee. When Dee indicated that she did not want to talk, the officer ended the interview. The officer's actions are legally proper.

EXAMPLE: After walking away from Dee's home, Officer Doff detains a suspect who fits the description of the robber. Officer Doff questions the suspect but neglects to first issue a *"Miranda* warning." Even assuming that the warning was necessary for the suspect's statements to the officer to be admissible in evidence in a later court case, Officer Doff is not liable to the suspect for civil damages. (*Chavez v. Martinez*, U.S. Sup. Ct. 2003.) In other words, suspects cannot recover money from police officers simply because the officers' questioning violates *Miranda.* On the other hand, suspects' civil rights are violated—and suspects can sue and receive money damages—when police officers use "egregious" questioning methods, such as torture or other methods of brutality.

Don't police officers always have to read people the "*Miranda* rights" before questioning them?

No. A *Miranda* warning is required only if a suspect is in custody and the police intend to interrogate the suspect. In other words, both "custody" and "interrogation" have to occur for *Miranda* rights to kick in. And even then, the only "penalty" for a police officer's failure to issue a *Miranda* warning is normally that a suspect's statement is inadmissible in evidence at trial. A statement made to a police officer by a person who is not in custody, or a statement made voluntarily rather than in response to police interrogation, is admissible in evidence at trial even if no *Miranda* warning was given.

EXAMPLE: Officer Dave Bouncer is investigating a barroom brawl. The bartender indicates that a patron named Bob Sawyer might be able to identify the instigator of the brawl. When Officer Bouncer interviews Bob, Bob makes statements implicating himself in the brawl. Officer Bouncer did not read Bob his *Miranda* rights. Nevertheless, if Bob is charged with a crime concerning the brawl, Bob's statements to Officer Bouncer will be admissible as evidence. At the time Officer Bouncer spoke to Bob, Bob was not in custody.

Delay the Interview

People who are uncertain about whether to talk to a police officer needn't feel trapped into giving an immediate "yes" or "no." Being confronted by a police officer tends to make many people nervous and anxious, which diminishes their ability to provide accurate information. A good alternative is to delay the interview by saying something such as, "I didn't expect this. I choose to remain silent now, perhaps I will talk to you another time." Among other things, delay gives a person a chance to talk to a lawyer, and perhaps have the lawyer present during the interview, if the person ultimately decides to talk. (By clearly invoking the right to remain silent, people can prevent prosecutors from trying to offer evidence of their refusal to answer questions at trial.)

Can people who think they are innocent of wrongdoing do themselves any harm by talking to a police officer?

Quite possibly. It is often perfectly sensible and socially desirable for innocent people to cooperate in a police investigation. However, talking to police officers always entails risks. Below are several important questions people should consider before agreeing to a police interview.

Can people who haven't done anything wrong harm their interests if they are unsure about the events a police officer is asking about?

Unfortunately, people who haven't done anything wrong are sometimes mistakenly accused of crimes. Equally unfortunately, these same innocent people may unwittingly add to the evidence against them if they talk to police officers before they are prepared to do so. An innocent person who is unprepared to talk about certain events may become confused and answer incorrectly, especially when confronted by police officers. Upon realizing the mistake, the person may then want to provide the correct information and "set the record straight." But the police (or a judge or jury) may regard the change of story in itself as suspicious and indicative of guilt. Thus, even people who want to cooperate with police officers ought to make sure that they are prepared to do so. Someone who is unsure about what to do might ask the officer to return at a later time.

Might the police learn about any unrelated crimes as a result of an interview?

People may talk to police officers because they are confident that they can demonstrate they are not involved in the crimes that the officers are investigating. However, they may unwittingly disclose information implicating themselves in other criminal activity.

> **EXAMPLE:** While voluntarily answering a police officer's questions and denying any involvement in a burglary, Sol Itary nervously mentions that he was using illegal drugs with someone else at another location when the burglary took place. If Sol is charged with possession of illegal drugs based on other evidence, the prosecution can offer Sol's statement to the officer into evidence because Sol voluntarily spoke to the officer.

Recording Statements Made to Police Officers

People who want to cooperate with police officers but fear that the police will distort their statements can insist that the officers record the conversation or prepare a written summary of it for the person to sign. The recording or summary minimizes a police officer's opportunity to distort at a later time. But a potential downside to having the statement recorded is that a defendant will have to live with it if the case goes to trial.

Might previous contacts with the police lead officers to distort what someone has said?

People who think that they may be police targets (perhaps because they have a criminal record) should be especially careful about voluntarily talking to a police officer. Police officers sometimes distort people's oral statements, either because the officers are lying or because they have heard only what they want to hear. By repeating in court only part of a person's statement or changing a few words around, a police officer may make an innocent remark seem incriminating.

> **EXAMPLE:** A humorous example of police officer distortion occurred in the 1992 comedy film, *My Cousin Vinny*. In the film, a police officer questions a college student who has been arrested for killing a grocery store clerk. The stunned student, who at first thought that he had been arrested for shoplifting a can of tuna fish, repeats in a dazed, questioning voice, "I shot the clerk?" In court, however, the police officer makes it sound as if the student confessed to the murder by testifying that the student asserted, "I shot the clerk." In real life, of course, police officer distortion is no laughing matter.

Do people ever get in trouble because they don't know the law governing the events an officer is asking about?

People sometimes unwittingly provide evidence of their own guilt because they inaccurately believe that their behavior does not amount to criminal conduct. They may think they are explaining their innocence, while the police officers are using their explanation to amass evidence of a crime.

> **EXAMPLE:** Moe gets into a fistfight with Curly, which results in a severe cut to Curly's head. A police officer contacts Moe, seeking his version of the fight. Thinking that he acted in self-defense, Moe fully describes his version of events. However, as the police officer interprets Moe's story, Moe used excessive force, and the officer arrests Moe for aggravated assault. Had Moe more clearly understood the law, he might not have talked to the police officer.

Can people help themselves by answering a police officer's questions?

Yes. Police officers may be as interested in clearing the innocent as in convicting the guilty. People can often clear their names as well as help the police find the real perpetrators by answering a few straightforward questions. For example, assume that Wally, a possible suspect, can demonstrate that "I was at dinner with Andre" at the moment a crime was committed. Wally both removes himself as a suspect and enables the police to concentrate their efforts elsewhere.

And legal rights aside, the truth on the street is that people often can make life easier for themselves by cooperating with police officers—as long as they don't have a good reason not to. "Contempt of cop" has resulted in the arrest and even physical injury of more than one innocent person.

When innocent people who are pulled over or questioned by police officers stand on their rights too forcefully, events can sometimes get out of control rather quickly.

Lie Detector Tests

Police officers sometimes ask suspects to take lie detector tests to "clear their names." In general, suspects should refuse to take lie detector tests. Police sometimes use the tests as tools for obtaining confessions, falsely telling suspects that because they flunked they might as well confess. Moreover, lie detector tests are notoriously inaccurate. Innocent people often test guilty. Though lie detector test results are not usually admissible in court, even a false "guilty" result may prompt the police to make an arrest.

Can people implicate themselves further by trying to talk their way out of a bad situation?

Yes! The golden rule of defense is that suspects who think that they may be implicated in a crime should keep their mouths tightly shut. Suspects all too frequently unwittingly reveal information that later can be used as evidence of guilt. The right to not incriminate oneself, guaranteed by the Fifth Amendment to the U.S. Constitution, is especially powerful in this situation, and a suspect should normally politely invoke the right to remain silent, at least until consulting with an attorney.

Is it risky to provide false information to a police officer?

Yes. When people lie to the police or otherwise intentionally assist a known criminal to avoid arrest, they may be charged as "accessories after the fact." They can also be charged with obstruction of justice.

Obviously, whether to furnish information leading to the arrest of a relative or friend is a personal decision. However, a person who chooses not to do so should simply decline to answer an officer's questions rather than lie. Rarely, if ever, would someone who simply declines to give information to a police officer qualify as an accessory after the fact.

> **EXAMPLE:** Cain comes running into his brother Abel's house, and tells Abel that he, Cain, just robbed a market and that the police might be on his tail. A few minutes later, a police officer knocks on Abel's door and asks him if Cain is in the house. Abel responds, "No, he left town permanently to go back east weeks ago." Abel is subject to criminal prosecution as an accessory after the fact. By affirmatively misleading the police, he has aided Cain in avoiding arrest.

Police Questioning of Arrestees

This section deals with police attempts to question suspects who are in custody. It explains the *Miranda* rule and the circumstances when it does and does not apply.

When is a suspect "in custody" for purposes of the *Miranda* rule?

A suspect is in the custody of a police officer when, under all the circumstances, a reasonable person in the suspect's place would understand that he or she is not free to terminate an interrogation and leave. In *California v. Beheler* (1983), the U.S. Supreme Court stated that a person is in custody when a person's "freedom of action is curtailed to a degree associated with formal arrest."

The physical space in which questioning takes place does not necessarily determine whether a person is "in custody."

Even if police officers question a prisoner in a prison conference room, the prisoner is not "in custody" if the officers advise him that he is free to stop the questioning and return to his prison cell. (*Howes v. Fields*, U.S. Sup. Ct. 2012.)

A police officer does not have to issue *Miranda* warnings to a person who is not in custody. Thus, a suspect who is not in custody under this test and answers a police officer's questions cannot seek to exclude the answers from evidence based on the officer's failure to precede the interrogation with *Miranda* warnings. However, if the suspect is a minor (typically, under the age of 18), age can be relevant in determining whether the suspect is in "custody." A child's age is a factor that affects how a reasonable person in the suspect's position would have perceived his or her freedom to leave. (*J.D.B. v. North Carolina*, U.S. Sup. Ct. 2011.)

What is a *"Miranda* warning"?

When police officers make an arrest, they commonly interrogate (question) the arrestee. Usually they are trying to strengthen the prosecution's case by getting the arrestee to provide evidence of guilt. An interrogation may have other purposes as well, such as developing leads to additional suspects.

By voluntarily answering police questions after arrest, a suspect gives up two rights granted by the U.S. Constitution:

- the Fifth Amendment right to remain silent, and
- the Sixth Amendment right to have a lawyer present during the questioning.

Although people are entitled to voluntarily give up these and other rights, the courts have long recognized that voluntariness depends on knowledge and free will, and that people questioned by the police while they are in custody frequently have neither.

To remedy this situation, the U.S. Supreme Court ruled in the case of *Miranda v. Arizona* (1966) that information obtained by police officers through the questioning of a suspect in police custody may be admitted as evidence at trial only if the questioning was preceded by certain cautions known collectively as a *Miranda* warning. Accordingly, police officers usually begin their questioning of a person in custody by first making the following statements:

- You have the right to remain silent.
- If you do say anything, what you say can be used against you in a court of law.

- You have the right to consult with a lawyer and have that lawyer present during any questioning.
- If you cannot afford a lawyer, one will be appointed for you if you so desire.
- If you choose to talk to the police officer, you have the right to stop the interview at any time.

If a suspect is in police custody, it doesn't matter whether the interrogation takes place in a jail or at the scene of a crime, on a busy downtown street, or in the middle of an open field. Other than routine automobile stops and brief on-the-street detentions, once a police officer deprives a suspect of freedom of action in any way, the suspect is in police custody and *Miranda* is activated.

> **EXAMPLE:** Cathy Yi is arrested for assault. At the police station, Officer Rozmus seeks to question Yi about the events leading up to the assault. Yi does not have to answer the officer's questions. She has a constitutional right to remain silent. If Officer Rozmus fails to give Yi the *Miranda* warning before questioning begins, then nothing Yi says is admissible in evidence.

What happens if a suspect who is in custody isn't given a *Miranda* warning and answers a police officer's questions?

If a police officer questions a suspect who is in custody without giving the suspect the *Miranda* warning, nothing the suspect says can be used against the suspect at trial. The purpose of this "exclusionary rule" is to deter the police from violating the *Miranda* rule, which the U.S. Supreme Court has said is required by the Constitution. (*Dickerson v. U.S.*, U.S. Sup. Ct. 2000.)

The *Miranda* Case

Ernesto Miranda was arrested for kidnapping and raping a young woman in Arizona. Ten days after the rape took place, the victim picked Miranda out of a lineup and identified him as her attacker. The police took Miranda into an interrogation room and questioned him for two hours. Eventually, Miranda broke down and confessed in writing to committing the rape. The police did not physically abuse Miranda or trick him into confessing. At trial, the prosecution offered Miranda's confession into evidence, and he was convicted. On appeal, the U.S. Supreme Court overturned the conviction and granted Miranda a new trial. The Supreme Court decided that the confession should not have been admitted into evidence at Miranda's trial because the police had not advised him of his right to remain silent and to consult with counsel. Miranda was convicted again after a second trial, even though the prosecution was not able to offer his confession into evidence.

Can the government ever use statements that the police obtained in violation of *Miranda*?

Yes, assuming that the only reason the statement is inadmissible is the *Miranda* violation and not other forms of police misconduct such as physical coercion.

If a defendant gives testimony at trial that conflicts with a statement made to the police, the prosecutor can offer a statement elicited in violation of *Miranda* into evidence to impeach (attack) the defendant's credibility. (*Kansas v. Ventris*, U.S. Sup. Ct. 2009.) Similarly, rules in many jurisdictions allow prosecutors to offer statements obtained in violation of *Miranda* against defendants in sentencing hearings. (*U.S. v. Nichols*, 4th Cir., 2006.) For example, assume that in an improperly obtained statement, a defendant admits to the police that he was armed with a weapon when he committed a crime. The defendant's confession may not be admissible at trial to prove his guilt, but the prosecutor may offer it into evidence during sentencing to try to obtain a harsher sentence.

Also, the government may be able to use the "fruits" of statements taken in violation of *Miranda*. If police officers learn about evidence by taking a defendant's statement in violation of *Miranda*, that evidence might be admissible against the defendant. Here are some common examples:

- In sufficiently dangerous situations, the "public safety" exception allows police officers to question suspects about weapons without giving a *Miranda* warning. If the interrogation leads the police to a weapon, the weapon can be offered into evidence against the suspect at trial. (*N.Y. v. Quarles*, U.S. Sup. Ct. 1984.)
- Dangerous situation or not, any tangible evidence ("physical fruits," such as a threatening note or the loot

from a robbery) that the police learn about through questioning that violates *Miranda* can generally be used against a suspect in court. (*U.S. v. Patane*, U.S. Sup. Ct. 2004.)

- If a statement taken in violation of *Miranda* leads the police to another witness, that witness can testify against the suspect at trial. (*Michigan v. Tucker*, U.S. Sup. Ct. 1974.)
- The "inevitable discovery" doctrine means that if the police would have eventually found tangible evidence on their own, the evidence can be used against a suspect at trial even if they actually found out about it through questioning that violates *Miranda*.

These interpretations of the *Miranda* rule give the police an incentive to violate the rule. Moreover, they mean that suspects have to protect themselves.

Suspects who think that what they say can't be used against them at trial because they weren't given *Miranda* warnings need to understand that these "fruits" of their improperly obtained statements may well be admissible in evidence.

EXAMPLE: Mal Addy is arrested for assault with a deadly weapon. The police question Addy without giving him a *Miranda* warning. Addy confesses to the crime and tells the police where he hid the knife that he used in the attack. The police then locate the knife. The prosecutor cannot offer Addy's confession into evidence at trial. However, the knife can be used at trial because the knife is a tangible object, not a statement.

EXAMPLE: Same case. While the police question Addy without giving him a *Miranda* warning, he tells them that he has illegal drugs in the backpack that he was carrying when he was arrested. The illegal drugs are admissible in evidence against Addy despite the *Miranda* violation, because the police would have inevitably found the drugs when they inventoried the contents of the backpack during the booking process.

Are there circumstances in which a statement by a suspect can't be used against that suspect even if a *Miranda* warning is given?

Yes, but only in unusual circumstances. If a police officer gives a suspect a *Miranda* warning and then physically coerces the suspect into talking (say, by refusing the suspect's requests for medicine that the suspect has to take), the resulting statement cannot be used against the suspect.

A confession following the giving of a *Miranda* warning also cannot be used against a suspect if it's the result of a ploy known as "question first, warn later." Police using this technique question a suspect without giving a *Miranda* warning. If a suspect confesses, the police then give a *Miranda* warning and convince the suspect that, having already confessed, the suspect should waive (give up) the right to remain silent and repeat the confession. Even though the second confession follows a *Miranda* warning, neither the first nor the second confession can be used against the suspect at trial. (*Missouri v. Seibert*, U.S. Sup. Ct. 2004.)

> ### Police Officers May Mischaracterize a Custodial Situation in Court
>
> Police officers generally believe that suspects are more likely to speak with them voluntarily in the absence of a *Miranda* warning. Thus, police officers have an incentive not to give the warning. One way they may attempt to evade the *Miranda* rule is by delaying the arrest of a suspect until after they're through with the questioning. If an officer can convince a judge that the officer was engaged only in general questioning and would have let the suspect walk away had the suspect chosen to do so, anything the suspect says to the officer can be used against the suspect at trial despite the lack of *Miranda* warnings.

Are charges automatically dismissed when police officers have questioned suspects without issuing *Miranda* warnings?

No. One popular misconception about the criminal justice system is that a case has to be thrown out of court if the police fail to give the *Miranda* warning to people they arrest. What *Miranda* says is that the warning is necessary if the police interrogate a suspect in custody and a prosecutor wants to offer the suspect's statements into evidence at trial. This means that the failure to give the *Miranda* warning is utterly irrelevant to the case if:

- the suspect is not in custody
- the police do not interrogate the suspect, or

- the police do interrogate the suspect, but the prosecution does not try to use the suspect's responses as evidence.

In essence, if the prosecution can win its case without using the improperly obtained statements, a *Miranda* violation will not cause dismissal of the case.

Is it ever a good idea for an arrestee to talk to the police without a lawyer present?

No. Talking to the police is almost always hazardous to the health of a defense case, and defense attorneys almost universally advise their clients to invoke the right to remain silent until the attorney has assessed the charges and counseled the client about case strategy.

How do suspects assert the right to remain silent or the right to a lawyer when being questioned by the police?

Suspects do not need to use a precise set of words to indicate that they want to remain silent. But the decision to remain silent should be clear. A suspect who responds to a *Miranda* warning by asking a police officer, "Should I contact a lawyer?" has not indicated a clear intent to remain silent. But arrestees clearly invoke their *Miranda* rights by saying things like the following:

- "I don't want to talk to you; I want to talk to an attorney."
- "I refuse to speak with you."
- "I invoke my privilege against self-incrimination."
- "I claim my *Miranda* rights."

In general, if the police continue to question an arrestee who says anything like the above, they have violated *Miranda*. As a result, nothing the arrestee says after that point is admissible in evidence.

Even though they don't have to mention the *Miranda* case or use a particular phrase to invoke their rights, suspects who want to prevent police questioning have to speak up and assert their desire to remain silent. If suspects fail to tell the police that they want to remain silent or talk to a lawyer, the police have the right to question them. (*Berghuis v. Thompkins*, U.S. Sup. Ct. 2010.) (The dissenting justices in *Berghuis* pointed out the irony of a rule that requires defendants to speak up to claim their right to remain silent.)

EXAMPLE: Police officers arrest Sy Lentz for murder and advise him of his *Miranda* rights. When Sy remains silent, the officers question him. After three hours of questioning, Sy answers "Yes" to an officer's question about whether he had prayed for forgiveness for shooting the victim. The prosecutor can offer the question and Sy's response into evidence at trial to prove that Sy is guilty of murder. Sy did not demand a lawyer or tell the police that he refused to talk to them. Sy's silence allowed the police to continue to question him, and his eventual answer is admissible at trial.

Can prosecutors ever offer a suspect's silence into evidence at trial?

Yes. If a suspect who has not been arrested and who has not been given *Miranda* warnings does not respond to a police officer's questions, the suspect's silence can be admissible at trial as evidence of guilt. Suspects have to in some way explicitly invoke the right to remain silent. If they don't, a prosecutor can use their silence in response to police officer inquiries as evidence of guilt. (*Salinas v. Texas*, U.S. Sup. Ct. 2013.)

> **EXAMPLE:** Officer Jones suspects that Adams, who isn't yet under arrest, was involved in an armed robbery. Adams says nothing in response to Officer Jones's questions about his where-abouts at the time of the robbery. At trial, Adams's silence is admissible evidence of his participation in the robbery. To demonstrate that he remained silent because he has a constitutional right to do so, Adams would have had to say something like "I claim my right to remain silent." (A 2014 California Supreme Court case, *People v. Tom*, allows the prosecution to argue that the silence of a suspect who has been arrested, but who hasn't been read the *Miranda* warnings or been interrogated, is likewise evidence of guilt.)

Does the *Miranda* rule apply to pre-arrest questioning of suspects by police officers?

Not necessarily. *Miranda* applies only to "custodial" questioning. A person is not in custody unless a police officer has "deprived a [person] of his freedom of action in a significant way." Whether a suspect is in custody and therefore not free to leave is an objective issue that judges decide without taking into account a suspect's inexperience or psychological condition. (*Yarborough v. Alvarado*, U.S. Sup. Ct. 2004.)

When it decided the *Miranda* case, the Supreme Court said that its ruling did not apply to "general on-the-scene questioning as to facts surrounding a crime or other general questioning of citizens in the fact-finding process." Thus, unless a person is in custody, an officer can question him or her without giving the *Miranda* warning, and whatever the person says is admissible in evidence.

> **EXAMPLE:** Officer Roy Altie responds to a call to investigate a purse-snatching incident. The officer learns from the victim that the culprit was a white male, about 5'10" tall, weighing about 175 pounds and wearing a lightcolored sweatshirt. About ten minutes later, about a mile from where the pursesnatching took place, Officer Altie sees a man generally fitting the attacker's description walking alone. Officer Altie realizes that he lacks sufficient evidence to make an arrest, and approaches the man merely to question him about his activities and whereabouts during the preceding one-half hour. Officer Altie need not precede the questioning with the *Miranda* warning. Officer Altie was engaged in general onthescene questioning.

If charges have been filed and counsel has been appointed, can police officers ever question suspects when their lawyers aren't present?

Yes. In order to claim the benefits of *Miranda*, defendants generally have to tell police officers that they do not want to speak to them or that they want to have their lawyer present before talking with the police. By itself, the fact that a judge has appointed a lawyer to represent a defendant does not prevent the police from questioning the defendant. (*Montejo v. Louisiana*, U.S. Sup. Ct. 2009.)

> **EXAMPLE:** Montejo is charged with murder. An arraignment judge appoints a lawyer to represent him. Later, police officers visit him in jail and advise him of his *Miranda* rights. Montejo doesn't invoke his right to remain silent and doesn't demand that his lawyer be present for questioning. Instead, Montejo cooperates with the police and writes a letter admitting to the killing. The prosecutor can introduce the letter into evidence to prove that Montejo committed the murder.

> **EXAMPLE:** In the same scenario, assume that Montejo had told the police that he wouldn't talk to them unless his lawyer was present. However, the police refused to take "No" for an answer, and kept badgering Montejo until he finally agreed to talk to them. Montejo then wrote a letter admitting to the killing. In this situation, the prosecutor could not introduce the letter into evidence to prove that Montejo committed the murder. Once he invoked his *Miranda* rights, the police had no right to continue to talk to him.

Do the police have to give the *Miranda* warning to drivers who are pulled over for traffic violations?

The U.S. Supreme Court has acknowledged that a traffic stop involves significant restraint of a driver's freedom. But it has ruled that a typical roadside detention doesn't place the driver "in custody" because it doesn't involve the kind of restraint that's typical of a formal arrest (for example, handcuffing). That isn't to say, however, that a traffic stop can't evolve into a full-blown arrest that requires *Miranda* warnings for further questioning.

Prior to police questioning, are statements that suspects make voluntarily to police officers admissible in evidence?

In general, yes. *Miranda* applies only to statements that are the product of police questioning. If an arrestee volunteers information to a police officer, the information is admissible in evidence.

> **EXAMPLE:** After failing a series of sobriety tests, Ina Bryate is arrested for drunk driving. As the officer is taking her toward the police vehicle, Ina says, "I couldn't possibly be drunk. I only had a few beers at the sorority party." Before Ina said this, the officer had neither given her a *Miranda* warning nor questioned her. Ina's statements are admissible in evidence. Ina spoke voluntarily; the officer did not question her. Thus, the fact that Ina had not been given a *Miranda* warning does not bar admission of her statement into evidence.

What does it mean to "waive" the *Miranda* rights?

Suspects waive (give up) their *Miranda* rights by talking to police officers after having been advised that they have the right not to. To avoid disputes in court about whether *Miranda* warnings were given and waived, police officers often ask suspects who indicate a willingness to talk to sign waiver forms acknowledging that they've received advisement of and understood their *Miranda* rights, and that they want to talk to the police anyway.

But police officers do not have to obtain either oral or written waivers from suspects after advising them of their *Miranda* rights. Police officers can continue to question suspects who fail to assert their right to remain silent or to have a lawyer present. Judges can infer a waiver of *Miranda* rights when suspects fail to assert them.

> **EXAMPLE:** Police officers advise robbery suspect Lou Slipps of his *Miranda* rights. When Lou remains silent, the officers proceed to question him. They tell him that the evidence against him is already very strong, and that the best thing he can do to help himself is confess. After about 90 minutes of interrogation, Lou tells the officers that he didn't mean to injure the robbery victim so badly. Lou's statement is admissible in evidence. Because Lou never asserted his *Miranda* rights, he waived them and allowed the police to continue interrogating him.

If suspects have invoked their *Miranda* rights, can police officers ever interrogate them at a later time?

Yes. Remember the old aphorism, "If at first you don't succeed, try, try again?" In the context of police interrogations, the aphorism means that police officers can

sometimes question suspects who have previously invoked their *Miranda* rights. In general, a suspect who has invoked the right to the presence of counsel during custodial interrogation can't be interrogated further until counsel is available or the suspect initiates conversation with the police. But if a break of at least 14 days takes place, during which the suspect was not in custody, police officers can renew questioning. At the subsequent interview, if the suspect waives his or her *Miranda* rights, his or her new statements will probably be admissible in evidence. (*Maryland v. Shatzer*, U.S. Sup. Ct. 2010.)

> **EXAMPLE:** Police officers advise robbery suspect Lou Slipps of his *Miranda* rights. When Lou insists on talking to a lawyer before talking to the police, the officers stop talking to him and return him to his jail cell. Eighteen days later, the police officers bring Lou from his cell to an interrogation room, and again read him his *Miranda* rights. This time Lou agrees to talk to them, and he states that he didn't mean to injure the robbery victim so badly. Lou's statement is admissible in evidence. Because the police officers waited at least two weeks after Lou first asserted his *Miranda* rights to question him again, his agreement to talk to them was valid and what he said is admissible against him in court.

What is the "booking question exception" to *Miranda*?

When suspects are booked into jail, a jailer (often called a booking officer) typically asks them routine questions about their health and outside relationships. To protect the safety of jailers and inmates alike, suspects with communicable illnesses or gang affiliations may need to be housed in special sections of a jail. Booking questioning does not constitute an interrogation, and a booking officer does not have to give *Miranda* warnings to suspects. As a result, incriminating statements that a suspect makes in response to routine booking questioning is likely to be admissible in evidence. (*Pennsylvania v. Muniz*, U.S. Sup. Ct. 1990.)

> **EXAMPLE:** Following routine booking practice, Officer Booker asks a suspect arrested for carjacking whether he is affiliated with any gangs. The suspect states that he is a member of the 823 Coyotes. If the suspect's membership in the gang is relevant to his guilt, the prosecutor may call Booker to testify to the suspect's statement, even though Booker did not give *Miranda* warnings to the suspect before questioning him.

Following a waiver of *Miranda* rights, can suspects change their mind and invoke the rights to remain silent and to talk to a lawyer?

Yes. Suspects can invoke their right to silence at any time, even if they have begun talking to the police. Of course, statements made before invoking the right to silence are admissible, so deciding to remain silent after previously answering questions may be the equivalent of locking the barn door after the horse has run away. To stop police questioning, a suspect merely has

to say something like, "I'm invoking the right to remain silent," or, "I want to talk to a lawyer before we go any further." If the police continue to question a suspect who invokes *Miranda*, nothing the suspect says after indicating a desire to halt the interview is admissible in evidence.

Has the *Miranda* rule had a negative effect on crime clearance rates?

When *Miranda* was decided, police and prosecutors predicted a dire effect on their ability to secure convictions. In a 1998 book about *Miranda*, Professor Richard Leo estimated that at least 80% of suspects waive their *Miranda* rights and voluntarily talk to the police. However, an empirical analysis of *Miranda's* possible effect on police officers' "crime clearance rates" (crime solving) during the period 1950–2012 determined that clearance rates for violent and property crimes declined during that period. The analysis found that a portion of that reduction was a result of *Miranda*. (See Cassell and Fowles, "Still Handcuffing the Cops? A Review of 50 Years of Empirical Evidence of *Miranda's* Harmful Effects on Law Enforcement" in Vol. 97 of the *Boston University Law Review* at p. 625 (2017).)

The following psychological factors that police regularly use to their advantage explain why suspects often make "voluntary" confessions that they later regret:

- Suspects who are in custody are psychologically vulnerable. Many suspects are intimidated by jail conditions, and talk in order to please the jailers who are suddenly in control of their lives.

- Police often lead a suspect to believe that a confession or cooperation in naming other suspects will result in leniency. Although courts generally consider this to be improper police conduct (see, for example, United States v. Johnson, 6th Cir., U.S. Court of Appeals (2003)), the police will usually deny that they promised leniency, and the judge will usually believe them.

- Police use the "good cop–bad cop" routine. Suspects believe the good cop is on their side, and so they gratefully and voluntarily talk to that officer.

- Many suspects talk voluntarily in the belief that only explicit confessions will be admissible in evidence. They are mistaken. Anything they say to the police, even if it seems to be in their favor, is admissible in evidence.

- Police may make suspects feel that their situations are already hopeless. For example, police officers may tell a suspect that he failed a lie detector test, that a codefendant confessed and incriminated the suspect, or that the police have a videotape of the suspect committing the crime. Even if the police lied, the confession is usually admissible in evidence.

How the Police Can Benefit From Delayed *Miranda* Warnings

Crafty police officers may intentionally delay giving *Miranda* warnings to suspects following an arrest for at least two reasons:

- If they don't interrogate the suspect, police officers don't have to give *Miranda* warnings. In the absence of the warnings, some suspects will blurt out voluntary statements that the prosecution can then offer into evidence at trial. For example, instead of immediately interrogating a suspect, a police officer may reveal the evidence that the officer has thus far gathered from other sources. Figuring that there's nothing to be gained from silence, the suspect may indicate a willingness to confess. The officer can then advise the suspect

of his *Miranda* rights, making the subsequent confession admissible in evidence against the defendant at trial. (*U.S. v. Gonzalez-Lauzan*, 11th Cir. 2006.)

- Even if a suspect remains silent, the prosecution can sometimes use that silence against the suspect at trial. Assume that a suspect who remained silent after arrest testifies in essence that, "I didn't do it." The prosecution may be able to attack the suspect's credibility (believability) by having the arresting officer testify to her silence following arrest. The prosecution's argument would be, "If the suspect really didn't do it, why didn't she immediately say that to the arresting officer?"

- Taking advantage of a suspect's pangs of guilt, police officers may emphasize the harm that the suspect has caused to the victim, and stress that the suspect can begin to repay the victim by owning up to the misdeed. A resulting confession turns the suspect's feeling of moral guilt into legal guilt.
- Police sometimes emphasize that a confession will speed things up. Many suspects, especially first-time offenders, want to put a criminal charge behind them quickly. To them, a confession represents the shortest line between two points.
- Police officers tell suspects, "This is a chance to make sure that the district attorney hears your side of the story." Then, in an effort to minimize their guilt, suspects often furnish evidence that eventually helps convict them.
- When two or more suspects commit a crime, officers sometimes extract confessions by falsely telling some suspects that the police regard them as witnesses rather than culprits.

Judges may rule that police officers improperly interrogated suspects without warning them of their *Miranda* rights when officers who are trying to be coy or tricky make comments that are the functional equivalent of interrogation. For instance, assume that an officer talks to an in-custody suspect known to the officer to be religiously observant about how a crime violates the Ten Commandments. If the discussion of the Ten Commandments leads to the suspect confessing to the crime, a judge may decide that the discussion amounted to an interrogation by the officer. In the absence of a *Miranda* warning, therefore, the suspect's confession would not be admissible in evidence.

Empty Promises

Police officers use a subtle form of coercion when they make empty promises of leniency. Police officers may recommend a light sentence, but at the end of the day, it's prosecutors and judges who normally determine punishment, based on statutory requirements and political expediency.

EXAMPLE: Dee Nyal is arrested and charged with burglary. At the police station, Dee waives her *Miranda* rights and voluntarily tells the police that she was at the movies when the burglary took place. At trial, the prosecutor wants to offer Dee's statement to the police into evidence to show it was false, because the movie Dee said she watched was not playing on the night of the burglary. Dee protests that what she said to the police shouldn't be admissible because she didn't make a confession. However, because Dee waived her *Miranda* rights, the statement is admissible, regardless of whether she made the statement to help herself or to admit guilt.

EXAMPLE: Len Scap is arrested for murder. The police give Len his *Miranda* warning, then tell him that he might as well confess because the police found his fingerprints at the crime scene and have an eyewitness who can easily identify him. Feeling all is lost, Len confesses to the murder. It turns out that the police lied to Len—they had neither his fingerprints nor an eyewitness. Len's confession is probably admissible in evidence. Judges generally rule that confessions are voluntary even if they are obtained by the police through trickery. (*Frazier v. Cupp*, U.S. Sup. Ct. 1969.)

But trickery can go too far. A documentary entitled *Scenes of a Crime* (2011) covers in detail the interrogation of a father who eventually confessed to killing his infant son. Convicted largely on the basis of the confession, the father went to prison. In 2014, New York's highest appeals court unanimously held that the deception of the interrogating officers made the father's confession involuntary. As but one example of their deception, the interrogating officers implored the father to confess in order to save his son's life even though the boy had already died. Upon retrial, the father was acquitted.

If a boss or landlord questions someone about illegal activity, can the response be used as evidence if there was no *Miranda* warning?

Yes. *Miranda* applies only to questioning by the police or other governmental officials.

If the police plant an informant in a jail cell, are statements that a suspect makes to the informant admissible in evidence?

If a jailed suspect has been formally charged with a crime, the police violate the suspect's right to counsel by planting a police informant in the suspect's cell in the hope that the suspect will make damaging statements to the informant. Nevertheless, if a suspect testifies at trial and contradicts a statement the suspect made to a planted police informant, prosecutors can offer the contradictory statement into evidence. Allowing impeachment in these circumstances promotes the integrity of the trial process. (*Kansas v. Ventris*, U.S. Sup. Ct. 2009.)

EXAMPLE: Ventris is in jail, charged with murder. Hoping to develop additional evidence against him, the police place an undercover informant in Ventris's jail cell. The informant is prepared to testify that Ventris admitted committing the murder. At trial, Ventris testifies that his girlfriend committed the murder. The prosecutor calls the informant to testify to Ventris's admission that he was the murderer. Because Ventris's trial testimony contradicted his jailhouse statement to the informant, the prosecution can offer the statement into evidence to impeach his credibility.

False Confessions and the "Central Park Jogger" Case

Confessions carry great weight with juries because most people believe that innocent people don't confess to serious crimes. However, the psychological factors noted above are so powerful that they can produce false confessions. Research carried out by The Innocence Project indicates that about 25% of suspects who were convicted and later proved innocent (usually based on DNA testing) had confessed their guilt. One of the most infamous examples of erroneous convictions based largely on false confessions occurred in the Central Park Jogger case. In 1989, a woman was raped and horribly beaten while jogging in New York's Central Park. Police officers extracted confessions from five teenage boys, and the boys were convicted and sentenced to prison even though their stories varied and DNA testing failed to link any of them to the attack. Thirteen years later, an individual named Reyes confessed that he alone had attacked the jogger. Reyes's confession provided details known only to the police, and DNA testing confirmed that Reyes was the source of the semen found at the crime scene. The innocent teenage boys' convictions were vacated. *The Central Park Five* (2012) is a documentary film about the case. The case is also dramatized in a 2019 television miniseries, *When They See Us*.

Besides *Miranda*, are there other restrictions placed on the police when they seek information from arrested suspects?

Yes. Confessions that are deemed to be involuntary are not allowed as evidence. Under this rule, the police are not allowed to use brutality, physical threats, or other means of intimidation to coerce suspects into confessing. If the police obtain information by any of these illegal means, the information is not admissible, whether or not they read the suspect the *Miranda* warning. In addition, under the "fruit of the poisonous tree" rule, any evidence that the police obtain as the result of the coerced confession would be equally inadmissible.

EXAMPLE: Clark Kent is arrested for indecent exposure. After he is booked, the police read him his *Miranda* rights. The police then proceed to question Clark over a 36-hour period, keeping him in solitary confinement when they are not questioning him and withholding almost all food and water. Clark finally agrees to talk to the police and confesses to the crime. Clark's statements are inadmissible in evidence. Clark did not freely and voluntarily waive his *Miranda* rights, because the interrogation methods were highly coercive.

EXAMPLE: Moe Money is charged with obtaining money by fraudulent means. Following the *Miranda* warning, Moe voluntarily agrees to talk to the police and denies any fraudulent conduct. The police then tell Moe that they will arrest his wife and bring her to the station for questioning. Moe tells the police that his wife is pregnant but very ill, and has been instructed by her doctor to remain in bed as much as possible to protect her health and that of the baby. The police tell Moe that's his problem, that they're going to arrest his wife unless he confesses. They say, "The health of your wife and your kid is up to you." If Moe then confesses, the confession would not be admissible in evidence. Moe's confession was involuntary. This is especially true if the police lacked probable cause to arrest Moe's wife and threatened to arrest her only to coerce Moe into talking. (*Rogers v. Richmond*, U.S. Sup. Ct. 1961.)

EXAMPLE: Sarah Bellum is arrested for armed robbery, and confesses after receiving *Miranda* warnings. Defense evidence shows that Sarah is intellectually disabled, with a mental age of nine. In addition, she suffers from attention deficit disorder and depression. Nevertheless, her confession is probably voluntary.

Private Individuals May Sometimes Be Police Agents for Purposes of *Miranda*

Courts sometimes hold private individuals to the same *Miranda* standards as police officers if the individuals act in concert with the police. For example, assume that the police arrest Rose Ettastone for embezzlement from the bank that employs her. Hoping to find out how Rose carried out the scheme, the police ask the bank manager to come down to the jail and interview Rose. Rose tells the bank manager details of the scheme, which the prosecutor wants to offer into evidence. Because the manager was acting as a police agent, he would have had to advise Rose of her *Miranda* rights before interviewing her if the statements were to be admitted as evidence.

Recent years have seen an explosion of private security guards. Because private security guards are not governmental employees, rules such as *Miranda* have generally not been applied to them.

EXAMPLE: Same case, except that this time Sarah's evidence is that at the time of her confession, the police had just awakened her from a deep sleep produced by her having ingested three tranquilizers a few hours earlier. The police testify that Sarah was fully awake and lucid. Her confession is again likely voluntary. While the drugs may have further impaired Sarah's already diminished cognitive functions, she was not legally incapable of making a voluntary confession.

The Police Usually Win "Swearing Contests"

Defendants' claims that they were coerced into talking often turn into swearing contests, with the police contending that everything was honest and aboveboard. Defendants who are physically coerced by police into talking can support their claims with, for example, photos of marks and bruises. But actual police brutality in this context is unusual, and defendants cannot usually offer independent evidence to support their claims of psychological coercion. Judges, believing that defendants have a greater motivation to lie than police officers, usually side with the police and conclude that no coercion took place.

How do intoxication or mental limitations affect the voluntariness of a confession?

Very little. Defendants often ask judges to rule that their confessions were involuntary on the grounds that they were drunk, were high on drugs, or had mental limitations when they confessed. Unless the defendant was practically unconscious at the time of confessing, however, judges usually decide that confessions are voluntary—despite the existence of factors that strongly suggest an opposite conclusion. (*United States v. Curtis*, 344 F.3d 1057 (10th Cir. 2003).)

> **EXAMPLE:** Same case, except that this time Sarah's evidence is that she confessed to armed robbery while in an ambulance on the way to the hospital. At the time she confessed, she was in pain from injuries she suffered when she was captured, she was under the effects of tranquilizers she had ingested just prior to the robbery, and she passed out a number of times during the interrogation. Under these more extreme circumstances, Sarah's confession is probably not voluntary. Her physical condition was so impaired that she was legally incapable of confessing voluntarily.

Search and Seizure

The Fourth Amendment to the U.S. Constitution limits the power of the police to make arrests, search people and their property, and seize objects, documents, and contraband (such as illegal drugs or weapons). These limits are the bedrock of "search and seizure law."

Search and seizure law is constantly in flux and so complex that entire books are devoted to it. This chapter reviews basic search and seizure rules.

The Constitutional Background

This section provides an overview of the limitations on searches and seizures provided by the Fourth Amendment to the U.S. Constitution.

What is the connection between the Fourth Amendment and privacy?

Decisions of the United States Supreme Court link the Fourth Amendment's prohibition of "unreasonable searches and seizures" to privacy. As a general rule, a "search" occurs only if a person has a "legitimate expectation of privacy" in the place or thing that a police officer searches. (*Katz v. U.S.*, U.S. Sup. Ct. 1967.) The legitimacy of an expectation of privacy rests on two factors:

- Does a person subjectively (that is, in the person's own mind) expect that a place or thing is private?
- Is a person's subjective expectation objectively reasonable, meaning that society as a whole is willing to honor it?

The answer to both questions has to be "yes" for police activity to constitute a search. If a judge determines that a search has taken place, the judge goes on to determine its reasonableness.

A government official's activity can also unlawfully interfere with privacy if an officer trespasses into a person's physical space. (*U.S. v. Jones*, U.S. Sup. Ct. 2012.) In *Jones,* police officers tracked a suspect's movements by attaching a hidden Global Positioning System (GPS) device to the suspect's car. The officers' actions constituted a search for purposes of the Fourth Amendment because the officers trespassed onto the suspect's private property.

Searches by private individuals might be wrongful but they do not implicate the Fourth Amendment. For example, people are not entitled to Fourth Amendment protection against searches conducted by private employers, landlords, and private security officers. This means, for example, that evidence discovered by such searches and then turned over to the police may be offered into evidence at trial, even though the same search would not have been legal if done by a government agent.

> **EXAMPLE:** Police officers look through the contents of a trash bin behind an apartment complex. No search has occurred, because people generally have no legitimate expectation of privacy in their trash.

EXAMPLE: Thinking that they might uncover evidence of criminal activity, police officers place a camera in a public restroom. The activity constitutes a search, because people generally have a subjective and objectively reasonable belief that a restroom is a private place.

EXAMPLE: A jewelry store security guard randomly checks the purses and pockets of people as they are about to leave the store. No search takes place. Private security guards are not government officials, so their activities are not subject to Fourth Amendment restraints. And suppose such a search reveals a shoplifter? When the guard calls the police and presents them with evidence of shoplifting, the police may arrest the individual and use the merchandise as evidence of the crime.

EXAMPLE: Police Officer Friday stops a vehicle for a traffic violation. While speaking to the driver through an open window, Friday observes and seizes a sawed-off shotgun lying on the passenger seat. No search takes place, as the driver has no legitimate expectation of privacy for objects in plain view.

EXAMPLE: Officer Friday makes a traffic stop and asks the driver for permission to look in the trunk. The driver says, "Sure" and unlocks the trunk. Friday seizes a baggie of marijuana in the trunk and arrests the driver. Friday's activities do not constitute a Fourth Amendment search, because although the driver might initially have had a legitimate expectation that the contents of the trunk were private, the driver gave up that expectation by willingly agreeing to let the officer take a look.

The Text of the Fourth Amendment

The right of the people to be secure in their persons, houses, papers, and effects, against unreasonable searches and seizures, shall not be violated, and no Warrants shall issue, but upon probable cause, supported by Oath or affirmation, and particularly describing the place to be searched, and the persons or things to be seized.

Can police officers enter private dwellings without a warrant to make arrests or look for evidence of a crime?

Privacy interests are highest in people's homes. As a result, and subject to exceptions that this chapter discusses, police officers can't make warrantless entries into private dwellings to make an arrest or conduct a search.

For Fourth Amendment purposes, dwellings include houses and their yards (which are sometimes called "curtilage"), apartments, hotel rooms, tents, and the like.

EXAMPLE: Police officers see a car parked in the driveway of a private home. Because the car fits the description of one seen leaving the scene of a recent burglary, the officers go up the driveway and conduct a warrantless search of the car. Though the mobility of cars often allows police officers to search them without needing to obtain a warrant, the officers violated the Fourth Amendment by going onto private property to search the car. (*Collins v. Virginia*, U.S. Sup. Ct. 2018.)

EXAMPLE: Johnson knocks down a passerby, robs him, and runs off. A police officer sees the robbery and chases Johnson to his house. The officer enters the house and arrests Johnson. The warrantless entry into the house and arrest are legal because the officer saw the suspect commit the crime and was "in hot pursuit."

What is the status of electronic tracking technology under the Fourth Amendment?

Current technology makes it possible for government officials to trace individuals' movements electronically. The electronic signals that are emitted into the public airwaves by GPS devices and cellphones are byproducts of the ordinary use of these electronic devices. Because the signals are in the public space, police officers have the capacity to keep tabs on people without physically trespassing into their personal space or possessions. For example, police officers can track people's locations and movements by monitoring signals from their mobile phones or the GPS devices in their cars.

But the ability to do something technologically doesn't mean that it's legal. Legislatures and judges have not yet agreed upon widely accepted guidelines for evaluating when government officials' monitoring of electronic signals is allowed under the Fourth Amendment. The ability to track someone electronically did not exist when the Bill of Rights was adopted in the 18th century, but this doesn't mean that guidelines cannot be developed—after all, the 18th century also did not envision a telephone, yet courts and legislatures have developed complex rules concerning the government's access to a person's phone conversations. An example of courts having to adjust to new tracking technology is the U.S. Supreme Court's decision in *Grady v. North Carolina* (2015). The Court held that a search occurs when the government monitors sex offenders by attaching electronic tracking devices to their bodies. Whether the search is constitutional under the Fourth Amendment depends on its reasonableness.

EXAMPLE: Suspecting that Katzin has carried out a series of burglaries, police officers attach a GPS tracking device to his van. They use the device to monitor the van's movements. The officers pull the van over near the scene of a burglary and arrest Katzin when they find stolen loot in the van. The officers are required to obtain a search warrant before attaching the GPS device to the van, so the search was improper. (*U.S. v. Katzin*, 3d Cir. 2013.)

Do police officers need search warrants to get cellphone location information that shows suspects' movements?

Cellphone towers use the electronic signals that cellphones constantly emit to monitor the phones' locations. As a result, police officers can trace people's movements by accessing their cellphone companies' records. In *Carpenter v. U.S.* (2018), the U.S. Supreme Court decided that people have a privacy interest in this information. So, unless an emergency situation exists, police officers have to obtain search warrants before they can get access to people's cellphone company records.

> **EXAMPLE:** A robber holds up the Trust Bank. The police want to look through cellphone company records to see if any ex-cons who had been previously convicted of bank robbery were in the vicinity of Trust Bank prior to the robbery. The police will have to obtain search warrants for anyone whose cellphone company records they want to examine. To obtain a search warrant, the police will have to show a judge that they have enough evidence against an individual to constitute probable cause to believe that the individual committed the robbery.

How do the concepts of "reasonable suspicion" and "probable cause" affect police officers' powers?

When police officers have information that gives them "reasonable suspicion" that a person has committed a crime, the officers can briefly detain the person for a cursory investigation that is less than an arrest or complete search. If they also have reason to believe the detained person may be armed and dangerous, they can conduct a limited pat-down to check for concealed weapons.

Stronger information that gives officers "probable cause" to suspect that people have committed a crime allows police officers to arrest and search them. Depending on the circumstances, police officers may first need to obtain arrest and search warrants.

Can police officers detain people who they mistakenly believe have broken the law?

Yes—so long as the officer's mistake is objectively reasonable. (*Heien v. North Carolina*, U.S. Sup. Ct. 2014.)

> **EXAMPLE:** A police officer believes that a state's law makes it illegal to drive unless both of a car's taillights are working. In fact, state law is uncertain: The law may require only one taillight to be working. An officer pulls a driver over for driving with only one working taillight, and while talking to the driver notices packages of illegal drugs on the back seat. The officer then arrests the driver for possession of illegal drugs. Even if a judge decides that the driver did not break the taillight law, the officer's mistake was objectively reasonable, so the stop of the driver was valid. So was the arrest, because the officer had a right to be in the place from which the illegal drugs were plainly visible.

EXAMPLE: Assume the same facts as above, except that the officer does not see any illegal drugs inside the car. Instead, after stopping the driver (mistakenly, remember) for the taillight violation, the officer orders the driver to open the trunk. Inside the trunk, the officer sees a package of illegal drugs and arrests the driver. Now the arrest is illegal. The stop of the driver is still valid, but a taillight violation does not allow an officer to search a car's trunk.

How can an illegal search affect a criminal case?

In *Mapp v. Ohio* (1961), the Supreme Court established the "exclusionary rule." This rule provides that items seized in violation of the Fourth Amendment cannot be used as evidence against defendants in a criminal prosecution, state or federal. To this day, some commentators continue to criticize the *Mapp* case on the ground that it unfairly "lets the criminal go free because the constable has erred." In recent years, the U.S. Supreme Court has appeared to agree with these commentators with decisions that narrow the scope of the exclusionary rule. But supporters of *Mapp* argue that excluding illegally seized evidence is necessary to deter police from conducting illegal searches. According to this deterrence argument, the police won't conduct improper searches if they know the resulting evidence will be barred from the trial.

EXAMPLE: Officer Joe Friday notices teenager Bunny Schwartz walking in a mall. Officer Friday demands to look inside Bunny's purse. The officer finds three pairs of earrings with the price tags still attached. A mall jewelry store owner identifies the earrings as having been stolen minutes earlier, when Bunny was the only customer in the store. A judge rules that Officer Friday's search of Bunny's purse was improper. As a result, the charges against Bunny will have to be dropped. Because the search of her purse was illegal, the earrings are not admissible in evidence against her. The prosecution has no case without the earrings, so the charges must be dismissed. Realizing that Bunny went free ought to deter Officer Friday from conducting illegal searches in the future.

If the police conduct an illegal search, do criminal charges have to be dismissed?

No. A judge will exclude evidence that the police seized or learned about as the result of an illegal search. But if a prosecutor has enough other evidence to prove a defendant guilty, the case can continue.

EXAMPLE: Dick McCallous is charged with possession of stolen property: cleaning products stolen from a local janitorial supply business. Half of the missing janitorial products that McCallous is charged with possessing were discovered by the police in the course of a warrantless search of McCallous's home after they had properly arrested McCallous for possession of the other half. In response to a defense motion to exclude evidence, the judge rules that the police illegally seized the janitorial products from McCallous's home, but that the other products were seized properly. The prosecution of McCallous can go forward, but only as to illegal possession of the products that were properly seized.

If a police officer finds contraband or evidence of crime, does that validate an illegal search?

No. A search can't be justified by what it turns up. If a search is illegal to begin with, the products of that search, no matter how incriminating, are inadmissible in evidence.

Can illegally seized evidence be used in court for any purpose?

Yes. Cases decided after *Mapp* have established that the Fourth Amendment is not a complete bar to the use of illegally seized evidence. For example, a judge may consider illegally seized evidence when deciding on an appropriate sentence following the defendant's conviction, and illegally seized evidence is generally admissible in civil cases and deportation cases. In some circumstances, a prosecutor can also use improperly seized evidence to impeach (attack the credibility of) a witness who testifies during a court proceeding.

> **EXAMPLE:** Flo Kane is on trial for possessing illegal drugs. During a pretrial hearing, the trial judge ruled that the police had illegally seized a gun from Flo's bedroom, and that the prosecutor could not admit the gun into evidence. While testifying, Flo states, "I've never had a gun in my house." This

testimony allows the prosecutor to use the illegally seized gun to attack the credibility of Flo's testimony. Even though the search wasn't legal, the prosecutor may show Flo the illegally seized gun and ask her a question such as, "This gun was in your bedroom, correct?", or, "Your testimony that you've never had a gun in your house was incorrect, wasn't it?"

Do Fourth Amendment protections apply in every state?

Basically, yes. The Fourth Amendment provides rights for defendants that are binding on every state. In addition, many state constitutions contain language similar to that in the Fourth Amendment, and a state can validly interpret its own constitution to give defendants greater protection—but not less—than the Fourth Amendment provides.

What is the "fruit of the poisonous tree" doctrine?

The colorful rule known as the "fruit of the poisonous tree" doctrine makes inadmissible any evidence that police officers seize or any information that police officers obtain as a direct result of an improper search or seizure. The tree is the evidence that the police illegally seize in the first place; the fruit is the evidence that results from the illegally seized evidence. Both tree and fruit are inadmissible at trial. The fruit of the poisonous tree doctrine removes what would otherwise be a big incentive for police officers to conduct illegal searches.

EXAMPLE: Officer Wiley arrests Hy Lowe for selling phony telephone cards. A judge ruled that Officer Wiley had illegally entered Lowe's home and improperly seized a map showing the location where Lowe hid the phone cards. Officer Wiley then used the map to find and seize the phone cards. At trial, neither the map (the poisonous tree) nor the phone cards (the fruit) are admissible in evidence.

Can defendants plead guilty but reserve the right to challenge a search and have the guilty plea set aside if the search is held to be illegal?

In most states, by pleading guilty, a defendant waives (gives up) any claim that evidence was illegally seized. This rule can be a dilemma for defendants who unsuccessfully challenge the legality of a search at the trial court level, for these reasons:

- After a defendant's unsuccessful challenge to the admissibility of seized evidence, a guilty verdict may be an all-but-certain result at trial.
- To save the time and expense of a useless trial, the defendant may decide to plead guilty.
- By pleading guilty, however, the defendant loses the right to appeal the trial court's decision on the search and seizure issue.

Some states do allow defendants, under the right circumstances, to plead guilty while reserving the ability to challenge the seizure of evidence on appeal.

Search Warrants

This section explains what search warrants are and when they are necessary.

What is a search warrant?

A search warrant is an order signed by a judge that authorizes police officers to search for particular objects or materials at a specified location and time. For example, a warrant may authorize the search of "the premises at 11359 Happy Glade Avenue between the hours of 8 a.m. to 6 p.m.," and direct the police to search for and seize "cash, betting slips, record books, and every other means used in connection with placing bets on horse races and other sporting events." Police officers can take reasonable steps to protect themselves when conducting a search, such as handcuffing occupants while searching a house for weapons. (*Muehler v. Mena,* U.S. Sup. Ct. 2005.)

How do police officers obtain search warrants?

Police officers obtain warrants by providing a judge or magistrate with information indicating that probable cause for issuance of a warrant exists. Usually, the police provide the information in the form of written statements under oath, called affidavits, which report either their own observations or those of private citizens or police undercover informants. In many areas, a judicial officer is available 24 hours a day to issue warrants. A magistrate who believes that an affidavit establishes "probable cause" to conduct a search will issue a warrant. The suspect, who may be connected with the place to be searched, is not present when the warrant is issued and therefore cannot contest whether there is probable cause before the magistrate signs the warrant. However, the suspect can later challenge the validity of the warrant with a pretrial motion. (A sample affidavit for search warrant and a sample search warrant are at the end of this chapter.)

Police officers can also obtain an *anticipatory* search warrant—a warrant that issues before contraband arrives at the location to be searched—if they can show probable cause. (*U.S. v. Grubbs*, U.S. Sup. Ct. 2006.) For example, if the police demonstrate to a magistrate that illegal drugs are about to be shipped to a suspect's home, they can get a warrant that allows the police to search the home once the drugs are delivered.

How much information do police officers need to establish probable cause for a search warrant?

The Fourth Amendment doesn't define probable cause. It is an imprecise term, but its general meaning is that a "fair probability" exists that the police will find the described evidence of crime or contraband in the place to be searched. What is clear (after some 200 years of court interpretations) is that the affidavits police officers submit to judges have to identify objectively suspicious activities rather than simply recite the officers' subjective beliefs.

The affidavits have to establish more than a suspicion that criminal activity is afoot, but do not have to show proof beyond a reasonable doubt.

The information in an affidavit need not be in a form that would be admissible at trial. For example, a judge or magistrate may consider hearsay evidence that seems reliable, even if a judge might exclude it at trial. However, the circumstances set forth in an affidavit, viewed as a whole, should demonstrate the reliability of the information. (*Illinois v. Gates,* U.S. Sup. Ct. 1983.) In general, when deciding whether to issue a search warrant, a judge or magistrate will likely consider information in an affidavit reliable if it comes from any of these sources:

- a confidential police informant whose past reliability has been established or who has firsthand knowledge of illegal goings-on
- an informant who implicates himself or herself as well as the suspect
- an informant whose information appears to be correct after at least partial verification by the police
- a victim of a crime related to the search
- a witness to the crime related to the search, or
- another police officer.

EXAMPLE: Hoping to obtain a warrant to search Olive Martini's backyard, a police officer submits an affidavit to a magistrate. The affidavit states that "the undersigned is informed that Olive operates an illegal still in her backyard." The magistrate should not issue a search warrant based on this affidavit. Because the affidavit is too vague and the source of the information is unstated, there's no way for the magistrate to evaluate its reliability. The affidavit doesn't establish probable cause.

EXAMPLE: Same case. The affidavit states that "I am a social acquaintance of Olive Martini. On three occasions in the past two weeks, I have attended parties at Martini's house. On each occasion, I have personally observed Martini serving alcohol from a still in her backyard. I have personally tasted the drink and know it to be alcoholic with an impertinent aftertaste. I had no connection to the police when I attended these parties." This affidavit is reliable enough to establish probable cause for issuance of a warrant authorizing the police to search Martini's backyard. The affidavit provides detailed, firsthand information from an ordinary witness (without police connections) that indicates criminal activity is taking place.

"No Entry While We Obtain a Warrant"

It may take an hour or two (or longer) for police officers to obtain a warrant. To prevent suspects from destroying evidence inside homes while the police are waiting for a judge to issue a warrant, the police may station themselves outside homes and prevent suspects from entering them. (*Illinois v. McArthur*, U.S. Sup. Ct. 2001.)

What happens if a police officer makes a good-faith search pursuant to a warrant that shouldn't have been issued in the first place?

In *U.S. v. Leon* (1984), the U.S. Supreme Court ruled that if the police conduct a search in good-faith reliance on a warrant, the search is valid and the evidence is admissible, even if the warrant was in fact invalid through no fault of the police. The Court reasoned that:

- It makes no sense to condemn the results of a search when police officers have done everything reasonable to comply with Fourth Amendment requirements.
- The purpose of the rule excluding the results of an invalid search as evidence is to curb the police, not a judge. If a judge makes a mistake, excluding the evidence wouldn't serve any deterrent purpose.

For example, assume that a judge decides that an affidavit submitted by a police officer establishes probable cause to issue a warrant. Even if a reviewing court later disagrees and decides that the warrant shouldn't have been issued in the first place, the officer's search in good-faith reliance on the warrant will probably be considered valid, and whatever the search turns up will then be admissible in evidence. If, however, the warrant is issued on the basis of statements in the affidavit that the police knew to be untrue or made recklessly without proper regard for their truth, the evidence from a search based on the warrant may later be excluded. In this situation, the evidence would be excluded based on the police officer's actions, not on error by the judge.

EXAMPLE: Officer Furlong searches a residence for evidence of illegal bookmaking pursuant to a search warrant. The officer obtained the warrant by submitting an affidavit containing statements the officer knew to be false. The search is not valid because the police did not act in good faith. Officer Furlong used a false affidavit to obtain the warrant. Whatever the search turns up would not be admissible in evidence.

EXAMPLE: Officer Cal Ebrate stops a motorist for a traffic violation. A computer check of the driver's license reveals an arrest warrant for the driver. Officer Ebrate places the driver under arrest, searches the car, and finds illegal drugs. It later turns out that the computer record was wrong, and that no arrest warrant actually existed. Here, the officer acted in good-faith reliance on the computer record. Thus, the arrest and search were proper and the drugs are admissible in evidence against the driver, even though the record was wrong. (*Arizona v. Evans*, U.S. Sup. Ct. 1995; *Herring v. U.S.*, U.S. Sup. Ct. 2009.)

If the police have a warrant to search a backyard for marijuana plants, can they legally search the inside of the house as well?

No. The police can search only the place described in a warrant, and usually can seize only whatever property the warrant describes. The police cannot search a house if the warrant specifies the backyard, nor can they search for weapons if the warrant specifies marijuana plants. However, this does not mean that police officers can seize only items listed in the warrant. Should police officers come across contraband or evidence of a crime that is not listed in the warrant while properly searching for stuff that is listed, they can lawfully seize the unlisted items.

Can police officers search someone not named in a warrant?

Normally, the police can search only the person named in a warrant. Without probable cause, a police officer cannot search other persons who happen to be present at the scene of a search. However, if an officer has reason to suspect that an onlooker is also engaged in criminal activity, the officer might be able to "frisk" the onlooker for weapons. (But see "'Stop and Frisk' Searches," below.)

If police officers knock and demand to enter a home, what should a resident do?

Lawyers often advise people in this situation to do the following:

- ask, through the door, to see a search (or arrest) warrant
- ask the officers to display the warrant in some way that doesn't involve opening the door all the way (like through a peephole)
- to inspect a warrant further, open the door, step outside, and close the door
- allow the officers to enter upon seeing what looks like a legitimate warrant

- if there's no warrant, tell the officers politely, but loudly so anyone else around can hear, that they may not enter the home
- invoke the right to remain silent
- call an attorney for help as soon as possible
- while the officers are in the home, after asking for permission, observe the officers' activities
- make notes about everything that happened (including identifying information like officer names and badge numbers)
- ask others around to carefully watch what's going on, and
- do not interfere with the officers' search.

Why shouldn't people interfere with officers, even ones who enter without a warrant? Here are a few reasons:

- It is much safer to challenge a police officer's actions in court than in a home.
- Interfering with a police officer's search can lead to criminal charges.
- Perhaps a valid warrant has been issued, even though the officer does not have it. If so, the officer probably has the right to enter. (*United States v. Hector*, 9th Cir. 2007.)
- The officer may have a legal right to enter without a warrant. Police officers sometimes have the right to conduct searches and make arrests without a warrant.

"Well, Look What We Have Here"

The rule that police officers can seize items not listed in a search warrant in the course of searching for items that are listed creates obvious disincentives for police to list all the items they hope to find. For example, perhaps a police officer suspects that a defendant carries a weapon, but can't establish probable cause to search for it. No problem. The officer can obtain a search warrant for other items, and then seize a weapon if the officer comes upon it in the course of the search. The defendant's only hope of invalidating the seizure of the weapon would be to convince a judge that the officer did not just happen to come across the weapon, but in fact searched for it.

For example, assume that a search warrant authorizes police to search for shotguns. Carrying out the search, a police officer finds cocaine inside a small box in the defendant's sock drawer. The defendant is arrested and charged with possession of cocaine. The judge might rule that the drugs are inadmissible in evidence and dismiss the charges, because the police officer searched a container that could not possibly conceal a shotgun. The outcome might be different if the warrant authorized a search for shotguns and ammunition, however. This authorization would legitimate the search of the box, as long as it was big enough to hold shotgun shells.

Can nationwide search warrants expand the government's ability to engage in "cybersleuthing"?

Yes. If government agents convince a federal judge that probable cause exists to believe that suspects are engaged in a widespread Internet-based criminal scheme (such as infecting millions of computers with "malware"), the judge can issue a search warrant that allows the government to hack into computers all across the country. (See Fed. Rule of Crim. Proc. 41.)

Consent Searches

This section discusses when a warrantless search may be legally justified because the person in control of the property is said to have agreed to it.

If a person agrees to a search, is the search legal even if a police officer doesn't have a warrant or probable cause to search?

Yes. If a person freely and voluntarily agrees to a search, the search is valid and whatever the officers find is admissible in evidence.

For example, assume that Officer Mayer knocks on the door of Caryn-Sue's house. Officer Mayer suspects that Caryn-Sue is part of a group of suspects who are making pirated DVDs, but the officer lacks probable cause to search her house or arrest her. When Caryn-Sue answers the door, the following conversation takes place:

Officer: Good afternoon. I'm Officer Mayer. Is your name Caryn-Sue?

Caryn-Sue: Yes, it is. What can I do for you, officer?

Officer: I'm investigating the production of pirated DVDs, and I'd like to talk to you.

Caryn-Sue: Well, I'm not sure I can help you. I'm not under arrest or anything, am I?

Officer: No, but you may have information that can help the investigation. Do you mind if I come in and look around?

Caryn-Sue: I'm in the middle of a couple of things. Could you come back later?

Officer: If that's necessary. But it won't take long.

Caryn-Sue: We might as well get it over with if you can hurry. Look around all you want, there's nothing here of interest to you.

Officer Mayer enters Caryn-Sue's house, and in a corner of her living room closet notices hundreds of blank DVDs. The officer arrests Caryn-Sue for producing pirated DVDs and seizes the blank DVDs.

Under these circumstances, a judge would undoubtedly rule that the officer legally seized the blank DVDs. Though the officer had neither a warrant nor probable cause to search Caryn-Sue's house, Officer Mayer's search was valid because Caryn-Sue agreed to let the officer search her house. The fact that the officer was politely insistent on entering the house does not overcome the fact that Caryn-Sue consented to the entry before it was made.

"Knock and Notice" (or "Knock and Announce") Laws

Generally, police officers executing a search warrant on a residence must knock on the door, announce their presence, and give someone inside a chance to open the door. The rule protects the safety, privacy, and dignity of the person whose home is to be searched, as well as of the police officers. The Fourth Amendment has been interpreted to require the knock and notice procedure (*Wilson v. Arkansas*, U.S. Sup. Ct. 1995), and federal law also requires it (18 U.S.C. § 3109).

However, police officers don't have to follow the knock and notice procedure if they reasonably fear that it will result in violence or destruction of evidence, or if the procedure seems futile under the circumstances. (*Richards v. Wisconsin*, U.S. Sup. Ct. 1997.) Moreover, after knocking and announcing their presence, police officers need only delay entry for a reasonable time before entering, which can be only a few seconds depending on the circumstances. (*U.S. v. Banks*, U.S. Sup. Ct. 2003.)

The "exclusionary rule" does not apply to violations of the knock and notice rule. (*Hudson v. Michigan*, U.S. Sup. Ct. 2006.) (Not all state courts completely agree with that proposition, though.) This generally means that evidence is admissible at trial even if it was gathered by police officers who violated the knock and notice rule when carrying out an otherwise valid search.

Do police officers have to advise people of the right to refuse to consent to a search?

No. No equivalent to *Miranda* warnings exists in the search and seizure area. Police officers do not have to warn people that they have a right to refuse consent to a search. (*U.S. v. Drayton*, U.S. Sup. Ct. 2002; *Ohio v. Robinette*, U.S. Sup. Ct. 1996.)

> **EXAMPLE:** Jaime Costello is sitting on a park bench. Officer Abbot approaches Costello and asks to look through his backpack. Costello replies, "Sure, go ahead, I guess I can't stop you." The officer finds illegal drugs in the backpack and arrests him. The search was valid because Costello gave his consent. Officer Abbot had no duty to clear up Costello's misconception that he had no choice but to consent. Thus, the drugs are admissible in evidence.

> **EXAMPLE:** Officer Nemir boards a public bus as part of a routine drug and weapons search and asks George, "Mind if I check you?" George agrees, and a pat down suggests hard objects similar to drug packages. George is arrested, and a further search reveals that George had taped cocaine in both thigh areas. The search was valid because George gave his consent. The cocaine is admissible in evidence.

If a police officer tricks or coerces someone into consenting to a search, does the consent make the search legal?

Generally, no. To constitute a valid consent to search, the consent must be given "freely and voluntarily." If a police officer wrangles consent through trickery or coercion, the consent does not validate the search. Often, a defendant challenges a search on the grounds that consent was not voluntary, only to have a police officer testify to a conflicting version of events that establishes valid consent. In these conflict situations, judges tend to believe police officers unless defendants can support their claims through the testimony of other witnesses.

> **EXAMPLE:** In our earlier example, assume that before Caryn-Sue consents to Officer Mayer's entry into her home, Officer Mayer falsely told her, "It will do you no good to refuse me entry. I've got a warrant, so I'm prepared to come in whether or not you consent." Caryn-Sue replies, "If you've got a warrant, I might as well let you in. Look around all you want." In these circumstances, because of the officer's false claim of having a warrant, Caryn-Sue's consent to the search wasn't voluntary. However, it may be Caryn-Sue's word against the officer's as to whether the officer tricked her into consenting.

> **EXAMPLE:** Undercover cop Jones, posing as an employee of the gas company, asks Casey to allow him into Casey's home to check for an alleged gas leak. Casey agrees. Jones enters and sees drugs and drug paraphernalia in the kitchen. Jones's entry into and search

of Casey's home is invalid. Consent that is obtained by fraud is not considered voluntary, and Jones's story that he was a gas company employee is fraud.

> **EXAMPLE:** Same case, but this time Jones has been posing as a parent in Casey's son's school and has made friends with Casey independent of his undercover mission. Casey invites his "friend" Jones in to play cards. Once inside the home, undercover agent Jones unexpectedly sees illegal drugs. He seizes the drugs and arrests Casey. In this situation, Casey was not tricked or coerced in any way to let Jones in. He just didn't know who his friend really was. The Constitution does not protect people from the consequences of having what courts call a "false friend." Jones's behavior was valid.

If someone opens the door to talk to a police officer who doesn't have a warrant and the officer enters without permission and searches, is the search valid?

No. Merely opening the door to a police officer does not constitute consent to entry and search. Thus, whatever such a search turns up would be inadmissible in evidence. Of course, if contraband or evidence of a crime is in "plain view" from the doorway, the officer may be able to seize it. (See "The Plain View Doctrine," below.)

Can someone consent to a limited police search of only one room?

Technically, yes. Where only limited consent is given, that limitation is supposed to be honored. But if the police, in the course of making a limited search, see evidence of illegal activity elsewhere, they may properly search and seize it. Also, once in a home, the police are very skilled at obtaining consent from the homeowner to expand the scope of the search.

EXAMPLE: Officer Zack asks permission to search Mike's residence for marijuana plants. Mike agrees. Officer Zack proceeds with the search, goes into Mike's desk, and reviews some of the documents he finds there. The search is invalid under the Fourth Amendment. Mike agreed only to the limited search for marijuana plants, and there were obviously no such plants in the documents that Officer Zack reviewed.

EXAMPLE: Officer Zack asks, and Mike agrees, to allow a search of Mike's home for narcotics. In the course of the search, the officer finds a closet containing an illegal weapon, which the officer seizes. The search is valid. The weapon was readily seen in a place where narcotics might be found.

Is consent to a search valid if it's a product of feeling intimidated by the presence of a police officer?

Yes. Many people are intimidated by police officers, and may even perceive a request to search as a command. However, as long as an officer does not engage in threatening behavior, judges will not set aside otherwise genuine consent.

EXAMPLE: The owner of a massage parlor agrees to allow police officers to search her business premises. At the time the owner consents, she has been handcuffed, she is in the presence of seven male police officers, the officers had already physically subdued and pointed a gun at an employee, the officers had threatened to tear up the premises, and the owner was of foreign descent and unfamiliar with the American criminal process. Even in these circumstances, a court upheld the owner's consent. (*State v. Kyong Cha Kim*, 779 P.2d 512 (Montana 1989). Despite the outcome of this case, another judge in another jurisdiction might find this type of police conduct so coercive or threatening as to make the consent involuntary.

If one roommate consents to a police search and the search turns up evidence that incriminates another roommate, can the evidence be used against the second roommate?

The answer often depends on whether the suspect is present when the other person gives consent. If the suspect is personally present and refuses to consent when the police ask for permission to search, the search is invalid. Even if the person who shares the residence has agreed to the search, the suspect's refusal means that evidence cannot be used against the suspect. (*Georgia v. Randolph*, U.S. Sup. Ct. 2006.) If the police have probable cause to arrest the occupant who objects to the search, an officer can arrest and remove the objecting occupant, then search the residence based on the consent of the other occupant. (*Fernandez v. California*, U.S. Sup. Ct. 2014.)

If a spouse, roommate, or cotenant agrees to a search in a suspect's absence, and the search turns up evidence that incriminates the suspect, the evidence might well be admissible in evidence at trial. An adult in rightful possession of a house or apartment usually has legal authority to consent to a search of the entire premises. But if there are two or more separate tenants in one dwelling, courts often rule that one tenant has no power to consent to a search of the areas exclusively controlled by the other tenants (for instance, their separate bedrooms).

A tricky twist is that the other person's consent will be considered valid if the police reasonably believe that person has the authority to consent—even if that belief turns out to be wrong.

> **EXAMPLE:** Bob's ex-wife Jan knows where Bob hides his cocaine. She calls the police and tells them about the cocaine. She directs them to Bob's house. When they get there, she opens the door with a key (she never returned it to Bob when she moved out). She puts her purse on the entry hall table, opens the hall closet, and puts on a sweater that appears to be hers. She then leads the police to the place where Bob stores his cocaine. As far as the police know, Jan lives in the apartment and has full authority to consent to the search. Even though Jan and the police entered the apartment without Bob's permission, the search did not violate Bob's Fourth Amendment rights. The police reasonably (though mistakenly) thought that Jan had the authority to consent to the search.

Can a landlord validly consent to a police officer's request to search a tenant's apartment?

No. The landlord is not considered to be in possession of an apartment leased to a tenant, and therefore lacks authority to consent to a search of leased premises.

Can the police search someone's hotel room without a warrant?

The general rule is, no. Again, however, an exception (such as consent or an emergency) may exist that would justify a warrantless hotel room search.

Is an employer's consent to a police search of an employee's workspace valid?

Probably. An employer can validly consent to a search of company premises. An employer's consent extends to employees' work areas, such as desks and machinery. However, police officers might need a warrant to search a clearly private area, such as an employee's clothes locker.

Can a child consent to a police search of a home while the parents are away?

This depends primarily on the child's age. The younger the child, the less authority the child would have to consent to a search. A state might, for example, require a child to be at least 12 to consent, with the child appearing to be "in charge" of the house at the time.

The Plain View Doctrine

This section covers warrantless searches and seizures that are considered valid because the police officer initially spotted contraband or evidence that was in the officer's plain view.

If a police officer enters a home legally, can the officer seize illegal drugs that are on a countertop?

Yes. A police officer does not need a warrant to seize contraband or evidence that is in plain view from where the officer has a right to be. An officer's seizure of an object in plain view does not violate the Fourth Amendment because the officer has not conducted a search.

> **EXAMPLE:** During daylight hours, Officer Mendoza stops a car for having an expired license plate. When Officer Mendoza approaches the driver, the officer sees a packet of what appears to be illegal drugs on the front seat of the car. The officer seizes the packet and arrests the driver. The seizure was legal because the drugs were in plain view. Though the officer had no probable cause to search the car at the moment the officer pulled the car over, seeing the illegal drugs on the front seat gave the officer a valid basis for the seizure.

> **EXAMPLE:** Same case, except that the traffic stop occurs at night and Officer Mendoza sees the packet of drugs on the front seat only after shining a flashlight into the interior of the car. The seizure of the drugs is still legal. As long as police officers are standing where they have a right to be, objects that they see with the aid of a flashlight are in plain view.

> **EXAMPLE:** Officer Tanaka pulls a car over for running a red light. When the driver rolls down the window, Officer Tanaka detects a strong odor of marijuana emanating from inside the car. The officer orders the driver out of the car and conducts a search. Underneath the driver's seat, the officer finds and seizes a pouch filled with marijuana. The seizure is legal. Smelling the marijuana gave Officer Tanaka probable cause to believe that the car contained illegal drugs (under what has come to be called the "plain smell" doctrine). The officer could therefore conduct an immediate search, without having to obtain a search warrant first.

If a police officer illegally enters a house and observes evidence in plain view, can the officer seize the evidence?

No. A police officer can seize objects in plain view only if the officer has a legal right to be in the place from which the objects can be seen or smelled. If an officer has no legal right to be where the evidence or contraband is spotted, the plain view doctrine doesn't apply.

> **EXAMPLE:** Two police officers in a helicopter fly over the backyard of a home as they are returning from the scene of a highway collision. Aided by binoculars, one of the officers sees a large number of marijuana plants growing in a greenhouse in the backyard. The officers report what they have seen, a search warrant is obtained, and the occupant of the house is arrested and charged with growing illegal drugs for sale. The officers' search of the backyard was

legal. The police officers had a right to be in public airspace, and the occupant had no reasonable expectation of privacy for what could be seen from that space. (Maybe this is an example of "plane view.") The outcome might be different if the police officer had spotted the plants from a space station using advanced technology spying equipment. The homeowner might reasonably expect that the backyard would not be subjected to that type of surveillance.

"Dropsy" Cases

The plain view doctrine has the potential to be abused by police officers looking for a way to get drugs or other incriminating evidence admitted at trial, even if the contraband was seized through searches that might not withstand judicial scrutiny. To eliminate the Fourth Amendment problem, an officer might testify that the defendants dropped the contraband on the ground just before they were arrested. Voilà, the contraband was in plain view. Over the years, an amazing number of defendants have developed dropsy problems!

Warrantless Searches Incident to Arrest

This section deals with warrantless searches that are considered valid because they were made in the course of making a valid arrest.

Can officers legally search someone they have arrested?

Yes. Police officers do not need a warrant to make a search "incident to an arrest." After an arrest, police officers have the right to protect themselves by searching for weapons and to protect the legal case against the suspect by searching for evidence that the suspect might try to destroy. Assuming that the officer has probable cause to make the arrest in the first place, a search of the person and the person's immediate surroundings following the arrest is valid, and any evidence uncovered is admissible at trial.

If probable cause exists, the Fourth Amendment allows police officers to arrest and search suspects for committing minor offenses that usually result in citations rather than arrests. (*Virginia v. Moore*, U.S. Sup. Ct. 2008.)

Can the police take DNA samples from arrested suspects?

In many cases, yes. The police can take DNA samples from suspects who are arrested for serious crimes regardless of whether they are ever charged with a crime or are charged and found not guilty. (*Maryland v. King*, U.S. Sup. Ct. 2013.) The U.S. Supreme Court has justified the DNA "search" as a method of identifying suspects who have been arrested. But the dissenters argued that this justification is silly, and that the real reason that police want to take DNA samples from arrestees is to see if they can use the samples in "fishing expeditions" to find out whether arrestees committed older unsolved crimes.

Can a jailer strip search an arrestee who is locked up for a minor offense?

Yes. To prevent items such as illegal drugs, alcohol, and weapons from being brought into jails, jailers have the right to conduct random and warrantless strip searches of all arrestees who are booked into jail— even those who are brought in for a minor offense, and even those who are arrested mistakenly, based on an expired warrant. (*Florence v. Burlington*, U.S. Sup. Ct. 2012.)

Statutes in many jurisdictions narrow the scope of *Florence v. Burlington* by limiting the offenses for which jailers can strip search arrestees. For example, one statute establishes a general rule that people arrested for a traffic, regulatory, or misdemeanor offense cannot be strip-searched. The rule allows strip searches if an arrest is for a violent offense, or if a weapon or illegal drugs are involved.

If an arrest takes place on the street or in a shopping mall, can the arresting officer search the arrested person's dwelling or car?

No. To justify a search as incident to an arrest, a spatial relationship must exist between the arrest and the search. The general rule is that the police may search the arrested person and the area within that person's immediate control. (*Chimel v. California*, U.S. Sup. Ct. 1969.) For example, an arresting officer may search not only a suspect's clothes, but also a suspect's wallet or purse. If an arrest takes place in a kitchen, the arresting officer can probably search the kitchen, but not the rest of the house. If an arrest takes place outside a house, the arresting officer cannot search the house at all. To conduct a search broader in scope than a defendant and the area within the defendant's immediate control, an officer would have to obtain a warrant.

> **EXAMPLE:** Officer Montoya arrests Sarah Adams for driving under the influence of drugs. Before taking Sarah to jail, Officer Montoya takes Sarah's key and enters her apartment. Inside, Officer Montoya finds a number of computers. He checks their serial numbers and finds out that they have been stolen. Officer Montoya seizes the computers as evidence and adds possession of stolen property to the charges against Sarah. The computers are not admissible in evidence. The officer should have obtained a search warrant before entering Sarah's apartment. Because Officer Montoya had no right to be inside the house in the first place, it doesn't matter that the computers were in plain view once he was inside.

Don't Go Back in the House

When the police arrest suspects outside their residences and have no basis for making a "protective sweep," officers may try to expand the scope of a permissible search by offering to let suspects go inside to get a change of clothes or feed a pet before taking the suspect to jail. While accompanying the suspect inside the residence, officers can seize whatever may be in plain view (for instance, drugs). Thus, suspects may wisely refuse an invitation by the arresting officers to let the suspect enter the residence, and instead rely on their friends if they need clothes or pet care.

If someone is arrested in a car, or shortly after leaving it, do the police need a warrant to search the interior of the car?

No. If the police arrest a suspect in or around a car, they don't need a warrant to search its interior. (*Thornton v. U.S.,* U.S. Sup. Ct. 2004.) They probably would need a warrant to search the trunk, however. If a police officer arrests a driver for violating a traffic rule, the officer cannot search the car without a warrant unless the officer has reason to believe that the car contains a weapon or evidence of crime that someone other than the driver might take. (*Arizona v. Gant*, U.S. Sup. Ct. 2009.)

Can the police conduct a warrantless search of the information stored in an arrestee's cellphone?

No. Unless emergency ("exigent") circumstances exist, an arrest does not justify the search of the contents of a mobile phone (or a similar electronic device). The police would have to obtain a search warrant by describing facts that satisfy a judge or magistrate that probable cause for a search exists. (*Riley v. California*, U.S. Sup. Ct. 2013.) The U.S. Supreme Court's *Riley* opinion emphasized the impact on privacy that would result if warrantless searches of mobile phones were valid, because people generally have access to vast quantities of personal information through their mobile phones. (The same rule should apply to electronic devices that are similar to mobile phones, such as laptops and tablets.)

Even if a police officer obtains a warrant to search a suspect's cellphone, courts differ as to whether the suspect has to provide the pass code that unlocks the phone. Equally unclear is whether a police officer can compel a suspect to unlock a phone that is protected with facial recognition software or other locking tools. Decisions about these matters will require judges to balance suspects' privacy interests against the social interest in uncovering evidence of crime.

If an arrest takes place outside a home, can the police go inside to look for accomplices?

Sometimes. Police officers can make protective sweeps following an arrest. (*Maryland v. Buie,* U.S. Sup. Ct. 1990.) When making a protective sweep, police officers can walk through a residence and make a cursory visual inspection of places where an accomplice might be hiding. For example, police officers could look under beds and inside closets. To justify making a protective sweep, police officers must have a reasonable belief that a dangerous accomplice might be hiding inside a residence. If a sweep is lawful, the police can legally seize contraband or evidence of crime that is in plain view.

> **EXAMPLE:** Police officers have warrants to arrest Fox and Mulder for armed bank robbery. Fox and Mulder live together in a house. Officers Spock and Kirk stake out the house and arrest Fox coming up the

driveway. With Fox in custody, Officer Spock goes into the house to conduct a protective sweep. Spock goes into a bedroom, lifts up a mattress and seizes a gun hidden between the mattress and the box spring. Witnesses later identify the gun as the one used in the bank robbery. Spock did not lawfully seize the gun. Because Fox and Mulder lived together, Fox was arrested outside the house, and they were suspected of committing a violent crime together, Spock probably had the right to make a protective sweep to look for Mulder. However, although Spock had a right to look under the bed, Spock had no right to lift up the mattress because nothing suggested that Mulder might be hiding between the mattress and box spring. After making sure that Mulder wasn't in the house, the officers should have secured the house and gotten a search warrant.

If an arrest takes place inside a home, can the police search the home?

They can to a certain extent. They may search the person arrested and the area within that person's immediate control. Immediate control is interpreted broadly to include any place a suspect may lunge to obtain a weapon. If the alleged crime is particularly violent, or if the police have reason to believe other armed suspects may be in the residence, the police may do a protective sweep to search any place such accomplices may be hiding. Also, while they are making a lawful arrest or protective sweep, the police may typically search and seize anything that is in plain

view and appears to be related to criminal activity.

Do guests have the same privacy rights as homeowners or tenants?

The answer depends on why the guests are there. If the guests are there for a brief commercial transaction or an illegal purpose and are not staying overnight, then they do not have the same privacy rights as social overnight guests and may not be able to successfully challenge a police search that took place in their host's home. (*Minnesota v. Carter*, U.S. Sup. Ct. 1998.)

> **EXAMPLE:** Mark hosts a weekly poker game at his apartment. One night the game included his neighbor Bobby. After a neighbor complained about a strange smell coming from Mark's apartment, the police arrived and, although they didn't have a warrant, searched the premises. In a cabinet in the bathroom, they found a baggie of illegal drugs belonging to Bobby. Bobby is arrested and charged with possession of illegal drugs. Bobby cannot exclude the drugs from evidence. As a temporary social guest who was not staying overnight, Bobby has no privacy right in the search of Mark's apartment.

Is a search following an illegal arrest valid?

No. If an officer lacks probable cause to make an arrest, the invalid arrest cannot validate a search. Any evidence found during a search following an improper arrest is generally inadmissible in evidence.

If an officer's search of an arrestee turns up evidence of an entirely different crime, is the evidence admissible at trial?

Yes. An officer can seize whatever evidence a proper search incident to an arrest turns up. As long as the search is valid, it doesn't matter if a seized object has nothing to do with the crime for which the defendant was arrested.

Can an arrest justify a search if a police officer improperly detains a person before finding out about a basis for making a legitimate arrest?

Yes. The "attenuation rule" means that, if the connection between unlawful police behavior and evidence is remote enough or interrupted, the evidence is admissible. The "attenuation rule" chips away at the exclusionary rule because a search can result in admissible evidence even if the search starts with an improper stop.

> **EXAMPLE:** A police officer improperly detains Strieff, who is leaving the house of a suspected drug dealer. After learning that Strieff has an outstanding arrest warrant, the officer places Strieff under arrest and searches him. The search turns up illegal drugs. The drugs are admissible in evidence against Strieff, because the arrest warrant attenuated the improper detention. (*Utah v. Strieff*, U.S. Supreme Court 2016.)

"Stop and Frisk" Searches

This section describes when police officers may conduct a limited search of a person for the purpose of assuring the officers' safety.

What is the "stop and frisk" rule?

The U.S. Supreme Court sanctioned stop and frisk searches in *Terry v. Ohio* (1968). A police officer need only have a reasonable suspicion of criminal behavior to detain and question a person (the "stop"). For self-protection, an officer who reasonably suspects that he's in danger can at the same time carry out a limited pat-down search for weapons (the "frisk"). This rule applies whether the suspects are on foot or in a car. A "reasonable suspicion" requires more than a hunch or a mere distrust; the officer must have objective grounds, based on all of the circumstances, to suspect that a person is involved in criminal activity.

> **EXAMPLE:** Officer Crosby sees Stills and Nash talking normally on a street corner. Having a hunch that a drug transaction may be underway, the officer detains and frisks the pair. The officer finds a gun in Nash's pocket and arrests him. Under these circumstances, Officer Crosby had no right to detain Stills and Nash in the first place. A "hunch" doesn't authorize detention; an officer must have "articulable facts supporting a reasonable suspicion." (*U.S. v. Hensley*, U.S. Sup. Ct. 1985.) Because the initial detention was improper, the frisk incident to that detention was also improper, and the result of the frisk—the gun—is inadmissible.

> **EXAMPLE:** Officer Jacks sees Jill hiding under the steps of an apartment building. As the officer approaches, Jill runs away. Officer Jacks chases and detains Jill. She is fidgety, looks angry, and is moving her hands toward her pockets. Officer Jacks pats her down for

weapons. The officer removes a hard object that turns out to be a plastic envelope containing burglar's tools. Officer Jacks can legally seize the tools because Jacks had a reasonable basis for suspecting that Jill was engaged in criminal activity and that she was dangerous. The officer had the right to detain Jill, pat her down, and remove an object that might have been a weapon.

EXAMPLE: Officer Ross spots Wade's minivan on a little-used road sometimes frequented by drug smugglers. Wade is driving at a time when border patrol officers commonly change shifts. Officer Ross, who knows that drug smugglers often use minivans, runs a check on the vehicle and finds that it is registered to an address in a block notorious for drug smuggling. Officer Ross stops Wade and asks to search the van, and Wade consents. A subsequent search of the minivan reveals 130 pounds of marijuana. Under these circumstances, Officer Ross had a reasonable suspicion that Wade was engaged in illegal behavior. Because the stop was legal and the resulting search was consensual, the marijuana is admissible as evidence. (*U.S. v. Arvizu*, U.S. Sup. Ct. 2002.)

What's the difference between a search and a frisk?

A search is more extensive. An officer conducting a full search can probe extensively for any type of contraband or evidence. A frisk allows officers only to conduct a cursory pat-down and to seize weapons

(such as guns and knives), objects that feel like weapons, or objects that an officer can tell from a plain feel are contraband. (*Minnesota v. Dickerson*, U.S. Sup. Ct. 1993.)

EXAMPLE: Officer Mace pulls over a driver who resembles a suspect wanted for armed bank robbery. Officer Mace asks the driver to get out of the car, then frisks the driver. The officer feels a soft packet in the driver's back pocket. With the packet still in the driver's pocket, the officer pokes a finger through the packaging into the packet, rubs powder from the packet onto his finger, removes his finger, and decides from the powder's appearance and smell that it is an illegal drug. The officer removes the packet and arrests the driver for possession of illegal drugs. The contents of the packet are not admissible in evidence. The officer had reasonable grounds for detaining the driver, but lacked probable cause to arrest the driver and conduct a full search. Therefore, all the officer could do was frisk the driver and seize either a weapon or contraband in plain feel. Because the soft packet could not reasonably have been mistaken for a weapon, and the officer had to manipulate the packet before deciding that it contained illegal drugs, the officer had no right to remove it from the driver's pocket.

EXAMPLE: Same case, except that Officer Mace testifies that, "When I frisked the driver, I felt a packet of little pebbles that felt like rock cocaine, so I seized it." Under these circumstances the rock cocaine is admissible in evidence. The officer could tell from a plain feel that the packet contained illegal drugs, so the seizure is valid. (Note: Police officers are generally very "up" on the law of search and seizure and know what a judge needs to hear in order to uphold a particular seizure and admit the evidence in court.)

Does the stop and frisk rule give police officers the right to regularly detain and hassle people based on their appearance or ethnicity?

No. Regardless of the way a person looks, the type of neighborhood, or the time of day, an officer can detain someone only if the officer can point to objective circumstances showing a reasonable basis that the person is engaged in suspicious behavior. Undoubtedly, however, some police officers illegally use stop and frisk to harass "undesirables," confident that they can later articulate enough circumstances to justify the detention. Again, for their own personal safety, people who believe that they are unfair targets of police harassment should put their claims before a judge rather than act belligerently on the street.

If a police officer sees a person toss away a packet, can the officer pick the packet up and arrest the person who tossed it if it contains illegal drugs?

Yes. The officer neither detained the person nor conducted a search. The officer had the right to pick up whatever was tossed away and to make an arrest when the object turned out to be illegal drugs.

Searches of Cars and Occupants

Based on the mobility of cars and the potential risks of traffic stops both for police officers and drivers, judges are reluctant to second-guess an officer's decision to pull a driver over and search the driver and passengers.

What are the basic "dos and don'ts" for police officers who pull drivers over for traffic violations?

Police officers who detain motorists for traffic violations typically issue tickets and allow them to proceed. However, if they have probable cause to believe that motorists have committed a traffic offense, police officers have the power to arrest and search motorists. (*Virginia v. Moore*, U.S. Sup. Ct. 2009.) Even if they plan only to issue a ticket, police officers can order drivers and any passengers to get out of a car. If police officers "reasonably believe" that drivers or passengers might be carrying weapons, they can conduct a short "frisk" (pat down the car's occupants). (*Maryland v. Wilson*, U.S. Sup. Ct. 1998.) However, police officers cannot search a car without a warrant based on a traffic violation unless they have reason to believe that the car contains a weapon or evidence of crime that someone other than the driver might dispose of. (*Arizona v. Gant*, U.S. Sup. Ct. 2009.) A traffic stop generally continues until the police officer says that the driver is free to leave. Before telling the driver that a stop has ended, police officers can briefly question the driver and passengers about matters unrelated to the purpose of the stop. (*Arizona v. Johnson*, U.S. Sup. Ct. 2009.)

On the other hand, police officers cannot use traffic stops as a pretext to launch extensive investigations. Unless the police have probable cause to believe that a car or its trunk contains weapons or contraband, the police cannot search a car that has been pulled over for a traffic violation. Similarly, unless police officers have probable cause to believe that a driver or passenger has committed a serious crime, the officers cannot use the stop as a pretext to interrogate the car's occupants about other possible crimes.

> **EXAMPLE:** Officer Colombo pulls a car over for making an illegal left turn. Inside the car are four teenagers. The officer has no reason to believe that criminal activity has taken place. Nevertheless, Officer Colombo orders the driver and passengers out of the car. As one of the passengers gets out of the car, a packet of cocaine falls out of his shirt pocket. Officer Colombo arrests that teenager for possession of illegal drugs. The arrest and seizure of the drugs is valid. Officer Colombo had the right to order the occupants out of the car. Once the packet of cocaine fell out of the teenager's pocket and was in plain view, Officer Colombo had the right to make the arrest.

> **EXAMPLE:** Officer Colombo pulls a car over for making an illegal left turn. Inside the car are four teenagers. The officer has no reason to believe that any of the occupants are armed or involved in criminal activity. Nevertheless, Officer Colombo orders the driver and passengers out of the car and frisks them. During the frisk, the officer feels what he believes to be a weapon in the jacket pocket of one of the teenagers. The officer reaches in, pulls out a packet of cocaine, and arrests the teenager for possession of illegal drugs. The arrest is invalid. Officer Colombo had the right to order the car's occupants out of the car, but had no basis to conduct a frisk. And, because a frisk can't be justified by what it turns up, the arrest based on the illegal frisk is itself illegal. (See "'Stop and Frisk' Searches," above.)

> **EXAMPLE:** Officer Colombo pulls a car over for making an illegal left turn. Inside the car are four teenagers. The officer had received a police radio call indicating that four youths had robbed a liquor store and escaped in a car resembling the one pulled over. Based on that information, Officer Colombo orders the driver and passengers out of the car and frisks them. In the course of one of the frisks, the officer feels what he believes to be a weapon in the jacket pocket of one of the teenagers. The officer reaches in, pulls out a packet of cocaine, and arrests the teenager for possession of illegal drugs. It turns out that none of the car's occupants were connected to the liquor store robbery. The arrest and seizure of the drugs were nonetheless valid. The radio call gave Officer Colombo reason to suspect that the car's occupants had been involved in the robbery, which gave the officer the right to frisk the occupants. The officer could then seize the drugs discovered during the frisk and arrest their owner.

When Can Police Use Checkpoints?

In recent years, police forces in many communities have set up roadblocks—also called checkpoints—at which police officers stop and inspect all drivers and vehicles passing along a road. Because the police typically lack probable cause to believe that any particular driver who is stopped has broken a law, checkpoints could violate the Fourth Amendment.

For a checkpoint to be valid, the police must follow the same procedures with respect to all motorists on a route; they cannot discriminatorily target any particular driver. Even if the police follow the same procedures for all drivers, a roadblock may still be illegal if its purpose is not closely tied to highway safety and instead is directed only at general crime control. A few U.S. Supreme Court cases illustrate this distinction:

- "Sobriety" checkpoints are valid. The goal of improving highway safety, combined with checkpoints' minimal intrusiveness, means that police officers can stop drivers at checkpoints and detain those suspected of driving under the influence. (*Michigan State Police v. Sitz*, U.S. Sup. Ct. 1990.)

- "Illegal immigrant" checkpoints in areas near border crossings are also generally valid. (*U.S. v. Martinez-Fuerte*, U.S. Sup. Ct. 1976.)

- "Narcotics checkpoints" set up to detect illegal drugs are not valid. The goal of apprehending people carrying drugs— while socially beneficial—is not sufficiently tied to roadway safety to overcome the Fourth Amendment prohibition of unreasonable searches and seizures. (*Indianapolis v. Edmond*, U.S. Sup. Ct. 2000.)

- "Investigatory checkpoints" are often lawful. If the police set up a roadblock in order to gather evidence to help solve a crime, they can temporarily stop and question motorists in the same area and around the same time of day that the crime occurred. The police can also lawfully arrest a driver for drunk driving if the driver enters an investigatory checkpoint while under the influence of alcohol. (*Illinois v. Lidster*, U.S. Sup. Ct. 2004.)

What is an "inventory search"?

Police officers may arrest drivers for a nonroutine traffic violation such as a DUI, reckless driving, or a violation of child restraint laws. If the owner can reach a responsible adult who can come for the car, an officer may leave it parked and locked. Otherwise, the police may have the car towed to an impound lot and inventory its contents. The inventory promotes the safety of the impound lot (maybe the car contains explosives or a weapon) and protects the police against claims that a driver's property was stolen from the car.

In the course of inventorying a car's contents, the police may find objects that constitute evidence of criminal activity or contraband, such as illegal drugs or weapons. If so, the police can legally seize the objects. But an inventory search is not necessarily a blank check for the police to rummage through all of a driver's belongings. For example, an arrest for a DUI would not necessarily justify an inventory search of a trunk or a locked glove compartment.

Can police officers pull a car over for a traffic violation when their true motive is to find evidence of criminal activity?

Yes. Judges generally ignore police officers' subjective motivation when evaluating the legality of their conduct. If a police officer has a valid basis for detaining a motorist (even a nitpicky one like a broken taillight), the stop is valid no matter what the officer's subjective purposes might be. (*Whren v. U.S.*, U.S. Sup. Ct. 1996; *Arkansas v. Sullivan*, U.S. Sup. Ct. 2001.) However, police officers cannot search a car without a warrant based only on a traffic violation unless they have reason to believe that the car contains a weapon or evidence of crime that someone other than the driver might dispose of. (*Arizona v. Gant*, U.S. Sup. Ct. 2009.)

EXAMPLE: Officer Colombo sees an old, battered car being driven at night by an unkempt driver in a wealthy section of town, and suspects that the driver might be planning to commit a crime. The officer notices that the light over the car's rear license plate isn't illuminated. The officer uses that minor traffic violation as an excuse to pull the car over and sees illegal drugs on the passenger seat. Officer Colombo then arrests the driver for possession of illegal drugs. The arrest and seizure of the drugs were valid.

Whatever his motivation, the minor infraction gave Officer Colombo the right to stop the vehicle. Seeing the drugs in plain view gave the officer the right to make the arrest.

"Driving While Black"

Many drivers are convinced that the police stop them simply because they have dark skin. In other words, they are pulled over solely because they are "driving while Black." The police uniformly deny that this occurs, but some do admit to acting on the basis of criminal profiles that often include racial or ethnic factors. For instance, cars driven by people who appear to be of Hispanic descent arguably are more likely to be stopped near the Mexico–U.S. border—because of suspicion of illegal immigration activity—than are cars driven by folks with other characteristics. Similarly, cars driven by African Americans may be more susceptible to a stop in neighborhoods populated by rich Caucasian people than those driven by people with Caucasian characteristics, especially if the hour is late and the car is an expensive model.

As long as the police have a legitimate reason to stop the vehicle (such as a minor traffic violation), then the stop generally doesn't violate the Fourth Amendment, even if the real reason for the stop is the person's race or ethnic background. (*Whren v. U.S.*, U.S. Sup. Ct. 1996.) However, the *Whren* case also suggests that this sort of police behavior may violate the Fourteenth Amendment's guarantee of equal protection of the law to all U.S. citizens.

Can police officers pull a car over based on information provided by an anonymous tipster?

Yes. Just as "reasonable suspicion" that a person committed a crime can justify a police officer's "stop and frisk" search, credible information from an anonymous tipster can constitute "reasonable suspicion" that allows a police officer to make an investigatory traffic stop. (*Navarette v. California*, U.S. Sup. Ct. 2014.)

> **EXAMPLE:** An anonymous 911 caller identifies the make, model, and license plate number of a car that drove her off the road. A patrol officer makes an investigatory stop of the driver of a car that matched the caller's description. Even though the officer did not personally observe suspicious driving, the officer had the right under the Fourth Amendment to pull the driver over for investigation. The caller's detailed and personal observations gave the officer reason to suspect that the driver was intoxicated. When the officer finds a large package of marijuana in the car, the officer has probable cause to seize the package and arrest the driver.

> **EXAMPLE:** Unbeknownst to the patrol officer, the 911 caller in the above example decided to take revenge against the driver—who the caller knew was transporting illegal drugs—by making up a phony story about being driven off the road. Because the information appears to be credible, the officer's investigatory stop of the driver, the seizure of the marijuana, and the arrest of the driver are all valid.

Does a traffic stop constitute a seizure of a car's passengers as well as of its driver?

Yes. When police officers pull cars over, neither the drivers nor the passengers generally believe that they are free to simply walk off. Therefore, for purposes of the Fourth Amendment, police officers who carry out traffic stops "seize" all of a car's occupants. (*Brendlin v. California*, U.S. Sup. Ct. 2007.) This allows drivers and passengers alike to challenge the legality of a stop and any ensuing searches and arrests. It also gives police officers the same power over passengers as over drivers. For example, officers may run the criminal histories of all of a car's occupants.

If the police have probable cause to search a car, do they have to obtain a warrant first?

No. Cars are not like dwellings. If the police have probable cause to search a car, they may do so. They do not need a warrant, even if they have adequate time to obtain one. (*Maryland v. Dyson*, U.S. Sup. Ct. 1999.) The basic reasons for this exception to the warrant rule are that cars can easily be moved, and courts have held that people don't have the same expectation of privacy in their vehicles as they do in their places of residence.

> **EXAMPLE:** Officer Ness receives information from a reliable informant that Jones has just purchased a large shipment of illegal weapons. The informant tells the officer that the weapons are in Jones's car, and gives the officer a full description of the car and the location to which Jones is taking the weapons. With this information, Officer Ness has probable

cause to obtain a search warrant. However, instead of obtaining a warrant, Officer Ness goes directly to the location, searches Jones's car, finds the weapons, and places Jones under arrest. The arrest and seizure were probably valid. Officer Ness had probable cause to believe that contraband was present in the car and was therefore entitled to search it without first obtaining a warrant.

If the police have probable cause to search a car, can they also search objects belonging to passengers?

Yes. Once they have probable cause to search a car, the police don't have to worry about whether the objects they are searching belong to the driver or the passengers. The officers have the right to

---

Safe and Sane Stopping Procedures

These few tips can help drivers who have been pulled over by police stay safe and get on their way as soon as possible:

- Drivers who become aware that a police officer has signaled to pull over should slow down, use the turn signal, and pull off the road (usually to the right) when it is safe to do so.
- Drivers should next turn off the engine, turn on the interior light (if it is dark out), and then keep their hands on the steering wheel. This should lessen officers' fears for their own safety. (Remember they know nothing about the driver, and a driver knows nothing about information known to a police officer about cars and occupants involved in recent crimes.)
- Drivers should avoid actions that suggest that they might be hiding something. An officer who sees a driver lean forward may think that the driver has hidden an object under the front seat. This may be enough for the officer to order the driver out of the car, pat the driver down, and search under the front seat.

- Drivers should stay in the car unless asked by the officer to get out.
- Drivers should obey officers' instructions. Until an officer allows a driver to drive off, the officer is in charge of the situation.
- Drivers should answer questions, but should not volunteer information or "mouth off." Drivers should save any arguments for the courtroom.
- If an officer questions a driver about crimes or activities unrelated to the traffic stop and the driver doesn't want to answer, the driver should politely say something like, "I know I have a right to remain silent, and I prefer not to answer that question."
- Drivers should tell any passengers to follow these same rules.
- Drivers should remember that police often have equipment that visually records traffic stops.
- A driver who has reason to doubt that the person who made the traffic stop is a police officer should ask to talk to a supervisor or tell the officer, "I will follow you to the police station."

search any object that might be capable of concealing whatever the police are searching for. (*Wyoming v. Houghton*, U.S. Sup. Ct. 1999.) If the search turns up incriminating evidence (such as drugs or loot from a crime), the police can arrest the driver and the passengers. (*Maryland v. Pringle*, U.S. Sup. Ct. 2003.)

EXAMPLE: Officer Colombo pulls a car over for making an illegal left turn. Inside the car are four teenagers. The officer notices a hypodermic syringe and traces of drugs in the driver's shirt pocket. The officer orders all the passengers out of the car, frisks them, and begins to search the car looking for drugs. The officer picks up a purse from the back seat, which one of the occupants identifies as hers. Officer Colombo opens the purse, finds drugs inside, and places the purse's owner under arrest. The arrest and drug seizure were valid. Because Officer Colombo had the right to search the car, the officer also had the right to search items belonging to any passengers, as long as the item could reasonably contain drugs.

EXAMPLE: Officer Colombo pulls a car over for making an illegal left turn. Inside the car are four teenagers. The officer notices an illegal automatic weapon sticking out under the front passenger seat. Officer Colombo orders all the passengers out of the car, frisks them, and begins to search the car looking for other evidence of weapons. The officer picks up a wallet from the back seat, which one of the occupants identifies as his. Officer Colombo carefully searches the wallet and finds drugs inside. He places the wallet's owner under arrest. This arrest and seizure are probably not valid. Because Officer Colombo had the right to search the car, the officer also had the right to search property belonging to its passengers if that property could reasonably contain the objects the police are searching for (in this case, weapons). Because no weapon could be concealed in the wallet, the search of the wallet was arguably illegal and the arrest based on it invalid.

Can a police officer who stops a motorist for a traffic violation have a police dog sniff around the car for illegal substances such as drugs?

Yes. Even if a police officer has no reason to believe that a car contains an illegal substance, the officer can use a trained "sniffer dog" to check for illegal substances. Any illegal substances that the officer finds with the dog's help can be used against the motorist at trial. (*Illinois v. Caballes*, U.S. Sup. Ct. 2005.)

At the same time, a police stop that takes longer than necessary to address the reason for the stop violates the Fourth Amendment. So, suppose an officer witnesses a simple traffic violation and doesn't have reasonable suspicion of other wrongdoing. It's illegal for that officer to have a dog sniff for drugs after completing the tasks related to the traffic infraction. (*Rodriguez v. U.S.*, U.S. Sup. Ct. 2015.)

Are the rules for car searches different for rental cars?

No. Drivers of rental cars have a reasonable expectation of privacy, even if they are not listed on the car rental agreement. (*Byrd v. U.S.*, U.S. Sup. Ct. 2018.)

Do police officers need a warrant to test the blood alcohol level of suspected drunk drivers?

When police officers stop a driver for a DUI offense (driving under the influence), they do not need a warrant to "search" a driver's blood alcohol level by requiring the driver to blow into a breathalyzer machine. However, a police officer generally does have to obtain a warrant in order to require a driver to submit to a blood draw, as this is a more physically intrusive search. (*Birchfield v. North Dakota*, U.S. Sup. Ct. 2016.)

Are the rules for car searches different near the U.S. borders?

Yes. The government has a unique interest in policing its borders at and around border crossings. At the border, police officers can search cars and their occupants even if they have no reason to be suspicious. That right to search in the absence of suspicion even extends to a vehicle's gas tank. (*U.S. v. Flores-Montano*, U.S. Sup. Ct. 2004.)

Warrantless Searches or Entries Under Emergency (Exigent) Circumstances

This section discusses emergency circumstances in which concerns for public safety and the need to preserve evidence allow police officers to conduct a warrantless search.

What are some examples of emergency situations that eliminate the need for search warrants?

Here are some situations in which most judges would uphold a warrantless search or entry into a residence:

- An officer checks a hurt motorist for possible injuries following a collision and finds illegal drugs.
- Following a street drug arrest, an officer runs into the house after the suspect shouts into the house, "Eddie, quick, flush our stash down the toilet." The officer arrests Eddie and seizes the stash.
- A police officer in hot pursuit of a fleeing armed robbery suspect continues the chase into the suspect's house, where the officer arrests and searches the suspect.
- A police officer on routine patrol hears shouts and screams coming from a residence, rushes in, and arrests a suspect for domestic violence.
- A police officer responding to a "loud party" complaint observes underage drinking and fighting going on inside the residence where the party is taking place. (*Brigham City v. Stuart*, U.S. Sup. Ct. 2006.)
- A police officer arrests a passed-out drunk driving suspect and wants medical staff to take a blood sample from the suspect before the alcohol level drops. (*Mitchell v. Wisconsin*, U.S. Sup. Ct. 2019.)

In these types of emergency situations, an officer's duty to protect people and preserve evidence outweighs the warrant requirement.

Can a judge decide after the fact that a claimed emergency did not justify a warrantless search?

Yes. If a judge later decides that an officer had time to obtain a search warrant without risking injury to people or the loss of evidence, the judge should refuse to allow into evidence whatever was seized in the course of the warrantless search. Judges always have the final word on whether police officers should have obtained warrants.

EXAMPLE: Responding to a call from a neighbor, Officer Jules finds a three-year-old wandering around an apartment building without adult supervision. The neighbor, Jim Roman, tells the officer that the child lives alone with her mother, that the mother left about two hours earlier, and that the child has been outside alone ever since. Officer Jules knocks on the mother's door a number of times. Getting no response, he breaks in and looks through the apartment. There he finds stolen food stamps in the bedroom. The food stamps are probably not admissible in evidence against the mother. Officer Jules was not faced with an emergency situation at the time of the search. The child was safely in custody, and the officer had no reason to suspect that the mother or anyone else was inside the apartment. Officer Jules should have gone to a judge to try to establish probable cause for the issuance of a search warrant.

EXAMPLE: Officer McNab arrests Ruby, who is alone in her apartment, for stealing jewelry. Officer McNab immediately searches Ruby's apartment and finds a number of pieces of stolen jewelry in a shoebox in a corner of Ruby's basement. A judge should not admit the jewelry into evidence. No exigent circumstances justify the warrantless search. Officer McNab had time to obtain a search warrant, because no one else was in the apartment to destroy or get rid of the evidence. If necessary, a police officer could secure the apartment until a warrant was issued. (Nor could the search be justified as incident to an arrest, because Officer McNab's search went beyond Ruby's immediate surroundings.)

Miscellaneous Warrantless Searches

This section explains whether the police need a warrant in some common search scenarios not covered above.

Can police secretly listen in on telephone conversations without a search warrant?

No. People reasonably expect their telephone conversations to be private, whether made from home, on a mobile phone, or from a public telephone booth. Police need a search warrant before recording or listening in on telephone conversations. (*Katz v. U.S.*, U.S. Sup. Ct. 1967.) Federal laws enacted in 1996 extend the general privacy in telephone conversations to electronic devices like cellphones and email. (18 U.S.C. § 2510.)

Under the Patriot Act, the National Security Administration claims the power to listen in on private conversations that may involve domestic terrorism. How widespread this domestic surveillance is—and the legality of such surveillance—remains a subject of debate.

Do the police need a warrant to search trash?

No. People generally do not have a reasonable expectation of privacy in garbage that they leave out for collection. (*California v. Greenwood,* U.S. Sup. Ct. 1988.)

> **EXAMPLE:** Fausto prunes his marijuana plants, placing the dead leaves and stems in a kitchen garbage bag, which he later puts in a garbage can outside his home for collection on trash day. Without Fausto's knowledge, the local police have asked the trash collector to deliver Fausto's trash directly to them rather than mixing it with other trash. The police search the trash, find the leaves and stems, and seize them as evidence. Fausto is charged with marijuana cultivation, a felony. The police procedures in this case did not violate Fausto's rights under the Fourth Amendment. Trash put out for collection is not within the Fourth Amendment's zone of protection. Because the trash is freely accessible to others (such as scavengers, snoops, and the police) the owner has no reasonable expectation of privacy in it.

Does the Fourth Amendment protect backyards as well as the inside of dwellings?

Yes. However, as a practical matter, a person's privacy in the backyard is harder to protect than privacy inside the home. For instance, there is no privacy in the yard if members of the public can see into it from a location where they have a right to be.

> **EXAMPLE:** Officer Alex pulls into an alley behind Joshua's house, stops his car, and climbs on the car roof to see over a high fence into Joshua's backyard. He spots a number of stacked boxes in an open shed. He shines his flashlight on the boxes and sees that they appear to contain electronic components. Officer Alex is aware of a recent burglary in which similar components were stolen. Officer Alex obtains a search warrant and returns to Joshua's house for a closer look. The components in the boxes match the description of the stolen ones, and Joshua is charged with the crime of receiving stolen property. Officer Alex did not violate Joshua's Fourth Amendment rights. Officer Alex was in a public place where he had a right to be. Climbing onto the car and using his flashlight doesn't make the search invalid because anyone driving in a high truck in the daytime could have made the same observations.

Can police officers surveil fields surrounding rural houses?

Yes. As long as the police are in a place they have a right to be, they can use virtually any type of surveillance device to observe the property. However, police officers cannot intrude into the typically enclosed area around a home called the "curtilage." Moreover, they can't trespass onto property to obtain a better view. Furthermore, the police cannot use specialized heat-scanning devices to obtain evidence of criminal activity inside a home. (*Kyllo v. U.S.,* U.S. Sup. Ct. 2001.)

Can public school officials search students without a warrant?

Public school students have fewer Fourth Amendment protections than adults. School officials do not need probable cause or search warrants; they can search students and their possessions as long as they have a reasonable basis for conducting the search, and the search is appropriate based on the age of the student and what's being sought. For example, if a school official has a reasonable belief that a student has a weapon, drugs, or other illegal substances, the official may pat down the student's clothes or request that the student empty pockets or any personal belongings such as backpacks.

> EXAMPLE: A junior high school student tells the school's vice principal that someone in a group of five to six children brought a gun to school. The vice principal searches the clothes and backpacks of all the students in the group. The vice principal finds a gun and calls the police. The search is valid, and the gun is admissible in evidence. The student's initial report gave the vice principal a reasonable basis to conduct the search.

> EXAMPLE: School authorities get a report that 13-year-old Savana Redding is distributing over-the-counter pills to other students in violation of school policy. The authorities search Savana's backpack and other personal belongings but find nothing. A school nurse then takes Savana into a private room and conducts a modified strip search. Savana has to remove and shake out her bra and loosen the elastic around her

underwear. The initial search of Savana's belongings is legitimate, but the strip search is not. The strip search of a 13-year-old girl in these circumstances is excessively intrusive, especially as no immediate risk of harm exists and school officials have no information suggesting that the pills might be hidden in her bra. (*Safford Unified School District v. Redding,* U.S. Sup. Ct. 2009.)

Can public school officials require drug testing for students participating in extracurricular activities?

Yes, public school officials may conduct drug tests on any student who is engaged in extracurricular school activities, even if the officials have no reason to think that a student is using drugs. (*Board of Education v. Earls,* U.S. Sup. Ct. 2002.)

> EXAMPLE: The Fidelity School District requires all middle school students participating in extracurricular activities to consent to urinalysis testing for drugs. Jack refuses and is prohibited from working on the yearbook. The school's policy is legitimate. Drug testing of high school and middle school students participating in extracurricular activities—even nonathletic activities—is a reasonable means of preventing drug use among schoolchildren and does not violate the Fourth Amendment.

Can a government agency force job applicants to take a drug test before hiring them?

Possibly. The U.S. Supreme Court has upheld drug tests for prospective federal government employees. (*National Treasury*

Employees' Union v. Von Raab, U.S. Sup. Ct. 1989.) The court has likewise upheld drug testing of current employees, even in the absence of a reasonable basis to suspect that an employee might be using drugs. The legality of drug testing in the employment context depends in part on the type of work carried out by the agency. The more an agency's work involves public safety or sensitive government policies, the more likely a court is to uphold drug testing.

Can police officers use high-tech devices to search for evidence of criminal activity within a residence?

No. Without a warrant, police cannot use high-tech "sense-enhancing" technology that is not in general use to collect information regarding the interior of a home or to monitor a person's conduct within his or her home.

> **EXAMPLE:** The police suspect that Wheeler is illegally growing marijuana inside his home. Knowing that indoor marijuana growers often rely on lamps that emit unusually high levels of heat, the police scan the outside of Wheeler's home with a thermal imager, a high-tech device that scans for heat. The scan indicates that portions of Wheeler's walls and roof are unusually hot. The police cannot use this information to obtain a search warrant to search Wheeler's home and find marijuana being grown inside. In fact, the use of the thermal imager constitutes an illegal "search" of Wheeler's home. Wheeler had a reasonable expectation of privacy in his home. By intruding into Wheeler's privacy

by means of a high-technology device not in general use, the police conducted an illegal search. Unless the police have probable cause to obtain a search warrant without using the information gained by using the thermal imager, a search would be illegal and the evidence inadmissible. (*Kyllo v. U.S.*, U.S. Sup. Ct. 2001.)

Can police officers bring a sniffer dog onto private property in an effort to detect illegal drugs?

Police officers who bring a sniffer dog onto private property to detect drugs conduct a search that is invalid unless the officers have probable cause to believe that illegal drugs are present. (*Florida v. Jardines*, U.S. Sup. Ct. 2013.)

> **EXAMPLE:** Responding to an anonymous tip that George was growing marijuana illegally in his house, police officers brought a trained sniffer dog onto George's front porch. Based on the dog's positive reaction, the officers obtained a search warrant and seized marijuana plants inside the house. The prosecution cannot use the plants as evidence. At the time the officers brought the dog onto the front porch they lacked probable cause to believe that the plants were in the house. The information they gathered (the dog's positive reactions) therefore should not have been used to support the warrant. As a result, the search warrant was invalid and the officers had no right to search George's house. (Remember, an illegal search cannot be justified by what it produces.) By contrast, had the police

brought the dog onto George's front porch in response to information provided by a reliable informant rather than an unknown tipster, the search warrant and seizure of the plants would have been valid. Similarly, if the dog had "alerted" to the presence of the plants when the officers were on the sidewalk walking past George's house, probable cause to believe marijuana plants were in the house would have existed and the search warrant and subsequent seizure of the plants would have been valid.

Can shops legally use closed-circuit cameras in dressing rooms?

Yes. Shops and other private enterprises are not government agencies and are therefore not subject to the Fourth Amendment.

Can an animal's distress justify a police officer's warrantless entry onto private property?

Yes. Court rulings in many states allow police officers to enter private property in emergency circumstances in order to rescue dogs (and perhaps other animals) whose lives are in immediate danger. (*Commonwealth v. Duncan*, Mass. Sup. Ct. 2014.)

Can police officers conduct warrantless searches of people on probation?

Probably. Probation normally comes with strings attached, including the requirement to submit to searches by peace officers, whether or not they have a warrant. This condition of probation allows police or probation officers to conduct warrantless searches of probationers based on "reasonable suspicion" (not "probable cause") that the probationers are in possession of contraband such as drugs or of other evidence of criminal activity. (*U.S. v. Knights*, U.S. Sup. Ct. 2001.)

Searches Performed by Private Security Guards

Private security personnel outnumber police officers in the United States. As a result, whether shopping in a supermarket or a pharmacy, working in an office building, or visiting a friend in a housing project, a person may be more likely to be confronted by a security guard than by a police officer. The Fourth Amendment does not apply to searches carried out by nongovernmental employees such as private security guards. For example, assume that a shopping mall security guard acting on a pure hunch (that is, lacking probable cause or even a reasonable suspicion) searches a teenager's backpack. Inside the backpack, the guard finds a baggie containing illegal drugs. The guard can detain the teenager, call the police, and turn the drugs over to a police officer. The drugs are admissible in evidence because the search was conducted by a private security guard.

EXAMPLE: Mark was convicted of a drug offense and placed on probation subject to a condition that he submit to searches of himself, his house, his vehicle, and any of his other possessions at any time by any law enforcement officer, without the need for a warrant. While Mark is on probation, a police officer observes him carrying objects that closely resemble items that were recently reported stolen from a nearby home. The officer later searches Mark's home, finds other stolen objects, and places Mark under arrest. The search of Mark's home was valid. The police officer reasonably suspected that Mark might be in possession of stolen goods. Because Mark is on probation and subject to a condition that he submit to searches, the officer does not need probable cause to justify the search.

Can government officers search passengers in airports, subways, and other mass transit locales even if they have no reason to suspect them of criminal activity?

Yes. Because of concerns about terrorism and other forms of mass violence, so-called warrantless "special needs" or "administrative" searches are valid so long as they are reasonably limited in scope. For example:

- Airport screening searches are valid because they help to protect airline passengers from terrorism and they are minimally intrusive. (*U.S. v. Hartwell*, 3d Cir. 2006.)
- New York subway rules authorizing random searches of subway passengers are valid because they allow officers to search only for explosives, and riders are advised when they enter a subway station that they are subject to search and are subject to arrest if they enter a station and refuse a search request. (*MacWade v. Kelly*, 2d Cir. 2006.)
- Searches of passengers' bags and vehicles on the Lake Champlain ferry (between Vermont and New York) are valid even though a rural ferry may be a less likely target of an attack than an urban subway system. (*Cassidy v. Chertoff*, 2d Cir. 2006.)

What is an administrative search?

Administrative searches occur when government officials conduct routine examinations of commercial premises and business records to ensure that businesses are complying with applicable rules and regulations. As a general rule, business operators have no right to refuse officials' requests to conduct administrative searches, and officials don't have to obtain search warrants before conducting them. For example, a health inspector wouldn't have to obtain a warrant in order to examine the maintenance records of a restaurant's food-storage equipment. On the other hand, hotel or motel operators must be afforded an opportunity to seek review of police officers' demands to examine records pertaining to their registered guests before they are subject to arrest for refusal to turn over the records. As a result, officers may have to obtain "administrative search warrants" before carrying out some types of searches. (*City of L.A. v. Patel*, U.S. Sup. Ct. 2015.)

Sample Affidavit for Search Warrant

United States District Court
FOR THE
Eastern District of Missouri

UNITED STATES OF AMERICA

vs.

John Doe

Docket No. _____A_____

Case No. _____11246_____

AFFIDAVIT FOR
SEARCH WARRANT

BEFORE Michael J. Thumb, Federal Courthouse, St. Louis, Missouri
Name of Judge or Federal Magistrate   *Address of Judge or Federal Magistrate*

The undersigned being duly sworn deposes and says:

That he has reason to believe that (on the person of) Occupants, and (on the premises known as) 935 Bay Street, St. Louis, Missouri, described as a two-story, residential dwelling, white in color and of wood frame construction ....

in the Eastern   District of Missouri

there is now being concealed certain property, namely   *here describe property*

Counterfeit bank notes, money orders, and securities, and plates, stones, and other paraphernalia used in counterfeiting and forgery,

which are   *here give alleged grounds for search and seizure*

in violation of 18 U.S. Code §§ 471–474

And that the facts tending to establish the foregoing grounds for issuance of a Search Warrant are as follows: (1) Pursuant to my employment with the Federal Bureau of Investigation, I received information from a reliable informant that a group of persons were conducting an illegal counterfeiting operation out of a house at 935 Bay Street, St. Louis, Missouri. (2) Acting on this information, agents of the FBI placed the house at 935 Bay Street under around-the-clock surveillance. During the course of this surveillance officers observed a number of facts tending to establish the existence of an illegal counterfeiting operation. These include: observation of torn and defective counterfeit notes discarded in the trash in the alley behind the house at 935 Bay Street, and pick-up and delivery of parcels at irregular hours of the night by persons known to the FBI as having records for distribution of counterfeit money.

Mary M. Dunton, Special Agent
Signature of Affiant

Federal Bureau of Investigation
Official Title, if any.

Sworn to before me, and subscribed in my presence   December 3rd, 20xx

Michael J. Thumb
Judge or Federal Magistrate

Sample Search Warrant

United States District Court

FOR THE

Eastern District of Missouri

UNITED STATES OF AMERICA

vs.

John Doe

Docket No. ___A___

Case No. ___11246___

SEARCH WARRANT

To Any sheriff, constable, marshall, police officer, or investigative officer of the United States of America.

Affidavit(s) having been made before me by
Special Agent, Mary M. Dunton

that she has been reason to believe that { on the person of / on the premises known as }

on the occupants of, and

on the premises known as 935 Bay Street, St. Louis, Missouri
described as a two-story, residential dwelling, white in color and of wood frame
construction ....

in the **Eastern**   District of **Missouri**

there is now being concealed certain property, namely

Counterfeit bank notes, money orders, and securities, and plates, stones, and other paraphernalia used in counterfeiting and forgery,

and as I am satisfied that there is probable cause to believe that the property so described is being concealed on the person or premises above described and that the foregoing grounds for application for issuance of the search warrant exist.

You are hereby commanded to search within a period of __10__ (not to exceed 10 days) the person or place named for the property specified, serving this warrant and making the search at anytime in the day or night[1] and if the property be found there to seize it, leaving a copy of this warrant and a receipt for the property taken, and prepare a written inventory of the property seized and promptly return this warrant and bring the property before me as required by law.

Dated this **3rd** day of **December, 20xx**

Michael J. Thumb
Judge or Federal Magistrate

[1] The Federal Rules of Criminal Procedure provide: "The warrant shall be served in the daytime, unless the issuing authority, by appropriate provision in the warrant, and for reasonable cause shown, authorizes its execution at times other than daytime." (Rule 41(C))

Arrest: When It Happens, What It Means

An arrest occurs when police officers take a suspect into custody. The moment of arrest often comes well before the suspect actually arrives at a jail. An arrest may begin as a temporary detention followed by a frisk or a search.

As interpreted by courts, the U.S. Constitution's Fourth Amendment authorizes an arrest only if the police have probable cause to believe that a crime was committed and that the suspect did it. This probable cause requirement restrains the power of the police to deprive people of liberty. It prevents the type of random roundup of "undesirables" that sometimes occurs in other countries.

Arresting Material Witnesses

A "material witness" is an individual who is not a suspect but who can provide important evidence implicating a suspect in a crime. If the police can convince a judge that a material witness in an important case will likely flee the jurisdiction before the case can come to trial, the judge can authorize the police to arrest the witness and keep the witness in jail until the case concludes.

Legislatures and courts have picked up where the Fourth Amendment leaves off, developing rules about how, when, and why people can be arrested. This chapter reviews the most important arrest procedures.

Common Consequences of Arrest

In addition to depriving a person of liberty, an arrest often triggers a variety of other events. Some of these are:

- The arrested person will have an official record of arrest, which may have to be reported to employers and licensing agencies, such as a state board of dentistry.
- Arrested people who are taken to jail commonly try to secure quick release by posting bail or convincing a judge to order release on their "own recognizance." (See Chapter 5.)
- The arresting police officer will usually issue *Miranda* warnings before questioning the arrestee.
- The arrestee—and sometimes the arrestee's car or home, depending on where the arrest occurs—may be searched.
- Any contraband or evidence of a crime may be seized for later use in court.
- An arrested person who remains in jail after the arrest will be taken before a judge as quickly as practicable for a hearing typically called an "arraignment" or "initial appearance."

General Arrest Principles

This section describes the basic legal principles governing arrests.

When exactly is a person under arrest?

An arrest occurs when a police officer takes a person into custody. However, arrest is not synonymous with being taken to jail. The following common situations illustrate the scope of an arrest:

- A driver is stopped for a routine traffic violation. The driver might technically be considered under arrest because the driver is not free to leave until the officer has written a ticket (or if it's the driver's lucky day, only issued a warning). But the arrest is temporary. Assuming the officer has no basis to suspect that the driver is engaged in criminal activity other than the traffic violation, the officer usually releases the driver once the driver produces identification and signs a promise to appear in court (assuming a ticket was written). Traffic stop arrests do not become part of a person's arrest record, and do not count as arrests for the purpose of answering the question, "Have you ever been arrested?" (on a job or license application, for example).

- A shopper in a mall is stopped by a police officer who says, "I'd like to know whether you saw the robbery that took place a few minutes ago in the jewelry store." No arrest has taken place. People questioned by police officers are not under arrest unless the officers indicate that they are not free to leave—and even in that case, the person may only be under "detention." (For reasons of personal safety, however, the shopper should not simply walk away from the officer without the officer's permission.) Even if the officer refuses permission, thereby detaining the shopper, this isn't a formal arrest if the shopper is allowed to leave after the questioning and is not charged with a crime.

- A police officer yells, "Hold it right there, you're under arrest!" to a suspect who assaulted someone on the street. The suspect flees. The suspect has not been arrested because the suspect has neither been taken into custody nor voluntarily submitted to the police officer's authority.

- A police officer yells, "Hold it right there, you're under arrest!" to two suspects who assaulted someone on the street. As the officer handcuffs Suspect 1, the officer tells Suspect 2, "Stay right there and don't move." Suspect 2 does not move. By submitting to the police officer's authority, Suspect 2 has been arrested, even though Suspect 2 has not physically been taken into custody.

- A store security guard has arrested someone for shoplifting and turns the suspect over to a police officer. The police officer issues a citation instructing the suspect to appear in court on a charge of petty theft. The suspect has been arrested, but does not have to go to jail.

Can people be charged with a crime without being arrested?

Yes. An alternative procedure—called "citation"—exists in most states. In lieu of arresting people for traffic offenses (like speeding) and minor misdemeanors (such as shoplifting), officers can issue citations. A citation is a notice to appear in court. By signing the citation, a person promises to appear in court on or before the date specified in the notice in exchange for remaining at liberty.

Need for Citation Procedures in Urban Areas

The jails in many urban areas are overcrowded. In some cases, jails are subject to court orders limiting the number of inmates they can hold. Because of this, many police departments instruct their officers to issue citations to suspects who in the past would have been arrested. One unfortunate by-product of this is that some suspects who might benefit from going to jail and "cooling off" remain free, and thus may pose a danger to themselves and to the persons who called the police.

Does the Constitution limit the power of the police to make arrests?

Yes. To be lawful, all arrests must comply with the Fourth Amendment to the U.S. Constitution. That amendment protects people against "unreasonable searches and seizures" and provides that warrants can issue only on a showing of probable cause. Arrests are covered by this Fourth Amendment provision because they are a type of seizure (of the body).

As interpreted by the courts, the Fourth Amendment generally requires police officers to obtain arrest warrants only when they enter a suspect's dwelling to make an arrest. (*Payton v. New York,* U.S. Sup. Ct. 1980.) However, the police do not need an arrest warrant in emergency situations such as when they pursue a fleeing suspect into a dwelling.

What does "probable cause" mean?

The Fourth Amendment makes "probable cause" the key term in the arrest process. The police need probable cause to make an arrest, whether they are asking a judge to issue an arrest warrant or justifying an arrest after it has been made. Some principles of probable cause are well settled:

- To establish probable cause, police officers must be able to point to objective factual circumstances leading them to believe that a suspect committed a crime. A police officer can't establish probable cause by saying something like, "I just had a hunch that the defendant was a crook."
- Judges, not police officers, have the last word on whether probable cause exists. A police officer may be sincere in believing that the facts on the ground establish probable cause. But if a judge examines that same information and disagrees, then probable cause does not exist

(or did not exist, if the question is being decided after an arrest is made).

- Probable cause to arrest may have existed at the time of the arrest, even if the police later turn out to be wrong. Put differently, an arrest is valid as long as it is based on probable cause, even if the arrested person is innocent. In this situation, probable cause protects the police against a civil suit for false arrest if the charges are later dismissed or the defendant is acquitted at trial.

Probationers and Parolees

The probable cause requirement for arrest does not generally apply to people who are on probation or parole. A common condition placed on probationers and parolees is that they must submit to arrest and search without probable cause. This doesn't mean that police officers can arrest probationers and parolees on a whim, or simply to hassle them, however. Police officers generally must have a "reasonable suspicion" (a less strict standard than probable cause) that a probationer or parolee is involved in criminal activity in order to make an arrest. (*Samson v. California*, U.S. Sup. Ct. 2006; *U.S. v. Knights*, U.S. Sup. Ct. 2001.)

These principles leave open the most important issue concerning probable cause: How much information do police officers need to convince a judge to issue an arrest warrant or to justify a warrantless arrest? In general, probable cause requires more than a mere suspicion that a suspect committed a crime, but not as much information as would be required to prove a suspect guilty beyond a reasonable doubt.

Because it is an abstract concept, a firm definition of probable cause is impossible. The Fourth Amendment doesn't provide a definition, so it's up to judges to interpret the meaning of probable cause on a case-by-case basis, taking into account:

- what the judge thinks the amendment's drafters meant by the term "probable cause"
- previous judges' interpretations in similar fact situations, and
- the judge's attitude about the proper balance between community safety and individual liberty.

Judges help to define the meaning of probable cause each time they issue a warrant or decide a case in which the issue arises.

> **EXAMPLE:** Officer Furman arrives at Simpson's Jewelry store moments after it's been robbed. Officer Furman sees broken glass inside the jewelry store. A man claiming to be Simpson, the owner, tells the officer that a man approximately 6'5" tall and weighing over 300 pounds held up the store at gunpoint and escaped with rings and watches in a small brown paper bag. A few minutes later, less than a mile away from the jewelry store, Officer Furman pulls a car over for speeding. The driver matches the description of the robber, and on the seat next to the driver are a small brown paper bag and a couple of

watches with the price tags attached. Though Officer Furman did not see the robbery itself, the driver matches the unusual physical description of the robber and has the property that Simpson said was missing. Furman has probable cause to arrest the driver.

EXAMPLE: Same case. Assume that the person claiming to be Simpson, the jewelry store owner, was actually the robber's accomplice. The accomplice gave Officer Furman a phony description and then fled after the officer drove off. The driver pulled over by the officer for speeding later is able to prove that he is the lawful owner of the watches that the officer saw on the seat. In this scenario, Officer Furman had no reason to doubt the word of the person claiming to be Simpson, and the broken glass corroborated "Simpson's" statement that a robbery had occurred. Thus, the officer had probable cause to make the arrest, even though the information turned out to be incorrect.

EXAMPLE: Officer Seesit pulls over a car and its three occupants for speeding. The officer searches the car with the driver's consent and finds baggies of cocaine stashed behind an armrest in the back seat. All three occupants of the car say that they didn't know that the cocaine was in the car. Seesit has probable cause to arrest the car's occupants. In the absence of evidence demonstrating that the cocaine belonged to a specific occupant, the officer could reasonably conclude that all of them knew about and possessed the cocaine. (*Maryland v. Pringle,* U.S. Sup. Ct. 2003.)

What happens if a judge decides that a police officer lacked probable cause to make an arrest?

A judge will not issue an arrest warrant unless the judge believes there is probable cause. However, police officers are authorized to make warrantless arrests without getting a judge's permission, unless they arrest the suspect at his or her home. When officers do make warrantless arrests, judges may later decide that the police lacked probable cause to make the arrest and order the charges dismissed and the suspect released. A judge's determination that the police lacked probable cause to make an arrest may have the following consequences:

- Exclusion of evidence. Any evidence seized by the police in connection with an illegal arrest typically cannot be used as evidence in court.
- Civil tort action. An improperly arrested person may be able to sue the arresting officer (and the city or other government entity that employed the officer) for damages in a civil lawsuit. In practice, civil tort actions against police officers for improper arrest tend to succeed only when a cop physically abuses a suspect in the course of an improper arrest.
- Removal of the record of arrest from the arrested person's records. This may require the filing of a petition with the court requesting removal of the arrest record.

Probable Cause Formed After the Arrest

If a judge decides that the police lacked probable cause at the time of the arrest, that does not always mean that a defendant is in the clear. By the time a judge makes that decision, the police may have gathered enough additional information to have probable cause. If so, a defendant might be released, only to be immediately and properly rearrested based on the additional information.

CAUTION

Resisting even an improper arrest is dangerous. Legislators and judges don't want arrestees resisting police officers and do want issues like probable cause litigated in court—rather than in the streets. In some states, an arrestee can't use force to resist an appropriately forceful arrest, even if there's no proper basis for the arrest (like probable cause). But, in some states, someone being unlawfully arrested has a right to use reasonable force to resist.

Of course, even where resisting unlawful arrest with reasonable force is legal, resisting at all is generally not a good idea. One reason is that the arrest might be lawful even if the arrestee is innocent. For another, circumstances can quickly unravel to the point that the arrestee is seriously injured or earns additional criminal charges.

Also, keep in mind that the definition of resisting arrest varies from state to state, but that someone can typically commit the offense even without using force. Further, someone might be

guilty of resisting arrest even if the officer isn't trying to apply handcuffs or otherwise enforce an actual arrest. Depending on the statute, the crime may be complete where the person fails to obey an officer's lawful order.

Arrest Warrants

This section describes arrest warrant procedures.

What is an arrest warrant?

An arrest warrant is an official document, signed by a judge (or magistrate), which authorizes a police officer to arrest the person or people named in the warrant. Warrants typically identify the crime for which an arrest has been authorized, and may restrict the manner in which an arrest may be made. For example, a warrant may state that a suspect can be arrested "only between the hours of 6 a.m. and 6 p.m." Finally, some warrants also specify the bail that a defendant must post to regain freedom following arrest. If the warrant is for a previous failure of the suspect to appear in court—called a bench warrant—it will probably specify that the arrested person may not be released on bail at all (sometimes termed a "no-bail warrant").

Do police officers always need to obtain arrest warrants before making arrests?

No. As long as a police officer has probable cause to believe that a felony was committed and that the arrestee committed it, a warrantless arrest usually is valid. In general, police officers need to obtain arrest warrants only to make an arrest for a misdemeanor crime that they did not personally witness or to enter a suspect's dwelling in a non-emergency situation to make an arrest.

How do the police obtain an arrest warrant?

To obtain a warrant, a police officer typically submits a written affidavit to a judge or magistrate. The affidavit, given under oath, must recite sufficient factual information to establish probable cause that a crime was committed and that the person named in the warrant committed it. A description so broad that it could apply to hundreds of people will not suffice. For instance, a judge will not issue a warrant to arrest "Rich Johnson" based on an affidavit that "a liquor store was held up by a bald potbellied man of medium height, and Rich Johnson matches that description." That description doesn't establish probable cause to believe that Rich Johnson robbed the liquor store, because the vague description would apply to numerous people. On the other hand, probable cause to arrest Rich Johnson probably would be adequate if the affidavit included the factual information that "the liquor store clerk and three witnesses identified a photo of Rich Johnson as the person who held up the liquor store."

If the Arrest Warrant Contains Incorrect Information

Sometimes, arrest warrants contain factual mistakes. For example, the suspect's name might be misspelled or the wrong crime might be specified. Ideally, the police should show the warrant to the suspect. And, if the suspect is able to prove that the officer has the wrong person, then the officer should not proceed. As a practical matter, however, a police officer might not show a warrant to a suspect. In that kind of situation, any mistakes as to identity would have to be sorted out later. And clerical errors like misspelling an arrestee's name, do not invalidate a warrant.

Warrantless Arrests

This section describes situations in which police officers do not need warrants to make arrests.

Do police officers need probable cause to make a warrantless arrest?

Yes. When police officers make a warrantless arrest, a judge does not have a chance to determine ahead of time whether the police have probable cause to make the arrest. Nevertheless, the Fourth Amendment probable cause requirement remains the same. For a suspect to remain in custody following an arrest, the police must speedily satisfy a judge or magistrate that they had probable cause to make the arrest. (*Gerstein v. Pugh,* U.S. Sup. Ct. 1975.)

When can a police officer legally make a warrantless arrest?

If they have probable cause to make an arrest, police officers can legally make warrantless arrests in these two circumstances:

- When the crime is committed in the officer's presence. For example, a police officer, on routine patrol, sees a driver strike a pedestrian and drive off without stopping (the crime of "hit and run"). The police officer can pursue and arrest the driver.
- When the officer has probable cause to believe that the suspect committed a felony, whether or not the deed was done in the officer's presence.

EXAMPLE: While on routine patrol, Officer Martin comes upon Fred Rowan, who possesses —and apparently is under the influence of—cocaine. Rowan tells Officer Martin that he bought the cocaine moments earlier from a man around the corner wearing a dark business suit and white loafers. Peering around the corner, Officer Martin sees a suspect matching that description standing on the street. Martin has probable cause to place the suspect described by Rowan in custody. The officer did not personally see the suspect sell cocaine to Rowan. But selling drugs is a felony, and Rowan's appearance and information give the officer probable cause to believe that the suspect had committed that crime.

EXAMPLE: Officer Winter is told by Mr. Summer, a security guard in an electronics store, that Summer personally saw a red-haired teenage girl wearing a leather jacket bearing the logo "Cafe Rock Hard" and tennis shoes leave the store with a boxed phone charger without paying for it. A few hours later, Officer Winter sees a red-haired girl dressed as Summer described sitting in a café charging her phone. Officer Winter cannot arrest the teenager. Even if she is guilty, the information given to Officer Winter indicates that the most serious crime she could have committed is the misdemeanor commonly called shoplifting. Officer Winter did not personally see the act, so he would need to submit an affidavit to a magistrate and obtain an arrest warrant before making an arrest. The officer can, however, issue her a citation ordering her to appear in court to answer to a misdemeanor shoplifting charge. If the suspect had stolen numerous items worth more than several hundred dollars, however, Officer Winter could make the arrest on probable cause because it would be classified as a felony rather than a misdemeanor.

The bottom line: Warrantless arrests are generally okay if probable cause exists, except for a misdemeanor not committed in the officer's presence.

Can the police make a warrantless arrest for a minor offense that is punishable only by a small fine?

Yes. If a police officer has probable cause to believe that an offense has been committed in the officer's presence, the officer can make an arrest even if the crime is very minor and punishable only by a small fine. (*Atwater v. Lago Vista*, U.S. Sup. Ct. 2001.) As a practical matter, police officers rarely make arrests in these situations. However, in the Supreme Court's opinion, a rule by which the validity of an arrest depends on the seriousness of an offense would be too difficult for police officers to follow because they would have to know the punishment for every criminal offense.

> **EXAMPLE:** Officer Buckle spots Whip Lash driving without a seat belt. In the state where the offense occurs, driving without a seat belt is punishable only by a small fine. Whip can't get any jail time even if he is found guilty of the offense. The offense was committed in Buckle's presence, so Buckle can arrest Whip without a warrant and take him to jail even though the offense is minor and doesn't carry jail time.

Can the police make a warrantless entry into a home in order to make an arrest?

Police officers generally need to obtain arrest warrants before arresting suspects in their homes. (*Payton v. New York*, U.S. Sup. Ct. 1980.) If necessary, another officer can be posted outside to prevent the suspect's escape during the time it takes to obtain the warrant.

However, warrantless in-home arrests are valid if "exigent circumstances" exist that make it impracticable for the police to obtain a warrant. Examples of exigent circumstances are:

- A police officer who is in hot pursuit of a fleeing suspect who runs into a house or apartment will not generally be required to break off the chase and obtain a warrant.

> **EXAMPLE:** Officer Hernandez arrests Frick for taking part in a string of burglaries. After Frick is taken into custody, he confesses and names Frack as the other person who took part in the burglaries. Frick also tells Officer Hernandez where Frack lives. Officer Hernandez cannot proceed immediately to Frack's house, demand admittance, and arrest Frack. Officer Hernandez must first get a warrant for Frack's arrest. Officer Hernandez is not in hot pursuit of Frack, and no other emergency circumstances justify the officer's going into Frack's home without a warrant.

- A police officer who reasonably believes that someone in the home is in danger and gains entry for that reason may then arrest someone without a warrant.
- A police officer who is let into the home by someone answering the door may make the arrest without a warrant.

Arrests and Civil Protests

People have a First Amendment right to engage in peaceful public protests. But police can arrest protesters without a warrant in some circumstances, as when protests turn violent, block traffic, or spill over onto private property. Government agencies can also require protesters to obtain a permit before engaging in a mass demonstration that can interfere with the right of others to move about freely. The ACLU's website provides an overview of rules that protect the free speech and public assembly rights of demonstrators and the rights of the government to protect public safety.

Use of Force When Making Arrests

This section explains what force the police are permitted to use when making an arrest.

Do the police have to knock before entering a home to make an arrest?

When police officers enter a home to arrest a suspect pursuant to a warrant, they are generally supposed to announce their presence by following "knock and notice" rules. While the rules can vary from state to state, police officers usually need not announce their presence in advance if they:

- are in hot pursuit of a fleeing suspect
- reasonably believe that someone is being harmed in the house
- have reasonable grounds to suspect that announcing their presence might put them in danger, or

- have reasonable grounds to suspect that announcing their presence would allow a suspect to escape or destroy evidence.

The Fourth Amendment has been interpreted to require the knock and notice procedure. (*Wilson v. Arkansas*, U.S. Sup. Ct. 1995.) However, the U.S. Supreme Court has held that violations of the rule do not require judges to exclude evidence or dismiss criminal charges. (*Hudson v. Michigan*, U.S. Sup. Ct. 2006.) (Some states decline to follow *Hudson* and in some circumstances require that evidence be suppressed if it was a product of a violation of knock and notice rules.)

How much force can police officers use when making arrests?

Police officers are generally allowed to use *reasonable force* to take a person into custody. For example, if a suspect's only resistance consists of a momentary attempt to run away or a token push, a police officer would not be justified in beating the suspect senseless. Officers who use unnecessary force may be criminally prosecuted and may also have to pay civil damages to the injured suspect.

Courts decide whether an officer's use of force was unreasonable on a case-by-case basis, taking into account the severity of the crime, whether the suspect posed a threat, and whether the suspect was resisting or attempting to flee. (*Graham v. Connor*, U.S. Sup. Ct. 1989.)

In a perfect world, suspects informed that they were under arrest would meekly submit to a police officer's authority. But then again, a perfect world would contain neither suspects nor police officers. In the world we live in, suspects sometimes try to flee or fight off arrest. In such situations, police officers can use force (and sometimes even deadly force) to make an arrest.

The amount of force that police officers can use when making an arrest is a subject of much concern and controversy. Police officers often seek discretion to use as much force as they—at the time of the arrest—think necessary, to protect both society and their personal safety. But citizens' groups, especially those made up of ethnic or racial minorities, often oppose any extension of police officers' authority to use force, on the ground that the police are too likely to use force discriminatorily against minorities.

EXAMPLE: Officer Smitts and his partner observe Delany punch somebody outside a bar and then run away. The officers give chase. When they catch up, Delany struggles and strikes at the officers in an effort to escape. While Officer Smitts applies a chokehold, the partner manages to handcuff Delany and manacle his legs. However, Officer Smitts continues to apply the chokehold for another minute, until Delany passes out. Officer Smitts used excessive force. Once Delany was shackled, there was no further need for the chokehold.

Can police officers legally use deadly force to make an arrest?

Sometimes. A police officer may use deadly force to capture a suspect only if a suspect threatens an officer with a weapon or an officer has probable cause to believe that the suspect has committed a violent felony. (*Tennessee v. Garner,* U.S. Sup. Ct. 1985.) The police can also use deadly force to protect the life of a third person. But police officers cannot routinely use deadly force whenever they seek to arrest a suspect for committing a felony. This reflects the public policy that it's better for police to allow some felony suspects to escape rather than kill them.

EXAMPLE: Officer Fish sees a suspect take a camera from an outdoor sales stall and run off without paying for it. The officer calls for the suspect to stop, but the suspect continues to run away. Because Officer Fish has personally seen the suspect commit a misdemeanor, Fish has probable cause to make an arrest. But Fish cannot shoot the suspect or use other serious force. If the suspect refuses to halt and Fish cannot chase down the suspect, Fish would have to try to make an arrest at a later time.

Can police officers use deadly force to terminate high-speed car chases?

Yes. Motorists who drive off at high speed instead of stopping in response to a police officer's blinking lights and siren often place the lives of other drivers and pedestrians at risk. To prevent harm to innocent bystanders, police officers have the right to use deadly force to put an end to the car chase and arrest fleeing motorists. (*Plumhoff v. Rickard*, U.S. Sup. Ct. 2014.)

Should Police Officers Fire Into Moving Vehicles?

A car driven in a police officer's direction can be a deadly weapon. An officer may shoot at it in self-defense. Or an officer may fire into a moving vehicle to prevent a dangerous suspect from escaping. Either situation creates serious hazards for passersby. Moreover, in the "heat of battle," an officer may overreact.

To try to protect police officers, suspects, and the public from unwarranted shootings, many police departments have developed policies to guide police officers' decisions about when to fire into moving vehicles. One common guideline advises officers to get out of the way of a moving vehicle when they can safely do so. Another recommendation is that police officers not fire into vehicles unless the people inside have weapons that create a serious risk of harm to the officers or others. While policies such as these may be helpful, they cannot eliminate the risk of shootings that in retrospect were unjustified; speeding cars tend to force officers into immediate and emotional decisions.

Can arrestees defend themselves against police officers' use of excessive force?

If police officers use excessive force in the course of making an arrest, arrestees may be entitled to use self-defense to protect themselves. It doesn't matter whether an officer has probable cause to make the arrest in the first place. The use of more force than is reasonably necessary to make an arrest is improper. However, an arrestee should use self-defense only when absolutely necessary to prevent severe injury or death. Judges and jurors are likely to blame any escalation in violence on an arrestee, so self-defense should always be considered a last-ditch option.

Citizens' Arrests

This section examines the power of lay people (non–law enforcement officers) to make an arrest without being held liable for false imprisonment.

Is it legal for an ordinary citizen to make an arrest?

All states authorize private citizens to make arrests. For example, a car owner may arrest a teenager trying to break into her car, or a store security guard may arrest a shoplifter.

Always Consider the Police Officer's Perspective

The probable cause rule allows police officers to act based on the information available to them, even if it later turns out that the information is wrong. Thus, even people who believe that they are innocent should act cautiously if stopped by police officers; the officers may have information causing them to think a person is dangerous.

For example, assume that a young man with red hair driving a late model convertible is pulled over by a police officer. The driver, confident that he's done nothing wrong, is indignant and belligerent. He gets out of the car and shakes his fists at the officer. But unknown to the driver, the police officer has information that five minutes earlier, a young red-headed man robbed a nearby convenience store at gunpoint and escaped in a late model convertible. The officer may interpret the young man's belligerence as a threat and decide to use force. The officer would probably have the right to do so, even though the young man is innocent and has no weapon.

The moral: People should keep their hands in view at all times so that the police don't think they are hiding any weapons. (When police officers are investigated for shooting unarmed suspects, they can often credibly claim that they thought the suspect was armed and reaching for a weapon.) And they should act courteously toward police officers, because they don't know what the officers know.

"Here Comes the Posse!"

The posse is a familiar staple in most westerns. Yet, reminiscent of the Wild West, in emergency situations, law enforcement officers can still conscript private citizens into serving on posses to capture suspects. Though the laws are rarely enforced, a citizen who refuses an officer's order to join a posse can technically be guilty of a misdemeanor.

Do private citizens have the same arrest powers as police officers?

No. In order to encourage citizens to leave arrests to the professionals, laws in almost all states afford less protection to private citizens who make mistakes during the arrest process than they do to police officers.

Most states authorize private citizens to make arrests if:

- they personally observe the commission of a crime
- the person arrested has actually committed a felony, even if not in the private citizen's presence, or
- a felony has in fact been committed, and the private citizen has probable cause to believe that the arrested person committed it.

Compare these rules to those that apply to police officers. As long as they act on probable cause, police officers are not civilly liable for mistakenly arresting an innocent person. But if a private citizen makes an arrest for a felony not committed in the citizen's presence, the citizen had better not mistakenly arrest an innocent person. If a private citizen is mistaken—that is, if it turns out that the arrested person did not commit a felony, or that nobody committed a felony, or that the private citizen had no reasonable basis to believe that the arrested person committed a felony—then the private citizen may be civilly liable to the arrested person for false imprisonment.

> **EXAMPLE:** While eating lunch in the park, Ella Mentry overhears two people talking about a plan to rob Haro's Jewelry Store. As the two people walk away, Ella realizes that one of the speakers is her next-door neighbor Nick. About an hour later, Ella sees a crowd and two police officers gathered in front of Haro's Jewelry Store. Ella immediately rushes to Nick's house, tells him that he is under arrest for robbery, and calls the police. It turns out, however, that Haro's was not robbed; the police and crowd had gathered for a diamond-cutting demonstration. Ella is civilly liable to Nick for false imprisonment. If Nick decides to sue, a court may order Ella to pay damages to compensate him for the time, trouble, and distress of the improper arrest. As a private citizen, Ella is not protected by probable cause.

Arrest Powers of Private Security Guards

The private security industry has grown in recent years. Most security guards have only the same legal rights as ordinary citizens when it comes to the power to make arrests. In some areas, however, local governments have given security guards a few police powers, including issuing traffic tickets and making arrests for nonviolent misdemeanors such as trespassing (entering someone else's property without permission). Just because the Constitution doesn't apply to private security guards, however, does not mean citizens have no legal rights if security guards' actions are inappropriate. For example, if a private security guard wrongfully detains, harasses, or physically injures a suspect, the injured person may have sufficient grounds to sue the security guard for a number of different torts (civil wrongs), including false imprisonment and battery.

Additionally, especially if the security guard works for a company that receives government funding, the injured citizen may have a valid federal civil rights violation claim. But remember: It is much safer to bring grievances to court after the fact than to challenge an armed security guard.

EXAMPLE: Same case. Assume that after overhearing Nick talking about a plan to rob Haro's, Ella tells Officer Chang what she heard. About an hour later, Officer Chang sees a large crowd gathered in front of Haro's and sees the person who turns out to be Nick running away from the store. Officer Chang runs after and arrests Nick. Again, it turns out that Haro's was not robbed. Officer Chang is not civilly liable to Nick for false imprisonment, as he had probable cause to believe that Nick committed a robbery. Though he was wrong, probable cause protects the officer against a suit for false imprisonment.

CAUTION

Private citizens are at great legal risk if they try to use deadly force to make an arrest. Courts are especially hostile toward private citizens who use deadly force to make arrests. Courts are rightly fearful that any encouragement of private citizens' use of deadly force will lead to armed vigilantes roaming the streets and lessening public safety. Thus, a private citizen's use of deadly force while making a citizen's arrest is not justified unless the citizen accurately believed that the use of deadly force was necessary to protect the citizen or others from extreme harm or death. Private citizens who are mistaken may be both sued civilly and prosecuted criminally.

Are there any other factors people should consider before making a citizen's arrest?

Legal problems aside, the biggest peril to keep in mind is the danger of confronting criminals. Police officers are highly trained and have excellent physical skills, yet even they are sometimes injured or killed when making arrests. Unless they are certain of their physical security, private citizens should turn their information over to the police rather than personally make arrests. And if they do make an arrest, private citizens must call the police and turn the suspect over as soon as possible.

EXAMPLE: Wachit, a store security guard, arrests a suspected shoplifter and calls the police. In response to Wachit's request, a police officer arrests the suspect. Even though the officer did not personally witness the theft, the warantless arrest is valid. Yes, a rule forbids police officers from making warrantless arrests for misdemeanors that are not committed in their presence. However, in this scenario, the security guard is the one who made the arrest. Wachit will fill out an arrest report, and the officer will take the suspect into custody as Wachit's representative.

Eyewitness Identification:
Psychology and Procedures

The popular media have made most people familiar with common tools of forensic science, such as fingerprint analysis, DNA analysis, and ballistics. Yet, in thousands of criminal cases per year, the prosecution's main evidence consists of eyewitness identification. And in over half the cases in which innocent people are set free after being wrongly convicted, sometimes after serving many years in prison, mistaken eyewitnesses were the cause. For better or worse, eyewitness identification often determines the outcome of criminal cases.

Because of the importance of eyewitness identification, evidence rules allow eyewitnesses not only to identify suspects at trial, but also to testify about pretrial identifications. The evidence of multiple identifications tends to strengthen a prosecutor's case. And, because of the problem of mistaken identifications, defendants are allowed to educate jurors about factors tending to undercut the accuracy of eyewitness identifications. With so much riding on the accuracy of eyewitness identification rather than forensic science, the principles and policies governing this type of evidence are critical to our system of justice.

An Overview of Eyewitness Identification Procedures

When eyewitnesses to a crime are available, the police typically want to find out as soon as possible whether they can identify the culprit. This section briefly describes common identification procedures and how those procedures can affect eyewitnesses' trial testimony.

What are the common pretrial identification procedures?

The three most common identification procedures are:

- **Lineups.** A lineup typically consists of five to six people. Usually one is the suspect, while the others may be police officers or other "decoys" who bear a resemblance to the suspect or fit the description that the eyewitnesses gave to the police. Generally the police hold a lineup after they've made an arrest, and they want to know whether the eyewitnesses can identify the suspect ("make a positive identification").

- **Showups.** A showup is a one-on-one identification procedure. The eyewitness views a single suspect, perhaps at a police station or sometimes at the crime scene. Again, the police generally conduct a showup after they've identified and arrested a possibly guilty suspect.

- **Photo identifications.** This procedure calls for eyewitnesses to view photographs, typically head shots (called "mug shots") in a police department's files. The police may resort to photo identifications when they don't have enough information to make an arrest. The eyewitness's positive identification of a suspect's photo is what allows the police to make an arrest.

In addition to identifying suspects, each of these procedures can also help to clear a suspect. For example, if an eyewitness fails to make a positive identification at a lineup, the police may release a suspect.

At trial, can eyewitnesses testify to pretrial identifications?

Yes. Typically, eyewitnesses testify about their ability to view the suspect during the crime itself, and then point to the defendant in the courtroom as the perpetrator. In addition, evidence rules in all states allow eyewitnesses to bolster their in-court identifications by testifying about their pretrial identifications (at a lineup, for example). For example, an eyewitness may testify as follows:

Question: And what happened when you came to the police station the day after the robbery?

Answer: Officer Smith sat me at a computer and asked me to look through photos and tell him if I recognized anyone.

Question: And did you recognize anyone?

Answer: Yes, as soon as I saw the photo of the defendant. I must have looked at 50 or 60 photos by that time, but when I came to the defendant's photo, I stopped looking and immediately told the officer that this was the robber.

Of course, the defense can ask questions about an eyewitness's failure to make a positive identification when the eyewitness had an opportunity to do so. For example,

a portion of a defense attorney's cross-examination of an eyewitness may go as follows:

Question: You've testified today that the defendant is the person who robbed the bank, right?

Answer: Yes.

Question: But you attended a lineup less than two weeks after the robbery, right?

Answer: That's true.

Question: And the defendant was in that lineup, wasn't he?

Answer: He was.

Question: Yet at that time you told the police that you didn't recognize anyone in the lineup as the robber, didn't you?

Answer: That's correct, but …

Question: Thank you. You've answered my question.

Are there safeguards against unduly suggestive pretrial identification procedures?

Yes. While the risks of mistaken identifications can probably never be overcome entirely, various safeguards lessen the chance that suggestive pretrial identification procedures will promote mistakes. Among the common safeguards are:

- Police officers are trained not to suggest, directly or indirectly, whom they want an eyewitness to identify. For example, eyewitnesses viewing a lineup should only be asked if they recognize anyone, and should not be told whether the suspect is in the lineup.

- Lineups are photographed, and records are kept as to which photos were shown to eyewitnesses. Thus, if the defendant was displayed in an unfair way that could lead an eyewitness to pick the defendant out of a group, the defense will have an opportunity to point that out. For instance, if an eyewitness described the perpetrator as "tall," and the defendant was noticeably taller than anyone else in a lineup, the defense may convince a judge that the lineup was unfair.

- The police keep eyewitnesses apart from each other during pretrial identification procedures. This eliminates the risk that at a lineup, one eyewitness will identify "the third person from the left" as the culprit simply because this witness saw or heard another eyewitness make that same identification.

- If a judge concludes that a pretrial identification procedure was unfair, an eyewitness cannot testify at trial to having identified the defendant before trial. In an extreme case, a judge may decide that a pretrial identification was botched so badly that an eyewitness won't even be allowed to make an identification at trial.

EXAMPLE: Shortly after receiving a report of a convenience store robbery, the police arrest Stan Desside, who generally matches the clerk's description. Bringing Desside to the store, the police tell the clerk, "This guy matches the description you gave. He's got a record a mile long, and his alibi doesn't hold water. Just tell us we've got the right guy, and we'll haul him off to jail so you won't have problems from him again." The clerk then says, "Good work. He's got to be the one who robbed me." Desside is then charged with robbing the store. In this extreme example, the police virtually told the clerk to identify Desside as the culprit. The judge should rule that the clerk can't testify to the out-of-court identification. Moreover, the risk is so great that the unfair procedure tainted the clerk's memory that the clerk shouldn't even be allowed to identify Desside at trial.

The Psychology of Eyewitness Identification

Cognitive psychologists have conducted literally thousands of experiments examining factors that might affect the accuracy of eyewitness identifications. This section summarizes some of what they've learned about eyewitness identification and discusses the type of testimony that eyewitness identification experts typically give at trial.

Is there reason to be skeptical of eyewitness identifications?

Yes. Numerous experiments (often with subjects watching video recordings of simulated crimes) have demonstrated that observers' perceptions and memories are often incorrect. Even eyewitnesses who say things like "I'll never forget that face" are often wrong. The human memory does not act like a computer, accurately recording, storing, and retrieving images on demand. Like all of us, eyewitnesses construct and interpret what they see while events are happening. The process continues while images are stored in eyewitnesses' memories and when they're called upon to "retrieve" the image when a police officer asks, "Do you recognize this person?" As one expert put it, "Some memories are elaborations created by witnesses over time based on their own rationalizations for what must have happened and suggestions from others." (E. Geiselman, *Eyewitness Expert Testimony*, pp. 74–75.)

What factors tend to cause eyewitnesses to identify the wrong person?

Some of the factors associated with mistaken identifications are matters of common sense and everyday experience. For example, all of us recognize the difficulty of making an accurate identification based on a quick glance as opposed to a long look. Similarly, one does not have to be a cognitive scientist to know that lighting, distance, and an eyewitness's physical condition (for example, just awakened) can also cause an eyewitness to identify the wrong person. Below are some of the less obvious factors that have been evaluated in research studies:

- **Stress.** While many people tend to believe that "stress sharpens the senses," research consistently shows that people who are under stress when they observe an event are more likely to misidentify the culprit. And, of course, being a crime victim or witnessing a crime can cause great stress.
- **Presence of a weapon.** Eyewitnesses confronted by a weapon are apt to focus on the weapon rather than the person holding it.

Find the Defendant

Inside the courtroom, witnesses ordinarily have no trouble figuring out whom to identify: It's the person sitting next to the defense attorney. Arranging for a truer test of an eyewitness's credibility, famed defense lawyer Johnnie Cochran, Jr., on at least one occasion got a judge to allow the defendant to be seated among the spectators. A decoy sat next to Cochran at counsel table. When the eyewitness was asked to "look around the courtroom and tell us if you see the perpetrator," the arrangement forced the eyewitness to carefully consider before answering. Much earlier in the 20th century, legendary Los Angeles lawyer Earl Rogers did the same thing, actually having the defendant switch places with a courtroom spectator while Rogers cross-examined the eyewitness. Rogers stood so as to block the witness's view of the switch.

- **Confidence level.** Eyewitnesses who express great confidence in their identifications are no more accurate than those who admit to uncertainty. Confident eyewitnesses sometimes have higher error rates.
- **Cross-racial identification.** Eyewitnesses are less accurate when asked to identify someone of a different race. This factor affects members of all racial groups.
- **Pressure to choose.** Eyewitnesses are more likely to make mistakes when they feel pressure to make an

identification, even if they are told that they don't have to make a choice.

- **Influence after the fact.** Eyewitnesses are more likely to make mistakes when they rehash events with other observers. In these situations, witnesses may alter their memories so that they can be in agreement with others.
- **Transference.** Eyewitnesses may make a mistaken identification because they saw the person they identify on a different occasion.
- **Multiple perpetrators.** Identification accuracy decreases as the number of people involved in an event increases.
- **Absence of an "employment boost."** Eyewitnesses who regularly interact with the public (store cashiers, bank tellers) are no better at making identifications than other people.

How do judges and jurors find out about factors that may lead to mistaken identifications?

Many cognitive psychologists not only conduct research experiments, but also qualify as expert witnesses and testify at trial. Based on the factors surrounding the commission of a crime, they can testify to how those factors might have affected eyewitnesses' ability to make an accurate identification.

Defendants who can't afford to hire a cognitive psychologist as an expert may ask a judge to appoint an expert at government expense. However, few court systems have enough money to allow judges to appoint eyewitness identification experts in every case in which their testimony is relevant. A less expensive option is for a judge to give a jury instruction that summarizes factors that might affect an eyewitness's accuracy.

When they testify at trial, do eyewitness identification experts give an opinion about whether the identifications in that case are accurate?

No. Qualified experts can "educate the jury" by talking generally about factors that studies have shown tend to lead to inaccurate identifications. But experts have no way of assessing whether a particular eyewitness is accurate.

> **EXAMPLE:** Sal Mander, a Caucasian male, is on trial for robbing Delores, an African American female. After Delores identifies Sal as her attacker, Mander's eyewitness identification expert testifies about factors that existed at the time of the robbery that might cast doubt on Delores's ability to observe and recall accurately. However, the expert cannot testify, "In my opinion, there's less than a 50% chance that Delores's identification is accurate." Eyewitness identification experts can talk about factors that have been associated with mistaken identifications in research studies, but experts themselves admit that they cannot assess the accuracy of any particular identification.

Lineups

This section describes issues related to lineups, one of the most frequently used pretrial identification procedures.

In addition to witnesses and those in the lineup, who else may be present?

Police officers and often a prosecutor attend lineups. A defense attorney may be present as well, because a suspect who has been formally charged with a crime has a right to be represented by a lawyer at a lineup. (*Kirby v. Illinois,* U.S. Sup. Ct. 1972.) In large cities, public defender offices may have an attorney available to attend a lineup 24/7. The defense lawyer may also bring an investigator, a paralegal, a law clerk, or another observer to act as a witness in a later court hearing in case the lineup procedures are unfair to the defendant. To avoid having to provide a suspect with counsel, the police may try to convince a suspect to participate voluntarily in a lineup before charges are filed.

Can suspects be required to participate in a lineup?

Yes. The police can force an arrestee to participate in a lineup. Judges do not consider this a violation of the Fifth Amendment privilege against self-incrimination because, in a lineup, suspects do not provide "testimony." (*U.S. v. Wade*, U.S. Sup. Ct. 1967.)

As a condition of granting bail or "release O.R.", a judge may require a suspect to participate in a lineup. However, being released from jail may reduce a suspect's chance of having to participate in a lineup because making the arrangements entails extra work for the police.

Blind and Sequential Lineups

Erroneous eyewitness identifications are the leading cause of improper convictions. Blind and sequential lineups are two procedures that might reduce the risk of erroneous identifications.

In blind lineups, the police investigator conducting a lineup does not know which of the people in the lineup is thought to be the suspect. A lineup is "double-blind" if the investigator tells eyewitnesses that the investigator does not know whether the suspect is in the lineup. These procedures reduce the risk that an investigator will provide subconscious hints as to a suspect's identity.

With sequential lineups, eyewitnesses view individuals one at a time instead of in groups of five or six. Eyewitnesses must "pass" on one possible suspect before seeing another one. Sequential lineups may reduce the risk that an uncertain eyewitness will simply pick out the person in a group who most closely resembles the actual culprit.

Unless they have a court order, the police cannot compel suspects who have not been arrested to participate in a lineup. The police may ask such suspects for voluntary participation, arguing that "this is our chance to clear you." While that may be true, even people who are confident of their innocence should think carefully—and perhaps talk to a lawyer—before agreeing to participate in a lineup voluntarily; after all, witnesses can make mistakes. On the other hand, the police may regard refusal as evidence of guilt and investigate the suspect's activities more aggressively.

Can suspects demand that the police conduct a lineup?

Laws in many states give suspects the right to demand a lineup. Suspects and their attorneys should think carefully before demanding a lineup, however. The advantage of participating in a lineup is that if eyewitnesses are unable to make a positive identification, the police may drop their investigation of a suspect. Yet suspects also risk a positive identification that strengthens the case against them.

During a lineup, do suspects see or have contact with eyewitnesses?

No. One-way mirrors or bright lights typically make it impossible for suspects to see witnesses. Even if contact is possible, suspects should not try to talk to witnesses. Even a plaintive "Tell them I'm innocent" may lead a witness to look extra hard at a suspect and identify the suspect as the perpetrator. The police may also construe a suspect's attempt to talk to a witness as intimidation and charge the suspect with a separate crime!

Can the police dictate what participants wear and say during a lineup?

Yes. Dressing the lineup participants as the culprit was dressed, and having them speak words that the culprit used, can increase the likelihood that an eyewitness's identification (or failure to identify) is accurate. Of course, for the lineup to be fair, conditions must be the same for all lineup participants.

> **EXAMPLE:** Ann Ekdote is arrested for burglarizing a home. Wilma, the next-door neighbor, tells the police that the burglar was a woman who wore large sunglasses, carried a big shopping bag, and yelled "It's all mine" while running out of the house. The police arrest Ann and ask Wilma to view her in a lineup. The police can dress Ann in large sunglasses and have her carry a big shopping bag if the items match Wilma's description, as long as all of the lineup participants are displayed to Wilma in the same way. The police can also require each lineup participant to yell, "It's all mine." It wouldn't be wise for Ann to refuse. Because the other participants will do as the police request, Ann is likely to draw more attention to herself by refusing to repeat the words (or by whispering them). Moreover, the prosecution can use Ann's refusal as further evidence of her guilt at trial.

What happens after a lineup is over?

A positive identification makes it likely that a suspect will be formally charged with a crime (if charges have not already been filed). And the prosecution can bolster its case for plea bargaining purposes or at trial by showing that the eyewitness identified the defendant at a lineup.

An eyewitness's inability to make an ID doesn't necessarily mean that a suspect will be freed. The prosecutor may conduct additional lineups for other eyewitnesses, or may decide to move the case ahead based on forensic evidence such as fingerprints and DNA analysis.

What features might incline a judge to rule that a lineup was unfair?

Judges are likely to decide that lineups are unfair or impermissibly suggestive in the following types of circumstances:

- The suspect is the only person in the lineup who closely resembles the eyewitnesses' description.
- The police drop not-so-subtle hints as to whom the eyewitnesses should identify by handcuffing the suspect while the decoys' hands are free.
- The police allow eyewitnesses to confer with each other before or during the lineup.
- The police instruct an eyewitness along the lines of "Pay particular attention to Number 3."

Events occurring before a lineup starts can also render it unfair. For example, assume that while the eyewitnesses are waiting outside the room where the lineup will take place, the police "accidentally" walk the handcuffed suspect past the eyewitnesses. Such a ploy would impermissibly indicate who the officers think is guilty.

Whether mistakes like these are intentional or accidental, they taint the resulting identifications. When such mistakes occur, eyewitnesses should not be allowed to repeat their lineup identifications at trial. If a judge determines that a lineup was so impermissibly suggestive that it must have influenced eyewitnesses' recollections of the events themselves, eyewitnesses should not be permitted to identify defendants at trial either.

How can a defense lawyer's presence safeguard a suspect's rights at a lineup?

A defense lawyer's presence is likely to deter impermissibly suggestive police behavior. In addition, a defense lawyer may:

- **Object to unfair elements and suggest fairer ones.** For example, a lawyer who notices eyewitnesses starting to confer with each other might ask the police officers to separate them.
- **Make a record of unfair aspects for use in a later court challenge to the lineup identifications.** For example, the lawyer may take a photo of the eyewitnesses conferring with each other or note that the angle of the lighting in the lineup room made the defendant stand out.
- **Observe the eyewitnesses' demeanor and attitudes.** The lawyer might get insights into how convincing the eyewitnesses might be at trial and how confident they are in their own identifications. (Eyewitnesses who are uncertain at the time of a lineup sometimes retract their identifications before trial.)

- **Observe conversations that the eyewitnesses have with the police or a prosecutor.** Ostensibly, the attorney's task is to ensure that the eyewitnesses aren't improperly coached. But the attorney can also be alert to anything witnesses say that might detract from the believability of their identifications. For example, an eyewitness may tell a police officer, "I'm as nervous now as during the holdup. It's really hard for me to pay attention." That's the kind of statement that an attorney can mention to a prosecutor during plea-bargaining discussions, because it indicates that the witness's identification may be mistaken. And if the case goes to trial, the defense attorney can cross-examine the witness as follows:

  Question: You were as nervous at the lineup as during the holdup, correct?
  Answer: I guess so, yes.

  Question: And that nervousness made it hard for you to pay attention to what was happening, right?
  Answer: I wouldn't say that.

  Question: Well, at the lineup, didn't you tell Officer Meachem that you were so nervous that it was hard for you to pay attention?
  Answer: Yes, I suppose I did say that.

- **Interview the eyewitnesses.** While defense attorneys are typically observers rather than active participants, they may have an opportunity to question the eye-witnesses. While victims and witnesses have no obligation to agree to an interview, the presence of police officers sometimes makes them comfortable talking to a defense attorney (especially if they hope that they can convince the lawyer that the suspect should plead guilty so they don't have to come back to court). If so, the attorney may gain helpful information about their ability to observe the culprit and how well the suspect corresponds to the descriptions given to the police.

Is it a good idea for people who haven't been charged with a crime to try to clear themselves by agreeing to a police request to participate voluntarily in a lineup?

Innocent people may reasonably decide to participate voluntarily in a lineup without being represented by a lawyer, as long as they recognize the risk that eyewitnesses will mistakenly identify them. After all, the alternatives—that police may continue to investigate their activities or resort to photo identifications—may be even less palatable. But criminal defense lawyers are likely to advise people who insist that they are innocent not to participate voluntarily in a lineup. If a serious criminal charge is possible, even people who think they did nothing wrong should seek legal advice before agreeing to participate voluntarily in a lineup.

EXAMPLE: Warren Tees is an ex-felon who resembles the description of a man who held up a liquor store. The police lack probable cause to arrest Warren. They are suspicious of him because of his past record, however, so they ask him to volunteer to take part in a lineup. Warren knows that he did not hold up the liquor store, he does not have a right to appointed counsel, and he cannot afford to hire an attorney. Warren has to decide for himself whether the risk that an unfair procedure will cause him to be mistakenly identified justifies the expense of a lawyer. If Warren refuses to be in a lineup, the police may regard that as suspicious and keep investigating his whereabouts at the time of the robbery. Moreover, if Warren doesn't agree to a lineup, the police can instead show the eyewitnesses a mug shot of him, which may create an even greater danger of mistaken identification.

How can suspects who don't have an attorney present protect their rights during a lineup?

Suspects who have already been charged with a crime have a right to have counsel present at a lineup, and should tell the police that they want a lawyer present, orally and in writing if possible, before the lineup gets underway. Suspects should not sign a "Waiver of Attorney," which allows the police to conduct a lineup without having an attorney present. If the police refuse to wait for an attorney and go ahead with a lineup, the suspect should participate in it and later file a motion to suppress any resulting identification.

If no attorney is present, lineup participants can help protect their right to a fair lineup by paying attention to the lineup procedures and writing down as soon after the lineup as possible any elements that seemed unfair. For example, an individual should make note of an unusually small number of participants. If a lineup consists of only three or four participants, a judge may later decide that the prosecution can't offer evidence of an identification at trial. Likewise, participants should be alert to ways in which they either looked or were dressed differently from the other participants, as well as to any conversations they overhear between the police and eyewitnesses.

Any notes that suspects make of their lineup observations should be marked "Privileged—For My Attorney Only" and not shown to anyone except a lawyer.

Types of Nontestimonial Evidence

Lineups are not the only nontestimonial activities in which an arrested person might have to participate. The police can compel arrestees to be photographed, to provide fingerprints, and to give samples of their blood, hair, voice, handwriting, and other physical characteristics. (*Schmerber v. California*, U.S. Sup. Ct. 1967.) Arrestees can demand that qualified medical professionals perform invasive tests and can also ask that their attorneys be present. An arrestee who cannot afford to hire an attorney should ask the court to appoint one before testing takes place. An attorney's presence can help ensure that a test is done fairly and compassionately. For example, a police officer is unlikely to engage in improper coaching when a defense lawyer is looking on.

Showups

Showups bring suspects and witnesses or victims together in face-to-face meetings.

What's the difference between a lineup and a showup?

A showup, like a lineup, is a form of eyewitness identification. At a showup, a witness or victim is normally confronted with only one person rather than a group of people. And whereas lineups almost always take place in police stations, showups may occur in a station or in the field, even at the crime scene. A crime-scene showup is especially likely when the police capture a suspect shortly after a crime.

Are showup identifications less reliable than other identifications?

Showups often take place soon after a crime, meaning that memory is less of a problem. But on the other hand, witnesses may still be under great stress when the police return soon after a crime with a suspect in tow. And nothing, short of telling the witness who committed the crime, could be more suggestive than presenting a single, in-custody person for identification. Further, regardless of what police officers say, an unsure witness might feel pressure to point the finger at the person on display.

In a 2017 report, Cal State Los Angeles detailed the results of testing regarding the reliability of showup identifications. In what was reported as a first-of-its-kind experiment, witnesses were led to believe they were part of an actual police

investigation and that their identification would result in the arrest of the suspect.

The study had several findings, including the following:

- Where officers didn't give a proper admonishment (in essence, advising the witness not to assume the suspect committed the crime), the false-identification rate was "exceedingly high."
- Where witnesses were exposed to information suggesting the police thought they had the right suspect (for example, overhearing a loud radio dispatch call that an officer had nabbed the perpetrator), false identification occurred approximately 50% of the time.

The study basically concluded that showups are tremendously unreliable. (See http://psycnet.apa.org/journals/law/23/1/1.)

Do suspects have a right to have an attorney present at showups?

Because showups almost always take place before charges are filed, suspects have no right to have an attorney present.

Might suspects have to participate in both a showup and a lineup?

Yes, it's possible that the police will require a suspect to participate in both a showup and a lineup. They might, for instance, conduct the initial showup, then arrange for a lineup after the filing of charges. At least theoretically, the lineup can substantiate the showup identification and provide a basis to determine whether additional witnesses can also identify the suspect as the perpetrator.

Photo (Mug Shot) Identifications

Police may seek identifications by having victims and witnesses look at photographs ("mug shots") rather than people.

How do police officers gather the photos to use in a mug shot identification?

Police officers typically enter witness descriptions of a perpetrator into a mug shot computer database. For instance, investigating a home break-in case, an officer might search for photos that fit the description of: "Asian male, 25-30 years old, 150-175 pounds, prior arrest for home break-ins." The computer then creates a file consisting of all the mug shots in the database tending to fit the description.

What happens during photo identifications?

Typically, the police ask victims and witnesses to come to the police station and try to identify a suspect by looking at photographs. The witnesses may look through computer files, large books of photos or smaller groupings of six photos commonly called "six packs." The photos are almost always mug shots, so witnesses are aware that the people they are looking at have criminal records.

Why do the police use photo identifications?

The police use photo identifications when they lack probable cause to make an arrest. Because the process is nonintrusive, the police can display photos to eyewitnesses whether or not they have any information tying any of those people to a crime. Thus, photo identifications are in essence a search for a suspect.

Are photo identifications generally considered reliable?

The risk of error has led many big city police departments to curtail or even abandon the use of photo identifications. Some police departments try to reduce the chance of error by intentionally including photos of "fillers" who are known to be innocent in photo arrays. The use of fillers reduces the risk that witnesses will tire of looking at photos and end up picking a photo that simply seems the best fit.

Do suspects have a right to have an attorney present at a photo identification?

No. (*U.S. v. Ash,* U.S. Sup. Ct. 1973.) Photo identifications often take place before charges are filed, and even suspects have no right to be present.

If neither suspects nor attorneys are present, how can the fairness of photo identifications be challenged?

The police are supposed to keep records of which photographs are shown to eyewitnesses, and the order in which they are shown. The defense can see the photos themselves prior to trial. Thus, if a photo display is unfair (for example, the defendant was the only person in a six pack who was fully facing the camera or the only person whose picture was in color), the defense can seek to suppress the identification.

Tricking Suspects Into Confessing

Police officers sometimes tell suspects that they might as well confess, because witnesses have already identified them from a photo as the perpetrator. Even if no identification has taken place, a resulting confession will normally be admissible in evidence because police are allowed to use this type of trickery.

Motions to Suppress Identifications

A motion to suppress an identification is a common defense method of seeking a judge's ruling that a pretrial identification is inadmissible in evidence because the process was unfair.

By what standard do judges decide whether a pretrial identification procedure was unfair?

The general rule is that a pretrial identification is admissible in evidence unless the procedure was "so unnecessarily suggestive of the defendant's guilt that it created a substantial likelihood of misidentification." (*Neil v. Biggers,* U.S. Sup. Ct. 1972.) This standard makes it difficult for defendants to knock out prior identifications. For example, trial courts do not have to routinely hold hearings to determine the reliability of pretrial identifications. (*Perry v. New Hampshire*, U.S. Sup. Ct. 2012.) As a result, juries often hear evidence of

pretrial identifications. Defendants typically bring up the same factors they raised in an unsuccessful attempt to get a judge to suppress an identification when arguing to jurors that an identification is unworthy of belief.

> **EXAMPLE:** While describing to Police Officer A the man whom she saw breaking into a car, eyewitness Blandon sees a man standing next to Police Officer B. Blandon tells Officer A, "That's the man who broke into the car." The identification is not unnecessarily suggestive, because the police did not arrange to have Blandon observe the suspect next to the police officer. (*Perry v. New Hampshire*, U.S. Sup. Ct. 2012.)

What options does a judge have when ruling on a motion to suppress an identification?

Judges' rulings on motions to suppress identifications typically consist of one of the following:

- When eyewitnesses identify suspects prior to trial more than once, a judge may limit how many identifications the witnesses can refer to at trial even if all the procedures were fair. For example, if an eyewitness identifies a suspect at a photo lineup and later in an actual lineup, the judge may rule that the witness may testify to only one of the identifications (in addition to the in-court identification during trial, of course). This option means that prosecutors can't automatically "pile on" identification testimony.

- A judge may rule that an eyewitness may not testify to a pretrial identification because it was conducted unfairly. For example, a judge may rule that a witness cannot testify to identifying a suspect at a showup because a police officer told the witness, "We're confident that this is the right guy."

- A judge may rule that an unfair identification procedure so tainted an eyewitness's memory that the witness cannot testify to the pretrial identification and also cannot identify the defendant at trial. If such a ruling eliminates the prosecution's only evidence of a perpetrator's identity, the ruling requires that charges be dismissed. Such extreme rulings are rare, however.

Booking and Bail: Checking In and Out of Jail

Many suspects are taken to jail upon arrest. Usually their first priority is to get out. Other than the old movie method of ordering a cake with a hacksaw in it, the usual method of leaving jail after arrest is posting bail. This chapter covers the bail system and its alternative to Monopoly's "Get Out of Jail Free" card, "own recognizance release" (also known as "release O.R.").

The Booking Process

Booking officers process arrested suspects into a jail system, using the procedures explained below.

What usually happens when arrested people are taken to jail?

As fans of crime dramas know, suspects taken to jail are normally booked shortly after arrival. Few booking officers were trained behind the reception desk of a luxury hotel. However, just as hotel registration cards provide information about hotel guests, so too do booking records provide information about the people who have to check into jail.

Because booking creates an official arrest record, arrested suspects who can post bail immediately often can't be released until after the booking process is complete. Even suspects who receive citations in lieu of being taken to jail often must go through a booking process within a few days of their arrest.

Why Some Suspects Are Taken to Jail While Others Remain Free

While many suspects are taken to jail upon arrest, others receive citations to appear in court and are allowed to remain free in the interim. The factors that influence a police officer's decision about taking an arrestee to jail include:

- **The seriousness of the crime.** Suspects arrested for petty misdemeanors (such as shoplifting) are less likely to be jailed than those charged with felonies or crimes of violence.
- **The suspect's mental and physical condition.** Police officers often jail suspects who cause a disturbance during the arrest process. Likewise, suspects who are a danger to themselves or others (such as a suspect who is under the influence of drugs or alcohol) are likely to be jailed upon arrest.
- **Jail conditions.** Many jails are overcrowded, forcing police to cite and release suspects who might otherwise be taken to jail.
- **Police department policies.** Police officers often have discretion to decide whether to jail a suspect, and each police department sets its own policies.

What usually happens during the booking process?

The booking process is highly impersonal, and typically includes the following steps:

Step 1: Recording the suspect's name and the crime for which the suspect was arrested. In olden days, this information became part of a handwritten police blotter; now virtually all booking records are computerized.

Step 2: Taking a "mug shot," perhaps the only photo guaranteed to be less flattering than the one on the suspect's driver's license.

Use of Mug Shots

Mug shots have a variety of possible uses. For instance, a mug shot can help to determine which of two people with the same name was arrested. A mug shot can also help to establish a suspect's physical condition at the time of arrest. The suspect's physical condition at arrest can be relevant to a claim of police use of unlawful force or to whether the suspect had been in an altercation before being arrested. Also, police officers may show mug shots to victims and witnesses to identify perpetrators.

Step 3: Taking the suspect's clothing and personal property (such as a wallet, purse, or keys) into police custody. At a suspect's request, some booking officers allow suspects to keep small non-dangerous personal items like a wristwatch. Any articles taken from the suspect must be returned upon release from jail, unless they constitute contraband or evidence of a crime.

EXAMPLE: Sticky Fingers is arrested for stealing a wireless router. The police seize the router at the scene of the arrest. During the booking process, the police find a packet of illegal drugs and a stolen camera in Fingers's backpack. These items will not be returned to Fingers upon his release on bail. The router and the camera are evidence of the crime of shoplifting. The drugs are illegal contraband; the police can take them regardless of whether drug charges are filed against Fingers.

Arrested Suspects Should Get Receipts for Personal Items

During booking, suspects should request a receipt for all personal items taken by a booking officer. The receipt should describe the unique characteristics of any items of special value (for instance, "one Swiss Army knife, autographed by the Swiss Army"). Insisting on a written receipt is one way suspects can ensure that the police ultimately return all confiscated personal property and clothing.

Step 4: Taking fingerprints. Fingerprints are a standard part of a booking record, and are typically entered into a nationwide database maintained by the FBI and accessible to most local, state, and federal police agencies. Comparing fingerprints left at the scene of a crime to those already in the database helps police officers identify perpetrators of crimes.

Step 5: Taking DNA samples. Booking procedures increasingly include DNA sampling. In *Maryland v. King* (2013), the U.S. Supreme Court ruled that jailers can take DNA samples from suspects who are arrested for serious crimes. Typically, jailers take DNA samples by swabbing the inside of suspects' mouths. DNA samples are entered into a national database. Police agencies across the country can use the DNA database to try to identify culprits who committed unsolved crimes in their jurisdiction.

Step 6: Conducting a full body search. Officers routinely make cursory pat-down inspections at the time of arrest. Far more intrusive is the strip search that is often part of the booking process. To prevent weapons and drugs from entering a jail, booking officers frequently require arrestees to remove all their clothing and submit to a full body search. Jailers are allowed to conduct random and routine strip searches, regardless of the nature of the arrestee's alleged offense, and even when there's no suspicion that an arrestee has contraband. (*Florence v. Burlington*, U.S. Sup. Ct. 2012.)

Statutes in many jurisdictions narrow the scope of *Florence v. Burlington* by limiting the offenses for which jailers can strip search arrestees. For example, a state law may provide that suspects arrested for traffic, regulatory, or misdemeanor offenses cannot be strip-searched. Strip searches are more common when arrests are for violent offenses, or if a weapon or illegal drugs are involved.

Step 7: Checking for warrants. The booking officer checks to see if an arrestee has any other charges pending, ranging from unpaid parking tickets to murder charges in other states. Suspects with warrants pending are normally not eligible for bail.

Step 8: Health screening. To protect the health and safety of jail officials and other inmates, the booking process may include X-rays (to detect tuberculosis) and blood tests (to detect sexually transmitted diseases, such as gonorrhea and AIDS).

Step 9: Eliciting information relevant to incarceration conditions. To reduce the likelihood of violence and injuries, jail officials often ask arrestees about gang affiliations, former gang affiliations, and other outside relationships. Depending on the answers, an inmate may have to be placed in protective custody or housed in one section of a jail rather than another. Routine questioning along these lines might or might not constitute an "interrogation" that requires officers to give a *Miranda* warning to the suspect.

Information that suspects disclose in response to a booking officer's questions can be admissible in evidence under the "routine-booking-question" exception to *Miranda*. But incriminating information that an arrestee gives in response to a jailer's question about gang affiliation may not be admissible in evidence at trial if the defendant hasn't been "*Mirandized*." (*Pennsylvania v. Muniz*, 496 U.S. 582 (1990), *People v. Elizalde*, 61 Cal.4th 523 (2015).)

! CAUTION

Additional criminal charges can result from items found during the booking process. While searching a suspect's clothing, backpack, and body cavities, officers sometimes find drugs or stolen goods. Such items can form the basis for additional criminal charges.

How long does booking take?

Booking may take hours. It depends on how many of the standard booking procedures are conducted, the number of arrestees being booked at the same time, and the number of police officers involved.

Are arrestees entitled to legal representation during the booking process?

No. Defendants in criminal cases have a constitutional right to legal representation at every critical stage of the proceeding, but courts regard booking as a routine administrative procedure, not a crucial event warranting legal counsel.

! CAUTION

The lack of representation by a lawyer during booking can damage the defense case. The booking process is impersonal, long, and humiliating, which leaves arrestees extremely vulnerable. With no attorney to provide comfort and advice, suspects are prone to start talking to the police officers who suddenly hold sway over them. These voluntary statements can often be used as evidence in court. Therefore, regardless of the psychological pressures of booking, suspects are well advised to say nothing about their case until they've spoken to an attorney.

Free Phone Calls

Laws in many states allow suspects to make one or more free local calls as soon as booking is completed. Suspects typically call attorneys, bail bond sellers, or friends and relatives, in an effort to make bail or at least hear a friendly voice. However, suspects need to be very careful about what they say over the phone, because police officers and other people may overhear their conversations or even monitor the calls.

EXAMPLE: Cliff Hangar is arrested and taken to jail. He refuses to participate in the booking process, demanding that the police let him phone for a lawyer. However, the police do not have to allow Cliff to call a lawyer until the completion of the booking process. Until then, Cliff should just answer the booking officer's questions, and should not talk about his case.

How can people find out whether someone has been taken to jail?

Police officers normally take arrested suspects to the closest jail. However, the closest jail may be filled to capacity, or gender considerations may lead a police officer to transport an arrestee to a more distant jail. The quickest way to find out if someone has been taken to jail, and, if so, which jail, may be to contact a bail bond office and ask the bonding agent for information. A bonding agent may not receive information until after the booking process is over, but bonding agents are generally "wired in" to jail procedures and can get information as soon as it is available. When speaking to a bonding agent, make sure to ask for the arrestee's booking number. Most bail bond agents will help whether or not a caller agrees to purchase a bail bond.

People can also seek information in person, directly from a jail facility. Ask to speak to a desk officer (who might be called a watch commander) to find out whether a particular person has been arrested and is in the jail. A local jurisdiction's website might also provide information on locating recent arrestees. For example, a city government website might have a page that informs people that they can call a number to find out if a person has been arrested and taken to jail.

When making inquiries, remember that people may be booked under a name that they don't usually use. For example, a woman's driver's license may have been issued in her married name even though she has gotten divorced and no longer uses her married name in everyday interactions. So if an initial inquiry comes up empty, family members or friends have to consider other names an arrestee might have been booked under.

What can people do if a family member or friend with mental or physical health issues is arrested and taken to jail?

Most jails routinely assess newly arrested people for mental and physical health issues. If an arrestee has physical or mental health issues and there isn't a lawyer who can make sure the arrestee's needs are met, a family member or friend can advise police officers and jailers about the person's condition, including specific diagnoses and need for medications. If personal contact with an arrestee is possible (in person or over the phone), the arrestee should be told to discuss the condition (but not the facts of the case) with police officers.

Family members and friends of an arrestee with physical or mental issues should get in touch with the arrestee's lawyer, if the arrestee already has one. They should seek guidance from the lawyer as to how to get the arrestee's needs met. If speaking with a lawyer isn't possible, family members and friends may:

- ask jail officials if the family member or friend can bring medications to the jail facility.
- inform jail officials that an arrestee needs to be seen by a jail physician or taken to a hospital, clinic, or detox facility.
- if the arrestee is likely to remain in jail for an extended period of time, ask whether a medical or mental health caseworker can be assigned to the arrestee.

Family members or friends of an arrestee with special needs might also fill out a jail's inmate health form if one is available. If not, they may prepare a personal note advising jailers of the arrestee's:

- name, birth date, and booking number
- diagnosis

- doctor contact information, and
- needed medications (drug name, dose, and time to be taken). If known, mention a drug's side effects and the likely effects of missed dosages.

People who submit such information should be sure not to write anything about the charges and to include only medical information. They should keep a copy of what they have written and give a copy to the arrestee's lawyer.

Arranging for Bail

Bail is often the first thing on an arrested person's mind. This section explains how courts arrive at a bail amount and how suspects can make bail.

What is bail?

Bail is cash or its equivalent (such as a bail bond) that a court accepts in exchange for allowing a defendant to remain at liberty until a case concludes. Bail creates a financial incentive for defendants to make all required court appearances. Should a defendant fail to appear in court, the bail is forfeited (that is, the court keeps the cash or collects on the bond) and the judge issues an arrest warrant. Bail jumping (not returning to court when required) is itself a crime.

If people charged with crimes are presumed innocent, why can they be forced to stay in jail if they can't post bail?

The basic purpose of requiring defendants to post bail in order to secure their release from jail pending trial is to ensure that they will show up in court until their cases are over. Judges may refuse to set bail for defendants who are serious "flight risks," perhaps because they have a record of failing to appear. Judges may also consider the seriousness of the charges and the need to protect society when deciding whether to set bail, and how much bail to require.

At the same time, many commentators argue that the bail system keeps far too many people in jail unfairly. Poor people who are "bailable" may remain in jail while their cases slowly wind through the court system, simply because they can't afford to post bail. In fact, some courts have ruled that bail systems that ignore defendants' ability to afford bail are unconstitutional because they deny poor people equal protection of the law or due process of law.

Bail reform efforts are underway in many jurisdictions. California appeared to become the first state to eliminate cash bail with a law scheduled to go into effect in late 2019 that made pretrial freedom dependent on algorithm scores and judges' decisions rather than ability to pay. The bail bond industry sought to overturn the law, though, and the fate of the new law was ultimately set to be decided by voters in 2020.

Somewhat in keeping with the potential California law, judges in some localities look to formulas that use factors such as age and criminal history to provide a more objective assessment of a defendant's flight risk and danger to the community—though the formulas themselves have been criticized for perpetuating unfair stereotypes.

Bail reform efforts have been boosted by the economic savings that governments obtain by reducing the size of jail populations. However, the question of whether bail policies can be liberalized without endangering communities is highly contested.

> **EXAMPLE:** In 2006, nursing assistant Ramon Gaspar was charged with sexually assaulting patients. He was released on bail, and fled to Guatemala. After more than a decade on the run, Gaspar was captured in 2017 and returned to Los Angeles. A judge set new bail at $1 million. The possibility of Gaspar's release on bail after his previous flight outraged his alleged assault victims.

Collateral for a Bail Bond

Often, bail bond sellers ask for collateral in addition to the cost of the bail bond. This means that the bond seller must be given a financial interest in enough real property (such as a house) or personal property (such as a car) to cover the bond seller's loss if the arrested person jumps bail, leaving the bond seller liable for the full amount of bail. Collateral adds to the cost of a bail bond by tying up the collateralized property until the case concludes. This means, for example, a person is not free to sell property while it serves as collateral. Moreover, bond sellers often refuse to do business with an arrested person who lacks the ability to post collateral.

What will courts and jails accept as bail?

Bail is usually posted in one of the following ways:

- By paying the full amount of the bail. For instance, if the police or a court set bail at $1,000, a defendant may post (pay) this amount in cash or with a credit card.
- By purchasing a bond from a bail bond seller, who typically charges a nonrefundable premium of about 10% of the amount of bail. For example, if the police or a court set bail at $1,000, a defendant can usually purchase a bail bond for $100. The bail bond seller has to forfeit the full bail amount to the court if the defendant who purchased the bond fails to appear in court.

Court-Financed Bail

Some states offer a hybrid between posting full cash bail and buying a bail bond from a private bail bond seller. Under the hybrid system, a qualifying arrested person pays a fee of 10% of the full cash bail directly to the court; collateral may also be required. Unlike when a bail bond is purchased from a private seller, the 10% fee (less an administrative charge) is eventually returned if the arrested person makes all required court appearances. Of course, if a defendant fails to appear at a required hearing, the defendant is liable for the full cash bail amount, as well as being subject to rearrest and a new criminal charge of bail jumping.

- By depositing with the court property worth at least the full amount of the bail in some courts. For example, if the police or court set bail at $1,000, and a suspect owns a fancy watch worth at least that amount, the defendant may be able to use the watch to post bail.

Is an arrestee better off buying a bail bond or posting the full cash amount?

For defendants who make all scheduled court appearances, posting full cash bail is cheaper than buying a bail bond. At the conclusion of the case, the defendant who posts full cash bail gets the money back (sometimes less a small administrative fee). Cash bail is refunded regardless of whether a defendant is convicted after a trial, pleads guilty before trial, or gets the charges dismissed. But defendants who buy a bail bond are out the purchase price regardless of the outcome of a case. The cost of a bail bond is a bail bond seller's nonrefundable fee. Moreover, a bail bond may be valid only for a limited time, perhaps a year. If a case drags on past that time, the defendant may have to pay a second fee.

> **EXAMPLE:** Cala Mari is arrested for drunk driving and taken to jail. Bail is set at $1,000. Cala posts this amount and makes all required court appearances. She eventually pleads guilty to reckless driving. At the end of the case, all (or almost all) of the bail money will be returned to Cala. By contrast, had Cala paid

$100 for a bail bond, the bail bond seller would not return that money to her.

Does an arrestee need to hire a lawyer to arrange for a bail bond?

No. Arrestees can arrange for bail themselves. They can either post cash bail personally or phone a bail bond seller and arrange for a bond.

Is It Wise for Relatives and Friends to Post Bail?

A true test of a relative's or friend's trust in a suspect can arise when the suspect calls from jail and says something like, "I need you to post bail for me." A relative or friend who posts full cash bail for a suspect may lose it all if the suspect jumps bail. If the friend or relative purchases a bail bond and the suspect jumps bail, the bail bond agency will demand payment of the full amount of the bond.

Even if the suspect makes all required appearances, the bail bond purchaser is out the bond seller's fee and may have property tied up as collateral. Finally, people who post bail for a suspect may have to appear in court and answer questions under oath as to where they got the money used to post the bail. Thus, before agreeing to post bail for a suspect, friends or relatives have to consider their own financial needs, the risk of the suspect jumping bail, and the likelihood that the suspect will repay any out-of-pocket costs (such as the bond seller's fee).

Can a jailed suspect's relatives or friends post bail?

Yes. Relatives or friends can come to a jail or court and post cash bail for an arrested person or purchase a bond from a bail bond seller.

How are bail amounts determined?

Judges ordinarily set a bail amount at a suspect's first court appearance after an arrest, which may be either a bail hearing or an arraignment. Judges normally adhere to standard practices (for example, setting bail in the amount of $500 for nonviolent petty misdemeanors). However, judges can raise or lower the standard bail, or waive bail altogether and grant release O.R., based on the circumstances of an individual case.

In addition to the seriousness of the charged crime, the amount of bail usually depends on factors such as a defendant's past criminal record, whether a defendant is employed, and whether a defendant has close ties to relatives and the community.

Judges may legally deny bail altogether in some circumstances. For example, if another jurisdiction has placed a warrant (hold) on a defendant, a judge is likely to keep the defendant in custody at least long enough for the other jurisdiction to pursue its charge. And bail may be denied to a defendant who is likely to flee the jurisdiction before the case concludes.

In many areas of the country, defendants can post bail with the police even before they are brought to court for a bail hearing or an arraignment. Many jails have posted bail schedules, which specify bail amounts for common crimes. An arrested defendant can obtain release immediately after booking by paying the amount of bail set forth in the jailhouse bail schedule.

EXAMPLE: Rosie Olla is arrested and charged with managing a large prostitution ring. Rosie is a naturalized American citizen born in Spain, and her family still lives in Barcelona. While searching Rosie after her arrest, the police found that she was carrying a passport and $5,000 in cash. Under these circumstances, a judge will probably be very reluctant to set bail for Rosie. Her family background and the fact that she was carrying a passport and a large amount of cash suggest that Rosie may flee to Spain if she is released on bail. Unless Rosie can explain to the judge why she was carrying the passport and cash, and can also demonstrate strong ties to the local community, a judge is likely to deny her request for bail.

Duty Judges

As an alternative or in addition to jailhouse bail schedules, some areas have duty judges. A duty judge is available to fix bail over the phone, without the necessity for a formal court hearing. Like a jailhouse bail schedule, using a duty judge is an option for arrested persons who are anxious to bail out of jail before going to court.

What are the typical rates in a bail schedule?

Bail schedules can vary considerably according to locality, type of crime, and residency. Most jurisdictions post their bail schedules online.

As a general rule, bail for offenses classified as felonies is five to ten times the bail required for misdemeanors. Also, the more serious and dangerous the crime, the higher the amount of bail is likely to be. For example, a county might have a standard presumptive bail of the following amounts for the following offenses:

- Murder: no bail
- Voluntary manslaughter: $100,000
- Involuntary manslaughter: $25,000

As a general rule, a jailhouse bail schedule is inflexible. The police will not accept bail other than as set forth in a schedule; suspects hoping to pay less must go before a judge.

Bail and Police Arrest Practices

Unfortunately for many suspects who want to bail out of jail quickly, the police tend to arrest suspects for the most serious criminal charge that can possibly be supported by the facts at their disposal. For instance, the police may treat possession of a small amount of marijuana (a misdemeanor in many states) as an arrest for possession of marijuana with intent to sell (a felony in all states). Even though the felony arrest will often be reduced to a misdemeanor charge later in the case, it is a felony for the purposes of the bail schedule, and bail will be set accordingly.

EXAMPLE: Rand Omly is arrested and jailed for possession of cocaine. According to the locality's bail schedule, Omly has to post bail in the amount of $10,000 to secure his release. The police are unlikely to accept a lower bail amount even if Omly has never previously been arrested, lives in the area, and has a family and a job. To lower the bail amount, Omly will have to wait to go before a judge and argue his special circumstances.

Are there times when someone might be better off waiting for a judge to set bail than paying the amount set forth in a bail schedule?

Bail schedules treat all suspects alike. But suspects with no previous arrests and strong ties to the community (for example, a job and family) may convince a judge to set much lower bail than the bail schedule provides—or even to grant own recognizance release. In this situation, by remaining in jail a day or two before appearing in court, a suspect might save a considerable amount of money. For example, if the bail schedule fixes bail at $10,000, a bond will cost $1,000 in a nonrefundable fee. If a day later the judge fixes bail at $1,000, the bond would then cost only $100. This means that by waiting for the judge to act, the defendant (or the defendant's family or friends) would save $900.

Of course, each individual suspect, and the suspect's family and friends, will have to weigh the opportunity to save money by asking the judge to lower the bail against the hardship of remaining in jail longer than is absolutely necessary.

How soon after an arrest will a suspect be taken to court?

Most jurisdictions require that an arrested person be taken "without unnecessary delay" before the nearest available magistrate. This first court appearance will be either a bail hearing or an arraignment, or both. The general rule is that an arraignment should take place within 48 hours of the time that a suspect is booked into jail. But many suspects who do not post stationhouse bail stay in jail for up to 72 hours before they are brought before a judge. So long as the police and prosecutors do not circumvent the 48-hour policy simply for punitive reasons, the delay rarely carries legal consequences.

On the other hand, a suspect arrested in the morning may sometimes be able to see a judge that afternoon if the prosecutor's office is quick with its paperwork.

Can people represent themselves at bail hearings?

Yes, but suspects typically benefit from legal representation at a bail hearing. Experienced attorneys know the factors that particular judges find important when considering a request for lowered bail or O.R. release. In addition, attorneys normally discuss cases with prosecutors before the bail hearing, and sometimes can assure the judge that the charges are not as serious as they look on paper. An attorney may also be able to organize a presentation that impresses the judge—for instance, a lawyer might arrange for family members, a boss, and supportive members of the community to be present and prepared to speak on the defendant's behalf at the court appearance. Finally, the simple truth is that judges often take attorneys' arguments more seriously than they do those of self-represented defendants.

What factors can self-representing defendants talk about when requesting lower bail or release O.R.?

Just like lawyers, self-represented defendants seeking lower or no bail should try to emphasize circumstances such as:

- **The defendant doesn't pose a physical danger to the community.** Obviously, this argument applies primarily to defendants charged with nonviolent crimes.
- **The defendant has no previous criminal record,** or has a minimal past record and made all required appearances associated with those charges.
- **The defendant has strong ties to the community,** such as a family and a job. (Judges are often impressed when family members and an employer personally appear to support a defendant at a bail hearing.)

Are there limits on how much bail a judge can require?

The Eighth Amendment to the U.S. Constitution (which is binding on all states) requires that the amount of bail not be excessive. What this means is that bail should not be a way to raise money for the state or to punish a person for being suspected of committing a crime. Nor can the police use bail to keep a suspect in jail simply to give themselves more time to gather evidence. Because a suspect is innocent until proven guilty, the amount of bail should be no more than reasonably necessary to keep the suspect from fleeing the jurisdiction before the case is over.

Despite these policies, many judges set unaffordably high bail in some types of cases to keep suspected offenders in jail pending trial. Judges can lose elections when defendants they've released on bail commit new crimes, but rarely take political heat for keeping a suspect behind bars. High bail is particularly likely when a defendant poses a danger to the community or has committed an offense against a family member. A judge may also set higher bail if a defendant is likely to flee the jurisdiction before trial or has a prior criminal record. Although some legal commentators argue that preventive detention—keeping a defendant in jail out of fear that the defendant is dangerous— violates the Eighth Amendment, the U.S. Supreme Court upheld the practice in *U.S. v. Salerno* (1987).

Because of terrorism concerns, foreign nationals may face special obstacles in the bail-setting process. Arrested foreign nationals may need to contact a lawyer with experience in both criminal law and immigration issues, and may also want to contact their country's consulate.

EXAMPLE: Rex Kars is charged with felony hit-and-run driving. At a bail setting hearing, the judge sets bail at $5,000. Kars argues that the bail is excessive, as he cannot afford to post that amount in cash nor does he have sufficient collateral to purchase a bail bond. However, while a judge can consider Kars's personal history and financial ability when setting bail, the fact that Kars cannot afford to pay the bail that is set does not necessarily make it excessive.

EXAMPLE: Holly Woode is arrested for stealing two blouses from a clothing store (petty theft). During a bail hearing, the judge tells Holly, "In my opinion, once a petty thief always a petty thief. If I let you out on bail, you'll probably just go on stealing." With that, the judge denies bail to Holly. (Alternatively, the judge sets bail so high that Holly clearly has no way of paying it.) The judge's decision is arbitrary and invalid. The crime that Holly is accused of committing is not one of violence, so preventive detention is unnecessary. Moreover, the judge's comments are based only on the judge's predisposition, not on information about Holly. Holly can file a petition for *habeas corpus* asking another judge to set reasonable bail. (She might have additional legal options). (See Chapter 23.)

Once a judge sets bail, can it be changed?

Yes. Judges have the power to raise or lower the amount of bail if new information emerges.

EXAMPLE: Phil Errup, an unemployed electrician, is charged with assault and battery. A judge initially sets bail in the amount of $10,000, commenting that Phil's lack of employment makes him a risk to flee. Phil cannot afford the bail, so he remains in jail. A week later, an electrical contractor agrees to hire Phil to work on a job, and to continue to employ Phil at least until the charges are finally resolved. This new information might lead the judge to lower the bail amount. Because the judge was influenced in part by Phil's unemployment, the job is a changed circumstance that might incline the judge (or a different judge) to lower the bail. Phil can file a Motion for Reconsideration of Bail and ask the electrical contractor either to attend the court hearing or send a letter to the court verifying the job offer.

EXAMPLE: Jenna Furr is charged with possession of cocaine. A judge initially sets bail in the amount of $1,000. Jenna posts bail and is released from jail. A week later, the district attorney receives new information that six months earlier, Jenna was charged with possession of illegal drugs in another state, and fled the state before the case was over. Upon the district attorney's request, the judge might schedule a new bail hearing, order Jenna to attend, and increase her bail or revoke it altogether.

Can release on bail be accompanied by restrictions on behavior?

Yes. Judges have the power to place restrictions on defendants as a condition of releasing them on bail. For example, depending on the offense charged, a defendant may have to agree to:

- abstain from excessive use of alcohol or drugs, and from possession of weapons

- avoid contact with a victim or witnesses
- report regularly to a law enforcement officer
- enroll in an anger management program
- maintain or seek employment
- maintain or seek an educational program, and
- remain in the custody of a designated relative or other person (perhaps under "house arrest").

What happens if a defendant violates a condition of bail?

Judges can revoke the bail of a suspect who violates a condition of bail. For example, if a suspect who is ordered to enroll in a counseling program fails to do so, the judge can revoke the suspect's bail and issue a warrant for the suspect's arrest. Or, if the judge does not consider the violation to be overly serious, the judge may simply raise the amount of bail (or require bail from a suspect previously released O.R.).

What happens if a defendant who has bailed out fails to show up in court?

This is a big no-no. Defendants who fail to appear at a scheduled court appearance may suffer both financial and criminal penalties. That is, a violator will forfeit the amount of bail and, in most states, may also be charged with a separate crime. If the person is ever arrested and detained again in the future—once the current case is resolved—the bail in that future case probably will be impossibly high, because the judge will consider the person a bail risk.

EXAMPLE: Della Ware is free on $1,000 bail after posting the full cash amount with the court. The judge orders Della to attend a pretrial settlement conference. However, Della fails to attend and does not explain her absence to her lawyer. As a result, Della will forfeit the entire $1,000 to the court. Della may also find herself charged with the crime of bail jumping, in addition to the crime she was charged with in the first place. A warrant will go out for her arrest, and when she's picked up neither the police nor a judge or magistrate are likely to offer her a second chance to post bail.

What if defendants such as Della fail to make a required court appearance and a bail bond seller has to pay the full bail amount to the court? Because the seller probably required Della to post collateral, the bond seller may sell her car or fancy watch or whatever property she pledged as security for the bond. In addition, if the collateral is insufficient, the bond seller can hire a bounty hunter to find Della, arrest her, and bring her back to the court's jurisdiction so that the bond seller no longer has to pay the full amount of the bail to the court (or gets the money back, if it has already been paid). If she skips bail, Della will have two groups after her—the police and the bail bond seller/bounty hunter. As you can see, it would be better for Della to just make all her required court appearances once she bails out.

Should defendants pay to bail out if they will probably do jail time anyway?

If a defendant is convicted of a crime and sentenced to jail, the sentence will normally be reduced by the number of days that person was detained in jail prior to conviction. (This is called "credit for time served.") Thus, a suspect who expects to receive a jail sentence may consider saving the cost of a bail bond and in effect begin serving the sentence prior to conviction.

From an economic standpoint, forgoing bail in such a situation may make sense. But in practice it's usually to a suspect's benefit to seek pretrial release. One obvious reason is that the suspect may be wrong about receiving a jail sentence upon conviction. Many jails are overcrowded, and suspects who in the past might have been incarcerated are now allowed to remain free even if they are convicted.

A second reason to bail out is that jail conditions are normally worse for inmates awaiting sentencing than they are for inmates who have already been sentenced. For example, people serving jail sentences may have access to exercise facilities and the jail's law library, and may be given work opportunities and other privileges. Prior to sentencing, these options may not be available.

Third, defendants who are released prior to trial run no danger of making statements to jailers or even other inmates that can be used against them if their cases ultimately go to trial.

Fourth, prosecutors usually move cases along more slowly when defendants are not in custody. As a result, witnesses can become less reliable and cases can get stale, so that bailed-out defendants can wind up with better deals. As at least one defense attorney liked to say, "Justice delayed is justice."

Finally, defendants who bail out have a chance to undertake constructive activities that may lead a prosecutor or a judge to dismiss or at least reduce the charges against them or lessen their punishment.

> **EXAMPLE:** Harold is charged with driving under the influence. Harold bails out of jail, starts attending AA meetings, and begins a counseling program for people with addiction problems offered through a community mental health center. Weeks later, when Harold and his attorney meet with the prosecutor, Harold has a record of the AA meetings he's attended and a letter from the head of the counseling program praising Harold's attendance and efforts. The prosecutor may be impressed enough with Harold's selfhelp efforts to place Harold on informal probation and dismiss the drunk driving charge after six months if Harold completes (or remains in) the counseling program and has no further arrests during that period.

Own Recognizance Release (Release O.R.)

Own recognizance release is the criminal justice system's version of Monopoly's Get Out of Jail Free card.

What does it mean to be released O.R.?

Simply put, O.R. release is no-cost bail. Defendants released on their own recognizance need only sign a written promise to appear in court as required. No bail has to be paid, either to the court or to a bail bond seller. However, all other aspects of bail remain the same. That is, a judge can place conditions on a defendant released O.R. (such as to check in regularly with a probation officer and to abstain from the use of drugs or alcohol) and order the arrest of a defendant who fails to show up in court when required.

How will a judge decide if a defendant is eligible for O.R. release?

Judges have nearly absolute discretion when it comes to deciding whether to require bail or release a suspect O.R. Generally, the same factors that might incline a judge to set low bail may persuade the judge to grant release O.R. Thus, factors favoring O.R. release include a suspect's good past record, longtime residence in a community, support of family members, and employment.

Sample Release Order and Bond Form

UNITED STATES DISTRICT COURT FOR THE CENTRAL DISTRICT OF CALIFORNIA

UNITED STATES OF AMERICA.	CASE NUMBER	
Plaintiff.	COMPLAINT	INDICTMENT/INFORMATION
V.		
Defendant/Material Witness		

VERIFICATION OF BAIL:
BAIL FIXED BY COURT FOR DEFENDANT/WITNESS:

IN CASE NO. _____

IN THE AMOUNT OF $ _____

CLERK, U.S. DISTRICT COURT

BY: _____
Deputy Clerk

Violation of Title ____ Section ____

TYPE OF BOND

☐ PERSONAL RECOGNIZANCE (Signature only - no dollar amount)
☐ UNSECURED APPEARANCE BOND IN AMOUNT OF $_____
☐ APPEARANCE BOND IN THE AMOUNT $_____
☐ WITH CASE DEPOSIT (amount or %) _____
   ☐ WITH AFFIDAVIT OF SURETY (No Justification) (Form CR-4)
   ☐ WITH JUSTIFICATION AFFIDAVIT OF SURETY (Form CR-3)
   ☐ AND WITH DEEDING OF PROPERTY OR ☐
☐ COLLATERAL BOND IN THE AMOUNT OF $ _____
(Cash or Negotiable Securities)
☐ CORPORATE SURETY BOND IN AMOUNT OF $ _____
(Corporate Surety Bond requires separate form)

PRECONDITIONS TO RELEASE

☐ You are to surrender to the Clerk of Court all passports issued to you and not apply for the issuance of a passport during the pendency of this case.
☐ Bail is subject to Nebbia Hearing.

ADDITIONAL CONDITIONS OF RELEASE

☐ Travel is restricted to _____
☐ You are to reside with _____
☐ Pretrial Services supervision   [   ] Intensive
☐ You are not to use illegal drugs and are to cooperate with Pretrial Services in a drug treatment and testing program.
☐ You are to participate in a residential drug/alcohol treatment program as approved by Pretrial Services.
☐ Other conditions: _____

GENERAL CONDITIONS OF RELEASE

I will appear in person in accordance with any and all directions and orders relating to my appearance in the above entitled matter as may be given or issued by the Court or any judicial officer thereof, in that Court or before any Magistrate Judge thereof, or in any other United States District Court to which I may be removed or to which the case may be transferred.
I understand the next ordered appearance is at _____ p.m.
                                           (Place)   (Date/Time)
I will abide by any judgment entered in this matter by surrendering myself to serve any sentence imposed and will obey any order or direction in connection with such judgment as the Court may prescribe.
I will not leave the State of California except upon order of this Court, and I will immediately inform the Court, the United States Attorney and my counsel in writing of any change in my residence address or telephone number so that I may be reached at all times.
I will not commit a Federal, State, or local crime during the period of release.
I will not intimidate any witness, juror or officer of the court, or obstruct the criminal investigation in this case in violation of Title 18 USC Section 1503 and 1510. Additionally, I will not tamper with, harass or retaliate against any alleged witness, victim or informant in this case in violation of Title 18 USC Section 1512 and 1513.

ACKNOWLEDGEMENT OF DEFENDANT/MATERIAL WITNESS

AS CONDITION OF MY RELEASE ON THIS BOND, PURSUANT TO TITLE 18 OF THE UNITED STATES CODE. I HAVE READ OR HAVE HAD INTERPRETED TO ME AND UNDERSTAND THE GENERAL CONDITIONS OF RELEASE. THE PRECONDITIONS AND ADDITIONAL CONDITIONS OF RELEASE AS CHECKED ABOVE AND AGREE TO COMPLY WITH ALL CONDITIONS OF RELEASE IMPOSED ON ME AND TO BE BOUND BY THE PROVISIONS OF LOCAL CRIMINAL RULES 5.2, 5.4 AND 5.5.
FURTHERMORE, IT IS AGREED & UNDERSTOOD THAT THIS IS A CONTINUING BOND (INCLUDING ANY PROCEEDINGS ON APPEAL OR REVIEW) WHICH SHALL CONTINUE IN FULL FORCE & EFFECT UNTIL SUCH TIME AS DULY EXONERATED.
I UNDERSTAND THAT VIOLATION OF ANY OF THE GENERAL AND/OR ADDITIONAL CONDITIONS OF RELEASE AS GIVEN ON THE FACE OF THIS BOND MAY RESULT IN A REVOCATION OF RELEASE, AN ORDER OF DETENTION AND A NEW PROSECUTION FOR AN ADDITIONAL OFFENSE WHICH COULD RESULT IN A TERM OF IMPRISONMENT AND/OR FINE.
I FURTHER UNDERSTAND THAT IF I FAIL TO OBEY AND PERFORM ANY OF THE GENERAL AND/OR ADDITIONAL CONDITIONS OF RELEASE AS GIVEN ON THE FACE OF THE BOND, THIS BOND MAY BE FORFEITED TO THE UNITED STATES OF AMERICA. IF SAID FORFEITURE IS NOT SET ASIDE, JUDGMENT MAY BE SUMMARILY ENTERED IN THIS COURT AGAINST MYSELF AND EACH SURETY, JOINTLY AND SEVERALLY, FOR THE BOND AMOUNT, TOGETHER WITH INTEREST AND COSTS, AND EXECUTION OF THE JUDGMENT MAY BE ISSUED OR PAYMENT SECURED AS PROVIDED BY THE FEDERAL RULES OF CRIMINAL PROCEDURE AND OTHER LAWS OF THE UNITED STATES AND ANY CASH, REAL OR PERSONAL PROPERTY OR THE COLLATERAL PREVIOUSLY POSTED IN CONNECTION WITH THIS BOND MAY BE FORFEITED.

DATE: _____

_____ Defendant/Material Witness' Signature   ( )_____ Telephone Number

_____ Address (please print)   City, State and Zip Code

☐ Check if Interpreter is used: I have interpreted into the _____ language all of the above conditions of release and have been told by the defendant that he or she understands all the conditions of release.

Date: _____

_____ Interpreter's signature

APPROVED: _____   DATE: _____
     UNITED STATES MAGISTRATE JUDGE

IF CASH DEPOSITED: RECEIPT # _____ FOR $ _____
(This bond may require surety agreements and affidavits pursuant to Local Criminal Rules 5.2 or 5.3)

Can a self-represented defendant ask for release O.R.?

Yes. In fact, a defendant should request release O.R. if there is any reasonable chance that the judge will grant the request. If the judge denies the O.R. request, the defendant can seek low bail as an alternative.

What is an O.R. officer?

Many communities rely on O.R. officers to help judges decide whether to release suspects O.R. (in some areas, O.R. officers are called pretrial officers). When a defendant requests release O.R., a judge may ask an O.R. officer to do a quick check of a defendant's general background, past criminal record, and ties to the community. The O.R. officer will then make a nonbinding recommendation to the judge. If possible, a defendant should ask an employer, religious leader, and others who can speak positively of the defendant to contact an O.R. officer or contact the court directly to support the O.R. request.

Release Order and Bond Form

Many courts use a checklist that covers all possible options available to the judge when deciding the status of a defendant pending trial. A sample form used is provided above.

From Suspect to Defendant

To be "charged" with a crime means to be formally accused of that crime. Police officers usually start the charging process with an arrest or citation. They then send copies of their reports to a prosecutor's office staffed by government lawyers whose job it is to initiate and prosecute criminal cases. The prosecutor is supposed to either:

- make an independent decision as to what charges should be filed, or
- enlist the help of citizens serving as grand jurors in deciding what charges to file.

Crime and Criminal Cases

This section reviews some basics about crime, including what makes certain acts criminal, the difference between civil and criminal cases, and the general categories of crime.

What are the hallmarks of a criminal case?

There are two different types of court cases: criminal and civil. A criminal case takes place when the government seeks to punish an offender for an act that has been classified as a crime by Congress, by a state legislature, or by a municipality. A civil case, on the other hand, usually involves a dispute over the rights and duties that people and organizations legally owe to each other. Among the important differences between criminal and civil cases are these:

- In a criminal case, a prosecutor, not the victim, institutes and controls the case. The prosecutor may file criminal charges even if the victim doesn't approve, or may refuse to file criminal charges despite the victim's desire that criminal charges be filed. This method of initiating the case contrasts with civil cases, where the injured party is the one who decides whether to sue and what claims to make.
- People convicted of crimes may pay a fine or be incarcerated or both. People held liable in civil cases may have to pay money damages or give up property, but do not go to jail or prison. (The U.S. doesn't have debtors' prisons for those who can't pay a civil judgment.)
- In criminal cases, government-paid lawyers represent defendants who want but can't afford an attorney. Parties in civil cases, on the other hand, usually have to represent themselves or pay for their own lawyers.
- In criminal cases, the prosecutor has to prove a defendant's guilt beyond a reasonable doubt. In a civil case, the plaintiff only has to show by a preponderance of the evidence that the defendant is liable for damages.
- Defendants in criminal cases almost always are entitled to a jury trial. A party to a civil action is entitled to a jury trial in some types of cases, but not in others.

CAUTION
The same conduct may violate both criminal and civil laws. A defendant whose actions violate both criminal and civil rules may be criminally prosecuted by the state and civilly sued by a victim for monetary damages. For instance, in 1995, O. J. Simpson was prosecuted for murder and found not guilty. In an entirely separate case, Simpson was also sued in a civil case for wrongful death by the victims' families. At the close of the civil case in 1997, Simpson was found "liable" (the civil equivalent to guilty, meaning responsible for) for the victims' deaths and ordered to pay millions of dollars in damages.

Are crimes classified according to their seriousness?

Yes. Like boxes of soap powder, criminal laws come in an array of shapes and sizes. The seriousness of a charge depends on whether it's a felony, a misdemeanor, or an infraction:

- Felonies are the most serious kinds of crimes. Generally, a crime is considered a felony when it is punishable by more than a year in a state prison (also called a penitentiary). Examples of felonies are murder, rape, burglary, and the sale of illegal drugs.
- Misdemeanors are less serious crimes, and are typically punishable by up to a year in county jail. Common misdemeanors include shoplifting, drunk driving, assault, and possession of an unregistered firearm. Often, an offense that is a misdemeanor the first time a person commits it becomes a felony the second time around.

What Makes a Crime a Crime?

In the United States, an act is a crime because Congress or a state or local legislative body has defined it as such. But why are some acts defined as crimes while others aren't? While whole books have been written on this subject, here are a few straightforward reasons why crimes are crimes:

- Many acts that we consider crimes today were considered crimes under English law when we became a country. In large part, we adopted that law as our own.
- Many crimes have their origin in moral precepts that originally were enforced by churches and taken over by the secular state.
- Acts carried out with an antisocial or malicious intent usually are considered worthy of punishment.
- Acts that may have been acceptable at one time (such as physical punishment of a child, drinking while driving, or domestic violence) are redefined as crimes when societal groups convince lawmakers to criminalize such acts.

At bottom, what is and is not a crime is, to an extent, arbitrary and a reflection of who has the power to decide. But with some notable exceptions—for example, drug laws—most common crimes have been considered crimes for centuries, and most people agree that they should be.

"Wobblers"

Prosecutors and judges sometimes are authorized by a criminal statute to treat the criminal behavior defined in the statute as either a felony or a misdemeanor. Such crimes are often referred to as "wobblers." For example, under a wobbler statute that allows assault to be charged as a felony or a misdemeanor, the prosecutor usually will decide which charge to bring on the basis of the severity of the injury to the victim and the nature of the defendant's intent and past criminal record. Similarly, after hearing evidence of a crime charged as a felony under such a statute, a judge may decide to reduce the charge to a misdemeanor.

- Infractions are still less serious violations, like those involving traffic laws, which typically subject a person to nothing more than a monetary fine. Defendants charged with infractions usually have no right to a jury trial or a court-appointed lawyer.
- Municipal laws, also called ordinances, are enacted by and are effective only in a particular city or county. For example, a city ordinance may forbid overnight parking or prohibit smoking in elevators. Violators of municipal laws are typically fined.

What's the difference between state and federal crimes?

States and the federal government both enact criminal laws. Some offenses, like routine drunk driving, would be state crimes, covered by state laws, whereas assaulting a federal officer, like an FBI agent, would likely be a federal offense no matter where it is committed.

But, as with many aspects of the law, even these divisions are not so clear-cut. To commit the crime of assaulting a federal officer (18 U.S.C. § 111), among other things, the victim must have been engaged in the performance of official duties at the time of the assault. If the victim was an off-duty FBI agent, the case might well be governed by a state assault statute.

Also, the same conduct may violate both federal and state laws. A well-known case involving federal and state criminal trials stemming from the same incident involved four California law enforcement officers accused of beating motorist Rodney King. The officers were tried and acquitted in state court on assault charges and were tried and convicted in federal court for having violated Rodney King's civil rights.

To Charge or Not to Charge, That Is the Question

Police officers make arrests, but prosecutors decide whether to file formal charges against suspects. This section explains how charges are filed and what factors typically influence prosecutors' charging decisions.

What are statutes of limitation?

Statutes of limitation establish time limits for starting criminal proceedings. Statutes of limitation generally start to "run" on the date that crimes are committed. If the applicable time limit expires before criminal proceedings begin, charges cannot be filed.

The time limits that statutes of limitation establish vary from one state to another and according to the seriousness of a crime. In general, the more serious a crime, the more time a state has to begin criminal proceedings. By way of example, here are some time limits set forth in Section 1.06 of the "Model Penal Code," which are similar to those of many states:

- murder charges: no time limit
- serious felony charges: six years
- misdemeanor charges: two years, and
- petty misdemeanors and infractions: six months.

States cannot retroactively change the rules to allow prosecution of crimes that are already barred by an existing statute of limitation. For example, assume that Will sexually molests a teenager named Joe. Joe doesn't report what happened for many years. By the time he tells the police about the molestation, the statute of limitations has expired. The legislature cannot enact a new law that would allow the state more time to prosecute Will. (*Stogner v. California*, U.S. Sup. Ct. 2003.)

> **EXAMPLE:** Larry breaks into a neighbor's house and steals an Italian lamp that he has always wanted for his own apartment. The neighbor reports the burglary to the police. However, the police misplace the report and, as a result, don't begin investigating the crime until many months later. By the time the police arrest Larry and the prosecutor is ready to begin criminal proceedings, the state's three-year statute of limitations on burglary has expired. As a result, Larry cannot be prosecuted for burglary. If the prosecutor were to begin criminal proceedings, Larry would be entitled to have the case dismissed.

> **EXAMPLE:** Same case. Assume that after committing the burglary, Larry moves to another state for three years. A few months after he returns, the police arrest him for burglary. In these circumstances, the state's three-year statute of limitations does not prevent Larry's prosecution for burglary. For statute of limitation purposes, the clock is ticking only during the time that a suspect remains in the state where the crime was committed and has a fixed place of residence or work. Thus, the statute of limitations was not running down during the three years that Larry was in a different state.

Victims' Right to Consult on Charges

Laws in a few jurisdictions provide a limited right for victims to consult with prosecutors about the charging decision. For example, a law might require prosecutors to notify victims if the prosecutors intend not to file charges and to give those victims a chance to consult before the decision not to file becomes final. Ultimately, however, prosecutors have the final say about whether to file charges and what charges to file.

Note: Statutes of limitation, which establish time limits for starting criminal proceedings, are distinguished from the Sixth Amendment right to a speedy trial, which applies to the length of time between the beginning of criminal proceedings and cases going to trial.

Who decides what criminal charges to file?

Prosecutors decide whether to charge suspects with crimes and what charges to file. Arrest and prosecution functions are separated primarily to protect citizens against the arbitrary exercise of police power. Police officers usually make arrests based only on whether they have good reason (probable cause) to believe a crime has been committed. By contrast, prosecutors can file formal charges only if they believe that they can prove a suspect guilty beyond a reasonable doubt. Prosecutors can also take a broader perspective. They have what is called "prosecutorial discretion." Prosecutors can look at all the circumstances of a case, including the suspect's past criminal record, when deciding whether to go forward with criminal charges.

Prosecutors can file charges on all crimes for which the police arrested a suspect, can file charges that are more or less severe than the charges leveled by the police, or can decide not to file any charges at all. (*U.S. v. Batchelder*, U.S. Sup. Ct. 1979.)

How much time goes by between arrests and the filing of charges?

If suspects are in custody, speedy-trial laws typically require prosecutors to file charges, if at all, within 72 hours of arrest. Some jurisdictions require prosecutors to charge a suspect even sooner, like within 48 hours. However, prosecutors' initial charging decisions are subject to change. For example, a prosecutor may not make a final decision on charges until after a preliminary hearing, which may take place more than a month after arrest.

Use of Arrest Reports in Criminal Cases

Arrest reports are almost always one-sided. They recite only what the police claim took place and may include only witness statements that support the police theory. While they are generally not admissible as evidence in a trial, arrest reports can have a major impact in criminal cases. Not only do arrest reports often determine what charges prosecutors file, but they also may play a key role in how much bail is required, the outcome of preliminary hearings (where hearsay evidence is often admissible), the willingness of the prosecutor to plea bargain, and trial tactics (for instance, the police report can be used to discredit testimony of the police officer who prepared the report).

How do prosecutors decide what crimes to charge?

Typically, prosecutors base their initial charging decisions on the documents sent to them by the arresting police officers (usually called police or arrest reports). Arrest reports summarize the events leading up to arrests and provide numerous other details, such as dates, time, location, weather conditions, and witnesses' names and addresses.

How do prosecutors obtain arrest reports?

Police officers and prosecutors work closely together. The police complete an arrest report soon after they make an arrest and then quickly forward the report to a prosecutor assigned to do case intake. The intake prosecutor decides whether to formally file charges (or to submit the evidence to a grand jury) and what charges to file.

Does a prosecutor ever conduct an independent investigation before deciding what charges to file?

In some parts of the country, prosecutors may personally talk to police officers, victims, and witnesses before filing charges. (Prosecutors do not normally talk to the suspect, especially if the suspect is already represented by counsel.) In most places, however, and in big cities especially, prosecutors who make charging decisions are likely to be too harried to conduct independent investigations. For instance, a single intake prosecutor may process

200–300 cases a day. Thus, prosecutors usually make charging decisions based on little more than a cursory review of a police report and a defendant's criminal history. If laboratory testing was done (such as in under-the-influence cases), prosecutors may also check the results of those tests before filing charges.

Prosecutors May Also File Charges to Satisfy Important Political Constituencies

Most chief prosecutors are elected officials. Many of them view their position as a stepping-stone to higher office. Their charging decisions are often, therefore, affected by public opinion or important support groups. For example, a prosecutor may file charges on every shoplifting case, no matter how weak, to curry favor with local store owners who want to get the word out that shoplifters will be prosecuted. Similarly, political realities may lead prosecutors to adopt a "no deals" policy in domestic abuse situations. Deputy or assistant prosecutors may feel that appearing tough will help their careers, either within the prosecutor's office or later if they want to become judges. Experienced defense attorneys understand that prosecutors must sometimes be seen as taking a strong stand publicly, even though they may be willing to respond to weaknesses in individual cases at a later stage of the process.

As a result, prosecutors' decisions typically rely almost entirely on police officers' decisions and efforts. Many prosecutors view their role as house counsel for the local police department. One reason is that prosecutors would be out of business without police. A second is that every time a prosecutor decides not to file charges, the prosecutor is implicitly, if not directly, snubbing the arresting officer. The prosecutor is saying to the officer in effect, "You didn't have enough evidence to make this arrest," or "You didn't follow correct procedures"; at least, that's what the officer often hears. Rather than having to play this role with the police, a prosecutor may go along with the officer's assessment and let the court and the defense worry about preventing any resulting injustice.

EXAMPLE: Officer Bremer pulls Opie over for failing to stop at a stop sign. The officer sees a small packet of illegal narcotics on the passenger seat next to Opie. The officer arrests Opie, and decides that the packet contains a sufficient amount of narcotics to support a charge that Opie possessed the narcotics for the purpose of sale, a much more serious crime than simple possession. Though the prosecutor would be content to secure a conviction for simple possession, the prosecutor charges Opie with possession for sale.

EXAMPLE: Officer Krupke arrests Bernardo Gutierrez, a Puerto Rican man, for interfering with a police officer's duties. Krupke claims that Bernardo physically tried to prevent Krupke from making an arrest. Bernardo claims that he did nothing wrong, but simply tried to tell Krupke that he was arresting an innocent person. The prosecutors know that Krupke has a bad attitude toward racial and ethnic minorities. Here, the intake prosecutor may fear that dropping the charges would invite Bernardo to file a suit for false arrest against the police. Also, the prosecutor's office would not be able to work with Krupke in the future if they didn't follow through on his arrests. However, the intake prosecutor might also alert the police department to a problem officer and ask for a review of Krupke's performance. However, the intake prosecutor might also alert the police department to a problem officer and ask for a review of Krupke's performance.

Why might prosecutors decide not to file charges against arrestees?

Intake prosecutors may decline to file charges for a number of reasons. Among the most common are:

- **An offense is trivial or low priority.** Prosecutor offices may view certain types of crimes as insignificant or not worth pursuing. For example, a prosecutor may decline to prosecute all cases involving possession of very small quantities of illegal drugs. Or the prosecutor may decide not to pursue charges against a group of protesters arrested at a local political rally.

Mediating Minor Nonviolent Criminal Cases

In some locations, minor criminal complaints are diverted out of the court system before prosecutors file charges. The alleged offender and complainant are brought together to discuss their problem, sometimes with a facilitator or mediator, to come up with some sort of solution. If you're interested, ask your defense attorney or public defender whether mediation is available in your jurisdiction.

- **The prosecutor believes that the facts do not support guilt beyond a reasonable doubt.** The prosecutor's ultimate role is to seek justice. If the prosecution has insufficient evidence to prove guilt beyond a reasonable doubt, a suspect should not be charged with a crime.

EXAMPLE: The main witness against a suspect is the suspect's cellmate, who in the past has committed perjury in order to obtain a shorter sentence. A prosecutor might decide that the cellmate's credibility is too doubtful to support the filing of charges against the suspect.

- **The victim asks that no charges be brought.** Charging decisions are for prosecutors, not victims. However, if victims ask prosecutors not to bring charges and make it perfectly clear that they will not cooperate, prosecutors often won't file charges. In past years, this type of situation was common in domestic violence situations. When abused partners or family members told police officers and prosecutors that they did not want to go forward, charges would be either not filed or dropped. In recent years, the law enforcement community has taken domestic abuse allegations more seriously. If they have admissible evidence of abuse apart from the victim that proves guilt beyond a reasonable doubt, prosecutors now bring and prosecute domestic abuse charges even if victims don't want to pursue the case.

Civil Compromise

Defense lawyers often try to prevent the filing of criminal charges by arranging for a civil compromise. Much like mediated agreements, the defendant agrees to reimburse a victim for damages. In return, the victim asks a prosecutor not to file charges. This option gives some arrestees a ticket out of the criminal justice system that may not be available to those who can't afford it.

- **The prosecutor views the suspect as a good person.** Occasionally, a prosecutor will decide that a basically good person made a stupid mistake that shouldn't result in a consequence as severe as a criminal charge. In such a situation, the prosecutor will refuse to prosecute, either in the interests of justice or because it would be a waste of resources (time and money) to charge such a person with a crime, even though the initial arrest was valid.

EXAMPLE: Lib Erty, a teenager, stood with a group of five girlfriends at a store cosmetics counter. A security guard saw two of the girls take some lipsticks and leave without paying for them. The guard detained all the girls and called the police. A police officer arrested them, including Lib, for shoplifting. After reviewing the case, the intake prosecutor believes that Lib did not take anything herself and was not aware that the other girls planned to steal the items. The prosecutor also learns that Lib has no prior criminal record, and that her chances for a college scholarship might be jeopardized if she is convicted of a crime. Under all the circumstances, the prosecutor decides that it would not be in the interests of justice to prosecute Lib. However, the store manager and police officer want the prosecutor to prosecute all the girls to send the teenage community a strong message that shoplifting will not be tolerated. The prosecutor may decide not to charge Lib with a crime. The prosecutor can consider the views of citizens and police, but the ultimate decision of whom to formally charge with crimes is the prosecutor's alone to make.

- **The prosecutor wants to convict a "big fish."** Commonly, a prosecutor will drop charges against a less culpable suspect in exchange for that suspect's testimony against a more important perpetrator.

Can a prosecutor file charges and then later decide to dismiss them?

Yes. Prosecutors have the power to *nolle prosequi* (withdraw) charges any time before a verdict is entered. In most jurisdictions, however, prosecutors need a judge's permission to *nolle pros* a case. (See Federal Rule of Criminal Procedures 48(a).) Especially in cases of great notoriety, judges may refuse to grant permission.

How does a suspect's criminal record affect charging decisions?

A past criminal record ("priors"), even for a different crime, makes it more likely that charges will be filed, and may affect the severity of those charges. For example, a shoplifting charge against a defendant with a prior shoplifting conviction may be filed as a felony instead of a misdemeanor (where the laws support that type of escalation). Similarly, a charge of drunk driving with a prior always carries a more severe penalty than a first charge of drunk driving.

Prosecutors May Extort Agreements Not to Sue

Defendants who have been wrongfully arrested can seek money damages by bringing civil suits for false arrest against the arresting officer, and sometimes against the city or county employing the officer. So, even if a prosecutor realizes that a bust was bad, the prosecutor might file criminal charges anyway, to head off a civil suit, and then drop the criminal charges only if the defendant agrees not to sue for false arrest. Some judges would consider the prosecutor's motive to be improper. But other judges would hold the defendant to the agreement, and throw out a false arrest civil suit by a defendant who had previously agreed not to sue. Clearly, an accused person considering suing for false arrest must speak with an attorney before agreeing to forgo a civil suit in exchange for a dismissal of charges.

The Mechanics of Charging

This section examines the typical process by which an arrest becomes a formal charge.

Is the charging process always the same?

No. Prosecutors may follow one of two procedures, depending largely on local policies and the seriousness of a crime:

- If a crime is a misdemeanor, a prosecutor often files an accusatory pleading directly in court. This pleading may be called a criminal complaint, an information, or a petition.
- If a crime is a felony, charges may be brought either in the form of an accusatory pleading (as with misdemeanors) or by an indictment handed down by a grand jury. Some states require prosecutors to use grand juries in felony cases. Other states allow prosecutors to decide which procedure to use. The Fifth Amendment to the U.S. Constitution requires the federal government to use grand juries in all felony cases.

How much can people learn about the prosecution's case by reading the charging document?

Very little. The initial charging document is usually little more than a formality. It often doesn't divulge specifics about the prosecution's case, but simply identifies the defendant and the crime or crimes with which the defendant is charged. An intake prosecutor simply inserts this information into a preprinted form. (See the sample criminal complaint at the end of this chapter.)

Will the complaint or information indicate whether the prosecutor is using a past criminal record as a basis for a more severe charge?

Generally, yes. When prosecutors use prior convictions to increase the severity of a charge, those prior convictions usually are alleged in the accusatory pleading. (A section called "Allegations of Prior Convictions" is included in the sample criminal complaint at the end of this chapter.) Charging documents also set forth circumstances that would result in a more severe sentence upon conviction, such as the use of a weapon during the commission of a crime.

Defendants Should Carefully Review Allegations of Prior Convictions

Prosecutors sometimes make mistakes in listing prior convictions, and such mistakes can be terribly costly to defendants. Defendants therefore must review the priors listed and consult with counsel about possible strategies to strike (convince a judge not to consider) some or all prior convictions.

Can people be charged with more than one crime for committing the same act?

Yes. A complaint may separate what seems like a single criminal act into separate criminal charges. For example, a bank robber who assaults five customers while trying to flee the scene of the crime may be charged with the robbery and five separate assaults. Similarly, a defendant arrested for drunk driving may be charged with two separate crimes: violating the "per se" statute that prohibits driving with a blood alcohol level at or over the legal limit, and violating a separate statute that prohibits driving under the influence of drugs or alcohol.

Although defendants may be convicted of separate charges for the same act, they usually can't be punished separately for each charge. As a general rule, the government may not punish a defendant more than once for the same conduct. What constitutes the exact same conduct can be a tricky question, one best left to experienced defense lawyers.

EXAMPLE: Shamon Yu is charged with kidnapping and rape. Yu allegedly grabbed his victim, drove her to a secluded spot ten miles away, and raped her. Yu can be sentenced separately for the kidnapping and the rape. Though everything that Yu did might seem a single criminal act, he committed two separate crimes and could be punished for each separately.

EXAMPLE: Bea Sotted is arrested for drunk driving. Bea faces two charges: violating a per se rule (driving with a blood alcohol level at or over the state's legal limit, regardless of whether driving is affected), and driving under the influence. If Bea is convicted of both crimes, however, she can receive only a single sentence because both crimes are based on the same criminal act.

What is "overcharging"?

Defense lawyers and defendants often argue that prosecutors "overcharge." The claim is that prosecutors charge defendants with very serious crimes not because they seek to obtain convictions for those crimes, but instead because they seek to scare defendants into pleading guilty to less serious charges. Police departments often arrest suspects for the most serious crimes that facts can possibly support; overcharging demonstrates prosecutors' support for the police and potentially deters arrestees from filing civil claims against the police.

> **EXAMPLE:** John George was arrested for robbing Paul Starr. John was arrested at Paul's home, after Paul tripped a silent alarm that summoned the police. John was charged with robbery (taking property from Paul by force or fear), burglary (breaking and entering into Paul's home), larceny (taking property, in essence "stealing" from Paul), and carrying a concealed weapon, all based on the same event, the one robbery. The prosecutor might have chosen to file multiple charges to promote the likelihood that John will plead guilty to one or two of the offenses in exchange for dismissal of the others.

> **EXAMPLE:** Charles "Chuckles" Lorettian was caught by the police spray painting his tag ("laughs") inside an abandoned warehouse. Chuckles was charged with malicious mischief (a misdemeanor) for the graffiti and with burglary (a felony) for breaking and entering into a building for the purpose of stealing property. Chuckles is young and has no prior convictions. The prosecutor may be reluctant to convict Chuckles of a felony because he is young, the warehouse was abandoned and empty, and Chuckles has a clean record, but including the felony charge may help the prosecutor convince Chuckles to plead guilty to the misdemeanor.

Grand Juries

Grand juries, described in this section, serve as a check on prosecutors' power to charge people with crimes.

What are grand juries?

Grand juries are similar to regular trial juries (technically called "petit juries") in that they are made up of randomly selected individuals who listen to evidence. However, there are some important differences between the two types of juries:

- Petit juries decide whether defendants are guilty beyond a reasonable doubt. Grand juries decide whether probable cause exists to believe suspects guilty and issue indictments (that is, to charge suspects with crimes).
- Grand juries meet in secret proceedings. Petit juries serve in public trials.
- Petit jurors usually serve for a short period, as little as ten days unless they serve on a longer trial. Grand jurors serve for longer periods that typically coincide with a term of court, often six to 18 months.
- Grand juries generally have 15–23 people, 16–23 in federal courts. (See Federal Rule of Criminal Procedure 6(a).) By contrast, a petit jury usually consists of six to 12 people.
- Petit juries generally have to be unanimous to convict a defendant. Grand juries need not be unanimous to indict. In the federal system, for example, an indictment may be

returned if 12 or more jurors agree to indict. (See Federal Rule of Criminal Procedure 6(f).)

What happens in a grand jury indictment proceeding?

A prosecutor presents a bill (the charges) to the grand jury and introduces evidence— usually the minimum necessary, in the prosecutor's opinion, to secure an indictment. The proceedings are secret and are held without a suspect or a defense lawyer present. Indicted suspects can sometimes later obtain transcripts of grand jury proceedings, a big reason why prosecutors like to present as little evidence as possible. The prosecutor may call a suspect or other witnesses to testify. (Any witnesses who think that they might be a target of investigation have a right not to answer questions.) If the grand jury decides to indict, it returns what is called a "true bill." If not, the grand jury returns a "no bill." However, the prosecutor may eventually file charges even after a grand jury returns a no bill. Prosecutors can return to the same grand jury with more evidence, present the same evidence to a second grand jury, or (in jurisdictions that give prosecutors a choice) bypass the grand jury altogether and file a criminal complaint.

Do grand juries usually indict?

Yes. The grand jury does not make its decision in the context of an adversary proceeding. Rather, grand jurors see and hear only what prosecutors put before them. (Prosecutors technically have an obligation to present "exculpatory" evidence—evidence that suggests that a defendant might not be guilty—though there might not be much other than the prosecutor's conscience to enforce this rule. (*U.S. v. Williams,* U.S. Sup. Ct. 1992.)

In part because there's no one on the "other side" to contest the prosecutor's evidence, grand juries almost always return an indictment as requested by the prosecutor. According to a U.S. Department of Justice study on plea bargaining, "Grand juries are notorious for being 'rubberstamps' for the prosecutor for virtually all routine criminal matters." (*Plea Bargaining: Critical Issues and Common Practices*, by William F. McDonald, (U.S. DOJ, National Institute of Justice, 1983).)

Why might a prosecutor ask a grand jury to issue an indictment rather than simply file a criminal complaint or information in court?

Where they have a choice, prosecutors often prefer grand juries because grand jury proceedings are secret. When prosecutors file an information, they are usually required to convince a judge in a public preliminary hearing that they have enough evidence to secure a conviction. Also, during a preliminary hearing, the defendant can see and cross-examine prosecution witnesses.

When do prosecutors subpoena witnesses to testify at a grand jury proceeding?

Prosecutors typically subpoena witnesses to appear before a grand jury either because:

- a prosecutor believes that a witness has information about a crime committed by a third party, and wants to elicit that information to secure an indictment against the third party, or
- a prosecutor regards a witness as a target (a person suspected of crime) and wants to develop evidence against the witness.

People called before a grand jury as witnesses do not have to be warned that they are or may become targets. *Miranda*-type warnings are not required, and, unless they are specifically given immunity, any testimony witnesses provide to a grand jury may be used against them in a later prosecution.

How can people find out if they are a target of a grand jury proceeding?

Defense lawyers can often confer with the prosecutor to find out whether a client is the target of a grand jury investigation. If so, the defense lawyer may try to work out a deal in which the target agrees to testify before the grand jury in exchange for immunity from prosecution.

Can witnesses be represented by counsel at a grand jury proceeding?

No. Defense lawyers are typically not permitted to accompany clients into the grand jury room. Grand jury proceedings are closed, and witnesses are not entitled to be represented by counsel during the proceedings. Lawyers may, however, remain in a nearby hallway, and witnesses may leave the room to consult with their lawyers if they are concerned that the answer to a question may incriminate them. Lawyers sometimes advise clients to exercise this right before answering every question. For example, a witness might repeatedly say, "I respectfully request permission to leave the room to consult with my lawyer before I answer that question."

Do witnesses have to answer a prosecutor's questions during a grand jury proceeding?

Under the Fifth Amendment to the U.S. Constitution, a witness does not have to answer questions if, in the witness's opinion, the answers might tend to incriminate the witness (by providing evidence of criminal activity). To claim the privilege, a witness should simply say, "I respectfully decline to answer based on my state and federal privileges against self-incrimination." (A witness who has been able to consult with a lawyer should follow the lawyer's advice.) The prosecutor can negate the Fifth Amendment by granting the witness immunity from prosecution. Prosecutors often develop evidence against the big fish in a criminal scheme by granting immunity to the little fish. Without immunity, the little fish could legally refuse to testify.

Diversion

Diversion is a process that allows suspects to avoid a conviction by agreeing to and fulfilling the terms of a type of informal probation.

Do prosecutors have any options other than charging suspects with crimes or dropping charges?

Yes. Cases can be diverted out of the criminal justice system. Defendants whose cases are diverted typically have to participate in a treatment or rehabilitation program. Because criminal charges are normally dropped when a defendant successfully completes a diversion program, diversion allows defendants to escape the consequences and stigma of a criminal conviction.

Can a police officer divert a case even before a suspect is booked into jail?

Possibly. Some jurisdictions (especially in large metropolitan areas) authorize police officers to take suspects who might otherwise be taken to jail and charged with low-level crimes to take them instead to "sobering centers," mental health facilities, or other social support agencies. The idea is to replace the costly "revolving door" consequences of criminalization with a more therapeutic approach that may reduce recidivism and help people get well.

Does the chance of getting into a diversion program depend on the charged crime?

Yes, although eligibility rules vary from one locality to another. Diversion programs are most often available to defendants charged with misdemeanors and nonviolent felonies involving drugs or alcohol. In some jurisdictions, diversion may be available to defendants charged with domestic violence, child abuse or neglect, traffic-related offenses, or even writing bad checks.

Apart from the charge, what factors affect eligibility for diversion?

Diversion eligibility often depends on two factors:

- A defendant's past criminal record. For example, in drug cases, a locality may offer diversion only to defendants with no prior drug convictions. Again, however, eligibility rules vary, and another locality may extend diversion to previously convicted defendants who have successfully completed probation or parole.
- A recommendation from a probation officer that a defendant is a fit candidate for diversion—that is, that a defendant is likely to benefit from and succeed at a treatment program.

Do defendants have to arrange for diversion at any specific time?

Sometimes. In many jurisdictions, however, diversion can remain an option up until the time of trial.

Sample Criminal Complaint

IN THE MUNICIPAL COURT OF LOS ANGELES JUDICIAL DISTRICT
COUNTY OF LOS ANGELES, STATE OF CALIFORNIA

THE PEOPLE OF THE STATE OF CALIFORNIA,	)	MISDEMEANOR COMPLAINT
	)	
	)	
Plaintiff,	)	CASE NO.
vs.	)	
	)	EDWARD M. KRINGLE, Clerk
	)	Court Administrator
	)	By _____
	)	Deputy Clerk
	)	
RANDY EVEN	)	Issued by
	)	JOHN K. BUGLE, City Attorney
	)	
Defendant(s).)		By B. ZAPPA
_____)		Deputy City Attorney

COUNT I

Comes now the undersigned and states that he is informed and believes, and upon such information and belief declares: That on or about MARCH 13, 20xx at and in the City of Los Angeles, in the County of Los Angeles, State of California, a misdemeanor, to wit, violation of the first paragraph of Subsection (a) of Section 23152 of the California Vehicle Code was committed by the above-named defendant(s) (whose true name(s) to affiant is (are) unknown), who at the time and place last aforesaid, did willfully and unlawfully drive a vehicle while being under the influence of alcoholic beverage and a drug and under the combined influence of an alcoholic beverage and a drug.

ALLEGATIONS OF PRIOR CONVICTIONS

Affiant further alleges that the defendant was convicted of having violated the following section(s) of the California Vehicle Code, said violation(s) and conviction(s) having occurred on or about the following date(s):

Code Section	Violation Date	Conviction Date	Docket No.	Court No.
NONE KNOWN				

COUNT II

For a further, separate and second cause of action being a different offense, belonging to the same class of crimes and offenses set forth in Count I hereof, affiant further alleges that on or about MARCH 13, 20xx at and in the City of Los Angeles, in the County of Los Angeles, State of California, a misdemeanor, to wit:

Sample Criminal Complaint (continued)

Violation of Subdivision (b) of Section 23152 of the California Vehicle Code was committed by the above-named defendant(s) (whose true name(s) to affiant is (are) unknown), who at the time and place last aforesaid, did willfully and unlawfully drive a vehicle with 0.08 percent or more, by weight, of alcohol in his or her blood.

The allegations of prior convictions listed in Count I of this complaint are hereby incorporated by reference as allegations of prior convictions for the purposes of this Count of the complaint.

All of which is contrary to the law and against the peace and dignity of the People of the State of California. Declarant and complainant therefore prays that a warrant may be issued for the arrest of said defendant(s) and that he may be dealt with according to law.

Attached hereto and incorporated by reference as though fully set forth are written statements and reports, consisting of pages, which constitute the basis upon which I make the within allegations.

A declaration in support of the issuance of such warrant is submitted.

Executed at Los Angeles, California, on March 19, 20xx.

I declare under penalty of perjury that the foregoing is true and correct.

_____

Declarant and Complainant

INFORMAL DISCOVERY NOTICE

TO THE ABOVE-NAMED DEFENDANT(S) AND/OR ATTORNEY(S) FOR DEFENDANT(S):

Plaintiff, the People of the State of California, hereby requests discovery/disclosure from the defendant(s) and his or her attorney(s) in this case pursuant to Penal Code Sections 1054.3 and 1054.5.

YOU ARE HEREBY NOTIFIED that if complete disclosure is not made within 15 days of this request, plaintiff will seek—on or before the next court date, or as soon as practicable thereafter—a court order enforcing the provisions of Penal Code Section 1054.5, subdivisions (b) and (c). This is an ongoing request for any of the listed items which become known to the defendant(s) and his or her attorney(s) after the date of compliance.

The written statements and reports attached hereto constitute discoverable materials designated in Penal Code Section 1054.1 Any additional material discoverable pursuant to Penal Code Section 1054.1 that becomes known to plaintiff will be provided to the defense.

If prior to or during trial, as a result of this request plaintiff obtains additional evidence or material subject to disclosure under a previous defense request or court order pursuant to Penal Code Section 1054.1, plaintiff will disclose the existence of that evidence or material within a reasonable time.

DISCOVERY MATERIALS SHOULD BE DELIVERED TO A DEPUTY CITY ATTORNEY IN MASTER CALENDAR COURT ON THE FIRST TRIAL DATE.

How can someone arrange for diversion?

Prosecutors sometimes voluntarily offer diversion to defendants who are clearly eligible under a community's guidelines. Defense counsel may also suggest diversion to prosecutors, sometimes even before formal charges are filed. Finally, defense counsel may wait until a defendant's first court appearance and ask the judge to order an evaluation for diversion.

A defendant who is referred for diversion in any of these ways then meets with a probation officer, who may conduct an investigation and prepare a report as to the defendant's suitability for diversion. The report may specify the type of program that is most suitable for the defendant. Judges normally follow a probation officer's recommendation.

Is it possible to appeal a judge's denial of diversion?

Defendants who are denied diversion and ultimately convicted can appeal a judge's refusal to admit them to a diversion program. However, these appeals rarely succeed.

What happens if a case is diverted?

Diverted defendants usually have to complete a diversion program. Diversion programs range from periodic counseling to live-in treatment programs.

Who pays the cost of a diversion program?

Probably. Defendants often have to pay a fee both to the court and to the treatment center. The cost of the diversion program can sometimes be more than a fine. However, the defendant hopefully benefits from the treatment and from avoiding a criminal record.

What happens when a defendant completes a diversion program?

In most states, charges are dropped when defendants successfully complete a diversion program. Thus, diverted defendants avoid a conviction. However, diversion programs vary, and in some jurisdictions successful completion of a diversion program does not expunge the record of arrest.

Those who do not complete the assigned program or meet conditions set by the treatment center, and those who are arrested on other charges during their term of diversion, will likely have the diversion revoked and the original charges reinstated. Sometimes, the judge will conduct a hearing before deciding whether to revoke diversion.

How is a sentence to complete a drug treatment program different from diversion?

Convicted defendants may have to attend drug and alcohol treatment programs as part of their sentence. But that is different from diversion. Defendants who plead or are found guilty and are formally sentenced have criminal records; no treatment program takes that away. But, if defendants are diverted, the criminal prosecution is actually suspended. They won't have a record of conviction if they successfully complete the program.

Criminal Defense Lawyers

One of the most immediate concerns for people charged with crimes is how to secure legal representation. This chapter discusses the different types of criminal defense attorneys and also addresses self-representation.

 RESOURCE
Find a lawyer at www.nolo.com/lawyers. Asking for a referral to an attorney from a trusted family member or friend can be a good way to find legal consultation or representation. You might also want to check out Nolo's Lawyer Directory, which offers comprehensive profiles of lawyers sorted by practice area. Visit www.nolo.com/lawyers. (There's more on finding a lawyer later in this chapter.)

Should a Defendant Have a Lawyer?

Defendants charged with crimes are almost always best served by obtaining a lawyer.

Are all criminal defendants represented by lawyers?

Not all are, but most criminal defendants choose to be represented by a lawyer, especially when jail or a prison sentence is a possible result. It is very difficult for defendants to represent themselves competently. While there are no firm statistics on how many people choose to represent themselves in criminal cases, estimates are well below 1%.

Why is legal representation so important?

Even with potentially high costs for legal representation, a defendant faced with the possibility of going to jail or prison should almost always be represented by counsel.

No matter how smart or well educated a person is, the criminal justice system makes it virtually impossible for most people to represent themselves competently. Each criminal case is unique, and only a specialist who is experienced in assessing the particulars of a case—and in dealing with the many variables that come up in every case—can provide the type of representation that every criminal defendant needs to receive if justice is to be done.

Criminal defense lawyers do much more than simply question witnesses in court. For example, defense lawyers:

- Negotiate "deals" with prosecutors, often arranging for reduced charges and lesser sentences. By contrast, prosecutors may be uncooperative with self-represented defendants.
- Suggest sentences tailored to clients' specific circumstances, which may in turn lessen clients' likelihood of committing future crimes.
- Help defendants cope with the feelings of fear, embarrassment, reduced self-esteem, and anxiety that criminal charges tend to produce in many people.

- Provide defendants with a reality check—a knowledgeable, objective perspective on their situation and what is likely to happen should their cases go to trial. This perspective is vital for defendants trying to decide whether to accept a prosecutor's offered plea bargain.
- Are familiar with important legal rules that people representing themselves would find almost impossible to locate on their own, because many criminal law rules are hidden away in court interpretations of federal and state statutes and constitutions. For example, understanding what may constitute an unreasonable search and seizure often requires familiarity with a vast array of state and federal appellate court opinions.
- Are familiar with local court customs and procedures that are not written down anywhere. For example, a defense lawyer might know which prosecutor has the real authority to settle a case and what kinds of arguments are likely to appeal to that prosecutor.
- Understand the possible hidden "downstream" costs of pleading guilty that a self-represented person might never think about.
- Devote time to a case that a defendant cannot afford to spend. Defendants who have jobs lack the time (and energy) to devote to such time-consuming

Thinking Outside the Box

Self-representation is made more difficult by the typical gulf between paper and practice in criminal cases. Books set forth the laws that define crimes, fix punishments, and establish courtroom procedures. But, the practice of criminal law can't be understood by reading books alone, even this one. To experienced criminal defense attorneys, the criminal law appears much the same as a droplet of water appears to a biologist under a microscope— a teeming world with life forms and molecules interacting unpredictably. For example, prosecutorial discretion—the power of prosecutors to decide whether to file criminal charges, and what charges to file—determines much of what actually happens in the criminal courts. Which prosecutor has the power to make decisions, and when those decisions are made, can greatly affect the outcome of a case. An act that looks on paper to constitute one specific crime can be recast as a variety of other crimes, some more and others less serious. What in a statute appears to be a fixed sentence for a particular crime can be negotiated into a variety of alternatives. In other words, the world of criminal law is vast, hidden, and shifting, and defendants enter it alone at their peril.

activities as gathering and examining documents and doing legal research.

- Gather information from prosecution witnesses. Witnesses often fear people accused of crimes and therefore refuse to speak to people representing themselves. Witnesses are more likely to talk to defense attorneys or their investigators.

- Hire and manage investigators. Investigators may be able to believably impeach (contradict) prosecution witnesses who embellish their stories at trial. By contrast, it is far less effective for a defendant to testify

that "the prosecution witness told me something different before trial."

Are indigent criminal defendants entitled to be represented by government-paid lawyers?

Yes. Paradoxically, the biggest reason that most defendants are represented by lawyers in criminal cases is that most defendants can't afford to hire their own private defense attorneys. When defendants are considered to be legally indigent—as most are—the court is constitutionally required to provide them with legal representation at government expense if jail or prison is a possible outcome of the case.

The Hidden Downstream Costs of Convictions

Convictions can have negative consequences far beyond the penalties imposed by law for a particular offense. For example:

- Although the actual sentence for a first-time drunk driving charge may be a $500 fine and loss of a driver's license for six months, a future drunk driving conviction may require a mandatory jail sentence. Even more dramatically, people who have a previous conviction for certain violent offenses are at risk of greatly harsher sentences under many states' "three strikes" legislation if they are convicted of any felony in the future, even a nonviolent one.

- Conviction of a crime in which an offender's property was used in the commission of the crime may result in

that property being taken away by the government in a civil forfeiture proceeding. For instance, assume that Charlie pleads guilty to selling marijuana out of his Rolls-Royce. In addition to being fined and/or jailed, Charlie may later find that the government has decided to take his car. Civil forfeiture proceedings following criminal convictions do not violate the constitutional rule against double jeopardy. (*U.S. v. Ursery*, U.S. Sup. Ct. 1996.)

- Conviction of even a misdemeanor may result in a noncitizen's deportation.

- Other common hidden costs include difficulty in securing employment, renting an apartment, and obtaining credit, as well as living with the stigma of a conviction.

Indigent Defendants Are Not Always Entitled to Free Legal Representation

Indigent defendants are entitled to free legal representation only if there is an actual risk of a jail or prison sentence. (*Alabama v. Shelton*, U.S. Sup. Ct. 2002.) For example, indigent defendants charged with minor traffic offenses are not entitled to free legal services. And, if a judge agrees at the start of a defendant's case not to impose a jail or prison sentence, no lawyer need be appointed. However, most judges prefer to appoint a lawyer rather than promise no jail time in advance.

Court-Appointed Defense Attorneys

Most criminal defendants are represented by court-appointed lawyers who are paid by the government.

How do people qualify for free legal services?

Normally, a defendant who wants a lawyer at government expense must:

- ask the court to appoint a lawyer, and
- provide financial information under oath, either in a financial eligibility questionnaire or in oral responses to questions posed by the judge.

Unfortunately, it is impossible to say with certainty who will qualify for a court-appointed lawyer. Each state (or even county) has its own rules about who qualifies as indigent for the purpose of getting a free lawyer.

The seriousness of a charge can affect a judge's decision as to whether a defendant is eligible for a free lawyer. For example, a judge may decide that a wage-earner charged with shoplifting has sufficient income and property to hire a private defense attorney, because the cost of such representation is likely to be relatively low. But the judge may decide that the same person is indigent and qualifies for a court-appointed lawyer if the person is charged with a complex and serious felony.

Can a judge order a defendant to pay a portion of the cost of a government-paid lawyer?

Most states provide for partial indigency. This means that a judge may allow a defendant who exceeds the indigency guidelines but cannot afford the full cost of a private lawyer to receive the services of a court-appointed attorney. At the conclusion of the case, the judge can require the defendant to reimburse the state or county for a portion of the costs of representation. Typically, the reimbursement rate will be much lower than the standard hourly fees charged by private defense attorneys in that community.

Will a judge consider relatives' financial resources when deciding whether a defendant is eligible for free legal services?

No. Defendants are not legally required to ask relatives for money to hire an attorney.

With rare exceptions, judges determine indigency only according to the income and property of the defendant. Adult defendants who are otherwise indigent remain eligible for court-appointed lawyers even if they have parents or other relatives who could afford to pay for a private attorney.

Will anyone check up on the accuracy of the financial information in an application for a free lawyer?

Perhaps. To protect the limited funds available for court-appointed lawyers, judges sometimes order audits on the accuracy of defendants' financial eligibility questionnaires. Because these documents must be filled out under oath, defendants who make materially false claims can be prosecuted for offenses like perjury. However, such prosecutions are rare. More likely, the consequence will be that the court will revoke the appointment of the lawyer and require the defendant to reimburse the government for legal services already rendered.

What is a Public Defender office?

Most criminal defendants are legally indigent and can't afford to pay for an attorney. On the other hand, the state can't legally prosecute indigents unless it provides them with an attorney. To satisfy this requirement, many states have set up public defender offices. Typically, each local office has a chief public defender (who may be either elected or appointed)

and a number of assistant public defenders ("P.D.s"). P.D.s are fully licensed lawyers whose sole job is to represent indigent defendants in criminal cases. Because they typically appear in the same courts on a daily basis, P.D.s can gain a lot of experience in a short period of time.

The P.D. is part of the same government-financed criminal justice community that includes the judge, prosecutor, police, and court personnel. As a result, defendants sometimes fear that a P.D. will pull punches in order to stay friendly with judges and prosecutors. However, most private attorneys—not just P.D.s—have regular contacts with judges and prosecutors. All defense attorneys, whether private or government paid, can maintain cordial relationships with judges and prosecutors while vigorously representing their clients' interests.

Some P.D. offices assign the same P.D. to a defendant's case from beginning to end. In other P.D. offices, the P.D.s are specialized. One P.D. may handle arraignments, another settlement conferences, another trials, and so forth. Under this latter method, a single defendant may be represented by a number of P.D.s as a case moves from beginning to end. This second approach can sometimes result in defendants feeling lost in the shuffle, especially if there isn't close communication between the different P.D.s as the case moves from one phase to the next.

Availability of Free Legal Assistance by Nonprofit Groups

Indigent persons can sometimes get free legal assistance in civil cases from various civil rights organizations. For example, an indigent person who wants to sue a city for stopping her from handing out political leaflets might seek help from the ACLU. However, such free legal assistance is rarely available to criminal defendants. In part because a system of government-appointed attorneys is already in place, few civil rights organizations represent indigent criminal defendants. However, defendants should not entirely discount the possibility. For instance, a woman charged with assault who claims that she was defending herself after years of physical abuse might seek legal help from a women's advocacy group.

How are panel attorneys different from public defenders?

Panel attorneys are private attorneys who agree to devote part or all of their practice to representing indigent defendants at government expense. Panel attorneys often handle most of the criminal cases in states that have not set up public defender offices. When a judge appoints an attorney for a defendant, the judge appoints the panel attorney whose turn it is to be in the judge's courtroom. Usually, the same panel attorney continues to represent a defendant until the case concludes.

Will judges usually appoint one lawyer to represent two codefendants?

Conflict-of-interest rules almost always prevent one attorney from representing two defendants. As a result, jurisdictions with public defender offices usually maintain panels of private counsel whom judges appoint to represent those indigent defendants the P.D. is not able to represent, because of a conflict of interest. Or a jurisdiction might have what's often called an "alternate defender office"—an office that provides representation in cases in which the public defender's office has a conflict of interest.

A P.D. would not be allowed to represent a defendant because of a conflict of interest in situations that include the following:

- Two defendants are charged with jointly committing a crime. Even if both are indigent, the public defender's office cannot represent both because each defendant may try to point the finger at the other as being more to blame.
- The victim is a former public defender client. In this situation, the P.D. would have two conflicting duties: (1) to vigorously represent the current client's interests, and (2) to not disclose any information learned from the previous client in confidence. To fulfill the duty of vigorous representation in the current case, the P.D. would have to use any information known about the victim that might put the victim's testimony in

doubt. Yet this could easily violate the duty owed by the P.D. to the previous client (the victim in the present case) to not use that information. Note: In this situation, public defender offices sometimes avoid conflict of interest problems by following a "don't peek" policy. Under this policy, a P.D. stays on a case by promising not to look in the P.D. office's files to dig up nasty but confidential information against a former client.

Do defendants have a say in which lawyer a judge appoints to represent them?

Generally, no. In communities served by public defender offices, a judge simply appoints the public defender's office to represent indigent defendants. The individual P.D. who actually provides the representation is normally the P.D. who happens to be assigned to the courtroom in which a defendant's case is heard. Similarly, panel attorneys are often appointed according to which panel attorney is available for assignment in the courtroom in which a defendant's case is heard.

Do court-appointed attorneys provide competent legal representation?

Despite the severe fiscal constraints on their offices, public defenders usually provide representation that is at least as competent as that provided by private defense attorneys.

Additionally, public defender jobs tend to be so competitive that P.D. offices can select highly qualified attorneys. True, many P.D.s stay for a few years, gain intensive experience, and then leave for the supposedly greener pastures of private practice. However, most public defender offices offer excellent training programs, so that even recently arrived P.D.s can rapidly build expertise.

Despite these good points, there is much that is wrong with many appointed-counsel programs:

- **Too much work, not enough money.** Regardless of the competence of individual court-appointed attorneys, they are often asked to perform too much work for not enough money. This is especially true of public defender programs. Local politicians don't win many votes by expanding the budget for court-appointed lawyers to keep up with the growth in criminal prosecutions. For example, courts in Louisiana and Minnesota have ruled that the system of free legal defense services in those states is so badly underfunded that it is unconstitutional. And in a 1996 California case, *Williams v. Superior Court,* the court noted that a deputy public defender was representing 21 defendants whose cases were beyond the time limit to take them to trial—yet was eligible for additional assignments.

Caseload Guidelines Are Often Incompatible With Quality Representation

Even nationally approved caseload guidelines sound staggering. Under those guidelines, one attorney may handle 150 felonies in addition to 400 misdemeanors, 200 juvenile cases, or 25 appeals in a year. Even assuming compliance with these guidelines, indigent defendants may languish in jail for a week or more before they see an attorney. And high caseloads often force court-appointed lawyers to give short shrift to individual cases and pressure defendants to plead guilty.

- **Don't rock the boat.** Court-appointed lawyers often appear in the same courtrooms day in and day out, and therefore know their way around the courthouse better than other criminal defense attorneys in the area. This can be a boon for one defendant but bad news for another. For example, the court-appointed attorney may use that familiarity to achieve the best result possible for one client, yet resist rocking the boat in another case to maintain friendly relationships with the judges and prosecutors he or she has to work with every day. The danger is perhaps most acute with panel attorneys. Panel attorneys may owe their jobs to the judges who appoint them, and some panel attorneys may fear that taking a position that offends a judge could be seen as biting the hand that feeds them.

EXAMPLE: Hedda Drynk is charged with drunk driving and is represented by Joe Riley, a court-appointed panel attorney. Hedda's case has been assigned to Judge Hawk for trial. Hedda has a previous conviction for reckless driving, and Riley knows that Judge Hawk is especially stern on second-time offenders. Riley could automatically have the case assigned to another judge by filing an affidavit asserting that Judge Hawk cannot give his client a fair shake. However, Riley might fail to file the affidavit out of fear that Judge Hawk will take revenge if he finds out that Riley has challenged his fairness. When Riley's current panel term expires, Riley may find that he has been replaced by another lawyer. Judge Hawk could not properly remove Riley from the panel for exercising this entirely proper procedure. However, Riley would have difficulty proving that this is the reason he was removed, and Riley might prefer not to rock the boat.

Should a defendant get a second opinion on advice from a court-appointed lawyer?

Defendants who think their court-appointed attorneys are not representing them adequately out of a fear of rocking the boat or any other reason should consider:

- Checking the court-appointed lawyer's advice with a private defense attorney. Even a legally-indigent defendant may be able to pay for a short second opinion consultation with a private defense attorney. Or, a defendant may have friends who can check with an attorney who has represented them.

- Talking to other defendants facing similar charges to find out if their attorneys have provided different advice. Note, though, that because each case is unique, advice for different defendants—even those charged with the same crime—may vary greatly and still be valid. Also remember that the conversation will not be confidential and can be disclosed to the prosecution.

Defendants need to remember that what they tell friends, family members (other than a spouse), cellmates, jailers, and others about their case is not confidential. Any of these people could be called as witnesses to testify to a defendant's disclosures.

Panel Attorneys Are Good, Too

In the past, many private defense attorneys shunned panel work. As a result, panel attorneys were often like bookends: either novice lawyers with no other source of clients, or older lawyers for whom panel work was a way to ease into retirement. However, private defense attorneys now tend to look at panel work as a plum assignment that can supplement their private practices. They are sure to get paid and, because they appear in court regularly, they can quickly build their reputations. Hence, judges in many areas can be quite picky, and panel attorneys are often experienced and highly competent.

Can a defendant who is unhappy with a court-appointed lawyer get a replacement?

Defendants sometimes ask judges to fire their appointed counsel (P.D. or panel attorney) and appoint a new one. Often, the stated reason is something like, "My attorney and I don't see eye to eye about case strategy" or "My attorney won't talk to me." However, judges rarely grant such requests, believing that most of them stem from frustration with the system or a desire to delay an all-but-certain conviction rather than the reason actually stated by the defendant. Most indigent defendants must therefore either accept whatever lawyer the judge appoints or represent themselves if they are qualified to do so. The right to counsel of choice does not extend to defendants who require appointed attorneys. (*U.S. v. Gonzales-Lopez*, U.S. Sup. Ct. 2006.)

However, if a defendant is able to offer concrete proof that communications with a court-appointed lawyer have completely broken down, the defendant may be able to successfully pursue a Motion for Substitution of Attorney. (The lawyer may join in the motion!)

A Court-Appointed Attorney May Voluntarily Agree to a Substitution

Instead of asking a judge to order a change of a court-appointed attorney, a defendant may have better luck asking the attorney to agree to the change. Rather than continue to represent a defendant with whom communications have broken down, court-appointed attorneys might honor such a request, and judges might go along.

Private Defense Attorneys

This section covers private criminal defense attorneys: who they are, how to find them, and what they charge.

What are private criminal defense attorneys like?

Defendants who want to be represented by an attorney, and can secure a qualified private attorney on their own, have a Sixth Amendment right to be represented by the attorney of their choice. (*U.S. v. Gonzales-Lopez*, U.S. Sup. Ct. 2006.)

Private criminal defense lawyers tend to practice either on their own or in small partnerships, and in a specific geographical setting. By contrast, attorneys who handle civil cases tend to congregate in large corporate law firms with branch offices in many cities. (Criminal defense attorneys may also work in multinational corporate law firms, typically representing clients charged with white-collar crimes.)

Here are some other differences between private criminal and civil attorneys:

- Big-firm civil attorneys tend to represent companies who do business all over the country or the world. Criminal defense lawyers tend to represent individuals whose problems are quite local.
- Companies represented by big-firm civil lawyers have a continual need for legal advice and representation. Individual criminal defendants tend to be one-shot players with nonrecurring or sporadic legal needs.

- The typical private criminal defense attorney has had several years of experience working for the government before going into private practice, either as a prosecutor (often, a district attorney or city attorney) or as a public defender.

EXAMPLE: Carson O'Genic is charged with hit-and-run driving, a felony. Carson wants to hire her own attorney, and a friend strongly recommends an attorney named Brette Simon. Carson is impressed with Brette but worried that Brette spent seven years as a prosecutor with the district attorney's office before becoming a defense attorney. Carson's concern is that Brette is prosecution oriented and may not do everything she can for Carson. However, Brette's previous prosecutorial experience alone should not cause Carson to hire a different attorney. Many excellent criminal defense attorneys have previous prosecutorial experience. If anything, Brette's years as a prosecutor are likely to benefit Carson. Brette is apt to be familiar with the district attorney's policies and practices, and may know just whom to talk to in an effort to resolve the matter in Carson's favor.

How can a jailed defendant find a private criminal defense lawyer?

While they are in jail, defendants have to overcome two obstacles to hire a lawyer:

- **Paying the lawyer's fee.** Criminal defense lawyers often want the bulk of their money up front, which means that defendants often have to come up with some upfront cash in fairly short order and may have to borrow from family members or friends.

- **Finding a satisfactory lawyer.** If an arrested suspect has previously been satisfactorily represented by a criminal defense lawyer, that is usually the lawyer the suspect should call.

Bailing out of Jail, Then Shopping for a Lawyer

It may be difficult to find and hire a good lawyer while in jail. The atmosphere is usually psychologically oppressive, a defendant can't comparison-shop, and the police and other defendants are notoriously poor judges of lawyers' competence. Defendants who can quickly bail out of jail on their own are often better off doing so, and then hiring a lawyer.

But how should other arrested suspects proceed? Probably the most fruitful approach is to get a referral from one or more of the following sources:

- **Civil practitioners.** Defendants who know an attorney in civil practice can ask that attorney to recommend a criminal defense lawyer. (Some civil practitioners, of course, are also competent to represent clients in criminal matters, at least for the limited purpose of arranging for release from jail following an arrest.)
- **Family members or friends,** who may either know of a criminal defense lawyer or at least have the time to pursue additional reference sources,

such as family clergy, doctors, or other professionals.

- **Bail bond sellers,** who are usually in regular contact with private defense lawyers.

If none of these resources pan out, and only as a last resort, defendants may consider referrals from other jailed suspects who are satisfied with their lawyers.

Does a defendant have to hire a lawyer selected by a relative or friend to get them out of jail?

No. Defendants who are in jail commonly ask relatives or friends to contact a lawyer for help in securing a speedy release. But a defendant doesn't have to hire that lawyer. If the attorney wants to be paid for arranging for bail, the attorney will normally have to look to the relative or friend who contacted the lawyer.

How should out-of-custody defendants find a private criminal defense lawyer?

Many defendants facing criminal charges are not in custody at the time they seek to hire an attorney. Either the police issue them a citation and a court date and never take them to jail, or they bail out of jail on their own, without first hiring an attorney.

Like defendants who are in custody, defendants who are not in jail can seek referrals from civil lawyers, friends and relatives, and bail bond sellers. However, nonjailed defendants have additional options. The additional sources include:

- **Lawyer Directories.** The publisher of this book, Nolo, has a free and easy- to-use online directory of lawyers, organized by location and area of expertise. Access Nolo's Lawyer Directory at www.nolo.com/lawyers. You can also find lawyer directories at Martindale-Hubbell's website (www.martindale.com) and Lawyers.com.

- **A local bar association's lawyer referral panel.** Attorneys are usually recommended according to their experience and the type and seriousness of a criminal charge.
- **Courthouse visits.** Defendants can visit a local courthouse and sit through a few criminal hearings. If a particular lawyer impresses a defendant, the defendant can ask for that lawyer's card (after the hearing has concluded) and then call for an appointment.

How can a defendant know if a particular lawyer is the right one?

No matter what the source of a lawyer referral, defendants should always personally interview a lawyer before hiring one. Out-of-custody defendants should consider "comparison shopping" by speaking with at least two lawyers before hiring one. A private defense attorney will often consult with a potential client at no charge, and a personal interview increases the likelihood that the defendant will be satisfied with the attorney's services.

A personal interview is desirable because a successful attorney-client relationship depends on more than just an attorney's background and legal skills.

An effective lawyer-client relationship is a true partnership, with both partners actively involved in making decisions. Because there's no guarantee that a lawyer who works well with one client will work equally well with another, even a strong recommendation from a trusted friend is not a substitute for a personal consultation.

A defendant should try to hire an attorney with experience in the courthouse where the defendant's case is pending. Though the same laws may be in effect throughout a state, procedures vary from one courthouse to another. For example, the D.A. in one county may have a no-plea-bargaining policy with respect to a certain offense, while the D.A. in a neighboring county may have no such policy. Defendants should prefer attorneys who have experience with local procedures and personnel.

A defendant should also try to find an attorney who has represented defendants charged with the same or very similar offenses. Modern criminal law is so complex that many lawyers specialize in particular types of offenses. For example, one may specialize in drunk driving, another in drug offenses, and another in white-collar crimes (generally referring to nonviolent, money-related crimes, such as tax fraud or embezzlement).

It is perfectly appropriate for a defendant to inquire during the initial consultation about the attorney's experience. A defendant should expect a competent criminal defense attorney to discuss experience and general strategies.

EXAMPLE: Zach Michaels is charged with driving under the influence of alcohol (drunk driving). Zach might ask the lawyer he's thinking of retaining such questions as:

"Have you represented people who have been charged with drunk driving?"

"What percentage of your practice involves representing people charged with drunk driving?"

"Are you certified as a specialist in drunk driving cases?" (Some states allow attorneys to qualify as specialists in specific areas of practice; others do not.)

"What percentage of your practice involves appearing in the court that my case will be assigned to?"

Because most private lawyers have years of criminal law experience either as a prosecutor or as a P.D. before going into private practice, defendants should not have to sacrifice quality to find attorneys who have local experience with their types of cases.

A defendant's lawyer speaks for the defendant. No matter how highly recommended a lawyer may be, it is also important that the lawyer be someone with whom the defendant is personally comfortable. The best attorney-client relationships are those in which clients are full partners in the decision-making process, and defendants should try to hire lawyers who see them as partners, not as case files.

Thus, defendants should ask themselves questions such as these when considering whether to hire a particular lawyer:

- "Does the attorney seem to be someone I can work with and talk openly to?"
- "Does the attorney explain things in a way that I can understand?"
- "Does the lawyer show personal concern and a genuine desire to want to help?"
- "Do the lawyer's concerns extend to my overall personal situation, rather than just the crime with which I'm charged?"
- "Does the lawyer appear to be a person who will engender trust in prosecutors, judges, and, if necessary, jurors?"

Should a defendant expect a lawyer to guarantee a good result?

No. Toasters come with guarantees; attorneys don't. Defendants should be wary of lawyers who guarantee satisfactory outcomes. Too much of what may happen is beyond a defense lawyer's control for a hard guarantee to make sense. A lawyer who guarantees an outcome may simply be trying a hard-sell tactic to induce the defendant to hire him or her.

If a lawyer is a member of a law firm, might other lawyers work on a defendant's case?

Yes. Lawyers often delegate work to colleagues in a law firm. For example, a lawyer may ask a law student (a "law clerk") or a paralegal assistant to do legal research, and ask an associate lawyer to appear with the client at a pretrial conference with the D.A. These are common lawyer practices, and they help lawyers hold down legal fees. (Clients who pay by the hour ordinarily pay less for an hour of a law clerk's or a paralegal's time than for an attorney's time.) However, these practices are appropriate only if the client knows about them in advance and agrees. Therefore, before retaining a lawyer a defendant should take the following steps:

- Find out whether the lawyer is currently involved in any unusually complex cases. If the lawyer is in the middle of a month-long jury trial, the lawyer is more likely to assign work to an associate.
- Ask whether the lawyer's practice is to assign work to an associate.

Defendants should also take the time to read a lawyer's retainer agreement before signing it. If it provides for work done by people other than the lawyer, a defendant may seek to amend it. (For example, if an agreement allows a lawyer to delegate work to colleagues, an amendment may state, "Unless otherwise agreed to in advance, Lawyer will be personally present at all court appearances.")

What's a private criminal defense lawyer likely to cost?

More than most people feel comfortable paying. However, as is so often the case in legal matters, a definitive answer to this question is impossible. Attorneys set their own fees, which vary according to such factors as:

- **The probable complexity of the case.** Most attorneys charge more for felonies than for misdemeanors, because felonies carry greater penalties, often require more court appearances, and so on.
- **The attorney's experience.** Generally, less-experienced attorneys set lower fees than their more experienced colleagues.
- **Geography.** Just as gasoline and butter cost more in some parts of the country than others, so do attorneys.

Because of factors such as these, standard legal fees do not exist. Most defendants can expect to pay much more for full representation than for consultation or a single court appearance. For example, a defendant charged with a misdemeanor should not be surprised by a legal fee in the neighborhood of $2,000–$3,000, with the cost being considerably higher if the case goes to trial. Moreover, most attorneys want all or a substantial portion of their fees paid up front (in advance).

Even before a defendant is convicted, some criminal charges allow the government to freeze money and other assets that were allegedly acquired illegally. A "freeze" order is valid even if it impinges on the right to counsel by depriving defendants of the money they would otherwise use to hire a private attorney. (*Kaley v. U.S.*, U.S. Sup. Ct. 2014.) However, an unreasonably large freeze order might violate the "excessive fines" ban of the U.S. Constitution. (*Timbs v. Indiana*, U.S. Sup. Ct. 2019).

How do criminal defense lawyers decide how much to charge?

Criminal defense lawyers usually charge either by the hour or by the case. Increasingly, the latter type of billing arrangement is more common in criminal cases.

Hourly billing

Defendants who are billed by the hour pay for the actual time their lawyers devote to their cases—say, $300 per hour. They may also pay for expenses a lawyer incurs in the course of the representation, such as copying fees, subpoena fees, and so on.

From the defendant's standpoint, there are advantages and disadvantages to hourly billing. The most important advantage is that defendants who pay by the hour benefit if a case concludes quickly. However, if the case becomes unexpectedly complicated, it can get very costly. Moreover, hourly fees give attorneys a financial incentive to devote more time to a case than it may warrant or the defendant is prepared to pay. Also, most criminal defense attorneys set a minimum retainer fee that they keep even if a case is resolved with one phone call.

Fortunately, experienced criminal defense attorneys usually can anticipate how many hours they are likely to spend on a case, and a defendant should not agree to an hourly charge without getting the attorney's good-faith estimate of how much time the case is likely to take.

Beware Super-Low Hourly Rates
With legal fees so high, most defendants understandably want to pay as little as possible for effective representation. However, a low hourly rate can be misleading. An experienced attorney with a high hourly rate may be able to resolve a case more quickly and satisfactorily than a novice with a much lower hourly rate, and therefore be less expensive in the long run.

Case billing

Lawyers who charge by the case represent defendants for a fixed fee. For example, a lawyer may set a fee of $2,500 for a defendant charged with drunk driving. The fee would not change according to the number of hours the lawyer devotes to the case.

As with hourly billing, the case billing approach has its advantages and disadvantages. The primary advantage is certainty. Defendants know going in what their cost will be, and the attorney bears the risk of unforeseen complications. However, a defendant may feel ripped off if the case settles very quickly. (In some quick settlement circumstances, attorneys will refund a portion of their fee. But many will not, and a client should not expect a refund if the case is resolved quickly.) Also, the fee may cover only the pretrial phase of the case; the attorney may require an additional substantial fee to actually try the case.

As with other types of information, the defendant should clarify this point before hiring the attorney.

Hourly Fee With a Cap

A defendant may also agree to pay an hourly fee but only up to an agreed-upon fixed sum. After that amount, the lawyer finishes the representation at no extra cost to a defendant. This approach combines the advantages of both of the fee arrangements discussed above while minimizing the disadvantages.

What is a retainer fee?

Whether they bill by the hour or by the case, criminal defense lawyers typically want defendants to pay a retainer fee up front, before the attorney begins working on the case. For example, a lawyer who bills at the rate of $200 an hour may want clients to pay up front for 20 hours of the lawyer's time, or $4,000. The lawyer will send the client regular statements showing how much time the lawyer has spent on the case, what was done, and how much of the retainer has thus far been used. If the balance in a defendant's account approaches zero, the lawyer will probably ask the defendant for an additional payment (unless the lawyer is working for a set fee). The lawyer will refund to the defendant whatever portion of the retainer remains at the end of the case.

Do criminal defense lawyers work on a contingency fee basis?

No. Lawyers who work on a contingency basis take their fees from money their clients recover as damages; if the clients collect nothing, the lawyers get nothing. Defendants in criminal cases don't recover money damages if they win, so there's no pot of money from which an attorney can collect fees. Furthermore, while contingency fees are common in some types of civil cases (particularly personal injury cases), contingency fees are considered unethical and are not permitted in criminal cases.

How do defendants know what legal services a lawyer's fees cover?

Defendants should carefully examine the terms of the attorney-client agreement they are asked to sign. At one time, this would have been difficult, because many attorney-client arrangements were oral and based on handshakes. Today, after reaching agreement with a defendant about fees, a lawyer will almost certainly ask the defendant to sign a written retainer agreement or fee agreement. The agreement is a written contract, fully enforceable in court, which specifies the attorney's fee and the services the lawyer will perform for that fee. (A sample retainer agreement is at the end of this chapter.)

Knowing the amount of an attorney's fee is one thing; knowing what services it covers is quite another. Many defendants who are fully aware of what their attorneys will charge are surprised when their attorneys inform them that they will have to pay extra for services that the defendants thought were included in the fee.

For example, the reality is that most cases are settled before trial. Because of this, a fee agreement may include an attorney's services only up until the time of trial. A defendant who wants to go to trial may therefore get a jolt when the attorney says, "My additional fee to take the case to trial will be $$$." Other extras that may come as a surprise to a defendant include:

- the cost of a private investigator
- expert witness fees
- the costs of copying documents and subpoenaing witnesses, and
- fees (often for a new attorney) to handle an appeal from a conviction.

There are no standard agreements. Just because one attorney performed a set of legal services for one all-inclusive fee does not mean that another attorney will do likewise. The key for defendants is to read retainer agreements carefully and ask their attorneys to explain possible extras.

 CAUTION
Beware flat fees that include expenses. Some lawyers include the cost for expenses like investigation, subpoenas, and photocopying within a flat fee for representation. This sounds like a great plan for a client because it suggests cost certainty. But with this kind of arrangement, the lawyer might hesitate to incur important expenses because they would come out of his or her—rather than the client's—pocket.

When Changing Lawyers Might Unfairly Prejudice the Prosecution's Case

A defendant's right to change lawyers must be weighed against the court's and prosecutor's right to keep the case moving on schedule. Assume, for example, that a defendant seeks to change attorneys on the eve of trial. The new attorney is likely to agree to represent the defendant only if the trial is delayed so that the new attorney can prepare. The prosecutor may oppose delay, perhaps because the prosecution witnesses will not be available to testify at a later date. In these circumstances, the judge may deny the defendant's request to delay the trial. This would mean—realistically—that the defendant would have to stay with the original attorney rather than bring in an unprepared new attorney.

Can I change lawyers if I'm unhappy with the one I hired?

Yes. Defendants who hire their own attorneys generally have the right to discharge them without court approval. A defendant does not need to show good cause or even justify the decision to the lawyer. (Most attorney-client agreements explicitly advise clients that they have the right to discharge their attorneys.) After discharging a lawyer, a defendant can hire another. Of course, the decision to change lawyers can be costly. In addition to paying the new lawyer, the defendant will have to pay the original lawyer whatever portion of the fee the original lawyer has earned.

Note that a judge may refuse to allow a change of lawyers if it would unreasonably delay a case to the detriment of the court, the prosecutor, the victim, and the witnesses.

What can clients do if they think a lawyer overcharged them?

In many states, bar associations (that is, organized groups of lawyers) can protect defendants against fee gouging. Many lawyer-client fee agreements provide for arbitration in case of a dispute between attorney and client over fees. Often, a state's bar association selects the arbitrator. Many arbitrators are very sensitive to fee gouging, and may reduce the fee of an attorney whose charges are out of line with others in the same geographical area.

Negotiating a Reduced or Alternative Fee

Many attorneys will settle with clients who are unable to pay their full fees—especially when the alternative is a hearing before a bar association arbitrator. Before filing a claim with the state bar, a defendant should seek a friendly resolution with the lawyer. The lawyer may well agree to extend payments or reduce the fee.

Can defendants who retain private lawyers change lawyers in mid-case?

Often, yes. Defendants who hire their own attorneys generally have the right to.

How can defendants be sure that they have an attorney's undivided loyalty?

Attorneys have a duty of loyalty to their clients and should not take on a case if representing the defendant would cause a conflict with other cases handled by that lawyer, or the lawyer's own personal or business interests. (See Rule 1.7, ABA Model Rules of Professional Conduct.)

Here are the types of questions that defendants can ask to make sure that they have a lawyer's loyalty:

- "Even though my mom (or uncle, etc.) is paying your fees, am I the one with whom you will discuss all important case strategies, including plea bargains?" No matter who is paying a lawyer's fee (even if the government is paying the fee), a lawyer's duty is to the client and not to whoever is paying the bills. For example, a lawyer cannot disclose a defendant's confidential communications to the person paying the defendant's fee. And it's up to the defendant, not the fee payer, to decide whether the defendant will plead guilty.
- "I'm charged with embezzling money from the city department where I worked, and I think I'm being made a scapegoat for political reasons. Do you represent any local agencies or politicians that will prevent you from showing who's really responsible for the money that disappeared?" Defense attorneys often try to show that others are responsible for the

crimes with which their clients are charged, and defendants do not want to be represented by lawyers whose hands may be tied.

- "If I decide that I want to go to trial, will you support that decision?" Sometimes attorneys take cases expecting them to settle and have no real desire to go to trial. As a result, a lawyer's advice may reflect the lawyer's agenda rather than the client's. (See *McCoy v. Louisiana*, U.S. Sup. Ct. 2018)

Public Defenders and the Duty of Loyalty

No less than private attorneys, public defenders owe a duty of loyalty to their clients. However, many P.D.s have far more cases than they can reasonably handle. As a result, P.D.s may resemble sausage makers—they try to stuff all their clients into the same mold. For example, many P.D.s routinely recommend that their clients accept standard deals, regardless of the clients' individual circumstances. The reason is that P.D.s may see their duty of loyalty as owed to their clientele as a whole, and spending a lot of time on one client's case would mean neglecting too many other clients. Nevertheless, P.D.s do give some cases more priority than others, and defendants should seek to ensure that their cases receive individualized attention.

EXAMPLE: Attorney Frieda Mann represents Jen Delein, who is charged with the unauthorized practice of law. Jen insists that she's not guilty and wants to go to trial. However, in an effort to get more court referrals, Mann is trying to establish a reputation in the local courts as a lawyer who can settle cases before trial. Therefore, Mann repeatedly urges Jen to plead guilty in exchange for a very small penalty and no jail time. By putting her own interests above her client's, Mann has violated her duty of loyalty to Jen. Mann's primary motive is to develop her law practice rather than to represent her client. Jen should ask Mann to return all or most of the money she has already paid, and hire a different lawyer. If Mann fails to return Jen's money, Jen should file a complaint with her state or local bar association.

Self-Representation

There's an old saying that "He who represents himself has a fool for a client." Nevertheless, a small percentage of criminal defendants do choose to represent themselves. This section explains rules about self-representation.

 CAUTION
Few defendants are capable of representing themselves competently. See "Should a Defendant Have a Lawyer?" above, to better understand why self-representation can be so difficult and risky. Also, as accurate, detailed, and helpful as we try to be in this book, the complexity of the criminal justice system and variations in rules and processes from one locale to another mean that the book does not purport to be a guide to self-representation.

A Famous Case of Self-Representation

Occasionally, high-profile defendants choose self-representation—though generally without much success. One of the most famous cases of self-representation involved Colin Ferguson, the so-called "Long Island Railroad Killer." Ferguson was tried in 1995 for gunning down six commuters on the Long Island Railroad. Though he faced life in prison without possibility of parole, Ferguson insisted on representing himself at trial. There was a huge public outcry against allowing him to do so, especially from people who thought that it would be cruel to allow Ferguson to personally question survivors of the attack. Nevertheless, the judge ruled that Ferguson was legally capable of waiving his right to an attorney and participating in the trial, and allowed him to represent himself. The jury convicted him on all counts after a short deliberation.

If the criminal justice system is so complex, why do some defendants choose to represent themselves?

Statistically, few defendants represent themselves in criminal cases. Those who do, do so for a variety of reasons:

- Some defendants who have the financial ability to hire lawyers decide not to because they think that the likely punishment is not severe enough to warrant the expense.
- Some defendants believe (often mistakenly) that their court-appointed or even hired attorneys in previous cases were ineffective, and figure they can do just as well by representing themselves.
- Some defendants believe that lawyers are part of an overall oppressive system and try to make a political statement by representing themselves.
- Some defendants want to take responsibility for their own destiny.
- Some defendants who are in jail pending trial can gain privileges through self-representation, such as access to the jail's law library. Also, not bound by lawyers' ethical codes, self-represented defendants can delay proceedings and sometimes wreak havoc on an already overloaded system by repeatedly filing motions.

Does a judge have to let defendants represent themselves?

No. Defendants cannot represent themselves unless a judge determines that they are competent to do so. The community as a whole has an interest in achieving justice. A trial in which an incompetent defendant self-represents does not constitute a fair trial.

The case that established that defendants have a right to represent themselves was *Faretta v. California*, U.S. Sup. Ct. 1975. The *Faretta* case said that a judge must allow self-representation if a defendant is competent to understand and participate in the court proceedings.

To determine competence, the judge often weighs factors such as:

- the defendant's age
- the defendant's level of education
- the defendant's familiarity with English, and
- the seriousness of the crime with which the defendant is charged.

Standby (Advisory) Counsel

A judge may appoint a standby lawyer at government expense to help a pro se indigent defendant who faces serious charges or who, although competent to self-represent, unduly delays or disrupts an orderly courtroom process. Standby counsel provide guidance and advice and may have to take over the defense if necessary. The presence of standby counsel reflects the public's interest in a fair process and judges' interests in handling cases in an efficient and orderly manner.

No single factor determines the result, and a defendant doesn't need the legal skills of a professional lawyer to qualify for self-representation. As long as a defendant is competent, knowingly gives up the right to an attorney, and understands court proceedings, the defendant is entitled to self-represent. However, a judge has the power to decide that a defendant is mentally competent to stand trial, yet not competent enough to self-represent. (*Indiana v. Edwards*, U.S. Sup. Ct. 2008.)

EXAMPLE: Ella Mental is charged with burglary. Ella has only a grade school education, and she has been in and out of mental institutions for much of her life. Ella tells the judge that she wants to represent herself in the burglary case. The judge allows Ella to do so, on the ground that Ella has been convicted of various crimes three times in the past and is thus familiar enough with criminal law to represent herself. Ella goes to trial, and her questions to prosecution witnesses are garbled and for the most part ruled improper by the judge. Ella is convicted. The judge should not have allowed Ella to represent herself. The mere fact that Ella has three prior convictions does not demonstrate that she is capable of knowingly giving up her right to an attorney and representing herself. In view of her limited education, her history of mental problems, and her inability to participate meaningfully in the trial, the judge should have ignored Ella's wishes and appointed a lawyer to represent her.

EXAMPLE: Lexi Khan is charged with assault and battery, and wants to represent herself. Lexi speaks English, but English is her second language and she has trouble understanding some words. She also has trouble reading a law book that the judge asks her to read. In the arraignment court, Lexi refused to enter a plea, and repeatedly said that the whole system is biased and that she wanted nothing to do with it. Over Lexi's objection, the judge appoints an attorney to represent her. Taking all the circumstances into account, the judge properly exercised discretion when denying Lexi's request for self-representation. In view of Lexi's language difficulties and refusal to participate in the arraignment proceedings, Lexi is not capable of representing herself at trial in a meaningful way.

EXAMPLE: Dane Gerous is charged with aggravated sexual assault, and asks to represent himself. The judge's questioning reveals that Dane did not finish high school, and has no previous legal experience. However, Dane accurately summarizes the charge that he is facing. Also, when the judge reads a statute to Dane, he is able to explain what it means in his own words. The judge should allow Dane to represent himself. The charge is serious, and the judge may believe that Dane would be better off with a lawyer. However, Dane has demonstrated sufficient ability to understand and participate in the proceedings, and thus he has a right to represent himself.

Can a defendant be represented by a nonattorney relative or friend?

No. Only licensed attorneys can represent defendants in court. For example, one spouse who is not a lawyer can't represent another spouse, and a nonlawyer parent can't represent a child. No matter how much a defendant trusts and respects a relative or friend, defendants must choose between self-representation and representation by an attorney.

Does a power of attorney give a nonattorney relative or friend the ability to represent a defendant?

The answer is still no. A "power of attorney" is a document that can enable a relative or friend to handle a defendant's property (such as a house or a bank account) as an "attorney in fact." A power of attorney can even designate one person to make health care decisions for another. But a power of attorney cannot convey the right to represent a defendant in a criminal case. State and federal statutes give lawyers a monopoly on this activity. This is true even though one of the powers often set out in a power of attorney document allows the attorney in fact to prosecute and defend actions in court; this has been interpreted to give the attorney in fact power to *hire* an actual licensed attorney to do the court work.

Can defendants start out representing themselves, then hire counsel if they get in over their heads?

Yes. Just as defendants can generally substitute one attorney for another (as discussed above), defendants representing themselves can substitute an attorney for themselves. Though often risky, some defendants choose to represent themselves in the hope of working out a quick deal with a prosecutor, and then hire an attorney if a speedy resolution is not possible.

How should defendants go about deciding whether to represent themselves?

As a general rule, the less severe the charged crime, the more sensible self-representation may be. Defendants charged with minor traffic offenses should rarely hire an attorney; defendants charged with misdemeanors and felonies should rarely be without one.

The most difficult decisions involve less serious misdemeanors such as drunk in public, possession of small amounts of drugs, shoplifting, and the like. Hiring an attorney in these situations may make sense because jail time and a fine are possibilities, and convictions may carry hidden costs. Common hidden costs include more severe punishment for a second conviction; difficulty in securing employment, renting an apartment, and obtaining credit; and living with the stigma of a conviction. On the other hand, first-time offenders are not usually sentenced to jail, and judges and prosecutors often offer standard deals to all defendants for these types of offenses, whether or not they are represented by counsel.

The most critical piece of information that defendants should try to learn before deciding whether to hire an attorney is what the likely—rather than possible—punishment would be upon conviction.

> **EXAMPLE:** A law states that the offense of shooting a deer out of season is punishable by a $1,000 fine and six months' imprisonment. However, the actual punishment routinely meted out for a first offense may be a $50 fine and an administrative suspension of the offender's hunting permit. Comparing the likely sentence to the costs of an attorney, the defendant may choose self-representation.

> **EXAMPLE:** Jay is charged with DUI. According to the statute, upon conviction, he may lose his license for up to a year, be sent to jail for up to six months, and have to pay a $2,000

fine. Jay learns that his judge does not send first offenders like him (whose blood alcohol reading was barely over the limit) to jail. Instead, the judge routinely imposes a fine of $400 and requires driving school. Balancing the likely consequences of a conviction against the cost of an attorney (and the substantial possibility that a conviction will result anyway), Jay might decide to plead guilty without hiring an attorney.

How Does a Defendant Find out About a Likely Sentence?

It can be hard for a defendant to find out what sentence a judge is likely to hand out in a given case. This information can't be found in statutes or court rules. Rather, information about a likely sentencing is part of the hidden law that lawyers learn from being in the trenches. Defendants who want to know what the punishment is likely to be upon conviction might take the following steps:

- Pay to consult a private defense attorney. Experienced attorneys can often make well-informed punishment predictions.
- Check with an attorney in the local public defender's office. Public defenders often have an "attorney of the day" or "duty attorney" assigned to answer questions, who probably is aware of the "standard sentence" for various crimes.
- Contact a trusted person (such as a family member or friend) who might know of an attorney with criminal experience who might be able to provide information about a likely sentence.

Sample Retainer Agreement

NOTICE: FEES IN THIS CONTRACT ARE NEGOTIABLE; ATTORNEY FEES ARE NOT SET BY LAW

1. **IDENTIFICATION OF PARTIES.** This agreement, executed in duplicate with each party receiving an executed original, is made between _[name of attorney]_ , hereafter referred to as "Attorney," and _[name of client]_ , hereafter referred to as "Client."

   This agreement is required by Business and Professions Code Section 6148 and is intended to fulfill the requirements of that section.

   [Option 1: One fee for case through sentencing]

2. **LEGAL SERVICES TO BE PROVIDED.** The legal services to be provided by Attorney to Client are as follows: Representation in Case No. _[number]_ , _[court, e.g., San Bernardino County Superior Court]_ , now set for arraignment on _[date]_ , through disposition, whether by trial, sentencing, or otherwise. No promises or representations have been made, express or implied, regarding the results in this case.

3. **LEGAL SERVICES SPECIFICALLY EXCLUDED.** Legal services that are not to be provided by Attorney under this agreement specifically include, but are not limited to, the following: _[List services excluded, e.g., representation following a mistrial or granting of a motion for a new trial, appellate work, work on any petition for an extraordinary writ, and representation on any other case (including cases related to this case, such as any later probation or parole revocation).]_

   If client wishes Attorney to provide any legal services not included under this agreement, a separate written agreement between Attorney and Client will be required.

4. **ATTORNEY FEES.** Client will pay to Attorney the fixed sum of _[dollar amount]_ for attorney fees for the legal services to be provided under this agreement, payment in full on or before _[date]_ . This payment is nonrefundable even if Client pleads guilty or the case is dismissed.

   [Option 2: Fee structure for case up to trial]

2. **LEGAL SERVICES TO BE PROVIDED.** The legal services to be provided by attorney to client are as follows: making court appearances concerning client's release from custody, plea negotiations, and setting a trial date; preparation of case for trial; and work on plea

Sample Retainer Agreement (continued)

negotiations, including discussions with prosecution. No promises or representations have been made, express or implied, regarding the results in this case.

3. LEGAL SERVICES SPECIFICALLY EXCLUDED. This contract does not cover payment for attorney services for the following:

   Appeals to _[the superior court appellate department/the court of appeal/the California Supreme Court/any federal court]_ .

   Writs or similar proceedings to any court.

   Representation in any administrative hearing, even if related to this case.

   Representation in any _[probation/parole]_ violation arising out of any case, even if the revocation is triggered by this case.

   [Representation at the preliminary hearing in this case.]

   Representation at the trial in this case.

   Representation at evidentiary hearings in this case.

   Representation at the sentencing hearing in this case.

   Representation at a retrial in this case.

   Representation if this case is dismissed and then recharged.

   As the case progresses, Attorney will notify Client of any proceedings not covered by this contract that require a new contract and the payment of additional fees.

4. ATTORNEY FEES. Client will pay to Attorney the sum of _[dollar amount]_ for attorney fees for the legal services to be provided under this agreement, payable in full on or before _[date]_ . This payment is nonrefundable even if Client pleads guilty or the case is dismissed on the first day Attorney makes a court appearance.

5. RESPONSIBILITIES OF ATTORNEY AND CLIENT. Attorney will perform the legal services called for under this agreement, keep Client informed of progress and developments, and respond promptly to Client's inquiries. Client will be truthful and cooperative with Attorney; keep Attorney reasonably informed of developments and of Client's address, telephone number, and whereabouts; and timely make any payments required by this agreement.

6. COSTS. Client will pay all "costs" in connection with Attorney's representation of Client under this agreement. Costs are separate from attorney fees. Costs include, but are not

Sample Retainer Agreement (continued)

limited to, expert fees and expenses, investigation costs, long-distance telephone charges, messenger service fees, photocopying expenses, and process server fees. Costs will be advanced by Attorney and then billed to Client, unless the costs can be met out of client deposits that are intended to cover costs.

7. DEPOSIT. Client will pay to Attorney an initial deposit of _[dollar amount]_ to be received by Attorney on or before _[date]_ , and to be applied against costs incurred by Client. This amount will be deposited by Attorney in an interest-bearing trust account. Client authorizes Attorney to withdraw the principal from the trust account to pay costs as they are incurred by client. Any interest earned will be paid, as required by law, to the State Bar of California to fund legal services for indigent persons. If, at the termination of services under this agreement, the total amount incurred by Client for costs is less than the amount of the initial deposit, the difference will be refunded to Client.

    Attorney will notify Client whenever the full amount of any deposit has been applied to costs incurred by Client. Within 15 days after each notification is mailed, client will pay to Attorney an additional deposit in the same amount, and to be applied in the same manner, as the initial one. Deposit of such additional amounts and payment of any interest earned will be made in the same manner as for the initial deposit. Client authorizes Attorney to withdraw the principal from the trust account to pay costs as they are incurred by Client. If, at the terminations of services under this agreement, the total amount incurred by Client for costs is less than the total amount of all deposits, the difference will be refunded to Client.

8. STATEMENTS AND FACTS. Attorney will send client a monthly statement indicating costs incurred and their basis, any amounts applied from deposits, and any current balance owed. If no costs are incurred for a particular month or if they are minimal, the statement will be held and combined with that for the following month unless a statement is requested by Client. Any balance will be paid in full within 30 days after the statement is mailed.

9. ERRORS AND OMISSIONS INSURANCE COVERAGE. Attorney maintains errors and omissions insurance coverage that would apply to the services to be rendered under this agreement. The policy limits of the coverage are _[dollar amount]_ per occurrence up to a maximum of _[dollar amount]_ per policy term.

    This statement is required by Business and Professions Code Section 6148.

10. EFFECTIVE DATE OF AGREEMENT. The effective date of this agreement will be the date when, having been executed by Client, one copy of the agreement is received by Attorney

Sample Retainer Agreement (continued)

and Attorney receives the payment required by Paragraph 4 of this agreement and the initial deposit required by Paragraph 7, provided that the copy, payment, and deposit are received on or before __[date]__ , or Attorney accepts late receipt.

The foregoing is agreed to by:

Date: _____   [Signature of client]   _____

                                    [Typed name]   _____
                                    Client

Date: _____   [Signature of attorney]   _____

                                    [Typed name]   _____
                                    Attorney

Understanding the Attorney-Client Relationship in a Criminal Case

Most defendants are represented by criminal defense lawyers. This chapter focuses on the attorney-client relationship and examines the legal and ethical obligations that lawyers owe to clients. Defendants need to understand these obligations to work effectively with the lawyers who represent them.

 RESOURCES
Want to know more about legal ethics? For a more detailed description of the ethical and legal obligations of lawyers to their clients, consult a professional responsibility treatise such as *Professional Responsibility of the Criminal Lawyer,* by John Wesley Hall, Jr., usually available in academic and large public law libraries.

How Effective Lawyer-Client Relationships Benefit Society

Regardless of its impact on the outcome of a particular case, an effective lawyer-client relationship often produces important long-range social benefits. Defendants who feel that they got "the shaft" from their own lawyers may lose respect for the entire criminal justice system and as a result be at risk of future antisocial behavior. By contrast, defendants whose own efforts contribute to an effective attorney-client relationship are more likely to feel empowered by the system and may thus be less likely to break the law in the future.

Confidentiality

This section covers the confidentiality of lawyer-client communications, which is the basis of an effective professional relationship.

 CAUTION
The words "Privileged and Confidential" should appear on all communications to a lawyer whether by letter, email, or other means. This shows that a communication is intended to remain private.

Can lawyers repeat what clients tell them to other people without the clients' permission?

No, with one important exception (discussed below). The most basic principle underlying the lawyer-client relationship is that lawyer-client communications are privileged, or confidential. This means that lawyers cannot reveal clients' oral or written statements (nor lawyers' own statements to clients) to anyone, including prosecutors, employers, friends, or family members, without their clients' consent. It doesn't matter whether defendants confess their guilt or insist on their innocence: Attorney-client communications are confidential. Both court-appointed lawyers and private defense attorneys are equally bound to maintain client confidences.

EXAMPLE: Heidi Hemp is charged with possession of illegal drugs. At the request of Heidi's mother, attorney Joe Lawless talks with Heidi in jail and offers to represent her. Heidi decides not to hire Lawless, and instead retains Bill Mucho as her lawyer after she bails out. At trial, the prosecutor calls Lawless as a witness and asks him to reveal what Heidi told him in their jail conversation. Lawless cannot testify. Lawless spoke to Heidi in his capacity as an attorney, so their conversation is confidential even though Heidi decided to hire a different attorney.

EXAMPLE: Same case. Heidi tells her lawyer that the drugs belonged to her, and that she bought them for the first time during a period of great stress in her life, just after she lost her job. Heidi authorizes her lawyer to reveal this information to the D.A., hoping to achieve a favorable plea bargain. However, the D.A. refuses to reduce the charges, and the case goes to trial. Cross-examining Heidi, the D.A. asks, "Isn't it true that you admitted to your lawyer that the drugs were yours?" This is not a proper question. Heidi authorized her lawyer to reveal her confidential statement to the D.A. But a statement made for the purpose of plea bargaining is also confidential, so the D.A. cannot refer to it at trial.

EXAMPLE: Same case. Soon after her arrest, Heidi speaks to her mother in jail. Heidi's case goes to trial, and the prosecutor calls Heidi's mother as a witness and asks her to reveal what Heidi told her. Heidi's mother would have to answer questions under oath about what Heidi said to her. Most states have not created privileges for conversations between parents and children.

 CAUTION

Clients' statements to lawyers concerning an intention to commit a crime or a fraud in the future are usually not confidential. Statements like these are an exception to the attorney-client privilege, and judges can compel lawyers to testify about them. (See below.)

If you discuss your case with your attorney in public, loud enough for others to overhear, can those others testify to what you said?

Yes. Lawyer-client communications are privileged and can't be testified to in court only if they are made in a context where it is reasonable to expect that they would remain confidential. (*Katz v. U.S.*, U.S. Sup. Ct. 1967.) A client who talks to a lawyer in such a loud voice that others can overhear what is said has no reasonable expectation of privacy and thus waives (gives up) the privilege. Similarly, people who talk about their cases on cellphones in public places risk losing confidentiality.

Are jailhouse conversations between lawyers and clients confidential?

Jailhouse conversations between defendants and their attorneys are considered confidential as long as the discussion takes place in a private area of the jail, and the attorney and defendant do not speak so loudly that jailers or other inmates can overhear what is said. Also, defendants must be very careful not to allow jailers or other prisoners to overhear what they say on the telephone. These "snitches" sometimes eavesdrop, and then claim that they were able to overhear incriminating information because the defendant spoke in a loud voice. (Inmate "snitches" often try to curry favor with prosecutors through such tactics.) If a judge believes them, the privilege is lost and a jailer or another prisoner can testify to a client's remarks.

> ⓘ CAUTION
> **If a jailer warns a prisoner that phone calls are or may be monitored, then phone conversations between prisoners and their lawyers may not be privileged.** If a jailer monitors a phone call and overhears a prisoner make a damaging admission to the prisoner's lawyer, then the jailer can probably testify to the defendant's statement in court.

If a relative or friend is present when a client talks with a lawyer, is the conversation still confidential?

Clients who bring strangers (people who are not part of the attorney-client relationship) into a meeting risk losing the right to claim that the meeting was confidential. This means that the D.A. might be able to ask the stranger or even the defendant about what was said during the meeting. However, the lawyer can maintain the privilege by convincing a judge that it was necessary to include the stranger in the conversation.

EXAMPLE: Geri Attrix is charged with filing fraudulent income tax returns. Geri brings her son, who helped her prepare the returns in question, to the meeting with her lawyer. Geri's conversation with her lawyer is probably confidential, despite her son's presence. Because Geri's son helped her prepare the tax returns, his input is necessary for the lawyer to gain a full understanding of the case.

If clients tell other people what they told a lawyer, is the conversation with the lawyer still confidential?

No. Blabbermouth clients waive (give up) the confidentiality of lawyer-client communications if they disclose those statements to someone else (other than a spouse, because a separate privilege exists for spousal communications). Clients have no reasonable expectation of privacy in conversations they reveal to others.

EXAMPLE: Benny Dikshun is charged with possession of stolen merchandise. The day after discussing the case with his lawyer, Benny discusses it with a neighbor. As long as Benny does not say something to his neighbor like, "Here's what I told my lawyer yesterday ...," the attorney-client communications remain confidential. However, Benny's conversation with the neighbor is not confidential, and the prosecutor can properly ask the neighbor to testify to what Benny told him.

Can clients conceal harmful evidence by giving it to their lawyers?

Usually, no. Clients might want to conceal harmful evidence like a weapon used in an attack or an incriminating document by giving it to their lawyers. Because what they say to their lawyers is confidential, many clients assume that this protection extends to objects, too, so that if they give objects to their lawyers, the police can't seize them.

However, if an object is an instrumentality of a crime (the means used to commit a crime, such as a knife used in a stabbing), a lawyer has to turn it over to the police. Clients can't conceal instrumentalities of crime by giving them to their attorneys.

> **EXAMPLE:** Sly Sims rushes into the office of attorney, Sue Menow, and hands her a knife. Sly tells Sue, "This is the blade that I stuck Gibson with. Keep it safe so the cops don't find it." Sly is eventually arrested and charged with stabbing Gibson. Sue has to turn the knife over to the police because it is the instrumentality of a crime. However, Sue must keep what Sly told her confidential, so she would have to turn over the knife anonymously. Sue could not reveal how she acquired the knife or her conversation with Sly.

> **EXAMPLE:** Same case. Assume that instead of handing Sue a knife, Sly Sims phones her and says, "I tossed the knife into the bushes behind the bowling alley on 8th Avenue." Sue goes to the location, looks at the knife, and leaves it exactly where it is. Sue does not have to tell the police where the knife is. Because Sue did not move the knife, she did not interfere with the police's ability to find the knife on their own. And she cannot reveal what Sly Sims told her, because that is confidential.

> **EXAMPLE:** Same case. Again, Sue gets a phone call from Sly Sims telling her the location of a knife used in a stabbing. Sue goes to the location and removes the knife so that she can have it tested. Because Sue removed physical evidence from its original location, she has an obligation to turn it over to the police. She probably also has to reveal exactly where she found it (see *Alhambra Police Officers Ass'n v. City of Alhambra Police Dep't.*, California 2003), but doesn't have to say how she knew where it was.

> **EXAMPLE:** Same case. After stabbing Gibson, Sly Sims comes into Sue's office and hands her a letter Gibson wrote, threatening that he would reveal a past indiscretion unless Sly paid him money. Sly asks Sue to keep the letter to prevent the police from finding out that he had a motive to stab Gibson. Sue probably does not have to turn the letter over to the police. The letter is not a crime instrumentality; it was not the means by which Sly committed the crime. Thus, Sue can treat the letter as confidential.

Is there a privilege for clients' statements to lawyers about crimes the clients plan to commit in the future?

No. The confidentiality of attorney-client communications usually does not extend to statements pertaining to future fraudulent or criminal conduct. The government can compel a defense lawyer to testify to a client's statement about such conduct. And, in emergency or life-threatening situations, a lawyer might have to reveal a client's statement—for example, a comment about a plan to kill someone—to the police before the possible event occurs.

> **EXAMPLE:** (Based on the John Grisham book and film, *A Time to Kill*): Two defendants are arrested for brutally raping Carl Lee's daughter. Carl Lee tells Jake, a lawyer and friend, of his plan to kill his daughter's attackers, and asks Jake to represent him after he's arrested. At this point, Jake should urge Carl Lee not to take the law into his own hands. But if Carl Lee insists that he will take personal revenge against the defendants, Jake should report the threat to the police so that they can prevent harm both to Carl Lee and to the attackers. In many states, Jake's failure to report Carl Lee's threat would be an ethical violation that could lead to Jake's suspension or disbarment.

Is the fact that the defendant has met with an attorney considered to be confidential?

No. Attorney-client confidentiality mainly extends to communications, so details such as the following are normally not considered confidential:

- the dates and times of attorney-client meetings
- the identities of people who were present during such meetings, and
- the amount of the attorney's fee (and who paid it).

Prosecutors do not routinely seek such information. Its relevance is often limited to

conspiracy cases, when a prosecutor wants the information to show that a number of people were part of the same conspiracy. When the information is relevant, attorneys usually must disclose it upon request.

Client-Centered Decision Making

While attorneys can give advice, clients have the ultimate right to make many important case-related decisions.

Should clients expect lawyers to involve them in important decisions?

Yes. Lawyers' ethical responsibilities require them to involve clients in decision making. For example, Rule 1.4 of the ABA Model Rules of Professional Conduct states, "A lawyer shall explain a matter to the extent necessary to permit the client to make informed decisions regarding the representation." Moreover, Standard 4-5.2 of the ABA Standards for Criminal Justice lists a number of decisions that "are to be made by the accused after full consultation with counsel."

Don't be fooled by movie and TV defense attorneys who often say things to clients like, "Here's what you are going to do." As lawyers' ethical codes recognize, cases belong to defendants, not to their attorneys. After all, the client and not the attorney pays the fine or serves the time. Lawyers provide counsel and advice, and defendants have the right to make important case decisions.

On the other hand, lawyers are not "mouthpieces." They are not required to fulfill all of their clients' demands, especially if doing so would conflict with ethical rules or the lawyers' own professionalism.

Are there specific decisions that defendants have the right to make?

Yes. Standard 4-5.2 of the ABA Standards for Criminal Justice identifies decisions that defendants are entitled to make, after consultation with attorneys. They include:

- what plea to enter (usually, guilty or not guilty)
- whether to accept a plea bargain
- whether to waive (give up) a jury trial
- whether to personally testify at trial, and
- whether to appeal.

Decisions about these matters are entrusted to clients not only because the matters are important, but also because lawyers normally have time to consult with their clients before the decisions are made. "Consultation" is a key term. Before making any decision, defendants should insist on meeting with their attorneys to review their options and the likely consequences of each.

> **EXAMPLE:** Solomon, an Armenian national, is charged with selling illegal drugs and is considering whether to plead guilty. This is Solomon's decision to make. Because of Solomon's status as a noncitizen legal resident of the United States, however, Solomon's attorney has to advise him that if he pleads guilty, he is subject to deportation. (*Padilla v. Kentucky*, U.S. Sup. Ct. 2010.)

> **EXAMPLE:** Garza pleads guilty as part of a plea bargain in which Garza agreed to give up his right to appeal. Nevertheless, after Garza instructed his attorney to appeal, the lawyer's refusal to file the appeal constituted ineffective assistance of counsel. (*Garza v. Idaho*, U.S. Sup. Ct. 2019.)

Are there other important decisions that defendants might want to make?

Because each case is unique, no bright dividing line separates important decisions that are for defendants to make from other decisions that lawyers can be expected to make. Generally, a decision is important if it is likely to have a substantial legal or nonlegal impact on a client.

Two lawyers handling the same case may sometimes reasonably disagree about whether to leave a particular decision to a defendant. In the final analysis, defendants who want to have as much involvement as possible in making decisions should do the following:

- repeatedly tell their attorneys that they want to participate in the decision making whenever feasible
- include in their lawyers' fee agreements a clause allocating decision making to the defendant whenever feasible
- insist that their lawyers counsel them about the availability and consequences of various options, and
- put their words into actions by making decisions expeditiously as the opportunities arise.

Should defendants expect to make all case-related decisions?

No. It simply isn't feasible for defendants to make all case-related decisions. Many tactical decisions, such as how to question potential jurors and cross-examine prosecution witnesses, rely heavily on an attorney's professional skills and experience. Decisions like these also have to be made on the fly, which puts them largely beyond the control of defendants. In the heat of trial, attorneys can't stop the proceedings and meet with their clients to make decisions about what questions to ask or objections to make.

Nevertheless, Standard 4-5.2 does provide that defense attorneys should make strategic and tactical decisions "after consultation with the client where feasible and appropriate." It lists the following examples:

- what witnesses to call
- whether and how to cross-examine witnesses
- what jurors to accept or strike
- what trial motions to make, and
- what evidence to introduce.

Many attorneys think these decisions should be entirely in their hands. Thus, clients who want a voice in as many decisions as possible should discuss their wishes with their attorneys at the outset of and throughout the lawyer-client relationship.

> **EXAMPLE:** (Based again on the film *A Time to Kill*): Carl Lee is charged with murder for shooting and killing two men who brutally raped his daughter. In the course of the shooting, Carl Lee also accidentally wounded a policeman, causing the policeman to lose a leg. During cross-examination of the policeman, Carl Lee wants his lawyer, Jake, to ask the policeman whether Carl Lee should be punished for killing the rapists. Jake does not want to ask the question, fearing that the policeman will want to see Carl Lee punished for causing him to lose a leg. When Carl Lee finally convinces Jake to ask the question, the policeman dramatically supports Carl Lee's actions. Nevertheless, Jake probably did not have an ethical duty to comply with Carl Lee's wishes and ask the question. In the heat of trial, lawyers normally have the tactical authority to decide what questions to ask. Besides, the witness's opinion about the legitimacy of Carl Lee's actions is irrelevant so the question is probably improper.

Does a defendant have the right to reject a lawyer's advice to accept a plea bargain and go to trial?

When lawyers and defendants can't agree about an issue as fundamental as whether to go to trial, it's normally the defendant's desire that prevails. Assuming that a defendant's decision is neither unethical nor illegal ("My decision is to bump off the prosecution witness"), the lawyer is the defendant's agent and must either carry out the defendant's decision or convince the judge to allow the lawyer to withdraw from the case. But defendants should not obstinately refuse their attorneys' advice. Defendants should ask questions to make sure that they understand the advice and why the lawyers think it's in their best interests before making a decision.

EXAMPLE: Ida Dunit is charged with aggravated assault, and has insisted to her lawyer that she struck the alleged victim in self-defense. One day, Ida's lawyer phones her to say that he's worked out a good deal with the prosecutor: If Ida pleads guilty (or nolo contendere) to simple assault, the prosecutor will recommend that Ida be sentenced only to time served (the jail time she already served while waiting to make bail), and a small fine. However, Ida believes that she is not guilty and is not sure that she wants to accept the deal. Ida can tell the lawyer to turn down the deal. Despite what the lawyer said, the lawyer has no power to make a deal without Ida's personal approval. However, Ida can expect a letter from the lawyer outlining the deal and stating that Ida has decided to reject it in spite of the lawyer's recommendation that she accept it.

Do defense lawyers have to inform prosecutors of defendants' plea bargaining proposals?

Like the decision about whether to go to trial, defendants are entitled to decide whether to offer or accept plea bargains. To enforce this right, defense attorneys are ethically required to:

- relay a client's offer to plead guilty to the prosecutor, and
- relay a prosecutor's plea offer to the client.

It doesn't matter if the defense attorney believes that the defendant's offer won't be accepted or the prosecutor's counteroffer is unacceptable.

The Ethical Rule Governing Disclosure of Plea Bargain Offers

Comment to Rule 1.4, ABA Model Rules of Professional Conduct, states: "A lawyer who receives ... a proffered plea bargain in a criminal case should promptly inform the client of its substance unless prior discussions with the client have left it clear that the proposal will be unacceptable."

What information should clients have in order to make intelligent decisions?

Before making an important decision, a defendant is entitled to know what alternatives are reasonably available and, as far as can be predicted, the likely consequences of each alternative.

For example, assume that a defendant is charged with assault with a deadly weapon. The defense attorney tells the defendant, "The D.A. is willing to accept a guilty plea to simple assault and recommend a sentence of six months in county jail and a fine of $500. The decision is yours—what do you want to do?"

The defendant's response should be something like, "Let's review the options and try to figure out the likely consequences of each one." Here, the defendant and the attorney should readily identify at least three possible options:

- plead guilty now
- plead guilty later, or
- refuse to plead guilty and go to trial.

Before making a decision, the defendant and attorney should discuss the likely consequences of each option. For example, the defendant may ask questions such as:

- "Is there a chance that I'll get a better deal if I wait until closer to the trial to plead guilty?"
- "What sentence am I likely to receive if I go to trial and I'm convicted of assault with a deadly weapon?"
- "I'm trying to get a job. Do you think a conviction for assault with a deadly weapon will look worse than one for plain assault?"

Defendants should not count on having perfect information about the likely consequences of each option. For instance, a defense attorney may have to respond to the second question above by saying, "It's really hard to predict what the sentence will be for a conviction of assault with a deadly weapon. The judge to whom we've been assigned is very unpredictable, and a lot will depend on the recommendation in the probation report that will be prepared following the guilty plea."

Nevertheless, the attorney should provide as much information as possible on the likely consequences of all available options, so the defendant can make the best decision under the circumstances.

To make sure that they carefully consider their options and consequences before making a decision, defendants should consider writing them down. Make a heading for each option, and underneath note the likely consequences of that option.

EXAMPLE: Penny Seagram is charged with drunk driving. At the time of her arraignment, Penny's lawyer tells her, "The D.A. will dismiss the drunk driving charge and allow you to plead guilty to reckless driving. You will pay a fine of $400, avoid any jail time, give up your driver's license for three months, and be on probation for a year. I think it's a pretty good deal, but it's up to you. Should we take the deal?" Penny should insist on a more thorough discussion with her lawyer before making a decision. Most likely, Penny's lawyer can postpone the arraignment for a week on condition that the D.A. keep the offer open for that length of time. In the meantime, Penny can review her options and alternatives with her lawyer.

Defendants Can Raise Options and Consequences

Attorneys are not always the drivers and defendants always the passengers in an effective attorney-client relationship. Defendants should not hesitate to bring up options and consequences on their own. In fact, when it comes to nonlegal consequences (such as the impact of a conviction on a defendant's job or family), defendants often can make more accurate predictions than attorneys. For example, assume that a stockbroker charged with making unauthorized trades has to decide whether to plead guilty to a lesser charge. The defendant may be in the best position to predict the effect of a conviction of a lesser offense on the defendant's license.

Can defense lawyers ethically advise clients about what decisions are in the clients' best interests?

Yes. Attorneys have a professional obligation to offer "candid advice." (Rule 2.1, ABA Model Rules of Professional Conduct.) Attorneys should offer their best professional judgment, not simply tell defendants what they want to hear.

> **EXAMPLE:** Carrie Oka is charged with drunk driving. The prosecutor has offered Carrie a chance to plead guilty to a lesser charge of reckless driving. Carrie says she wants to go to trial, mentioning various reasons why she is confident that a jury will disbelieve the police officer's testimony about how Carrie was driving. Carrie's lawyer is sympathetic to some of her arguments, but believes on balance that a judge or jury will believe the police officer, that the prosecutor's offer is a good one, and that Carrie should take it. Even after Carrie has indicated her desire to refuse the prosecutor's offer, her lawyer can still advise her to accept it. Defendants all too often see their cases through rose-colored glasses. Carrie's lawyer has an obligation to provide dispassionate advice. In the end, however, the lawyer should follow her wishes.

Is it ethical for a lawyer to withdraw from a case because a defendant refuses to accept the lawyer's advice?

Occasionally, lawyers and defendants have such strongly opposing views that the lawyer cannot effectively carry out the defendant's desired strategy. In such a situation, the attorney may seek to withdraw as the defendant's counsel, or the defendant may seek to have the attorney replaced. Whether a judge will grant either request depends on whether the prosecution will be prejudiced or the proceedings will be unnecessarily delayed or disrupted.

> **EXAMPLE:** Denise Baylout is charged with burglary and is represented by a public defender. Unfortunately, Denise and her attorney do not always agree on the best strategy. Denise also thinks that her attorney is cold and aloof and not committed to her defense. Denise asks the judge to appoint a different public defender. However, a change of counsel in this context is very unlikely. Defendants who hire private counsel can replace them at will, as long as doing so doesn't unduly delay proceedings. But defendants who are represented at government expense generally get whomever the judge appoints or a public defender's office assigns. Unless attorney-client communications have broken down to such an extent that Denise cannot get a fair trial, the judge will probably refuse to appoint a new attorney.

Is a client's inability to continue to pay a private lawyer's fee legitimate grounds for the lawyer to withdraw from the case?

Possibly, subject to approval by the judge. Professional rules in many states allow a lawyer to withdraw from a case if a client fails to pay the lawyer's fees, or if continuing to represent the client causes financial hardship to the lawyer. However, before a judge permits a lawyer to withdraw from a case, the lawyer usually has to give sufficient advance warning to give the client time to hire a new attorney. And a judge might not permit the attorney to withdraw at all under any of these circumstances:

- The attorney seeks to withdraw on the eve of trial.
- The attorney has put in so much work on a case that the client would be prejudiced by having to start all over with another lawyer.
- The client has already paid substantial legal fees to a lawyer and is financially unable to pay additional fees.

Keeping Clients "In the Know"

This section covers the ethical rules that require lawyers to keep clients informed about the progress of a case.

Do lawyers have to inform clients about important case-related developments?

Yes. Defendants frequently grouse to friends after a case is over, "My lawyer didn't tell me what was going on." To prevent this from happening, defendants should insist that their lawyers adhere to their ethical obligation to inform them about the progress of cases.

As defined by ethical rules, a lawyer's duty to keep clients informed has two primary components:

- to advise defendants of important case developments (such as a prosecutor's offered plea bargain or locating an important defense witness), and
- to respond reasonably promptly to defendants' requests for information.

Keeping Clients Informed

ABA Standard for Criminal Justice 4-3.8 states: "Defense counsel should keep the client informed of the developments in the case and the progress of preparing the defense and should promptly comply with reasonable requests for information." (See also Rule 1.4, ABA Model Rules of Professional Conduct.)

Do clients frequently complain that their lawyers fail to keep them adequately informed about case-related developments?

Yes. Without labeling either party to the relationship "wrong," lawyers and clients may have different perspectives on the lawyer's duty to inform the defendant of case developments.

> **EXAMPLE:** Anita Consult's arraignment has just concluded; she and her attorney Sol Vent are supposed to return to court in a month. As they are leaving the courthouse, attorney Vent tells defendant Anita, "I'm going to set up a meeting with the D.A. in the next few days to try to work things out; I'll let you know what happens." As it turns out, Vent

and the D.A. can't get together for three weeks. Vent does not bother to tell this to Anita. Anita is upset with Vent. Having heard nothing, Anita worries that the case may have been settled without her knowledge, or that the D.A. refused to meet with Vent. Because no developments took place, Vent probably did not violate the ethical rule requiring an attorney to keep his client informed. However, because Vent indicated that he would be speaking to the D.A. in the next several days, it certainly would have been wise, from a customer service standpoint, to inform Anita about the delay.

Are there steps clients can take to encourage lawyers to inform them promptly of case-related developments?

The duty to keep clients informed rests on attorneys, not clients. But on the theory that if the attorney screws up it's the client who usually suffers, here are a couple of steps that defendants can take to try to secure effective communication with their lawyers:

- Establish, in advance, a clear understanding about case updates. If an attorney's practice is to initiate contact only when a development occurs, the attorney should communicate that to the client at the outset of the representation. If a client wants (and can pay for) regular updates regardless of whether developments have taken place, that too can be spelled out in advance—even included in a written retainer agreement. A defendant can indicate a willingness to accept case

updates not only from the lawyer personally, but also from the lawyer's paralegal assistant and other law office personnel.

Representing Guilty Defendants

Criminal defense lawyers frequently have to deal with the potentially onerous task of representing defendants who they know are guilty.

Can lawyers zealously represent clients they know are guilty?

Definitely. Defense attorneys are ethically bound to zealously represent all clients, the guilty as well as the innocent. (See Canon 7, ABA Model Code of Professional Responsibility.) Perhaps no one has put the duty so eloquently as Henry VIII's soon-to-be-beheaded ex-Chancellor Sir Thomas More, who, before going to the scaffold, insisted, "I'd give the Devil benefit of law, for mine own safety's sake." A vigorous defense is necessary to protect the innocent and to ensure that judges and citizens—and not the police—have the ultimate power to decide who is guilty of a crime.

Moreover, defense lawyers may not know for sure whether a defendant committed a charged crime. Just because a defendant says "I did it" doesn't make it so. The defendant may be lying to take the rap for someone else, or may be guilty only of a different and lesser crime than the charged crime. Or a defendant may have done the act in question, but may have a valid defense.

For these reasons among others, defense lawyers often do not ask clients if they committed the crime. Instead, lawyers use the facts and a client's circumstances to obtain the best plea bargain possible, or put on the best defense possible and leave the question of guilt to the judge or jury.

At trial, can defense lawyers ethically argue that defendants they know to be guilty should be acquitted?

Yes. The key is the difference between factual guilt (what the defendant actually did) and legal guilt (what a prosecutor can prove). A good criminal defense lawyer asks not, "Did my client do it?" but rather, "Can the government prove that my client did it?" No matter what the defendant has done, a defendant is not legally guilty until a prosecutor offers enough evidence to persuade a judge or jury to convict. However, the defense lawyer may not lie to the judge or jury by specifically stating that the defendant did not do something the lawyer knows the defendant did do. Rather, the lawyer's trial tactics and arguments must focus on the government's failure to prove all the elements of the crime.

> **EXAMPLE:** Sam Anella is charged with shoplifting. Sam admits to his lawyer that he took a watch, as charged. Sam's lawyer realizes that the store's hidden camera videotape is fuzzy and practically useless as prosecution evidence. In addition, Sam's lawyer learns that the store's security guard was at the end of a long overtime shift and had been drinking alcohol. Sam's lawyer can

use these facts in an argument for Sam's acquittal. Before trial, Sam's lawyer can argue to the D.A. that the D.A.'s case is too weak to prosecute. At trial, Sam's lawyer can argue to a judge or jury to acquit Sam. No matter what Sam has done, Sam is not legally guilty unless the prosecutor can prove it beyond a reasonable doubt. But Sam's lawyer cannot ethically state in his argument that Sam "didn't do it," only that the D.A. didn't prove that Sam did do it. While the line between ethical and unethical behavior may seem like—indeed, is—a fine one, it is a line that criminal defense lawyers walk every day on the job.

Competent Clients

This section explains how defendants can help their attorneys provide the most effective defense possible.

What is a competent client?

Competent clients share in the responsibility for an effective attorney-client relationship. Competent clients needn't possess an attorney's knowledge and skills. Instead, competent clients:

- understand, and hold attorneys to, the ethical duties outlined in this chapter
- participate in making important case decisions, and
- follow through on their attorneys' advice by, for example, making and showing up to appointments with counselors, dressing respectfully when coming to court appearances, and

keeping quiet when the lawyer tells them not to speak about the facts of the alleged crime. Some of these actions may lead to better outcomes, such as reduced sentences or even dropped charges. Other actions, such as attending counseling, may lend support to an argument that a defendant has already begun rehabilitation in the event of a conviction.

Just as educated patients elicit better information and often better medical care from their doctors, competent clients tend to receive better communication and improved legal representation from their lawyers.

Can clients benefit by attending court sessions unrelated to their cases?

Sure. Courtrooms are public places, and defendants can learn a lot simply by

---

How to Become an Unpopular Defense Lawyer

Criminal defense attorneys may vigorously defend guilty clients, but as a couple of examples make clear, they might risk committing professional suicide by the tactics they choose in doing so. Way back in 1840, Charles Phillips, one of the finest British barristers of his era, defended Benjamin Courvoisier against a charge that Courvoisier brutally murdered his employer, wealthy man-about-town Lord Russell. Courvoisier privately confessed to Phillips that he was guilty. Nevertheless, Phillips's aggressive cross-examinations suggested that the police officers were liars and that other members of Lord Russell's staff might have killed him. Courvoisier was convicted and executed. But when it became generally known that Phillips had known that his client was guilty, Phillips became a pariah to the profession and the public.

Moving forward to 2002, San Diego lawyer Steven Feldman got the "Phillips treatment" when he represented David Westerfield, who was charged with molesting and murdering seven-year-old Danielle van Dam. Feldman knew privately that Westerfield was guilty. Nevertheless, at trial Feldman aggressively attacked Danielle's parents. He offered evidence that they frequently invited strangers into their home for sex orgies, and suggested that one of the strangers could have been the killer. Westerfield was convicted and sentenced to death. Yet like Phillips, Feldman was viciously attacked in the media. TV commentators and members of the public called for his disbarment.

Although Phillips and Feldman gave their clients the best defense possible, their experiences suggest that defense lawyers may risk their reputations and perhaps their careers by the tactics they choose in some cases.

taking an hour or two to watch a court in session. Defendants can examine the demeanor and dress of other defendants, and identify what seems to impress or put off the judges. Defendants can then mirror effective behavior during their own court appearances.

Is it wise for clients to engage in legal research?

Competent clients need not play amateur lawyer or second-guess every bit of legal advice their lawyers give. But defendants should understand the charges against them and the basic procedures followed by the local criminal courts. The procedures described in this book are a good starting point. Defendants should also read the statutes they are accused of violating and understand how courts have interpreted those statutes.

RESOURCES

Help with legal research. For an extended discussion of research tools—and how to use them—consult *Legal Research: How to Find & Understand the Law*, by the Editors of Nolo (Nolo).

A Walk Through Criminal Court

Contrary to the popular notion of courthouses as solemn places—much like churches where people are quiet, well-dressed, and respectful—state courts devoted to criminal cases can resemble train stations during rush hour: crowded, confusing, and noisy. The "action" happens in the courtroom and in the halls outside; the people seem (and often are) tense and scared.

The reality is that criminal court is the last place most people want to be, except perhaps the lawyers and court staff who work there. For anyone else who must go, however, the best way to cope is to first learn what's what, who's who, and how things work.

The Courthouse

Courthouse architecture often incorporates classical features to suggest that courthouses are important public spaces. But newer courthouses tend to look less like the Parthenon and more like a modern office building. To enter a courthouse, people usually have to pass through security and metal detectors, and so need to leave plenty of time to get where they want to go.

How can people find out where they are supposed to go?

Courthouses usually have guards or directories near the main entrance. Either can help defendants, witnesses, or anyone else who wants to attend court to "Department J,"

"Judge Paul's courtroom," the "Court Clerk's" office, or any other location.

Finding the Right Courthouse

Obviously, before visitors can find the right courtroom, they need to be in the right courthouse. Criminal courts are often located in the same building as civil courts, but, especially in large urban areas, they may be in a different building. People who have to or want to attend criminal court proceedings need to be sure they are in the correct courthouse.

What happens in the courthouse clerk's office?

The clerk's office is the courthouse's central nervous system. Here, documents relating to all the cases in the court are filed and stored. The courthouse clerk's office may also issue subpoenas (orders to appear in court), collect fines, and manage other administrative details. Courthouse clerks also work with the courtroom clerks who are assigned to individual courtrooms.

Do courthouses have legal research sections?

Courthouses often had law libraries that were open to the public. The availability of online legal databases has doomed many books and many of these library spaces to extinction.

Do judges normally sit in the same courtroom every day?

Most judges conduct open-court hearings in the same courtroom every day, though some are assigned to different courtrooms on different days. Visitors should check with the courthouse clerk's office if they are unsure where a particular judge is sitting on a particular day. If there is a line at the courthouse clerk's office, visitors might look on the walls and doors, where clerks often post daily lists of all the cases to be heard in each courtroom. Those lists typically also include the names of the judges that will hear the cases.

Other than courtrooms, what other offices are often located in courthouses?

Courthouses also may provide business offices for:

- court personnel, such as judges, secretaries, and clerks
- court-related officials, including prosecutors and public defenders, and
- law enforcement agencies, such as a marshal's and a sheriff's office.

Courthouses in which criminal matters are handled also have jails. Visitors won't usually see them, because they are typically located behind courtrooms, in basements, or on a separate floor. These jails (sometimes called "holding cells," "pens," or "bullpens") provide a temporary place to keep in-custody defendants when they go to court. Most often, they are for day use only.

The Courtroom

This section offers a general orientation to the courtroom.

Are all courtrooms created alike?

No. Courtrooms differ in both process and substance.

Process. To help metropolitan courts deal with a large volume of cases efficiently, courtrooms located in a single courthouse may specialize in distinct stages of the criminal justice process. For example, defendants' first court appearances may be in a courtroom in which only arraignments and bail hearings take place. As cases proceed, later appearances may take place in separate courtrooms devoted to pretrial motions, guilty pleas, and trials. The courtrooms of appellate court judges are often in separate courthouses.

Substance. Courtrooms in the same courthouse may also differ according to types of cases. For example, misdemeanor trials may take place in one courtroom and felony trials in another. And cases involving illegal drugs may be dealt with in one courtroom, cases in which the defendants are military veterans in another, and cases in which the defendants are under 25 or 21 years old in yet another. Arrangements such as these enable judges, lawyers and court personnel to develop specialized expertise and resources.

Where do spectators go to observe court proceedings?

Most courtrooms have a spectator area in the back, often separated by a "bar" or partition from the rest of the courtroom. Members of the public, including those who come to court to support a family member or friend, sit in this area.

Where's Justice?

Because so much activity relating to criminal cases goes on outside the courtroom—and because of the general loss of confidence in the legal system that was prevalent among certain segments of the community at the time—famous 1960s comedian/ social commentator Lenny Bruce was fond of saying, "In the halls of justice, the only justice is in the halls."

Where do defendants sit while they wait for their case to be called?

Defendants who are free on bail usually sit in the spectator area of a courtroom until their cases are called by the courtroom clerk, bailiff, or judge. In-custody defendants wait in holding cells and are escorted into the courtroom by a bailiff.

Should defendants stand when they are inside a courtroom?

Defendants should sit or stand as directed by their attorneys (if they have counsel)

or by the judge, courtroom clerk, or bailiff. The custom is different in different proceedings and different courtrooms. For example, during a short arraignment or bail hearing, defendants typically stand next to counsel. However, at trial or a hearing on a motion they may sit at counsel table in the area at the front of the courtroom.

Where will the lawyers be?

Again, it depends on the proceeding. In pretrial hearings, lawyers may stand directly in front of the judge. In trials, however, lawyers usually sit or stand at counsel table, with the prosecutor usually on the side closer to the jury box.

Most lawyers stand when addressing the judge or questioning witnesses.

Who sits in the rows of seats near the judge?

Jurors sit in those seats, called the "jury box," during jury trials. The jury box may remain empty during nonjury proceedings (or when a jury is deliberating), or the judge may use it to seat lawyers or in-custody defendants during arraignments and motions.

What is "the bench?"

The judge's bench is the raised wooden desk or podium at the front of the courtroom. Attorneys and defendants alike should not go near the bench unless they ask for and receive the judge's permission to "approach the bench." This forbidden territory includes the "well," the space between counsel table and the bench, where the courtroom clerk and the court reporter may sit.

What is a judge's "chambers?"

Typically, judges have private offices called "chambers" adjacent to a courtroom. A judge and the attorneys talk in chambers during a trial or another proceeding, especially if they want to go "off the record" and have a quiet place to confer. Also, some judges prefer to hold plea bargaining negotiations in chambers.

Attorneys may request that in-chambers conferences be put "on the record" if they become uncomfortable with what is being said. This means the conference will be recorded word for word by a court reporter and preserved for possible later review.

What do empty courtrooms signify?

Courtrooms may be empty for a variety of reasons. One is that a jurisdiction may lack the funds to hire enough judicial officers to provide adequate justice. Another is that the judicial officer and lawyers assigned to a courtroom are discussing cases and resolving motions in chambers rather than in the courtroom.

The Courtroom Players

A jingle on the long-running children's TV show *Mr. Rogers* asked, "Who are the people in your neighborhood?" If a neighborhood includes a courthouse for criminal cases, this section explains who those people are likely to be.

What do judges do?

The judge, the man or woman seated at the bench wearing a black robe, typically performs some or all of the following functions:

- conducts hearings and makes rulings concerning pretrial business such as preliminary hearings and motions
- presides over trials
- makes legal rulings during trials, such as whether to admit or exclude particular evidence
- decides on the guilt or innocence of the defendant when the defendant has opted for a nonjury trial (called a "bench trial")
- instructs the jury (if there is one) on the law they must follow to decide the defendant's guilt or innocence, and
- pronounces sentence on convicted defendants following a guilty verdict or negotiated guilty plea.

Especially in metropolitan areas, judges may be assigned to hear only pretrial motions, conduct only misdemeanor trials, or handle only preliminary hearings in felony cases.

Are there other words that mean the same thing as "judge"?

Judicial titles can be misleading. For example, at the top of the judicial power ladder, the term "justice" often refers to the judges who are part of a jurisdiction's highest court, such as the U.S. Supreme

Court or a state's supreme court. At the lower end of the ladder, "justices of the peace" are appointed in some states to set bail or preside over criminal cases that don't involve jail or prison time. While justices of the peace may be trained in legal rules and processes, they are not necessarily lawyers.

"Commissioners" and "magistrates" are typically lawyers appointed by the judges in a court system (for example, U.S. magistrates are appointed by federal district court judges) to act as judges. The judges may delegate full judicial authority to magistrates and commissioners or limit them to certain types of cases or certain functions within cases. For example, a magistrate might have authority to set bail, conduct arraignments, and issue search and arrest warrants, but not to conduct trials.

What do courtroom clerks do?

Courtroom clerks are court officials who work for particular judges. Courtroom clerks have many duties. Typically, they:

- Verify that the parties are present in court. If a defendant fails to come to court when required, the courtroom clerk may assist the judge in preparing a bench warrant for that defendant's arrest.
- Prepare and maintain the court calendar (sometimes called the "docket"), which lists the dates and times for trials and other matters.
- Prepare court orders for the judge to sign, such as an order granting a motion to exclude evidence.

- Keep custody of exhibits entered as evidence in a case and administer oaths to witnesses, jurors, and interpreters.
- Obtain for the judge's reference and keep custody of case files maintained and stored in the courthouse clerk's office.
- Assist the judge during a hearing or trial by marking and handling documents and other exhibits.

What Are Case Files?

A case file holds all of the legal papers (indictments, bail orders, and other documents) relating to the case, which have been "filed," that is, delivered to the court's custody to be stored as permanent, usually public records.

What do "law clerks" do?

Law clerks are lawyers (or law students) who assist judges by conducting legal research, preparing memos, or drafting orders.

Who are "bailiffs?"

Bailiffs are police officers (often deputy sheriffs) who protect other courtroom personnel and maintain order and decorum inside courtrooms. A bailiff's wide range of duties may include quieting down or removing disruptive spectators, bringing defendants in custody from holding cells to the courtroom, handling exhibits, and escorting jurors to and from deliberation rooms.

Are court reporters present in courtrooms?

Court reporters are frequently present during trials, although they have sometimes given way to audio recording equipment. Court reporters or recording equipment are often absent from courtrooms devoted to pretrial motions or other nontrial proceedings.

What do interpreters do?

At all critical stages of cases, judges appoint translators for defendants, victims, witnesses, and others who have a limited ability to speak and understand English. Large metropolitan areas may need help translating 90 or even more languages. Under the Americans With Disabilities Act, hearing-impaired individuals may obtain sign language interpreters.

Defendants who have interpreters should communicate through them at all times. For example, suppose Jim has a translator. Even if he thinks that he understands a question without waiting for it to be translated and can answer it in English, he should listen to the translation before answering and should answer in his primary language.

The presence of an interpreter does not affect the confidentiality of attorney-client communications.

EXAMPLE: Su has been charged with shoplifting for trying to steal an expensive dress. Su's first language is Mandarin and her knowledge of English is quite limited. Su claims that she walked out of the store with the dress in the mistaken belief that the dress store clerk had agreed to let her take it to a tailor and get an estimate for alterations before deciding whether to buy it. Su is not really sure why she was arrested when she walked out of the store, and has not been able to understand fully what the police officers have said to her. When in court, Su should ask for assistance from an interpreter. Even if Su's lawyer speaks Mandarin fluently, the lawyer cannot participate in courtroom proceedings while simultaneously translating for Su. (If Su knows someone who can interpret for her, she can ask the judge to appoint that person.) If Su speaks to her lawyer through the interpreter, both the lawyer and the interpreter have a duty not to reveal the conversation to anyone without Su's permission.

Where do the jurors come from and what do they do?

Jurors are randomly drawn from a court's geographical area—typically from voter and/or motor vehicle registration lists. They listen to evidence and deliberate toward an appropriate verdict based on instructions that judges give them. Criminal juries typically consist of 12 jurors (plus alternates, who take over for any disqualified jurors). However, as few as six jurors are legally permissible, at least in trials involving less serious offenses. In criminal cases, jurors are instructed that they may convict a defendant only if the prosecution has proved the person guilty beyond a reasonable doubt.

Jurors do not make legal rulings, such as deciding whether an item of evidence is admissible. And jurors usually do not decide what sentence a defendant should receive in case of a conviction, capital punishment cases being an exception.

It is increasingly common for judges to involve jurors in the questioning of witnesses. Before excusing witnesses, many judges invite jurors to submit written questions. After reviewing the jurors' proposed questions with attorneys from both sides, the judge decides which questions (if any) to ask.

The Difference Between Trial and Appellate Courts

In both state and federal courts, there are trial courts (lower courts, where cases are first heard) and higher or appellate courts, which review decisions of the trial courts. To appeal a case means to petition an appellate court to overturn or modify the decision of the lower or trial court. Often, a defendant can successfully appeal a case only if the judge in the trial court made a mistake about the law that affected the outcome of the case. Appellate courts normally won't reconsider the evidence and try to second-guess the verdict. (But there may be other grounds for successful appeal, like "ineffective assistance of counsel" or newly discovered evidence.)

In the federal court system, the courts, in order from lowest to highest, are district courts, circuit courts of appeal, and the United States Supreme Court (the highest federal court).

While most criminal actions (such as theft, drunk driving, and murder) are processed in state courts, many crimes are handled in the federal courts, including those occurring on federal property and crimes taking place in more than one state (such as interstate drug trafficking).

In the state systems, the names of criminal courts vary greatly from state to state. In some states, the lowest level of criminal courts (often hearing bail motions and arraignments) may be called magistrate courts, police courts, or traffic courts. The next level of courts may be called municipal courts, superior courts, or county courts, and the highest court is often (but not always) the state supreme court. (There are typically intermediate appellate courts, too.) Check a public or law library or an online government site to find out more about a state's court structure.

Most Cases Don't Involve Juries

Juries are not formed unless and until a case goes to trial. At least 90% of criminal cases end in plea bargains (never getting to trial), and many trials are handled by judges alone, so most criminal cases go from start to finish without the involvement of a jury.

Who are the parties in a criminal case?

In criminal cases, the parties are the state or federal government bringing the charges (also known as the People or the State) and the defendant(s), the person or people accused of the charged crimes.

Who are *pro se* defendants?

A self-represented defendant typically is referred to as a *pro se* (pronounced pro say) defendant, from the Latin meaning "[f]or oneself," or a *pro per* defendant (or just a *pro per*), from the Latin term "*in propria persona*," defined as "[f]or one's own person." (*Black's Law Dictionary.*) Because the Latin phraseology can get daunting, some members of the legal self-help movement prefer the plain-English term, "self-represented."

Who are the lawyers who handle criminal cases?

Prosecuting lawyers represent the governmental entity that has charged a defendant with a crime. For example, a prosecutor representing the federal government is likely to be a U.S. attorney, while the prosecutor representing a state may be a district attorney. A defense lawyer may be in private practice, a public defender, or a member of a panel of defense lawyers. Only licensed attorneys can serve as prosecutors or defense counsel.

During trials, lawyers question witnesses, offer exhibits, argue the merits of their positions to judges and jurors, object to arguably inadmissible evidence, prepare proposed jury instructions, and generally handle all aspects of a case for the party they represent. Lawyers also carry out a variety of pre- and post-trial tasks, such as interviewing percipient and expert witnesses, visiting crime scenes, conducting legal research, drafting and arguing motions, and engaging in plea bargaining discussions.

Do defense lawyers speak for their clients?

Most of the time, defense lawyers speak for their clients inside courtrooms. However, defendants may speak for themselves in a few instances, such as when they enter a plea, when they testify, and when they address the judge during sentencing. Represented defendants should always consult with their lawyers before addressing a judge directly.

Outside of court, lawyers also speak for their clients. Under lawyers' professional rules, clients must communicate with represented opposing parties through their lawyers rather than directly. So prosecutors, for instance, contact the lawyers of repre-sented defendants to discuss cases, not the defendants themselves.

> ! **CAUTION**
> **Keep your mouth shut.** With some minor exceptions (such as giving one's name and address if arrested), a suspect accused of a crime should not speak to anyone without first talking to a lawyer.

What other people are likely to be in courtrooms?

The other people who are likely to be in a criminal courtroom are:

- The police officers who arrested the accused or the officers investigating the crime. They may be in court to testify about the arrest or investigation, or to advise a prosecutor about case-related events.
- Victims. For many years regarded as peripheral, victims now play a greater role in the criminal justice process. Frequently, they attend every court session to observe. Some victims assist in identifying suspects. And, victims may speak to the judge during sentencing about the crime's impact on their lives and the type of sentence they consider appropriate. Personnel from both governmental and nonprofit victim/witness assistance programs may counsel and accompany a victim or witness to court.
- Probation officers, who may be assigned to investigate the defendant's background and prepare a report to help the judge decide on a sentence.
- Family and friends lending moral support to the defendant or victim.
- Reporters for newspapers and radio and television stations.
- Courthouse groupies. Even total strangers may come to the courtroom to watch; most court proceedings are open to the public.

Courtroom Behavior

As in all social settings, how people appear and behave in the courtroom can affect how other people see them. The opinion of some of these other people (such as the judge and jury) will be very important. This section offers a few tips on making the best possible impression.

Are most people anxious when they have to go to court?

Most definitely. For most non-regulars, criminal courtrooms are intimidating. And it's no wonder. Judges and lawyers use unfamiliar legal terms, the proceedings are formal and ritualistic, and the outcomes affect people's lives, sometimes forever. Defendants, victims, witnesses, family members, and friends all are likely to be nervous and unsure of themselves.

The best way for people to cope is to ask questions, prepare, and perhaps observe other cases.

What is appropriate courtroom attire?

In general, proper courtroom attire displays respect for the system of justice. Most courts have a specific dress code; such a code might prohibit hats (except for religious purposes), shorts, tank tops, and bare feet.

Prosecutors and defense lawyers typically give courtroom attire advice to people who are unfamiliar with courtroom proceedings. The advice extends to family members and friends in the spectator section—judges and jurors can see them and may draw positive or negative inferences based on their attire. In general, lawyers advise people to dress conservatively. They may advise "business casual," or "dress as if going to an important job interview." While customs may differ from one locality to another, modest attire is almost always a good choice.

How should defendants behave toward courtroom personnel?

Defendants should go out of their way to be courteous to everyone, especially to court personnel, and even when court isn't in session. That said, it's usually improper to engage people like prosecutors, witnesses (including police officers), and especially victims, in conversation. (Depending on the circumstances, it might even be illegal for a defendant to approach or talk to a witness or victim.)

For defendants, a bit of courtesy can go a long way. In many ways, the system of justice is biased against the accused. One of this country's most honored legal principles is that people are presumed innocent until they are proven guilty beyond a reasonable doubt. But many people just don't buy it anymore. Or, they do in theory, but in practice they don't trust (or consciously or unconsciously fear and dislike) anyone even accused of a crime. One reminder of this is the number of times defense lawyers are asked, "How can you defend those people?" (This is the title of one public defender's memoirs.)

We certainly hope that on a large scale, this attitude will change. But in the meantime, accused people should know that, in practice, they may well face a presumption of guilt rather than the presumption of innocence to which they technically are entitled. Hopefully, the simple suggestions above and many more throughout this book will help people accused of crime cope with what is often a deck stacked against them.

How should defendants address a judge?

There are certain times when represented defendants must talk directly to the judge —for example, when a plea is entered or during sentencing, defendants may speak on their own behalf. The most important thing for a defendant to remember in these situations is to be polite and, if appropriate, to show genuine remorse.

In addition, it is critical to follow certain basic rules and customs, among them the following:

- Stand when addressing the judge. Those unable to stand for medical reasons should mention that to the judge at the outset so that remaining seated is not interpreted as a sign of disrespect.
- Call the judge "Your Honor"—not "Judge," not "Sir," and especially not "Ma'am." In court, by long-running tradition, "Your Honor" is the neutral, respectful term used by all. It is a term judges expect and one they like to hear.
- Speak slowly and clearly, directly into the microphone if one is provided. If not, stand tall and project so that the judge, attorneys, and court reporter can hear easily. (On the other hand, don't yell.)
- Represented defendants should speak only when asked to and, if possible, only after getting a go-ahead or guidance from their attorney as to what to say. Be careful to wait until counsel and the judge finish before speaking. (Before court, defendants should review with their attorney how to handle prompts to speak. For example, a defense lawyer might remind a defendant not to look at the lawyer for direction when responding to a judge's questions.)
- Keep emotions in check. Angry expressions, emotional gestures, and the like can be disastrous, even when a defendant is seated and silent. Likewise, laughing or appearing smug or nonchalant is to be avoided at all costs.

Do defendants need to take special precautions when in a courthouse?

Inside a courtroom, defendants should not discuss their cases with witnesses, reporters, family members, or anyone other than their lawyers. Defendants should take special care not to say anything, even to their own lawyers, in a public place, such as a cafeteria, a bathroom, or an elevator, where they may be overheard.

Arraignment

An arrangement is the usually brief hearing that commonly starts the courtroom phase of a criminal prosecution. A typical arraignment consists of some or all of the following:

- The suspect—now called the defendant—is given a written accusation prepared by the prosecutor's office.
- A judge appoints an attorney at the request of an unrepresented defendant.
- The defendant responds to the written charges, usually orally and almost always with a "not-guilty" plea.
- The judge sets a tentative schedule for later courtroom proceedings, such as a pretrial conference, a preliminary hearing, a hearing on pretrial motions, and the trial itself.
- The judge decides unresolved bail issues (bail may be set, raised, or lowered, or the defendant may be released O.R.).

Arraignment Basics

An arraignment is often the first step in what can be a lengthy criminal justice process.

When does an arraignment take place?

Arraignments are usually held within 48 hours of a suspect's arrest (excluding weekends and holidays) if the suspect is in jail. If the suspect has bailed out or was issued a citation, the arraignment typically occurs several weeks later. The exact timing of arraignment varies from one locality to another.

All states must adhere to the U.S. Supreme Court's ruling that an arraignment should take place "as quickly as possible" after arrest. (*Mallory v. U.S.*, U.S. Sup. Ct. 1957.)

Why are speedy arraignments required under the U.S. Constitution?

The requirement that a suspect be arraigned shortly after arrest is intended to protect the suspect. A quick arraignment before a judge means that suspects can't be required to languish in jail while the police rummage around for enough evidence of criminal activity to support a charge.

Is an arraignment usually delayed for suspects who bail out of jail before going to court?

Yes. By bailing out, a suspect can probably count on the arraignment being delayed for at least two weeks. The delay is rarely of legal consequence, because speedy arraignments are intended primarily to benefit jailed suspects. However, in an unusual case, a bailed-out suspect might still ask the judge to dismiss charges because of a delayed arraignment. To be successful, the suspect would have to demonstrate that the delay was extraordinary, that it was not the suspect's fault, and that it ruined the suspect's opportunity to present an effective defense (perhaps because it led to the destruction of crucial defense evidence).

The Tactical Advantages of Delay

In most cases, delays help defendants. Prosecution witnesses may forget what they saw and heard, prosecutors might lose evidence, and cases simply lose momentum. The older a case, the easier it often is to negotiate a plea bargain favorable to the defense. Also, delays give the defendant a chance to undertake counseling, get a job, or otherwise establish a pattern of behavior that can favorably impress the judge at a later sentencing (if one occurs).

As with all general rules, however, there are exceptions. In 1995, in the famous O.J. Simpson criminal trial, the defense pushed for the earliest possible trial date. The defense strategy substantially reduced the prosecution's ability to prepare to try an extraordinarily complex case.

How does an arraignment compare to a trial?

Life inside an arraignment courtroom tends to be far more hectic than at trial. The court's calendar (the cases a judge will hear on a given day) is likely to be crowded, and the judge often has to move quickly from one case to the next. The courtroom will be buzzing with prosecutors, defense attorneys, and defendants, all waiting for the judge to call their cases. Sometimes, a judge will interrupt one case to make a ruling or take a plea on another. No juries are present at arraignment.

In addition to the often hectic atmosphere of an arraignment courtroom, judges, clerks, prosecutors, and defense counsel can sound as if they are speaking in a strange code. They routinely refer to courtroom procedures by statute numbers or the names of the cases that mandated the procedures. For example, an attorney might tell the defendant, "We're going to have a *McDonald* conference with the D.A.," or "We'll schedule a 605 motion." The latter remark doesn't mean that the motion will be heard on an interstate highway. The attorney may simply be referring to a hearing to review a lab analysis of alleged drugs. Defendants confused by unfamiliar jargon should always ask for a translation.

EXAMPLE: Al Dente appears at an arraignment on drunk driving charges. After Al enters a not guilty plea, the judge asks, "Do you want me to set this for a 605 conference?" Al represents himself for purposes of this hearing, does not understand what this means, but is fearful of displaying his ignorance in open court. Nevertheless, Al should ask the judge to explain what a "605 conference" is. The opinions of court personnel and others as to Al's legal knowledge are much less important than Al making an intelligent decision about his case. If Al is excessively image conscious, he can ask to "approach the bench." If the judge agrees, Al can go up to the judge and ask his question out of earshot of other people in the courtroom.

Where Defendants Sit During Arraignments

During arraignment, defendants who were unable to make bail (known as "custodies") will be brought into the courtroom by a sheriff from holding cells located behind the courtroom, and often will be seated in the jury box if the courtroom has one. If there is no place to put them, they will be ushered in one at a time. Defendants who were given a citation or released on bail or O.R. enter the courtroom through the public doors and sit in the spectator area until their cases are called.

What happens during a typical arraignment?

The primary purpose of an arraignment is to give the defendant written notice of the charged crime(s) and take the defendant's plea. In addition, the judge may do any of the following.

Appoint counsel. The judge will appoint an attorney to represent an indigent defendant if jail time is a possible outcome. Defendants who are ineligible for court-appointed counsel and need additional time to hire an attorney can ask the judge to "continue" (delay) the arraignment for a week or so.

Hear a bail motion. Whether or not they had an earlier bail hearing, defendants can ask the arraignment judge to review their bail status (for example, to reduce the bail or convert bail to O.R. release). Similarly, if bail has been posted, the prosecutor may argue that newly discovered information justifies revoking or raising the amount to assure the defendant's appearance or protect the public.

Set a date to hear pretrial motions. Defendants and their attorneys may raise legal issues at arraignment that the judge may wish to consider in the future, when both sides have had an opportunity to make and respond to motions setting forth their arguments. For example, the defendant may file a motion claiming that the case has been filed in the wrong court or that the activity in which the defendant was engaged doesn't constitute a crime.

One Arraignment and Out

An arraignment can be the first and last court appearance for a defendant who pleads guilty (or *nolo contendere*, which is the same as "no contest"). In simple cases, the arraignment judge may accept a guilty plea and sentence the defendant immediately according to an agreement worked out by the defendant and the prosecutor. In more complex cases, or cases where significant jail time is a possibility, the judge may accept the plea but set a future date for sentencing.

Criminal defense attorneys routinely discourage their clients from pleading guilty at the arraignment. However, there might be instances when a guilty plea could conceivably get the best result for the defendant.

Set dates for upcoming hearings not involving motions. Depending on a state's procedures and whether the charge involves a felony or a misdemeanor, the judge may schedule a number of upcoming hearings. For example, in one case an arraignment judge may schedule a preliminary hearing; in another, the judge may schedule a plea bargaining settlement discussion.

Why might a defendant ask to "continue" an arraignment to a later date?

Defendants who are uncertain about whether to represent themselves at arraignment may buy additional time to make a decision by asking for a continuance (postponement). Judges routinely grant continuances of at least a week to give the defendant a chance to hire an attorney. In return, the defendant may have to "waive time," meaning the defendant gives up the right to be arraigned within statutory time limits. The continuance does not obligate the defendant to hire an attorney. The defendant can typically appear at the next scheduled date for the arraignment and self-represent or ask for a court-appointed lawyer.

To obtain a continuance, the defendant usually must appear in court on the date set for arraignment and ask the judge for more time to find an attorney. However, a defendant who wants a continuance and finds it inconvenient to appear in court on the date set for arraignment should contact the arraignment court clerk ahead of time to find out if an informal continuance is possible.

Can defendants appear at arraignments through their lawyer?

Many states excuse defendants from having to appear at arraignment if their attorneys are present. However, even these states are likely to impose some limitations. For example, many states excuse defendants from personally attending arraignments only if the defendants are charged with misdemeanors; defendants charged with felonies have to appear in court, with or without an attorney.

A defendant may have to appear in court personally in order to plead guilty or enter a no-contest plea. Constitutional considerations require the judge to question the defendant face to face before accepting a plea that results in a conviction. The judge needs to determine for the record that:

- a factual basis for the plea exists (that is, the defendant admits to facts that justify conviction of the crime charged)
- the defendant is pleading guilty voluntarily (that is, the plea is not the result of illegal threats or promises)
- the defendant is aware of all the rights he or she is giving up by pleading guilty or no contest (such as the right to a jury trial, the right to cross-examine adverse witnesses, and the right against self-incrimination), and
- the defendant understands the charges and recognizes the potential consequences of the guilty or no-contest plea.

Do prosecutors ever dismiss charges prior to an arraignment?

Yes. But unfortunately, this possibility generally exists only for defendants who hire private attorneys prior to arraignment. Defendants who are represented by court-appointed counsel often do not even have counsel appointed until the time of arraignment. And a self-represented defendant should not risk additional legal difficulties by discussing the case with a prosecutor before arraignment (assuming that a prosecutor would agree to meet with the defendant in the first place).

Defendants who hire private counsel before arraignment have a chance to derail the case for several reasons. First, in most parts of the country, intake prosecutors (not the police) are supposed to analyze cases to make sure that there is evidence of guilt and that prosecution is in the interests of justice. Frequently, however, the caseload is so heavy that reviews are cursory, and weak cases sometimes slip into the pipeline. If an attorney can convince a prosecutor of the weaknesses in the case, the case may get dismissed.

Second, prior to arraignment, no one in the prosecutor's office has invested a lot of time or money in the case, and there is no need to justify the effort with at least some kind of conviction.

Third, intake prosecutors normally work in offices tucked away from the courtroom spotlight. Courtroom prosecutors, however, who arraign and try cases, have to take heat from judges if they show up in court with weak cases.

Finally, especially in urban areas, courtroom dockets (schedules) are crowded. By quickly disposing of weak cases, prosecutors can devote the little time they have to more serious cases.

For all these reasons, if defense counsel can point out weaknesses that the intake prosecutor did not consider, or convince the prosecutor that further proceedings would not be in the interests of justice, a prearraignment meeting between the defendant's attorney and the prosecutor may result in the case being derailed before arraignment.

> **EXAMPLE:** Redd Emption was arrested for carrying a concealed weapon. Rushing to make an airplane, Redd forgot that the gun he was supposed to leave at his house was still in his backpack. He was arrested when the airport metal detector revealed the gun. Redd has no prior arrests. The only reason that he had the gun in the first place is that a series of robberies had taken place in his apartment building, and his father had loaned him the gun for protection. Redd is out on bail and is scheduled for arraignment in a week. Thinking that his arrest is a misunderstanding, Redd is uncertain about whether to hire an attorney. However, a private attorney may be able to get the case dismissed before the arraignment. Redd's attorney may be able to contact the arraignment prosecutor to seek a mutually agreeable outcome. Redd's attorney can point out information that the intake prosecutor may not have been aware of— Redd didn't own the gun; he had borrowed

it for protection, and inadvertently had it in his backpack. Though Redd may technically be guilty as charged, these factors may convince the prosecutor that trying Redd is not in the interests of justice. As a result, the prosecutor may agree to dismiss the case or offer Redd diversion (that is, agree to temporarily not file the charges and end the case permanently if Redd stays out of trouble for a period of time).

If a case is dismissed at arraignment, does the "double jeopardy" rule prevent a prosecutor from charging the defendant with the same crime?

No. As long as the statute of limitations (the period of time within which a case can be filed following a crime) has not run out, the police can rearrest defendants whose cases have been dismissed at arraignment. Defendants are not considered to be "in jeopardy" for purposes of the double jeopardy rule until the trial actually begins. Dismissal followed by rearrest can be expensive—a defendant may have to obtain a second bail bond and pay a second fee.

How do defendants who remain in custody get from a jail to an arraignment court?

Jailed suspects get free rides to arraignments, courtesy of the local sheriff. Upon arriving at the courthouse, jailed suspects are put into "holding cells" or "pens" located near the courtroom. They are called into court singly or as a group, depending

on local practice. They usually remain in jail attire for the arraignment, as no jury is present.

What happens if a bailed-out defendant is late or can't make it to court for a scheduled arraignment?

Defendants who cannot for any reason appear in court as scheduled MUST contact either their attorneys (if they are already represented) or the courtroom clerk (if they are not) as soon as possible. As long as a defendant notifies the clerk in advance and has a valid reason to be late or absent, a judge is likely to delay an arraignment or continue it to a later date. (A defendant might need a doctor's note, for example, to prove the lateness or absence was justified.) But if the defendant fails to contact the court and is absent from the courtroom when the judge calls the defendant's case, the judge may immediately revoke bail and issue a warrant for the defendant's arrest.

How do indigent defendants obtain lawyers at arraignments?

Defendants who think they may financially qualify for a court-appointed attorney should ask the judge to appoint one when their case is called. A defendant may say something like, "Your Honor, I want to talk to a lawyer before I do anything." The judge will delay the arraignment until the public defender or panel attorney on duty in the courtroom has a chance to talk with the defendant.

Is there a "pecking order" for arraignments?

Arraignment judges typically call cases in the following order:

- cases in which defendants are represented by private counsel
- non-custody defendants who are representing themselves, and
- defendants who are represented by a public defender or other court-appointed counsel, or defendants who are in custody.

This order awards first preference to private attorney cases and lowest priority to public defender cases, perhaps on the grounds that public defender clients are not paying for their attorneys' time and public defenders often have to spend the whole day in court anyway.

Attacking Prior Convictions

Most states have laws that punish defendants more severely for repeat offenses. The most extreme examples of this policy are laws mandating up to a life sentence for anyone convicted of a third qualifying offense (the so-called "three strikes" laws). When faced with this type of statute, the defense will obviously benefit if it can invalidate an earlier conviction (called "striking a prior"). A frequent way to attack a prior conviction based on a guilty plea has been to show that the plea was not knowingly or intelligently made and that the defendant therefore gave up constitutional rights out of ignorance.

What constitutional rights do defendants waive by pleading guilty or no contest at arraignment?

Criminal defendants have a variety of constitutional rights—most fundamentally the right to trial by jury, the right to present their own witnesses, and the right to confront and cross-examine prosecution witnesses. By pleading guilty or *nolo contendere* ("no contest," a type of guilty plea), defendants give up these rights. Especially if the judge plans to sentence the defendant to jail, the judge usually will insist that the defendant give up these rights "on the record" in open court. This explicit waiver insulates the conviction that results from the plea from later being declared invalid.

Can defendants benefit from the presence of relatives at arraignment?

Though arraignments tend to be brief and perfunctory, defendants often derive psychological support from the presence of relatives, close friends, and employers. Their very presence can produce tangible benefits if the defendant is seeking lower bail or release O.R. Seeing that defendants retain the support of others notwithstanding their arrest may incline the judge to exercise discretion in a defendant's favor, if possible.

Is it possible to have two arraignments in the same case?

Yes, in felony cases, if the state operates a two-tiered system of trial courts. One arraignment takes place in the lower tier, and a second arraignment in the higher-tier court if the lower-tier court decides in a preliminary hearing that the case should proceed as a felony.

Self-Representation at Arraignment

Self-representation at arraignment is possible but often risky, for the reasons explained below.

Is it a good idea for defendants to represent themselves at arraignment?

Many defendants are capable of representing themselves at an arraignment. They can plead not guilty and even ask the judge to reduce bail. During the interval between the arraignment and the next court appearance (rarely less than two weeks and often longer), the defendant can decide whether to hire a lawyer for post-arraignment proceedings.

Nevertheless, it's not a good idea for most defendants to go it alone at the arraignment. For example, if a technical defect exists in the prosecution's case, the defendant may have the right to raise the defect only prior to entering a plea. Also, a particular prosecutor's office may have a policy of offering the best deals to defendants who plead guilty (or no contest) at their arraignments. Defendants who intend at some point to plead guilty but are unaware of such a policy may suffer a harsher punishment by putting off the guilty plea until after the arraignment.

Finally, arraignment judges are more likely to lower bail when defendants have legal representation. Thus, most defendants considering self-representation should postpone the arraignment by asking the judge for a continuance, and then consult with a criminal defense lawyer before deciding to self-represent.

What should bailed-out defendants do when they enter a courthouse for an arraignment?

Defendants first need to make sure they are in the correct courtroom, and then check in with the court clerk or bailiff.

Can a self-represented defendant ask for priority in calling a case?

Normally, arraignment judges give priority to private attorney cases. This means that the judge tends to handle all "private attorney matters" before hearing other cases. Self-represented defendants who have a special reason why their cases should be taken out of order can request priority. To make a priority request, the defendant should notify the courtroom clerk or bailiff at the time of checking in of the need for priority. If the request is valid, the clerk or bailiff will inform the judge, who may call the case along with the private attorney cases.

What happens when a case is called?

Subject to local variation, most arraignments tend to unfold as follows: When the judge calls a defendant's case, the bailiff directs the defendant where to stand. The judge reads the charge; at that time a defendant who has not already gotten one usually receives a written copy of the complaint (the charge(s)). The judge then asks the defendant if he or she has an attorney or wants the court to appoint one. As mentioned, defendants usually plead not guilty at arraignment. However, a self-represented defendant alternatively may:

- ask for a continuance of a week or two
- in unusual circumstances, make a motion to dismiss the case, or
- in unusual circumstances, plead guilty (or no contest).

Assuming that the defendant enters a not guilty plea, the judge typically schedules the next court appearance. The next appearance may entail a pretrial conference, a preliminary examination, or a trial date, depending on local procedures and whether the case involves a felony or a misdemeanor. In the event of a guilty plea, the judge may pronounce sentence immediately, or schedule a later sentencing hearing, which occurs after a probation officer investigates a defendant's background and submits a report.

If the arraignment is combined with a bail hearing, which is typical, the judge will set bail at some point in the course of the arraignment. If the defendant's bail status has already been determined, the judge normally concludes the arraignment by continuing that same status.

If a defendant is already out on bail, might the issue of bail arise at arraignment?

Yes. Judges often conclude arraignments by continuing defendants on the same bail status they had prior to arraignment. However, the arraignment judge has the power to reset bail, either lower or higher. Bailed-out defendants can ask the arraignment judge to release them O.R. or lower the bail in order to free up cash and collateral for other purposes (including hiring an attorney). Unfortunately, even if the judge lowers the bail or grants the defendant O.R., the bail premium already paid to the bail bond seller cannot be recaptured.

The Effect of a No-Contest (*Nolo Contendere*) Plea

For criminal law purposes, no-contest pleas and guilty pleas have an identical effect. In jurisdictions that allow no-contest pleas (and not all do), the effect of such a plea is usually limited to criminal cases. This is because no-contest pleas are usually inadmissible as evidence in civil cases. This can make it possible for a criminal defendant who might later face a lawsuit brought by the victim for civil damages to plea bargain a criminal case without giving a potential adversary ammunition to use against the defendant in a civil case. However, the rule on the effect of no-contest pleas on civil cases is not the same in all states. In California, for example, convictions based on no-contest pleas for crimes that can be punished as felonies are dismissible in civil cases.

It is also possible that the prosecutor will seek higher bail (for instance, because the defendant has a criminal record). If the arraignment judge does increase a bailed-out defendant's bail, the defendant can be returned to custody until the higher bail is met. Self-representing defendants who have any reason to fear an increase in bail should come to the arraignment prepared to pay the additional cost. For example, a defendant might ask a bail bond seller to come to court and immediately post bond for the higher amount.

Do jailed defendants have the right to represent themselves at arraignment?

Yes. Of course, defendants who are in custody at the time of arraignment are likely to ask a judge to set bail (if this has not already occurred at an earlier bail hearing) or to lower the bail previously set. A defendant's bail status is always subject to review, and defendants should never hesitate to inform judges of changed circumstances (for example, a job offer) that might lead the judge to reduce bail.

Developing the Defense Strategy

This chapter examines the crucial process by which defendants and their lawyers formulate a defense strategy. A defense strategy typically emerges as a defense attorney finds out about the prosecution's evidence and a defendant's version of events. The process of developing a defense strategy is fluid, and it varies from one case to another. For example, the attorney's tentative theory of defense will influence the topics the attorney asks about. The defendant's answers to those questions may in turn affect the attorney's defense strategy.

This does not mean that defendants and their attorneys collaborate to make up false stories. For various reasons explained in this chapter, defendants usually benefit from telling their attorneys the truth as the defendants perceive it. However, multiple versions of truth can coexist in the defense of criminal charges. For instance, assume that a woman is charged with murdering her boyfriend. The "truth" may be that the defendant acted in self-defense, that the boyfriend abused the defendant physically and verbally in the months preceding the killing, or both. A defense strategy is a product of a defendant and defense attorney fitting together the version of the truth that is most likely to produce a satisfactory defense outcome (a verdict of not guilty, a verdict of guilty of a lesser charge, or an acceptable plea bargain).

Overcoming a Failure to Communicate

The process by which an attorney works with a defendant to develop the defendant's version of events, and the impact of the defendant's version on the overall defense strategy, usually can be seen and understood only during confidential attorney-client meetings. Few books for nonlawyers address this process, and few nonlawyers understand it. Hopefully, the information in this chapter will make it easier for defendants to work harmoniously with their attorneys to develop an accurate and effective defense strategy.

Overview

This section discusses a process by which defendants and their lawyers often develop a defense version of events.

What is the most fundamental rule of attorney-client relationships?

Lawyer-client conversations are confidential. The law "privileges" these conversations, so that unless clients agree, lawyers cannot tell anyone what clients tell them.

For example, a prosecutor cannot ask a lawyer a question such as, "Did your client tell you she is guilty?" As this chapter describes, what clients tell lawyers can of course affect case strategy. But clients' private statements to lawyers are to remain private and the lawyers cannot reveal them to anyone.

What is a defendant's version of events?

A version of events is simply the defendant's account of the events leading up to the defendant's arrest. However, a version of events is not like a diamond, lying intact in the ground waiting to be found. Instead, defendants and their attorneys usually piece the defendant's version together—over the course of one or more interviews—based on the defendant's recollections and objectively verifiable facts, and informed by the lawyer's knowledge of the laws and defenses that apply to the type of behavior in question.

The result of this cooperation between the defendant and the attorney is hopefully a full and accurate defense story that is consistent with the truth and can withstand any challenge that the prosecution may mount.

Who controls the defense strategy —clients or lawyers?

While many defense lawyers are experienced "pros," many of the most important defense strategies are for clients to make. For example, clients have the right to decide:

- Whether to plead guilty or go to trial.
- Whether to have a judge or jury trial.
- Whether to testify in their own defense or remain silent at trial.

Even when defense lawyers believe it to be in their clients' best interest to admit guilt, clients have the right to insist on their innocence. Clients have the right to prevent their lawyers from making a strategic choice to admit guilt. (*McCoy v. Louisiana*, U.S. Sup. Ct. 2018.)

Is it ethical for lawyers to help defendants arrive at their version of events?

Yes. A story may be told in a variety of ways, and each of those stories may be accurate. By way of analogy, consider two maps of the United States, one in which the states are depicted according to geographical boundaries, the other in which the states are depicted according to density of population. The maps will look different, yet both will be accurate. It's up to an attorney and a defendant to develop together the most legally helpful, accurate version of events relevant to the case. The result will hopefully have such characteristics as:

- **Consistency with objectively verifiable evidence.** For example, if the police found the defendant's fingerprints at the scene of a crime, hopefully the defendant's version accounts for the presence of the fingerprints. ("Defendant was at the apartment the day before the burglary.")
- **The potential to gain the sympathy of a judge or jury.** For example, the defendant's version may demonstrate that he or she tried to withdraw from the criminal activity in question and prevent it from happening.

- **Explaining why events took place as the defendant claims.** For example, if the defendant claims to have been out of town on the date of the crime, the defendant's version explains why the defendant was out of town.

As may be apparent, the account of events a defendant might tell spontaneously could omit these and other elements that are both accurate and helpful. This is why defendants and their attorneys have to work together to develop a version of events that will best benefit the defense.

What kinds of versions of events do defendants tell their attorneys?

While no two defendants will ever come up with a factually identical version of events, a defendant's account almost always falls into one of three broad categories:

- **"Confession" story.** Defendants who tell their lawyers confession stories admit that they did what the prosecution claims: "Yes, I did break into the house through a window and steal the computer."
- **"Complete denial" story.** Defendants who tell their lawyers complete denial stories assert that the prosecution's claims are totally false. An "alibi" is a familiar type of complete denial story: "I was out of town with a friend when the burglary they say I committed took place. I have no idea what they're talking about."
- **"Admit and explain" story.** This story falls between the "confession" and "complete denial" stories. Defendants

who tell "admit and explain" stories agree that part of the prosecution's claims are accurate, but assert legally critical differences: "I did go into the house and take the computer, but I went in through the front door with a key after the person who lived there gave me permission to borrow the computer."

How does a defendant's version of events affect the defense strategy?

The ultimate defense strategy grows out of, but is not the same as, a defendant's version of events, regardless of which of the three broad categories above it falls into. When formulating a defense strategy, an attorney also considers such factors as the reliability of defense and prosecution witnesses, community attitudes toward crime and the police, and a defendant's moral culpability. A defense attorney uses these factors to develop a "theory of the case" that is consistent with provable facts and explains events in a way that favors the defense.

For example, assume that a defendant is charged with burglary. The prosecution's evidence consists of the defendant's confession to the police shortly after the defendant's arrest, and an eyewitness who "is pretty sure that the defendant was among the burglars." The defendant has told his attorney that a couple of the defendant's friends planned and carried out the burglary, that he had never been in trouble but stupidly went along with them so as to look good in their eyes, and that the police didn't tell him that he had a right to remain silent or have an attorney present during questioning.

This is in essence a "confession" story. Nevertheless, the defendant and the defense attorney may adopt a defense theory that "overzealous police officers tried to paper over weak eyewitness identification evidence by improperly extracting a confession from a naive suspect." This theory is consistent with the defendant's version of events, and it describes events in a way that favors the defense.

Pursuing this strategy, the defense attorney might file a pretrial motion seeking to bar the prosecution from offering the confession into evidence because the police failed to comply with *Miranda* procedures. In addition, the defense attorney might develop arguments that the eyewitness identification evidence is too weak to prove guilt beyond a reasonable doubt. The goal of this strategy may be either to achieve a not guilty verdict at trial, or to weaken the prosecutor's case enough to persuade the prosecutor to agree to the defense's desired plea bargain. (The attorney's goal at trial may even be a "hung jury." Even if the defendant is convicted, the defense attorney may rely on the defendant's lack of a prior criminal record, and the fact that he was a dupe who passively participated in a crime orchestrated by others, to argue for minimum punishment.

As long as they tell the truth, should defendants talk to the police officers who arrest them?

Even assuming that they want to tell the truth, almost all suspects should talk to a defense attorney before talking to the police. In part, this is because the police may accidentally or purposefully distort a suspect's statement at trial. More over, many suspects are too nervous and unaware of the law to tell the police an accurate story that will also benefit their defense. Because there are many ways to accurately recount a series of events, suspects are almost always better off talking to an attorney before talking to the police.

Does the defense have to reveal its version of events to prosecutors prior to trial?

Because the defense version of events is developed in the course of confidential attorney-client conversations, it can remain confidential until the defendant discloses it or the attorney discloses it with the defendant's permission, usually in the context of plea bargaining. However, in most states, the prosecutor has the right to know before trial if the defendant will be presenting an alibi or insanity defense.

Also, the defense may have to provide the prosecution with the identities of defense witnesses and any written statements they've made. By reading the statements or interviewing the witnesses, the prosecutor may be able to glean many aspects of the defendant's story.

Although the details of the defendant's version of events need not be disclosed, except as noted, the general contours of the story tend to be imparted to the prosecution early in the case, when the possibility of a plea bargain is first discussed. Just how much of a defense story should be disclosed prior to trial to facilitate a possible plea bargain (or in some jurisdictions, a court-engineered settlement) will depend on such factors as:

- how likely it is that disclosure will result in a settlement favorable to the defendant
- whether the defense will gain from keeping the story under wraps as long as possible, and
- how obvious the story is or how much of the story is already known to the prosecution.

How the Defendant's Version of Events May Limit Defense Strategies

Defense lawyers are also "officers of the court" who have a responsibility to uphold legal ethical rules. As explained in this section, these rules may limit the type of defense an attorney can present in a particular case.

Can a defendant tell one story to the defense lawyer and testify to a different story at trial?

No. Attorneys may not knowingly encourage or help a witness to give perjured testimony (testimony that the attorney knows to be false). (See Rule 3.3, ABA Model Rules of Professional Conduct.) If a defendant has told an attorney one version of events, the defendant cannot change the version for trial just because a different story would be stronger. This means that defendants have to be careful when giving their version to their lawyers, because a defendant may have to live with that version should the case go to trial (or get another lawyer if he or she is in a position to do so).

EXAMPLE: Rusty Nails is charged with assault and battery. Rusty has repeatedly insisted to his attorney that it's a case of mistaken identity, and that he was nowhere near the bar where the attack took place. In the course of investigation, Rusty's lawyer talks to two of his friends who say that they saw the fight and that Rusty acted in self-defense. Rusty cannot testify to self-defense at trial unless he can satisfactorily explain the sudden change of story (for instance, "I was nervous," or, "I lied at first because I was afraid you wouldn't believe the truth"); Rusty's lawyer may conclude that Rusty's self-defense testimony constitutes perjury. If Rusty plans to stick to the self-defense story on the stand, Rusty's lawyer might be unable to call Rusty as a witness.

Can a lawyer call witnesses to testify to an untrue version of events that indicates that the client is not guilty?

No. It doesn't matter whether the person who will give false testimony is a defendant or a defense witness. In either event, ethical rules forbid attorneys from calling witnesses who they know will perjure themselves.

EXAMPLE: In the Rusty Nails example above, neither Nails nor his two friends can testify that Nails acted in self-defense. If Nails would be committing perjury by testifying to self-defense, then so would his witnesses. The ethical constraint on the attorney is the same.

Ethical Rules and Self-Represented Defendants

Self-represented defendants are not subject to the ethical rules constraining attorneys. There-fore, a self-represented defendant who testi-fies untruthfully is not subject to the discipline that attorneys might face if they assisted in such behavior. Nevertheless, an untruthful self-represented defendant runs the risk of a perjury charge, as well as being given a harsher sentence. If a conviction results and the judge concludes that the defendant lied, he or she may choose to unofficially punish the defendant by imposing a stiffer sentence than might otherwise have been the case.

Can a defendant testify to a version of events that has changed over the course of attorney-client meetings?

Yes. Defendants are not forever locked in to the first versions of events they tell their lawyers. Defendants can and often do change what they initially tell their attorneys. For example, a defendant might recall additional information or realize after talking to others or seeing photos that the first version was inaccurate. A defense attorney's first commitment is to the client, and the attorney will not conclude that a defendant's modified version of events is untruthful unless the circumstances leave the attorney no other choice. As long as the attorney is subjectively satisfied that helping the client formulate a different version is not a breach of professional ethics, the attorney can present the defendant's modified version at trial.

EXAMPLE: Rusty Nails remains charged with assault and battery. As before, Rusty's initial version is that it's a case of mistaken identity, and that he was nowhere near the bar where the attack took place. Some time later, Rusty tells his lawyer that the truth is that he acted in self-defense. Rusty explains that he did not initially admit to participating in the fight because he had promised his girlfriend not to go near the bar where the fight took place. Rusty has decided to tell the truth now and patch up things with the girlfriend later. Rusty may testify to self-defense at trial. His explanation for the changed story is plausible enough for almost any defense attorney. Even if the defense attorney subjectively distrusts Rusty's new version, the attorney has sufficient grounds to help Rusty tell it while avoiding an ethics violation.

Can lawyers "coach" defendants to help them testify more credibly at trial?

Defense lawyers have a duty to help defendants formulate the strongest defense story possible. To that end, lawyers can and do coach defendants in a variety of ways.

For instance, attorneys can:

- use interviewing techniques that stimu-late memory, such as asking defendants to relate events chronologically
- conduct interviews at the scene of important events, or

- ask defendants to write down in their own words their versions of important events. (To maintain the confidentiality of what they've written, defendants should write "Privileged and Confidential Document—For My Attorney Only" at the top of the first page, and if possible hand whatever they've written directly to their attorneys.)

In addition, attorneys can coach defendants by fully explaining the charges against them, and by imparting as much as is known of the prosecution's story. Defendants need such information if they are to tell an accurate version that does not leave out information potentially helpful to the defense.

For example, assume that Rhoda is charged with the crime of "receiving stolen goods." Before seeking to elicit Rhoda's version, Rhoda's lawyer may ethically tell her something along these lines:

"Rhoda, you're charged with receiving stolen property. What that means in plain English is that you personally are not charged with stealing anything; the claim is that you obtained property even though you knew for a fact that someone else had stolen it. Now, I'd like to find out from you as much as you can tell me about what happened. But first let me tell you that the police report and a brief talk I had with the D.A. indicate that they claim you are a middleperson in a ring that deals in stolen watches. A couple of guys named Bernie and Chuck supposedly steal watches from warehouses and drop off some of the cartons in your garage, and you later distribute them to jewelry stores around town. They've got the names of some of the stores you supposedly deal with. Unless you have any questions, why don't you tell me what you know about all this?"

Subjective Interpretations of Ethical Rules

It would be misleading to suggest that all criminal defense attorneys subscribe to the same view of their ethical obligations regarding perjured testimony. In fact, some believe that any limitation on their right to present testimony interferes with a defendant's right to an effective defense. Most defense attorneys agree that it's wrong to present perjured testimony, but are likely to vary when it comes to making a subjective judgment as to whether proposed testimony is perjured.

As a practical matter, attorneys who decide to elicit perjured testimony in violation of their ethical responsibilities are rarely caught. Usually, the only witness to the ethical lapse is the defendant, who has little incentive to rat on an attorney whose strategy, while unethical, was effective. About the only time that abuses come to light is when defendants who are unhappy with the outcomes of their cases complain about their attorneys. Even then, proving that an attorney broke ethical rules is difficult. To many judges and prosecutors, convicted defendants who complain about their lawyers come across as people just looking to blame someone else for their troubles.

EXAMPLE: As before, Rusty Nails is charged with assault and battery growing out of a barroom brawl. When Nails meets with his attorney, the attorney tells him, "They've got you charged with assault and battery, but I've talked to a couple of people and I think we can make a good case for self-defense. Now, I'm going to tell you exactly what to say, and if you want me to represent you, you better do as I tell you." The attorney's instruction violates ethical rules by making up a story for Rusty to tell. The attorney would be subject to discipline if the client revealed what happened. A defendant confronted by such an approach should look for another attorney as soon as possible. An attorney who will so cavalierly violate one ethical rule is likely to violate others, including the one mandating loyalty to the client's case.

EXAMPLE: Same case. Before asking Nails to give his version of events, Nails's lawyer says, "Before talking to you, I asked my investigator to stop by the cafe and talk to a couple of the employees. They remember that the guy you hit took a swing at you first, so it looks like we might have a good case for self-defense. But before I know if this will fly, I'll need to know from you what happened." Though some defense attorneys might dissent, most would probably agree that the defense attorney has acted unethically by telegraphing the story that the attorney expects the client to tell. The attorney should stick to telling Nails what he's charged with and summarizing what he knows of the prosecution's evidence, and then carefully elicit Nails's story.

Can a prosecutor attack the credibility of a defendant's testimony with conflicting statements the defendant made to the police?

Yes. When a defendant's story at trial varies in some way from the story he or she told to the police, prosecutors typically call a police officer as a witness to testify to the inconsistencies. The prosecutor can then argue to the judge or jury that the changes in story mean that the defendant is unworthy of belief. This is another reason that defendants should always talk to their attorneys before talking to the police.

Hollywood's Take on How Defense Attorneys Help Develop the Defense Story

A dramatic example of an attorney struggling with the ethics of how much information to give a defendant before asking for the defendant's version is the lecture scene in the classic courtroom film, *Anatomy of a Murder*. In the film, a defendant is charged with murder. The defendant admits the shooting, but claims that it was the result of an "irresistible impulse" caused by his wife's telling him that the deceased had raped and beaten her. After some urging by his old mentor, the defense attorney delivers to the defendant a short lecture on the possible defenses to murder, explains which don't apply, and then asks the defendant to consider the remaining defense when telling his story of why he shot the deceased. Attorneys disagree as to whether the lawyer in the film overstepped ethical bounds.

When Attorneys Ignore a Defendant's Version of Events

Defense lawyers may choose not to ask defendants for their version of events, for the reasons explained below.

Do attorneys routinely ask defendants for their versions of events as soon as possible?

No. Experienced defense attorneys know that many defendants who have just been arrested and jailed are not in a psychological condition to relate accurate stories. An attorney may also be concerned that guards or other prisoners may try to eavesdrop. Instead, the attorney may cover only the defendant's more pressing needs. For example, during an initial jailhouse interview an attorney may do no more than:

- reassure the defendant that the attorney's sole obligation is to the defendant, and that the attorney will do everything possible to secure a satisfactory outcome
- explain the charges and bail proce- dures, and advise the defendant that the immediate priority is to seek the defendant's release on bail or on his or her own recognizance (O.R.)
- ask if the attorney can help take care of any of the defendant's personal matters until the client bails out of jail, such as canceling a business meeting or phoning relatives, and
- advise the defendant to say nothing to the police or any other person before meeting with the attorney.

Do defense lawyers sometimes choose not to ask defendants for their version of events?

Paradoxically, despite the frequent importance of defense stories, some experienced and successful criminal defense attorneys make it a practice not to ask for the defendant's version unless there is a good reason to know it. Because it is up to the prosecution to prove a defendant guilty beyond a reasonable doubt, these defense attorneys prefer to focus their efforts on contesting the prosecution's case rather than on proving the truth of the defendant's story. For these attorneys, the danger of having ethical roadblocks to putting on an effective defense outweighs the benefits of knowing the defendant's version.

> **EXAMPLE:** Return to the case of Rusty Nails, who is charged with assault and battery. The defense attorney never asks for Nails's story. Two employees of the café where the fight took place tell the attorney that the so-called victim threw the first punch, and that Nails hit back in self-defense. The employees admit to the attorney that they do not like the victim, and the attorney suspects that they may not be telling the truth. The attorney can nevertheless call the employees as witnesses at trial. The employees' story does not conflict with anything that Nails said, because the defense attorney never asked for Nails's version of events. And defense attorneys can call witnesses who they only suspect may not be telling the truth (as opposed to those who they know are lying), because credibility is for the judge or jury to decide, not the defense attorney.

Can defendants help their lawyers undermine the credibility of prosecution witnesses?

Yes. Even if the defense attorney does not develop the defendant's affirmative story, the attorney may enlist the defendant's help in disproving the prosecutor's case. For example, a defense attorney may go line by line through a police report or the statement of a prosecution witness with a defendant and ask, "Can we disprove that?" By seeking out only information that casts doubt on the prosecution's case, the defense attorney can involve the defendant in the defense effort without asking for the defendant's complete story.

Initial Interviews by Court-Appointed Lawyers

Because of large caseloads, court-appointed lawyers often ask defendants about their version of events during an initial meeting immediately prior to arraignment. Their goal may be to identify and dispose of "guilties" as quickly as possible (often through quick plea bargains) in order to devote the bulk of their time to cases that may go to trial.

Should defendants tell their stories to their lawyers even if the lawyers don't ask them to?

No. An attorney's lack of interest in a defendant's account of events is usually a strategic decision not to find out information that might hamstring an effective defense.

The Importance of Honesty in Developing a Defense Strategy

In the defense of criminal cases as in so many other areas of life, honesty is almost always the best policy. This section explains why.

If defendants admit to their lawyers that they are guilty, can the lawyers nonetheless argue that they are not guilty?

Yes. The duty of defense attorneys to zealously represent clients extends to the guilty as well as the innocent. Thus, even if they know that a client is guilty, defense attorneys can cross-examine prosecution witnesses and argue that the prosecution has failed to prove guilt beyond a reasonable doubt. This is because the defense has the right, in our justice system, to raise every possible doubt about the prosecution's case, whether the defendant committed a crime or not. Guilt or innocence is for a judge or jury to determine, not the defense attorney.

Also, the goal for a criminal defense attorney may be "getting help" rather than "getting off." Instead of engaging in an ultimately fruitless fight against criminal charges, an attorney may best serve a defendant by arranging for help that begins to turn a defendant's life in a more positive direction. An honest admission of guilt is often the first step in the right direction.

Can it help an attorney to know that a client is guilty?

Yes. Defendants can usually achieve the best outcomes by telling their attorneys the truth.

By concealing evidence or providing mis-information, defendants may prevent their attorneys from mounting the most effective possible response to the prosecution's evidence. Ironically, innocent defendants who conceal information because they believe it makes them look guilty often end up doing more harm to their cases than good.

> **EXAMPLE:** Cal Amity, a former police officer, is charged with murdering his fiancée after she refused to move with him to another state. The prosecution claims that, on the morning that he resigned as a police officer, Amity took a gun with him when he went to meet his fiancée at the café where she worked. He then shot his fiancée when she refused to leave with him. Amity insists to his lawyer that he shot his fiancée by accident after she pulled a gun on him; he didn't take a gun with him when he went to talk to his fiancée. At trial, however, the prosecution surprises the defense by calling two police officers who testify that they saw Amity leaving the station after he resigned with a gun tucked in his waistband. Amity later admits to his lawyer that he had the gun on him all along. Amity's delay in telling the truth to his lawyer has hurt his case. Had Amity's attorney known that Amity was carrying the gun, the attorney might well have been able to show that Amity was carrying the gun for a different reason than because he intended to kill his fiancée. For example, perhaps Amity carried it out of force of habit: Police officers routinely carry guns when off duty, so Amity continued this habit even though he had just resigned. But by concealing evidence, Amity makes it difficult for his attorney to effectively respond to the prosecution's evidence, even if the shooting really was accidental.

> **EXAMPLE:** Will Hurt is charged with assault and battery on Ken Tusion. Hurt tells his attorney that Tusion attacked him, and that he hit Tusion in self-defense. Hurt also denies any previous problems between him and Tusion. At trial, the prosecution offers evidence that a few days before the fight, Hurt got angry with Tusion for trying to date Hurt's girlfriend. Hurt should have mentioned the earlier incident to his attorney. By failing to disclose the earlier incident to his attorney, Hurt allows the prosecution to surprise the attorney at trial. Had Hurt told the truth, the attorney might have been able to negate the importance of the earlier incident.

It's Possible to Be Guilty and Still Come Out Ahead

Another reason to tell attorneys the truth is that the truth may reveal the defendant to be guilty, but only of a less serious offense. For example, a defendant's truthful story may reveal that a defendant charged with assault with a deadly weapon is at most guilty of simple assault, a much less serious crime. If the defendant lies and insists on complete innocence, the defense attorney may be unable to arrive at a realistic plea bargain. And if the case goes to trial, the defense attorney may not be able to ask the jury to convict on the lesser offense rather than the greater offense, because the facts that would allow such a result were not disclosed by the defendant to his attorney.

The ultimate decision is up to the defendant. If the defendant believes herself guilty, should she admit guilt to the lawyer? If the defendant believes herself innocent, should she conceal harmful evidence from the lawyer? Defendants have to decide for themselves. They should understand, however, that it's likely they'll do more harm than good by concealing the truth.

> **EXAMPLE:** Cal Purnia is charged with shoplifting. Unwilling to admit guilt to his lawyer, Cal makes up a phony story. Cal tells his lawyer that he came into the store with the watch that he is charged with stealing, and gives the lawyer what looks like a receipt for its purchase, dated about a month before the theft. Cal's lawyer shows the receipt to the D.A. and asks the D.A. to dismiss the charges. The D.A. refuses and shows Cal's lawyer film from a hidden camera clearly showing Cal stealing the watch. Because of Cal's phony story, the D.A. refuses to plea bargain and takes the case to trial. Cal is convicted and given a substantial fine. Cal's attorney could probably have achieved a better outcome had Cal not tried to rely on the phony receipt. The lawyer might have arranged for Cal to enroll in a counseling program. That might have led the D.A. to reduce the charges and place Cal on probation. By lying, Cal prevented his lawyer from providing effective representation.

Criminal Laws and Their Language

This chapter explains and interprets criminal laws. Criminal laws are often hard to understand for several reasons:

- They may include unfamiliar concepts, such as the term "malice aforethought" in many murder statutes.
- Familiar concepts, such as "maliciously" or "recklessly," are often used differently in criminal laws. These are what lawyers call "terms of art." That is, they are common terms that take on special meanings when used in the law.
- The legal definition of a crime is often different from its popular meaning. For example, if Yolanda comes home to find that her house was broken into, she's likely to yell, "I've been robbed!" No, she hasn't. Yolanda's house may have been burgled, but technically Yolanda wasn't robbed.
- Laws may vary from one state to another. For example, possession of a small amount of marijuana is illegal in some states but permissible in others.
- Verdicts often depend on how judges and jurors subjectively interpret vague, abstract rules regarding defendants' mental states. For example, a killing may not be a crime at all or it may be first-degree murder, depending on how a jury evaluates the defendant's thought processes before the killing.

As a result, though "ignorance of the law is no excuse," people are often justifiably uncertain about the meaning of many criminal rules.

The chapter focuses on:

- the meaning of the legal language in common criminal statutes
- how to distinguish similar offenses, such as murder and manslaughter, from each other, and
- how to work backward from a statute's legal language to the type of evidence that a prosecutor is likely to offer to prove a violation of the statute.

 RESOURCES

Learning the law. For detailed information about conducting legal research, check out *Legal Research: How to Find & Understand the Law,* by the Editors of Nolo (Nolo). The book discusses in great detail—and in an easy-to-understand way—the use of research tools.

Mens Rea

In our criminal justice system, *mens rea* is the moral foundation for finding people guilty and punishing them.

What does *mens rea* mean?

Mens rea (mens-REE-a) is Latin for "guilty mind." The *mens rea* concept expresses the belief that people should be punished (fined or imprisoned) only when they have acted with an intent or purpose that makes them morally blameworthy.

Do criminal laws mention the the term *mens rea*?

No. *Mens rea* is never identified as a distinct element of a crime. Instead, immoral conduct is almost always the underlying justification for the enactment of a criminal law. In the legal system's eyes, people who intentionally engage in the behavior prohibited by a law have *mens rea*; they are morally blameworthy. For example, a murder law may prohibit "the intentional and unlawful killing of one human being by another human being." Under this law, one who intentionally and unlawfully kills

another person had the mental state, or *mens rea,* at the time of the killing to be morally blameworthy for that death.

Can a criminal law be valid even if it doesn't require *mens rea*?

Yes, though such laws are relatively few in number. Laws that don't require *mens rea*— that is, laws that punish people regardless of their state of mind—are called "strict liability" laws. The usual justification for a strict liability law is that the social benefits of stringent enforcement outweigh the harm of punishing

---

What Is the Criminal Law?

The criminal law is actually a complex web of rules, laws, and policies that can vary from one jurisdiction to another. The primary components of the criminal law are:

- **Substantive laws:** Rules that define crimes (such as murder) and defenses (such as self-defense).
- **Rules of criminal procedure:** Rules that govern the processes by which crimes are prosecuted and defended, such as what an arraignment consists of and when it takes place.
- **Federal criminal laws:** Laws enacted by Congress that are within the scope of federal authority as set forth in the federal Constitution. Examples are laws that make it a federal crime to transport illegal drugs across state lines, rob a federally chartered bank, or commit mail fraud.

- **State criminal laws:** Laws made by state legislatures that apply to crimes committed within a state.
- **Municipal laws:** Laws that apply within a city or county, such as anti-dumping rules and curfews.
- **Case law:** Rules that come from judicial opinions.
- **Constitutional provisions:** Rules that come from the federal Constitution or a state's constitution. When these constitutional rules conflict with laws, the rules prevail.
- **Evidence rules:** Rules that determine the evidence that prosecutors and defendants can offer at trial, such as the hearsay rule.
- **Court rules:** Local rules that govern courthouse policy and procedures, such as when courts are open and where documents are filed and maintained.

a person who may be morally blameless. Examples of strict liability laws include:

- Statutory rape laws, which, in some states, make it illegal to have sexual intercourse with a minor, even if the defendant honestly and reasonably believed that the sexual partner was old enough to consent legally to sexual intercourse.
- Sale of alcohol to minors laws, which, in many states, punish store clerks who sell alcohol to minors even if the clerks reasonably believe that the minors are old enough to buy liquor.

Strict liability laws like these punish defendants who make honest mistakes and therefore may be morally innocent. Because the legal consequences of innocent mistakes can be so great in certain circumstances, people who find themselves in situations governed by strict liability rules need to take special precautions before acting.

Do people who commit an illegal act by mistake have *mens rea*?

Not necessarily. In most cases, moral blame attaches when a person *intentionally* engages in conduct that is illegal. The corollary of this principle is that people who *unintentionally* engage in illegal conduct may be morally innocent. People can unintentionally break the law when they make a mistake of fact. A person who breaks the law because he or she honestly misperceives reality lacks *mens rea* and should not be charged with or convicted of a crime. (Mistake of fact is often irrelevant

to guilt under strict liability laws, because they are not based on *mens rea*.)

EXAMPLE: John owes Barbara $100. At a party, John tells Barbara that the money he owes her is in a desk drawer and that she should take it. Assuming that it adds up to $100, Barbara puts the wad of money that she finds in the desk drawer in her purse and leaves the party. The next day, John realizes that the $200 he had in his desk drawer is missing. Barbara is not guilty of stealing $100 if a judge or jury believes that Barbara honestly thought that she was only taking $100. Barbara's honest mistake indicates that she did not have a guilty mind. Because theft is a *mens rea* crime, not a strict liability crime, Barbara is not guilty.

EXAMPLE: Jane borrows a raincoat from Jean. Unbeknownst to Jane, one of the pockets contains a packet of illegal drugs. A police officer standing in a mall sees Jane take off the raincoat and the packet of drugs falls out of the pocket. The officer then arrests Jane. Jane is not guilty of possession of illegal drugs. She lacked *mens rea* because she didn't know that the drugs were in the borrowed raincoat.

Can reckless conduct amount to *mens rea*?

Yes. Ordinary carelessness is not a crime. For example, negligent drivers are not usually criminally prosecuted, though they may have to pay civil damages to those harmed by their negligence.

However, more-than-ordinary careless-ness can demonstrate *mens rea*. Common terms for morally blameworthy carelessness are "recklessness" and "criminal negligence." Unfortunately, no clear line separates non-criminal negligence from recklessness and criminal negligence. In general, carelessness can rise to the level of recklessness and amount to a crime when a person disregards a substantial and unjustifiable risk. Indefinite language like that doesn't necessarily create a clear line between ordinary and criminal carelessness. Police officers and prosecutors have to make the initial decisions about whether to charge a careless person with a crime. At that point, it's up to judges and juries to evaluate a person's conduct according to community standards and decide whether the behavior is dangerous enough to demonstrate a morally blameworthy mental state (*mens rea*).

> **EXAMPLE:** Eddie gets a slingshot for his 25th birthday. He is so excited that he runs into the street, picks up a small rock, and, without aiming, shoots the rock as far as he can. The rock hits and severely injures Marsha as she crosses the street about 40 yards away. The street tends to be a busy one, and Eddie has lived on the street for 15 years. Eddie's conduct demonstrates *mens rea*.
>
> He may not have intended to injure Marsha. However, he acted recklessly. He knew from experience that people were likely to be out walking on his street, and nevertheless fired off an object capable of causing severe physical injury. Eddie's conduct is morally blameworthy.

> **EXAMPLE:** Merrie gets a slingshot for her 25th birthday. She is so excited that she runs to an open field near her house, picks up a small rock, and without aiming shoots the rock as far as she can. The rock hits and severely injures Michael as he walks across the field about 40 yards away. The field is surrounded by a fence displaying a number of "No Trespassing" signs, and the incident took place at midnight. Merrie's conduct does not demonstrate *mens rea*. Under the circumstances, she could reasonably believe that the field would be deserted and that no one would be hurt by the rock. Even if her conduct is unreasonable, it is not so reckless that it demonstrates *mens rea*.

Mistake of Law vs. Mistake of Fact

Make no mistake: Mistake of fact can negate *mens rea*, but "mistake of law"—that is, not knowing the law—usually cannot. People who intentionally commit illegal acts are almost always guilty, even if they honestly don't realize that what they are doing is illegal. For example, if Jo sells cocaine in the honest but mistaken belief that it is sugar, Jo may lack *mens rea*. However, if Jo sells cocaine in the honest but mistaken belief that it is legal to do so, Jo is considered morally blameworthy. Perhaps the best explanation for the difference is that if a mistake of law allowed people to escape punishment, the legal system would be encouraging people to remain ignorant of legal rules.

EXAMPLE: Good friends Smith and Wesson go deer hunting. When they stop for lunch, Smith has a couple of beers. An hour later, Smith shoots in the direction of moving branches, thinking he's shooting at a deer. He hits Wesson instead, killing him. Smith's conduct probably constitutes criminal negligence. Smith should know that drinking alcohol is especially dangerous when he is carrying a loaded weapon. Also, Smith should have known that his hunting companion was likely to be in the vicinity. Smith's reckless disregard of a substantial and unjustifiable risk demonstrates *mens rea*.

Can a young child have *mens rea*?

It depends on the age of the child and the state where the act takes place. Laws in all states exempt very young children from criminal responsibility. These laws assume that very young children do not have the capacity for *mens rea*. However, the *mens rea* age limit varies from state to state. Some states exempt only children under the age of seven. Other states have a presumption that even older children (perhaps up to age 14) lack *mens rea*, but leave room for judges to determine that a particular youthful offender did have *mens rea*.

Children who are legally old enough to have *mens rea* may be guilty of crimes, but be eligible to be treated as juveniles rather than as adults.

The Meaning of Frequently Used Legal Language

Lawyers often refer to words used in legal rules as "terms of art." This doesn't mean that the words are colorful or attractive. Rather, "term of art" serves as a warning that a commonly used word may take on an uncommon meaning when it's used in a legal rule. This section defines a handful of these terms as they are used in criminal law.

What does the term "knowing" or "knowingly" mean?

Many laws punish only violators who knowingly engage in illegal conduct. The "knowingly" requirement indicates that a crime involves *mens rea*, and prevents people who make innocent mistakes from being convicted of crimes. What a person has to know to be guilty of a crime depends on the behavior that a law makes illegal. For example:

- A drug law makes it illegal for a person to knowingly import an illegal drug (often referred to as a controlled substance) into the United States. To convict a defendant of this crime, the prosecution would have to prove that the defendant knew that the substance brought into the United States was an illegal drug.
- Another drug law makes it illegal to furnish drug paraphernalia with knowledge that it will be used to cultivate or ingest an illegal drug. To convict a defendant of this crime, the prosecution would have to prove that a defendant who sold or supplied drug paraphernalia knew the improper purposes to which the paraphernalia would be put.
- A perjury law makes it illegal for a witness to testify to any material

matter that the witness knows to be false. To prove perjury, the prosecution would have to prove that the witness knew when testifying that the testimony was false.

- A school safety law makes it illegal for a person to knowingly possess a firearm in a school zone. To prove a violation of this law, the prosecution would have to prove both that the defendant knew that he was carrying a gun and that he was in a school zone.

EXAMPLE: Donald, an Oregon resident, vacations in Canada. As Donald is about to leave Canada, his friend Brandi gives him a satchel. Brandi tells Donald that the satchel contains wedding presents for Brandi's friend who lives in Oregon, and that the friend will collect the satchel from Donald in a few days. After he crosses the border, a police officer finds the satchel in Donald's car. The officer opens it and finds that it contains packages of cocaine. Donald is charged with knowingly importing illegal drugs. If his story is true, Donald did not knowingly import drugs into the United States. If Donald did not know that the satchel contained illegal drugs, he did not knowingly import them and therefore lacked *mens rea*. Of course, Donald might reasonably expect judges and jurors to have a skeptical attitude toward his somewhat fishy story. What's more, "willful blindness"—deliberately avoiding knowledge of a key fact or circumstance—can at times serve as a substitute for actual knowledge. In other words, if Donald had good reason to know the satchel contained drugs and didn't look in it because he wanted to be able to deny that

he knew what was in it, he might be guilty of knowingly importing illegal drugs.

How can the government possibly prove what a defendant knew?

A defendant might confess to a police officer or admit knowledge in a phone call or a text message. However, in most cases the government has to offer circumstantial evidence of a defendant's knowledge. That is, the government offers evidence of circumstances surrounding the defendant's actions and asks the judge or jury to infer the defendant's knowledge from those circumstances. For example, in Donald's case above, the government might offer the following circumstantial evidence to show that Donald knew that the satchel contained illegal drugs:

- Brandi (or others) had on an earlier occasion asked Donald to carry presents across the border in a satchel; on this earlier occasion, Donald found out that the satchel contained illegal drugs.
- Donald had tried to conceal the satchel in his car.
- The satchel was too heavy (or too light) to account for the presents that Brandi told Donald it contained.
- The satchel emitted a strong odor of drugs.
- Donald is a drug user.
- Donald was aware that Brandi's friend was a drug user.

What are "specific intent" crimes?

Specific intent laws require the government do more than show that a defendant acted knowingly. Specific intent laws require the government to prove that a defendant had a particular purpose in mind when engaging in illegal conduct. Each specific intent law identifies the particular purpose that the government has to prove. For example:

- Many theft laws require the government to prove that a defendant took property with the intent to permanently deprive a person of the property. To convict a defendant of theft, the government has to prove that a thief's plan was to forever part a victim from the stolen property. For example, a culprit who drives off in another's car without permission and returns it a few hours later might be convicted only of joyriding. However, the same culprit who drives off in another's car without permission and takes it across the country probably demonstrates a specific intent to permanently deprive the owner of the car and would be guilty of the more serious crime of car theft.

- Insurance fraud laws often require proof that a defendant destroyed insured property with the intent to defraud the insurer. To convict a defendant of insurance fraud, a prosecutor has to prove that a defendant's purpose in destroying insured property was to collect money from the property's insurer. For instance, a prosecutor might offer evidence that the owner of a decaying factory hired an arsonist to set fire to it and then filed an insurance claim.

- A serious drug crime involves possession of drugs with the intent to sell them. To prove this crime, a prosecutor would have to prove that a defendant intended to sell the drugs found in the defendant's possession rather than keep them for his own use. For example, the prosecutor might offer evidence that the drugs were bundled into separate packages, that the defendant also owned a set of scales commonly used by drug pushers to weigh drugs, and that customers were frequently seen going in and out of the apartment.

EXAMPLE: Red Handed is charged with stealing a laptop computer. The prosecutor offers evidence that Red took a laptop from an electronics shop without paying for it and tried to pawn it the next day. Red's effort to pawn the laptop the day after taking it is strong circumstantial evidence that Red planned to permanently deprive the electronics shop of its possession.

EXAMPLE: Hank O'Hare is charged with kidnapping with intent to commit rape. The victim testifies that as she was walking home one evening, O'Hare jumped out from behind some bushes, grabbed her, and pushed her into his car. Inside his car, O'Hare covered the victim's mouth and secured her hands with adhesive tape. O'Hare drove around for 15 minutes before the victim managed to free her hands and escape from the car. O'Hare is clearly guilty of the lesser (but still very serious) crime of kidnapping. However, the circumstantial evidence is probably not strong enough to prove that O'Hare kidnapped the victim for the purpose of committing a rape. However, any one of the following items of evidence would be legally sufficient to prove that O'Hare kidnapped the victim with the intent of committing rape: (1) statements by O'Hare to the victim (or to O'Hare's cronies) indicating his sexual intent; (2) O'Hare's sexual touching of the victim before she managed to escape; or (3) evidence that O'Hare had previously used the same "m.o." (methods) to kidnap and rape other young women on previous occasions.

What does the term "maliciously" mean?

In everyday usage, people often use the term malicious to mean spiteful or wicked. In most criminal statutes, however, "malicious" is simply synonymous with "intentionally" and "knowingly." As a result, the term "maliciously" usually adds nothing to the general *mens rea* requirement.

> **EXAMPLE:** Red Brown is charged with spray-painting graffiti on Wood Siding's house. The statute under which Red is charged requires that the prosecution prove that Red acted maliciously. The prosecution has to prove only that Red intentionally sprayed paint on Wood's house. The fact that Red may have done it as a joke is irrelevant.

Sometimes, the word "malicious" can mean that a defendant who acted in a highly reckless manner may be guilty, even without acting "intentionally" or "knowingly."

> **EXAMPLE:** Buhr Nying has just finished raking a flurry of fall leaves that have dried and been piling up for weeks. Nying raked them toward the space between Nying's and Nying's neighbor's home, thinking that Nying would put them in the trash cans several days later, when the trash is collected. Nying noticed that it was a particularly windy day, so he went inside his home, got a jacket, cigarettes, and a beer, and sat on his stoop smoking to relax after the hard work of raking leaves. Nying threw the butts of his cigarettes on his lawn without extinguishing them, and they landed on dried leaves that blew toward the neighbor's home. Nying went inside his home and the pile of leaves caught fire, burning down his neighbor's house. Nying may well be guilty of arson, even if he did not intend to burn his neighbor's home, if the state statute defines that crime as "the malicious burning of the dwelling house of another." His action of throwing lit cigarettes toward dried leaves on a windy day in close proximity to neighboring houses would be considered highly reckless.

How does the term "willfully" affect the meaning of a statute?

As with "maliciously," the term "willfully" usually adds nothing to the general *mens rea* requirement. In most statutes, to commit an illegal act willfully is simply to commit it intentionally. For example, consider these statutes:

- "It is unlawful to willfully disturb another person by loud and unreasonable noise."

- "Anyone who willfully encourages another to commit suicide is guilty of a felony."

Each of these statutes merely requires the government to show that a person intentionally committed the act made illegal by the statute.

> **EXAMPLE:** Raye Dio deliberately cranks up the volume on her stereo at 3 a.m. The volume is so high that it wakes up a number of other tenants, who call the police. Raye acted willfully because she knew that she was playing her stereo at a high volume. If Raye is seriously hard of hearing, she may not have realized that what seems like a normal volume to her is in reality unreasonably loud. If so, Raye did not knowingly create unreasonable noise and so did not behave willfully. However, if Raye persists in playing her stereo loudly even after the neighbors have advised her that the volume is unreasonably loud, Raye may be guilty of disturbing the peace notwithstanding her hearing problem. She has acted willfully, especially because reasonable alternatives (such as headphones) are available.

Less commonly, the term "willfully" in a statute has been interpreted to require the government to prove not only that a person acted intentionally, but also that the person intended to break the law. (This is an unusual instance in which ignorance of the law actually IS an excuse!) For example, in one case, a federal law made it illegal to willfully bring in to the country more than $10,000 in cash without declaring it to customs officials. The U.S. Supreme Court decided that to convict a person of violating this law, the government had to prove that the person knew the law's requirements. (*Ratzlaf v. U.S.*, U.S. Sup. Ct. 1994.) This more exacting interpretation of "willfully" preserves the *mens rea* foundation of criminal law where, as in the cash-declaring law, many people might be morally innocent yet break the law.

How does the term "feloniously" affect the meaning of a statute?

The term "felonious" is sometimes included in a law when prohibited conduct can in some circumstances be legal. Its presence is a reminder that a law applies only to a prohibited form of conduct. For example, consider this law:

"Anyone who feloniously takes the property of another is guilty of theft."

Taking another's property is often perfectly legal. For example, a woman may give her sister general permission to wear her sweaters. And shoppers certainly commit no crime when they take an item off a shelf when deciding whether to buy it. The statute makes only felonious taking illegal—that is, taking property without permission and with the intent to permanently deprive another of the property.

What does the term "motive" mean?

Motive refers to the reason why a person committed an illegal act. For example, a person's need to raise money quickly to pay off a bookie may be the motive for a robbery; revenge for a personal affront may be the motive for a physical attack. Prosecutors often offer motive evidence as circumstantial evidence that a defendant acted intentionally or knowingly. The reason is that, like most people, judges and jurors believe in cause and effect. They will be more likely to believe that a defendant had *mens rea* if they know that the defendant had a motive to commit an illegal act.

Does the government have to prove motive?

No. While prosecutors frequently do offer motive evidence, they are not required to do so. By the same token, defendants may offer evidence showing that they had no motive to commit a crime, and then argue that the lack of a motive demonstrates reasonable doubt of guilt.

> **EXAMPLE:** Lucretia Borgia is charged with murdering her husband, Sid. The government offers evidence that Lucretia had begun secretly dating another man in the months before Sid died. Lucretia offers evidence that under the terms of Sid's father's will, Lucretia would inherit $1 million, but only if Sid was alive when the father died. Sid's father was still alive at the time of Sid's death. The government's evidence suggests that Lucretia had an emotional motive to knock off Sid; Lucretia's evidence suggests that she had a financial motive not to. It's up to the judge or jury to weigh the conflicting motive evidence together with all the other evidence in the case and arrive at a verdict.

Crimes and the Constitution

While the U.S. Congress and state legislatures have broad powers to define crimes, courts have the ultimate power to decide whether a criminal statute is constitutional. For example, the U.S. Supreme Court decided that a District of Columbia law banning the possession of handguns was invalid because it violated the Second Amendment. (*District of Columbia v. Heller*, 2008.) The federal government still has wide powers to control weapons. For example, it can ban specific types of weapons, it can ban weapons in particular places (such as around airports and schools), and it can prevent certain people (such as ex-felons and people who have been convicted of crimes involving domestic violence) from owning weapons.

Derivative Criminal Responsibility

This section looks at situations in which someone who did not commit the primary criminal act may still be guilty of a crime.

Who is an accomplice?

An accomplice is someone who intentionally helps another person commit a crime. Even if an accomplice does not participate in carrying out the crime, the accomplice's precrime assistance makes an accomplice just as guilty, in the eyes of the law, as the person who actually carries out the crime. For example, assume that Lars Senny breaks into a warehouse and steals property belonging to the warehouse owner. Hal Perr would be Lars's accomplice and just as guilty as Lars if Hal took any of the following steps to help Lars commit the theft:

- Hal works in the warehouse and drugged the warehouse night watchman before leaving work on the day of the theft.
- Hal cut the wires to the burglar alarm (or cut a hole in the fence) so that Lars could enter the warehouse without being detected.
- Hal has a blueprint of the warehouse, and he met with Lars a week before the theft to review warehouse layouts and exit routes.
- Hal rented a U-Haul truck and left it parked outside the warehouse on the night of the robbery.
- Hal agreed to babysit for Lars's infant child so that Lars could break into the warehouse.

Does an accomplice need *mens rea* to be guilty of a crime?

Yes. To prove that a defendant is an accomplice, the government must prove that the defendant intentionally aided in the commission of a crime. This means that the defendant must realize that the principal is going to commit a crime and must intend to assist in the effort.

> **EXAMPLE:** Jill Lester manages a warehouse. Jill takes Lars Senny on a tour of the warehouse after Lars informs the warehouse owner that he is interested in purchasing it. The night of the tour, Lars uses the information he gained from Jill to successfully enter the warehouse and steal property. Because Jill did not intentionally help Lars commit the theft, Jill lacked *mens rea* and did not commit a crime.

The Accomplices in the Oklahoma City Bombing Tragedy

In 1995, a bomb exploded in front of the federal building in Oklahoma City; 168 people were killed and more than 500 were injured. A jury convicted Timothy McVeigh of first-degree murder for carrying out the bombing. McVeigh was sentenced to death. McVeigh was executed in 2001. A separate jury convicted Terry Nichols of conspiracy for helping McVeigh plan the bombing and gather bomb components. However, the jury acquitted Nichols of murder because of its uncertainty over whether Nichols realized that McVeigh planned to carry out the bombing at a time when the federal building was open for business. Nichols was sentenced to life in prison in June 1998. Michael Fortier, another accomplice, was sentenced to 12 years in prison in May 1998 after pleading guilty to four charges, including failure to warn authorities of the bomb plot and transporting stolen weapons. In part, Fortier's lighter sentence was due to his cooperation with the government; he provided crucial testimony that helped convict McVeigh and Nichols.

Barbara Graham: The Executed Accomplice

In 1953, Barbara Graham was convicted in California of helping three others murder and rob a widow. Graham's role consisted mainly of helping her cohorts gain entry into the widow's home. Graham was sentenced to death, though she may not have participated in the actual killing. She was executed in 1955 after two last-minute stays of executions were lifted, becoming one of four women ever executed in California. The case was dramatized in the 1958 film *I Want To Live!* for which Susan Hayward won the Academy Award for Best Actress.

EXAMPLE: Les Sorr rents a room in his apartment house to Les See. See tells Sorr, "I'm glad the apartment is available. That store across the street cheated me and I can shoot out the windows from here." Sorr replies, "I hope you don't do that." See does in fact shoot out the store windows from inside the apartment. Sorr is probably not guilty as See's accomplice in the shooting. Sorr intended only to rent the apartment, not to help See commit a crime. But if Sorr had responded by raising the rent by $50 because of the desirability of the location for See, Sorr would probably qualify as an accomplice because he benefited from See's criminal act.

Accomplices, Accessories, Aiders and Abettors, and Principals

To distinguish the criminal culpability of one crime helper from another, the common law has developed specialized terms for the various ways in which one could be a party to the crime. For instance, a principal in the first degree is the person who actually carries out a crime. A principal in the second degree (an aider and abettor) is a helper who is present at a crime scene but in a passive role, such as acting as a lookout. An accessory before the fact is a helper who is not present at the crime scene.

While some state laws retain the common law terminology, few states make any distinction between the criminal liability of crime perpetrators and their accomplices. All can be punished equally, whether they actually commit the crime or only help bring it about.

What is an accessory after the fact?

An accessory after the fact is someone who, knowing that another person has already committed a felony (generally, the crime has to be a felony), helps that person avoid arrest or trial. Perhaps because an accessory after the fact becomes involved only after a crime has already occurred, accessories after the fact typically face lesser punishment than accomplices or principals.

EXAMPLE: Abbe Citron is driving past the Last National Bank when she sees her husband Alan run out of the bank carrying a bag of cash and being chased by a security guard. Alan jumps into Abbe's car and asks her to drive him to a secret hideaway. She does so. Abbe is an accomplice, just as guilty as Alan of the bank robbery, because she helped Alan to escape. Abbe does not qualify for the lesser crime of being an accessory after the fact because Alan had not yet finished committing the crime of bank robbery when Abbe assisted him. A crime is not finished until the criminal has reached a place of temporary or permanent safety.

EXAMPLE: As in the previous example, Alan has robbed the Last National Bank. Alan runs home, tells Abbe what he did and hides in the basement. A short time later, when the police come looking for Alan, Abbe tells them that she has not seen Alan and does not know where he is. Abbe is guilty of being an accessory after the fact to bank robbery. Abbe is not an accomplice because Alan had finished committing the crime before Abbe tried to help him evade capture.

EXAMPLE: Tippycanoe and Tyler meet at a movie theater. Once inside, Tippycanoe shows Tyler a bag of candy and snack food, tells Tyler that he stole it from a shop, and offers some to Tyler. Between them, Tippycanoe and Tyler finish the whole bag. Tyler is not guilty of being an accessory after the fact. Tyler helped Tippycanoe to conceal the crime by eating some of the stolen food. However, Tippycanoe's crime was petty theft, which is almost certainly a misdemeanor and not a felony. In most states, an accessory after the fact is guilty of a crime only if the underlying crime is a felony.

The Law's Suspicious Attitude Toward Accomplice Testimony

Judges have historically taken the testimony of accomplices with a grain of salt because of accomplices' obvious motive to minimize their own responsibility (and punishment) by shifting most of the blame to somebody else. As a safeguard, most states have a rule that a defendant cannot be convicted merely upon the testimony of an accomplice. If a prosecution witness qualifies as an accomplice, the prosecution has to corroborate the witness's testimony with independent evidence linking the defendant to a crime.

Who are conspirators?

Conspirators are two or more people who agree to commit a crime. (The distinction between accomplices and conspirators is that the former are helpers, while each conspirator is a principal.) Conspiracy is a controversial crime, in part because conspirators can be guilty even if the crime that they agree to commit never occurs. As a result, conspirators can be punished for their illegal plans rather than for what they actually do. To provide some protection against convicting people purely for their private thoughts, most states provide that conspirators are not guilty of the crime of conspiracy unless at least one of them commits an overt act. An "overt act" is an activity that goes beyond mere planning or preparation and in some way puts the conspiracy plot in motion.

> **EXAMPLE:** Bonnie and Clyde agree to rob the Last National Bank. The night before the planned robbery, Bonnie brags about the plan to a friend, who notifies the police. Bonnie and Clyde are arrested early the next morning, before they can carry out their plan. Bonnie and Clyde are not guilty of conspiracy. They formed a mental plan but took no overt act toward its completion.

> **EXAMPLE:** Same case. Before bragging about her plan to the friend, Bonnie had called the Last National Bank to ask what time it would open the next morning. Bonnie's phone call, though not itself a crime, is an overt act that helped put the conspiracy into motion. Bonnie and Clyde can be convicted of conspiracy even though the robbery never occurred.

Overt Acts Can Be Trivial

States that require prosecutors to prove overt acts in conspiracy cases add little to the prosecution's burden. Almost any objectively provable act, even one that standing alone is entirely innocent, can be sufficient to prove a conspiracy. Writing a letter, making a phone call, attending a lawful meeting, and hiring a lawyer are examples of overt acts that have satisfied conspiracy statutes.

How does the government prove that a conspiracy exists?

Few conspiracies are reduced to writing. As when trying to prove intent or knowledge, a prosecutor usually relies on circumstantial evidence of conspiracy. Just as a person might infer the existence of a fire from smoke, prosecutors ask judges and juries to infer from the conspirators' behavior that an illegal agreement gave rise to that behavior.

> **EXAMPLE:** Laurel and Hardy drive through the streets of a city. They pass three piano stores. Each time, Laurel stops the car, and Hardy gets out with a hammer, walks into the piano store, and smashes a piano to bits. Laurel and Hardy are conspirators because their behavior suggests that they are carrying out a plan to which they agreed earlier.

Can conspirators receive double punishment?

Yes. Conspiracy is itself a crime. As a result, conspirators can be convicted both of conspiracy and of the crime they carry out in furtherance of the conspiracy. For instance, assume that Bonnie and Clyde conspire to rob a bank, then actually rob it. Bonnie and Clyde can be convicted and separately punished for conspiracy and for bank robbery.

Can a conspirator be convicted of crimes committed by coconspirators?

Yes. Another broad feature of conspiracy law in most states is that each conspirator is legally responsible for crimes committed by any other conspirators, as long as those crimes fall within the scope of the conspiracy. Because the precise goal of a conspiracy is rarely written down, a conspirator's criminal liability can easily be far greater than the conspirator anticipated. A conspirator may intend to take part only in a single crime, yet be responsible for additional crimes committed by coconspirators who intended for the conspiracy to encompass a number of crimes.

EXAMPLE: Bonnie and Clyde agree to rob the Last National Bank. Bonnie waits in the getaway car while Clyde holds up the bank. To prevent being captured, Clyde shoots and severely wounds a bank security guard. Bonnie can be convicted of both bank robbery and shooting the security guard. A successful getaway is an inherent part of a crime scheme. Because shooting the security guard furthers the purpose of Bonnie and Clyde's conspiracy, Bonnie and Clyde are equally responsible for the shooting.

EXAMPLE: Bonnie and Clyde rob the Last National Bank. The same evening, they divide up the money and go their separate ways. The next morning, Bonnie robs the Next to Last National Bank. Clyde is not legally responsible for the Next to Last National Bank robbery. Bonnie and Clyde were conspirators only for the limited purpose of robbing the Last National Bank. That plan was carried out—the money had already been divided and the conspirators had gone their separate ways. The robbery that Bonnie carried out the next morning was therefore not in furtherance of the original plan, and Clyde is not legally responsible for it.

EXAMPLE: Bonnie, Clyde, Barker, and Dillinger get together and plan to each rob a bank on the same day and later divide up the total proceeds equally. Dillinger later recruits Capone, who helps Dillinger rob a bank. Each robber, including Capone, can be convicted of the robberies committed by the other robbers. The conspiracy encompassed all the bank robberies, so each conspirator is legally responsible for each of them. Even though Capone may only have agreed to help Dillinger, Capone is bound by the conspiracy's wider scope.

Murder and Manslaughter

This section explains the important but often subtle distinctions between murder and manslaughter, and between different degrees of those crimes. Often, a defendant's conduct could easily fit into either category. A judge's or jury's verdict in these cases may be less dependent on the abstract language of the rules than on their judgment about just how morally blameworthy a defendant is.

Is homicide the same thing as murder?

No. A homicide is any killing of a human being by another human being. Many homicides are legal, such as a justifiable killing of a suspect by the police and a killing committed in self-defense.

What is murder?

Murder is an intentional killing that is:

- unlawful (in other words, the killing isn't legally justified), and
- committed with "malice aforethought."

Malice aforethought doesn't mean that a killer has to have acted out of spite or hate. Malice aforethought exists if a killer intends to kill a person. In addition, in most states malice aforethought isn't limited to intentional killings. Malice aforethought can also exist if:

- a killer intentionally inflicts very serious bodily harm that causes a victim's death, or
- a killer's behavior, which demonstrates extreme reckless disregard for the value of human life, results in a victim's death.

Under this scheme, intent to do serious bodily harm and extreme reckless disregard are legally equivalent to an intent to kill. To be consistent, from here on we'll refer to murders as intentional killings.

If a victim is dead in any event, why distinguish between first-degree and second-degree murder?

Even within the universe of those who kill unlawfully and with malice aforethought, the law regards some killers as more dangerous and morally blameworthy than others; this group can be convicted of first-degree murder. Unlawful and intentional killings that don't constitute first-degree murder are second-degree murder.

The rules vary somewhat from state to state as to what circumstances make an intentional killing first-degree murder. The following circumstances are common:

- The killing is deliberate and premeditated. In other words, the killer plans the crime ahead of time. For example, premeditation exists if a wife goes to the store, buys a lethal dose of rat poison, and puts it in her husband's tea.
- The victim is a peace officer, a judge, or an elected representative.
- The killer uses an explosive device such as a bomb.

What is the felony-murder rule?

Felony-murder rules typically provide that when a death occurs during the commission of a dangerous felony, a felon is guilty of murder. If two individuals carry out a dangerous felony jointly, each may be convicted of murder under the rule, even when only one of them was the actual killer. Indeed, in some jurisdictions a felon may be convicted of murder even if a death that occurs during the course of a felony is accidental and unintended, or carried out by someone other than the felon. The rule thus substitutes commission of a dangerous felony for the element of "intent" that a murder conviction usually requires. Under the rule, a felony may continue for as long as a felon actively seeks to escape detection or arrest.

> **EXAMPLE:** While Clyde is in a bank pulling off an armed robbery, the bank's security guard shoots at Clyde but kills a customer instead. In some states, Clyde may be prosecuted for murder because

the customer's death is attributable to his commission of a dangerous felony. Other states would not apply the felony murder rule to Clyde because the security guard was not a coparticipant in the robbery.

EXAMPLE: A company's bookkeeper has a sudden heart attack and dies after observing a trusted employee stealing company funds. The felony-murder rule does not apply because embezzlement is not a dangerous felony.

EXAMPLE: At Bob's request, Heidi, Ellie's caregiver, leaves a window in Ellie's house unlocked so that Bob can climb through it and steal a valuable painting that Ellie owns. In the course of trying to steal the painting, Bob kills Ellie. In most states, Bob and Heidi might both be convicted of murder because Bob killed Ellie while committing a felony. However, Heidi could not be convicted of murder under a 2018 California law because she did not participate in the killing and was not a major participant in the crime.

Does the felony-murder rule apply to a death that occurs while a felon is trying to escape?

Yes. A crime generally encompasses the period during which a culprit actively seeks to escape capture. A death that occurs during a felon's escape from the scene of a dangerous felony is thus punishable as murder under the felony-murder rule. Once an escape is complete and a felon has arrived at a place of temporary safety, the felony-murder rule ceases to apply.

EXAMPLE: Jeff breaks into an appliance warehouse and steals a truckload of refrigerators. With the stolen appliances in the back of his truck, Jeff accelerates when he sees a police car behind him. The acceleration causes a refrigerator to fall off the truck and into the path of the police car. The police officer swerves to avoid the refrigerator, collides with another truck, and dies. If the jury decides that Jeff was actively escaping from the warehouse burglary at the time he saw the police officer, the felony-murder rule applies and the jury may convict Jeff of murder. But if the jury decides that the burglary was complete and Jeff had already reached a place of temporary safety when the officer's car came up behind him, the felony-murder rule would not apply.

Is the punishment for first-degree murder usually more severe than for second-degree murder?

Yes. Many states have mandatory minimum sentences for murder, and the mandatory minimum for first-degree murder is almost always higher than for second-degree murder. Defendants convicted of first-degree murder can also be eligible for the death penalty in jurisdictions in which it is in force. Defendants convicted of second-degree murder are often sentenced to a term of years rather than to life in prison, and are almost always eligible for parole.

What is the difference between murder and manslaughter?

Manslaughter (in some states called third-degree murder) is an unlawful killing that does not involve malice aforethought (intent to kill). The absence of malice aforethought means that manslaughter involves less moral blame than either first- or second-degree murder. Thus, while manslaughter is a serious crime, the punishment for manslaughter is generally less than for murder.

Do degrees of manslaughter exist, as they do for murder?

Yes, though the two degrees of manslaughter are usually referred to as voluntary and involuntary manslaughter.

Voluntary manslaughter is often called a "heat of passion" crime. Voluntary manslaughter often arises when a person is suddenly provoked (in circumstances that are likely to provoke many reasonable people) and kills in the heat of passion

The "Nanny" Case: Murder or Manslaughter?

The subtle distinctions between murder and manslaughter were at the heart of a controversial and internationally televised nanny trial in Massachusetts. A 19-year-old British au pair babysitter was charged with second-degree murder for killing an infant that had been left in her care. The prosecution claimed that she shook the baby so violently that he died. In crimespeak, the prosecution claimed that the babysitter's behavior demonstrated extreme reckless disregard for human life. The defense claimed that the baby died as the result of an unforeseeable reaction to normal shaking, so she committed no crime. Under Massachusetts law, the defense could have asked the judge to instruct the jury about involuntary manslaughter, which would have allowed the jury to conclude that the babysitter was criminally negligent for shaking the baby too hard.

However, the defense asked the judge not to instruct on involuntary manslaughter, gambling that the jury would acquit the babysitter altogether rather than convict her of murder. (Other states don't allow the defense to play tactical games like this one, and require the judge to instruct on every verdict reasonably warranted by the evidence.)

The defense lost the gamble. The jury convicted the babysitter of second-degree murder, which carried a mandatory minimum sentence of 15 years in prison. A few weeks later, the defense asked the judge either to acquit the babysitter or reduce the verdict to involuntary manslaughter. The judge did the latter, sentenced the babysitter to time served, and freed her from prison immediately. The Massachusetts Supreme Court upheld the judge's decision in June 1998.

aroused by the provocation. That the killing is not considered murder is a concession to human weakness. Killers who act in the heat of passion may kill intentionally, but the emotional context prevents them from being fully in control of their actions. As a result, the heat of passion reduces their moral blameworthiness.

The common example of voluntary manslaughter involves a husband who comes home unexpectedly to find his wife committing adultery. If the husband is provoked into such a heat of passion that he kills the paramour right then and there, a judge or jury might very well consider the killing to be voluntary manslaughter.

A killing can constitute involuntary manslaughter when a person's reckless disregard of a substantial risk results in another's death. Because involuntary manslaughter involves carelessness and not purposeful killing, it is a less serious crime than murder or voluntary manslaughter.

The subtleties between the degrees of murder and manslaughter reach their peak with involuntary manslaughter. Suppose that Rosencrantz is driving a car and runs over and kills Guildenstern. Rosencrantz might be:

- Not guilty of a crime at all. If Guildenstern's family sues Rosencrantz in a civil case, Rosencrantz might have to pay damages to Guildenstern's heirs if Rosencrantz was negligent—that is, if Rosencrantz failed to use ordinary care.
- Convicted of involuntary manslaughter. This might happen if Rosencrantz recklessly disregarded a substantial risk, meaning that Rosencrantz was more than ordinarily negligent. For example, a judge or jury might convict Rosencrantz of involuntary manslaughter if Rosencrantz killed Guildenstern while driving under the influence of alcohol.
- Convicted of second-degree murder. If Rosencrantz's behavior demonstrated such an extreme reckless disregard for human life that a judge or jury decides that it shows malice aforethought, he might be convicted of second-degree murder. For example, if Rosencrantz doesn't just kill Guildenstern as a result of drunk driving, but does so with a stolen car after his license had been taken away for previous drunk driving convictions, a judge or jury might convict Rosencrantz of second-degree murder.

EXAMPLE: Fast Boyle is walking along a busy street. Clay bumps into Boyle and continues walking without saying "Sorry." Angered by Clay's rudeness, Boyle immediately pulls out a gun and kills Clay. Boyle is guilty of second-degree murder, because he killed Clay intentionally. A judge or jury is unlikely to conclude that the killing was premeditated, which would elevate the shooting to first-degree murder. On the other hand, this was not a heat of passion killing that might reduce the conviction to voluntary manslaughter. While Boyle might personally have been provoked into killing Clay, the circumstances were not so extreme that many ordinary and reasonable people would have been provoked to kill.

EXAMPLE: Same case, except that instead of shooting Clay, Boyle pulled out a knife and threw it at Clay, intending just to hurt him and teach him a lesson. However, the knife punctured Clay's liver and he bled to death. Boyle is again guilty of second-degree murder. Boyle may not have intended to kill Clay. Nevertheless, Boyle intended to inflict a very serious bodily injury on Clay, and that injury caused Clay's death. In most states, malice aforethought would be implied from Boyle's intent to do serious harm.

EXAMPLE: Standing next to each other in a bookstore a few feet away from the top of a flight of stairs, Marks and Spencer argue over the proper interpretation of free will in Hobbes's philosophy. The argument becomes increasingly animated until Spencer points a finger at Marks and Marks pushes Spencer backwards. The push is hard enough to cause Spencer to fall backwards and down the stairs. Spencer dies from the resulting injuries. Marks would probably be guilty of involuntary manslaughter. It was criminally negligent of Marks to shove a person standing near the top of a stairway. But the circumstances don't suggest that Marks's behavior was so reckless as to demonstrate extreme indifference to human life, which would have elevated the crime to second-degree murder.

EXAMPLE: Lew Manion comes home to find that his wife Lee has been badly beaten and sexually abused. Manion takes Lee to the hospital. On the way, Lee tells Manion that her attacker was Barnett, the owner of a tavern that she and Manion occasionally visit. After driving Lee home from the hospital about four hours later, Manion goes to a gunshop and buys a gun. Manion then goes to the tavern, shoots Barnett, and kills him. Manion could be convicted of first-degree murder because his purchase of the gun suggests that the shooting was intentional and premeditated. Voluntary manslaughter is a somewhat less likely alternative. Most judges and jurors are likely to think that enough time elapsed between the time Manion found out about Lee's injuries and the time he shot Barnett for any heat of passion to have cooled. Manion should have steered clear of the gun shop and reported the crime to the police.

Sexual Violence

This section describes common crimes that involve sexual violence, including rape, domestic violence, and sex crimes against children.

What is rape?

Rape is unlawful (nonconsensual) sexual intercourse, often accomplished by means of force or fear. For purposes of rape laws, sexual intercourse occurs at the moment of sexual penetration, however slight.

Forcible rape occurs when someone uses violence or threats of violence to coerce a victim into sexual intercourse. In most states, however, rape can also occur in a number of other ways. For example, rape generally also consists of sexual intercourse occurring under these conditions:

- the rapist prevents a victim from resisting by plying the victim with alcohol or drugs

- the rapist poses as a public official and threatens to arrest or deport the victim unless the victim agrees to sexual intercourse, or
- the rapist knows that the victim has a disorder or disability that prevents the victim from legally consenting to sexual intercourse.

EXAMPLE: Amanda goes out to dinner with her boss Fred. After dinner Fred suggests that "we go back to my office and enjoy ourselves." Amanda has heard that Fred has been violent in the past. Fearing both that Fred may hurt her and that her career may suffer if she doesn't go along, Amanda agrees to go back to the office and engages in sexual intercourse with Fred. No rape has occurred. Fred neither used force nor threatened harm to Amanda. Her subjective fear based on what she has heard about Fred doesn't invalidate her consent. Of course, Amanda may have a valid civil claim against Fred and the company for workplace sexual harassment.

EXAMPLE: Belinda is sleeping when Stan breaks into her apartment, pulls out a knife, and threatens to use it unless Belinda agrees to sexual intercourse. Belinda pleads with Stan to leave, but he refuses and begins to strike her. Eventually Belinda hands Stan a condom and says, "At least use protection." Stan uses the condom while having sexual intercourse with Belinda. Stan is guilty of rape. The sexual intercourse was forcible, not consensual. Belinda's request that Stan use a condom is not evidence of consent, but rather an effort to suffer as little future harm as possible.

Can a husband be guilty of raping his wife?

Yes. If sexual intercourse is nonconsensual within the meaning of the rape laws, the fact that the parties are married is irrelevant. Of course, the fact that the alleged rapist is her husband may make it more difficult for a wife to convince the police or a judge or jury that rape rather than consensual intercourse took place.

Can a woman be guilty of rape?

Yes, though such cases are rare. In a few instances, females have been convicted of rape when they have been the accomplices of males and have lured a victim to a place where a rapist awaits.

Dramatic Changes in Rape Evidence Rules

Until the mid-1970s, evidence rules tended to discourage rape victims from reporting the crime. Since then, largely as the result of political pressure from women's rights groups and their allies, there have been two dramatic shifts in rape evidence laws favorable to rape victims. First, rape shield laws often prevent defendants from inquiring into rape victims' sexual histories. (See Federal Rule of Evidence 412.) Second, in most states, the general rule forbidding evidence of defendants' past crimes has been abandoned in sexual offense cases. When a defendant is charged with rape or another sexual offense, the prosecution can offer evidence of the defendant's past sexual offenses. (See Federal Rule of Evidence 413.)

Do degrees of rape exist?

In many states, yes. First-degree rape may consist of rape accompanied by severe physical injuries. First-degree rape carries a harsher punishment than second-degree rape, which may involve no physical injuries beyond the rape itself.

What is the difference between "stranger rape" and "date rape"?

"Stranger rape" occurs when a rape victim is attacked by a previously unknown person. For example, an assailant who violently drags a passerby into a secluded spot and rapes her commits a stranger rape. Date rape (sometimes called "acquaintance rape") occurs when the rapist and the rape victim have an existing social relationship, and the rapist strikes in the course of that relationship. For example, a date rapist may turn "heavy petting" into rape by ignoring a woman's repeated pleas that she does not want to engage in sexual intercourse. Date rape is far more common than stranger rape. While both are equally illegal, the ambiguities that are inherent in many social situations make date rape a far more difficult crime to prove than stranger rape.

What is statutory rape?

Statutory rape is sexual intercourse with a minor, defined in many states as someone who is under age 18 at the time the intercourse takes place. The minor's stated or apparent consent to intercourse is irrelevant. Statutory rape laws tend to be strict liability laws that make a minor legally incapable of consenting to sexual intercourse. The assumption behind statutory rape laws is that someone under the age of consent does not have the mature mental capacity to voluntarily consent to intercourse.

Can a minor be guilty of statutory rape of another minor?

In some states, if two minors engage in sexual intercourse, both could be prosecuted for statutory rape. Many states' laws, however, make concessions to the frequency of sexual intercourse among minors in modern society and include close-in-age exceptions. Such provisions eliminate penalties for intercourse between minors, or reduce the charge from a felony to a misdemeanor, as long as the partners are no more than a specified number of years apart in age. In many states, the close-in-age exception applies to minors who have an age difference of less than three years.

What is domestic violence?

Domestic violence is a catchall term for violence that occurs between people who have an intimate personal relationship. They may be married, living together, or even just dating. They may be heterosexual, lesbian, or gay. While anyone can become a domestic violence perpetrator or victim, serious injuries resulting from domestic violence typically result from men attacking women. Though murder and rape can be forms of domestic violence, most often, domestic violence consists of lesser forms of physical abuse, such as hitting. Stalking can also be a form of domestic violence.

Many states define domestic violence as its own crime. As a result, a suspect who strikes a "significant other" may be charged with domestic violence instead of, or in addition to, other crimes, such as assault and battery. Recognizing that domestic abusers take advantage of their victims' trust and confidence, convictions for domestic violence often result in harsher punishment compared to similar crimes committed against strangers.

Is it true that most acts of domestic violence go unreported?

Yes. Women, who are usually the victims of domestic violence, are often reluctant to report the abuse. Abused women may hope that the abuse was an isolated act that will not be repeated. Or they may be fearful that reporting the violence will only goad their attackers into further violence. If a woman and her children are dependent on their abuser's income, she may fear that reporting the violence will result in loss of financial support. Understandable though such reactions may be, they combine to produce estimates that most crimes of domestic violence go unreported.

Is domestic violence an easy crime to prosecute?

Generally, no. Even when victims of domestic violence report attacks to the police, prosecutors often are unable to convict abusers because so many victims refuse to testify against their attackers at trial.

As defendants have a constitutional right to confront and cross-examine their accusers, prosecutors cannot offer domestic violence victims' statements to the police into evidence in lieu of the victims' testimony. As a result, charges often have to be dismissed. (*Davis v. Washington*, U.S. Sup. Ct. 2006.)

The combination of failing to report and refusing to cooperate with prosecutors makes domestic violence one of the hardest crimes to prosecute successfully. Thus, many abusers remain free to continue their pattern of abuse.

Are there special evidence rules that help prosecutors convict perpetrators of domestic violence?

Some states have special rules for domestic violence cases that allow prosecutors to offer evidence that defendants charged with domestic violence have committed other acts of domestic violence. These rules are an exception to the general rule that prosecutors can't offer evidence of defendants' past crimes.

Also, an abuser might attack or threaten a victim for the purpose of frightening the victim into refusing to testify at trial for earlier acts of abuse. If this happens, an abuser waives (gives up) the right to confront and cross-examine the victim at trial, and police officers may testify to the victim's pretrial description of what happened. (*Giles v. California*, U.S. Sup. Ct. 2008.)

Apart from prosecuting abusers, what other help is available to domestic violence victims?

Domestic violence victims may call 911; statements made to 911 operators may be admissible in court to prove that a domestic abuser is guilty. (*Davis v. Washington*, U.S. Sup. Ct. 2006.) Many localities also have domestic violence hotlines. People who have reason to fear becoming victims of domestic violence should always know how to contact a domestic violence hotline. People who have been subjected to domestic violence may also go to court and secure a protective order. An abuser who violates the terms of a protective order (for example, by showing up at a victim's home or place of work) may be arrested and charged with a crime. Finally, a federal gun control law makes it illegal for people who have been convicted of crimes involving domestic violence to own or have guns. (For a discussion of the law, see *United States v. Hayes*, U.S. Sup. Ct. 2009 and *Voisine v. U.S.*, U.S. Sup. Ct. 2016.)

People in domestic violence situations can find help online. Nolo maintains a victim resources page at www.nolo.com/legal-encyclopedia/resources-for-victims-of-crime.html. That page lists organizations for victims in various situations, including the following domestic violence resources:

- The National Domestic Violence Hotline (www.thehotline.org)
- Rape, Abuse & Incest National Network (www.rainn.org)
- DomesticShelters.org (www.domesticshelters.org)

 CAUTION

Be mindful when looking for help with abuse. When looking for help as a victim of abuse, remember to consider how private your computer, Internet, and phone use are. Consider whether there's anything you can and should do to prevent someone else from learning that you're doing research or seeking help. Some victims, for instance, might use the same computer or device as the abuser or might have a phone plan that allows the abuser to see the calls they make and receive. Other kinds of technology, like home security cameras and GPS in phones and cars, can also allow for monitoring by the abuser.

Is child sexual abuse a pervasive problem?

Common estimates are that as many as a third of females and a fifth of males in the United States experience sexual violence or at least sexualized touching before the age of 18. However, the practice of many researchers to lump together abuse of young children with consensual sexual conduct of older teenagers makes the prevalence of sexual abuse of young children uncertain. Despite the popular image of the pedophile as a "stranger with candy" who lures victims into a secluded area, most sexual abusers know their victims. Most sexual abusers are male.

What constitutes a crime of child sexual abuse?

Because children are legally incapable of consenting to sexual activity, virtually any form of sexual activity involving a child is likely to constitute sexual abuse. The distinct crimes that constitute child sexual abuse are of two general types, sexual assault and sexual exploitation.

Some types of violent child sexual abuse (such as rape and oral copulation) are the same as adult crimes. But all states also have special laws criminalizing less violent types of sexual abuse of children. Examples of such laws include various forms of sexual molestation, such as fondling and touching a child's private parts for purposes of sexual gratification, indecent exposure (exposing one's genitals to a child), luring a child into a secluded area for sexual purposes, and displaying pornography or exposing a child to other sexual behavior.

Sexual exploitation includes possessing or distributing pictures of minors engaged in obscene acts, coercing minors into engaging in prostitution, and pressuring children into engaging in sexual conduct.

Is child sexual abuse an underreported crime?

Yes. Young children especially may not realize that an adult's conduct constitutes sexual abuse. Also, children are often fearful of telling an adult that they have been molested. One reason is that the molester is often a family member or trusted friend; another is that molesters often try to silence their victims with threats. Children also may be too embarrassed or ashamed to report that they have been abused.

Do laws exist that are directed specifically at child sexual abuse?

Many laws are directed specifically at child sexual abuse. For example, many professionals, such as teachers and physicians, have a legal obligation to report suspected child sexual abuse. During child abuse prosecutions, judges may appoint lawyers called "guardians ad litem" to represent the interests of the minors. Also, prosecutors can offer evidence that a defendant charged with child sexual abuse has committed other similar acts of abuse, regardless of whether the defendant was convicted of or even charged with committing the other abusive acts.

Defendants convicted of sexual abuse of minors are often punished more harshly than defendants who sexually abuse other adults. If they are proved to represent a continuing threat to children's safety, sexual abusers may be kept in prison for longer than their original sentences. Sexual abusers may also have to register with the police once they are released from prison and may face restrictions on where they can live. For example, the Adam Walsh Child Protection and Safety Act of 2006 established national registration requirements; failure to register is a felony.

"Revenge Porn": Illegal?

In recent years, state legislatures have begun to enact what are known as "revenge porn" or "cyber exploitation" laws. The idea behind these laws is to stop people from, and punish them for, publicizing sexual images of former significant others. California enacted the first law ever aimed at revenge porn in 2013.

Cyber exploitation is an evolving area of law. Legislatures throughout the country have debated whether to enact or refine revenge porn laws. Meanwhile, some First Amendment advocates argue that the laws infringe free speech rights. They also assert that the laws are too broad—that they could be used to punish people who haven't engaged in behavior one would actually consider revenge porn.

Is it a crime to possess or distribute child pornography?

Yes. Laws prohibit the possession or distribution of pictures showing children engaged in sexually explicit activity. The laws cover printed and electronic pornography, and transmission from one person to another is illegal regardless of whether the sender charges a fee or sends it for free.

Possession of *virtual* child pornography, in which the images are generated by computers—for example, computer-generated animations—is not always illegal. (*Ashcroft v. Free Speech Coalition*, U.S. Sup. Ct. 2002.)

However, the Supreme Court has found that a law making it illegal to knowingly offer to distribute child pornography (whether the children depicted are real or virtual) is constitutional. (*United States v. Williams*, U.S. Sup. Ct. 2008.)

Assault and Battery

Assault and battery laws punish perpetrators of various types of violence. Traditionally an offender committed an assault by placing a victim in fear of immediate bodily harm, and a battery by striking or offensively touching a victim. While many current laws refer to the crime of "assault and battery," an offender can be convicted of assault even if a victim is not struck or harmed.

> **EXAMPLE:** Snider and Mantle had recently threatened each other. Shortly thereafter, Snider and Mantle are walking towards each other, and when they are close, Snider brandishes the baseball bat he is carrying and yells at Mantle. Snider has assaulted Mantle even if he does not strike Mantle with the bat.

What is aggravated assault?

"Simple" assault and battery is usually prosecuted as a misdemeanor when a victim suffers little or no physical harm. Aggravated assault is a felony that often occurs when offenders use weapons or cause serious injuries. State laws may distinguish among first-, second-, and third-degree assault, with first degree being the most serious.

What is assault with a deadly weapon?

Assault with a deadly weapon is an extremely serious felony, akin to the crimes of attempted murder and assault with intent to kill. An assault or battery accomplished with the use of any type of object that is capable of causing serious injury or death can give rise to a charge of assault with a deadly weapon.

> **EXAMPLE:** A police officer stops a motorist for running a stop sign. The officer approaches the car from the rear. To prevent the officer from finding the cache of illegal drugs in the back seat, the motorist backs the car up rapidly in the direction of the officer. The officer avoids injury by jumping out of the way, and the motorist drives off. The motorists may be charged with assault with a deadly weapon, attempted murder, or assault with intent to kill.

Motor Vehicle Crimes

Motor vehicles can be the target of a crime (as in grand theft auto), the instrumentality of a crime (as in vehicular homicide), or the situs of a crime (as in reckless driving). Many breaches of the law involving cars, such as moving violations, are infractions that are punishable only by fines. This section examines common crimes involving automobiles that can result in misdemeanor or felony convictions. (See Chapter 25 for a discussion of the crime of driving under the influence, or "DUI.")

What is hit-and-run?

Hit-and-run laws require motorists to remain at the scene of accidents in which they are involved, whether the accidents result in property damage, injuries, or death. The crime of hit-and-run typically involves a motorist being involved in an accident and failing to:

- stop at the accident scene
- provide identification, or
- offer help to any person injured as a result of the accident.

A motorist is required to remain at the scene of an accident even if another driver's negligence or recklessness caused the accident.

Typically, the motorist must have been aware of the collision to be guilty of hit-and-run. (Being unaware of a crash is normally a tough defense.)

If a motorist damages an unoccupied vehicle or other property, hit-and-run laws typically require the motorist to notify the police and leave accurate identifying information in a place where the property owner is likely to find it.

Hit-and-run can be charged as either a misdemeanor or a felony, but it is especially likely to be charged as a felony if a motorist fails to remain at the scene of an accident that results in injury or death.

What is vehicular manslaughter?

Motorists can be charged with vehicular manslaughter when their reckless or grossly negligent driving results in a victim's death.

For example, vehicular manslaughter charges might result from an accident in which a driver strikes and kills a pedestrian while sending a text message. Vehicular manslaughter is often a "wobbler" crime that is treated as a misdemeanor or a felony, depending on factors such as a motorist's past driving record and the degree of carelessness.

> **EXAMPLE:** Already on probation after pleading guilty to DUI six months earlier, Bill is involved in an accident in which his car runs a red light and collides with another car; the driver of the other car dies. Testing shows that Bill was driving while under the influence of alcohol at the time of the accident. Bill's extremely reckless driving may result in a charge of murder rather than a lesser charge of vehicular manslaughter.

What is grand theft auto?

Misdemeanor "petty theft" becomes the felony of grand theft when a theft exceeds a statutory amount, often $500 to $1000 depending on the state. The term "grand theft auto" signifies the policy in most states to treat theft of a car as felony grand theft regardless of the vehicle's value. The same policy often applies to all motorized vehicles, so that theft of a motorcycle or boat also constitutes grand theft.

In order to convict an offender of grand theft auto, a prosecutor must often prove that the offender:

- took or drove away a motor vehicle
- that belonged to someone else

- with the intent to permanently deprive the owner of the vehicle.

The crime of grand theft auto can be carried out in many ways. For example, a thief might break into a parked car, hotwire it, and drive it away, or drive off in a car that the owner left momentarily with the motor running.

> **EXAMPLE:** Sally buys a "junker" as a surprise gift for her son Al, who loves to work on old cars. Before Sally can give him the car, a thief steals it and sells it to a "chop shop" for parts. The thief has committed felony grand theft auto, even if the state's general grand theft law provides that a theft must involve more than $500 to constitute a felony. It does not matter that the thief did not keep the car, because selling it to the chop shop permanently deprived Sally and Al of the vehicle.

What is reckless driving?

Reckless driving is often defined as driving that demonstrates "willful or wanton disregard for the safety of others." For example, a motorist might be given an ordinary ticket for exceeding the speed limit on a freeway by 10 m.p.h. But the motorist might be charged with reckless driving for exceeding the speed limit by 25 m.p.h. and weaving in and out of lanes. Reckless driving is usually a misdemeanor, but a felony charge might result if reckless driving results in significant property damage or physical injuries.

Narcotics Offenses

Federal and state laws criminalize a wide variety of drug-related crimes. Laws often refer to drugs as "controlled substances." A variety of "schedules" may group drugs according to their chemical properties; the seriousness of a drug charge can vary according to the schedule the drug is a part of.

A common defense in drug cases has to do with the legality of the search that led to police officers seizing the drugs—for a discussion of search and seizure laws and procedures, see Chapter 2.

Many jurisdictions have created drug courts that have developed alternatives to jail, especially for first-time offenders.

The sections below identify common types of drug-related crimes.

What is possession of paraphernalia?

The use of illegal drugs often involves paraphernalia such as syringes, pipes, and bongs. Possession of drug-related paraphernalia is often itself a crime.

What is drug possession?

Drug possession laws typically distinguish between "simple possession" and "possession for sale or distribution." Simple possession laws apply to offenders who possess illegal drugs such as marijuana, methamphetamine, cocaine, and heroin for personal use. Some states, though, have decriminalized possession of small quantities of marijuana. The federal government, on the other hand, has not.

Simple possession is often a misdemeanor. Felony charges for possession for sale or distribution result when police officers uncover a large quantity of illegal drugs, often accompanied by non-narcotic "drug cutting" substances and packaging materials such as baggies. Possession-for-sale charges can result even when the police find a small amount of drugs, as where they also find items like scales and packaging materials.

What is drug cultivation?

Marijuana is the most common privately cultivated illegal drug. While most states continue to criminalize cultivation of marijuana, some states allow cultivation of small quantities of marijuana for personal or medical use. Federal laws, however, criminalize the cultivation of marijuana, creating potential conflicts between federal and state drug laws.

What is drug trafficking?

Drug trafficking is normally a felony that involves either the importation of illegal drugs into the United States from another country or the shipment of illegal drugs from one state to another. Trafficking is one of the most serious forms of illegal drug activity; conviction may result in several years in prison.

What is being under the influence?

"Under the influence" laws punish offenders whose consumption of illegal (and sometimes legal) drugs make them a danger to themselves or others. "Drunk in public" laws are low-level offenses that allow police officers to remove inebriated persons from streets and other public places, often for their own safety. "Under the influence" offenses become far more serious offenses when inebriated drivers operate motor vehicles.

Burglary

Burglary laws generally protect homes, businesses, and personal safety.

What is burglary?

Burglary laws protect buildings. A burglary generally occurs when a culprit:

- breaks into and
- enters
- a building
- without consent, and
- with the intent to commit a felony or to steal property, even if the theft itself would only be a misdemeanor.

In Burglary Laws, Buildings Are Not Just Residences

In early common law days, the burglary laws applied only to homes—and then only if the burglary occurred at night. Burglary laws now extend to almost all kinds of structures, even portable ones like cars, boats, and mobile homes. Shops, barns, stables, and outhouses are some of the other structures covered by modern burglary laws. And, burglaries committed in broad daylight are now also considered criminal.

Burglary is thus a specific intent crime. What distinguishes the felony of burglary from less serious misdemeanors (such as trespassing) is that the prosecution in a burglary case has to prove that a defendant intended to commit a felony or theft inside a building at the very moment that the defendant entered it.

> **EXAMPLE:** Phil O'Nee is charged with burglary. The prosecution claims that Phil, wanting an engagement ring for his girlfriend, broke into a department store. Once inside, it was dark. Phil got scared and decided he'd just grab a bottle of perfume from the cosmetics area. He would give that to his girlfriend in the meantime, until he could get a ring. Phil admits taking the perfume, and asks the judge to convict him only of petty theft, a misdemeanor. If the prosecution proves that Phil intended to steal expensive jewelry when he broke into the store, Phil can be convicted of burglary (in addition to petty theft for stealing the perfume). One way the prosecution might prove Phil's intent to commit the felony of theft is to have a friend testify that Phil told him the week before the incident that Phil could not afford to buy an engagement ring so planned to steal one to surprise his girlfriend.

Does burglary require a forcible breaking and entry?

No. Years ago burglary laws were more rigid, and they required the government to prove that a defendant forced open a door, a window, or some other part of a building to gain entry. Now, going into a building without consent through an open window or an unlocked door constitutes a break and entry for purposes of almost all burglary statutes. Even a partial entry can constitute a burglary. For example, assume that the police arrest a suspect just as the suspect reaches her arm through an open window. If the other requirements are met, one arm in is sufficient entry to constitute a burglary.

Do degrees of burglary exist?

Yes. The danger of physical injury is greatest when a burglar enters an inhabited building, so, in many states, this constitutes first-degree burglary. Under some statutes, entry at night rather than in the daytime also constitutes first-degree burglary, regardless of whether the building is inhabited.

Any Felony Will Often Do for Burglary

The term "burglary" probably calls to mind a masked crook with a sack breaking into a residence and stealing personal property. In reality, the crime of burglary is broader than that. Entry into a building with the specific intent to commit any type of felony crime often satisfies burglary laws. For instance, a suspect may enter a building with the intent to burn it down or molest a child. Both are sufficient for burglary. This is why chronic petty thieves often end up with burglary convictions. By following their usual m.o. (*modus operandi*, or method of committing the crime), they make it easy for prosecutors to prove that they entered a shop with the intent to steal.

Is it a burglary if a person enters a building intending to commit a crime, but is arrested or scared off before the crime can take place?

Yes. With burglary, the key moment is the offender's entrance into a building. If, at that moment, the burglar intends to commit a felony or steal property inside the building, a burglary has taken place even if no other crime actually takes place. On the other hand, it isn't burglary (although it may be another crime) if a culprit first decides to commit a crime only after entering a building.

EXAMPLE: Klaus Santo enters the home of his ex-wife Wilma by climbing down her chimney. Santo has previously threatened to harm his wife, and he has a tire iron protruding from his back pocket. Wilma hears Santo coming, runs to a neighbor's house, and calls the police. The police arrest Santo as he tries to run away through the back door. Santo committed a burglary. He entered Wilma's house without consent. The prior threats and the tire iron in his back pocket are circumstantial evidence showing that at the moment Santo entered her house, he intended to attack Wilma with a deadly weapon.

EXAMPLE: Same case, except assume that Santo offers evidence at trial that when he came down Wilma's chimney, he'd been drinking heavily for three days and was too drunk to understand what he was doing. In some states, Santo's evidence would constitute a partial defense to a burglary charge. To be convicted of burglary, Santo must have had a specific intent to commit a felony. Some states would allow Santo to claim that he was so intoxicated that he was unable to form the required specific intent. The defense would be a partial one because Santo could still be convicted of the lesser crime of breaking into Wilma's home. (For more on the intoxication defense, see Chapter 13.)

EXAMPLE: Same case, except assume that Santo and Wilma are high school classmates on the eve of graduation. As a prank, Santo climbs down a chimney in Wilma's house, toilet papers the inside of Wilma's house, and leaves by the front door. Santo has not committed a burglary because his actions show that he did not enter Wilma's house with the intent to commit a felony or steal property. Nevertheless, Santo could be charged with less serious crimes, such as trespassing or, if he did some damage, malicious mischief.

Can possession of stolen items support a burglary conviction?

Yes. Even in the absence of an eyewitness identification, it is possible for the prosecution to offer enough circumstantial evidence to prove that a particular person broke into a house. As a fallback, a prosecutor might try to secure a conviction of the suspect for possession of stolen property.

EXAMPLE: Goldie Locks returns to her apartment one afternoon to find that her front door has been forced open. A number of items are missing, including Goldie's favorite chair that had been left to her by her great-aunt. Three weeks later, the police arrest Bear Withus on drug charges. Inside Bear's house, the police find Goldie's chair. In response to police questions, Bear claims that the chair had been given to him years earlier by a friend whose name he cannot remember. The circumstantial evidence (including Bear's false story to the police as to how and when he acquired the chair) could suggest that it was Bear who entered Goldie's apartment without permission and committed a theft once inside. Depending on all the evidence, Bear could be convicted of burglary.

Robbery

As explained below, robbery is a violent and serious felony.

What is robbery?

Robbery is a crime of both theft and violence. It consists of using force or fear to take personal property directly and permanently from another person. A classic and all-too-common example of robbery is the holdup of a convenience store. A robber pulls a gun (thus using force or fear, even if it's unloaded or a toy gun) and demands money from the clerk. Purse snatching can also constitute robbery if the victim is confronted by the robber.

EXAMPLE: Opper Tunist comes upon a person lying on the pavement, apparently passed out from the effects of alcohol. Seeing no one else around, Opper removes the wallet from the sleeper's pocket and runs away. Opper has not committed robbery, because he didn't use means of force or fear. Opper did, however, commit the crime of theft or larceny (taking the sleeper's property without permission).

Is robbery a specific intent crime?

Yes. Robbery is a type of theft, and as is often true with theft crimes, the government has to prove that a robber took property with the intent to forever deprive the victim of the stolen property.

How can the government prove that a thief intended to permanently deprive a victim of stolen property?

A prosecutor typically relies on circumstantial evidence to prove intent, as is true for other crimes that require proof of knowledge and other state of mind elements that can't be directly proven. In other words, a prosecutor asks a judge or jury to use common sense to infer a thief's intent from the circumstances under which property was stolen.

> **EXAMPLE:** Cal Lechter accosts Cora Spondent outside a baseball card show, believing that Cora had just bought the "Puddinhead Jones" card that Lechter wants for his collection. Lechter points a gun at Cora and says, "Give me the cards you just bought." Cora complies. Lechter flips through the cards, then asks, "Where's the Puddinhead Jones card?" Cora replies, "I don't know what you're talking about. I don't have it." Lechter then throws the cards to the ground in disgust and runs off. Lechter can be convicted of robbery because he took Cora's cards by means of force or fear, and the circumstances suggest that at the time he took the cards, he intended to permanently deprive Cora of the Puddinhead Jones card had Cora bought it.

Do degrees of robbery exist?

Yes. In some states, first-degree robbery consists of a robbery committed inside a residence, or against certain classes of people, such as taxicab drivers or passengers. Other robberies are second-degree robberies.

Theft

This section covers theft, the crime of taking personal property.

What is theft?

Theft (or larceny) is an umbrella term that applies to various methods of stealing personal property with the specific intent to permanently deprive the victim of possession. (Theft laws generally don't apply to land, because land can't be carried off. Of course, other laws protect landowners who are swindled out of their property.) In addition to the standard form of theft (that is, simply carrying off someone else's property), two other common forms of theft are:

- embezzlement, in which an employee or other personal representative diverts money or property intended for the employer or principal to his or her own personal use, and
- fraud (or false pretenses), which typically occurs when a thief tricks a victim into voluntarily handing over money or property.

EXAMPLE: Joy Rider sees a new Lexus parked on a residential street. The doors are unlocked and the keys are in the ignition. Never having driven a Lexus, Joy impulsively gets behind the wheel. Joy drives around for about ten minutes and leaves the car a block away from where she found it. Joy is probably not guilty of car theft. Because Joy returned the car close to where she found it only a short time after taking it, she probably lacked the intent to permanently deprive the victim of the car. Most states have enacted a less serious crime of joyriding (or operating a vehicle without the owner's consent) to cover these types of situations.

EXAMPLE: N.V. Uss is furious to learn that his ex-girlfriend has become engaged to another man. One day, Uss sees his ex-girlfriend sitting at a table in a restaurant, showing her engagement ring to a companion. Uss rushes up to the table, grabs the ring, runs outside and throws the ring into a sewer pipe. The ring is never found. Uss is guilty of theft of the ring. The fact that Uss did not keep the ring for himself is irrelevant. The gist of theft is permanently depriving a victim of the property that was stolen. Because Uss's actions suggest that he intended for his ex-girlfriend to do without the ring permanently, Uss is guilty of theft (and probably robbery as well because he took the ring directly from the victim).

EXAMPLE: Em Bezzler works behind the counter at an ice cream shop. Over a period of weeks, Em pocketed part of the money that customers gave her. Em hid her activities from the shop owner by failing to ring up some ice cream sales. Finally, the shop owner catches on, fires Em, and starts to call the police. Em immediately offers to return all the money that she took, with interest. Even if Em fully pays back the shop owner, she is guilty of embezzlement. Returning stolen property may count in a defendant's favor at the time of sentencing, but it is no defense to a theft or embezzlement charge. Em is guilty of theft because the circumstances suggest that she intended to permanently deprive the shop owner of the money at the time she took it.

What is the difference between grand theft and petty theft?

Theft can be grand theft and, therefore, more serious, for a variety of reasons. (Some states differentiate between theft offenses with degrees rather than with the "grand" and "petty" terminology.) Laws in many states deem a theft to be grand theft when:

- The property taken is worth more than a minimum amount, likely between $500-$1,000, depending on the state.
- Property is taken directly from a person, but by means other than force or fear. (If force or fear were used, the crime would be robbery.) An example would be picking the pocket of an unsuspecting victim.
- Particular types of property are taken. For example, the theft of cars and some types of animals is often grand theft regardless of their actual market value.

A theft that does not qualify as a grand theft is often considered petty theft.

CAUTION

"Petty with a prior" can be grand theft. A prior conviction for petty theft can elevate a second charge of petty theft from a misdemeanor to felony grand theft. If the prosecution intends to use the prior conviction as the basis for a more serious charge, the complaint or information must refer to the prior conviction. A prosecutor might also elevate a petty theft charge to a felony by charging the culprit with burglary, alleging that the culprit entered a shop with the intent to steal merchandise.

Is it theft for one who finds lost property to keep it?

Keeping lost property can qualify as theft if the finder could reasonably return the property to its owner. For example, if Sue is bicycling along a deserted lane and sees a $100 bill floating on a puddle next to the curb, Sue would not be guilty of theft if she kept it. However, it's different if Sue sees Charles drop a $100 bill as he is getting out of a car. Charles is unaware that he has dropped the money and begins to walk away. If Sue rides over, picks up the $100 bill and keeps it, Sue has likely committed theft because she knows that the money belongs to Charles, and she has a reasonable opportunity to return it to him. From a legal standpoint, Sue's keeping the money when she could easily return it to its rightful owner is what is known as a "constructive" taking.

Is it theft to steal property from a thief who has previously stolen it?

Yes. Theft is illegal even if the person from whom property is stolen had no right to the property in the first place. This rule is necessary to prevent successive thieves from taking the same property with no fear of punishment.

Is it theft to steal contraband such as illegal drugs or weapons?

Yes. Stealing contraband is illegal, even though the victim of the theft had no right to possess the property in the first place. Again, the rationale is to deter the act of theft, no matter what the character of the stolen property.

Is it illegal to buy or keep stolen property?

Yes. This crime is popularly known as receiving stolen goods. To convict a defendant of receiving stolen goods, the government has to prove that property in the defendant's possession was stolen, and that the defendant acquired the property knowing that it was stolen. As is typical when a statute requires proof of knowledge and other state of mind elements, the government usually has to rely on circumstantial evidence to try to prove a defendant's knowledge that property was stolen. Usually, the government's case relies on evidence that would have alerted any reasonable person that the items were "hot."

EXAMPLE: Hu Gnu is an avid collector of rock-and-roll memorabilia, and he subscribes to a number of websites devoted to such items. A few days after a theft of rock-and-roll items from a museum is widely reported on TV and in newspapers in Hu's hometown, Hu receives an email message offering to sell a collection of Beatles memorabilia at a very low price. The seller claims that a quick sale is necessary because the seller has suffered a number of business losses. In fact, the Beatles items were stolen from the museum. Hu buys the Beatles items. Circumstantial evidence suggests that Hu knew that he was buying "hot" merchandise. Hu is an experienced collector, the prices were very low, and the offer came on the heels of a widely reported museum theft. Hu is likely guilty of receiving stolen property.

EXAMPLE: Luke Otherway owns Pawn City and is in the business of lending money in exchange for taking possession of personal property. Rose Anfell is known to Luke as a drug user who often sleeps in the doorways of Pawn City and other shops. One day Rose brings two diamond rings into Pawn City, tells Luke that they were left to her by a distant relative, and asks to pawn them. Luke gives Rose $2,000 in exchange for the rings. Two days later, the police examine the rings and identify them as two of the rings stolen from a jewelry store the day before Rose brought the rings into Pawn City. Laws in many states obligate professional dealers in secondhand goods to investigate suspicious deals. Here, a woman known to Luke to be homeless and a drug user suddenly turns up in possession of two diamond rings and a fishy story about how she got them. Even though Luke did not actually know that the rings were stolen, and may not even have known about the jewelry store theft, the circumstances strongly suggested the possibility that the rings were stolen. As a pawnshop owner who failed to investigate how Rose got the rings, Luke is likely to be convicted of receiving stolen property.

Hate Crimes

Hate crime laws punish those who commit crimes against people who belong to distinct social groups that legislators have found to warrant special protection.

Do hate crime laws make it a crime to hate?

No. Hatred may be lamentable, but it is not against the law to have a mental attitude of hate towards specific people or groups. Moreover, in many circumstances, the First Amendment to the U.S. Constitution prevents punishment for expressing hatred toward specific individuals or social groups.

What is a hate crime?

While hate crime laws may vary from one state to another, in general, a hate crime occurs when an illegal act is committed because of a victim's race, color, religion, ancestry, national origin, disability, gender, or sexual orientation. (We'll call this "hate crime intent" or "hate crime purpose" in this section so as not to have to repeatedly refer to every possible illegal purpose.) This does not mean that every crime committed against a victim who belongs to one of the groups identified by a hate crime law is a hate crime. A hate crime occurs when an illegal act is committed *because* a victim belongs to one of the groups identified in a hate crime law.

> **EXAMPLE:** While an accomplice asks Jesse for directions, Fingers Malloy removes the wallet from Jesse's rear pocket and tries to run away. However, Fingers is captured less than a block away. Jesse immigrated to this country from Samoa about three years earlier. No evidence suggests that Fingers committed the crime because Jesse is from Samoa. Fingers may be guilty of theft, but he is not guilty of a hate crime.

> **EXAMPLE:** Same case as above, except that the prosecution offers evidence that Fingers intentionally singled out Jesse as a victim because Jesse came to this country from Samoa. Fingers can now be convicted of a hate crime.

What is the purpose of hate crime laws?

Hate crime laws seek to protect people who belong to groups that have frequently been the target of illegal acts. Hate crime laws also send a message that targeting these victims because of their status (for example, as gays or women or Muslims) is antithetical to maintaining a free and pluralistic society.

Are there different types of hate crime laws?

Yes. One form of hate crime law defines a type of illegal conduct that is punishable in and of itself. For example, interfering with a person's civil rights with a hate crime intent may itself be a crime, regardless of whether the perpetrator violates any other criminal laws. Thus, just as the crime of murder is distinct from that of theft, so may a hate crime be a separately defined crime.

A second form of hate crime law increases the punishment of those who commit other crimes with a hate crime purpose. For example, a crime that is ordinarily a misdemeanor may become a felony if a perpetrator commits it with a hate crime intent. Similarly, a felony that is ordinarily punishable by up to five years in state prison may become punishable by up to eight years in state prison if a perpetrator commits it with a hate crime intent.

Hate crime laws have been challenged by defendants on the ground that they violate their free speech rights, but thus far courts have generally upheld and enforced them. (For an example, see *Wisconsin v. Mitchell*, U.S. Sup. Ct. 1993.)

> **EXAMPLE:** The prosecution proves that Damian, a Caucasian ex-convict, fired several shots through the window of a neighbor's home that is owned by an African American family. Damian fired the shots into the home because the family was African American and Damian wanted to intimidate the owners into selling their home and moving out of the neighborhood. Damian may be convicted of committing a hate crime, because he attempted to interfere with an African American's right to own a home and did so because the family was African

American. Damian might also be convicted of the separate crimes of assault with a deadly weapon and being an ex-convict in possession of a firearm, and his sentence for committing these crimes may be increased because he committed them with a hate crime intent. (Even if Damian were convicted of three separate crimes, he would probably not have to serve separate sentences for each crime because he committed only a single illegal act. Another way to say this is that he would serve all the sentences concurrently.)

Who decides whether a defendant had the intent to commit a hate crime?

At trial, a defendant may be convicted of committing a hate crime only if the prosecutor proves beyond a reasonable doubt that an illegal act was committed with a hate crime intent. It is up to the jury, not the judge, to decide whether the defendant acted with a hate crime purpose. (*Apprendi v. New Jersey*, U.S. Sup. Ct. 2000.)

Proving that a defendant acted with a hate crime purpose can be difficult. A prosecutor normally must find and offer evidence that the defendant committed the illegal act because the victim belongs to a group identified in a hate crime law. The evidence might consist of a statement made by a defendant. For example, to show that an act is a hate crime because it was committed against a gay man, a prosecutor may offer evidence that a defendant told a friend something like, "I plan to attack the next person I see who is homosexual." Or, the prosecutor may offer evidence that a defendant committed a series of illegal acts against different victims, each of whom were members of an ethnic minority group identified in a hate crime law.

EXAMPLE: In July 2019, 19-year-old Santino Legan broke into the Gilroy Garlic Festival and used an assault rifle to kill three people and wound about a dozen others. Police officers killed Legan. Though no prosecution ensued, in the days following the tragic events police officers tried to understand whether Legan had committed hate crimes. Police officers interviewed people who knew Legan, brought in profilers, and combed through Legan's postings on social media sites.

White-Collar Crimes

The term "white-collar crime" usually refers to a type of complex crime in which a criminal doesn't use weapons, but instead uses computers, financial statements, and the trust of his or her victims to steal property. Offenders are often bankers, businesspeople, doctors, lawyers, and other professionals; hence the term "white collar." However, white-collar criminals may occupy any social position. Many modern computer-related white-collar crimes are even committed by juveniles.

What are some examples of white-collar crimes?

Common white-collar crimes include the following:

- **Securities fraud.** Example: Megafoods Inc. induces people to overpay for shares of its stock by concealing information that it has been losing money.

The Martha Stewart "Insider Trading" Case

Martha Stewart (famous for her TV shows and magazines devoted to decorating and food) was convicted of crimes related to insider trading in March 2004. Stewart had sold all of her stock in a company called ImClone Systems the day before ImClone publicly announced that it was virtually worthless. Stewart denied to government agents that she sold her stock based on a tip from ImClone's president. The government offered plenty of evidence that she had been tipped off in advance to ImClone's problems, and a jury convicted Stewart of obstruction of justice. ImClone's president had earlier pleaded guilty to insider trading and was sentenced to prison.

• **Insider trading.** Example 1: Megafoods' corporate officers find out that the government is going to file a huge lawsuit against the company the next day. They sell their shares of stock in Megafoods immediately, before the general public can find out about the lawsuit and drive the value of the shares way down. Example 2: During a round of golf, a Megabank executive tells Jones that Megabank is about to acquire Local Bank. Jones buys shares in Local Bank before Megabank publicly announces the acquisition, and sells the Local Bank shares a few months later for a large profit. Jones is guilty of insider trading. He bought and sold stock based on private information, and it is reasonable to conclude that the bank executive expected to receive a personal benefit from Jones in exchange for the tip—if not immediately, then in the future.

• **Credit card fraud.** Example: Jim runs up thousands of dollars in credit card charges, knowing that he cannot pay them back.

• **Bankruptcy fraud.** Example: Barbara runs up huge debts with the intention of declaring bankruptcy so that she will not have to pay back her creditors.

• **Telemarketing fraud.** Example: Bob phones people and solicits charitable donations, even though Bob keeps most of the money he collects for himself.

• **Embezzlement.** Example: Sally, an accountant working for Megafoods, underreports the money that the company has earned and puts the difference in her private bank account.

• **Money laundering.** Example: A husband and wife finance their bakery business with the money they earn by selling illegal drugs.

• **Home repair fraud.** Example: A repairman convinces a senior citizen that the roof of her house is about to collapse, takes a large down payment for materials, then is never seen again.

Based on information that white-collar criminals often carry out their schemes by sending out unsolicited electronic mail messages (a type of email popularly called "spam"), Congress enacted a new law in 2003—the "Controlling Assault of Non-Solicited Pornography and Marketing Act"—that severely punishes offenders who use spam to commit crimes such as fraud, identity theft, and child pornography.

> **EXAMPLE:** Daniel filed for bankruptcy, but did not list all of his assets on the forms he filed with the court. Concealing assets in bankruptcy proceedings with the intent to defraud creditors is a crime. On the other hand, if Daniel honestly forgot about an asset or did not know he owned it, then his actions may not be criminal.

> **EXAMPLE:** Laurie wanted to look really spiffy for an upcoming high school reunion. Laurie took her friend Taimie's credit card without her permission, went to the mall, and used it to pay for a brand new outfit. Laurie's unauthorized use of Taimie's credit card constitutes theft.

Is it illegal to refuse to pay income taxes?

Yes. Refusing to pay federal income taxes—whether motivated by anti-government attitudes or greed—is illegal. Possible consequences range from civil penalties, including fines and interest, to criminal

---

Concealment Often Results in Harsher Penalties

Individuals and companies suspected of committing white-collar crimes sometimes respond by trying to conceal information. For example, they may destroy records that they think are harmful or instruct employees to lie to government investigators. Frequently, such conduct only "compounds the crime" in various ways:

- To a government investigator or a judge or jury, evidence of concealment is seen as a sign of wrongdoing.
- Hiding information from government investigators may itself constitute a crime. Thus, even if the government can't prove that a white-collar crime had taken place, it may win by proving concealment of the evidence.
- Hiding information often dramatically increases the penalty for engaging in

white-collar crime. Judges may show mercy towards those who admit to wrongdoings and make efforts to make up for the harm they've caused. However, those who do everything they can to conceal their misdeeds are likely to face harsh criminal and civil penalties. They are also likely to suffer in the "court of public opinion." For example, Arthur Anderson was once one of the biggest accounting firms in the world. Faced with charges that it helped a company, Enron, produce false business statements, many of Arthur Anderson's managers ordered the destruction of records. The destruction came to light, and Arthur Anderson lost so much credibility with the public that it dissolved virtually overnight.

prosecution, and—in rare cases—jail time. There has been a long history of refusal to pay federal income taxes as a form of civil disobedience, dating back to Henry David Thoreau. The Vietnam War and attempts to build a border wall also led some to refuse to pay such taxes. In every era, the IRS and courts have consistently rejected as frivolous any arguments based on a taxpayer's asserted right to refuse to pay taxes.

Is white-collar crime often more difficult to detect and prove than violent "street crimes"?

Yes. White-collar crime often takes place noiselessly in private offices rather than out in public. The offenders are often educated and sophisticated, and they try to conceal their crimes in secret computer files, complex financial reports, offshore bank accounts, and the like. Thus, the "cop on the beat" is unlikely to uncover evidence of white-collar crime. Instead, detection of white-collar crime is often the domain of state and federal agencies that employ private (and often undercover) investigators, lawyers, accountants, and professionals. Also, the government hopes that "whistleblowers" will come forward to report their own organizations' misdeeds.

Can a corporation be guilty of committing a white-collar crime?

Yes. A corporation as well as its employees can be guilty of a crime. Of course, a corporation cannot be put in prison. However, corporations can be ordered to pay fines and provide restitution (payments to crime victims).

> ### Encouraging and Protecting "Whistleblowers"
>
> Whistleblowers are employees who report wrongdoing by the private businesses or government agencies for which they work. Whistleblowers often take the risk that their willingness to report on their colleagues' misdeeds will cause them to lose their jobs and be blacklisted from future jobs. However, they perform a valuable function, because as insiders they are privy to information that the government could not otherwise find out about.
>
> A federal law known as the False Claims Act, like similar laws in many states, encourages whistleblowing by providing that whistleblowers may be entitled to a portion of the money that white-collar criminals are ordered to pay to the government. False claims acts also protect whistleblowers from being fired for reporting illegal or fraudulent activities.

Do white-collar criminals "get off easy" compared to people who commit other types of crime?

A general perception exists that the punishment white-collar criminals tend to receive does not adequately reflect the harm they cause and the public trust they abuse. However, the accuracy of this perception is debatable. First, many white-collar criminals have received jail time in recent years, including: Bernard Madoff (150-year sentence for operating a long-term Ponzi scheme); Bernard Ebbers, former CEO of WorldCom (25 years); Martha Stewart; Timothy and John Rigas of Adelphia; and Enron's Andrew Fastow. Second, a seemingly light prison sentence may reflect an offender's willingness to make restitution to fraud victims. Because complex white-collar schemes can be difficult for the government to prove in court, a light sentence may also reflect an offender's willingness to provide information that enables the government to arrest others and prosecute them successfully.

> **EXAMPLE:** Don, a medical doctor, runs a busy clinic where he sees lots of patients. In order to see Medicare patients while earning what he considers to be an acceptable income, Don occasionally instructs his office manager, Mary, to bill Medicare: for more expensive tests than those he has actually performed; for services at his hourly rate even when patients were seen only by Nancy, his office nurse; and for reviewing X-rays that were already reviewed by a radiologist. Unbeknownst to Don, Mary falsified information when applying for Don's office to become a qualified Medicare provider. Nancy found out that the office overbills Medicare for services, but she likes her job so she plays along and keeps her mouth shut. Don and Mary both committed numerous acts of Medicare fraud and are subject to a fine and/or imprisonment. Don could also lose his license to practice medicine. Nancy did not commit a crime by failing to report Don's and Mary's misdeeds.
>
> If Nancy had instead reported Don and Mary to the government as soon as she learned of the fraud, and Don and Mary were found

guilty and required to pay fines, Nancy might have been entitled to a portion of the money. Moreover, Don and Mary could be ordered not to retaliate by harassing or firing Nancy.

On the other hand, if Nancy lies about what she knows to a Medicare or other government investigator, she might be guilty of the crimes of obstruction of justice or lying to federal authorities. Nancy might then be fined and might also lose her nursing license.

 RESOURCES
For more information on the False Claims Act. For an employee who suspects that other people in a company are violating the law, the following references can help:

- Taxpayers Against Fraud (www.taf.org)
- *The New Whistleblower's Handbook*, by Stephen Kohn, and
- *Civil False Claims and Qui Tam Actions*, by John T. Boese.

Also, a state's department of justice should have information on whether the state has a false claims act or equivalent law.

Are white-collar crimes more likely than crimes of violence to lead to civil lawsuits?

Yes. Perpetrators of white-collar crimes are more likely than violent criminals to have substantial assets. Thus, victims of white-collar crimes may have a good chance of collecting on the judgments they obtain in civil lawsuits. By contrast, violent criminals are often "judgment proof." They have so few assets that a civil judgment obtained by a crime victim is likely to be worthless.

How can targets of government investigations into fraud claims protect themselves?

People who think that they might be the target of a white-collar crime investigation should hire a lawyer with experience in these types of cases. White-collar crime investigations can be lengthy and complex. An investigation may involve requests for business and personal records that government officials are not entitled to obtain without a court order. In addition, white-collar offenses may lead to the government filing either civil or criminal charges, so laypeople usually need the help of experienced lawyers to know where they stand. Finally, government prosecutors may offer various forms of immunity in exchange for information, and potential targets of an investigation will likely need help to understand how to protect their interests during immunity negotiations.

How can consumers avoid becoming fraud victims?

Most people try to protect themselves from becoming victims of violent crime. For example, they lock the doors of their houses and cars and avoid walking alone at night in unfamiliar neighborhoods.

Consumers should exercise that same level of vigilance to avoid becoming victims of white-collar crime. There are a number of steps people can take, including:

- Realize that a get-rich-quick invest-ment program that sounds "too good to be true" probably is.
- If you are pressured into making a decision by being told that it's "now or never," choose "never."

- Don't be fooled into trusting seemingly friendly, honest-sounding people if you don't know them. Don't make decisions before you've checked their backgrounds and references.
- Don't give solicitors your credit card or Social Security number.
- If you are suspicious, end the dialogue quickly. Then, report what happened to your state's attorney general's or district attorney's office; these offices have consumer fraud divisions. You may also report suspected fraud to the FBI.
- Be wary of suspicious looking emails and be careful about the links you click and websites you visit.

Many community organizations, such as the Better Business Bureau (www.bbb. org) and AARP (www.aarp.org), publish information online about how consumers can avoid becoming fraud victims. Moreover, using keywords like "consumer fraud" will enable Internet users to pull up numerous websites with information on how they can protect themselves against specific types of fraudulent schemes. Among the websites are the Department of Justice's Fraud Section (www.justice.gov/criminal-fraud), the Office for Victims of Crime (www.ovc.gov), and the Directory of Crime Victim Services (https://ovc.ncjrs.gov/findvictimservices).

Also, the National Consumers League's Fraud.org has information on telemarketing, Internet fraud, fraud scams against the elderly, and more.

What is "identity theft"?

Identity theft consists of stealing another person's identifying information—for example, a Social Security number, credit card number, or bank account number—and using that information to take money or make purchases. Identity theft can not only cause direct financial losses, but it may also force victims to spend weeks trying to reestablish credit and their good names. Unless corrected, identity theft can hamper a victim's ability to obtain employment, college loans, or buy a car or home. Examples of identity theft include:

- electronically accessing a victim's computer (perhaps with the aid of "spyware") and then using passwords to access online bank accounts
- sifting through trash (sometimes called "dumpster diving") and finding account numbers on credit card receipts or bank statements
- making phone calls or sending emails to convince people to reveal their Social Security numbers or other data, and
- obtaining personal financial data via a phony email or website made to resemble a legitimate business (known as "phishing").

Identity theft can be a crime of unbelievable cruelty. In one scam, families of soldiers serving overseas were contacted by callers who falsely said that they represented the Red Cross and that they needed the family member's personal identifying information in order to get money to their loved one immediately. Many people were victimized, and the Red Cross responded by publicly announcing that it never asks for personal identifying information by phone.

What can people do if they suspect that their identity has been stolen?

An important resource is the Federal Trade Commission's website (www.identitytheft.gov).

How can people avoid becoming victims of identity theft?

Be familiar with the basic tools of online safety. Use virus protection, firewalls, and other basic safety methods. Change passwords often, don't share them with people, and choose unusual passwords. OnGuard Online (www.onguardonline.gov) is a government site offering information on computer safety.

People should shred bills and statements before throwing them away; any that are kept should be stored in a safe place. People should not give out personal information in response to unsolicited phone calls or emails. To verify the legitimacy of a request for identifying information or money, a local Better Business Bureau office is a good starting point.

Someone who hasn't changed addresses yet receives a "Move Validation Letter" from the post office or isn't getting expected bills should contact the postal service.

People should check their credit reports at least once a year to make sure an identity thief has not used their personal information to get credit. A free copy of a credit report is available annually from each of the three nationwide credit reporting bureaus at www.annualcreditreport.com.

EXAMPLE: Michele, while paying bills, realized that she had not received her monthly bill from the alarm security company. The absence of a bill was a red flag indicating that someone had tampered with Michele's identity. Michele phoned the company and found out that someone had changed the mailing address on her account. She followed up by contacting the Postal Inspection Service and determined that someone had falsely completed a change of address form. Because she acted promptly, Michele was able to correct the problem and was able to get her mail promptly rerouted back to her.

EXAMPLE: Kathi received yet another of those unsolicited "You are preapproved" notices for a new credit card, and she promptly threw it in the trash. She should have shredded the application so that an identity thief could not complete the application in her name.

Can business owners do anything to prevent their customers' identities from being stolen?

Yes. Business owners can lock cabinets in which written records are stored and encrypt electronic data. For other suggestions, consult a booklet on privacy protection published by the Federal Trade Commission (FTC) at www.ftc.gov/tips-advice/business-center/guidance/protecting-personal-information-guide-business.

Where can people find more information about identity theft?

Several government agencies have websites on identity theft, including the:

- Federal Trade Commission (FTC) (www.consumer.ftc.gov/features/feature-0014-identity-theft)
- U.S. Department of Justice (USDOJ) (https://ojp.gov/programs/identity theft.htm)
- Social Security Administration (SSA) (www.ssa.gov/pubs/EN-05-10064.pdf), and
- Consumer Financial Protection Bureau (www.consumerfinance.gov/ask-cfpb/what-is-identity-theft-en-1243).

As noted in the section on general fraud information above, many nongovernment organizations also have helpful information on identity theft prevention and the actions that identity theft victims might take. These include:

- the National Consumer League's Fraud.org
- the Better Business Bureau (www.bbb.org)
- AARP (www.aarp.org)
- the nonprofit Identity Theft Resource Center (www.idtheftcenter.org), and
- the nonprofit Privacy Rights Clearinghouse (www.privacyrights.org).

Common Defenses to Criminal Charges

Defendants have a constitutional right to try to create a reasonable doubt that they are guilty by attacking the prosecution's evidence and presenting evidence of their own. This does not mean that judges have to admit any evidence a defendant might want to offer, however.

For example, judges can exclude defense evidence because it constitutes inadmissible hearsay, because it is speculative, because it is unduly misleading, or because it violates rules of evidence. However, a state cannot arbitrarily take away a defendant's right to present a defense.

While myriad crimes exist, only a limited number of defenses are available. This chapter examines some common ones.

"Due Process" Defenses

In addition to the types of defenses described in this chapter, on rare occasions a court may decide that the Due Process clause in the Fourteenth Amendment to the U.S. Constitution prevents the government from criminalizing certain conduct. For example, the government cannot make it a crime for two adults of the same sex (or opposite sexes, for that matter) to engage in private, intimate sexual conduct. (*Lawrence v. Texas*, U.S. Sup. Ct. 2003.)

Prosecutor's Failure to Prove Guilt

This section covers the most frequently used defense in criminal trials: that the prosecution's evidence fails to prove the defendant's guilt beyond a reasonable doubt.

Why is failure to prove a defendant guilty beyond a reasonable doubt the most common defense argument?

The prosecution's burden of proof is the highest that the legal system imposes on a party to a lawsuit. If the prosecution can't meet its burden, the defendant must be found not guilty. At the same time, the defense has a right to remain silent. The defense often exercises that right to prevent exposure of the defendant's criminal record and to avoid the defendant being cross-examined by the prosecutor. Poking holes in the prosecutor's case is therefore often the best—and least risky—defense strategy available.

Can defendants argue that they are not guilty if they don't testify or call witnesses?

The defendant can sit silently through the entire trial and present no witnesses but still argue that the prosecution case is simply too weak to prove guilt beyond a reasonable doubt. Even if the defense presents no case of its own, the defense can strengthen the not guilty argument by cross-examining prosecution witnesses and poking as many holes in their stories as possible. Taken together, the defense argument goes, the holes create a reasonable doubt as to the defendant's guilt.

At the same time, the absence of a defense case denies the prosecution a target to poke holes at in return, as the prosecution generally is not permitted to comment on the fact that defendant chose to not testify or failed to put on witnesses.

Will They Infer Guilt from Silence?

Defendants have a constitutional right not to testify, and judges and jurors are legally prohibited from taking a defendant's silence as an indication of guilt. However, a risk exists that some jurors may disregard this rule, if only subconsciously. For defense attorneys and their clients, a defendant's decision as to whether to testify or remain silent is often a central tactical concern.

EXAMPLE: Noah Counting is charged with a nighttime burglary. The only evidence of his guilt is an eyewitness who thought she recognized Noah running out of the burglarized house about the time of the crime. Cross-examining this witness, Noah's attorney gets her to admit that she really couldn't be absolutely sure it was Noah. After the prosecution rests (finishes presenting its evidence), the defense must decide whether to put on its case. It can present a witness to testify that Noah and the witness were playing cards at the time of the burglary. However, the prosecution can attack the defense witness's credibility on several grounds. Also, the defense witness is easily rattled when asked questions. The defendant may reasonably decide not to put this witness on the stand. The prosecution eyewitness's testimony is so weak that it is unlikely to persuade a judge or jury of Noah's guilt beyond a reasonable doubt. By presenting its own shaky witness, the defense would risk making the prosecution's case look stronger by comparison.

Motion to Dismiss

A useful defense strategy is to make a motion to dismiss at the close of a shaky prosecution case. If the judge grants the motion, the case is over without the defendant having to choose whether to present evidence and create the risk of inadvertently strengthening the prosecutor's case.

How can the defense poke holes in the testimony of prosecution witnesses?

Cross-examining prosecution witnesses and bringing out weaknesses in their testimony requires skill and preparation. The aim is to undermine the credibility (believability) of the witness. The more the defense undercuts the government witnesses, the more likely it is that the judge or jury will form a reasonable doubt as to the defendant's guilt and be willing to acquit. The following are factors that the defense typically relies on when attempting to cast doubt on prosecution witnesses' testimony.

Bias

A prosecution witness has a motive to harm the defendant, and therefore is lying or grossly exaggerating.

> **EXAMPLE:** "You're making this up to get back at the defendant for firing you from your job, aren't you?"

Limited opportunity to observe

A prosecution witness's observations are mistaken because the lighting was bad, the witness was under the influence of drugs or alcohol, the witness was too far away, or for some other reason the witness may not have seen or heard things clearly.

> **EXAMPLE:** "You only got a side view of the robber from across the street, correct? And you'd drunk three beers in the hour before you saw the robbery, right?"

Faulty police methods

Evidence from police laboratories is unreliable because machines were not properly maintained, technicians were not properly trained, evidence was not carefully collected or stored, and so on.

> **EXAMPLE:** "You personally have no idea whether the Breathalyzer machine was operating properly, right?" "Lots of spectators were wandering in and out of the house while you were gathering evidence, weren't they?"

A prosecution witness cuts a deal

A prosecution witness lies to curry favor with the prosecution to get a good deal on criminal charges the witness is facing.

> **EXAMPLE:** "You're hoping to stay out of jail by testifying against the defendant, right?"

Implausible story

A prosecution witness's story is not believable (that is, it flies in the face of common experience).

> **EXAMPLE:** "Your reason for being out on the street at 3 a.m. is that you suddenly remembered you had to return a library book?"

Inconsistencies

A prosecution witness's story is unworthy of belief because it has changed over time.

> **EXAMPLE:** "Right after the robbery you told the police that the robber had no facial marks, right? But today you've testified that the robber had a scar on his right cheek, right?"

Of course, it is not always possible for the defense to find significant weaknesses in a prosecution witness's testimony. And the presence of a weakness or two does not automatically mean that the judge or jury will disbelieve the prosecution witness. However, confining the defense case to attacking the credibility of prosecution witnesses on cross-examination (for example, by showing that the witness has a conviction for a crime involving dishonesty), and then arguing reasonable doubt, is a frequent defense strategy.

Can defendants use the "weak case" argument if they testify or call witnesses?

Yes. Even when defendants testify or call witnesses, they typically still rely on the argument that the prosecution has failed to prove guilt beyond a reasonable doubt. It's important for defendants to realize that even when they present evidence, they usually are not legally obligated to convince the judge or jury that the defense story is accurate. The burden of proving guilt rests at all times on the prosecutor. As defense attorneys frequently remind judges and jurors, "It's not up to us to convince you that the defendant is innocent. The defendant is presumed innocent, and the burden remains on the prosecution to convince you beyond a reasonable doubt of guilt."

Can a defendant try to create a reasonable doubt by introducing evidence that someone else committed the charged crime?

Yes. A defendant can offer evidence that someone else committed the charged crime. However, in order to prevent defendants from "blowing smoke" by throwing blame at numerous possible suspects, evidence of third-party guilt is typically admissible only if the trial judge believes that the defendant's evidence is sufficient to raise a reasonable doubt about the defendant's guilt. Before they can offer evidence of third-party guilt, defendants generally have to produce evidence linking the third party to the crime. Rumors that the third party committed the charged crime, or even evidence that a third party had a motive to commit the crime, is not enough to create a reasonable doubt about the defendant's guilt.

Keeping the Jury's Attention Focused on the Prosecution's Weak Case

Sometimes, defense attorneys decide not to call witnesses for fear that jurors will erroneously think that the defense then assumes the burden of proving that its version of events is accurate. The benefits of not presenting a defense case—impressing on jurors the fact that the entire burden of proof is on the prosecution—*may* outweigh the risk that jurors will take the failure to call defense witnesses as evidence of guilt.

Criminal defendants have a constitutional right to present a defense. Therefore, a judge cannot forbid a defendant from offering evidence of third-party guilt simply because the judge believes that the prosecutor has presented an exceptionally strong case. (*Holmes v. South Carolina*, U.S. Sup. Ct. 2006.)

> **EXAMPLE:** Watson is charged with armed robbery. At trial, the victim identifies Watson as the attacker, and the prosecutor offers DNA evidence connecting Watson to the crime. Watson claims that Moriarty committed the robbery. Watson wants to offer evidence that a couple of years ago, Moriarty had claimed that the robbery victim failed to pay off a debt she owed him. At that time, Moriarty swore, "I'll get even with her if it's the last thing I do." However, the judge would not allow Watson to offer

the evidence about Moriarty. Watson's evidence shows that Moriarty may have had a motive to rob the victim, but does not otherwise connect Moriarty to the crime.

EXAMPLE: In the same case, in addition to offering the evidence above, Watson also wants to offer evidence from an eyewitness that Moriarty ran out of the victim's house carrying a gun around the time the robbery was committed. Watson's evidence not only shows that Moriarty had a motive to commit the crime, but also ties Moriarty directly to the crime scene. The evidence is admissible because it is sufficient to raise a reasonable doubt about Watson's guilt.

"Scotch Verdicts"

Juries in Scottish criminal trials have a choice of three verdicts: guilty (or "proven"), not proven, and not guilty. While the latter two verdicts both result in acquittal, the not proven verdict implies that while a defendant may be guilty, the prosecution failed to offer sufficient proof. A not guilty verdict allows Scottish jurors to signal their belief that a defendant is factually innocent. By contrast, U.S. juries have no way to declare a belief that a defendant is innocent. In the United States, every not guilty verdict leaves open the possibility that the jury believed that a defendant may be guilty but that the prosecution failed to offer sufficient proof.

"Partial" Defenses

The partial defenses covered in this section do not entirely acquit a defendant, but they reduce the seriousness of a conviction.

At the end of a trial, are the only options conviction and acquittal of the charged crime?

Not necessarily. Defendants may go to trial expecting to be convicted of something, and aim for conviction of a less serious crime than the one they're charged with. Conviction of lesser crimes is often a possibility because for most crimes, the prosecution has to prove a number of discrete elements. These elements are like building blocks. If the defendant can create reasonable doubt about a necessary block in the more serious offense, the defendant may be found guilty only of a lesser crime that requires proof of fewer blocks. When defendants can reasonably argue for lesser charges, they will offer "partial defenses," concentrating their attack on the prosecution's lack of proof for one element, the absence of which converts a serious charge into a lesser crime. For example:

- A defendant charged with the felony of assault with a deadly weapon may argue that the object used in the fight was not a dangerous weapon, and therefore that the evidence at most supports a conviction for simple assault, a misdemeanor.
- A defendant charged with the felony of possession of drugs for sale may argue that the defendant possessed

only a small quantity of drugs, and that therefore the evidence at most supports a conviction of possession of drugs for personal use, a misdemeanor.

- A defendant charged with the felony of car theft may argue that the evidence does not establish that the defendant intended to steal the car but rather supports a conviction for the lesser crime of borrowing the car without permission—that is, joyriding.
- A defendant charged with assault with intent to commit murder may offer evidence that she has a mental impairment that makes her incapable

of forming the intent to kill, and that therefore the evidence supports at most a conviction for the lesser crime of assault with a deadly weapon.

How and when do jurors find out about the possibility of convicting a defendant of a lesser crime?

The defense has two ways of informing jurors about the possibility of convicting the defendant of lesser crimes than what's been charged. One is through argument. At the close of the evidence, the defense argues that, at most, the prosecution's evidence supports conviction for a lesser crime.

The Common Partial Defense of Lack of Intent

In many serious crimes, the prosecution has to prove not only what a defendant did, but also that the defendant acted with a certain mental state, known as intent. For example, assume that the prosecution proves that Smith fired a gun and hit Wesson in the shoulder. Depending on what the prosecution can prove about Smith's intent in firing the gun, Smith may be:

- completely innocent (Smith fired the gun by accident)
- guilty of a minor misdemeanor (Smith fired the gun on purpose but had no way of anticipating that Wesson or any other people were around)
- guilty of assault with intent to commit great bodily injury, a serious felony (Smith was trying to wound but not kill Wesson), or

- guilty of attempted murder (Smith was actually trying to kill Wesson).

Because intent can be so critical to the outcome of a case, defendants often offer partial defenses designed to show that they didn't have the intent required for conviction of the more serious offenses. In one case, for example, a mother was charged with murder when she allegedly failed to secure her infant child in a car seat and then lost control of her car, resulting in the child's death. To prove the mother guilty of murder, the prosecution had to prove that the mother acted with such a high degree of recklessness that she was indifferent to human life, similar to an intent to kill. The jury concluded that the mother did not have that intent and convicted her only of a misdemeanor.

Second, the defense asks the trial judge to include a lesser-crime instruction with the rest of the jury instructions. If the judge agrees that the evidence could support conviction of a lesser crime, the judge may give an instruction along these lines:

"Jurors, Mr. Hatfield (the defendant) is charged with assault with a deadly weapon. To convict Mr. Hatfield of this crime, you must be convinced beyond a reasonable doubt that Mr. Hatfield struck Mr. McCoy with an object that is inherently dangerous to human life. If you are not convinced beyond a reasonable doubt that the object was inherently dangerous to life, then Mr. Hatfield can be guilty at most of the lesser crime of simple assault."

Can defendants argue both that they are not guilty of any crime and that if they are guilty of anything, it's only a lesser crime?

Legally, yes. For example, the defendant can argue, "I hit McCoy in self-defense, and therefore I'm not guilty of anything, but even if you decide that I didn't act in self-defense, you should decide that the object I used, a small stick, was not inherently dangerous to human life. Therefore I cannot be guilty of anything more than simple assault."

This kind of in-the-alternative argument can be hard for jurors to follow. Jurors may also be put off by the defendant's morally ambiguous argument that "I didn't do it, but if I did, it wasn't as bad as they say." Experienced defense attorneys often stick with what they consider the stronger argument rather than risk alienating or confusing the jury.

EXAMPLE: Harley Quinn is charged with armed robbery. Quinn can argue that the prosecution's evidence is too weak to prove beyond a reasonable doubt that the robber had a weapon. Quinn can also argue that he was not the robber, because he was out of town at the time it took place. The alibi defense is logically possible so long as Quinn doesn't claim any firsthand knowledge of the robbery.

Does the judge always have to instruct jurors about possible lesser crimes?

No. A judge will not give a lesser crime instruction unless the evidence supports the possibility that the defendant is guilty of a lesser crime. If a judge refuses to instruct on a lesser crime, then the defendant cannot argue it to a jury.

EXAMPLE: Dr. Crippin is charged with murdering her husband by drowning him in a bathtub. Dr. Crippin does not deny that her husband was intentionally murdered, but claims to have been out of town at the time the murder was committed. The defense story gives the jury only two choices: either Dr. Crippin committed the murder or someone else did. No evidence exists to support conviction of a lesser crime such as manslaughter, so the judge will not instruct the jurors about it.

Is it always in a defendant's interest for the judge to instruct the jury about a lesser crime?

No. Defendants are sometimes better off not having jurors consider the possibility of convicting them of a lesser crime. For example, assume that jurors are uncertain whether a defendant is guilty of a serious charge, and have the option of convicting the defendant of a lesser crime. After wrangling with the issue for several hours or days, jurors may compromise by convicting the defendant of the lesser crime. If these same jurors had to choose between convicting the defendant of the serious crime or acquitting the defendant, they might well choose to acquit. In this situation, the defendant could be worse off if the jurors had the option of a lesser charge. Therefore, whether or not to ask the judge to give a lesser crime instruction requires careful thought.

Can the judge give a lesser crime instruction over an objection by the defense?

Yes. Judges sometimes instruct jurors about lesser crimes on their own, regardless of the defendant's wishes. Appellate courts sometimes rebuke trial judges for not giving lesser crime instructions, even when defendants ask the trial judge not to give the instructions.

Can a defendant base a partial defense on something other than a lesser offense?

Yes. Sometimes the seriousness of a charge depends on the defendant's past criminal record. If the defendant can invalidate a past conviction, the defendant may be subject only to a lesser charge or a lesser punishment.

Self-Defense

Defendants accused of violent crimes frequently claim that they acted in self-defense. A legitimate self-defense claim legally justifies an acquittal.

In what kinds of cases can defendants argue self-defense?

Self-defense is a possible defense when the defendant is charged with a violent crime. Typical violent crimes include:

- battery (striking or offensively touching someone against his or her will)
- assault with a deadly weapon
- assault with intent to commit serious bodily injury
- manslaughter, and
- murder.

Does a defendant admit to striking an alleged victim when relying on a self-defense argument?

Yes. Inherent in the concept of self-defense is that the defendant did strike the alleged victim. The defense asserts that the striking was legally justified because the "victim" who was struck was in actuality the attacker, and the defendant had to strike to avoid physical harm. Thus, the basic issue in many self-defense cases boils down to, "Who started it?" An important secondary issue is whether the defendant's violence was a proportionate and necessary response.

Can defendants claim self-defense if they admit striking the first blow?

Yes. If a reasonable person would think that physical harm is in the immediate offing, the defendant can use reasonable force to prevent the attack. People do not have to wait until they are actually struck to act in self-defense.

> **EXAMPLE:** Attila and Genghis begin arguing after their cars collide. The argument gets heated, and Attila suddenly lifts his arm and forms his hand into a fist. Thinking that Attila is about to hit him, Genghis quickly knocks Attila to the ground and twists Attila's arm behind Attila's back. Under the circumstances, a reasonable person would think that Attila was about to hit Genghis. People don't have to wait to be hit before protecting themselves. Thus, Genghis acted in self-defense and is not guilty of a crime. In fact, the officer could arrest Attila for assaulting Genghis (making Genghis fear that he was about to be hit).

> **EXAMPLE:** Popeye sees Bluto walking down the street. They've had a few scuffles in the past. Though Bluto is paying no attention to Popeye, Popeye has a hunch that Bluto may trip him walking by. To prevent this, Popeye socks Bluto. Popeye does not have a valid self-defense claim, because the circumstances would not suggest to a reasonable person that Bluto was about to attack Popeye.

How much force can someone use in self-defense?

A person can use a reasonable amount of force in self-defense. How much force is reasonable depends on the circumstances of each situation—particularly the amount of force the alleged victim is using against the defendant. A defendant who acts in self-defense, but who uses more force than is reasonable for self-protection, is still guilty of a crime (anything from simple assault to murder, depending on how disproportionate the force is).

> **EXAMPLE:** David is charged with striking Goliath with a ketchup bottle. David claims that he and Goliath got into a verbal argument at a lodge meeting, Goliath gave David a light push, and David then picked up the ketchup bottle and smashed it over Goliath's head. A conclusion that David acted in self-defense is unlikely. A person acting in self-defense can only use as much force as is reasonable to prevent harm. A light push that causes no injury does not justify a beating with a glass bottle.

> **EXAMPLE:** David and Goliath get into an argument at a lodge meeting. Goliath raises his hand and opens his fist as if to slap David across the cheek with the palm of his hand. The lightning-quick David pulls out his gun and shoots Goliath in the chest. David's self-defense claim will fail—not because he acted preemptively, but because he used far more force than appropriate to defend against a slap of the face.

The Menendez Case—A Famous Claim of Imperfect Self-Defense

Some states allow a partial defense known as "imperfect self-defense." This defense reduces the charges of defendants who use force because they honestly (but mistakenly) believe that they are under attack.

In a highly publicized California case, the Menendez brothers were charged with murder for brutally killing their wealthy parents, and they relied on imperfect self-defense at trial. The brothers claimed that they killed their parents because the father had been so abusive in the past that they honestly (though incorrectly) believed that their father was planning to kill them. Had the jury accepted the brothers' imperfect self-defense, it would have reduced the crime to manslaughter. The first trial ended in a hung jury. The Menendez brothers were convicted of murder after a second trial and sentenced to life in prison.

When does the "stand your ground" defense apply?

Many states have some version of a "stand your ground" or "no retreat" rule. This kind of rule generally applies to someone who isn't an aggressor and who knows about—but doesn't take—an opportunity to safely retreat. It generally allows a person in that situation, who reasonably believes an attacker will cause him or her serious physical harm or death, to use deadly force against the attacker.

Other states require that innocent people who are aware that they can retreat in complete safety take the opportunity to retreat—instead of responding with deadly force to threats of deadly force.

Proponents of stand-your-ground laws argue that people who've done nothing wrong shouldn't have to run in fear from their attackers. Critics argue that these laws encourage violent encounters—they point out that, even without a stand-your-ground law, retreating isn't necessary when it would endanger the person being attacked.

Does the defense have the burden of proof of self-defense?

In many states, a defendant who offers evidence sufficient to support a self-defense claim doesn't have to prove to a judge or jury that the use of force was lawful. The burden to prove the defendant guilty beyond a reasonable doubt remains on the prosecution—it must prove beyond a reasonable doubt the elements of the crime and that the defendant didn't act in self-defense. In some states, however, a defendant who claims self-defense has the burden of proving (usually by a preponderance of the evidence) that the use of force was justified. Even in these states, though, if the defense doesn't convince the jury that the use of force was justified but the jury isn't convinced of guilt beyond a reasonable doubt, the jury must vote "not guilty."

Using Self-Defense to Expand the Scope of Admissible Evidence

Self-defense can make some evidence admissible that would not otherwise be allowed. For example, witnesses cannot ordinarily testify to rumors. But a defendant who claims self-defense can testify to any information that led the defendant to reasonably believe that the use of force was necessary. If one factor in that belief was a rumor that the victim was violent, the defendant can probably testify to the rumor.

Can a defendant support a self-defense claim with evidence of the alleged victim's violent character?

Yes. Defendants can support a self-defense claim with evidence that an alleged victim was prone to violence. Of course, it's open to the prosecution to produce evidence that the alleged victim was not prone to violence. Some states (such as California) go beyond this, and also allow the prosecution to offer evidence of the defendant's past history of violence. In these states, defendants have to think carefully before offering evidence of an alleged victim's violent past.

Battered Woman Syndrome

Traditionally, self-defense arises when defendants protect themselves against contemporaneous attacks. In a modern variation, women have argued that they acted in self-defense when they have struck or even killed their male spouses or partners even though their partners or spouses were not then attacking them. (For example, a woman might strike her partner or spouse while he is sleeping.)

Many states now extend self-defense—or at least imperfect self-defense—to these situations. These states authorize judges and juries to find that women have acted in self-defense when their male partners' or spouses' history of physical, sexual, and/or mental abuse has reasonably put the women in fear of serious harm or death in the near future. Many states also allow women to support their self-defense claims with testimony from psychological experts who testify to the characteristics of battered woman syndrome.

Alibi

This section covers the alibi defense, also known as the "somewhere else" defense.

What is an alibi defense?

The classic alibi defense relies on evidence that a defendant was somewhere other than the scene of the crime at the time it was committed. For example, assume that Freddie is accused of committing a burglary on Elm Street at midnight on Friday, September 13. Freddie's alibi defense might consist of testimony that at the time of the burglary, Freddie was watching *Casablanca* at the Maple Street Cinema.

Does the word "alibi" imply falsity?

Alibi is a perfectly respectable legal defense. Yet to some people, the term connotes a phony defense. Defense attorneys usually are careful to remind jurors that alibi is simply a legal term referring to evidence that a defendant was elsewhere at the time a crime was committed, and that it in no way suggests falsity.

Does a defendant have to testify to rely on an alibi defense?

No. The defense can call whomever it wants as witnesses. For example, a defendant who claims to have been at the movies with Ellen DeJenner at the time a crime was committed can call Ellen as a witness to testify to the alibi, whether or not the defendant takes the stand.

Supporting an Alibi Defense

Because some jurors may be suspicious of an alibi defense, alibi claims should be supported with as much independent evidence as possible. For example, a defendant who claims to have been in another town when a crime was committed might offer evidence such as:

- the testimony of a stranger who saw the defendant in the other town
- a receipt for the purchase of gasoline or another item from a gas station or store in the other town, or
- evidence that the defendant had a preexisting appointment to be in the other town.

Does the defense have the burden of proof with respect to an alibi defense?

No. Defendants who rely on alibis have to offer evidence to support their claims, but do not have to convince the judge or jury that they were elsewhere at the time the crime was committed. The burden is still squarely on the prosecution to prove beyond a reasonable doubt that the defendant who offers the alibi is nevertheless guilty. (Remember, however, that some jurors may erroneously think that the defendant takes on an affirmative burden simply by putting on a defense case, as explained above.)

Does the defense have to notify the prosecution before trial that it will present alibi evidence?

Many federal and state court jurisdictions require defendants to advise prosecutors prior to trial of the defendants' intention to rely on an alibi defense, and to supply the names and telephone numbers of their alibi witnesses. (See Federal Rule of Criminal Procedure 12.1.) The notice provisions allow prosecutors to ask the police to check out an alibi before trial and try to disprove it. For example, if Freddie will claim at trial that he was watching *Casablanca* at the Maple Street Cinema at the time the crime was committed, many states would require Freddie to advise the prosecutor of his intention to offer that evidence. The pretrial notice gives the police time to investigate, and perhaps allow the prosecution to counter the defense with evidence that *Treasure of the Sierra Madre* was the only film showing at the Maple Street Cinema that evening.

Insanity

Defendants who were legally insane at the time they committed a criminal act are not morally blameworthy, as explained below.

Why does the law allow a defendant to be found not guilty by reason of insanity?

The insanity defense is based on the principle that punishment for serious crime is justified only if defendants were capable of controlling their moral behavior and could appreciate the wrongfulness of their behavior at the time the crime was committed. Legally insane defendants who suffer from a mental disease are not immoral actors or are not in control of their actions, the reasoning goes, and so should not be criminally punished for acts committed because of the insanity.

The Insanity Defense Remains Controversial

Though the insanity defense was recognized in England as early as 1505, it remains controversial. Many people point out that a person killed by an insane person is just as dead as one killed by someone who is sane, and argue that people should be punished for the harms they cause regardless of their mental functioning. Opponents of the insanity defense also doubt the competence of psychiatrists, judges, and jurors to determine after the fact whether someone suffered from a mental disease at the time the crime was committed, and the connection, if any, between mental disease and the commission of crime. Perhaps due to popular dissatisfaction with the insanity defense, few defendants actually rely on it. And of the defendants who do, very few are actually found not guilty by reason of insanity.

What is a common definition of insanity?

The most popular definition is the "*M'Naghten* rule," established in England in the 1840s. Under the *M'Naghten* rule, defendants are not guilty by reason of insanity if at the time of a crime they were afflicted with a mental disease that caused them not to know what they were physically doing (lack of cognitive capacity) or not to know that what they were doing was wrong (lack of moral capacity).

States have the power to adopt their own insanity definitions. (See *Clark v. Arizona*, U.S. Sup. Ct. 2006.) For example, a state might recognize only "lack of moral capacity" aspect of *M'Naghten*. In such a state, defendants would be sane under the law if they understood that their actions were wrong.

Nine Insanity Defense Myths

Professor Michael Perlin has described nine myths that people tend to believe about the insanity defense but that social science researchers have proven to be totally without foundation.

1. **The insanity defense is overused.** It is rarely used.

2. **The insanity defense is used only in murder cases.** Roughly one-third of the cases in which an insanity plea is entered involve a murder charge.

3. **Defendants risk nothing by pleading insanity.** Defendants who plead insanity and are found guilty—in other words, defendants who try but fail to show they are legally insane—serve significantly longer sentences.

4. **Defendants who are found not guilty by reason of insanity are quickly released from custody.** They are generally locked up for twice as long as defendants who are convicted of the same offenses.

5. **Defendants found not guilty by reason of insanity serve less time in custody than defendants convicted of the same offenses.** Again, they tend to spend twice

as long in custody as defendants convicted of the same crimes.

6. **Most insanity trials feature "battles of the experts."** About 90% of the time, defense and prosecution experts are in agreement about a defendant's mental disease or defect.

7. **Defense attorneys overuse the insanity defense to "beat the rap."** Attorneys often enter an insanity plea in an effort to obtain mental health treatment for defendants.

8. **Insanity is a "rich man's defense."** The defense is most often used in cases involving indigent defendants.

9. **Defendants who plead insanity are usually claiming vague symptoms and "faking it."** Virtually all insanity defenses are based on schizophrenia or another specific major mental disorder.

(Perlin, Michael L., "The Insanity Defense: Nine Myths that Will Not Go Away." *The Insanity Defense: Multidisciplinary Views on Its History, Trends, and Controversies* (White, Mark D., Editor).)

EXAMPLE: Bentley and Craig are charged with murder after Craig kills a police officer who interrupts their attempt to rob a warehouse. Bentley's evidence shows that Bentley is mentally impaired; a head injury he suffered as a young child has left him with the mental ability of an eight-year-old. Also, Bentley didn't think that Craig should try to steal, but went along with Craig so that Craig would be his friend. To be considered insane in most states, a person has to be unable to distinguish right from wrong. Because Bentley knew that it was wrong to steal from the warehouse, the jury should conclude that he was sane. However, Bentley could have a partial defense. The jury could also conclude that Bentley's mental impairment rendered him incapable of forming an intent to kill, so that Bentley should be found guilty only of manslaughter.

Do courts use other definitions of insanity (besides the *M'Naghten* rule)?

Yes. Different definitions of insanity exist, with the result that a defendant who is not insane under one definition may be insane under another. For example, another common definition of insanity accepted in some states is known as "irresistible impulse." (This defense was the focus of the famous courtroom movie *Anatomy of a Murder.*) Defendants who acted because of an irresistible impulse knew that their actions were wrong, and thus would be considered sane under the *M'Naghten* rule. However, they may still be considered insane under the irresistible impulse rule if, at the time of the crime, they were afflicted with a mental disease that rendered them unable to control actions that they knew were wrong.

Are defendants who are found not guilty by reason of insanity set free?

No. Defendants found not guilty by reason of insanity usually are confined to mental institutions and are not released until a court determines that whatever insanity they experienced at the time of the crime is no longer present. Because judges do not want repeat performances from insane defendants, a defendant found not guilty by reason of insanity can easily spend more time in a mental institution than the defendant would have spent in prison if convicted of the crime.

Can defendants be found both guilty and insane?

Yes. Some states follow a "guilt first" procedure. In these states, a defendant's sanity is not determined until after a defendant has been found guilty of a crime. Then, if a defendant is found to have been insane when the crime that gave rise to the conviction was committed, the defendant is placed in a mental hospital. When (and if) the defendant's sanity is restored, the defendant goes to prison to serve any remaining time on the sentence.

Does an insanity defense require testimony from a psychiatrist?

In almost all cases involving insanity, yes. When a defendant enters a plea of not guilty by reason of insanity, a psychiatric expert examines the defendant on behalf of the defense. (One reason for this is that nearly all insanity tests that courts employ require a finding that the defendant suffered from a mental disease or defect, whatever other elements may or may not be required.) The psychiatrist's investigation will normally include the circumstances of the crime, the defendant's past history, and one or more personal interviews of the defendant. The prosecutor can, and usually will, request that the defendant be examined by a government psychiatrist. As Myth No. 6 in the sidebar above suggests, prosecution and defense psychiatric experts often agree on the basic question of whether a defendant has a mental disease

Competence to Stand Trial

Whether or not a defendant pleads insanity as a defense to criminal charges, an issue can arise as to a defendant's sanity at the time of trial. Defendants cannot be put on trial if they suffer from a mental disease that prevents them from understanding the proceedings and assisting in the preparation of the defense. If a defendant claims incompetence to stand trial, a judge will hold a hearing and take evidence concerning the defendant's current competence. (Insanity refers to a defendant's mental condition at the time the crime was allegedly committed; competence to stand trial evaluates a defendant's mental condition at the time of trial.) At this hearing, the defendant has the burden of proving incompetence to stand trial by a preponderance of the evidence. (*Cooper v. Oklahoma*, U.S. Sup. Ct. 1996.) If the judge decides that the defendant is mentally incompetent, the defendant will probably be placed in a mental institution until competency is reestablished. In what the U.S. Supreme Court has said are likely to be "rare" circumstances, prison officials can legally force prisoners to

take medications that would make them competent to stand trial. (*Sell v. United States*, U.S. Sup. Ct. 2003.) Once a prisoner regains competence, with or without the help of medication, the trial will take place.

Defendants can be mentally competent to stand trial, yet not sufficiently mentally competent to represent themselves. (*Indiana v. Edwards*, U.S. Sup. Ct. 2008.)

One good but extreme example of how competency to stand trial works involved the alleged mob boss Vincent "The Chin" Gigante, who was indicted for a variety of crimes including murder, mail fraud, and extortion. Gigante claimed that he was incompetent to stand trial, based in part on evidence that for years his life consisted only of wandering around the block where he lived in pajamas and a bathrobe. In 1996, a federal judge ruled that Gigante had engaged in an elaborate deception for more than 20 years and ordered him to stand trial. Gigante reportedly told other mobsters that "pretending to be crazy just wasn't worth it."

or defect. But psychiatric diagnoses are to some extent subjective, so disagreements between prosecution and defense experts can unfairly cause some people to doubt the reliability of psychiatric evidence.

However, while opposing psychiatrists may disagree about whether a defendant suffers from a mental disease or defect, Federal Rule of Evidence 704(b) prohibits psychiatrists from testifying directly either that a defendant was sane or insane.

Friends and Relatives as Defense Witnesses

Jurors tend to be suspicious of defense medical experts who pronounce a defendant insane based on a conversation or two and a review of records. The strongest evidence of insanity is often provided by friends and relatives who have known the defendant long enough to form a reliable opinion that the defendant is mentally ill. Most jurisdictions allow nonexpert witnesses to give an opinion regarding the sanity of a person with whom the witness is well acquainted.

Can judges appoint psychiatrists to examine indigent defendants who rely on an insanity defense?

Yes. An indigent criminal defendant who claims to have been insane at the time of an alleged offense and whose sanity is seriously in question is entitled to the assistance of a qualified mental health expert (typically a psychiatrist). The defense mental health expert must be independent from the prosecution. The defense expert's role is to assist in evaluation, preparation, and presentation of the defense case. (*McWilliams v. Dunn*, U.S. Sup. Ct. 2017.)

The Partial Defense of Diminished Capacity

Diminished capacity is a partial defense akin to insanity. Where it is allowed, diminished capacity can reduce the criminal responsibility of defendants whose acts are the result of mental defects that fall short of the legal definitions of insanity. Diminished capacity played a central role in an important California trial in the early 1980s, when a jury accepted a diminished capacity defense and convicted Dan White of manslaughter for killing San Francisco Mayor George Moscone and Harvey Milk, an openly gay county supervisor, in San Francisco. White relied on the so-called "Twinkie defense," claiming that eating food high in sugar content had left him temporarily unable to control his actions. The verdict so aroused the public's anger that California and other states abolished the diminished capacity defense.

Does the defense bear the burden of proving insanity?

Usually. The prosecution will still have the initial burden of proving guilt beyond a reasonable doubt. But after that, defendants wishing to raise an insanity defense in most states and in federal court will have the burden of convincing a judge or jury that they meet the requirements of that jurisdiction's insanity test. Normally, the defendant's burden is to prove insanity only by a preponderance of the evidence, the lower burden of proof commonly used in civil cases. However, some jurisdictions make things harder for defendants by requiring them to prove insanity by clear and convincing evidence, a burden of proof somewhere in between the lower preponderance and the higher reasonable doubt standards.

Does the defense have to notify the prosecution before trial that it will present an insanity defense?

Yes. As with the alibi defense, pretrial rules in many jurisdictions require defendants to advise prosecutors prior to trial that they will rely on an insanity defense at trial. (See Federal Rule of Criminal Procedure 12.2.) Prosecutors often respond by demanding that a defendant be examined by a government psychiatrist before trial.

Duress

Offenders may not be guilty if they commit crimes while under extreme duress.

What is the duress defense?

The duress defense arises when a defendant admits committing a crime, but offers evidence that he or she was genuinely threatened with immediate and serious physical harm if the crime were not carried out. In most states, the duress defense does not extend to killing innocent people.

EXAMPLE: Bob Alou is standing at a bus stop when he feels a gun pressed against his temple and hears a man whisper menacingly, "You're a dead man right now unless you grab the purse of the lady standing next to you and hand it to me." If Bob takes the purse and hands it to the gun holder, the circumstances are probably sufficient to establish the defense of duress.

EXAMPLE: In the same scenario, the man whispers menacingly to Bob, "You're a dead man right now unless you kill the lady standing next to you." Though Bob is subjected to the same level of duress in both examples, Bob cannot rely on a duress defense in this situation. If Bob kills the lady, he is guilty of murder in almost all states. A few states reduce the crime to manslaughter when a defendant kills under duress.

Necessity

The defense of "necessity" is also known as the "lesser of two evils" defense.

What is the defense of necessity?

The necessity defense arises when a person commits a relatively minor offense in order to avoid a greater and imminent peril. The defense vanishes if the peril is minor and the harm is great.

EXAMPLE: Pam panics when her young son's flu symptoms suddenly become severe and she cannot get through to a 911 operator. She drives her son to a hospital's emergency room even though a judge had previously suspended her driver's license for failure to pay parking tickets. Pam can invoke necessity as a defense to a charge of driving with a suspended license.

EXAMPLE: Honus Waggoner realizes that he dropped a cherished baseball card on a section of railroad track. To prevent a rapidly-approaching train from destroying the card, Honus shoves a large rock onto the tracks. The train hits the rock and derails; many passengers are injured. Honus cannot rely on the necessity defense because the gravity of the harm to the train and its passengers is huge compared to his threatened loss.

Is necessity a common defense?

No. The defense exists primarily in the writings and musings of law professors. The necessity defense most famously arose in an 1884 English case known as *Regina v. Dudley and Stephens.* In this case, four sailors who survived a shipwreck were stranded at sea in a small open boat. At sea for about three weeks and without food and water for a week, they were near death. Two of the sailors killed a third, who was chosen not by lot but because he was the youngest and also was weak from drinking seawater. The three remaining sailors ate his flesh, and survived until they were rescued four days later. Charged with murder, the two killers

relied on a defense of necessity. The jury rejected the defense and convicted them of murder. The judge sentenced the killers to death, but the government commuted the sentence to six months in prison.

Intoxication (Under the Influence of Drugs or Alcohol)

Defendants do not have a constitutional right to offer an intoxication defense. (*Montana v. Egelhoff,* U.S. Sup. Ct. 1996.) The voluntary ingestion of alcohol or drugs does not usually excuse a defendant's criminal behavior.

Is having been under the influence of drugs or alcohol a complete or partial defense to criminal charges?

Voluntary intoxication is rarely a complete defense to a criminal charge. People know (or should know) that alcohol and drugs may affect their ability to control their behavior. As a result, defendants who voluntarily consume alcohol or drugs and, because of that, commit a crime are subject to punishment to the same extent as defendants who commit crimes while stone cold sober.

EXAMPLE: Frank Lee is charged with sexually assaulting Terri Jones. Lee claims that he had been drinking heavily at a party on the night of the attack, and that his mental functioning was so impaired by the effects of alcohol that he lost control and attacked Jones. Lee cannot escape conviction and punishment by blaming his actions on intoxication.

However, voluntary intoxication may serve as a partial defense to crimes requiring a prosecutor to prove that a defendant acted with a specific intent. The intoxication does not entirely excuse the defendant's crime. But if intoxication produced mental impairment that rendered a defendant unable to form the required specific intent, the defendant might be convicted of a lesser crime. (Like insanity, this defense must usually be supported with medical or psychiatric testimony.)

Intoxication Defense Rules Vary

Rules governing the intoxication defense vary greatly from state to state and according to the charged crime. For example, a state might have any of the following rules:

- Voluntary intoxication can serve as a partial defense to any crime requiring specific intent.
- Voluntary intoxication can serve as a partial defense only in murder cases.
- Voluntary intoxication is not a defense to any criminal charge.

EXAMPLE: Buck Shot is charged with assault with intent to commit murder. The prosecution claims that Buck shot at Vic Timm with the intention of killing Timm, but missed. Buck admits firing the shot, but claims that he had no intention of killing Timm. Buck claims that about an hour before the shooting he'd ingested an illegal drug that so impaired his mind that he was incapable of forming an intent to kill Timm. The prosecution has charged Buck with a crime that requires the prosecutor to prove that Buck had a specific intent to kill Timm. If, because of drug consumption, Buck was incapable of forming an intent to kill, then in some states Buck could be found guilty only of a lesser crime, such as assault. (If Buck could somehow prove that he was so impaired that he didn't even recognize Timm was a person but honestly believed him to be a deer, for example, Buck might prevail in this type of argument. Again, even where this would be allowed, as the example indicates, it is hard to prove.)

Can *involuntary* consumption of drugs or alcohol serve as a complete or partial defense to criminal charges?

Yes. People might consume drugs or alcohol through no fault of their own and lose the ability to control their behavior. If a judge or jury agrees that a defendant consumed drugs or alcohol involuntarily, and because of the resulting mental impairment committed a crime, the defendant should be found not guilty. This defense conjures up images of someone forcing a drink down someone else's throat. More commonly, this defense applies when a person unknowingly consumes a drug or alcohol. For example, assume that Michele is at a party and that Cervantes slips a drug into Michele's drink that causes an intoxicating effect on Michele. Michele strikes and kills Marilyn while driving home from the party, and is charged with murder. If Michele can prove that she was unknowingly drugged, and her senses were impaired as a result, she may be acquitted entirely or at least convicted of a less serious offense.

Entrapment

Entrapment is an "I really and truly didn't want to do it" defense. This section explains the circumstances when entrapment can serve as a defense to criminal charges.

What is the connection between entrapment and predisposition?

The entrapment defense protects someone from a conviction if a government agent (often an undercover police officer or a police informant) induced the person to commit a crime.

However, someone's predisposition to commit a crime can negate the entrapment defense. Even if a government agent suggests a crime and participates in carrying it out, a predisposed defendant's entrapment defense is unlikely to succeed. Entrapment defenses are therefore difficult for defendants with prior convictions to win.

> **EXAMPLE:** Solely on the basis of a statement made by a confidential informant, a police officer suspects that Hy Poe is a drug dealer. Wearing a concealed recorder, the officer tries to buy illegal drugs from Hy. Hy refuses to sell any drugs, and claims to know nothing about drugs. The officer repeatedly pleads with Hy to sell drugs, indicating that the officer needs the drugs to treat a medical condition. Hy says that he thinks he knows someone who can

procure drugs, and arranges to meet the officer an hour later. Hy returns in an hour, offers to sell the drugs to the officer, and is immediately arrested. A judge or jury would be justified in concluding that the officer entrapped Hy by inducing Hy to commit a crime that Hy would not otherwise have committed. If so, Hy should be found not guilty.

> **EXAMPLE:** Same case. When the officer approaches Hy to buy illegal drugs, Hy replies, "This isn't a good place—we could be under surveillance from cops." The officer convinces Hy to conclude the drug deal in a secluded alley. The officer then arrests Hy. The officer talked Hy into selling the drugs, but Hy was evidently predisposed to the sale under the right circumstances. A judge or jury would be justified in convicting Hy.

Does the defense bear the burden of proving entrapment?

Yes. Defendants who claim that they were entrapped into committing illegal acts normally have the burden of convincing a judge or jury (by a preponderance of the evidence) that they were induced to commit crimes they were not predisposed to commit.

Jury Nullification

This section explains jury nullification, one of the criminal justice system's most carefully guarded secrets.

Does a jury have the power to find a defendant not guilty no matter how strong the evidence of guilt?

Yes. Jurors, not prosecutors, judges, or police officers, have the ultimate power to decide whether a defendant is guilty. As the conscience of the community, jurors can acquit a defendant even if they think the defendant really committed the charged crime. When jurors nullify a law by acquitting a defendant who has obviously broken it, judges and prosecutors can do nothing about it. A jury's not guilty verdict is final.

> **EXAMPLE:** Mother Hubbard is charged with child abuse for using a switch on her ten-year-old child, leaving welts on the child's arms and legs. Mother Hubbard testified that she used the switch only after trying many nonphysical punishments and seeing that her child was still on the verge of getting involved with gangs and drugs. The jury acquits Mother Hubbard. Jurors tell the judge that while they believed that Mother Hubbard used excessive force on her child, under all the circumstances it would be unjust to convict her of a crime. As the community's ultimate conscience, the jurors have the power to decide that Mother Hubbard is not guilty. Their not guilty verdict is final.

Judges and Nullification

Judges have the same power to nullify a law with a not guilty verdict. However, defendants who hope for a nullification outcome normally choose jury trials in the belief that jurors will be more sympathetic and feel less bound by the law.

Evidence That May Lead to Nullification

While defendants cannot offer a nullification defense, they can sometimes present a case in a way that leads jurors to consider nullification on their own. Cases that result in nullification often have these characteristics:

- The defendant acted out of strong moral convictions shared by jurors. For example, a defendant acted out of a desire to close a toxic waste dump, and jurors believe the goal to be legitimate.
- Evidence portrays a defendant in a sympathetic light. For example, jurors may sympathize with a defendant who broke the law trying to close a toxic waste dump only after making a number of legal efforts. (Note: Any sympathy evidence must be relevant to a valid defense. Judges don't admit evidence simply because it may arouse sympathy for a defendant.)
- Evidence arouses jurors' hostility to the government. For example, jurors may be hostile to police officers who were too aggressive when arresting a person engaged in a peaceful but illegal protest.
- The defendant is not charged with a crime of violence.

Can the defense argue nullification to the jury as a defense?

No. The defense cannot explicitly ask jurors to nullify the law. For example, a judge would quickly silence a defendant who said, "Jurors, I was only trying to protect my community against a poisonous waste dump. You should find me not guilty even if you think I did break the law." In fact, judges do not instruct jurors about their nullification power. Jurors who might consider a nullification verdict have to realize on their own that they have the power to nullify the law.

What are the most common situations in which a jury might nullify a law?

Jurors might consider a nullification if:

- The jurors believe a law to be politically unjust. For example, during Vietnam War protests in the 1970s, some jurors refused to convict war protestors who were charged with criminal trespass because they thought that a law banning nonviolent protests was unjust. In more recent times, jury nullification has occurred when defendants who nonviolently protest nuclear testing or toxic waste dumps are charged with crimes.
- The jurors believe that a valid law is being unjustly applied. For example, in the film *A Time to Kill*, jurors acquitted an African American father of murder after the father killed the two men who brutally raped his daughter. The jurors did not consider the murder law itself unjust. Instead, the jurors thought that it was not fair to apply that law to the father's conduct.

Should a defendant turn down a good plea bargain and hope for jury nullification?

No. Defendants who rely on jury nullification are usually disappointed. Jurors almost always limit their deliberations to whether a defendant committed the charged crime. Political overtones and feelings of sympathy or hostility notwithstanding, jurors rarely acquit a defendant they think is guilty as charged.

Discovery: Exchanging Information With the Prosecution

Discovery is the process through which defendants find out from the prosecution as much as they can about the prosecution's case. For example, through standard discovery techniques, a defendant can:

- get copies of the arresting officers' reports and statements made by prosecution witnesses, and
- examine evidence that the prosecution proposes to introduce at trial.

Traditionally, the prosecutor was not entitled to information about a defendant's case. But in recent years, discovery has become more of a two-way street. Just as defendants can discover information from prosecutors, so too can prosecutors sometimes find out about defense evidence.

Modern Discovery Policy

Pretrial disclosure of information through discovery can foster settlement and enhance the fairness of trials. This section explains the general role discovery plays in the criminal justice process.

Are real trials as full of surprises as movies and TV shows indicate?

Very rarely. Until recent years, prosecutors and defendants could guard evidence from each other with the same fervor that toddlers show in protecting toy trucks and dolls from their siblings. Now the attitude of legislators and judges is that cases will settle and the outcome of trials will be fairer if parties can anticipate the evidence that will emerge at trial.

Surprise evidence may produce fine drama, but it leads to poor justice. Thus, every jurisdiction has discovery rules obliging prosecutors to disclose evidence to defendants prior to trial. And, to a lesser extent, defendants have obligations to disclose evidence to prosecutors prior to trial.

Pleading Blind

Despite improvements in discovery procedure, defendants sometimes find themselves in the position of deciding whether to plead guilty without being aware of anywhere near all the evidence. In some states, prosecutors can wait until shortly before trial to turn over discovery. Having to decide whether to take a plea deal or take one's chances at trial and risk a much stiffer sentence without having the full picture can put a defendant in quite a bind.

The gradual trend in the U.S., however, might be moving toward more discovery rights for defendants. And some prosecuting offices provide more discovery or provide discovery earlier in the process than the law requires.

How does prosecution disclosure of evidence promote guilty pleas?

The rule compelling prosecutors to disclose anticipated evidence to the defense before trial promotes guilty pleas when the disclosure reveals the strength of the case. The defendants often realize that they will do better pleading guilty and "taking a deal" than going to trial. Discovery helps explain why about 95% of criminal cases result in defendants pleading guilty before trial.

Does discovery mean that the prosecution has to reveal its trial strategy to the defense?

No. Discovery rules generally distinguish between raw information (names of witnesses, police reports, drug or alcohol test results) and attorney theories and strategies. The latter is called "attorney work product." Prosecutors don't have to turn over their work product to defendants. Each side has to prepare its own case for trial, and can protect its intellectual labors against a lazy adversary.

> **EXAMPLE:** Vy Tummin is charged with assault and battery on a police officer. Vy claims that she reacted in self-defense to the police officer's use of illegal force. The prosecutor plans to show a videotape of the incident to the jury. The prosecutor also has prepared a file memorandum as a self-reminder about what portions of the tape to emphasize during the trial and why those portions are especially significant. Vy demands to see the videotape and all trial preparation memoranda written by the prosecutor. Discovery rules allow Vy to see the videotape. But the prosecutor will not have to turn over the memorandum. The memorandum is the prosecutor's work product, because it's the prosecutor's strategic analysis of the significance of evidence.

Discovery of Information Helpful to the Defense

As part of their obligation to pursue justice and promote fairness, prosecutors have a duty to reveal exculpatory information to the defense.

Do prosecutors have to turn over information that helps defendants?

Yes. Prosecutors have to provide defendants with "exculpatory" information. Exculpatory information is material information known to the prosecutor tending to prove that a defendant is not guilty of a charged crime. (*Brady v. Maryland*, U.S. Sup. Ct. 1963.) Exculpatory evidence is "material" if a reasonable probability exists that its disclosure would have changed a trial's outcome. If the prosecutor fails to turn over exculpatory information and the defendant is convicted, an appellate court can overturn the conviction if the defendant appeals and the exculpatory information that the prosecutor failed to disclose was important.

However, prosecutors are totally immune from personal liability if they improperly fail to turn over exculpatory information to the defense. (*Van de Kamp v. Goldstein*, U.S. Sup. Ct. 2009.) This means that defendants who have been convicted and imprisoned due to a prosecutor's failure to disclose exculpatory information typically can't sue the prosecutor for monetary damages. (Prosecutors can be open to lawsuits in certain limited situations. For example, there might be a viable suit where the prosecutor violated the law in the investigation of—rather than the prosecution of—a case.)

EXAMPLE: Maso Menos is charged with burglary. Two witnesses who saw Menos in a lineup identified him as the burglar. However, a third witness present at the same lineup stated that Menos was not the burglar. The prosecutor does not think that the third witness is telling the truth. Nevertheless, the prosecutor has to tell Menos about the third witness. It's not up to the prosecutor to decide who's telling the truth and who isn't. Information about the third witness is potentially helpful to Menos, so the prosecutor has to disclose it.

EXAMPLE: Mai O'Mai's conviction of a serious felony rested largely on the testimony of a single prosecution eyewitness. After the trial, O'Mai finds out that the prosecution failed to turn over two statements in which the eyewitness told the police before trial that he did not see any faces and would be unable to identify the culprit. The exculpatory statements were material, because there's a reasonable probability that their disclosure would have changed the trial's outcome, O'Mai's conviction should be reversed. (*Smith v. Cain*, U.S. Sup. Ct. 2012.)

How helpful to a case does information have to be before a prosecutor has to turn it over?

Information doesn't have to be so powerful that it proves the defendant conclusively innocent to qualify as exculpatory information. As long as information known to the prosecution might contribute to doubt about the defendant's guilt in the mind of a reasonable judge or juror, the prosecutor must reveal the information to the defendant. A "reasonable probability" means that the likelihood of a different result is great enough to undermine confidence in a guilty verdict's correctness. (*Smith v. Cain*, U.S. Sup. Ct. 2012.) Examples of exculpatory information that prosecutors have to turn over to defendants include:

- a prosecutor's promise of leniency to a witness in exchange for the witness's testimony, and
- a prosecution witness's previous conviction of a crime that a defendant could offer into evidence to attack the witness's credibility.

However, if a defendant pleads guilty, the prosecution might not have to turn over the past records of government informants. (*United States v. Ruiz*, U.S. Sup. Ct. 2002.)

EXAMPLE: Jane Austere is on trial for robbery of a small market; Jane's defense is mistaken identity. The prosecution's primary witness is Al Cohol, who identifies Jane as the robber. Jane is convicted. Jane then learns that the prosecutor knew prior to trial—but failed to tell Jan—that Cohol had undergone years of treatment for alcohol addiction. Jane asks the judge to set aside the conviction and order a new trial, based on the prosecution's failure to turn over this information. The prosecutor asks the judge to deny Jane's request, because she never specifically asked for information concerning Cohol's background. The judge should order a new trial. The information is important because Cohol's years of alcohol abuse might cast doubt on his ability to identify Jane. Prosecutors have to disclose important exculpatory information even if the defendant fails to ask for it. This makes sense: How can defendants ask for information if they don't know it exists?

EXAMPLE: Same case. In pretrial discussions with Cohol, the prosecutor learns that Cohol is a member of a white supremacist organization who uses derogatory epithets for members of minority groups. The prosecutor is personally repulsed by Cohol's activities and use of epithets, but does not reveal this information to Jane's lawyer. After her conviction, Jane learns about Cohol's background and use of racial and ethnic slurs. Jane submits a motion asking the judge to set aside the conviction and order a new trial based on the prosecution's failure to reveal this information to the defense prior to trial. The judge is unlikely to grant Jane's motion. In order to overturn Jane's conviction, the judge would have to decide that the information about Cohol was legally relevant and that it would tend to create a reasonable doubt in the mind of a rational juror. In the absence of evidence that Jane was a member of a group targeted by Cohol's white supremacist organization and that Cohol was an active member of the group, the judge is unlikely to rule that the prosecution had a duty to turn the information over to the defense.

Do prosecutors have to search for information that might help defendants?

No. Prosecutors have to turn over exculpatory information that they know about. However, prosecutors don't have to search for information that might help a defendant or even report every rumor that comes to the attention of the police.

If defendants don't know that helpful information exists, how can they find out whether a prosecutor has concealed it?

Though they have an ethical duty to achieve justice, not just to obtain convictions, prosecutors in an excess of zeal may fail to voluntarily reveal exculpatory information to the defense. Defense attorneys should always be alert to the possibility that exculpatory information exists. They may learn of it in one of the following ways:

- by finding a reference to helpful information in a document that the prosecutor has had to turn over for other reasons
- by asking witnesses and police officers who are willing to talk before trial whether they know of any information that might support the defense version of events, or

- by interviewing witnesses after the trial results in a conviction. At this time, prosecution witnesses may be less guarded in their comments and may reveal exculpatory information that they made available to the prosecution prior to trial. The defense would then have to go back to the trial judge to try to overturn the conviction based on the prosecution's failure to disclose that information.

Can defendants search police and prosecution files to see if they contain helpful information?

Defense attorneys often file pretrial motions asking a judge to force a prosecutor to give the defense access to police and prosecution files and records for the purpose of discovering information that might help the defense. Prosecutors typically refuse to grant access on the ground that the defense has no right to rummage around in prosecution files hoping to find helpful information.

Generally, the only time that a judge will force the police and prosecution to open up their files is when the defense can demonstrate in advance that the files are likely to contain information that is critical to the defendant's case. Judges will not allow a defendant to go on a "fishing expedition." But if the defendant's motion contains information demonstrating that a police officer's personnel file may include information about citizen complaints and disciplinary actions that relate to the defendant's claims, a judge is obliged to examine the personnel file and compel the prosecutor to turn

over its relevant portions to the defendant. In California, for example, the legal authority for defense motions seeking access to police officer personnel files includes Penal Code § 832.7; Evidence Code § 1043; *Pitchess v. Superior Court* (Cal. Sup. Ct. 1974); and *Garcia v. Superior Court* (Cal. Sup. Ct. 2007).

Discovery of Harmful Information

Discovery also gives defendants a preview of the evidence the prosecution will rely on to prove guilt at trial, as explained below.

What specific types of information do prosecutors have to turn over?

A typical state law might require that prosecutors disclose the following to the defense at least 30 days before trial:

- **Names and addresses.** The prosecution has to disclose the names and addresses of all people it intends to call as witnesses at trial.

When Lawyers Need Permission to Reveal Information to Their Clients

Recognizing the danger that may confront victims and witnesses were their addresses and phone numbers made available to certain defendants, many jurisdictions forbid defense attorneys from revealing this information to their clients without specific court authorization.

- **Statements by the defendant.** These include the defendant's statements to police officers after arrest.
- **Any "real evidence" that the police have seized as part of their investigation.** For instance, if a defendant is charged with assault with a deadly weapon, and the police seized a beer bottle with which the defendant allegedly struck the victim, the prosecutor must allow the defense to examine the beer bottle.
- **Felony convictions of witnesses.** The prosecution must disclose felony convictions of any important prosecution witnesses whose credibility will be at issue so that the defense can use the criminal records to impeach the witness.
- **Exculpatory evidence.**
- **Statements of any witnesses whom the prosecution intends to call at trial.** For example, if the police documented the statement of an eyewitness to the crime, and the prosecutor expects to call the eyewitness to testify at trial, the defense is entitled to a copy of the statement. Other material that falls under this category includes statements and reports of expert witnesses. This would include, for example, a blood-alcohol analysis by a laboratory technician that the prosecution intends to introduce in a drunk driving prosecution.

In addition to the foregoing items, the law might require that defense counsel be given various other forms of evidence, including but not limited to case-related photographs, videos, and recordings.

Local Discovery Variations

Despite the overall trend toward liberal discovery, discovery rules can vary greatly from one jurisdiction to another. For example, in federal courts, defendants are not entitled to see pretrial statements of government witnesses until after the witnesses have testified. (18 U.S.C. § 3500— the "Jencks Act".) An important benefit of criminal defense attorneys is their familiarity with local discovery rules.

Can defendants obtain copies of their "rap sheets" (records of arrests and convictions)?

Yes. Defendants are entitled to discovery of their own rap sheets. Defense attorneys examine these carefully, because they can be partially incorrect or incomplete. For example, a conviction on a defendant's rap sheet may belong to another person who has a similar name, or a conviction that shows up as a felony may have been only a misdemeanor, or charges dismissed long ago may show up as still pending. Correcting wrong information on a rap sheet may, for example, enable the defense to:

- deprive prosecutors of evidence with which to attack the credibility of a defendant who chooses to testify at trial, or
- obtain a more favorable plea offer from the prosecutor than would be possible in light of the uncorrected rap sheet.

Should the Defense Correct a Favorable but Erroneous Rap Sheet?

If a defendant notices that a rap sheet fails to mention an arrest or a conviction, should the defense bring the oversight to a prosecutor's attention? Generally, the answer is "no." It's not up to defendants to do the government's work. In rare instances, perhaps if the defense is certain that a prosecutor is bound to learn of the mistake before the case concludes, the defense might earn brownie points toward a favorable plea bargain by pointing out the mistake.

Can the defense get access to witnesses' grand jury testimony?

In many states, yes. Defendants are generally entitled to all pretrial statements of prosecution witnesses, whether given informally to police officers or formally under oath before a grand jury. A grand jury transcript will reveal prosecution witnesses' likely trial testimony and provide the defense with a basis for discrediting any witnesses who testify differently at trial than they did before the grand jury.

Do prosecutors have to turn over police reports?

Yes. Police reports (sometimes called arresting officers' reports) typically detail the events leading up to and even after a defendant's arrest. They may include the police officer's own observations, summaries of witness statements, and descriptions of seized evidence. The defense usually receives copies of police reports at the time of arraignment.

Will the prosecution turn over search and seizure materials?

Yes. The defense receives copies of arrest and search warrants, and accompanying affidavits (statements in support of the application for a warrant, given under oath). If the affidavits show that the police did not demonstrate probable cause for the issuance of a warrant, or lied about an important fact, the defense may have a viable motion challenging the legality of an arrest or the seizure of evidence.

Challenging Improper Arrests

Unless the police seized evidence in the course of an unlawful arrest, challenging the validity of an arrest warrant is often an act of futility. Even if the arrest was improper at the time, the prosecution has usually had sufficient time to gather additional evidence and secure another arrest warrant. However, a successful challenge to an arrest warrant can pay off if the police seized evidence when they made the arrest. Even if the police rearrest the defendant pursuant to a valid warrant, the prosecution may be unable to use the improperly seized evidence in court.

Reciprocal Discovery

Discovery has become a two-way street, with defendants obligated to reveal information to prosecutors. This section explains the defense's duty to provide information in discovery.

Can the judge order the defense to disclose evidence to the prosecutor?

Yes. Defendants have argued that forcing them to turn over evidence to the prosecutor in advance of trial violates their Fifth Amendment right to silence and their privilege against self-incrimination. However, judges have upheld so-called "reciprocal" discovery laws, which compel defendants to disclose some information to prosecutors before trial.

What information might the defense have to turn over to the prosecutor?

While each jurisdiction has its own reciprocal discovery rules, here are a few examples of reciprocal discovery laws:

- Upon demand by a prosecutor, the defense must give written notice of intent to offer any planned alibi defense and reveal the names and addresses of the alibi witnesses. If a defendant refuses to comply, then the defendant cannot offer the alibi defense or call the witnesses at trial.
- The defense must disclose to prosecutors (a) the names and addresses of all people other than the defendant it

plans to call as witnesses; (b) any relevant written or recorded statements made by any of these witnesses; (c) any experts' reports; and (d) any "real" evidence (tangible objects) that the defense intends to offer into evidence.
- Upon request by prosecutors, defendants must submit to reasonable physical or medical inspections of their bodies; permit the taking of samples such as handwriting, hair, and blood; and, if mental illness is in issue, submit to psychiatric examination.

Do Facebook pages and other social media sites provide free discovery to police and prosecutors?

Yes. People post personal information on social media sites such as Facebook, Instagram, and Snapchat. Police officers can troll these sites for information related to criminal charges or investigations and may find posts that prosecutors can use as evidence against defendants at trial. Here are just a few of many examples:

- Drug enforcement agents checking out a California suspect's social media site found photos showing the suspect surrounded by marijuana plants. The suspect bragged on the website that the plants were a cash crop.
- A defendant who was the son of a well-known California politician was charged with murder. Powerful friends who supported the defendant's release

on low bail submitted affidavits to the judge attesting to the defendant's good character. The prosecution rebutted these testimonials with photos the defendant had posted on his social network page, showing the defendant stabbing a frog and raising a knife over a kitten.

- Florida detectives arrested a few burglary suspects after finding photos of the suspects standing among the stolen items posted on their social networking sites.

- Texas authorities revoked the parole of convicted sex offenders who had created social network profiles that violated the terms of their parole.

Knowing that police officers often look for incriminating information on social media sites, some defense lawyers ask clients for their social network information. However, if they do find incriminating information about clients, the defense lawyers may be unable to remove it or advise their clients to remove it. Removal could constitute tampering with evidence, which is itself a crime.

Investigating the Facts

n addition to using discovery procedures to obtain evidence, the defense often gathers evidence on its own. Defense investigation methods can be as informal as phone calls and email exchanges with potential witnesses or as formal as a deposition under oath.

Interviewing Prosecution Witnesses

This section explains why it's important to interview the witnesses who will be testifying for the prosecution, and some common techniques for doing so. Defense lawyers and investigators often seek to interview prosecution witnesses, but defendants should rarely if ever try to do so personally.

How does it help the defense to interview prosecution witnesses?

The defense can gain three significant benefits from interviewing prosecution witnesses rather than relying only on their written statements:

- The defense can gauge witnesses' demeanor and credibility.
- Ferreting out details of prosecution witnesses' stories allows the defense time to think about how to poke holes in their testimony and counter their testimony with defense evidence.
- If the prosecution witness's testimony at trial differs significantly from what the witness told the defense before trial, the defense may be able to undermine the prosecution witness's

credibility by showing that the story changed from one telling to the next.

Why interview prosecution witnesses if the prosecution has to turn witness statements over to the defense?

Defendants cannot be certain the prosecution will play by the rules. Moreover, if a witness has only spoken orally to the police or prosecutor, there may be no evidence of that statement for the defense to obtain. Finally, witness statements prepared by the prosecution may not be an accurate guide to the testimony the witness will give at trial. Witness statements often are terse summaries, prepared by a police investigator for witnesses to sign, and don't fully portray what the witness has to say.

Is it legal for the defense to interview prosecution witnesses before trial?

Yes. Prosecutors do not own their witnesses, and they cannot prevent witnesses and crime victims from talking to the defense. It's up to individual witnesses, including victims, to decide whether to talk to the defense before trial.

Can defendants expect prosecution witnesses to talk voluntarily to someone from the defense team?

Prosecution witnesses do not normally voluntarily submit to defense interviews. Most prosecution witnesses are either the alleged crime victims or people who are closely identified with the prosecution (like police officers), and therefore have no wish to help the defense. However, rules in most jurisdictions forbid prosecutors from explicitly instructing witnesses not to talk to the defense.

Defendants Should Not Personally Interview Crime Victims

Whatever the defendant's intent, an alleged victim may interpret any personal contact from the defendant as a threat. If the victim reports the "threat" to the police, the defendant might wind up having bail revoked and facing an additional criminal charge. Therefore, unless an attorney arranges for the contact in advance, the defendant should never personally contact a victim.

"I Can't Tell You What to Do, But ..."

Prosecutors sometimes subtly evade the rule forbidding them to instruct witnesses not to talk to the defense by simply advising witnesses of the law. Prosecutors can say something like, "I'm not telling you what to do, but I can tell you that the law doesn't require you to talk with the defense if you don't want to." Prosecutors realize that this word to the wise is enough in most cases to discourage prosecution witnesses from cooperating with defense interview requests.

If voluntary cooperation is unlikely, how should the defense go about interviewing prosecution witnesses?

The defense has two ways to increase its chances of obtaining prosecution witness interviews before trial. However, both can be costly, and one is an option only in a few states. One possibility is for the defense to hire a private investigator. Private investigators specialize in finding and interviewing reluctant witnesses. The fact that many private investigators are former police officers enhances their chances of success. Private investigators can be costly, however, typically charging hourly fees plus expenses for their services. Many defendants simply can't afford to hire private investigators.

Public defender offices, which serve indigent defendants in many parts of the country, sometimes employ investigators as part of their staff. Demands on these investigators usually are very heavy, and it's up to the lawyers in the office, not an individual defendant, to decide which cases the investigators work on.

In some jurisdictions, a second way to interview a prosecution witness prior to trial is to serve the witness with a subpoena (a court order) compelling the witness to attend and answer questions at a deposition (an out- of-court session at which the witness can be questioned under oath). During a deposition, the witness is questioned under oath in front of a court reporter, who records the testimony and transcribes it into a booklet. Depositions can be expensive.

Depositions are common in civil cases, but far less frequent in criminal cases. While a few states don't, most states severely limit criminal defendants' ability to take depositions or bar criminal case depositions entirely.

Should defendants personally interview prosecution witnesses and save the cost of an investigator?

No. By personally interviewing prosecution witnesses, a defendant takes a risk that a witness will view the personal contact as threatening and report it to the police. Moreover, the defense can't do much about a sudden change in story at trial when it's the defendant who personally conducted the interview. To prove that the prosecution witness's story has changed, the defendant would have to testify. And even then, it would only be the defendant's word against that of the witness.

> **EXAMPLE:** Ruth Lessly is charged with trespass, but denies that she was among a group of youths who broke into a boarded-up house. Ruth personally contacts Bess, who lives next to the boarded-up house and who witnessed the break-in. Bess tells Ruth that she doesn't remember Ruth as one of the youths who broke into the house. Nevertheless, Bess might well report Ruth to the police, claiming that Ruth tried to threaten her into giving favorable testimony. And what if, at trial, Bess testifies that she is certain that Ruth was one of the trespassers? At this point, all Ruth can do is to testify that Bess changed her story, at the cost of giving

up her right to remain silent. Even if Ruth testifies to Bess's earlier statement, Bess is likely to deny making it. A judge or jury might choose to believe Bess rather than Ruth.

> **EXAMPLE:** Same case. Assume that a private investigator, rather than Ruth personally, interviews Bess before trial. When the investigator shows Bess a picture of Ruth, Bess tells the investigator that she doesn't remember Ruth as one of the youths who broke into the house. At trial, Bess identifies Ruth as one of the trespassers. The defense is now in a better position to attack Bess's testimony. By using an investigator, Ruth can't be accused of trying to intimidate Bess. Furthermore, the defense can call the investigator as a witness to testify to Bess's earlier remark that conflicts with her testimony. A judge or jury might well regard the investigator as more believable than Ruth. Also, Ruth can exercise her right to remain silent while still attacking Bess's credibility through the investigator's testimony.

Finding and Interviewing Defense Witnesses

Defense lawyers try to identify witnesses who can support their clients' stories and their characters, as discussed below.

What can defendants do to help identify potential defense witnesses?

Defendants should work with their lawyers as to what should and shouldn't be done to investigate a case. For example, as a starting point, defense lawyers often ask clients to provide information about bystanders who might have been at the scene of a crime or an arrest. Potentially helpful information includes a bystander's gender, physical appearance, manner of dress, and the like—anything that might help the defense locate and interview the person.

A defendant who is not in custody may also visit scenes of important events, ideally at the same time of day that the actual events took place. That way, defendants are more likely to recognize regular passersby who were on the scene earlier and can pass the information along to their lawyers.

A defendant can also contact friends, employers, and other people who might testify to the defendant's good character. Such evidence is often admissible at trial, and in a close case may tip the scales in the defendant's favor. And even if the defendant is ultimately convicted at trial, these people can be invaluable in convincing the judge to be lenient when sentencing the defendant.

Should defendants personally interview potential helpful witnesses?

Defendants represented by attorneys should let their attorneys or investigators interview potential witnesses. Attorneys and investigators are more likely to know which topics to probe. If the defense attorney agrees, it can be helpful for the defendant to accompany the attorney or investigator on an interview of a personal friend who wants to help the defendant. However, defendants should not be present at other interviews, because witnesses

may regard the defendant's presence as intimidation and report to the police that the defendant threatened them.

How else can defendants be involved in fact investigation?

Defendants who are not in custody can— in cooperation with their attorneys—use a few self-help techniques to assist their attorneys in the investigation. Some of these tasks include:

- Taking photographs. The defendant can photograph the scenes of important events. These photographs can become defense exhibits at trial. Or, the photos may raise issues that poke holes in the testimony of prosecution witnesses.
- Gathering receipts, records, and other documents from such places as government offices and private employers, if they will be helpful to the defense.
- Contacting counseling and community service agencies to find programs in which the defendant can enroll to learn how to control behaviors related to the crime. For example, a defendant with a substance abuse problem may start attending AA meetings. (Participation in such programs can be very persuasive when negotiating a plea or arguing for a lenient sentence.)

Studies suggest that, as a general rule, defendants who take an active role in their own defense do more than save money. They tend to achieve better outcomes than those who leave representation entirely in the hands of their attorneys.

What is a *subpoena duces tecum*?

A defense lawyer needing documents from uncooperative people or offices can serve them with *subpoenas duces tecum*. This rather forbidding term refers to a court order requiring a person or organization to deliver the documents, records, or objects designated in the subpoena to court. (See Federal Rule of Criminal Procedure 17.) The order is easy to get; in some courthouses *subpoenas duces tecum* are prestamped and a defense attorney need only fill in the blanks.

Using an "Early Return Date" on Subpoenas

It's to a defendant's advantage to look through subpoenaed documents before the actual date of trial. To make this possible, the defense attorney can put an early return date on a subpoena—that is, have the documents due in court before the actual date of trial. Then the attorney can examine or get copies of the documents before trial.

Do subpoenas always work to produce the requested evidence?

No. A person whose books or records are subpoenaed can ask a judge to "quash" (nullify) the subpoena. The usual ground for such a request is that the subpoena is so broad that compliance is impossible or too costly. Judges often respond by asking the defense to tailor the subpoena to specific records, and to describe the information the defense expects the records to contain. Judges may even throw the subpoena out in its entirety if it appears the defense is on a "fishing expedition." But, if a subpoena is valid and the person or business with the relevant records won't produce them, the defense may have to file a motion to compel compliance.

What is the role of expert witnesses in fact investigation?

Expert witnesses often play an important role in the investigation and trial of criminal cases. For example, an expert may:

- examine "real evidence," such as weapons and allegedly illegal drugs
- examine a defendant's physical or mental condition, or
- assess the investigation carried out by police crime lab technicians.

If a defendant is indigent, a judge may grant a defense attorney's request for the appointment of an expert to help the defense at government expense. Otherwise, defendants and their attorneys have to weigh the expenses of hiring an expert witness against the likelihood that an expert's investigation will be helpful during plea bargaining discussions or at trial.

Preliminary Hearings

The term "preliminary hearing" (sometimes called "probable cause hearing," "preliminary examination," "PX," or "prelim") refers to a hearing in which a judge decides whether probable cause exists to require a defendant to stand trial for a charged crime. At a prelim, a judge does not decide whether the defendant is guilty, but only whether the prosecution has presented enough evidence to justify a belief that a crime occurred and that the defendant committed it. If the judge decides that the prosecution has sufficient evidence, the defendant is "bound over," meaning that the court will retain jurisdiction over the defendant until the case is either taken to trial or settled.

The Judge Can Reduce the Charges

If the judge finds that there is insufficient evidence to hold the defendant to answer at trial for the charged crime, but there is enough evidence of a lesser crime, the judge may hold the defendant to answer—after the preliminary hearing—for that lesser crime.

In essence, a preliminary hearing provides an independent judicial review of the prosecutor's decision to prosecute. But because the preliminary hearing requires the prosecution to produce enough evidence to convince the judge that the case should proceed to trial, it also provides the defense with an excellent opportunity to probe the strength of the prosecution's case.

An Overview of Preliminary Hearings

Preliminary hearings are an alternative to grand juries in many jurisdictions. This section explains the purpose and logistics of preliminary hearings.

Do preliminary hearings always take place in criminal cases?

No. In some states, preliminary hearings take place only when defendants request them. In other states, they are held only in felony cases.

In many states, the prosecutor may eliminate the need for a preliminary hearing altogether by convening a grand jury and obtaining an indictment. And, for strategic reasons, defendants may waive (give up) their right to a preliminary hearing altogether and proceed directly to trial.

When do preliminary hearings take place?

A preliminary hearing typically takes place within weeks after an arraignment, when defendants are formally charged with crimes. For instance, under the Federal Speedy Trial Act, a preliminary hearing must normally be held within 30 days of the time the defendant is arrested. (See 18 U.S.C. § 3161.) Many states have similar time frames.

However, defendants can and often do "waive time"—that is, give up their right to a speedy trial—which allows the preliminary hearing to be delayed to a time more convenient for all the major players in the case. Delays in the processing of criminal charges often benefit defendants, which explains why defense attorneys often advise clients to waive time.

Are preliminary hearings open to the public?

Preliminary hearings usually take place in open court where the public, the defendant and defendant's family, any victims, the media, and any other interested people may all be present. In rare cases, however, a judge may decide to close the courtroom (for example, in the case of a sex crime where the victim is a child).

What happens during a preliminary hearing?

In some ways, preliminary hearings are previews of what the trial will be like, if the case gets that far (most don't). A prosecutor offers testimony from witnesses and may also introduce case-related evidence, such as a weapon. Typically, prosecutors present only enough evidence to convince the judge that there is probable cause to hold the defendant for trial.

The defense has the right to—and most often will—cross-examine prosecution witnesses both to discover additional case-related information and to evaluate their credibility. This helps the defense prepare to cross-examine these witnesses at trial and may also present defense attorneys with information that they can use to improve their positions in plea negotiations.

After the prosecution is finished with its presentation, the defense has the right to put on its own case, but is not required to do so—and usually doesn't.

In what important ways are preliminary hearings different from trials?

Preliminary hearings differ from trials in many important respects:

- Preliminary hearings are much shorter than trials. A typical prelim may take from a half hour to two hours, and some prelims only last a few minutes.
- Preliminary hearings are conducted in front of a judge alone, without a jury.
- The burden of proof, while still on the prosecution, is much lower during a preliminary hearing than it is during trial. At trial, the prosecution has the burden of proving each element of the charged offense(s) beyond a reasonable doubt. But at the prelim, the prosecution only has to show probable cause that the accused committed the charged crime(s).
- The goals differ. The goal of trial is to determine a defendant's guilt. The goal of a preliminary hearing is to screen: to weed out weak cases and protect defendants from unfounded prosecutions.

What procedural rules apply during preliminary hearings?

Many of the same procedural rules that govern trials apply in preliminary hearings. For example, ordinary witnesses (nonexperts) may testify only to what they have perceived; they may not speculate or testify to irrelevant information. On the other hand, hearsay evidence that would not be admissible at trial is often admissible during preliminary hearings.

What are the possible outcomes of a preliminary hearing?

A preliminary hearing usually has one of three outcomes:

- Most often, the defendant is held to answer, or "bound over" for trial on the original charge.
- Sometimes, when the charge is a felony, the judge may reduce the charge to a misdemeanor or a less serious felony.
- A small percentage of cases are dismissed by the judge (though the prosecution may usually refile them).

Why do preliminary hearings infrequently result in dismissal of charges?

The prosecution usually wins at the preliminary hearing stage of a case for a number of reasons:

- The burden of proof is low. The prosecution merely has to offer sufficient evidence to constitute probable cause that a defendant committed a charged crime. As long as the evidence offered by the prosecution is enough to logically justify a guilty verdict if the judge or jury believes it, the judge will let the prosecution take the case to trial.
- Judges tend to resolve doubts in favor of prosecutors.
- The prosecution usually can use evidence during the preliminary hearing (such as hearsay evidence) that would not be allowed during a trial.

- The defense typically does not put up a strenuous fight at this stage, most often for strategic reasons. Without putting on much or sometimes any evidence at all, it is difficult for the defense to rebut (or challenge) the prosecution's evidence sufficiently to convince the judge to rule against the prosecution at this preliminary stage of the proceedings.

If a judge finds probable cause to hold a defendant for trial, what happens next?

After a defendant is bound over for trial, a prosecutor typically files a separate document (often called an "information"), which signals the start of further court proceedings.

Defendants who are free on bail normally remain free following the prelim, but are often required to appear in court at the next scheduled hearing. In-custody defendants stay in jail awaiting their next court appearance, although they normally can renew their request for bail at the prelim. Bail is always reviewable, and a judge might grant bail if the actual facts (as presented at the prelim) are not as bad as the police report made them sound.

At this point, depending on the jurisdiction and the seriousness of the crime, a case is likely to proceed in one of these ways:

- The defendant may be arraigned a second time before a higher level court in states that have two tiers of courts.
- The parties may proceed directly to plea negotiations.

- A judge may set a later date for either a pretrial conference, trial, or both.

Is a preliminary hearing ever a substitute for trial?

Yes. Prosecutors and defense attorneys sometimes agree to "submit on the record." When this happens, a judge (not a jury) determines the defendant's guilt or innocence based on the judge's review of the preliminary hearing transcript. A prosecutor might agree to submit on the record when the case is weak but the prosecutor's office doesn't want to dismiss charges outright. If the judge then dismisses the case, the prosecutor can deflect criticism from angry victims or police officers to the judge.

More often, a case submitted on the record favors the prosecution rather than the defense, and in essence is a slow plea of guilty. In such cases, the defense knows that a guilty verdict is all but certain, but by submitting on the record, the defense can move the case more quickly to an appellate court or simply offer an out to a defendant whose case is hopeless but doesn't want to plead guilty or *nolo contendere*. (Defense attorneys can submit on the record only if the defendant agrees to waive trial.)

Might a prosecutor handle only the preliminary hearing phase of a case?

Yes. Prosecutors' functions can vary from one office and even from one case to another. A prosecutor may be in charge of all phases of a criminal prosecution, or a prosecutor may handle preliminary hearings only and leave other phases of

cases to other prosecutors. Where the latter practice is followed, the defense will have to deal with different prosecuting attorneys at different stages of the proceedings.

What's the advantage of a grand jury to a prosecutor?

Though judges most often favor the prosecution in preliminary hearings, grand juries—perhaps in part because they are not publicly scrutinized—are usually even more prosecution friendly. Moreover, the defense is not present during grand jury proceedings and therefore has no opportunity to cross-examine the witnesses called to testify by the prosecution.

Do Not Confuse Indictments and Convictions

When a defendant has been indicted, that means a grand jury has found probable cause to believe the defendant guilty. An indictment is a far cry from the judge or jury (a regular trial jury, called a "petit jury") actually convicting the defendant. A conviction happens only after a trial where charges have been proven beyond a reasonable doubt, or upon a plea of guilty or no contest.

Does the defense have any say in whether a prosecutor proceeds by way of grand jury or preliminary hearing?

When procedural laws allow the prosecution to decide between a grand jury and a preliminary hearing, the prosecution almost always controls the decision. In rare instances, the defense may force an open-court preliminary hearing by making a motion for a preliminary hearing to the court.

Defense Rights During Preliminary Hearings

Defendants enjoy a variety of procedural protections during preliminary hearings.

Do defendants have the right to be represented by counsel at a prelim?

Yes. Defendants have a right to be represented by counsel at a preliminary hearing. (*Coleman v. Alabama,* U.S. Sup. Ct. 1970.) If a defendant cannot afford to hire a lawyer, the court will appoint one.

Does the defendant have a right to remain silent at a prelim?

Yes. The defense has the right to remain silent at preliminary hearings. The defense usually opts not to put on evidence at the preliminary hearing. While that makes it more likely that a judge will rule for the prosecution, judges almost always rule in the prosecution's favor even when defendants present evidence. Thus, by presenting evidence, the defense runs the chance of unnecessarily giving the prosecution a preview of its trial strategy.

Can the testimony given at a preliminary hearing be used later in the case?

Yes. Just as at trial, testimony at a preliminary hearing is recorded, often by a court reporter.

Often, the testimony a witness gives at the preliminary hearing is the witness's first statement on the record regarding the facts of the case. And that statement may be useful to the defense if the witness tells a different story at trial.

> **EXAMPLE:** Daniel Marks is charged with driving under the influence (DUI). The arresting officer testifies at the preliminary hearing that Daniel had an open beer can on the front seat of the car. Later, at trial, the same officer testifies that there was an open beer can on the front seat and five empty beer cans on the floor near the back seat. The defense attorney can cross-examine the officer during trial and ask why, if there really were cans on the back floor, the officer "forgot" to mention those cans at the preliminary hearing.

Additionally, a judge may allow testimony given at a preliminary hearing to be entered in evidence at trial if the witness later becomes unavailable (for instance, dies or leaves the country).

> **EXAMPLE:** Same as above. Daniel Marks is charged with DUI. Daniel's friend Julia, a passenger in the car when Daniel was arrested, planned to go on a three-month trek to Nepal. Knowing of Julia's Nepal plans, Daniel's lawyer decides to put Julia on the stand at the preliminary hearing. After the arresting officer testified, Julia testified that she had purchased and brought along with her in Daniel's car a six-pack of canned diet soda. She explained that she was on a diet and often brought her own beverages with her. She further stated that she had held

the soda can Daniel had been drinking from when the policemen stopped them because Daniel needed to get his driver's license and couldn't do that while holding the can. Julia testified also that the remaining five cans of diet soda were on the back seat. The judge found probable cause to hold Daniel for trial and set a trial date (when Julia was scheduled to be in Nepal). Daniel, unwilling to plea bargain, insists he was only drinking soda and feels he was arrested because of his eccentric appearance (blue and green "punk" hair, multiple tattoos, and body piercings). At Daniel's trial, he can probably have Julia's exculpatory testimony read to the jury.

Victims and Prosecution Witnesses May Not Have to Testify at Preliminary Hearings

Many states no longer require prosecution witnesses to testify at or even attend prelims. Police officers can testify to what they've been told by victims and witnesses. Ordinarily this would violate the hearsay rule, but it is allowed because the purpose of the preliminary hearing is to determine probable cause rather than guilt. This practice undermines the common defense strategy of using the preliminary hearing as a way of testing the credibility of potential trial witnesses, because police officers often cannot answer questions the defense would have put to such witnesses, nor can defense lawyers assess the demeanor of witnesses who aren't there.

Although the defense does not typically present evidence at a preliminary hearing, the Daniel Marks example above demonstrates why it might be important on occasion for the defense to do so. Further, it can be very important for the defense to cross-examine a prosecution witness who presents damaging testimony at the preliminary hearing, because if that person becomes unavailable, the judge will usually allow the prosecution to use that evidence at trial.

Does the defense ever win at the preliminary hearing?

The defense might win and the case might be dismissed (or the charges reduced) at the close of a preliminary hearing if:

- The eyewitness identification of the defendant does not hold up under cross-examination, and there is no other credible evidence to show that the defendant committed the crime in question. This may cause the whole case against the defendant to unravel, and the judge may readily agree to dismiss the charges (or reduce them to a charge that doesn't require the eyewitness testimony).
- A key prosecution witness fails to show up or becomes reluctant to testify, perhaps because the defendant is a spouse, family member, or friend, and the prelim is being held in a state that requires the witness to attend rather than allowing the police to relate what the witness told them.

- The prosecution fails to offer evidence in support of each element of the crime charged. For example, to convict a suspect of grand theft, the prosecution usually must show that (1) the defendant, (2) took and carried away, (3) property with a value of more than $500, (4) belonging to another (person or company), (5) with the intention of depriving that person or company permanently of the property. In the prelim, the prosecution does not have to prove each of these elements beyond a reasonable doubt, but it does have to produce some evidence to substantiate each element. If the prosecution does not offer evidence as to one or more of the elements, the judge should dismiss the charge.

EXAMPLE: Mary North and a friend were arrested for grand theft for allegedly stealing a watch from Southstrom's department store. At the preliminary hearing, the prosecution puts on evidence to show that Mary and her friend were in the store the day a watch was stolen. A visual recording depicts Mary's friend putting a watch in her backpack. There is no visual recording of Mary. Mary was wearing pants with no pockets and was not carrying a purse, backpack, or anything else at the time. The prosecution presents no evidence whatsoever to show that Mary actually took anything. Mary's lawyer will make a motion asking the judge to dismiss the case on the basis that the prosecution failed to put on evidence for one critical element, namely that Mary participated in the theft of the watch. If the judge denies the motion to dismiss, Mary's lawyer can still try to negotiate a plea bargain with the prosecutor. The prosecutor may be willing to dismiss the charges altogether or reduce them significantly.

Common Defense and Prosecution Strategies

This section explains how prosecutors and defense attorneys typically try to use the preliminary hearing to strengthen their own cases without giving away too much information to the other side.

What can the prosecution and defense gain from a preliminary hearing in terms of their case strategies?

Officially, preliminary hearings protect defendants by weeding out baseless charges. Unofficially, however, each side may use a preliminary hearing to check out the other side's evidence. As a matter of course, both the defense and prosecution tend not to put on so much evidence that they show their whole hand. And, because the defense doesn't have to, it often doesn't put on any evidence at all.

What specifically can the defense gain from the preliminary hearing?

Even though the defense doesn't expect to see all the prosecution's cards, the preliminary hearing may give the defense a preview of how strong the prosecution's tangible evidence is, how persuasive the prosecution's witnesses are, and how believable those witnesses are likely to be should the case go to trial. The defense tries to size up how solid the government's case is as a whole.

Such information can be important to the defense, whether it ultimately settles the case in a plea bargain or proceeds to trial. If the prosecution's case seems weak—if, for example, prosecution witnesses change their earlier stories, forget important details, or are otherwise discredited—the defense may decide it's worthwhile to proceed to trial. The prosecution, on the other hand, may be prompted to offer a generous deal, or at least the defense may gain leverage to push for one. If, however, the government's case seems very strong, this information may help the defense decide to accept a plea bargain, even if it's not what the defense had hoped for, rather than wasting further energy and money fighting what looks to be a losing battle.

Because more than 90% of cases end before trial, it's clear that a primary defense goal at the preliminary hearing is to look for evidence it can use to get the best possible result at the plea bargaining table. For example, if an arresting officer's credibility can be undermined during the preliminary hearing, and that officer is the state's main (or only) witness, the prosecutor may be willing to offer a much better deal following the prelim than the

prosecutor would have if the officer had been a better (more believable) witness.

A Case of Destroying the Witness at the Preliminary Hearing

In the 1995 O.J. Simpson double murder criminal trial, the prosecution called the L.A. County coroner, among other witnesses, to testify at the preliminary hearing. The defense's cross-examination of the coroner revealed serious errors—for example, the coroner's office waited too long to examine the bodies and failed to adequately preserve certain evidence taken from the bodies. This cross-examination was so devastating that it forced the prosecution to change its plan to call the coroner to the stand during trial. Because everyone (in and out of court, as the preliminary hearing was nationally televised) saw how poorly the coroner performed during the prelim, the prosecution was forced to find another way to get at least some of the important evidence in without calling the coroner to the stand. They ended up calling another doctor from the coroner's office who, though he didn't actually perform the autopsies, was able to testify about the physical evidence.

Information gathered at the preliminary hearing will also help the defense if the case is one of the few that do go to trial. Whether or not the defense presents its own witnesses, the defense will usually vigorously cross-examine prosecution witnesses in the preliminary hearing. This cross-examination gives the defense an opportunity to see how the prosecution witnesses will hold up, and to pin them down as to what their testimony will be at trial. (If they change their testimony at trial, the preliminary hearing testimony can be used to impeach their credibility.)

Objections During Preliminary Hearings

Sometimes defense lawyers are required by local rules to object to evidence during a preliminary hearing in order to preserve their right to object to that same evidence later at trial. In the absence of such rules, however, defense lawyers often choose to remain silent and allow prosecutors to present inadmissible evidence at the preliminary hearing. Why? The defense lawyers are using the preliminary hearing as a discovery device—to learn all they can, good and bad, about the prosecution's case. Because there is no jury at the preliminary hearing to be prejudiced by the damaging evidence, it is often better, from the defense standpoint, to let the prosecution think it has a strong case than it is to educate the prosecution about the problems in the case (which only gives the prosecution a chance to correct the errors and strengthen its case for trial).

As useful as a vigorous cross-examination of prosecution witnesses may be, a sound alternative defense strategy is to cross-examine prosecution witnesses very briefly and politely. This serves two purposes:

- This may relax and lull a witness into admitting damaging evidence either then and there, or later when the defense attorney unexpectedly gets aggressive at trial.
- The defense may save evidence that hurts the witness's credibility and spring it on the witness at trial. Because the defense did not produce this evidence at the preliminary hearing, the witness may not be expecting it at the trial, and the surprise may fluster the witness and make him or her look bad in the eyes of the jury.

When does it make sense for the defense to waive a preliminary hearing?

The reasons the defense might waive the right to a preliminary hearing include:

- The defendant intends to plead guilty and wants to avoid publicity (and expense, if the defendant is represented by private counsel).
- The defendant is guilty of more than the charged offenses and fears further charges from the potentially damning evidence that may come out at the preliminary hearing. Also, if the facts

of the case are particularly nasty, and the defendant plans to plead guilty anyway, the less the sentencing judge hears about the facts, the better for the defendant.

- The prosecution's case is strong, and the defense fears that prosecution witnesses may become so entrenched in their positions once they testify under oath at a prelim that they may become angry (or angrier) with the defendant and possibly refuse later interviews requested by the defense as it prepares for trial.

- The prosecution intends to call witnesses at the prelim who may be unavailable at the time of trial. If the prelim goes forward, this testimony will be available in the form of transcripts from the prelim for the prosecution to use at trial. By waiving the prelim, the defendant may prevent the testimony from coming in when trial time rolls around.

- The defense wants to stall in the hopes that by the time the case comes to trial, the prosecution's witnesses will have either become available, forgotten, or become confused about what happened during the alleged crime. In this situation, the defense may waive the prelim and move for several continuances (delays) of the trial date.

Fundamental Trial Rights of the Defense

A familiar adage states that it's better to let 100 guilty people go free than convict one innocent person. This philosophy is reflected in a number of fundamental trial rights that defendants enjoy. Most of these rights trace their pedigree to the U.S. Constitution's Bill of Rights, and they act as an important restraint on governmental power over private citizens. This chapter describes these fundamental trial rights, which, taken together, form a large part of the "due process of law" guaranteed by the Fifth and Fourteenth Amendments to the U.S. Constitution.

The Defendant's Right to Due Process of Law

The Fifth Amendment to the U.S. Constitution provides in part that a person cannot "be deprived of life, liberty or property without due process of law." This due process clause is the basis for many of the rights afforded criminal defendants and procedures followed in criminal courts.

What is meant by the term "due process"?

"Due process" is an abstract term meaning nothing more nor less than what judges and lawmakers say it means. They generally have interpreted it to mean that criminal procedures are supposed to be fair and just. The term has two general dimensions:

- **Procedural due process.** This means that before criminal defendants can be punished, they must be given a legitimate opportunity to contest the charges against them. For example, they are entitled to notice of the charges long enough before trial to have a chance to prepare a defense, and they are entitled to be tried by fair and impartial judges and juries.
- **Substantive due process.** This means that any actions the government takes must further a legitimate governmental objective. No matter how fair the process, people can't be punished for reading books or making statements that government officials don't like.

Does the Fifth Amendment's due process clause apply to state governments?

The Fifth Amendment applies directly to the federal government only. However, the Fourteenth Amendment also has a due process clause, which includes the words "nor shall any State deprive any person of life, liberty or property without due process of law." The U.S. Supreme Court has interpreted the Fourteenth Amendment to make applicable to the states many of the rights set forth in the Bill of Rights. For example:

- The Fourth Amendment's prohibition of unreasonable searches and seizures was made applicable to the states by the case of *Mapp v. Ohio*, U.S. Sup. Ct. 1961.
- The Eighth Amendment's prohibition of cruel and unusual punishment was made applicable to the states by the case of *Robinson v. California*, U.S. Sup. Ct. 1962.

- The Sixth Amendment's guarantee of the right to counsel was made applicable to the states by the case of *Gideon v. Wainwright,* U.S. Sup. Ct. 1963.
- The Fifth Amendment's establishment of a privilege against self-incrimination was made applicable to the states by the case of *Malloy v. Hogan,* U.S. Sup. Ct. 1964.

The Fifth and Fourteenth Amendments' due process clauses also are the sources of rights not specifically spelled out in the Bill of Rights. For example:

- In *Rochin v. California* (U.S. Sup. Ct. 1952), the Court held that illegal narcotics pumped from a suspect's stomach against his will were inadmissible in court because the police procedures "shocked the conscience" and were "too close to the rack and the screw" to be permitted. However, not every bodily intrusion violates due process. For example, laws requiring blood samples have been upheld against claims that they violate due process.
- In *Stovall v. Denno* (U.S. Sup. Ct. 1967), the Court held that unduly suggestive lineup procedures could violate due process.

Does the due process clause prevent the use of involuntary confessions?

Yes. The due process clause has long been interpreted to prohibit the use in court of confessions that are involuntary, even if they may be factually truthful. For example, a confession is likely to be thrown out as involuntary if the police obtain it by using or threatening to use physical force. Likewise, a confession may be unlawfully obtained if the police violate a defendant's *Miranda* rights.

EXAMPLE: Jonah, a small man of foreign parentage and limited English skills, is approached on the street and questioned by two police officers. Seeing that the officers are carrying guns and sticks, and having heard reports of police brutality in his neighborhood, Jonah is completely intimidated and answers "Yes" to every police question, including whether Jonah committed a crime. The officers did not violate Jonah's due process rights. Though Jonah may have reason to fear the police officers, his confession was voluntary because the officers did nothing to overcome his free will.

EXAMPLE: Same case, except that when the officers approach Jonah they tap their gun holsters while telling him that, "It'll be best for you just to confess to doing the robbery last week at the drug store. We know your old Mama's been ill lately, and we don't know how she'll react to the news that her son's been badly hurt." Jonah then admits that he robbed the drug store. The officers' conduct violated Jonah's due process rights. The implied threat of violence to Jonah and its possible impact on his mother would likely amount to sufficient police coercion to overcome Jonah's free will.

EXAMPLE: Dad finds illegal drugs under his son's bed, beats his son, and makes him call the police and confess. Dad may have committed a crime himself, but unless Dad is working for the police, his conduct isn't a due process violation. Due process limitations apply only to the behavior of government agents like police officers, not private citizens.

What other procedures are governed by the due process clause?

Any aspect of the criminal justice system that arguably violates "fundamental fairness" raises potential due process concerns. Judges' willingness to use the due process clause to invalidate police and prosecution behavior can vary, however, and is probably less in an era when much of the populace wants to get tough on crime. Some of the other important procedures that are required or prohibited by the due process clause include the following:

- Due process is violated if the government's unreasonable and unexplained delay in charging a defendant with a crime substantially impairs a defendant's ability to mount a defense.
- Due process requires the government to disclose exculpatory information— that is, information tending to show that the defendant is not guilty—to the defense.
- Due process is violated if the government entraps a defendant into committing a crime.
- Due process requires judges to "recuse" themselves when the court

on which the judge sits is asked to rule on the merits of a petition by a defendant whom the judge had helped to prosecute before becoming a judge. (*Williams v. Pennsylvania*, U.S. Sup. Ct. 2016.) Even if they can't prove actual bias, defendants are entitled to have judges recuse themselves when circumstances suggest that the probability that a judge is actually biased is too high to be constitutionally tolerable. (*Rippo v. Baker*, U.S. Sup. Ct. 2017.)

- Due process requires judges to instruct juries that defendants are presumed innocent of the charges against them.
- Due process may be violated if a prosecutor's arguments include repeated factual errors, and are so angry and intemperate that they prevent the trial from being fair.
- Due process requires that a defendant's guilt be proven beyond a reasonable doubt.
- Due process requires that defendants have a fair opportunity to present evidence. Rules that unduly impinge on that right (for example, by preventing a defendant from offering evidence that another person committed the crime with which the defendant is charged) are invalid.
- Due process can affect what happens inside the courtroom during a jury trial. For example, forcing defendants to wear prison clothes rather than street clothes in the courtroom violates due process. (*Estelle v. Williams*, U.S.

Sup. Ct. 1976.) Whether courtroom spectators' conduct can result in a violation of defendants' due process rights varies among jurisdictions. For example, some courts have ruled that due process is violated when spectators watch a trial wearing ribbons or buttons displaying a victim's face. However, other courts have ruled that such spectator conduct does not violate due process. (*Carey v. Musladin*, U.S. Sup. Ct. 2006.)

The Prosecution's Burden of Proof

The prosecution has the burden of proving guilt beyond a reasonable doubt.

Is it up to the defense to convince a judge or jury of the defendant's innocence?

Absolutely not. The defendant is presumed innocent until the moment a judge or jury finds him or her guilty. It's up to the prosecution to offer enough evidence to convince the judge or jury that the defendant is guilty. Another way of saying this is that the prosecution has the burden of proof.

What exactly does the prosecution have to prove to meet its burden of proof?

Most crimes consist of two or more discrete elements. The prosecution has the burden of proving facts sufficient to satisfy each element of the charged crime. If the prosecution fails to meet its burden with respect to any one element, a defendant should be found not guilty of that crime.

EXAMPLE: Rob Banks is charged with burglary. Assume that the elements of burglary the prosecution has to prove are: (1) Rob (2) entered (3) a dwelling (4) belonging to another (5) without the owner's permission, and (6) with the intent to commit a crime. The jurors are convinced that the prosecution proved (1), (2), (4), (5), and (6), but do not think that the backyard shed that Rob broke into qualifies as a "dwelling." The jurors should find Rob not guilty. The prosecution has the burden of proving each and every element of the crime charged, and here it failed to meet its burden.

How strong a case does the prosecutor have to present to justify a conviction?

The prosecution has to prove the defendant's guilt beyond a reasonable doubt. This is the highest burden of proof the law can impose. (By contrast, a plaintiff in a civil case only has to prove a defendant liable by a preponderance of the evidence.) The term "beyond a reasonable doubt" has no precise meaning. Sometimes, for example, judges tell jurors that "beyond a reasonable doubt" means that jurors must be convinced of guilt to a "moral certainty" before they vote to convict. Though the meaning of "beyond a reasonable doubt" may be imprecise, it reminds judges and jurors that convicting defendants is serious business, and that the prosecution has to overcome all reasonable inferences favoring innocence. At the same time, any doubts should be based on the evidence; that is, the prosecution should not have to disprove all imaginary explanations that might negate guilt.

EXAMPLE: Ida Dunnit is charged with shoplifting. A store security guard and two customers testify that they saw Dunnit put two computer software packages in her purse and leave the store without paying for them. Dunnit offers no evidence at all. During deliberations, one of the jurors says, "I don't think that she's guilty. Who knows—the guard and the two customers may be lying because they're paying her back for something she did to them." The juror's misgivings do not constitute reasonable doubt. Because the juror can't point to any evidence suggesting that the witnesses are taking revenge on Dunnit by perjuring themselves, the juror's doubts are not reasonable. To satisfy its burden of proof, the government does not have to overcome every possible doubt, just rational doubts. However, the legal system cannot prevent a juror from misapplying the concept of reasonable doubt in favor of a defendant. In other words, this juror cannot be forced to convict Dunnit.

Defense lawyers have favorite and sometimes colorful methods of stressing the meaning of beyond a reasonable doubt during closing argument to juries. Some hold their arms away from their sides to resemble a scale, and then tip far to the side to indicate the magnitude of the prosecution's burden. And some use evocative language, such as, "The conscience of this state cannot sanction the conviction of any individual on speculation, on intuition, or on hunches. You are sworn to uphold the law. You are the people who promised during jury selection that you would not convict on speculation. That you would not convict unless the state proved its case beyond a reasonable doubt. You are the people who said that even if you thought deep down in your hearts that my client was guilty, but that the state had not proven its case beyond a reasonable doubt, you would not convict. That is the conscience of the community, and you are here to uphold it."

Whatever their individual methods, defense lawyers always emphasize to jurors the prosecution's heavy burden of proof.

Beyond a Reasonable Doubt

While each jurisdiction may phrase the prosecution's burden of proof somewhat differently, the following language (taken from a frequently given jury instruction) is typical: "A defendant in a criminal action is presumed to be innocent until the contrary is proved, and in case of a reasonable doubt whether his guilt is satisfactorily shown, he is entitled to a verdict of not guilty. This presumption places upon the State the burden of proving him guilty beyond a reasonable doubt. Reasonable doubt is not a mere possible doubt, because everything relating to human affairs, and depending on moral evidence, is open to some possible or imaginary doubt. It is that state of the case which, after the entire comparison and consideration of all the evidence, leaves the minds of the jurors in that condition that they cannot say that they feel an abiding conviction, to a moral certainty, of the truth of the charge."

Does the defense ever have the burden to prove anything?

Yes. The defense may have the burden of proving certain affirmative defenses. For example, if the defendant claims to be not guilty by reason of insanity, the defense may have the burden of proving that the insanity claim is accurate. However, when the defense has to prove something, its burden of proof is lighter than the government's beyond a reasonable doubt burden. For example, the defense has to convince a judge or jury of insanity only by a preponderance of the evidence or, in some jurisdictions, clear and convincing evidence.

The Defendant's Right to Remain Silent

This section explains how the defendant's right to remain silent actually plays out in a criminal case.

Does a defendant have to testify or offer evidence at trial?

No. The Fifth Amendment to the U.S. Constitution provides that a defendant cannot "be compelled in any criminal case to be a witness against himself." In short, the defendant has the right to sit mute. The prosecutor cannot call the defendant as a witness, nor can a judge or defense attorney force the defendant to testify if the defendant chooses to remain silent. The right to silence extends to a defendant's right not to present a defense at all. This constitutional right to silence is consistent with the prosecution's burden of proof. Even in the absolute absence of a defense case, the defendant must be found not guilty unless the prosecution offers evidence convincing a judge or jury that the defendant is guilty beyond a reasonable doubt.

What does the privilege against self-incrimination mean?

People have to come to court and testify in response to subpoenas. Failure to do so may be punished as contempt of court. But a witness may refuse to answer particular questions if the responses would tend to incriminate that witness.

EXAMPLE: Greta, a graduate student at Queens University, is subpoenaed as a witness in the criminal trial of Professor Victor for stealing university property. The police have evidence that Greta kept some of the items Professor Victor is charged with stealing. If the government can prove that Greta knew the items she kept were stolen, she could be found guilty of the crime of receiving stolen property. Because the prosecution might be able to use Greta's testimony against her in a future criminal proceeding, she has a right not to answer questions about the theft.

EXAMPLE: Same case. Greta has told the police that she witnessed Professor Victor's theft of university property, but did not try to prevent the theft or report it to the police. Greta's conduct may violate a portion of the university's code of conduct, and if so she may be placed on academic probation or even dismissed from the university. However, her failure to act is not a crime. Because her testimony could not be used against her in a criminal proceeding, Greta cannot properly refuse to answer based on the Fifth Amendment. Possible university penalties are not the same as criminal punishment. If Greta refuses the judge's order to testify, she can be held in contempt of court and incarcerated, possibly until she agrees to testify.

What do innocent defendants have to lose by testifying in their own defense?

Even an innocent defendant runs a variety of risks by testifying, including:

- The judge or a juror may react negatively to the defendant's demeanor.
- Either on direct or cross-examination, the defendant's testimony may accidentally strengthen the prosecution's case.
- The prosecution may be able to attack the defendant's character with the defendant's prior crimes and misdeeds. Such evidence often would be inadmissible if the defendant didn't testify.
- By testifying, the defendant allows the jury to compare the prosecution's story to the defendant's. Subconsciously, the jurors may base their decision on whichever story they find more convincing rather than hold true to the principle that they must find the defendant guilty beyond a reasonable doubt.

For these and other reasons, defense attorneys often advise their clients not to testify.

Might a judge or jury infer guilt from a defendant's silence?

This question is difficult to answer. Because the defendant has a constitutional right to remain silent and even to refuse to present a defense, the judge or jury may not infer guilt from the defendant's refusal to testify. (*Griffin v. California,* U.S. Sup. Ct. 1965.) In keeping with this rule, the prosecution may not argue or even imply that a defendant's silence is an indication of guilt. And upon request from the defense, the judge must instruct the jury that it cannot infer guilt from the defendant's silence. Jurors are at least sometimes capable of following such instructions. In the famous 1995 murder trial of O.J. Simpson, Simpson did not testify in his own defense and was nevertheless acquitted of murdering his ex-wife and her friend.

However, no matter what the legal rule, jurors are sometimes suspicious of a defendant who doesn't testify. A juror who is unsure how to vote once deliberations begin may be subconsciously (and negatively) affected by the defendant's failure to testify. Some jurors may even consciously disregard the judge's instructions by reasoning along these lines: "If I were innocent, I'd sure get on the stand, look the jurors in the eye, and testify to my innocence. Because this defendant was afraid to testify, the defendant must be guilty."

The bottom line is that defendants take risks whether they choose to testify or not. Standard 4-5.2 of the ABA Standards for

Criminal Justice instructs attorneys that the decision is for the defendant to make after full consultation. Defendants should carefully consult with their attorneys before deciding whether to testify.

EXAMPLE: At the conclusion of a trial in which the defendant neither testified nor called witnesses, Prosecutor Dustin Miojo says during closing argument, "The state's case is uncontradicted." A judge would probably rule that the comment is a fair characterization of the state of the evidence rather than an implication that the failure to present a defense indicates guilt. Had the prosecutor repeated the statement several times or made direct references to the defendant's silence, the judge would be more likely to rule that the prosecutor stepped over the line.

EXAMPLE: Mary Jane pleads guilty to selling marijuana. During the sentencing hearing, the prosecutor presents a witness who testifies that she saw Mary on numerous occasions selling marijuana to school children. Mary says nothing at the hearing, but her lawyer questions the witness and seriously attacks her credibility. The judge cannot impose a harsher sentence on Mary Jane based on her failure to respond to the witness testimony, because a harsher sentence would constitute drawing negative inferences from a defendant's silence during sentencing hearings. (*Mitchell v. U.S.*, U.S. Sup. Ct. 1999.)

Can suspects refuse a police officer's request for a bodily sample on the grounds that the result might be incriminating?

No. Only evidence that is considered testimonial or communicative—that is, evidence intended to express a person's thoughts—is protected under the Fifth Amendment privilege against self-incrimination. This exception means that the police can require suspects to provide evidence of a purely physical nature—provided that there's a proper basis for obtaining the evidence in the first place—without violating the Fifth Amendment. (*Schmerber v. California*, U.S. Sup. Ct. 1966.) Among the types of physical evidence that a defendant may be required to provide are documents, photographs, fingerprints, and samples of the defendant's voice, hair, saliva, urine, and breath. A suspect may also be required to participate in a lineup and wear certain clothing or repeat certain phrases (for the purpose of voice identification).

Can prosecutors negate witnesses' invocation of the Fifth Amendment right not to testify?

Yes. The prosecution can give a witness "immunity" in response to a legitimate refusal to testify based on the Fifth Amendment. The prosecutor can offer one of two forms of immunity, depending on factors such as the seriousness of the immunized witness's own criminal conduct:

- "Transactional" immunity means that the person given immunity cannot be prosecuted for any crimes related to the subject matter of the testimony.

- "Use" immunity means that the witness given immunity may in the future be prosecuted for a crime related to the subject matter of the witness's testimony, but the immunized testimony itself cannot be used in the future prosecution.

Prosecutors often give immunity to compel small fish to testify against big fish. For example, a prosecutor may give a small-time drug dealer immunity in exchange for the dealer's testimony against the drug lord from whom the dealer purchased the drugs. A witness who refuses to testify after being given immunity can be held in contempt of court by the judge and jailed.

The Defendant's Right to Confront Witnesses

This section explains the defendant's right to confront and cross-examine all prosecution witnesses, including those whose hearsay statements are offered into evidence at trial.

Is the defense entitled to cross-examine prosecution witnesses?

Yes. The Confrontation Clause of the Sixth Amendment gives defendants the right to confront the witnesses against them. Implicit in the right to confront witnesses is the right to cross-examine them. (*Douglas v. Alabama*, U.S. Sup. Ct. 1965.) Prosecution witnesses have to come to court, look the defendant in the eye, and subject themselves to questioning by the defense. The Sixth Amendment prevents secret trials and, subject to limited exceptions, forbids prosecutors from proving a defendant's guilt using oral or written statements from absent witnesses.

Police laboratory reports or affidavits describing the results of forensic tests (such as DNA typing and blood alcohol content) are testimonial. (*Melendez-Diaz v. Massachusetts*, U.S. Sup. Ct. 2009.) Thus, to introduce this type of evidence, prosecutors must usually call forensic analysts as witnesses at trial so that defendants can cross-examine them.

EXAMPLE: Bea Yussef is on trial for felony hit-and-run. A witness testified for the prosecution, then suddenly became ill and had to go to the hospital before Yussef's attorney could conduct cross-examination. The judge should strike the prosecution witness's direct testimony from the record and instruct the jury to disregard it. Even though Yussef's inability to cross-examine the witness is not due to any fault of the prosecution, the prosecution cannot rely on witnesses whom the defense has not had an opportunity to cross-examine. If the testimony was so important that jurors are unlikely to be able to erase it from their minds, the judge might have to stop the trial (declare a mistrial) and, if the prosecution wishes, start all over again.

Testimonial Hearsay and the Confrontation Clause

The Confrontation Clause guarantees that in criminal cases, defendants have the right to confront the witnesses against them. As a result, prosecutors cannot offer "testimonial" hearsay statements against defendants unless the person whose hearsay is offered (pursuant to an exception to the hearsay rule) testifies as a witness or unless the defendant has previously had a chance to cross-examine the person (say, during a preliminary hearing). (*Crawford v. Washington*, U.S. Sup. Ct. 2004.)

A hearsay statement is a statement made outside of the courtroom that's offered into evidence for its truth (that is, to prove the facts stated). Such a statement is testimonial when government agents elicit information in nonemergency situations in order to gather evidence for a criminal prosecution.

For example, information that a witness gives to a grand jury under oath is clearly testimonial (and often would not be admissible under the hearsay rule either). As a result, a prosecutor cannot offer grand jury testimony against a defendant if the person who gave the testimony does not testify at trial and the defendant has not otherwise had a chance to cross-examine the witness. Likewise, if police officers go to a crime scene and ask victims and witnesses to describe what happened, the witnesses' statements are likely to be testimonial and inadmissible at trial in the absence of a defendant's opportunity to cross-examine either at or before trial. (*Davis v. Washington*, U.S. Sup. Ct. 2006.)

On the other hand, statements that people make to 911 operators in the course of an "ongoing emergency" are not testimonial.

(*Davis v. Washington*, U.S. Sup. Ct. 2006.) A 911 operator is not gathering evidence, but rather is trying to figure out what is happening in an ongoing emergency. Similarly, if police officers interview a fatally wounded shooting victim when the shooter is still at large, an ongoing emergency exists and the victim's responses are not barred by the Confrontation Clause, even if the defendant doesn't get an opportunity to cross-examine. (*Michigan v. Bryant*, U.S. Sup. Ct. 2011.) However, if an emergency has passed, a 911 call may be testimonial. For instance, if a 911 caller reports a kidnapping after the victim has escaped to safety, the report is testimonial. (*State of Conn. v. Kirby*, Conn. Sup. Ct. 2006.)

In *Ohio v. Clark* (U.S. Sup. Ct. 2015), the Court held that the Confrontation Clause wasn't violated when a teacher testified to a three-year-old's statement identifying the man who caused his injuries. The Court stressed that (1) the abuse made for an "ongoing emergency," (2) the boy was too young to understand that what he said might be used as evidence, and (3) the teacher wasn't a law enforcement officer.

The U.S. Supreme Court is badly divided and has reached inconsistent conclusions over the question of whether police laboratory analysts who conduct forensic tests are "witnesses" whose statements are "testimonial" for purposes of the Confrontation Clause. In *Melendez-Diaz v. Massachusetts* (U.S. Sup. Ct. 2009), the prosecution offered into evidence a forensic analyst's report stating that the substance seized from a criminal defendant was cocaine. The Court decided by a narrow 5-4 margin that the analyst was a witness and that the report constituted testimonial

Testimonial Hearsay and the Confrontation Clause (continued)

hearsay. Under the Confrontation Clause, the prosecution had to produce the analyst as a witness at trial. Similarly, in *Bullcoming v. New Mexico* (U.S. Sup. Ct. 2011), involving the admissibility of an intoxication test, the Court ruled by the same narrow 5-4 margin that the prosecution's witness had to be the analyst who actually conducted the test, not a different analyst from the same lab who was familiar with testing procedures.

But the Court appeared to veer away from this rule in *Williams v. Illinois* (U.S. Sup. Ct. 2012), where the prosecution's forensic expert testified that a match existed between a rape defendant's DNA and DNA found at the crime scene. The Court ruled by a 5-4 margin that the Confrontation Clause didn't require the prosecution to call as a witness the forensic analyst who actually conducted the DNA analysis. Four Justices in the majority disagreed with *Melendez-Diaz* and *Bullcoming*, stating that forensic analysts are not "witnesses" for Confrontation Clause purposes. These four found themselves on the winning rather than on the losing side when a fifth Justice joined with them for a completely different reason: the DNA report was too informal to be "testimonial."

Thus, the Court is in disarray as to whether prosecutors have to call as witnesses the analysts who conduct forensic tests and prepare reports, or whether another witness with knowledge of testing procedures satisfies the Confrontation Clause. Courts all over the country await further guidance from the Supreme Court.

EXAMPLE: Mary Kontrary is charged with drunk driving. On the day set for her trial, the prosecutor announces that the arresting police officer is on vacation. In lieu of the police officer's testimony, the prosecutor asks the judge for permission to offer into evidence against Mary the officer's police report detailing the reasons for the arrest. Under the Confrontation Clause, Mary has a right to confront and cross-examine the police officer. The defense can't cross-examine a police report. Also, the police report does not fit within an exception to the hearsay rule. The judge should dismiss the case or allow the prosecution to delay the trial, time permitting.

Is it possible for defendants to be tried in their absence?

No, with rare exceptions. A defendant's own behavior can cause the defendant to lose the right to personal confrontation. A defendant who voluntarily fails to show up for trial can sometimes be tried *in absentia.* And, a defendant whose conduct repeatedly disrupts the trial may be removed from the court. (*Illinois v. Allen*, U.S. Sup. Ct. 1970.) Of course, the defendant's attorney would remain in the courtroom, if the defendant were represented.

EXAMPLE: Bea Yussef is still on trial for felony hit-and-run. Bea has a medical problem that causes her to be highly disruptive unless she has proper medication. Because Bea has been in jail, her doctor has been unable to adjust her medication. As a result, Bea becomes uncontrollable in court, and the court orders her removed. The judge is entitled to order Bea's removal if her outbursts constantly disrupt the trial (her attorney would remain). At the same time, removing Bea from her trial is a serious step, one that may prejudice the jury against her. The judge must permit Bea to return if medicine enables her to control her behavior.

EXAMPLE: Stan Desside is charged with assault and battery on Noah Way. Desside claims that he hit Way in self-defense. The prosecutor asks that Desside stay outside the courtroom while Way testifies, because Desside has threatened to attack Way again if Way testifies against him. The prosecutor's request is improper. The Confrontation Clause gives Desside the right to be personally present when Way testifies. However, based on the threat, the judge can issue a protective order requiring that Desside not annoy Way or come within a prescribed distance of him. Desside could be punished for contempt of court for violating the order regardless of whether or not he strikes Way.

Has a defendant's right to confront witnesses had an impact on domestic violence cases?

Yes. In an all-too-typical scenario, female victims of domestic violence refuse to cooperate with the police and prosecutors once the initial emergency has passed. At one time, prosecutors were nevertheless able to convict domestic abusers by having police officers testify to victims' hearsay statements describing defendants' abuse. However, many of these statements are "testimonial" and are no longer admissible

in evidence. (See *Davis v. Washington*, U.S. Sup. Ct. 2006.) As a result, unless domestic violence victims are willing to testify at trial, charges against their abusers often have to be dismissed.

Are there special confrontation rules for child sexual assault cases?

Yes. In recent years, legislators have been concerned about defendants who escape punishment for sexually molesting young children because the children are afraid to testify in the defendant's presence. To address this problem, many states have enacted special rules that authorize judges to allow children to testify via closed circuit TV. The defendant can see the child on a TV monitor, but the child cannot see the defendant. The defense attorney can be personally present where the child is testifying and can cross-examine the child. The U.S. Supreme Court has upheld the constitutionality of these special procedures. (*Maryland v. Craig*, U.S. Sup. Ct. 1990.)

The Defendant's (and the Media's) Right to a Public Trial

Public trials prevent secret injustices. This section explains the right of the public, the defendant, and the media to open court proceedings.

Can friends and family members attend a defendant's trial?

Yes. The Sixth Amendment guarantees public trials in criminal cases. This is an important right, because the attendance of friends, family, ordinary citizens, and the press can all help ensure that court proceedings are conducted fairly and that the defendant's rights are respected.

Can defendants prevent an alleged victim's family and friends from attending court proceedings?

No. The right to a public trial belongs not just to defendants but also to the prosecution, victims, and the public at large.

Can the judge limit the number of people who observe a trial?

Yes. As part of maintaining order in the courtroom, judges may restrict the number of people they allow in court, and judges may also order people who disrupt proceedings to leave the courtroom.

Does the media have a right to cover criminal proceedings?

Yes. The Supreme Court has recognized that one of the purposes of the First Amendment free speech clause is to protect speech about how the government operates. This includes media access to all open court criminal proceedings, trial and pretrial proceedings alike. (*Richmond Newspapers v. Virginia,* U.S. Sup. Ct. 1980; *Globe Newspaper Co. v. Superior Court,* U.S. Sup. Ct. 1982.)

The Supreme Court has also indicated that rarely, if ever, will the media be stopped from publishing information about what happens during public court proceedings, even if that information might be harmful to the

defendant's ability to get a fair trial. (*Nebraska Press Association v. Stuart,* U.S. Sup. Ct. 1976.)

Are there circumstances that might justify closing criminal proceedings to observers?

Yes, but only as a last resort and as a rare measure to protect an equally important competing right, such as the right to a fair trial or the privacy rights of a child.

> **EXAMPLE:** Steven Racci is charged with murdering his criminal law professor. In part because the professor, Kathi Rae, was a beautiful young woman and a frequent guest on law-related talk shows, the case has gotten enormous press coverage. Steven's lawyer has asked the court to close all pretrial proceedings, including the preliminary hearing, and the trial itself to the public. The defense lawyer argues that Steven's right to a fair trial is being denied by the press coverage, in particular because the press is reporting on "evidence" that may not be admitted at trial and so might poison the minds of potential jurors and the public against Steven. A defendant's right to a fair trial may outweigh the public's right to observe and obtain information about the trial. But a judge may not close a proceeding to the public unless it is necessary to prevent prejudice and alternative measures that would reasonably protect the defendant are unavailable. In Steven's case, alternatives exist, such as screening out those whose exposure to the pretrial publicity makes them unfit to serve as fair and impartial jurors. Thus, the judge should probably not close Steven's trial to the public.

The judge could also sequester jurors (separate them from the outside world) or order the jurors not to read or watch any news relating to the trial (judges normally give this order as a matter of course). The judge could also order a change of venue, moving the case to a locale less saturated with pretrial publicity.

EXAMPLE: Defense lawyer Bobbie Hulls requests that the court close the trial of his client, Eve Yule, who is on trial for allegedly molesting her young daughter. Though avoiding further harm to child abuse victims has been found sufficiently important to justify some court closures, the court must first explore other, less drastic, ways of preventing the alleged harm. Here, the court could allow the victim to testify in private and have the testimony transmitted to court via closed circuit TV. Or the judge could close only the portion of the trial when the daughter testifies.

EXAMPLE: Same case as above. Eve Yule is on trial for allegedly molesting her young daughter. During jury selection, both the prosecutor and defense counsel want to ask potential jurors potentially embarrassing questions about their intimate lives. Nevertheless, the judge need not bar public access to the courtroom. The judge has an alternative: allowing jurors who wish to do so to answer potentially embarrassing questions in the judge's chambers (with counsel present, of course), rather than in open court.

Sequestration Rules

Sequestration rules attempt to prevent witnesses from being influenced by the testimony of other witnesses. Sequestered witnesses have to stay outside the courtroom until it is their turn to testify, and they cannot discuss their testimony with other witnesses until those witnesses have been excused from giving further testimony. Thus, if a defendant's friends or relatives are going to testify, sequestration rules may prevent them from being physically present inside the courtroom for much of the trial.

Can judges limit the conduct and number of news media in the courtroom?

Yes. Judges have to protect defendants' rights to a fair trial, and can't allow the media's presence or activities to disrupt courtroom order. For example, in *Sheppard v. Maxwell* (U.S. Sup. Ct. 1966), the Supreme Court found the defendant's right to a fair trial had been denied in part because of "the carnival atmosphere at trial" caused by the media. In that case, crowds of news reporters were apparently so loud that it was difficult to hear witnesses and lawyers. Also, reporters were seated so close to the defendant that he could not speak confidentially with his lawyers.

Are TV cameras routinely allowed in courtrooms?

No. It is up to the judge. The media may televise a criminal trial at the judge's discretion, unless the defendant shows that the coverage will violate his or her right to fair trial. (*Chandler v. Florida,* U.S. Sup. Ct. 1981.) Some courts (such as the U.S. Supreme Court) have a policy of not televising proceedings. And, after the internationally followed 1995 televised murder trial of O.J. Simpson, many judges have become more reluctant to permit live televising of trials. The Simpson trial took nine months to complete, and television drew much of the blame for the length of the trial. In 1997, when Simpson faced a civil trial based on the same murders for which he had been tried criminally, the judge refused to allow TV cameras and the case was over in a few weeks.

Can the judge order a lawyer not to discuss a case with the media?

Yes. A trial judge faced with prejudicial publicity may protect the defendant's right to a fair trial by placing a "gag order" on attorneys, parties, and witnesses, preventing them from discussing a case outside the courtroom. Also, lawyers' ethical rules often limit the type and extent of commentary prosecutors and defense lawyers may make about an ongoing prosecution. For example, gag order or not, a prosecutor is not permitted to interfere with a defendant's right to a fair trial by disclosing negative facts about the defendant if the facts probably are not admissible as evidence.

Does the media have the right to investigate crimes?

The media may investigate all they want, as long as they are using lawful means, such as interviewing suspects or witnesses who voluntarily choose to talk or obtaining government documents under the Freedom of Information Act. However, the media does not have the right to force suspects to talk or submit to other procedures. A suspect, of course, does not have to (and usually should not) talk to anyone except his or her own defense lawyer. A suspect may have to submit to police identification procedures, such as appearing in a lineup or giving a blood sample, but has no obligation to give or say anything to the media.

Is it proper for reporters and photographers to enter a house along with the police officers who are searching it?

No. *Wilson v. Layne* (U.S. Sup. Ct. 1999) decided that a homeowner's Fourth Amendment search and seizure rights are violated when police officers allow newspeople who are on so-called "media ride-alongs" (riding with police officers to crime scenes) to accompany the officers into a home to observe and photograph searches or arrests. Police officers who commit such violations can be personally liable to a homeowner for money damages.

A Defendant's Right to a Jury Trial

The jury trial is one of the most enduring symbols of the U.S. criminal justice process.

Are criminal defendants always entitled to a jury trial?

The Sixth Amendment guarantees jury trials in all criminal prosecutions. However, this right does not extend to petty offenses. The U.S. Supreme Court has defined a petty offense as one that does not carry a sentence of more than six months in jail. (*Lewis v. U.S.*, U.S. Sup. Ct. 1996.) Because felonies and most misdemeanors carry possible maximum sentences of more than six months in jail, defendants are entitled to a trial by jury in most cases.

What happens if a defendant wants a judge trial, but the prosecutor wants a jury trial?

If either the prosecutor or the defendant wants a jury trial, then a jury trial there shall normally be, assuming the case is serious enough to warrant a jury trial in the first place.

If neither the prosecution nor the defense expresses a preference, will a judge or jury decide a case?

It depends on where the trial takes place. In federal court trials, defendants get jury trials unless they give written notice that they want a judge trial. (See Federal Rule of Criminal Procedure 23(a), which provides that a defendant entitled to a jury trial will have one unless the defendant agrees to waive (give up) a jury trial in writing, and the government and the judge accept the defendant's waiver.)

Many states have similar provisions. A few states, however, take the opposite approach, and provide that trial will be to a judge unless the defendant expressly requests a jury.

Why do juries mostly consist of 12 people?

The United States inherited its jury system from England, and in England juries have generally consisted of 12 people since the fourteenth century, for reasons nobody is quite sure of. Maybe that's how many spare chairs the first courtroom had. But a jury can constitutionally consist of as few as six people. (*Williams v. Florida*, U.S. Sup. Ct. 1970.) The size of juries tends to vary depending on the state and the seriousness of the charge. For example, a state might generally require 12-person juries for felony and misdemeanor trials but allow the prosecution and the defense to agree to less-than-12-person juries in misdemeanor cases. Another state might provide for six-person juries in noncapital cases and 12-person juries in capital cases.

Do all jurors have to vote the same way to produce a verdict in a criminal trial?

Not necessarily. Defendants tried by six-person juries can be convicted only if the jury is unanimous in favor of guilt. (*Ballew v. Georgia*, U.S. Sup. Ct. 1978.) But the U.S. Supreme Court has upheld a state law providing for less than unanimous verdicts by 12-person juries in non-death-penalty cases. Assuming that a state's law provides for less-than-unanimous verdicts in criminal cases, convictions based on nine out of 12 jurors voting for a guilty verdict are constitutionally valid. (*Johnson v. Louisiana*, U.S. Sup. Ct. 1972.)

Again, however, not all states provide for less-than-unanimous verdicts. Some states require unanimous verdicts in all criminal cases.

A "hung jury" results when less than the required number of jurors can agree on a verdict. For example, in a state that requires unanimous jury verdicts, a hung jury results if only 11 of the 12 jurors vote to convict a defendant. Hung juries often result in retrials, though prosecutors might decide not to proceed with a retrial if the majority of people on a hung jury voted to acquit the defendant.

A Defendant's Right to Counsel

Virtually all criminal defendants have legal representation, either privately retained or provided at government expense. This section is about a criminal defendant's right to be represented by an attorney during all important phases of the criminal justice process.

What is the basis of criminal defendants' right to legal representation?

The Sixth Amendment to the U.S. Constitution provides that "in all criminal prosecutions, the accused shall enjoy the right … to have the assistance of counsel for his defense."

Does the government have to appoint and pay for attorneys to represent indigent defendants?

A judge must appoint an attorney for an indigent defendant (a defendant who cannot afford to hire a private attorney) at government expense in criminal cases in which the defendant may be imprisoned. (*Scott v. Illinois,* U.S. Sup. Ct. 1979.) As a practical matter, judges routinely appoint attorneys for indigents in nearly all cases in which a jail sentence is a possibility. Otherwise, the judge would be locked into a non-jail sentence.

At what stage of a criminal case does the right to counsel begin?

An accused person's right to counsel becomes effective at the moment judicial proceedings begin. (*Michigan v. Jackson,* U.S. Sup. Ct. 1986.) When this moment occurs varies from one case to another. For example, if a criminal case begins with a grand jury indictment, the right to counsel goes into effect with the indictment (even though defendants may not know until they're arrested that they had been indicted). If an arraignment is the first step in a criminal case, then the right to counsel becomes effective at the time of arraignment. Once the right to counsel attaches to defendants, police officers generally cannot question them unless their attorneys are present or they waive (give up) the right to have an attorney present. (See Chapter 1 for information on the right to counsel after arrest, in the context of police interrogation.)

> **EXAMPLE:** Rose Peters is indicted by a grand jury for selling illegal drugs. Rose first finds out about the indictment the next day, when the police come to her apartment to arrest

her. While arresting Rose, the police question her and she admits that she's been involved in selling illegal drugs. The formal criminal proceedings against Rose began with the indictment. At that point she had the right to counsel. Therefore, police questioning in the absence of an attorney was improper, and anything Rose said cannot be introduced into evidence against her in court. (*Fellers v. United States*, U.S. Sup. Ct. 2004.)

EXAMPLE: Same case. After Rose is taken to jail, she waives her *Miranda* rights and agrees to answer the police officer's questions. She then repeats what she told the police officer at the time she was arrested, that she was involved in selling illegal drugs. Even though Rose waived her *Miranda* rights, the police officer's earlier improper conversation with Rose at the time of her arrest may render her jailhouse confession inadmissible.

Do lawyers control all case-related decisions?

No. Standard 4-5.2 of the ABA Standards for Criminal Justice reminds lawyers that certain fundamental decisions are for clients and not lawyers to make after adequate consultation. (Refer to Chapter 8 for more information.)

If a lawyer represents a defendant in connection with one offense, can police officers question the defendant about other offenses without the attorney's presence?

Yes. As long as a defendant has been *Mirandized*, the Sixth Amendment right to have counsel present doesn't extend to uncharged offenses even if the offenses are factually intertwined.

EXAMPLE: Robb was suspected of a burglary in which a man disappeared. Robb was indicted for burglary and an attorney was appointed to represent him. While on bail, Robb confessed to his father that he had killed the man. The father informed the police, who arrested Robb for murder. Robb was given his *Miranda* rights, waived his right to counsel, and confessed to the murder. The police have the right to question Robb about the murder charge without his attorney being present, because the Sixth Amendment is "offense specific." (*Texas v. Cobb*, U.S. Sup. Ct. 2001.) In other words, the Sixth Amendment precludes the police from questioning a *Mirandized* defendant only on the specific offense for which the attorney was retained. Thus, the confession to the murder is admissible in evidence against Robb.

Can a conviction be overturned because a defendant's lawyer was incompetent?

The U.S. Supreme Court has ruled that indigent defendants who are represented by appointed counsel and defendants who hire their own attorneys are entitled to adequate representation. (*Cuyler v. Sullivan*, U.S. Sup. Ct. 1980.) But defendants should not expect a conviction to be overturned just because the defendant's attorney made some mistakes. To result in a guilty verdict being overturned, an attorney's errors generally have to be so serious that they amount to a denial of a fair trial. (*Strickland v. Washington*, U.S. Sup. Ct. 1984.)

Below are examples of claims defendants have made against their attorneys that appellate courts have ruled do not justify throwing out a guilty verdict. (Each case, though, depends on its precise facts, and different courts might reach different outcomes on similar facts.)

- failing to call favorable witnesses at trial
- using cocaine during the time the representation was taking place
- failing to object to a judge's erroneous instruction to jurors concerning the burden of proof
- eliciting evidence very damaging to the defendant while cross-examining prosecution witnesses
- repeatedly advising a defendant who claimed innocence to plead guilty, and
- representing the defendant while being suspended from the practice of law for failure to pay state bar dues.

On the other hand, circumstances can be sufficiently shocking to justify throwing out a guilty verdict based on an attorney's incompetence. Judges have ruled that the following claims justify a reversal of a guilty verdict or a sentence:

- putting a law student intern in charge of the defense and leaving the courtroom while the case was going on
- acknowledging during closing argument that the defendant was guilty of a lesser crime without first securing the defendant's approval of this tactic
- during jury *voir dire* (questioning of potential jurors), failing to challenge two potential jurors who said they would be bothered by the defendant's failure to testify
- failing to investigate a defendant's personal background in a capital punishment case, because the information produced might lead jurors not to sentence the defendant to death (*Wiggins v. Smith,* U.S. Sup. Ct. 2003)
- eliciting testimony from an expert witness that people who have the same racial background as the defendant are more likely to be violent (*Buck v. Davis*, U.S. Sup. Ct. 2017), and
- repeatedly dozing off during trial proceedings. (*U.S. v. Ragin*, 4th Cir. 2016.)

The upshot of all these cases is that defendants should not rely on the appellate courts to ensure that they have the effective assistance of counsel. Understanding the foundations of the attorney-client relationship and insisting on good representation is key.

Does a defendant's right to adequate representation extend to plea bargaining?

Yes. (See Chapter 20.)

When can defendants represent themselves?

Defendants have a right to represent themselves if they are competent to do so. Defendants can be mentally competent to stand trial, yet not sufficiently mentally competent to represent themselves. (*Indiana v. Edwards*, U.S. Sup. Ct. 2008.) In some cases judges may appoint a lawyer as an adviser for a self-representing defendant, with the lawyer being ready to take over the defense if necessary.

In most cases, criminal defendants should either hire an attorney or, if they can't afford one, accept a court-appointed attorney. (For more on self-representation, see Chapter 7.)

A Defendant's Right to a Speedy Trial

Prosecutors can't unreasonably delay legal proceedings while incarcerated suspects languish in jail or bailed-out suspects go through life with criminal charges hanging over their heads.

Does the Constitution specify the timing of a trial?

No. The Sixth Amendment gives defendants a right to a "speedy trial," but it does not specify exact time limits. Thus, judges often have to decide on a case-by-case basis whether a defendant's trial has been so delayed that the case should be thrown out. In making this decision, judges look at the length of the delay, the reason for the delay, and whether the delay has prejudiced the defendant's position. In one case, for example, the U.S. Supreme Court held that a gap of five years between a defendant's arrest and trial did not violate the Constitution, because the defendant agreed to most of the delays. *(Barker v. Wingo,* U.S. Sup. Ct. 1972.)

Do any rules reinforce speedy trial rights?

Every jurisdiction has enacted statutes that set time limits for moving cases from the filing of the initial charge to trial. For example, federal court cases are governed by the Speedy Trial Act (18 U.S.C. § 3161). This law sets the following time limits:

- The government has to formally charge a defendant with a crime within 30 days of the defendant's arrest.
- The government should bring a case to trial not less than 30 nor more than 70 days after charging a defendant with a crime.

States have their own versions of the Speedy Trial Act. In one state, for example, a defendant might have the right to demand a trial within 60 days of being charged with a crime. In the absence of a demand, the prosecution in that state might have 90 days to bring a misdemeanor case to trial, and 175 days to bring a felony case to trial. In another state, the government might normally have 60 days from the filing of charges to bring felony cases to trial. The law in that state might provide that the prosecution has 30 days to bring a misdemeanor case to trial if a defendant is in custody and 45 days if the defendant isn't.

Do cases ever move slower than the rules seem to require?

Yes. Time limit rules are typically subject to a host of exceptions. For example, when computing the time before trial, delays caused by the absence of the defendant or an important witness may not count. Also, defendants and prosecutors often agree to delay proceedings. As a result, many cases take longer to conclude than a glance at the statutes would suggest.

What happens if the prosecutor waits too long to bring a case to trial?

The prosecution's failure to adhere to statutory time requirements generally results in dismissal of a case. However, if the applicable statute of limitations has not expired, the prosecution might be able to refile the charges and start a new case.

Is it usually in a defendant's interest to delay a trial for as long as possible?

Sure. The longer a case goes on, the more likely it is that the prosecution witnesses will become forgetful, move away, or lose interest in testifying. Prosecutors know this, of course, and often it is prosecutors who oppose defendants' requests for delays. That is why many states extend the right to a speedy trial to prosecutors as well as defendants.

Is it ever in a defendant's interest to ask for a trial as soon as possible after charges are filed?

Yes. A very speedy trial can be to a defendant's advantage in cases in which the prosecution has to do a lot of investigation and conduct scientific tests. A quick trial can force the prosecution to go to trial before it is really ready to do so. The defense used this tactic in the 1995 double murder trial of O.J. Simpson. The defense hastened the start of the trial by waiving various hearings it might have insisted on, most notably a hearing on the admissibility of DNA evidence. Many commentators cited the prosecution's possible unpreparedness as a factor that contributed to the jury's not guilty verdict.

The Defendant's Right Not to Be Placed in Double Jeopardy

Among the several clauses of the Fifth Amendment to the U.S. Constitution is this well-known provision: "nor shall any person be subject for the same offense to be twice put in jeopardy of life or limb." The Double Jeopardy Clause protects defendants from government harassment by preventing them from being put on trial or punished more than once for the same offense. Double jeopardy problems are unusual, because prosecutors usually want to wrap up all their charges in the same case.

When is a defendant considered to be "in jeopardy"?

In a jury trial, jeopardy begins when the petit jury (the jury that will decide the case, as opposed to a grand jury) is given an oath. (*Esteban Martinez v. Illinois*, U.S. Sup. Ct. 2014.) In a trial before a judge sitting without a jury, jeopardy begins when the first trial witness is sworn in. When a defendant enters into a plea bargain, jeopardy begins when the judge unconditionally accepts the defendant's guilty plea. Consider these scenarios:

- A prosecutor dismisses a case after a jury is selected but before it is given the oath, and then refiles the criminal charges and begins the case all over again. (A prosecutor might do this if an important witness were temporarily unavailable to testify.) The second case can go forward because the defendant was never formally in jeopardy.

- A suspect is subpoenaed to appear before a grand jury, which refuses to issue an indictment. The prosecutor secures additional evidence and again subpoenas the defendant to appear before the grand jury. The second subpoena is valid because the suspect was not formally in jeopardy earlier. (Of course, on both occasions the suspect could refuse to answer questions before the grand jury by invoking the Fifth Amendment.)

- In a trial before a judge, the prosecutor dismisses the case when its principal witness badly garbles his testimony. The case cannot be refiled because the defendant was in jeopardy once the first witness was sworn in. Therefore, trying the case again would be double jeopardy.

Can defendants face charges in both state and federal court for the same conduct?

Generally, yes. Defendants can properly be charged for the same conduct by different jurisdictions. (*Gamble v. U.S.*, U.S. Sup. Ct. 2019.) This happens only infrequently, however, because of limited government resources. For example, a suspect named Bufford Furrow was arrested in 1999 after shooting at a number of children in a Jewish day care center in California and killing a postal worker in the course of his escape. Furrow was indicted in federal court for murdering a federal employee and committing hate crimes in violation of federal civil rights laws. Furrow could also have been charged in a California state court with murder (for killing the postman) and attempted murder (for shooting at the children). Furrow's prosecution by both the federal and state governments would not violate the Double Jeopardy Clause because they are separate jurisdictions.

What is the "same offense" for purposes of the Double Jeopardy Clause?

The answer is complex because jurisdictions use two different tests, and the outcome of a double jeopardy claim can depend on which test a jurisdiction uses. Some states use a broad "same conduct" test, meaning that a prosecution is for the same offense if it is for a crime that arose from the same conduct that was the subject of a previous prosecution. Other states (and federal courts) use a narrower "same elements" test, meaning that a prosecution is for the same offense only if all the legal elements (sometimes called material facts or facts of consequence) of one crime are the same as the crime that was the subject of a previous prosecution.

> **EXAMPLE:** Jones was charged with the crime of robbery for accosting Hans Supp at gunpoint and taking his wallet. To prove robbery, the prosecution had to show that Jones took Supp's property by means of force or fear. However, Jones was found not guilty. The prosecutor now charges Jones with the crime of theft for taking Supp's wallet. Jones objects that the theft charge violates the Double Jeopardy Clause. The second charge

is clearly barred under the "same conduct" test because both the robbery and the theft charges grow out of Jones's attack on Supp. It is also barred under the narrower "same elements" test, because all of the elements in the crime of theft also are a part of the crime of robbery, for which Jones was already put in jeopardy.

EXAMPLE: Jones is charged with the crime of robbery for accosting Hans Supp in his office at gunpoint and taking his wallet. The judge dismisses the case after the prosecution's evidence fails to prove that Supp was in his office when Jones stole his wallet. The prosecutor now charges Jones with burglary, claiming that Jones entered Supp's office for the purpose of committing a theft. Jones objects that the burglary charge violates the Double Jeopardy Clause. The burglary charge violates the Double Jeopardy Clause if the court uses the same conduct test, because both charges arise from the same conduct. But the burglary charge does not violate double jeopardy under the same elements test, because the crimes of robbery and burglary each contain a legal element that is not part of the other crime. Robbery is theft through force or fear, an element that's not part of the crime of burglary. And burglary involves breaking into and entering a building, an element that's not part of the crime of robbery. Because the elements of the two crimes are different, Jones could be separately charged under the same elements test with both crimes, even though both grow out of the same conduct.

If a defendant's appeal results in an appellate court reversing a conviction, does retrial of the defendant violate the Double Jeopardy Clause?

If an appellate court reverses a guilty verdict, the defendant can usually be retried and, if convicted again, can even be given a harsher sentence than the one given at the first trial. For this reason, defendants who would have a good argument on appeal but who received an unusual and lenient sentence are sometimes wiser to forgo the appeal. (There's no guarantee of getting the same judge for the retrial.)

Reasons for prosecutors not retrying cases after an overturned conviction include:

- The appellate decision rested on the improper introduction of evidence, which the prosecution is barred from using in a second trial. If that evidence was essential to the prosecution's case, the government may decide that it does not have enough evidence to convince a jury of the defendant's guilt.
- The prosecutor and defendant strike a deal (a plea bargain). The case may be old and witnesses hard to relocate; the heat may be off the prosecutor to try the case; or there may be newer, more pressing cases that merit the government's attention.
- In any retrial, the double jeopardy rule prevents the government from pursuing a charge as to which a defendant was found not guilty during the first trial.

EXAMPLE. Ida Dunnit is tried on two charges: assault with a deadly weapon, and assault. The jury finds Ida not guilty of assault with a deadly weapon, and convicts her of the lesser crime of simple assault. Ida appeals, and the appeals court overturns the guilty verdict. The state can retry Ida, but only for simple assault. The not guilty verdict on the charge of assault with a deadly weapon is final.

On rare occasions, an appellate court reverses a conviction for a reason that prevents the state from retrying a defendant. For example, if an appellate court concludes that even the most favorable interpretation of the prosecution's evidence is insufficient as a matter of law to prove an element of a charged crime beyond a reasonable doubt, no retrial is possible following reversal of the conviction. Similarly, if an appellate court rules that evidence that was necessary to convict a defendant is inadmissible, the defendant cannot be tried again.

EXAMPLE. Jackson was convicted of the murder of a drug dealer. On appeal, he argued that the police stopped his car without a reasonable suspicion that he met the description of the assailant. Finding that the stop was motivated by racial bias, the appellate court ruled that the detention, and evidence that resulted from it, should have been suppressed. Because there was no other evidence linking the defendant to the crime, the court also ordered the case dismissed on the grounds of insufficient evidence.

Can a defendant be retried if the judge has declared a mistrial?

In most circumstances, yes. A judge may declare a mistrial and call a halt to a case if there is manifest necessity for such an action. For example, a judge may declare a mistrial if:

- the number of jurors falls below the number required by statute because of illness
- the defendant becomes ill and it is not feasible to interrupt the trial for the length of time necessary for the defendant to recover
- jurors engage in misconduct (such as by visiting the scene of the crime despite the judge's orders not to do so), or
- jurors are unable to reach a unanimous verdict after the judge gives them a reasonable amount of time to deliberate. (*Renico v. Lett*, U.S. Sup. Ct. 2010.)

EXAMPLE: Blueford is charged with murder and manslaughter. The jury foreperson reports to the judge that the jurors are unanimously opposed to convicting Blueford of murder, and are deadlocked on the manslaughter charge. The jurors continue to deliberate, but the judge declares a mistrial when the jury remains unable to reach a verdict. Double jeopardy principles allow the state to retry Blueford on both charges. The foreperson's report that the jurors were unanimously opposed to convicting Blueford of murder was not a formal acquittal of the charge; the jurors could have changed their minds when they resumed deliberations. (*Blueford v. Arkansas*, U.S. Sup. Ct. 2012.)

A judge may also declare a mistrial and order a new trial if the defense deliberately (or even mistakenly) makes a legal error that in the judge's view can't be undone by admonishing the jurors to disregard what they heard. For example, perhaps in violation of a judge's ruling, a defense lawyer in front of the jury refers to the key prosecution witness's prison record. If the judge concludes that the lawyer's remark makes a fair trial impossible, the judge will declare a mistrial. (The defense lawyer may also face disciplinary proceedings if circumstances suggest that the lawyer made the improper remark on purpose because the trial was going badly for the defendant.)

In unusual circumstances when the improper actions of prosecutors and judges result in mistrials, defendants cannot be retried. For example, let's say that a prosecutor, fearing that a trial is going badly, deliberately "leaks" improper information to a jury that prejudices the defendant's right to a fair trial. Or a highly impatient judge declares a mistrial based on a jury's failure to arrive at a verdict during the unreasonably short time period that the judge allotted to deliberations. In circumstances such as these, an appellate court may determine that a retrial of the defendant would violate double jeopardy.

If the defendant can show that the prosecutor deliberately created the conditions for the mistrial or that there was no manifest necessity for ending the trial, a retrial could be found to violate double jeopardy.

Can a defendant be sued in civil court and charged in criminal court for the same conduct?

Yes. The Double Jeopardy Clause forbids only successive criminal prosecutions growing out of the same conduct. For example, after O.J. Simpson was acquitted of murdering his ex-wife and her friend, their relatives filed a civil suit against him for actual and punitive damages caused by the killings. The civil suit raised no double jeopardy issues, even though punitive damages are a type of punishment, and Simpson was held civilly liable for the deaths.

Basic Evidence Rules in Criminal Trials

Rules of evidence are the trial system's equivalent of the rules of grammar. Just as grammar rules determine how we write, so too do evidence rules control courtroom procedures. Even defendants represented by lawyers can benefit from awareness of basic evidence rules by being able to understand and better participate in important strategic decisions. This chapter covers the evidence rules that tend to be most important in criminal trials.

Overview

Evidence rules limit not only what witnesses and lawyers can say during trials, but also how they can say it. This section explains the purpose and origins of rules of evidence.

What is the purpose of evidence rules?

Evidence rules guide the process by which information (evidence) flows from witnesses to a judge or jury. The rules control both the *content* of evidence and the *manner* in which witnesses testify (that is, how they relate the information that the law allows them to provide). To take a familiar manner rule, witnesses may testify only in response to questions rather than by telling a long uninterrupted narrative. An equally familiar yet often misunderstood content rule is the hearsay rule, which bars witnesses from testifying about certain statements made outside the courtroom.

Where do evidence rules come from?

Most evidence rules developed through "common law" judicial decisions. Like water droplets in caves that over the years formed stalactites, the evidence rulings made by individual judges gradually crystallized into rules that later judges followed.

Today, most court-developed evidence rules have been turned into statutes by Congress and state legislatures. California was among the first states to enact a comprehensive set of evidence laws, known as the California Evidence Code. The California code was a primary model for the Federal Rules of Evidence (FRE), a set of laws that governs trials in federal courts. About 40 states have enacted evidence rules based on the Federal Rules of Evidence. Because every jurisdiction's evidence rules are based on the common law and on each other, evidence rules are largely similar throughout the country.

Do judges still make evidence rules?

For the most part, no. With some exceptions, legislatures have taken over the development of evidence law. Lawmakers know that evidence rules can affect the outcomes of cases, and they want to have primary influence in shaping those rules. Of course, it's up to judges to interpret the evidence rules that legislators produce, and, in doing so, judges can substantially alter the scope and meaning of the rules. Judges' interpretations can in turn lead to statutory amendments either incorporating the new interpretations or specifically rejecting them. The frequent tug-of-war between judges and legislators to control evidence rules is alternatively fascinating and frustrating to many lawyers.

How do trial judges deal with the evidence rules within their courtrooms?

Many evidence rules consist of general guidelines, and judges have the power and responsibility to interpret the guidelines in the pursuit of justice in individual cases. For example, assume that an evidence rule provides that certain kinds of documents have to be shown to have been prepared in a trustworthy manner before a judge can admit them into evidence. The judge might require greater proof of trustworthiness in a trial involving two multinational corporations than in a trial involving a landlord-tenant dispute. Similarly, one judge may require more proof of trustworthiness than another judge.

Are the evidence rules in criminal cases different from those used in civil cases?

In most jurisdictions, no. The rules known as the Federal Rules of Evidence, for example, apply to both civil and criminal trials. However, certain evidence rules apply differently in criminal and civil cases. An example is Federal Rule of Evidence 404(a), which makes certain types of character evidence admissible only in criminal cases.

Do the same evidence rules apply to both judge and jury trials?

Yes. Again, most jurisdictions have only one set of evidence rules, applicable generally to all trials. In practice, however, judges tend to apply evidence rules much less strictly in cases tried before a judge than in jury cases. Many judges believe that, unlike a jury, they can sort out the legally admissible evidence from that which is not admissible when it comes time to make a decision. Also, information has to be disclosed to judges before they can decide whether or not it's admissible. Because judges hear about information whether or not it's admissible, a ruling excluding evidence is less significant in a judge-tried than in a jury-tried case. Sometimes defendants choose judge trials rather than jury trials because they hope that a judge will be subconsciously influenced by information that is technically inadmissible.

> **EXAMPLE:** Polly Anna is on trial for embezzling funds from the bank where she was formerly employed. Polly wants to attack the credibility of a key prosecution witness by showing that the witness has been previously convicted of a crime. However, because the conviction occurred some years ago and because the judge has discretion as to whether or not to admit evidence of the conviction, Polly's lawyer is uncertain about its admissibility. This uncertainty might be a factor inclining Polly toward a judge trial. Even if the judge were to exclude the conviction from evidence, the judge will at least know of the conviction and might be subtly influenced by it. By contrast, if the judge excludes evidence of the conviction in a jury trial, the jury will never hear about the conviction.

What are evidence mini-trials?

Judges often have to hear what witnesses have to say before deciding whether a jury should be permitted to hear the testimony.

Evidence that determines the admissibility of other evidence is called "foundational evidence," and the phases of trial involving foundational evidence are often called "mini-trials." In jury trials, to prevent jurors from finding out about evidence that the judge ultimately rules inadmissible, the jury usually is excused from the courtroom during mini-trials.

> **EXAMPLE:** Miguel Ito is on trial before a jury for burglary. The prosecution wants to offer into evidence a confession made by Miguel to a police officer shortly after Miguel's arrest. Miguel claims that the confession was taken in violation of the *Miranda* rule (the rule requiring suspects to be informed of their right to remain silent) and therefore is inadmissible. The judge will conduct a mini-trial. After listening to foundational evidence about the confession and whether the police followed the *Miranda* rules, the judge will decide whether to admit the confession into evidence. To prevent the jury from learning about the confession unless the judge rules it admissible, the jury will be excused from the courtroom during the mini-trial.

What are "limiting" instructions?

Limiting instructions come into play when, as is often the case, evidence is admissible for one purpose but not for another. A judge will often instruct ("admonish") jurors to consider the evidence only for the legitimate purpose, and ignore it for any other purpose. Following a limiting instruction can require mental dexterity that few people possess.

> **EXAMPLE:** In an assault case in which the defense is self-defense, the alleged victim testifies, "A day before the fight, my brother told me that the defendant had once killed a man." The judge admits the testimony because it would allow the jury to infer that the victim feared the defendant and therefore did not initiate the fight. At the same time, evidence rules forbid the jury from considering the testimony as evidence that the defendant actually had killed a man (for this purpose, the testimony would be inadmissible hearsay and perhaps also inadmissible as an attack on the defendant's character). The judge issues a limiting instruction warning the jurors not to consider the statement as evidence that the defendant actually killed a man: "You may consider the evidence you've just heard only for its possible effect on the alleged victim's state of mind. You may not consider the statement as evidence that the defendant actually killed a man." While limiting instructions such as this are common, their value is dubious because of the mental gymnastics required to follow them.

Do judges usually take the lead in enforcing evidence rules?

No. Unlike football and basketball referees, who call fouls without waiting for the fouled team to make a request, judges normally do not strike improper evidence on their own volition. Judges usually rule only when the defense or prosecution asks for a ruling by making an objection. To object, all the defense or prosecutor need do is to succinctly point out the reason for the error. For example, if the prosecutor asks a police officer to testify to a statement made by a witness shortly after the commission of a crime, the defense might say, "Objection, hearsay." If the judge finds that the objection is proper, the judge will sustain the objection.

Otherwise, the judge will overrule it. If the judge wants clarification of the objection, the judge will ask for it.

Might a defense lawyer decline to object to improper evidence for strategic reasons?

Making objections is as much an art as a science. Even if prosecution evidence is inadmissible, a defense attorney may decide not to object for any number of reasons. For example, the attorney might think the evidence is helpful to the defense, or might regard the evidence as so exaggerated that the jury will not believe it. The defense attorney may also decide that objecting will call further attention to damaging evidence, whereas the jury may let the testimony go in one ear and out the other if the attorney simply says nothing. Another concern is that if a defense attorney objects too much (even if the objections are valid), the jury will view him or her as a nuisance or obstructive. Finally, the defense attorney may think that an objection will lead jurors to think that the defense is trying to hide evidence that isn't all that important in the first place. In the heat of trial, defense attorneys typically have to make instantaneous decisions about whether to object; they rarely have time to consult with clients.

Rules Regulating the Content of Testimony

This section is about what kinds of evidence can and cannot be introduced into a criminal trial for the purpose of influencing the decision of the judge or jury. Evidence rules generally aim to weed out unreliable evidence and promote fairness.

What's the most basic evidence rule?

Relevance (as defined by Federal Rule of Evidence 402) is the basic building block of evidence rules. Only relevant evidence is admissible. For evidence to be relevant, a logical connection must exist between the evidence and the factual issue it is offered to prove or disprove. The connection needn't be so strong that any single item of evidence alone proves or disproves a fact. It's good enough if the piece of evidence constitutes a link in a chain of proof along with other pieces of evidence. (As the famous legal authority McCormick put it long ago, "A brick is not a wall.") The main limitation of the relevance rule is that the connection must be based on reason and logic rather than on bias and emotion.

> **EXAMPLE:** Ruby Ridge is charged with stealing makeup from a drugstore the night before Halloween. The prosecution wants to offer evidence that Ruby's mom had refused to buy her a Halloween costume. The evidence is relevant to prove that Ruby had a motive for stealing the makeup.

EXAMPLE: Same case. The prosecution also wants to call the drugstore manager to testify that the makeup department suffers more thefts than any other department of the drugstore. This testimony would be irrelevant because it does nothing to logically connect Ruby to the theft.

EXAMPLE: Lance Sellot is charged with drunk driving. The prosecution wants to offer evidence that Lance is a member of a violent street gang. The evidence is irrelevant because the crime charged has nothing to do with gang activities. No logical connection exists between gang membership and whether Lance was drunk at the time he was arrested. The evidence would appeal only to a judge's or jurors' prejudices and emotions.

EXAMPLE: Clare Voyant is charged with car theft. Clare was arrested in her home, and the prosecution wants to offer evidence that the arresting officer found marijuana and an unregistered handgun in Clare's home. No logical connection exists between car theft and possession of marijuana and a handgun. Again, the evidence would appeal only to a judge's or jurors' prejudices and emotions.

Is relevant evidence always admissible?

No. Evidence has to be relevant to have any chance of admissibility, but not all relevant evidence is admissible. Judges often exclude relevant evidence because of some other evidence rule. For example, evidence that is otherwise relevant may have a great potential to unfairly stir a judge's or jurors' emotions and prejudices. In such situations, the judge is supposed to balance the importance of the evidence against the risk of unfair prejudice. (Federal Rule of Evidence 403.) If the judge determines that the importance outweighs the risk of unfair prejudice, the judge admits the evidence. But if the judge determines that the risk of unfair prejudice substantially outweighs the relevance of the evidence, the judge excludes the evidence. Judges have lots of discretion when it comes to making such rulings. As a general rule, a judge is much more likely to exclude evidence as prejudicial in a jury trial than when the judge is hearing the case without a jury.

EXAMPLE: Kai Ping is charged with assaulting Kevin Pong with a knife; Ping claims self-defense. In a jury trial, the prosecution seeks to offer into evidence the following three items: (a) the knife allegedly used in the assault; (b) a photograph of Pong taken minutes after the fight, showing cuts on Pong's face and arms; and (c) the bloodstained T-shirt that Pong was wearing at the time of the fight. A judge is likely to admit the knife and the photograph into evidence, but exclude the shirt as unduly prejudicial. The size and shape of the knife and the nature of Pong's injuries are rationally related to the issue of whether Ping or Pong was the aggressor in the fight. But the bloody T-shirt has little probative value (that is, it isn't needed to understand what happened and therefore lacks importance to the case), and the sight of the bloody T-shirt may well inflame the jury against Ping.

What's the "personal knowledge" rule?

The "personal knowledge" rule (Federal Rule of Evidence 602) requires all witnesses (except expert witnesses) to testify based on firsthand information. For example, if Monty Vesuvius is going to testify that a defendant charged with drunk driving swilled down four martinis before jumping behind the wheel of a car, Vesuvius must actually have seen the defendant drink the martinis. Suppose Vesuvius says any of the following:

- "I assumed they were martinis because the defendant was drinking out of glasses that martinis are usually served in."
- "I figure the defendant drank them because of the four empty glasses on the defendant's table."
- "I know that the defendant drank the martinis because the bartender told me so."

Each statement shows that Vesuvius lacks personal knowledge and cannot testify to the issue of what the defendant drank. However, very little is required to show that personal knowledge existed. Most often, the judge will tilt toward letting questionable evidence in and leave it to the defense to bring out in cross-examination or closing argument just how shaky the evidence is.

> **EXAMPLE:** Babe Bear is charged with trespassing onto property owned by Goldie Locks; Bear's defense is mistaken identity. At trial, the prosecution wants Locks to identify Bear as the individual who ran out of her door when Locks came home after visiting her grandmother. In an evidence minitrial,

Bear offers evidence that Locks had been drinking wine and was inebriated when she came home. Bear's evidence also shows that Locks, who normally wears glasses, was not wearing them when she came home. Locks may make her identification, because she is testifying from personal knowledge—that is, she claims to have personally observed the events to which she is testifying. Whether the problems that Bear pointed out mean that Locks's testimony is not believable is a separate question—dealing with the weight of the evidence—that the judge or jury will have to decide at the end of the case.

> **EXAMPLE:** Sue Emmall is charged with possession of heroin. The prosecution plans to call Hy Enlow, Sue's next-door neighbor, to testify that Hy saw Sue holding a baggie of white powder that Hy believed to be cocaine. Hy can testify from personal knowledge that Sue was holding a baggie containing a white powder. However, only an expert drug analyst could testify to whether or not the powder is cocaine. Unless Hy were qualified as an expert, he could not testify to an opinion that the powder was cocaine.

Can defendants offer evidence of their good character?

Yes. The "mercy rule" allows a criminal defendant to offer evidence of his or her good character as a defense to criminal charges. (Federal Rule of Evidence 404.) For example, if the defendant is charged with embezzlement, the defendant could offer evidence that she is honest and law-abiding. (The evidence is relevant on the theory that honest and law-abiding people are less likely to steal money than people without this character trait.) Character evidence offered under the mercy rule is usually in the form of opinions from the defendant's close acquaintances. Like all other evidence, in order to be admissible, character evidence has to be relevant and based on personal knowledge. This means that the trait of the defendant's character to which a witness testifies must have some connection to the charged crime.

> **EXAMPLE:** Norman Bates is charged with assaulting Roseanne Fell. Bates can call a close friend to testify that, "In my opinion, Bates is a nonviolent person who wouldn't hurt a fly." The mercy rule allows Bates to offer character evidence suggesting that he has a propensity to be peaceful, making it less likely that he assaulted Fell. However, the friend could not testify that Bates is honest, because that character trait isn't related to the crime.

Does the defense incur any risks by offering evidence of the defendant's good character?

Most definitely, which is why defendants rarely take advantage of the mercy rule. The primary risks are these:

- The opinion of a defendant's good character usually comes from a close acquaintance and may not, for that reason, carry much weight with a judge or jury.

- The prosecution can cross-examine a defendant's good-character witness, in the process bringing out evidence of a defendant's past misdeeds that otherwise would have been inadmissible.
- Once the defendant introduces evidence of good character, the prosecution can call its own witnesses to testify to the defendant's bad character.

If the defense doesn't offer evidence of the defendant's good character, can the prosecutor offer evidence of the defendant's bad character?

In most situations, no. Evidence rules generally forbid prosecutors from presenting "bad" character evidence unless the defendant first opens the door by presenting evidence of good character. Character evidence is barred in this situation because it is too prejudicial. A judge or jury might convict a defendant for being a "bad person," even if the evidence that the defendant committed the charged crime is weak.

Can a defendant who claims to have acted in self-defense offer evidence of the alleged victim's violent character?

Yes. Federal Rule of Evidence 404 and most state rules allow defendants to offer evidence of a supposed victim's propensity to be violent or aggressive. But this is a dangerous tactic for defendants. Following a defendant's attack on a "victim's" character, the prosecutor can respond in two ways. One, the prosecutor can offer rebuttal evidence that supports the victim's peaceful character. Two, the prosecutor can offer evidence that the defendant has a propensity to be violent or aggressive. As a result, defense attorneys are often reluctant to attack a victim's character.

Can prosecutors and defense attorneys attack witnesses' credibility with character evidence?

Yes. Subject often to judicial discretion, evidence rules allow the prosecution and the defense to attack the credibility of adverse witnesses by offering evidence of past misdeeds involving dishonesty. (Federal Rules of Evidence 608, 609.) Usually, such testimony is of one of the following types:

- evidence that a witness has been convicted of a felony, or a misdemeanor involving dishonesty (such as theft)
- evidence in the form of a witness's opinion that another witness is dishonest, or
- evidence that a witness has committed specific acts showing dishonesty, such as lying on a job application.

Evidence concerning a witness's character is limited to the trait of honesty, because only that trait is relevant to the credibility of a witness's testimony. And once a witness's character has been attacked, the party that called the witness may respond with evidence of the witness's honesty.

Noncharacter "Bad Person" Evidence

Despite the rule barring prosecutors from offering evidence of a defendant's bad character, prosecutors routinely try to get around the rule by arguing that the bad person evidence is relevant for another reason. (Federal Rule of Evidence 404(b).) For example, a judge would probably permit a prosecutor trying to convict a defendant of assault to offer evidence that the defendant previously assaulted the same victim. A judge would probably rule that it is noncharacter evidence showing that the defendant had a grudge against the victim. A limiting instruction warning jurors not to use the evidence to make a judgment about the defendant's character would be appropriate.

Another noncharacter theory that prosecutors often use to present evidence of a defendant's past misdeeds is *modus operandi*, or "m.o." Under this theory, the prosecutor can offer evidence that the method a defendant used to commit past misdeeds is unique and nearly identical to the method the defendant allegedly used to commit the charged crime. Evidence of the past misdeeds is then admissible, not to paint the defendant as a bad person, but to show that the common m.o. points to the defendant as the perpetrator of the charged crime. Again, for whatever it's worth, a judge might give a limiting instruction.

The Tough Choice Facing Defendants Who Have Previously Been Convicted of Crimes

Defendants who wish to testify in their own defense and have previously been convicted of crimes are often faced with a difficult choice. If the defendant testifies, the prosecutor may be able to offer the defendant's prior conviction into evidence for the purpose of attacking the defendant's credibility as a witness. Even though the jury will be told that the conviction is relevant only to the defendant's credibility as a witness, the jury may well infer that the defendant is just a bad guy who deserves to be punished for that reason. By not testifying, the defendant usually can prevent the jury from finding out about the prior conviction (because the defendant's credibility as a witness is not in issue). But this may deprive the defense of valuable evidence, as well as arouse the suspicions of jurors who wonder why the defendant did not testify. For many defendants, neither option is appealing. This decision is one that defendants and their attorneys should make only after careful consultation.

Will a jury find out that a defendant offered to plead guilty to a reduced charge?

No. To encourage defendants to engage in plea bargaining, evidence rules provide that the prosecution cannot offer evidence that a defendant had offered to plead guilty before the trial started.

What are rape shield laws?

For many years, evidence rules permitted men on trial for rape to attack their female accusers' credibility by delving into the accusers' sexual histories. Typically, the questions were highly embarrassing; the threat of having to answer them scared many women into not reporting rape in the first place. Moreover, the relevance of previous sexual conduct to the victim's credibility or willingness to engage in sexual intercourse on a particular occasion was highly dubious. As the recognition of these problems grew, all jurisdictions enacted "rape shield laws" (see Federal Rule of Evidence 412), which prevent irrelevant inquiries into rape complainants' sexual histories.

What is hearsay?

Hearsay is an out-of-court statement (or conduct that is the equivalent of a statement or assertion) that is offered for its truth. Out-of-court statements are assertions made in a manner other than by witnesses in court, and their admissibility is governed by what is known everywhere as the "hearsay rule." The purpose of the hearsay rule is to prevent witnesses from testifying to statements made by absent people who can't be seen or cross-examined. In general, the hearsay rule excludes evidence of the "he said, she said" variety.

Nevertheless, as discussed below, out-of-court statements are often admissible in evidence despite the hearsay rule. Depending on the purpose for which an out-of-court statement is offered, the hearsay rule may not even apply. An out-of-court statement frequently qualifies as "nonhearsay," and is therefore admissible in evidence. The second reason is that the rule is so riddled with exceptions that even when the rule does apply, out-of-court statements are often "hearsay, but admissible."

Character Evidence in Sexual Assault Crimes

Legislatures and judges in many states believe that those who commit sexual assault crimes tend to repeat their crimes and that (especially when the victims are children) the crimes are very difficult to prove in court. As a result, many states have created special exceptions to the character evidence rules for sexual assault prosecutions. The exceptions allow prosecutors to offer evidence that defendants charged with sexual assault or child molestation have committed those crimes in the past. (Federal Rules of Evidence 413, 414.) The exception for past acts of child molestation was a major factor in the media-saturated trial of the late singer Michael Jackson in Santa Maria, California, in 2005. Jackson, an international celebrity, was accused of molesting a teenage boy at Jackson's "Neverland" ranch. The judge allowed the prosecutor to offer evidence that Jackson had previously molested a number of other young boys. The lurid details of the previous crimes consumed many more days of the trial than did the testimony focused on the charged crimes. Jackson was nevertheless acquitted of all charges.

While the hearsay rule gives defendants the right to confront and cross-examine prosecution witnesses, defendants can forfeit this right if prosecution witnesses fail to testify at trial because the defendant engaged in wrongdoing with the intent of inducing the witnesses not to testify. (See *Giles v. California*, U.S. Sup. Ct. 2008.)

EXAMPLE: Romeo is charged with attempting to kill his former girlfriend Juliet by giving her poison. Juliet survived and immediately told a police officer what happened. A few days before trial, acting on instructions from Romeo, Tybalt visits Juliet and tells her, "If you show up at trial and testify against Romeo, don't expect to survive." Juliet calls the prosecutor, says that she is too scared to testify, and disappears. Romeo has forfeited his right to cross-examine Juliet. He and Tybalt threatened Juliet with the intent of preventing her from testifying against Romeo. Because the threat succeeded in preventing Juliet from testifying, the judge will allow the police officer to testify to Juliet's hearsay statement describing how Romeo tried to kill her.

What determines whether an out-of-court statement is hearsay?

An assertion whose relevance does not depend on its truth is not hearsay, and therefore the hearsay rule does not apply. Thus, the first question when analyzing the admissibility of an out-of-court statement under the hearsay rule is, "What is the statement offered to prove?" If the statement is offered to prove something other than its truth, it is nonhearsay.

The Hearsay Rule Applies to Both Oral and Written Statements

Though the term "hearsay" implies that the rule applies only to oral statements, it applies to written statements as well. Statements in letters, emails, business reports, and other documents may be hearsay or not, depending on the use to which they are put. And just like oral statements, the contents of documents may be admissible under an exception to the hearsay rule.

EXAMPLE: Cole Slawson is charged with murdering Barbie Cue on September 6. Cole claims that Barbie was still alive on September 7, and therefore Cole could not have killed her on September 6. Cole calls Sal to testify that Barbie (whose voice she knows well) phoned her on September 7 and said, "I'm still alive." Sal's testimony is admissible as nonhearsay to support Cole's defense. Cole is not offering Barbie's statement (through the testimony of Sal) for its truth. It makes no difference whether Barbie's words are true or false. If Barbie utters any words on September 7 (even, "I'm dead"), she clearly could not have died on September 6.

EXAMPLE: Barr Nunn is charged with assaulting Slim Pickens with a deadly weapon. To prove that the object with which Nunn struck Pickens was a beer bottle, the prosecutor wants Violet to testify, "The day after the fight, the bartender told me that Nunn hit Pickens with a beer bottle." Violet's testimony is inadmissible hearsay. The bartender's statement is being offered for its truth. The statement is relevant to prove that Nunn used a beer bottle only if the words in the statement are true.

EXAMPLE: Same case. Nunn's defense is that he is not guilty because Pickens attacked first and Nunn acted in self-defense. To prove that Pickens would not have attacked Nunn, the prosecutor wants Violet to testify, "The night before the fight, Pickens told me that Nunn always carries a gun and is not afraid to use it." Violet's testimony does not constitute hearsay. Pickens's statement is relevant to show that he feared Nunn. If Pickens feared Nunn, Pickens might not attack him. Thus, even if the statement was inaccurate (that is, even if Nunn did not actually carry a gun), it nevertheless undermines Nunn's self-defense claim, and so it serves the nonhearsay purpose of showing the victim Pickens's state of mind.

EXAMPLE: Same case. Hearing the fight, a police officer rushes into the bar to find Slim Pickens lying on the floor, bleeding from a head wound. The police officer looks to the bartender and asks, "Who hit this man?" Without saying a word, the bartender points to Barr Nunn. The bartender's pointing to Nunn is the equivalent of the statement, "Nunn is the one who hit Pickens." Because the pointing would be relevant to the case only if it were true, it would be considered hearsay and not admissible in evidence— unless one of the exceptions applies.

Can prosecutors and defense lawyers avoid the hearsay rule by simply offering an out-of-court statement for something other than its truth?

It's not quite that simple. The out-of-court assertion has to be relevant for its non-truth purposes. Otherwise the assertion is inadmissible.

> **EXAMPLE:** As evidence that John committed a crime, the prosecution wants a police officer to testify, "Marcia told me that she saw John commit the crime." When the defense attorney objects on the ground of hearsay, the prosecutor responds, "I'm not offering this to prove that Marcia's statement was true, only that the police officer talked to Marcia." However, Marcia's statement is not admissible for a nonhearsay purpose. The fact that a police officer talked to Marcia is irrelevant to John's guilt or innocence. In these circumstances, if the prosecution cannot offer Marcia's out-of-court assertion for its truth, it cannot offer the assertion into evidence at all, because it isn't relevant in any other way.

Can witnesses testify to their own out-of-court statements?

The hearsay rule applies the same to all statements, whether made by other people or by a testifying witness. Thus, if the relevance of a witness's own statement depends on its truth, the hearsay rule would prevent the witness from testifying to the witness's own out-of-court statement, unless an exception to the hearsay rule applies.

Judges Have Discretion to Exclude Nonhearsay

The fact that an out-of-court statement may be relevant as nonhearsay is not an automatic ticket to admissibility. The judge can exclude nonhearsay if there's too great a risk that the jury will improperly consider the statement for its truth, and that risk substantially outweighs the importance of the nonhearsay use. An example of this arose in a famous 1930s case involving the murder trial of Dr. Shepard. Dr. Shepard was charged with poisoning his wife; he claimed that she committed suicide. The government offered into evidence a statement Mrs. Shepard made to her nurse shortly before Mrs. Shepard's death. According to the nurse, Mrs. Shepard said, "Dr. Shepard has poisoned me." The government claimed that the statement was admissible as nonhearsay: It wasn't offered for its truth, but as evidence that Mrs. Shepard was not in a suicidal frame of mind. (The government's theory was that people bent on suicide don't accuse others of killing them.) The U.S. Supreme Court said that while the statement might have been relevant as nonhearsay, it should have been excluded because its importance to that issue was outweighed by the great danger that the jury would regard it as true. In memorable words, Justice Cardozo wrote for the Court that "Discrimination so subtle is a feat beyond the compass of ordinary minds. The accusatory clang of those words would drown all weaker sounds." (*Shepard v. U.S.*, U.S. Sup. Ct. 1933.)

Are there exceptions to the rule excluding hearsay?

Yes—a lot! Expanding on the common law, all jurisdictions recognize various exceptions to the hearsay rule. Most of these exceptions exist because legislators who make the evidence rules think that out-of-court assertions made in specific circumstances are more likely to be reliable. So many exceptions exist that many judges and lawyers think that the rule should be rewritten to say, "Hearsay evidence is admissible, unless an attorney is too dumb to think of an exception." If an exception applies, an out-of-court statement is admissible even though its relevance depends on its truth.

Among the more colorful or popular exceptions are the following.

Excited utterances. This exception admits into evidence statements made under the stress or excitement of perceiving an unusual event. ("Excitement" here does not imply a positive or happy reaction; it can be startling or shocking.) The notion is that people are unlikely to lie when they describe a sudden and exciting event at the time the event occurs. For example, assume that a witness to a bank robbery says right after the robbery, "Oh my God, did you see that? The bank robber had a tattoo on his left ear!" This would qualify as an excited utterance, as it describes an obviously exciting situation and was made immediately afterward. By contrast, a California motorist's assertion, "That driver ran the red light," would probably not qualify as an excited utterance. An event has to be unusual to produce the necessary excitement. Excited utterances that victims make in response to police officer questioning may be admissible at trial against defendants, even though the defendants have no chance to cross-examine the victims. (*Michigan v. Bryant*, U.S. Sup. Ct. 2011.)

Dying declarations. This exception admits into evidence statements made under a sense of immediately impending death. The theory is that such statements are trustworthy because "people don't want to meet their Maker with a lie on their lips." Like excited utterances, dying declarations that victims make in response to police officer questioning may be admissible at trial against defendants, even though the defendants have no chance to cross-examine the victims. (*Michigan v. Bryant*, U.S. Sup. Ct. 2011.)

Opposing party statements. The hearsay exception for opposing party statements makes admissible a defendant's out-of-court statements when offered into evidence by the prosecutor. (Remember, defendants can't offer their own out-of-court statements into evidence.) For example, if a defendant waives her *Miranda* rights and talks to a police officer after she is arrested, the prosecutor can ask the police officer to testify to the defendant's statement.

Pretrial identifications. Prosecutors can elicit testimony as to witnesses' pretrial identifications. For example, a police officer could testify, "At a lineup, Jones pointed to the defendant and said, 'That's the robber.'" Or Jones could testify, "I looked through a bunch of photos and, when I saw a photo of the defendant, I told the cops, 'That's the robber.'"

Assertions of state of mind. This exception admits into evidence statements setting forth people's emotions, beliefs, intent, and so on. The exception rests in the importance of testimony about mental states in many criminal cases, and people's trustworthiness in describing such matters; for example, why would they lie? In the famous, though grisly, U.S. Supreme Court case that gave rise to this exception (*Hillmon v. Mutual Life Insurance*, U.S. Sup. Ct. 1892), the issue was the identity of a badly-burned corpse found near Crooked Creek, Kansas. Hillmon's widow claimed it was her husband; the insurance company claimed it was a man named Walters. The insurance company wanted to offer into evidence a letter written by Walters to his fiancée a few days before the corpse was found in which Walters said, "I'm going to Crooked Creek to meet up with Hillmon." The Court held that the letter was admissible to show Walters's intent to go to Crooked Creek. Walters's intent to go to Crooked Creek was relevant because it showed that Walters probably did go to Crooked Creek (thus increasing the chance that the corpse was his). The case was tried to a jury six different times over a period spanning 1882–1903, and ended only after the parties settled out of court. No legal determination of whether the corpse was Hillmon or Walters was ever arrived at. (For further information about this fascinating case, see Bergman and Wesson's chapter essay "I Am Going With a Man by the Name of Hillmon" in the book *Trial Stories*.)

Prior inconsistent statements. If a witness's testimony varies in some important way from prior out-of-court statements made by that witness, the prior statements are admissible in evidence. For example, a police officer testifies in court, "I heard what sounded like a smashed window, and I went to investigate." But the officer's police report prepared prior to trial states, "After being informed of a smashed window, I went to investigate." The statement in the police report is admissible as a prior inconsistent statement; the defendant may want to offer it into evidence to cast doubt on the accuracy of the officer's testimony.

Still Confused by the Hearsay Rule?

You're not alone! The ins and outs of the hearsay rule can be very complex; even experienced lawyers and judges sometimes find hearsay issues difficult to resolve. The discussion in this chapter should help a defendant discuss hearsay issues with his or her lawyer.

Business and government records. Written records reflecting regular business and government activities are often admissible under exceptions to the hearsay rule. Presumably, the regularity with which they are prepared, and the need for accurate records in this context, make them trustworthy.

Police Reports as a Government Record

A police report generally consists of an officer's account of events leading up to an arrest, and sometimes of a postarrest investigation. Because a police report often simply recounts statements by witnesses, and no exceptions apply to the witnesses' statements, police reports frequently are barred from evidence by the hearsay rule. However, sometimes, in state courts, a portion of a police report may be admitted into evidence as a government record. For example, if a police officer arrives at the scene of a hit-and-run, measures skid marks, and records the measurements in a police report pursuant to the officer's official duties, that portion of the police report may be admissible in evidence.

How is expert testimony different from regular testimony?

Experts have special education, training, or experience that allows them to testify to opinions on matters beyond everyday understanding. Experts are not limited by the personal knowledge rule. Experts may give opinions based on information provided by other witnesses or contained in written reports. Also, unlike other witnesses, experts can and usually do demand payment for testifying.

> **EXAMPLE:** Hap Hazard is on trial for robbery; the defense is an alibi. Hap wants the jury to understand the factors that he claims caused the eyewitnesses to mistakenly identify him as the robber. Hap can probably offer expert testimony to support this claim. Most courts have ruled that factors affecting witnesses' ability to observe and recollect are sufficiently beyond everyday understanding to allow experts to testify. In this case, Hap might hire a forensic cognitive psychologist to testify about factors that commonly lead to misidentifications.

How do indigent defendants secure the services of an expert witness?

Experts are expensive. It's not unusual for an expert to charge defendants a few thousand dollars for a day of testimony, with an additional fee for preparation time. Fees are less of a problem for prosecutors, because fingerprint experts, ballistics experts, and laboratory technicians who testify to such matters as blood alcohol levels in drunk driving cases often are already on the government payroll.

Court-appointed lawyers do not have the funding to hire an expert on every case. However, a court-appointed lawyer can petition a judge to appoint an expert. If a judge considers an expert's opinion legally necessary or helpful to a fair resolution of the case, the judge can appoint an expert at government expense. For example, an expert who might charge private clients $3,000 might have to accept $750 per day for a court-appointed case (assuming the expert agrees to participate at those rates).

> **EXAMPLE:** Nell Shrap is on trial for making a telephoned bomb threat. The prosecutor's primary evidence is an audiotape of the threat. A government voice identification expert will testify that the voice on the tape is Nell's. Nell is indigent. Nell's attorney can file a pretrial motion asking the court to appoint a voice identification expert at government expense. If the judge grants the motion, the defense expert can consult with Nell's attorney, check the procedures of the prosecutor's expert, and testify on Nell's behalf at trial.

Special Interest Organizations as Sources of Expert Witnesses

If a special interest organization believes that a defense has sufficient importance and legal justification, in high-publicity cases the organization may hire an expert to appear in support of the defendant. For example, assume that a woman charged with assaulting her husband relies on the defense of battered woman syndrome. Women's rights groups might be willing to provide an expert to testify on the defendant's behalf.

What is a "chain of custody"?

A chain of custody is the more complex foundation needed for the admissibility of certain types of exhibits as evidence. Exhibits are tangible objects that are relevant to the facts of a case. Stolen cosmetics in a shoplifting case; the drugs in an illegal possession of controlled substances case; the photograph of a broken window in a burglary case; the printout of a breathalyzer machine in a drunk driving case; all of these are exhibits once they are offered into evidence at trial. Proving that an exhibit is exactly what it is represented to be—the actual drugs found on the defendant or the very cosmetics stolen from the store— requires proof of who had possession of the exhibit at all times between the time the evidence was seized and the trial. Proving this chain of custody is especially necessary when exhibits are subject to alteration or are tested prior to trial.

Because criminal prosecutions typically depend on evidence gathered by police officers, it is prosecutors who generally need to establish a chain of custody. In turn, a typical defense strategy is to attack the sufficiency of the prosecutor's chain. If the defense succeeds in preventing the prosecutor from offering an exhibit into evidence, the judge might rule that the prosecutor has insufficient evidence to allow a case to continue.

For example, assume that Hy Immer is on trial for possessing illegal drugs. To prove Immer guilty, the prosecutor must offer the packet of powder that a police officer removed from Immer's pocket into evidence, and prove that the powder is an illegal drug. To establish the chain of custody for the packet, the prosecutor will have to do the following:

- show that the officer who seized the packet marked it in a way that enables the officer to distinguish it from similar items that may have been taken from other suspects
- prove that the police stored the packet in a way that provides reasonable assurance that nobody tampered with its contents
- call a qualified expert to testify to the chemical composition of the contents of the packet
- establish that the packet given to and tested by the expert is the one that the officer seized from Immer
- prove that the testing procedures were properly carried out, and
- prove that the packet tested by the expert is the same packet as the one the police bring to the trial.

Immer's attorney can challenge each and every step in this foundation. If the prosecutor cannot convince the judge that the foundation is adequate, the judge will rule the packet inadmissible and, in all probability, dismiss the case.

Rules Regulating the Manner of Testimony

As your mother may have told you, it's not just what you say, but also how you say it that counts. This section explains the rules that govern how information, testimony, and exhibits are actually turned into evidence that can be considered by the judge or jury.

Why does the prosecution get to go first in a trial?

The usual explanation is that the prosecution has the burden of proof. It is therefore fair to allow the prosecution to present its evidence first. Actually, this order can be an advantage to a defendant. The prosecution often has to present its case without knowing much about the defense's line of attack. However, the advantage is temporary, as the prosecution has a chance to respond to the defense evidence in a part of the trial called the rebuttal.

Can the defense lawyer rehearse testimony with defendants and witnesses?

On direct examination, a lawyer generally cannot use leading questions to signal the answers that the lawyer wants the witness to give. For example, assume that the defense lawyer wants a defense witness to testify that she arrived home at 9 p.m. The lawyer cannot ask, "Did you arrive home at 9 p.m.?" Instead, the lawyer would have to ask a less leading question such as, "What time did you arrive home?"

However, defense lawyers can use a variety of other methods to help defendants and defense witnesses testify in a truthful and accurate manner. First, defense lawyers can and should meet with their clients and witnesses before trial to review their testimony. And if the witness forgets something while testifying, the lawyer can show the witness a letter, report, or other document to refresh the witness's memory. Many judges will even permit lawyers to ask leading questions if a witness has had an obvious glitch in recall.

> **EXAMPLE:** Jesse James is charged with armed robbery; his defense is mistaken identity. The prosecutor calls Kit Carson as a witness and asks, "You saw the defendant rob the store, is that correct?" This is an improper leading question because it suggests the prosecutor's desired answer. Defense counsel can object and force the prosecutor to ask a nonleading question. For example, the prosecutor might properly ask, "Please look around the courtroom and tell us if you see the person whom you saw with a gun in the store."

When can lawyers ask leading questions?

On cross-examination, lawyers are allowed to ask leading questions. When cross-examining, prosecutors typically ask narrow questions that try to force defendants and their witnesses to provide information helpful to the prosecutors. Of course, defendants and their witnesses must testify truthfully at all times. But they must be careful to avoid going along with misleading information in the prosecutors' leading questions. For example, if a defense witness's story is that an incident occurred "at dusk," the witness should not meekly go along with the prosecutor's leading question, "It was really dark out there, wasn't it?"

To be sure that they testify as truthfully and accurately during a hostile cross-examination as during a friendly direct questioning, defendants and their witnesses should:

- listen carefully to the prosecutor's questions
- stay calm and not get into an argument with the prosecutor, and
- tell the judge if they are unable to answer a question. For example, a witness who lacks personal knowledge should say, "I don't know" rather than guess at an answer. And a witness who has to qualify a "yes" or "no" answer to make it accurate might say, "Your Honor, I can answer that question only if I'm allowed to explain my answer."

> **EXAMPLE:** Jesse James is still on trial for armed robbery. After witness Kit Carson testifies and identifies James as the robber, defense counsel cross-examines Carson. Defense counsel asks, "You had drunk three whiskeys within a half hour of entering the store, correct?" The question is leading but proper on cross-examination. The theory is that since Carson is likely to be hostile to the cross-examiner, Carson is unlikely to agree with the cross-examiner if the information is false.

How accurate are the portrayals of snarly, nasty lawyers in courtroom movies and TV shows?

How TV and film lawyers ask questions is largely a product of past history and the screenwriter's imagination. Attorneys are officers of the court, and they must respect the institution of trial regardless of their attitudes toward opposing witnesses. Lawyers also don't want the jury to think they are bullies, for fear that the jurors will then sympathize with the witness under attack. Defendants and defense witnesses who are confronted with unfairly aggressive prosecutorial questioning must remain cool and allow the defense attorney to object to the prosecutors' tactics. Defendants and their witnesses must also know how to protect themselves if defense counsel fails to object.

Common forms of improper questions include the following:

Argumentative questions (popularly known as "badgering the witness"). These questions do not ask for information. Instead, they are derisive comments or legal arguments put by the prosecutor in the form of questions. Typical argumentative questions are:

- "You expect the jury to believe that story?"
- "Shouldn't the jury believe the police officer who testified rather than you?"
- "With all the evidence against you, how can you deny that you stole the watch?"

Self-protection note: Defendants and their witnesses should not argue with the prosecutor. Instead, they can use an argumentative question as an opportunity to reinforce favorable testimony. For example, a witness might respond to the first question above by testifying, "I don't expect the jury to believe anything. I'm just here telling you what happened."

Questions that assume facts not in evidence. Prosecutors are supposed to ask questions, not testify. Questions that assume facts not in

evidence violate the rule by making factual assertions to which witnesses have no chance to respond. Consider these examples:

- "Most people are terrified at the sight of a weapon, yet you were calm at the time of the robbery?"
- "Even though there were at least ten people in front of the electronics counter, you recognized immediately that Jones was a security guard?"

Self-protection note: Defendants and their witnesses can respond to the prosecutor's assumed fact while reinforcing prior testimony. For example, to the first question a witness might say, "I can't tell you how most people react to a gun. All I can tell you is that on this occasion, I was calm." Similarly, in the second example a witness might testify, "I wasn't counting how many people were at the counter. I can only repeat that for the reasons I already gave, I immediately picked out Jones as a security guard."

Questions that misquote witnesses. During cross-examination, prosecutors sometimes refer to testimony that a witness has previously given. But they cannot try to alter the meaning of the testimony by misquoting it. Consider these examples:

- On direct examination, a defendant testifies, "I was at the movies with a friend at 9 p.m." The prosecutor asks, "You say that you were with a friend at some point in the evening?"
- On direct examination, a defense witness testifies, "I had a couple of beers." The prosecutor: "You admit that you were a bit high yourself, right?"

Self-protection note: Witnesses should remind prosecutors of their actual testimony. For example, the witness's response in the second case might be, "I didn't say that I was high; I said that I had a couple of beers."

Questions that ask witnesses to speculate or draw improper conclusions. These questions improperly ask witnesses to testify to matters outside their personal knowledge. Consider these examples:

- "If you had seen Stephanie on the corner, would you have tried to make a drug deal?"
- "Dressed as you were, would Katz have been pretty frightened of you when you walked in?"

Self-protection note: Witnesses should not speculate. They often lose credibility in front of a jury by speculating about things they know nothing about. Thus, in the second example, the witness might respond, "I can't speculate about how someone else might have felt."

Can witnesses be present in court to listen to the testimony of other witnesses?

Often, witnesses are "sequestered." Sequestered witnesses cannot watch the trial until they have finished testifying. However, unlike witnesses, defendants can't be excluded from a courtroom. Defendants have a constitutional right to be present throughout a trial. Defendants often take advantage of this right by testifying last. By testifying last, defendants can listen to all the other witnesses and direct their testimony to conflicts or ambiguities in the defense case.

Expert Witnesses, Scientific Evidence, and Specialized Knowledge

As scientific knowledge develops and specialized knowledge is increasingly relevant to issues that arise in criminal trials, testimony from forensic experts has become common in criminal trials. This section explains the rules that apply to forensic experts: witnesses whose testimony is based on specialized knowledge.

Does the personal knowledge rule apply to testimony from expert witnesses?

No. Lay witnesses (ordinary percipient witnesses) are limited to testifying about matters they have personally observed. But Federal Rule of Evidence 702 and compatible rules in the states allow experts to use their specialized knowledge to testify about matters that they haven't personally observed. For example, an accident reconstruction expert might use skidmarks and other information to testify to an opinion about the approximate speed of a car involved in an auto accident—even though the expert did not observe the accident.

What is scientific evidence?

Many forensic experts testify regarding scientific evidence, knowledge about which has been developed through a process known as the "scientific method." Common examples of scientific evidence include DNA analysis, hair and fiber comparisons, fingerprints, and voice identification evidence.

Is scientific knowledge the basis of all testimony from expert witnesses?

No. Any witness whose testimony is based on specialized information may qualify as an expert witness. For example, a police officer with years of experience with drug transactions may be able to testify that the manner in which drugs were packaged indicates that they were held for sale rather than for personal use.

What is the "helpfulness" standard?

An expert witness may testify based on specialized knowledge so long as the testimony is helpful to a judge or juror. For example, an expert in eyewitness identification may be able to testify to the factors that tend to undermine the accuracy of an identification, even though lay jurors and judges would be familiar with some of the factors based on their own experiences.

What is the "reliability" standard?

Testimony based on specialized knowledge is generally admissible if the principles on which experts rely and the methods that they use are reliable. (*Daubert v. Merrell Dow Pharmaceuticals*, U.S. Sup. Ct. 1993.) In federal courts and many state courts, judges are gatekeepers. It's up to judges to determine whether the principles and methodologies underlying an expert's field of expertise are reliable. The burden of proof is on the party calling an expert to convince a judge that the principles and methods leading to an expert's specialized knowledge are reliable. This is true whether an expert's testimony is based on scientific principles, such as those underlying DNA testing, or nonscientific principles, such as those underlying an expert jewelry appraiser's estimate of a gem's value. (*Kumho Tire Co. v. Carmichael*, U.S. Sup. Ct. 1999.)

> **EXAMPLE:** A purported expert witness claimed to have invented a "brain wave machine" that could detect whether actual memories resided in a person's brain. A defendant called the expert to testify in a case in which the defendant was charged with murder. The defendant had testified to an alibi, claiming to have been attending the opera at the time the murder took place. The defense then sought to have the expert testify that the expert had examined the defendant with the aid of his brain wave machine, and that the machine detected a memory within the defendant's brain of attending the opera at the time of the murder. The judge did not permit the expert to testify, ruling that the defense had not established the reliability of the brain wave machine.

What is the "general acceptance" test of reliability?

Not all jurisdictions follow the *Daubert* rule that judges are the gatekeepers who determine the reliability of testimony based on specialized knowledge. Some jurisdictions use the older "general acceptance" test, at least for novel scientific evidence. Under this test, judges defer to scientific communities. For an expert's testimony to be admissible, the scientific principles and methods underlying the testimony must be generally accepted by the relevant community of scientists. In effect, scientific communities rather than judges are the gatekeepers who determine whether scientific principles and methods are sufficiently reliable to allow an expert to testify.

What is the difference between "opinion" and "educational" experts?

Expert witnesses typically provide opinions about trial-related matters and explain the bases of those opinions. For example, a DNA expert may testify to the overwhelming probability that a defendant was the source of the blood that was found at a crime scene and explain how the expert arrived at that opinion.

"Junk Science"

Testimony from forensic experts has become a routine part of the criminal justice system. In turn, many judges and lawyers have become concerned about so-called junk science. There is no clear definition of junk science. Generally, the term applies when information offered by a prosecution or defense witness is claimed to have a scientific basis even though, judged by the standards of mainstream scientists, it doesn't. The fear is that juries will be easily bamboozled by pseudo-experts who will testify to anything for a price. The burden falls mainly on judges (very few of whom are trained in the scientific method) to distinguish between valid and invalid scientific testimony.

How reliable and accurate is expert testimony based on scientific principles and testing?

Expert scientific testimony may be inaccurate either because the underlying principles are wrong or because crime lab tests are unreliable or carried out sloppily. Here are some of the documented failures:

- The chief serologist of the West Virginia Police Crime Lab was found to have falsified test results in at least 134 cases over a ten-year period.
- A forensic chemist in the Oklahoma City Police Crime Laboratory was repeatedly rebuked by appellate courts for withholding exonerating test results from defense attorneys and for gross delays in providing defendants with test results.
- Experts have frequently connected defendants to crimes based on hair comparison analysis principles that are scientifically unreliable.
- A study of Houston's Police Crime Lab revealed so many problems with its procedures that a Texas state senator concluded that "the validity of almost any case that has relied upon evidence produced by the lab is questionable."
- The FBI Crime Laboratory, generally regarded as the country's premier forensic facility, admitted to a variety of mistakes. Technicians at the lab misidentified the explosive charge in the Oklahoma City bombing case, falsified DNA testing procedures, relied on a method of bullet lead analysis that lacked scientific validity,

and reported fingerprint matches when none existed.

- Testimony from "bite mark" experts (also known as "forensic odontologists") has been largely discredited. Bite mark experts would typically rely on a defendant's supposedly unique mouth structure as the basis of an opinion that a defendant was the source of teeth marks found on a victim's body. Factors such as the resiliency of skin and the difficulty of making a comparison based on less-than-full sets of teeth marks has led judges to reject the reliability of forensic odontology.

A 2009 report prepared by the prestigious National Academy of Sciences described the problems in U.S. crime labs and recommended a variety of reforms. These included standardization of testing procedures, increased training for lab technicians, and increased reliance on random proficiency testing.

Compared to other types of testimony on which prosecutors commonly rely (for example, eyewitness identification, confessions, and police informants), scientific evidence has the potential to be far more neutral and reliable. Hopefully, the scientific community will take the lead in enhancing the accuracy and reliability of expert testimony based on scientific testing.

Galileo's Return

Before the U.S. Supreme Court decided the case of *Daubert v. Merrell Dow Pharmaceuticals* in 1993, a party seeking to offer scientific evidence in most jurisdictions had to establish that a particular scientific methodology was "generally accepted" among scientists. Many critics thought this test was unduly conservative. They pointed out that this test would have prevented Galileo from testifying that the world was round, because the earth's roundness was not generally accepted among scientists in Galileo's day. Under *Daubert*, general acceptance is simply one of many factors a judge can consider when deciding whether to admit novel scientific evidence. However, a number of states, most notably California, still follow the general acceptance rule. The result is that new scientific approaches to crime detection often are not used for years after their development, until they win general acceptance in the scientific community.

Is DNA evidence routinely admissible at trial?

Yes. Judges accept testimony from properly qualified experts who provide opinions based on the universally accepted principle that every person (except an identical twin) has a unique molecular makeup. Different methodologies allow experts to identify the portions of DNA molecules that establish a person's uniqueness. The most common of these methodologies is RFLP, or the Restriction Fragment Length Polymorphism Technique. By comparing an individual's known DNA with a sample of DNA from a crime scene (for example, in a drop of blood or a strand of hair), an expert can give an opinion concerning the likelihood that both samples came from the same person.

Can DNA evidence ever benefit the defense?

Certainly. The defense may offer DNA evidence to establish that the defendant is not guilty of a charged crime by showing that DNA found on the victim could not have come from the defendant. DNA evidence has led to the belated release of several hundred incarcerated defendants who were wrongly convicted (usually based on eyewitness identification testimony that turned out to be wrong) before DNA technology was available for use in court.

Are the results of a polygraph (lie detector) test admissible at trial?

Usually, no. The theory underlying polygraph testing is that lying is stressful, and that this stress can be detected and recorded on a polygraph machine if a subject lies in response to the examiner's questions. Lie detectors are called polygraphs because the test consists of simultaneously monitoring several of a subject's physiological functions (breathing, pulse, and galvanic skin response) and printing out the results on graph paper, which in turn can demonstrate exactly when in the questioning period the greatest

stress occurred. If the period of greatest stress lines up with the key questions on the graph paper, this testing method presumes that a subject is lying.

Supporters of lie detector tests claim that the test is reliable because (1) very few people can control all three physiological functions at the same time, and (2) polygraph examiners run preexamination tests on subjects that enable the examiners to measure a particular subject's reaction to telling a lie. Critics of polygraph testing argue that (1) many subjects can indeed conceal stress even when they are aware that they are lying, and (2) there is no reliable way to distinguish the stress generated by the test and the stress generated by a particular lie.

Most jurisdictions continue to doubt the reliability of lie detector tests. Some states admit the results of polygraph tests at trial, at least if the prosecution and defendant stipulate (agree) prior to the test that its results will be admissible.

Is testimony from previously hypnotized witnesses admissible?

Police departments at one time commonly used hypnosis as an investigative tool. The hope was that crime victims or witnesses would be able to recall details while under hypnosis that they could not recall while fully conscious. At trial, prosecutors sought to elicit testimony to details that witnesses were able to recall while under hypnosis.

Today, many judges are skeptical of the reliability of details that emerge while a person is under hypnosis. For example, judges fear that some people will make up details in a subconscious effort to please the hypnotist, and that previously hypnotized witnesses will be impervious to cross-examination because they have faith in whatever they recalled while under hypnosis, regardless of its objective accuracy. Thus, some states do not allow previously hypnotized witnesses to testify at all, forcing police and prosecutors to choose between hypnotizing a witness to develop leads for investigation and using the witness at trial. Other states allow previously hypnotized witnesses to testify, but limit their testimony to information that the witnesses recalled and reported to the police prior to being hypnotized.

What is neutron activation analysis?

Neutron activation analysis (NAA) is a method of identifying, analyzing, and comparing numerous types of physical evidence. For example, the NAA technique can:

- detect gunshot residue on the hand of a person who recently fired a gun
- identify the color, brand, and composition of paint, and
- detect the presence of certain narcotics.

The NAA technique measures gamma rays emitted by a sample of material after that material has been bombarded with neutrons in a nuclear reactor. NAA analysis tends to be expensive, and therefore is used only when a case warrants it. Judges generally accept expert testimony concerning NAA results, though some judges still require a minitrial to establish the validity of NAA methodology.

What is the status of "shaken baby syndrome" testimony?

Prosecutors have called forensic medical experts to opine that defendants in relevant cases shook infants so violently that the infants died. The testimony is based on medical findings that shaken baby syndrome was the cause of death. An expert's opinion that shaken baby syndrome was the cause of an infant's death is based on three medical findings: retinal bleeding, bleeding in the protective layer of the infant's brain, and brain swelling.

Across the country, numerous defendants have been convicted and imprisoned based on shaken baby syndrome testimony. However, the reliability of the shaken baby diagnosis is unclear. Defense medical experts have testified that retinal bleeding, bleeding in the protective layer of an infant's brain, and brain swelling can be due to causes other than violent shaking. One hypothesis is that these injuries can occur from trauma in the birth process itself.

Shaken baby syndrome testimony remains controversial.

How may the authenticity of unusual documents be established?

Forensic experts known as "questioned document examiners" apply scientific techniques to explain when and how a particular document originated, and whether a signature or other handwriting on the document is authentic or a forgery. Judges routinely admit testimony from questioned document examiners into evidence. For example, questioned document examiners may:

- compare two handwriting samples and give an opinion as to whether the same person wrote both. For example, the testimony of questioned document examiners who looked at ransom notes was crucial to the 1932 conviction of Bruno Hauptmann for kidnapping and killing the Lindbergh baby. The experts testified that, among many other things, both Hauptmann and the author of the ransom notes wrote "t" in the word "the" in such a way that it resembled a "u."
- restore burned or water-damaged documents sufficiently to read them.

What does fingerprint evidence consist of?

Fingerprint evidence rests on two basic principles: (1) a person's "friction ridge patterns" don't change, and (2) no two people have the same pattern of friction ridges (even identical twins). Because judges routinely accept the reliability of these principles, parties seeking to offer fingerprint evidence at trial do not have to convince the judge of the validity of the methodology underlying fingerprint evidence.

Friction ridges (that are the same on each person's fingers and foot soles) contain rows of sweat pores. Sweat mixed with other body oils and dirt produces fingerprints on smooth surfaces. Fingerprint experts use powders and chemicals to make such prints visible. The age of fingerprints is almost impossible to determine. Therefore,

defendants often try to explain away evidence that their fingerprints were found at crime scenes by testifying that they were at the scene and left the prints at a time other than the time of a crime.

Police officers can use fingerprints to identify defendants and crime victims if a print matches one already on file. People's fingerprints can be on file for a variety of reasons. For example, people may be fingerprinted when they are arrested, or when they join certain occupations.

What are forensic pathologists?

Forensic pathologists, often coroners, testify to the time and causes of death. For example, based on medical training and pathological expertise, a forensic pathologist may testify that a victim found dead in water actually died from strangulation before entering the water. Or a pathologist may give an opinion as to the type of object used to deliver a blunt force injury.

Privileged (Confidential) Information

Privileges are evidence rules that prevent the disclosure of private communications made in the course of confidential relationships. If a legislature has determined that certain information is privileged, the goal of protecting the confidential relationship outweighs the goal of allowing the jury to hear "the whole truth." Privilege rules are complex and can vary greatly from one state to another; this section provides a brief overview of a few common privileges.

What are "privileged communications"?

Privileged communications are statements made in private, in the course of a relationship that is privileged under a state's laws. For example, states grant privileges for private communications between:

- attorneys and clients
- physicians (and other medical personnel) and patients
- spouses, and
- ministers and congregants.

Privilege laws encourage clients to talk freely and openly to attorneys, spouses to talk freely and openly to each other, and congregants to speak freely and openly to priests, ministers, rabbis, imams, and other religious representatives. States create privileges because lawmakers have decided that society has a greater interest in protecting these relationships than in placing before judges and jurors all the evidence that might be relevant to the case.

Additional privileges in some states protect other relationships that are deemed to have special value. Examples include relationships between:

- journalists and informants, and
- psychotherapists and patients.

EXAMPLE: When they are alone, Greg Airias admits to his father that he committed a burglary. Greg is later charged with burglary, and at trial the prosecutor calls the father as a witness and asks the father to testify to Greg's statement. Greg's father probably would have to answer the question. Few states have enacted a privilege for private communications between parents and children. If Greg's father refuses to testify, the judge would have the power to hold him in contempt of court and send him to jail for refusing a valid order to testify (although most judges would be reluctant to send Greg's father to jail in these circumstances).

What is the consequence of a judge's ruling that a communication is privileged?

The person protected by a privilege, known as the "holder" of a privilege (for example, a client who communicates with an attorney), has a right to refuse to disclose what was said. The other party to the communication (for example, the attorney to whom the client spoke) must also refuse to disclose what was said unless authorized by the holder of the privilege to speak. The privilege bars disclosure at every stage of a criminal case, including pretrial hearings, trial, and postconviction proceedings.

EXAMPLE: Sue Cherr receives medical treatment for a knife wound she received during a fight in a tavern. While she is being treated, Sue tells the doctor how she was wounded. Sue's private statements to her doctor would probably be privileged, meaning that the prosecutor could not ask either Sue or the doctor to disclose what Sue said. On the other hand, Sue can ask the doctor to testify to what she said if she thinks the testimony will help her defense. Sue is the holder of the privilege, so she has the power to waive it (give it up). Sue's statements to the doctor would be hearsay, but probably admissible under a common exception that makes admissible statements from patients to physicians pertaining to medical treatment.

Are there exceptions to confidentiality rules?

Yes. Nearly every privilege is subject to a variety of exceptions. For example:

- If a client seeks a lawyer's help in planning a future crime or fraud, the client's statements to the lawyer will not be privileged.
- No privilege exists for communications made in public places where they can be overheard.
- A privilege will cease to exist if the holder of a privilege discloses a privileged communication to a third party.

EXAMPLE: Lucy is charged with knowingly selling adulterated chocolates. In the courthouse elevator, she tells her lawyer Desi, "I should have known that they'd find out about the chemicals I added to that batch of chocolates." Fred, the other passenger in the elevator, overhears the statement. Fred can testify for the prosecution about what Lucy said to Desi. Lucy waived the attorney-client privilege by speaking to her lawyer loud enough to be overheard in a public area.

EXAMPLE: Same case, but this time Lucy made the statement to her lawyer Desi while alone with him in Desi's law office. When she leaves Desi's office and goes back to work, Lucy tells her coworker Ethel, "I told my lawyer about how worried I was that they'd find out that I put the chemicals in the batch of chocolates." Ethel can testify for the prosecution to what Lucy said to her. By revealing to Ethel what she told her lawyer, Lucy waived the attorney-client privilege.

What privileges commonly exist for spouses?

Two privileges exist for spouses. The "spousal communications" privilege protects communications between spouses. To be privileged, a communication must be made by one spouse to the other, in private, while the spouses are married. A communication made in these circumstances remains privileged even if the spouses have separated or divorced by the time a case goes to trial. Like the attorney-client and doctor-patient privileges, the privilege for spousal communications is subject to exceptions. In most states, for example, no privilege exists in prosecutions for spousal abuse.

A second "spousal testimony" privilege allows one spouse to refuse to testify against the other spouse without risk of punishment. The second privilege allows the spouse to refuse to testify even about events that occurred before the marriage. On the other hand, this second privilege does not exist if the parties are no longer married by the time a case comes to trial. (And in the early days of this privilege, one spouse had the power to forbid the other spouse from testifying. For example, a husband charged with bank robbery could prevent his wife from testifying that she saw him run into the house with the loot from the robbery, even if the wife wanted to testify against him. Almost all states have abolished this aspect of the privilege; each spouse has the right to decide whether to testify against the other spouse or rely on the privilege and refuse to testify.)

EXAMPLE: Hank O'Hare is charged with assaulting a customer in the dry cleaning store that he and his wife Hedda run. Hedda witnessed the fight between her husband and the customer. Hedda has a right not to testify at Hank's assault trial. In a few states, even if Hedda wanted to testify, Hank could prevent her from doing so. But if Hank and Hedda are divorced at the time of Hank's trial, the spousal testimony privilege does not exist and Hedda has no right to refuse to testify. If called as a witness by the prosecution, a divorced Hedda would have to testify.

Are there privileges that protect statements made by crime victims?

Yes. Crime victims often incur both physical and psychic injuries, and thus may receive medical treatment and/or psychological counseling. Statements made by crime victims to medical personnel, psychiatrists, and clinical psychologists are generally protected from disclosure by the same privilege rules that may protect defendants' statements from disclosure. In addition, many states have enacted a privilege for statements made by victims of sexual attacks to crisis counselors.

Defendants charged with crimes often argue that their constitutional rights to a fair trial and to confront the witnesses against them should outweigh these victim privileges. For example, a defendant may ask to see a crisis counselor's notes regarding statements made by an alleged sexual assault victim in order to discover whether the alleged victim told a different story to the counselor than to the police. Few privileges are absolute, and judges sometimes allow defendants access to crisis counselors' records, especially when a defendant has some evidence that an alleged victim has given conflicting accounts of events.

Motions and Their Role in Criminal Cases

This chapter describes motions that commonly arise during criminal cases. A motion is a formal request for a judge to issue an order or make a legal ruling. A motion may involve a simple scheduling matter, such as one party's desire to postpone a preliminary hearing (a Motion for a Continuance). Motions like this are typically made orally. Or, a motion may be supported by a written brief that discusses complex legal issues. For example, a defendant's Motion to Suppress Evidence may ask a judge to rule that crucial prosecution evidence is inadmissible at trial because the police seized it illegally. If a judge rules in the defendant's favor, the prosecution may have to dismiss charges.

 CAUTION

Motions can be confusing. This chapter highlights a few of the many important rules and procedures involved in preparing motions in a criminal case. But it is not a comprehensive guide, and rules and procedures can vary greatly from one court to another.

Basic Procedures

This section gives an overview of the typical procedures for bringing motions.

When during a criminal case are motions made?

Parties may make motions before, during, or after a trial. For example, a defendant's

Motion to Set Aside a Jury Verdict obviously can't be made until after trial, because there has to be a verdict to set aside. Before trial, defendants often file motions to attack the admissibility of prosecution evidence. A ruling in favor of the defense on such a motion may result in dismissal of charges or a willingness of a prosecutor to settle a case on terms more favorable to a defendant.

What is a typical process by which motions are made and resolved?

Motions often have three distinct stages:

Giving notice (advising an adversary of a forthcoming motion). Parties are entitled to know ahead of time that their adversaries intend to ask for a court order. Notice can be given orally or in writing, depending on the type of motion. To give notice orally, a defense attorney might say during a defendant's arraignment, "Your Honor, the defense intends to move for a ruling that the knife is inadmissible because the police officer seized it illegally." Written notice is given by preparing a Notice of Motion. The notice is filed with the court and served on the adversary.

Most jurisdictions require that the notice and accompanying papers:

- identify the hearing date when a judge will consider a motion's merits
- identify the specific order a party wants the judge to make
- set forth the facts giving rise to the motion (in writing, often in the form of an affidavit or declaration under penalty of perjury), and

- explain the legal basis for the request in a document that is sometimes called a "Memorandum of Points and Authorities." This document resembles an appellate brief, and may consist of many pages of legal arguments and case citations.

Hearing the motion. During the hearing, each party has a chance to make oral arguments in an effort to convince a judge to grant ("sustain") or deny the motion.

Judge's ruling. The judge hearing the motion may rule immediately after the argument, or the judge may "take the matter under submission" and issue a ruling days or even weeks later, and sometimes not until a trial is underway. In complex situations, the judge may invite the parties to submit further written legal arguments before making a ruling.

Motion practices can, though, vary from the above description. For example, parties may forgo oral argument or waive advance written notice of a motion.

Who can submit a motion?

Typically, only the actual parties to the case (the defense and prosecution) can file motions. Sometimes, others who want to assert rights may file motions. For example, in a high-profile case, a TV station may file a motion requesting that a judge allow the televising of pretrial and/or trial proceedings.

What happens during a motion hearing?

Hearings on motions are usually informal, and may last only a few minutes. A jury is not present. The judge normally has read the parties' briefs before the hearing, and therefore doesn't want the parties to simply repeat what they wrote. The judge may ask questions and give each side a chance to respond to those questions and each other's arguments.

Written Arguments Can Help Defendants

Even when not required to do so, many defense lawyers routinely support their motions with written briefs, for three reasons: (1) a judge may take written arguments more seriously; (2) judges often make up their minds based on written arguments, before the attorneys argue orally during a hearing; and (3) the defendant will have a better record on which to rely during an appeal if the judge denies the motion.

Can stipulations be used instead of motions?

Yes. Before making motions, defense lawyers often ask prosecutors (or vice versa) to stipulate (agree voluntarily) to a request. For example, a defense attorney who wants to continue (delay) a preliminary hearing may simply ask the prosecutor to agree to a new date. If the prosecutor agrees to the delay, the defense need not make a formal motion. Instead, the parties might simply file a written stipulation in court informing the court of the new date. However, some court rules require the judge to approve stipulations before they are put into effect.

Hallway Hearings

Because of large caseloads, criminal court procedures are often informal. A defense attorney and prosecutor may work out a continuance (or another pretrial issue) informally while standing in a hallway waiting for the judge to call the case. In most cases, judges merely rubber-stamp voluntary agreements. When an agreement results in a defendant waiving (giving up) legal rights, however, the judge often asks the defendant to personally waive the rights on the record. For example, a judge might ask the defendant to personally stipulate (agree) to a continuance to show that the defendant understands the right to a speedy trial and is giving up that right knowingly.

EXAMPLE: The prosecutor and defense lawyer agree to postpone the preliminary hearing of defendant Julie Daniels from March 8, the originally scheduled date, to April 25, a date that has been cleared with the court clerk. In many jurisdictions, one of the attorneys will prepare a stipulation and file it with the court.

Is it risky to file a motion just to delay the case?

Motions filed for the sole purpose of delay are considered frivolous (baseless or made for an improper purpose) and can lead to the offending party being sanctioned (punished) by the judge.

Can defense lawyers make motions without consulting their clients?

Attorneys often make decisions about what motions to file and when to file them without involving their clients. Often, the reason is motions raise tactical concerns that involve legal judgment. Also, an issue may arise so suddenly that the attorney has no time to consult the defendant. Defendants who want more hands-on involvement in their cases can ask their lawyers ahead of time to consult them whenever possible.

Pretrial Motions

This section describes several forms of pretrial motions.

Can a defendant in custody move for release while the case pends?

Yes. Defendants can seek pretrial release from custody. At least in states that still have the traditional bail system, they can typically do so through a Motion to Reduce Bail. Bail may have been set originally by a standard measure such as a stationhouse bail schedule. As a result, defendants may file motions to reduce bail based on their individual circumstances. Even if a judge has already set bail, the defendant may bring new circumstances to the judge's attention in a Motion to Reduce Bail. Such a motion is often made orally.

EXAMPLE: Ken Ahura was arrested for driving under the influence. Ken and his family recently moved from another state, and at the time of his arrest Ken was unemployed. Using a bail schedule, the police set Ken's bail at $10,000, far in excess of what he could afford. At Ken's first court appearance, Ken's lawyer should move for a reduction of bail. The lawyer would stress the hardship to Ken and his family of him being in jail, and any factors indicating that Ken will show up as necessary and abide by the conditions of bail. Even if the judge rejects Ken's first motion to reduce bail, Ken may make additional bail reduction motions if there is a change in circumstances, such as a job offer or someone who is well known and respected in the community coming forward and vouching for him.

How can defendants attack technical defects in charging documents?

A defendant can attack an improper complaint with a Motion to Dismiss for Vagueness or a Motion to Dismiss Based on Improper Jurisdiction. A criminal complaint must specify the crime(s) charged, the defendant(s) accused of the crime(s), and the authority for the prosecution to make such charge(s). The complaint must also allege that the defendant committed each and every element of the crime(s) charged. For example, the crime of larceny (theft) typically includes the following elements: (1) the taking and carrying away, (2) of someone else's property, (3) with the intent to deprive that person permanently of

the property in question. Theoretically, if the complaint fails to allege each of these elements, the judge may dismiss it.

Realistically, technical defects such as these are uncommon. Prosecutors use the same forms over and over, so it's unlikely that a form will be defective. Also, the prosecution is usually free to amend (change) any mistakes, so motions to dismiss based on technical violations are rarely useful. However, this is not always true. For example, a successful dismissal motion may prevent the prosecution from refiling charges if a statute of limitations (a law that requires a complaint to be filed within a specified time period) will expire before new charges can be filed.

What is a Motion for a Bill of Particulars?

The defense may file this motion in an effort to find out more information about the prosecution's case. A Bill of Particulars is typically a formal and specific statement of the charges; its purpose is to give the defendant more particular information to allow for appropriate case preparation. This type of motion is relatively uncommon today.

What is a Motion to Reduce Charges?

As the title suggests, a Motion to Reduce Charges asks a judge to rule that the facts do not warrant the severity of the charge. This is not a common motion, because (1) in misdemeanor cases, judges in most states do not normally review the evidence against a defendant prior to trial, and (2) in felony cases, most states have a procedure called a "preliminary hearing," in which the judge decides whether the prosecution's felony case is adequately supported by the evidence. More typically, defendants seek reduced charges by plea bargaining with prosecutors and offering to plead guilty to lesser crimes.

What is a Motion for Change of Venue?

A defense Motion for Change of Venue asks the judge to relocate the case to a different location. Generally, criminal court proceedings (pretrial and trial) take place in the county in which the alleged crime occurred. Defendants sometimes ask for a change of venue (location) when excess pretrial publicity makes it difficult to find unbiased jurors in the locality where a case is pending. If the judge agrees and determines that the defendant will be unable to get a fair trial because of the publicity, the judge may grant the motion.

Even where the defendant has received extensive negative publicity, the defense may choose not to ask to have the case moved because:

- the case may be sent to an even more undesirable location
- the defendant may end up far away from family and friends
- defense counsel may be at a disadvantage not having an office close by the courtroom, or
- the cost of a trial away from the defense attorney's home base may be more than the defendant can afford.

EXAMPLE: In 1858, soon-to-be-president Abraham Lincoln represented William "Duff" Armstrong, who was charged with murder. The alleged murder took place in Mason County, Illinois. Lincoln successfully moved for a change of venue, and the trial took place in Cass County, Illinois. Armstrong was acquitted of the charge of murder. The classic 1939 film, *Young Mr. Lincoln*, is loosely based on the case.

What is a Motion to Strike a Prior Conviction?

Defendants can seek to reduce the severity of charges by filing a Motion to Strike a Prior Conviction. Defendants with prior records are often sentenced much more harshly than first offenders and may even be charged with more serious offenses at the outset. For example, a misdemeanor may be filed as a felony if a defendant is a repeat offender. For these reasons, it may be especially critical to an effective defense to challenge the legitimacy of prior convictions.

The most common reason for a judge to strike a prior conviction is a procedural irregularity or constitutional violation associated with the prior conviction. For example, the defendant may have been denied counsel at a critical stage of the case that resulted in the prior conviction, or the defendant may have entered into a plea bargain unknowingly or because of coercive practices by the police. Sometimes, defense counsel can convince the judge in the current case that fairness requires the prior conviction to be disregarded—struck—where the defendant has since engaged in a long period of good behavior or formal rehabilitation.

Court Records Can Be Wrong

It is not unusual for rap sheets (records of prior convictions) to contain mistakes. For example, a misdemeanor conviction may have been erroneously recorded as a felony. As a routine matter, defense lawyers typically review conviction records for errors and sometimes have defendants review the records as well.

Why might the defense file a Motion for Discovery?

Defendants can file a Motion for Discovery to find out information in prosecutors' files. Such motions are in some sense unnecessary, as prosecutors have a legal duty to turn over any information that might help the defendant, even if the defendant fails to ask for it. And many prosecutors voluntarily hand over all the information that the defense is entitled to, such as police reports and lab tests. But perhaps a prosecutor refuses to turn over information pertaining to a confidential informant's past criminal record. If defense counsel thinks that the information is important and pertinent to the charge or the defense, a Motion for Discovery is an appropriate vehicle for seeking to obtain the information. (See below for more on information about confidential informants.)

What is a Motion to Preserve Evidence?

Defendants can file a Motion to Preserve Evidence to force prosecutors to preserve evidence long enough for the defense to run its own tests. For example, if a prosecutor's DNA expert concludes that a strong likelihood exists that the defendant was the source of the blood found at a crime scene, the defendant may want a judge to order the prosecutor to preserve the blood sample so that the defense can conduct its own test.

Can the defense find out if a prosecution witness is actually a government informant?

Defense attorneys can find out whether the prosecution is relying on a government informant by filing a Motion to Disclose Identity of a Confidential Informant. Defense attorneys often try to attack a witness's credibility by showing that the witness is a paid informant who has something to gain (frequently money or reduced charges in the informant's own case) by testifying against the defendant. With this motion, the defense may ask the court to order the prosecution to reveal an informant's identity and location. The prosecution may vigorously oppose this motion in order to protect the identity of the informant. If the judge grants the motion, the prosecution may choose to dismiss the case rather than lose a valuable police resource.

Can defendants access information in police officers' personnel files?

When a police officer's past conduct is relevant to the defense, the defendant may seek to gain access to portions of the officer's personnel file by filing what might be called a "Motion to Examine Police Officer's Personnel File." A state's law might require that the judge review the file and decide whether it reveals past wrongdoing by the officer that the defense is entitled to know about. For example, if a personnel file reveals that an officer has in the past used excessive force when making arrests, planted evidence, or exhibited racial prejudice, the judge may order the prosecution to provide this information to the defendant. The defense may be able to use such information to undermine the officer's credibility and weaken the prosecution's case. However, judges do not let defendants go on fishing expeditions into police officer files. Unless a defendant can demonstrate a specific purpose for the request, a judge is likely to deny this motion.

What is a Motion to Suppress Evidence?

One of the most common pretrial motions is a Motion to Suppress (exclude) improper evidence. This motion can request the exclusion of evidence obtained as a result of:

- an improperly obtained confession
- an improper search or arrest, or
- a tainted identification.

What is a Motion for a Speedy Trial?

Defendants are entitled to be tried relatively quickly unless they give up (waive) this right. A defendant can enforce his or her right to be tried in a timely fashion by filing a Motion for a Speedy Trial. The defense can file this motion to force the prosecutor to abide by rules limiting the amount of time that can pass before the defendant is brought to trial. Delays often benefit the defendant, as witnesses' memories fade, witnesses move, evidence is lost, and prosecutors lose momentum and are often more willing to make a deal. Therefore, defense lawyers typically don't insist on speedy trials.

What is a Motion *in Limine*?

In Limine (LIM-in-nay) is Latin for "at the very beginning." A defense lawyer may file this kind of motion in an effort to get a judge to rule before trial that prosecution evidence will not be admitted during the trial. By filing the motion before trial rather than waiting to object until the prosecution seeks to offer the evidence at trial, a defendant tries to prevent the jury from ever hearing about the evidence. Also, a judge's ruling on a Motion *in Limine* can help the defense plan trial strategy.

Motions *in Limine* are often made orally, though they may be supported with a Memorandum of Points and Authorities.

EXAMPLE: Steven Brack faces trial on bank robbery charges. Brack hopes to testify in his own defense, but is concerned that if he does so, the prosecution will seek to attack his credibility by offering into evidence his previous conviction for bank robbery. If the judge rules in response to his Motion *in Limine* that the prior conviction is inadmissible as unduly prejudicial, Brack is more likely to testify in his own defense.

Some judges routinely conduct pretrial conferences with counsel before jurors are selected, to handle procedural matters related to the trial, including any Motions *in Limine*.

Motions *in Limine* are a critical component of the typical criminal case. There are many ways to discredit witnesses. However, once a witness refers to damaging evidence, it's difficult for jurors to disregard what they've heard—to, as they say, "unring the bell." So much the better, therefore, to address disputed evidentiary issues in advance and not allow the bell to ring in the first place.

Motions During Trial

Attorneys often "go through the motions" during trials. Explained below are a few motions that might be made during trial.

Can the defense ask the judge to conduct part of the trial at the crime scene?

A defendant can ask a judge to escort jurors to an important crime scene by filing a Motion to Allow Jury to View the Crime Scene. Unfortunately, judges incur costs and delays by granting such motions. Thus, a defendant has to support such a motion with a strong argument about why the jurors should visit a scene and why alternatives (such as a photograph or visual recording) are inadequate.

What is a Motion to Strike Testimony?

Ideally, attorneys can object to improper evidence before jurors hear it. If the evidence is anticipated, the objection can be made in a Motion *in Limine*. But it's obviously impossible to anticipate everything a witness might say. When jurors do hear improper evidence, the defense can make a Motion to Strike Testimony, followed up by asking the judge to instruct the jurors to disregard the stricken testimony. (In extreme situations, the defense might even move for a mistrial.) Even though it is difficult for jurors to disregard something they have heard, it is important for defendants to move to strike improper testimony for at least three reasons:

- Even though the witness should not have made the statement in the first place, jurors can consider evidence unless it is formally stricken by the judge.
- If jurors ask for testimony to be read back while they are deliberating, they will not hear the stricken testimony.
- The instruction may hurt the credibility of a prosecution witness. When jurors are told to disregard portions of a witness's testimony, the jurors may perceive the witness as a partisan who is unwilling to follow the rules of trial.

What is a Motion to Dismiss?

Defense lawyers often make a Motion for Dismissal (or Acquittal) after the prosecution rests (concludes its presentation of evidence). This Motion asks a judge to rule that the prosecution hasn't made out a strong enough case to convict. Defense lawyers make this motion out of the presence of the jury so that if the judge denies the motion (which is usually very likely), the jury won't interpret the denial to mean that the judge thinks the defendant is guilty.

> **EXAMPLE:** Vic Trola is a public defender representing Yu Kaleili on kidnapping charges. The prosecution's main evidence was the victim's testimony that Kaleili intentionally forced the victim to enter his car and would not let her leave. During Trola's cross-examination, the victim admitted to entering Kaleili's car willingly. The victim also testified that Kaleili never tried to stop the victim from leaving the car; the victim stated that it was her "impression" that Kaleili would not permit her to leave. After the prosecution rested its case, Trola made a Motion for Dismissal, arguing that the prosecution had failed to prove an essential element of kidnapping: that Kaleili detained the victim against the victim's will. If the judge believes that a jury would be unjustified in concluding beyond a reasonable doubt that Kaleili detained the victim, the judge should grant the Motion to Dismiss.

Posttrial Motions

Trials may end, but the motion process can continue. This section covers motions that might be made after a verdict.

Deadline to Move for New Trial

Defendants who want to make a motion for a new trial must typically do so very soon after the jury reaches a verdict. In federal court, new trial motions must be made within seven days, unless they are based on newly discovered evidence, and even those must be made within three years after the final judgment. (See Federal Rule of Criminal Procedure 33.)

If a judge or jury finds a defendant not guilty, can the prosecutor move for a new trial?

No. If a jury or judge finds a defendant not guilty as to all charges, the prosecution can neither appeal the verdict nor ask the judge to set aside the verdict and order a new trial. A retrial would violate the defendant's constitutional right against double jeopardy. Even if the judge, the prosecutor, and half the nation think that a jury wrongly acquitted an obviously guilty defendant, a not guilty verdict is final. The only motion following a not guilty verdict is normally the defendant leaving the courtroom as quickly as possible.

What options does the defense have for challenging a guilty verdict?

Defendants who think they've been wrongfully convicted have a number of options, including the following.

The defendant can make a motion asking the trial judge to overturn the jury's guilty verdict and enter a verdict of not guilty. A judge who believes that a guilty verdict was unreasonable can change it to not guilty. Judges seldom acquit defendants in the face of a jury's guilty verdict, because the jury is supposed to decide factual disputes. (For more on this topic, see Chapter 21.)

 CAUTION

Postconviction law is complex. The law governing posttrial motions—and appeals and writs (see Chapter 23)—is both vast and confusing. If you've been convicted, you might have more options than what's discussed here. Attorneys specializing in post-conviction law and procedure are especially critical for defendants whose convictions may be invalid.

A defendant can move for a new trial—that is, ask the judge to set aside the jury's verdict and order a retrial. Defendants may move for new trials based on a variety of grounds. The broadest rules give judges the power to grant a new trial "if required in the interest of justice." (Federal Rule of Criminal Procedure 33.) Other rules identify specific grounds on which judges can grant new trials. For example, a rule may authorize judges to grant new trials for reasons including the following:

- The defendant has discovered new and important evidence that couldn't have been discovered prior to trial.
- The jurors engaged in misconduct during the trial.
- The judge or prosecutor committed an important legal error.
- The judge gave an improper jury instruction.

Defendants are not entitled to a perfect trial. Often, even when there are mistakes, judges consider them harmless error—not so serious as to require the setting aside of a verdict—if they probably had little or no effect on the jury when it reached its guilty verdict.

If the trial judge does grant the defense motion for a new trial, the prosecution can appeal and challenge the judge's decision. But the judges who hear appeals commonly allow trial judges wide discretion in their decisions to grant or deny new trial requests. Appellate judges know that they only review a written record, while the trial judge actually saw and heard the witnesses. Accordingly, appellate judges only reverse trial judges' decisions to grant new trials when the written record plainly shows the trial judge's decision was wrong (or "clearly erroneous," as appellate court judges like to say).

Defendants can appeal (ask a higher court to reverse the conviction) because of legal errors that took place during the trial.

EXAMPLE: Julio Daniels was convicted of burglarizing Shelly's Candy Shoppe. After the verdict, one juror told a reporter about the deliberations. The juror said that Juror No. 8 had gone to the shop, measured the opening in a broken window, and then returned to the deliberations and told fellow jurors that it was "plenty big enough for Daniels to get through," which led other jurors to convict. Another juror announced that she was confused, uncertain, and only wanted to do what was right, so if the other jurors were sure the defendant was guilty, she would also vote to convict. Another juror apparently made racial slurs about the defendant during deliberations, announcing he "knew" Julio Daniels was guilty because "all those people are criminals." The defense should obtain an affidavit from any and all jurors willing to give a factual account of what happened during the jury deliberations and move for a new trial. Juror misconduct is proper grounds for a new trial, and all of the following are prohibited:

- jurors considering evidence not presented in court (the juror in this example going to the scene of the crime, measuring the window and telling fellow jurors to consider the observations as fact)
- a juror deciding to convict just to go along with others and not out of personal conviction, and
- a juror basing a verdict on racial prejudice.

EXAMPLE: Anna Rose was convicted by a jury of burglary. John Fell testified for the prosecution and identified Anna as the burglar. Anna's attorney moves for a new trial based on Fell's having whispered after the verdict that he believed he'd made a mistake. Judges often believe that witnesses and even jurors suffer from postverdict remorse and too easily want to take back what they did or said. The judge might conclude that Fell's recantation is not believable or that the prosecution had sufficient evidence to convict Anna even without Fell's testimony, in which case any error would be harmless and the judge would deny Anna's motion.

When trial is to a judge sitting without a jury, what motions can the defense make to seek relief from a guilty verdict?

For many of the same reasons that a defendant may move for a new jury trial, a convicted defendant may ask the judge to:

- modify the verdict (for instance, change it from conviction on one charge to conviction on a lesser charge), or
- vacate the verdict (withdraw it altogether and order a new trial).

Because these motions ask judges to effectively overrule themselves, they are not usually successful. Nonetheless, in certain situations, such a motion might be worth a try—for instance, if new and important evidence is discovered that might persuade the judge to remedy an injustice.

When might newly discovered evidence justify setting aside a guilty verdict?

A judge may grant a new trial if the defense discovers new and helpful evidence that justifiably was not known about at the time of trial. Defense counsel's being on vacation and not having adequate time to prepare is not considered a good reason (though an "ineffective assistance of counsel" claim might be possible in that situation). But the recent surfacing of an alibi witness who had fled to another country may be. Another possible good reason is that scientific evidence that was not available at trial becomes available. Old cases have been reopened, for instance, to analyze blood samples with new DNA technology.

> EXAMPLE: Guy Goode was convicted of rape; his defense was mistaken identity. One year after Goode's conviction, scientists develop a new test that demonstrates that he was not the source of the semen found in the rape victim. The information qualifies as newly discovered evidence, because the test was unavailable at the time of Goode's trial. Moreover, the evidence is important: Had it been offered at the time of trial, it might well have produced a different verdict. Goode should move for a new trial.

Writ Proceedings in the Trial Court

Writs, discussed further in Chapter 23, are generally orders from higher courts to lower courts. In some states, defendants can seek special relief from the trial court itself through a proceeding called a writ *coram nobis*. For example, a defendant might use this writ to ask the trial court itself to reopen a case to review facts that the defendant could not present during trial, either because they were not known or for some other extraordinary reason (for instance, the defendant had been threatened and was afraid to present facts that could have produced an acquittal).

Plea Bargains: How Most Criminal Cases End

A plea bargain is an agreement between a defendant and a prosecutor in which the defendant typically agrees to plead guilty or no contest (*nolo contendere*) in exchange for an agreement by the prosecutor to drop one or more charges, reduce a charge to a less serious offense, or recommend to the judge a specific sentence acceptable to the defense.

As criminal courts become ever more crowded, prosecutors and judges alike feel increased pressure to move cases quickly through the system. Trials can take days, weeks, or sometimes months, while guilty pleas can often be arranged in minutes. Also, the outcome of any given trial is usually unpredictable, whereas a plea bargain provides both prosecution and defense with some control over the result—hopefully, one that both can live with.

For these reasons and others, and despite its many critics, plea bargaining is very common. More than 90% of convictions result from negotiated pleas. And though some commentators still view plea bargains as dirty little back-room secrets, explicit rules in most jurisdictions govern plea bargaining procedures. (See Federal Rule of Criminal Procedure 11(e).)

Plea Bargaining—Terminology and Timing

Let's start off with plea bargaining basics.

Are there other terms for a "plea bargain"?

A plea bargain may also be called a plea agreement, a negotiated plea, or simply a "deal."

Sentence Bargaining and Charge Bargaining

Plea bargaining can be divided into two primary types: sentence bargaining and charge bargaining. Sentence bargaining is a method of plea bargaining in which the prosecutor agrees to recommend a lighter sentence for specific charges in exchange for a defendant's guilty or no contest plea. Charge bargaining is a method where prosecutors agree to drop some charges or reduce a charge to a less serious offense in exchange for a plea by the defendant.

When does plea bargaining take place?

In most jurisdictions and courthouses, plea bargaining can take place at virtually any stage in the criminal justice process. Plea deals can be struck shortly after a defendant is arrested and before the prosecutor files criminal charges. At the opposite end of a case, a plea deal may be struck as a jury returns to a courtroom to announce its verdict. If a trial results in a hung jury, in which the jurors are split and cannot make the unanimous decision required, the prosecution and defense can (and frequently do) negotiate a plea rather than go through another trial. And plea deals are sometimes reached after a defendant is convicted while a case is on appeal.

The Pros and Cons of Plea Bargains

In online shopping and criminal cases alike, a "bargain" may not be as good as it initially seems. Defendants have to think through their alternatives before pleading guilty, considering the advantages and disadvantages explained below.

Does a guilty or no-contest plea result in a conviction?

Yes. A guilty or no-contest plea entered as a judge-approved plea bargain results in a criminal conviction; the defendant's guilt is established just as it would be after a trial. The conviction will show up on the defendant's criminal record (rap sheet). And, the defendant loses any rights or privileges, such as the right to vote, that the defendant would lose if convicted after trial.

What does it mean to plead "no contest" (*nolo contendere*) rather than guilty?

A no-contest or *nolo contendere* plea in essence says to the court, "I don't choose to contest the charges against me." The primary difference between a guilty and a no-contest plea is that if a victim sues a defendant in civil court, the no-contest plea often cannot be offered into evidence against the defendant as an admission of guilt. A guilty plea, on the other hand, does

serve as an admission of guilt and can be introduced in civil cases as evidence against the defendant.

Might a prosecutor agree to a guilty plea but not to a no-contest plea?

Yes. Defendants generally do not have a right to plead no contest, meaning that a guilty plea may be a defendant's only alternative to trial.

Why do most defendants plead guilty or no contest?

For most defendants, the principal benefit to plea bargaining is receiving a lighter sentence for a less severe charge than might result from a conviction at trial.

> **EXAMPLE:** Commander O.M. Pyre is charged with 20 counts of burglary after a spree of burglaries in his neighborhood. Assistant District Attorney Art Mills offers to drop the charges to two counts of burglary if Pyre pleads guilty right away. Pyre takes the deal, because his sentence will be shorter and he will be eligible for parole earlier than if he were convicted on every charge at trial.

Privately represented defendants who agree to plea bargains can save a bundle on attorneys' fees. It almost always takes a lot more time and effort to try a case than to negotiate a plea bargain, so defense counsel typically charge a much higher fee if a case goes to trial.

There may also be other benefits for defendants who plead guilty or no contest, such as the following.

Getting out of jail. In-custody defendants may be released from jail following the judge's acceptance of a plea, depending of course on the charge and the deal.

Benefits of Moving From Jail to Prison

One way a defendant might benefit from pleading guilty is by moving more quickly from jail to prison. Conditions in many jails are worse than in prisons. And as jails are primarily for short-term incarceration, prisons may have educational and work programs that jails lack.

Getting the matter over quickly. A plea of guilty or no-contest more quickly resolves what for most people is a stressful situation. Going to trial usually requires much more time in court than a plea bargain.

Having fewer and/or less serious offenses on one's record. Pleading guilty or no-contest in exchange for a reduction in the number of charges or the seriousness of the offenses can look a lot better on a defendant's record than the convictions that might result following trial. This can be particularly important if the defendant is convicted in the future. For example, a second DUI conviction may carry mandatory jail time, but if the first DUI offense had been bargained down to reckless driving, for example, there may be no jail time for the second DUI arrest (of course, it depends on the case and the jurisdiction). Even for people who are never rearrested,

getting a charge reduced from a felony to a misdemeanor, or from a felony that constitutes a strike under a "three strikes" law to one that doesn't, can be a critical benefit. Some professional licenses must be forfeited upon conviction of a felony. Future employers may not want to hire someone previously convicted of a felony. Felony convictions may be used in certain court proceedings (even civil cases) to discredit people who testify as witnesses. Felons can't own or possess firearms. And in many jurisdictions, felons can't vote.

Having a less socially stigmatizing offense on one's record. Prosecutors may reduce charges to less socially offensive ones in exchange for a guilty or no-contest plea. For example, a prosecutor may reduce a child molestation or rape case to an assault. Conviction of the lesser charge in this instance may allow the defendant to avoid having to register as a sex offender. Also, a lesser offense may lessen the likelihood that family members and friends will stigmatize a defendant. Of more immediate concern, sometimes defendants convicted of stigmatizing offenses are at a greater risk of being attacked in prison.

Avoiding publicity. Famous people, ordinary people who depend on their reputation in the community to earn a living, and people who don't want to bring further embarrassment to their families all may choose to plead guilty or no-contest to remove their names from the limelight as quickly as possible. While news of the plea itself may be public, the news is short-lived compared to news of a trial.

Avoiding deportation. Noncitizens who plead guilty may be deported after they have finished serving their misdemeanor or felony sentences. Defense lawyers must inform noncitizens that deportation is a potential consequence of a guilty plea. (*Padilla v. Kentucky*, U.S. Sup. Ct. 2010.) For noncitizens charged with crimes, therefore, pleading guilty to an offense that reduces the likelihood of deportation is another potential benefit of plea bargaining.

The 364-Day Misdemeanor Year. Some states have made the maximum imprisonment for many or all misdemeanors 364 days rather than 365. That change is designed to avoid deportation consequences that would have been triggered if the misdemeanor in question carried the possibility of, or if the misdemeanor defendant actually received, a full one-year sentence.

Factors That Affected Detective Fuhrman's Plea Bargain

Retired detective Mark Fuhrman, infamous for having denied using racial slurs during the O.J. Simpson criminal trial, pleaded no contest to perjury charges. Fuhrman apparently "didn't have the money to wage a long court battle and didn't want to put his family through such a trial." Said Fuhrman, "... I don't think the city of Los Angeles either deserves or could handle a trial like this ... I cut my losses and everybody else's." (From "Fuhrman Grants Interview, Apologizes for Slurs," *L.A. Times*, October 8, 1996, at B1.)

How does plea bargaining benefit judges and prosecutors?

For judges, the primary incentive to accept plea bargains is to move along crowded calendars. Most judges simply don't have time to try every case that comes through the door.

Additionally, because jails are over-crowded, judges may face the prospect of having to let convicted people (housed in the same facilities as those awaiting trial) out before they complete their sentences. Judges often reason that the quicker those offenders who are not likely to do much jail time anyway are "processed" out of jail (by plea bargains), the fewer problems with overcrowding, and the less frequently serious offenders will have to be released before their full sentence has been served.

The judge's concerns about clogged calendars are the prosecutor's concerns as well. When the judge is bogged down, the judge yells at prosecutors to move cases along quicker. To keep judges happy (and keep the machine rolling), prosecutors must keep "the bodies" moving (as criminal defendants are most unfortunately referred to by some courthouse regulars).

Prosecutors are, of course, also concerned for their own calendars. Clogged calendars mean that the prosecutor's staff is overworked. Plea bargains lighten the staff's caseload. Because plea bargains are much quicker and require less work than trials, they are also easier on the prosecutor's budget. With today's cutbacks on already slim resources, D.A.s feel they will have additional time and resources for more important cases if they conclude a large number of less serious cases with plea bargains.

Another benefit to the prosecution is an assured conviction. No matter how strong the evidence, no case is ever a slam dunk.

Plea bargains also allow prosecutors to protect government informants. Many informants have criminal records. If a case were to go to trial and the informant were to testify, the defense in many cases could impeach the informant with his or her past criminal history. But in the context of a plea bargain, the prosecution generally does not have to turn over an informant's criminal history to the defense. (*United States v. Ruiz*, U.S. Sup. Ct. 2002.)

Plea bargains also give prosecutors flexibility. For instance, they can offer a deal to someone who, though guilty, has given testimony about a codefendant or helped resolve some other unsolved case.

> **EXAMPLE:** Bran Dess, an experienced criminal with a long rap sheet, planned to rob Donna's Liquor store. He recruited Martha Stevens to be his lookout. Martha has no criminal history and is just 18. She merely stood guard; she was not armed and did not know Bran had a gun. As Bran threatened Donna and forced her to empty the cash from the register into his money bag, Bran's gun accidentally fired. Donna suffered serious but not fatal injuries; Bran and Martha fled. Martha later confessed to the police.

Bran pleads guilty to armed robbery and gets sentenced 25 years to life in prison— ironically, the same sentence he likely would have gotten after trial, because of his record and the nature of the robbery. Martha, however, though technically guilty of armed robbery, is offered a plea to larceny (theft), for which she may serve up to one year in prison, in exchange for her testimony against Bran. The prosecutor likely justified the deal by reasoning that Martha helped to get the really bad guy off the street and played only a minor role in the robbery, and that this was her first offense. These last two factors would ordinarily tend to lighten Martha's sentence even without her cooperation.

Finally, prosecutors may use plea bargains to circumvent laws they don't agree with. For instance, a prosecutor may disagree with laws prohibiting possession for personal use of small amounts of marijuana, so the prosecutor's office may have an unwritten policy of giving all such offenders "offers they can't refuse."

How might plea bargains benefit victims?

Victims can also benefit from plea bargains. A plea bargain ends a case and allows victims to avoid the stress of testifying and facing a perpetrator at a trial. While a victim may feel disappointed by a prosecutor agreeing to a deal, many victims are relieved to leave the past in the past and move on with their lives as soon as possible.

Can a plea bargain be based on a "civil compromise"?

Yes. A civil compromise typically results in dismissal of criminal charges against a defendant. For a civil compromise to occur, the following elements must generally be present:

- The charged crime must be a misdemeanor. Civil compromises of felony charges are rare.
- The defendant must compensate the victim for the damages caused by the illegal action.
- The victim must appear in court and assure the judge and prosecutor that the defendant has given fair compensation for the victim's losses.
- The judge and prosecutor must agree that the defendant has fairly compensated the victim. No matter a victim's wishes, judges and prosecutors will typically not allow a civil compromise to terminate a criminal case based on charges of domestic violence, elder abuse, or similar illegal acts, where the crime is a serious harm to society as a whole and not just to the individual victim.

EXAMPLE: As part of a college fraternity initiation stunt, Jim sprays graffiti onto the wall of a sorority house and is charged with misdemeanor vandalism. Jim apologizes and pays to have the graffiti removed and the wall repainted. The sorority president appears in court with Jim, tells the judge and prosecutor that Jim has taken care of the damage, and asks to have the vandalism charge dismissed. The judge and the prosecutor agree that the compensation is fair and the charge is dismissed. The compromise protects the sorority and saves Jim from having a conviction on his record.

The Plea Bargaining Process

Many cynics argue that like laws and sausages, plea bargains are best made out of public view. This section explains how plea bargains come about.

What happens in a plea bargain?

In a typical plea bargain, the defense lawyer and prosecutor confer, and one or the other proposes a deal. The negotiations can be lengthy and conducted only after both parties have had a chance to research and investigate the case. Or, they can be minute-long exchanges in the courthouse hallway.

EXAMPLE: Deputy Public Defender Cooper passes Assistant District Attorney Van Lowe in the hallway on their way into the courtroom. The following interchange takes place.

P.D. "Mornin', V.L. Got a good offer for me in the Reback case?"

D.A. "That's the assault case?"

P.D. "Yeah. Honor student, nice guy, got into a scrap with another guy at a fraternity party. He's been in since last night. How 'bout time served, probation, and completion of an anger management course?"

D.A. "Fine."

P.D. "Okay, what about the Bremer case?"

It is quite likely that a plea bargain in a misdemeanor assault case would take place this quickly and this informally, especially when the deal is between a prosecutor and court-appointed attorney who work with each other every day and trust each other. "Time served" means that the jail time will be just what the defendant has already spent in jail—in this case, overnight. Of course, the deal is not final until the defendant Reback agrees to it.

Can a lawyer arrange a plea bargain without the client?

Yes, but the decision about whether or not to accept the plea bargain ultimately rests with the client. For practical purposes, however, defense counsel often urge defendants to accept deals, convincing them they'll get a much harsher sentence if they go to trial (and they're often right). And defendants tend to take the deals that their attorneys recommend.

Does a defendant's right to effective assistance of counsel extend to plea bargaining?

Defendants have a Sixth Amendment right to effective assistance of counsel during plea bargaining. (*Missouri v. Frye* and *Lafler v. Cooper*, U.S. Sup. Ct. 2012.) Because more than 90% of criminal cases end with guilty or no-contest pleas, defendants need to be fully informed of the important ramifications of a plea.

EXAMPLE: Jones is charged with felony burglary. The prosecutor tells Jones's lawyer that Jones can plead guilty to a misdemeanor. However, the lawyer never tells Jones about the prosecutor's offer. Jones goes to trial and is convicted of felony burglary, and then learns that he could have pleaded guilty to a misdemeanor. As a result of the lawyer's ineffectiveness, Jones can have the conviction set aside.

EXAMPLE: Lee, a foreign national in the United States on a student visa, pleads guilty to a drug offense. Lee was unaware that the conviction made her eligible for deportation, and her lawyer neglected to mention this consequence to her. Because a competent lawyer would make sure that Lee knew that a conviction could result in her deportation, the lawyer provided ineffective assistance and Lee can have the conviction set aside. (*Padilla v. Kentucky*, U.S. Sup. Ct. 2010.) (In 2017, the Supreme Court found that a defendant showed a reasonable probability that he wouldn't have pleaded guilty had he known it would lead to mandatory deportation; therefore, his lawyer's erroneous advice on the deportation implications of the guilty plea made for ineffective assistance of counsel. (*Lee v. U.S.*, U.S. Sup. Ct. 2017.))

What role do judges play in plea bargaining?

It is up to the judge to impose sentence in a criminal case. On the other hand, it is up to the prosecutor to decide what charges to bring; the judge has no authority in that sphere except to dismiss a charge that the judge feels wasn't established by the prosecution. This means that a prosecutor may be able to agree to change the charges or even drop some charges in exchange for the defendant's plea without the judge being able to stop it. However, if the plea bargain involves the type of sentence to be imposed by the judge, the prosecutor cannot guarantee the result without the judge's agreement.

"Pleading to the Sheet"

In states like California, judges and lawyers may use the phrase "plead to the sheet" to describe the defendant pleading guilty to all charges filed by the government without any agreement with the prosecution about the sentence. Defendants may choose this option when they don't want to go to trial, but think that they can get a better sentence than the prosecution offered to recommend. Other phrases that may convey the same concept include "pleading straight up" and "open plea."

Here is yet another area where the advice of an experienced criminal law attorney is critical. Such a lawyer can explain the procedure and options and may be able to provide insight about the sentence the judge would impose.

Much of the time, plea bargaining negotiations take place privately between the defense lawyer and prosecutor, outside of court. The judge has no formal role until the plea is offered in open court. In some courts, however, the judge is actively involved in pushing both sides to negotiate, even facilitating negotiations in the judge's chambers (office). On occasion, the judge will provide guidance to the defense and prosecutor by indicating what sort of a sentence would be acceptable.

Do judges have to accept plea bargains?

No. In many courts, prosecutors agree to recommend the bargained-for sentence without obtaining an explicit agreement beforehand from the judge to accept the deal. But prosecutors typically know from past experience whether a judge can be counted on to accept a prosecutor's recommendation. If the judge rebels or simply doesn't follow the track record, and seeks to impose a harsher sentence than the one the defendant was led to expect, the defendant is usually allowed to withdraw the guilty plea. (If the case ultimately goes to trial, the jury will never find out that the defendant had sought to plead guilty.) But if the prosecutor has made it clear that the judge might not accept the recommendation, and the defendant pleads guilty anyway, the defendant may be stuck with the judge's sentence. In other words, sometimes bargaining for the prosecutor's recommendation will produce a sure result; other times, it simply means that the defendant can test what the judge is willing to do; and still other times, it guarantees nothing at all and risks a harsh sentence.

Do victims have a role in the plea bargaining process?

Many victims are dissatisfied when defendants are allowed to enter into plea bargains, feeling that the harms they suffered were disregarded and the defendants got off too easily. As a result of the efforts of victims' rights groups, laws in many states now allow victims to have a say in the plea bargaining process.

Some states require prosecutors to consult with victims before entering into plea bargains. In other states, victims have a legal right to come to court and address a judge personally before the judge decides whether to accept a plea bargain. Still a third possibility for victims in many states is to consult with the probation officer before the officer prepares the presentence reports that often influence a judge's sentencing decision.

What factors enter into a judge's decision to accept or reject a plea bargain?

As a practical matter, many judges go along with plea bargains as long as the agreed-upon sentences are within the range of what they consider fair. Usually this means determining whether, given the seriousness of the crime and the defendant's criminal record, the sentence seems appropriate in light of other sentences the judge has handed down. However, shifting community attitudes toward types of crimes can affect judges' sentencing policies. Also, sentencing guidelines adopted by legislatures can constrain judges' sentencing discretion.

Prosecutors Who Back Out of a Deal

Sometimes, prosecutors agree to certain deals out of court and then change their minds in front of the judge. In most places, the defendant caught in such a situation would have the right to simply withdraw a plea of guilty. To deter prosecutors from going back on a deal, the defense should have the agreed-to terms put in writing before going before the judge. If the prosecutor agrees only to make a recommendation or to not oppose the defense lawyer's request for a certain sentence, however, the court may refuse to allow the defendant to withdraw the plea. (See Federal Rule of Criminal Procedure 11(e) (2); *Santabello v. N.Y.*, U.S. Sup. Ct. 1971.)

What is a plea colloquy?

Before accepting guilty or no-contest pleas, judges typically engage defendants in a courtroom "colloquy." A judge questions the defendant briefly to make sure that a factual basis for the plea exists. (There are exceptions, though, as with an *Alford* plea—that's where a defendant claims to be innocent but pleads guilty because of the strength of the prosecution's evidence. (*North Carolina v. Alford*, U.S. Sup. Ct. 1970.)) Moreover, a judge will use the colloquy to make sure and put on the record that defendants are aware of the rights they are giving up by pleading guilty or no-contest. For a "knowing and intelligent" guilty plea to be made, defendants have to admit, know and understand:

- the conduct made punishable by the law
- the charges against them
- the consequences of the plea (both the sentence as it stands and the possible sentences that could be given were the defendant to have a trial), and
- the rights that they are waiving (giving up) by pleading guilty, including (1) the right to counsel if unrepresented, (2) the right to a jury trial, (3) the right not to incriminate themselves, and (4) the right to confront and cross-examine their accusers.

Defendants should also know that, if they are not U.S. citizens, they may risk deportation when they are convicted of a crime. Defendants are competent to waive counsel and plead guilty as long as they are capable of understanding the proceedings. (*Godinez v. Moran*, U.S. Sup. Ct. 1993.)

In some courts, defendants who plead guilty are asked to fill in or sign a form waiving their rights.

Usually the judge asks the defendant a fairly long list of questions to determine whether the plea is knowing and intelligent. For their part, defendants normally follow their attorneys' advice and avoid upsetting the plea bargaining apple cart by quietly answering "yes" to all the judge's questions.

Assuming the defendants' answers are satisfactory, judges typically accept the deal. In some cases, a judge may consult with the crime victim, ask a probation officer to prepare a presentence report, and listen to arguments from both the defense and prosecution before making sentencing decisions.

Pleas That Aren't Knowing and Intelligent

If a defendant entered into a plea without counsel and did not appear, from a later review of the record, to have made a knowing and intelligent plea, that defendant may have grounds to request that the conviction be stricken (removed) from the defendant's record, or at least not be considered in any future proceedings. Striking prior convictions can be important because offenders tend to be sentenced more severely with each repeat offense.

EXAMPLE: Assuming that Deputy Public Defender Cooper and Assistant District Attorney Van Lowe have agreed on the plea bargain in the Reback case from the previous example, the following might take place in the courtroom:

Clerk: "Court is now in session, the Honorable Judge Kevin Don presiding."

Judge: "In the matter of the *State vs. Reback*, Mr. Reback, how do you plead?"

Defendant Reback: "Guilty, Your Honor."

Judge: "Counsel, have you reached a settlement?"

D.A.: "Yes, Your Honor. The people have agreed to time served and probation, as long as Mr. Reback completes an approved anger management course."

Judge: "Mr. Reback, do you know that by pleading guilty you lose the right to a jury trial?"

Defendant Reback: "Yes, Your Honor."

Judge: "Do you give up that right?"

Defendant Reback: "Yes, Your Honor."

Judge: "Do you understand what giving up that right means?"

Defendant Reback: "Yes."

Judge: "Do you know that you are waiving the right to cross-examine your accusers?"

Defendant Reback: "Yes."

Judge: "Do you know that you are waiving your privilege against self-incrimination?"

Defendant Reback: "Yes."

Judge: "Did anyone force you into accepting this settlement?"

Defendant Reback: "No."

Judge: "Are you pleading guilty because you in fact struck the victim without legal provocation?"

Defendant Reback: "Yes."

Judge: "Mr. Reback, you are hereby sentenced to 12 hours in jail, which you have already served, and to two years' probation, on condition that you complete a court-approved anger management course."

What is a "trial penalty?"

A statute that allows for harsher punishment of defendants who ask for jury trials than for defendants who plead guilty is unconstitutional. (*U.S. v. Jackson*, U.S. Sup. Ct. 1968.)

However, trial judges often have discretion when it comes to sentencing, and appellate courts rarely second-guess discretionary punishments. Often, a judge's exercise of discretion results in harsher punishment meted out to defendants who go to trial and are convicted compared to the sentence that would have resulted from an offered plea deal. But harsher posttrial sentences don't necessarily constitute an unfair penalty on defendants who exercise their constitutional right to trial. The reverse perspective is that plea bargaining provides a benefit to defendants who signal remorse by pleading guilty or no-contest while providing defendants with an incentive to remove cases from the criminal justice system.

An unfortunate byproduct of a perceived trial penalty is innocent defendants potentially pleading guilty. A prosecutor whose evidence is weak may offer a deal rather than dismiss a charge. An innocent defendant, fearing a trial penalty, may take the deal rather than go to trial. Ultimately, the best remedy for a perceived trial penalty may be good-faith evaluation by prosecutors of the strength of their evidence and defendants' level of culpability.

The Strategy of Negotiating Plea Bargains

Just as in other negotiations, such as those of a buyer and seller in a real estate transaction, there are strategies involved in plea bargaining.

How does "over-charging" affect plea bargaining?

Prosecutors may create bargaining chips by "over-charging," initially charging defendants with the most serious charges possible. Over-charging creates incentives for defendants to plead guilty or no-contest to fewer or less serious (but ultimately more realistic) charges.

> **EXAMPLE:** Officer Rhett Cutler stopped Charlotte O'Hara for an unsafe lane change. While writing the ticket, Officer Cutler spotted what looked like a packet of illegal drugs on the back seat. O'Hara was arrested and ultimately charged with possession of illegal drugs for sale. By charging O'Hara with possession for sale, the prosecutor leaves wiggle room to drop the charge to "simple possession" in exchange for a guilty plea if the circumstances warrant the lesser charge.

Do defendants receive "cookie cutter" plea deals?

While an oft-heard phrase is "The punishment should fit the crime," plea bargains often reflect both the seriousness of charged crimes and defendants' unique characteristics. For example, a prosecutor's plea offer may reflect factors such as:

- whether the defendant has any prior convictions ("priors")
- the manner in which the offense was committed, and
- how strong the prosecution's case (evidence) is.

A comprehensive study of plea bargains, conducted in the mid-1980s, found that defense lawyers also look for specific characteristics of the defendant that may be used to argue for leniency in any given case. (See "Plea Bargaining: Critical Issues and Common Practices," U.S. Department of Justice, July 1985.)

One defense lawyer described plea bargaining as follows:

"Everyone in the system knows roughly what a given case is 'worth.' By balancing the seriousness of the crime and the defendant's record (how much time the prosecution wants the defendant to do), against the strength of the evidence and the skill of the defense lawyer (how likely the prosecution is to get a conviction), a specific deal is arrived at." (*How Can You Defend Those People: The Making of a Criminal Lawyer,* James S. Kunen.)

What is a "standard deal"?

For many common offenses, prosecutors in a given courthouse have worked out what is, in effect, a "price list," setting out the typical sentences for different offenses. For example, in one area, it may be the prosecutors' practice to uniformly reduce all first-time DUI (driving under the influence) offenses in which blood alcohol tests reveal a marginal or borderline level to a lesser offense, such as reckless driving. And, judges may hand down uniform sentences pursuant to the standard deals.

How can a defendant find out about a "standard deal?"

A layperson considering hiring a private attorney might want to know whether it's viable to self-represent, take a "standard deal," and save time and money. However, standard deals are typically not written down anywhere. Experienced defense lawyers (often public defenders and panel attorneys) typically know the "going price" in a particular jurisdiction for common charged crimes. Laypeople wanting to know if they can obtain a "standard deal" may try to check with a public defender or panel attorney, or consult even just once with a privately paid lawyer.

What other factors might influence the terms of a deal?

A number of other factors may influence particular plea bargains, including:

- the jurisdiction in which a case arises
- how congested a court's calendar is
- the policies of a prosecutor's office, and
- the philosophy of the judge.

Good defense lawyers should know this "lay of the land" information. Defense lawyers who are not personally familiar with these details tend to seek advice from colleagues who are more familiar with the local scoop. Such local factors can be critical. If the judge has a reputation for leniency (for a particular type of charge, at least), the defense lawyer may be able to get a better deal out of the prosecutor than if the judge has a get-tough reputation.

Defendants also tend to find themselves in stronger bargaining positions when their cases are to be heard in busier courts, such as those in large, metropolitan areas, where many judges' (and prosecutors') foremost concern is to get through their backlog.

Are defendants with lawyers likely to get better deals than defendants who represent themselves?

Yes. To get a good deal, a defense lawyer may have to lobby a prosecutor. And just as a child lobbying a parent for a later bedtime must curry favor and display honesty and reliability, so too must effective defense lawyers. Prosecutors are often more reasonable when discussing cases with defense lawyers they've come to know and trust compared to self-represented defendants who are strangers.

Defense lawyers are also more likely than self-represented defendants to be able to confer with prosecutors early on in cases, before prosecutors become entrenched in their positions.

And the reality is that most prosecutors are much more comfortable discussing cases with other lawyers than with self-represented defendants. In one study, prosecutors flatly admitted personal prejudice against unrepresented defendants. (See "Plea Bargaining: Critical Issues and Common Practices," U.S. Department of Justice, July 1985 at 43.) In misdemeanor cases in Texas, the study reported, unrepresented defendants discussed their cases directly with the prosecutors, "who generally advise[d] them to plead guilty to avoid being 'creamed' if they [went] to trial and in order to get probation or diversion right away." One prosecutor further admitted that in a weak case, "If there is a defense attorney, I'll dismiss it … If there is no attorney, I'll try to get the defendant to plead guilty."

How do defendants know whether to take a deal?

Plea bargaining is common because it provides benefits to both prosecutors and defendants. There is no way to know for sure, however, when the best time to take the deal is. Plea negotiations are something of a poker game, and defendants can't know for sure whether they will be dealt a better hand as a case progresses.

General wisdom suggests that it is often beneficial for defendants to hold off accepting initial offers. Underlying this theory is the idea that the more time that passes after the alleged offense, the weaker the state's case may become. Witnesses disappear and forget, and physical evidence may be lost. And all that time, the defense has a chance to build a better case. So, for some cases, the longer the defendant can hold out, the better the deal will be.

Some prosecutors have a hard-and-fast policy, however, of escalating their demands if an initial offer isn't accepted. Experienced defense lawyers are often aware of these hardball tactics, and may recommend that their clients accept such offers. Also, even if delays are beneficial

to the defense, waiting is usually easier for those defendants who are out on bail than it is for in-custody defendants.

Because of these variables, defendants should consult with their lawyers about strategies of waiting versus taking the deal or going to trial.

Do defense lawyers push clients to take deals because it's easier for the lawyers?

Many defendants have the perception that lawyers (especially those paid for by the government) just want to get them to plead guilty to make life easier for the lawyers. Often, before the first meeting with the client, the defense lawyer will have seen the police report, spoken with the D.A., and possibly even agreed upon a tentative plea bargain. In one study from years back, defendants reported most often hearing, as the first words their lawyers spoke, "I can get you … if you plead guilty." (See *American Criminal Justice: The Defendant's Perspective*, by Jonathan D. Casper.) Many defendants today echo this sentiment, believing that government lawyers don't care whether they are guilty or innocent.

It is true that it is less work for a lawyer when a client takes a plea. Therefore, defendants must make sure their lawyer works for their best interests, fairly explaining the pros and cons of any deals offered and not rushing or pressuring the defendant into accepting a deal. The final decision on whether or not to plead rests with the clients; defendants have a right to a trial if they want one.

EXAMPLE: Tonya Herding was caught on camera Thursday afternoon stealing clothes, jewelry, and perfume from Mays Department store. She was arrested at the store, taken to jail, and booked. Bail was set at $1,500, but Herding had no money to post bail. She told the police she would need a court-appointed lawyer. She spent the night in jail and was arraigned the next day. In court, just before her case was called, Herding met Nancy Herrigan, the P.D. assigned to the case. Herrigan told Herding she got a good deal and thought Herding should accept it to get out of jail. If Herding has people she can contact to lend her the money, she could probably get a bail bond for $150, and for another $150 or so she may be able to get a second opinion from a private defense lawyer. At a minimum, Herding should ask Herrigan to explain what the deal is and why it's a good one. Is it, for example, the standard deal for such offenses? She may also want to ask what Herrigan thinks of requesting a continuance and lobbying the D.A. further before accepting the first offer.

However, a perception that government-paid lawyers put their own interests first is more legend than reality. Public defenders are overly maligned. Plea deals that government-paid lawyers work out may tend to be just as good or better for defendants on the whole than the results private counsel obtain from going to trial. In other words, some private counsel may push to go to trial when it would be better for the defendant to take the deal.

Can defendants do anything if they suffer from buyer's remorse?

Plea bargains are usually binding. Defendants cannot get out of deals just because they changed their minds. In certain (albeit rare) circumstances, however, when it would be unfair to allow a deal to stand, defendants may be allowed to withdraw a guilty plea. Examples of such circumstances may include when a defendant:

- does not have the "effective assistance of counsel" in making the deal (see Chapter 17 for more on effective assistance of counsel)—for instance, the defendant was forced to plead before a public defender could be appointed
- is not informed of the underlying charges before agreeing to the deal
- does not voluntarily agree to the deal, or
- receives a sentence that differs from the agreed-upon deal.

The Trial Process

This chapter explains criminal trial procedures and tactics. While procedures can vary somewhat from one courtroom to another, the overview that this chapter provides can help all nonlawyers understand their role in the trial process.

Summary of the Trial Process

The many rituals associated with modern trials have developed over centuries. Because of America's common law heritage, all states and the federal government follow a largely uniform set of procedures. In summary form, those procedures are as follows.

Judge or jury: The defense and prosecution each decide whether to ask for a jury trial.

Select the jury: If a jury trial, the defense and prosecution select the jury through a question-and-answer process called *voir dire.*

Address evidence issues: The defense and prosecution ask the court in advance of trial to admit or exclude certain evidence (these requests are called Motions *in Limine*).

Opening statements: The prosecution and then the defense make opening statements to the judge or jury. (Criminal defense lawyers often choose not to make an opening statement until after the prosecution has rested its case. One reason for such delay is to avoid disclosing information to the prosecution.)

Prosecution case-in-chief: The prosecution presents its main case through direct examination of prosecution witnesses and introduction of any pertinent tangible exhibits, such as weapons, photos, and lab test results.

Cross-examination: The defense cross-examines the prosecution witnesses.

Redirect: The prosecution reexamines its witnesses (called redirect examination).

Prosecution rests: The prosecution rests its case.

Motion to dismiss: The defense has the option of making a motion asking the judge to dismiss the charges based on the prosecution's failure to prove guilt beyond a reasonable doubt. Dismissal is rare.

Defense case-in-chief: The defense presents its main case through direct examination of defense witnesses and introduction of any pertinent tangible exhibits.

Cross-examination: The prosecutor cross-examines the defense witnesses.

Redirect: The defense reexamines the defense witnesses.

Defense rests: The defense rests its case.

Prosecution rebuttal: The prosecutor offers new evidence to rebut (counter) the defense case.

Instructions settled: The prosecutor, defense lawyer, and judge finalize the jury instructions.

Prosecution closing argument: The prosecution makes its closing argument, summarizing the evidence as the prosecution sees it, and explaining why the jury should render a guilty verdict.

Defense closing argument: The defense makes its closing argument, summarizing the evidence as the defense sees it, and explaining why the jury should render a not guilty verdict (or at least a guilty verdict on a lesser charge).

Prosecution rebuttal argument: As the prosecution has the burden of proof, often the prosecutor has an opportunity to speak last and address arguments made by the defense.

Jury instructed: The judge instructs the jury about what law to apply to the case and how to carry out its duties. (Some judges "preinstruct" juries, reciting at least some of the instructions before closing argument or even at the beginning of the trial.)

Jury deliberations: The jury deliberates and tries to produce a verdict by (usually) unanimous agreement.

Posttrial motions following a guilty verdict: If the jury renders a guilty verdict, the defense often makes posttrial motions asking the judge to override the jury and either grant a new trial or order the defendant acquitted.

Sentencing if guilty verdict: Following a guilty verdict, the judge pronounces a sentence right away or delays sentencing for another day, often after the preparation of a sentencing report by a probation officer.

Appeal. A defendant can challenge the legal validity of a conviction in an appellate court. The prosecution cannot appeal from a not-guilty verdict; such a verdict is final.

Writ Proceeding. A defendant who can no longer appeal a conviction often can use a writ to challenge the validity of the conviction. (The challenge is sometimes many years after the conviction occurred.) The most common of these writs is the writ of *habeas corpus*. Some kinds of arguments can be made only via writ.

Choosing a Judge or Jury Trial

To be tried by a judge or a jury, that is often the question. This section explains the options.

Is a defendant entitled to a jury trial?

The U.S. Constitution guarantees the right to trial by jury in all but "petty" cases (by interpretation, cases in which the defendant cannot be imprisoned for more than six months). Defendants charged with felonies and serious misdemeanors are entitled to jury trials. Defendants charged with minor misdemeanors punishable only by fines— called infractions (for example, speeding)— are not.

Are defendants likely to be better off with a judge or a jury?

Defendants should normally opt for a jury trial unless they have a good reason to waive (give up) a jury and leave the decision to a judge sitting without a jury. Among the reasons this is often the best choice are that it allows defendants to:

- **Play the percentages.** Most jurisdictions require unanimous jury verdicts. For example, if a case is tried to a 12-person jury, the prosecutor has to convince all 12 of the defendant's guilt. A reasonable doubt in the mind of any single juror will prevent the defendant's conviction—assuming the juror acts conscientiously. By contrast, a judge offers the defense but one mind in which to raise a reasonable doubt.

- **Have a hand in selecting jurors.** Before the start of a jury trial, the defense can question and excuse (dismiss) some potential jurors during jury *voir dire*. In most states, however, unless it can prove actual bias on the part of the judge, the defense has to accept the judge assigned to the case.

The "One Free Bite" Rule

Some states allow the defense to dismiss a judge without having to prove that the judge is biased. The defense simply files an affidavit stating, in effect, "We want a different judge." But the defense can use this affidavit procedure only once; the defense must accept the next judge assigned to the case unless, of course, the defense can show actual bias.

Despite these reasons, the defense is sometimes better off with a judge trial. For example, the background of a certain judge might suggest sympathy for a defendant. Or, the success of the defense case may rest on a technical legal argument that a judge is more likely than a jury to accept.

Who should make the decision about judge or jury?

The judge-vs.-jury trial decision is an important one, and the defendant should normally make it after consulting with an attorney. (This is specified in Standard 4-5.2, ABA Standards for Criminal Justice.)

Usually, defense attorneys have greater access than defendants to information about judges, their backgrounds and their attitudes, and a better understanding of the technical merits of the case. But a defendant may be just as well equipped as the attorney to gauge the mood of the community toward the police and the type of crime with which the defendant is charged, and to assess the emotional appeal of the case.

The Jury Trial "Penalty"

Some judges apply an unwritten and unfair jury trial penalty policy, giving harsher sentences to defendants who opted for a jury rather than a judge trial. For example, in off-the-record conversations, judges often tell defense attorneys something like, "If your client takes a bench (judge) trial and is convicted, he's looking at a couple of years in jail. But if he insists on a jury trial, all bets are off." The implication is that defendants who put the system to the added time and expense of a jury trial will pay for it in their sentences. Before deciding on a judge or jury, defendants should try to find out what the risks are.

What happens if a defendant wants a judge trial and the prosecutor asks for a jury trial?

If either side—prosecutor or defense—requests a jury, then trial will be to a jury.

Does a defendant who asks for a jury trial have to pay jury fees?

No. Unlike in civil trials, in which the parties pay the jury fees, the government pays jury fees in criminal cases.

The Jury Waiver in the Leopold and Loeb Case

The trial of Leopold and Loeb took place in Chicago in the 1930s. Thinking themselves too smart to be caught, two wealthy and mentally disturbed young men killed a young boy just for the thrill of it. After their arrest, their parents hired the famous Clarence Darrow to defend them. Dramatically, Darrow waived a jury trial and pleaded his clients guilty. Under then-existing Illinois law, a judge (rather than a jury) then had to sentence Leopold and Loeb. Darrow figured that he had a better chance of saving his clients' lives in front of a judge. He was right; they were given life sentences, and Leopold was eventually paroled.

Jury *Voir Dire*

Voir dire (pronounced "vwar deer"), the process of questioning potential jurors, is a uniquely American feature of jury trials. The *voir dire* portion of a trial must generally be open to the public under the Sixth Amendment to the U.S. Constitution. (*Presley v. Georgia*, U.S. Sup. Ct. 2010.)

What is jury *voir dire*?

Voir dire is the jury selection process, during which potential jurors answer questions about their backgrounds and attitudes. The prosecutor and defense can challenge potential jurors whose answers demonstrate that they might not be fair and impartial. If a judge allows a challenge, the challenged juror is dismissed and replaced from a larger pool of potential jurors.

What kinds of questions can be put to potential jurors?

Some *voir dire* questions are routine; they are put to potential jurors in just about every criminal case. For example, potential jurors are typically asked whether they know the attorneys, the defendant, or any witnesses, where they work, and whether they have ties to law enforcement. Other questions are case specific. For example, if the defendant is charged with making a fraudulent insurance claim, potential jurors will undoubtedly be asked about their attitudes toward and experiences with insurance companies.

When *voir dire* questions may be invasive of a juror's privacy (as in a sexual violence case), judges often give potential jurors an option to answer in the judge's chambers, outside the presence of the other potential jurors.

Who asks the questions on *voir dire*—the judge or the attorney?

In the past, attorneys did all *voir dire* questioning, except the handful of routine questions that the judge would ask. In many state courts, this is still true. However, it's increasingly common for judges to do most of the questioning in an effort to speed up *voir dire* and prevent attorneys from using *voir dire* to build rapport with the jurors and plant ideas about their side of the case.

Especially in the federal courts, the prosecution and defense may be limited to submitting written questions that they want the judge to ask.

What does it mean to challenge potential jurors?

The defense and prosecution can each challenge potential jurors. A challenge is a request for the judge to dismiss a potential juror. The rules allow for two types of challenges: (1) challenges for cause, and (2) peremptory challenges.

A challenge for cause asks the judge to excuse a potential juror on the ground that the juror's answers demonstrate actual bias. Both sides are entitled to jurors who are fair and impartial. Jurors who are predisposed in favor of one side or the other cannot legally serve on a jury. For example, a judge will undoubtedly grant a defendant's challenge for cause if a potential juror says something like, "I think police officers do a marvelous job under almost impossible conditions. I'd find it very difficult to disbelieve any testimony a police officer gives." Such an answer shows that the juror is predisposed to believe a police officer

over the defendant, and is not, therefore, fair and impartial. Defendants often seek to exercise challenges for cause privately, perhaps in the judge's chambers. That way, if the judge denies the challenge, the defendant is not faced with an angry juror.

Constitutional Limits on Peremptory Challenges

As a general rule, attorneys can exercise peremptory challenges for whatever reason they choose. However, courts have ruled that attorneys cannot excuse potential jurors because of the jurors' race or gender. For example, if a defendant claims that a prosecutor has exercised a peremptory challenge against a prospective juror based on the juror's race, the prosecutor has to show that the challenge was based on a valid, race-neutral reason. (*Foster v. Chatman*, U.S. Sup. Ct. 2016.)

Peremptory challenges allow either side to excuse potential jurors even if their answers do not demonstrate actual bias. A defense lawyer or prosecutor who believes for whatever reason that a potential juror favors the adversary can use a peremptory challenge to excuse that juror.

For instance, if a defense attorney believes that viewers of a particular news channel are likely to be prosecution-minded, the attorney might use a peremptory challenge to excuse such a viewer.

Judges Do Not Often Grant Challenges for Cause

Even when a potential juror's background suggests probable partiality toward one side or the other, most judges will allow the juror to sit as long as the juror insists that he or she can give both sides a fair trial. For instance, assume that an alleged victim and a potential juror are both plumbers. The defendant may believe that the juror will subconsciously favor the prosecution. Nevertheless, if the potential juror swears to be open-minded and fair, the judge would probably deny the defendant's challenge for cause. The defense might then use one of its peremptory challenges to strike this juror.

The judge must grant a peremptory challenge, regardless of whether the judge believes the challenged juror is biased. However, each side gets only a limited number of peremptory challenges.

Alternate Jurors

In many cases, judges try to seat regular and alternate jurors. The alternates sit in throughout a trial, but will not step in and decide the case unless one of the regular jurors becomes ill or for some other reason has to be excused from the jury. Without an alternate, the judge in this situation might have to declare a mistrial and start a trial all over again.

How many juror challenges does each side get?

Each side has an unlimited number of challenges for cause. However, the number of peremptory challenges is very limited. For example, Federal Rule of Criminal Procedure 24 grants each side only three peremptory challenges in misdemeanor cases. Most states have similar limits. In cases involving murder and other very serious charges, each side may have as many as 20–25 peremptory challenges. Regardless of the number, the defense has to carefully save its peremptory challenges for those potential jurors whom they cannot successfully challenge for cause, but who are most likely to harbor biases in favor of the prosecution or otherwise be likely to favor the prosecution or reject the defense story.

EXAMPLE: Marcus Nieman is charged with stealing merchandise from Westrom's Department Store. Victoria Macy, a potential juror, is a store clerk at a different department store. In response to defense counsel's questions, Macy testifies that shoplifting hurts everyone because it leads stores to raise prices. Nieman's attorney challenges Macy for cause, but the judge denies the challenge when Macy insists that she can be fair to both sides and won't blindly accept a security guard's testimony. Whether Nieman should use a peremptory challenge to bump Macy off the jury is a difficult decision for Nieman (and his lawyer) to make. Nieman has only a few peremptory challenges in this misdemeanor case, so he has to think about whether other potential jurors (including those who might replace Macy) would be even less acceptable than Macy.

Do defendants or their lawyers decide which jurors to challenge?

Many defense attorneys think that deciding which jurors to challenge is a matter of professional craft that the defendant should leave to the attorney. Standard 4-5.2 of the ABA Standards for Criminal Justice supports the lawyers' attitude, though it advises attorneys to consult with clients before challenging potential jurors "where feasible and appropriate." Defendants are often at least as sensitive to potential jurors who give off "bad defense vibes" as are attorneys, and ordinarily defendants should ask their attorneys to consult them during jury selection.

Jury Consultants

Defendants who can pay for it often hire jury consultants to assist in the selection of jurors. Typically, jury consultants investigate people's attitudes in the locality where a trial will take place and develop profiles of jurors who are likely to favor either the defense or the prosecution. For example, a jury consultant may report that "college-educated females under the age of 35 are likely to favor the defense." The defense can take such information into account when deciding which jurors to challenge.

Can the defense use *voir dire* to preview its case?

Attorneys have often tried to use *voir dire* to begin persuading jurors to vote their way. The ensuing delays in starting trials were a major reason that judges in many areas took over *voir dire* questioning. Nevertheless, the defense can use even a limited questioning opportunity to "educate" jurors about the fundamental rules favoring defendants. Consider these questions that the defense might ask:

"Does each of you understand that the mere fact that Mr. Binder has been arrested and charged with a crime is not evidence of guilt?"

"Does anyone disagree with the principle that as she sits here now and through-out the entire trial, Ms. Ouspenskaya is presumed innocent unless and until the prosecution convinces you beyond a reasonable doubt of her guilt?"

The defendant would not really expect a potential juror to disagree with such basic principles. The questions emphasize to the jurors that the burden of proof favors defendants and that all defendants are presumed innocent until proven guilty.

Motions *in Limine*

This section explains Motions *in Limine*, which parties may use to seek pretrial rulings on the admissibility of important evidence.

What is the purpose of a defense Motion *in Limine*?

A defense Motion *in Limine* (which may be made in writing or orally) asks a judge to make a pretrial ruling that evidence a prosecutor intends to offer at trial is inadmissible. For example, a defendant might ask for a ruling that "the prosecution cannot refer to the fact that the defendant has previously been convicted of a crime." If the judge grants the Motion in Limine, neither the prosecutor nor prosecution witnesses can refer to the conviction during the trial.

If the defense doesn't make a Motion *in Limine*, can the defense make an objection to prosecution evidence during the trial?

Yes. The defense can wait until a prosecutor offers evidence during trial, and then object. But waiting until trial raises the danger that jurors will hear objectionable evidence before the defense has a chance to object. For example, testimony might unfold as follows:

Prosecutor: "Had you ever seen the defendant before?"

Witness: "Yes, the defendant was in a fight in a different bar the week before."

Defendant: "I object to any reference to an earlier fight, it's irrelevant."

Judge: "I agree. The testimony is stricken, and I instruct the jurors to disregard it."

Even though the judge upholds the defense objection and tells the jurors to disregard the improper evidence, some jurors may be influenced by it. As attorneys are wont to say, "It's hard to unring a bell." By making a Motion *in Limine*, the defense hopes to prevent jurors from hearing improper evidence in the first place.

And in cases where the judge rules that the evidence in question is admissible, it may still benefit the defendant to file a Motion *in Limine*. At least the defense knows ahead of time that the damaging evidence will be allowed in at trial, and can plan its strategy accordingly.

Can the judge delay ruling on a Motion *in Limine* until trial?

Yes, and judges often do so. The judge may want to wait until the trial is underway before ruling on the admissibility of evidence. Nevertheless, a Motion *in Limine* is a useful way for defendants to "red flag" an objection to important but potentially highly prejudicial prosecution evidence. If and when the prosecutor attempts to introduce the evidence, the judge will have been given notice by the pretrial motion that this is critical evidence and may be more willing to take the time during trial to carefully consider its admissibility.

Opening Statements

Opening statements are road maps. They provide overviews that help jurors understand the parties' legal claims.

What is an opening statement?

An opening statement is an opportunity for the defense and prosecution to describe what they plan to prove and what evidence they plan to offer. The prosecution and defense cases often emerge piecemeal from a number of witnesses, and are likely to be interrupted by court recesses, cross-examination, and the like. Thus, an opening statement allows each side to make it easier for the judge or jury to follow their case. Good opening statements are like road maps and movie previews. Like a road map, an opening statement tells a judge or jury where the defense or prosecution case is headed. And like a movie preview, a good opening statement whets a judge's or jury's appetite for the evidence to come.

Can evidence be introduced during an opening statement?

No. What is said during opening statement does not constitute evidence. The judge or jury cannot rely on facts referred to during the opening statements when deciding the case. For example, assume that during opening statement a prosecutor says, "You'll hear the defendant's next-door neighbor testify that the defendant drank three beers before leaving for work that morning." If the next-door neighbor does not testify, or testifies but fails to mention three beers, the judge or jurors cannot use the prosecutor's assertion as evidence that the defendant drank three beers. Rather, during closing argument the defense attorney would most likely attack the prosecution's case

by pointing out the prosecutor's failure to deliver the evidence promised in the opening statement.

If the prosecution's opening statement refers to highly prejudicial information that is not offered into evidence, the judge may uphold a defense request for a mistrial.

When does the defense make its opening statement?

In most jurisdictions, the defense can make an opening statement either immediately after the prosecutor's (before any witnesses testify) or after the prosecution's case-in-chief is over (before defense witnesses testify).

When given the choice, defense lawyers often choose the first option. Even though judges repeatedly admonish jurors not to evaluate a case until all the evidence is in, jurors weigh information as they hear it. This gives prosecutors a big advantage, because they get to present evidence first. Defense opening statements are one way to keep jurors' minds open until defendants get to present their evidence.

On the other hand, if the defense strategy is to defer certain key decisions—such as whether the defendant will testify—until after the prosecution case is finished, it may be better to defer the defense opening statement until the beginning of the defense case.

Can the prosecution or defense argue the merits of a case during an opening statement?

No. Because an opening statement serves only as a preview, neither the defense nor the prosecution can argue. For example, a defendant cannot explain why the defense case is stronger than the prosecution's.

Some judges allow more argument during the opening statement than other judges. Whatever leeway a judge allows a prosecutor should also be given to the defense.

> **EXAMPLE:** Rex Kars is on trial for assaulting Herman Shepherd. Kars claims that he acted in self-defense. The prosecutor makes the following remarks during opening statement: "Frank Enstein will testify that he saw the defendant Kars strike the first blow. I submit that Enstein is totally credible. He had the best view of anyone at the scene and is completely unbiased, and his testimony is more credible than any evidence the defendant will offer." The prosecutor is making an improper argument. Opening statement is limited to a preview of evidence; it is not the time to argue which side's evidence is more credible. The prosecution must wait until closing argument, when the jury has heard all the evidence, to make such points.

Prosecution's Case-in-Chief

The ball starts in the prosecution's court when it's time to present evidence.

Why does the prosecution get to put on its case first?

The prosecution goes first because it has the burden of convincing the judge or jury of the defendant's guilt. Until the prosecution puts on enough evidence to satisfy this burden, there's no reason for the defense to put on a case at all.

How can defendants find out what facts a prosecutor has to prove to obtain a conviction?

To figure out what the prosecutor has to prove, defendants have to very carefully analyze the criminal laws they are charged with violating. Often, the legal definition of a crime differs from its popular understanding. For example, in many jurisdictions drivers may be convicted of drunk driving simply because their blood alcohol level was at or exceeded the legal limit. The prosecution does not have to prove that alcohol affected their driving.

Most crimes consist of two or more discrete subcomponents called elements. To prove a defendant guilty, a prosecutor has to support each element with proof. If the prosecutor fails to prove any one element beyond a reasonable doubt, the defendant should be found not guilty.

For example, assume that Phil Thee is charged with grand theft. In many states, grand theft consists of the following elements:

- the defendant
- took property belonging to someone else
- worth more than $500
- with the intent to permanently deprive the owner of the property that was taken.

If the prosecution fails to offer enough evidence to satisfy each element during its case-in-chief, Phil must be acquitted. For instance, the prosecution may prove that Phil took someone's property, but fail to prove the property's value (Element 3). Or, the prosecution may prove the value of the taken property, but fail to prove that Phil intended to permanently deprive the owner of possession (Element 4). In either instance, the judge or jury would have to acquit Phil.

To obtain a verdict of not guilty, does the defense have to mount an attack on every element of the charged crime?

No. The prosecution has the burden of proving beyond a reasonable doubt each and every element of a charged crime. This means that if the defense raises a reasonable doubt as to any one element, the defendant must be found not guilty. This is why the defense typically focuses its attack on one or two elements.

For example, return to the case of Phil Thee, the defendant charged with grand theft. In response, Phil might attack just one of the elements that the prosecution has to prove. For example, Phil may concede that someone may have stolen property worth more than $500, but offer evidence that it wasn't he who stole it. Or, Phil may concede that he took property worth more than $500, but claim that he was borrowing it pursuant to an agreement he had made with its owner.

Direct Examination of Witnesses

Witness testimony emerges at trial through a traditional and stylized question and answer format. This section covers direct examination, the phase of trial in which the parties question their own witnesses.

What is the purpose of the oath that all witnesses take?

The purpose of the oath is to impress on witnesses the seriousness of testifying in court. By swearing to tell the truth, witnesses also subject themselves to perjury charges should they lie about an important matter. (Witnesses who for religious or other reasons do not care to take an oath and swear to tell the truth may instead "affirm" that they will testify truthfully. Whether a witness "swears" or "affirms" to tell the truth, the legal effect is the same.)

Rarity of Perjury Prosecutions

Witnesses bent on perjury may have little to fear from prosecutors. Perjury tends not to be a high priority crime for most prosecutors, in part because it can be difficult to prove actual knowledge of falsity. An exception to this might be in cases widely reported in the media. When a witness appears to commit perjury in full view of millions, prosecutors may have no choice other than filing perjury charges. An example of this was Detective Mark Fuhrman, who pleaded guilty to perjury after lying during the 1995 internationally televised murder trial of O.J. Simpson.

Does the question-and-answer format apply to testimony by defendants?

Yes. Testimony is supposed to emerge in question-and-answer form, not as an unbroken narrative. When witnesses respond to specific questions from attorneys, adversaries know ahead of time what general information the witness is likely to provide, and have time to object if necessary.

Can the defense decide the order in which its witnesses testify?

Yes. The defense can call witnesses in whatever order it chooses. However, the defendant often testifies last (if at all). Because the defendant cannot be excluded from the courtroom while other witnesses testify, a defendant who testifies last has the benefit of hearing what the other witnesses have said and listening to the prosecutor's cross-examinations.

Can the prosecutor call the defendant as a witness?

No. Under the Fifth Amendment to the U.S. Constitution, defendants have an absolute right not to be called as a witness nor to testify unless they choose to do so.

Cross-Examination

The right to question the opposing party's witnesses through cross-examination is the hallmark of the adversary system of justice.

What is cross-examination?

After a witness's direct examination concludes, the opposing side has an opportunity to ask questions. Cross-examination is an opportunity both to elicit evidence helpful to the cross-examiner, and to attack the credibility of the evidence that supports the adversary's claims.

What are leading questions?

Leading questions suggest a questioner's desired answer. Example: "The robber had a mustache, right?" Leading questions are proper during cross-examination but for the most part are improper during direct examination.

What kind of information does a cross-examining prosecutor want to get out of a defense witness?

A prosecutor's usual cross-examination goal is to undermine the credibility (believability) of testimony given by the defendant and other defense witnesses during direct examination. The defense can expect cross-examination to cover these possible areas:

- The witness's prior criminal record, if any, for the purpose of impeaching the witness's credibility. Prior arrests are not generally admissible in evidence, but prior convictions that arguably call into question the witness's honesty are, especially if the convictions are for felonies.
- Inconsistencies between the witness's testimony and any statements the witness gave to police officers or others.
- If the witness is the defendant, the defendant's motive to commit the crime. For example, if the defendant is charged with assault, the prosecutor might ask questions suggesting that the victim had insulted the defendant's family.

Tips for Witnesses

People whose testimony is needed in court are usually served with subpoenas, which are court orders. (See the sample subpoena at the end of this chapter.) Subpoenaed witnesses who fail to appear in court at the time and date indicated on the subpoena can be taken into custody. Witnesses should understand the following rules:

- Witnesses can and should discuss their testimony ahead of time with the attorney for the side that called them. Witnesses should know generally what questions will be put to them.

- Witnesses can talk informally to the attorney for the other side if they want to, but they do not have to.

- When testifying, witnesses should limit their answers to the questions asked. They should not volunteer additional information. Even if they are just trying to be helpful, what they say may be legally improper—and it may end up hurting rather than helping.

- Witnesses who don't understand a question should ask the questioner to rephrase it.

- Witnesses often needn't worry if they have a temporary loss of memory. After a witness replies, "I don't remember," evidence rules allow attorneys to show the witness letters, reports, memos, or any other documents to remind the witness of forgotten information. However, after having his or her memory stimulated in this manner (called "refreshing recollection"), the witness must still be able to testify from memory. If the witness says, after viewing a document, "You know, I still can't remember," the witness will not be allowed to simply testify to what's in the document.

- Witnesses who are worried about wasting time in court until they testify should ask the attorney who subpoenaed them about an "on call" procedure. Witnesses who are on call agree to be available to come to court and testify on short notice, but in the meantime can go about their daily tasks.

- Witnesses should keep their cool during cross-examination, and answer an adversary's questions in the same way they answered questions asked by the attorney for the side favored by their testimony—that is, make sure they understand the question and limit their answers to what the questions ask.

- Witnesses whose answers may subject them to criminal charges should assert their Fifth Amendment privilege against self-incrimination. (If possible, they should consult with a lawyer as soon as they become involved in the case.) Witnesses who are unsure about their potential exposure should tell a judge that they want to consult an attorney before answering questions.

- If the witness is the defendant, the defendant's physical ability to do whatever the defendant claims to have done. For example, the prosecutor may try to cast doubt on the defendant's claim to have gotten from one house to another in 15 minutes, or to have been able to observe the color of a car at night.
- A personal relationship suggesting that a witness might be biased in favor of the defendant.

Can the defense attorney help the defendant prepare for cross-examination?

Yes. Defense attorneys often play the part of a prosecutor and rehearse the prosecutor's likely cross-examination with defendants (and defense witnesses) before trial. Such rehearsals (often called "woodshedding of witnesses") are perfectly legal and proper.

After the prosecutor cross-examines a defense witness, can the defense attorney ask that witness additional questions?

Yes. This is known as redirect examination, and it gives the defendant or witness a chance to respond to the prosecutor's credibility attacks during cross-examination. For example, if the prosecutor asked the defendant about a prior inconsistent statement, the defendant will have a chance to explain the reason for the inconsistency. Also, redirect gives the defendant or other witness an opportunity to clarify portions of a story that may have gotten muddied during a prosecutor's misleading cross-examination.

Defense Motion to Dismiss

Once the prosecution has finished presenting its evidence, the defendant may file a motion to dismiss, asking the judge to dismiss the case before it reaches the jury.

Can a judge dismiss a case after the prosecution rests?

Yes. Even in a jury trial, the judge has the power to decide that the prosecution's evidence isn't strong enough to support a guilty verdict. The defense can ask the judge to exercise this power by making a Motion to Dismiss at the conclusion of the prosecution's case-in-chief. If this motion is granted, the defense won't have to present its own case. And the dismissal will operate as the legal equivalent of an acquittal, which means the defendant cannot be retried on the same charge.

Does the defense have anything to lose by making a Motion to Dismiss?

Generally, no. The motion is made out of the jury's presence. Therefore, even if the judge denies the motion, the jury is unaware that the judge has ruled that the prosecution's case is strong enough to justify a guilty verdict. However, to preserve their own reputations, defense attorneys usually don't move to dismiss if the prosecution's evidence, if believed, is obviously strong enough to justify a guilty verdict.

Defendant's Case-in-Chief

Once the prosecution has finished presenting its evidence, the defense has an opportunity to present evidence.

Are the questioning rules for the defense the same as for the prosecution?

Yes. Like prosecutors, the defense can call witnesses in whatever order they wish. Also, they must elicit testimony in question-and-answer form, and cannot ask leading questions of defense witnesses.

Is it always a good idea to present a defense case?

No. Sometimes the defendant's best argument is that the prosecution evidence is not strong enough to prove guilt beyond a reasonable doubt. In such situations, a defendant may choose to rest on the presumption of innocence and neither call witnesses nor present other evidence. This tactic may be riskier in a jury trial. Jurors are probably more prone than judges to think, "If the defendant had a good case, why didn't we get to hear it?" Thus, defendants should carefully review with their lawyers any decision to rest on the presumption.

> **EXAMPLE:** June Buggs is on trial for burglary. June's defense is mistaken identity; she claims to have been at home at the time of the burglary. The defense effectively undermined the credibility of the only prosecution witness who claimed to be able to identify June as the burglar. Moreover,

June was home alone at the time of the burglary, and has told her lawyer that her memory of the evening is impaired by the fact that she had been smoking marijuana. June should consider not presenting a defense case. The prosecution case is weak, and June may do her case more harm than good if she is unable to remember clearly what she was doing on the night of the burglary. Because her strongest argument may be the prosecution's inability to prove her guilty beyond a reasonable doubt, June may reasonably choose to rest on the presumption of innocence.

Can the prosecutor respond to the evidence presented by the defense?

Yes. After the defense "rests" (finishes presenting evidence), the prosecutor normally has a chance to offer "rebuttal" evidence. The prosecutor can offer rebuttal evidence only to attack evidence offered during the defense case. The prosecutor cannot use rebuttal to rehash the prosecutor's case-in-chief or put in new evidence unrelated to what the defense presents.

> **EXAMPLE:** Cara Way is on trial for grand theft. During the defense's case-in-chief, Cara's attorney calls Chia as an alibi witness to testify that Chia and Cara were at the movies at the time of the theft. On rebuttal, the prosecutor wants to call two witnesses: (1) Cain, to testify that Cain recently overheard Chia tell Cara, "If you're ever in trouble, you can count on me for an alibi," and (2) Abel, to testify that Cara was

the person he saw commit the burglary. (Abel already testified to this during the prosecution's case-in-chief.) Cain can testify as a rebuttal witness, because Cain's testimony attacks the evidence presented by Cara. Abel cannot testify, because his testimony wouldn't respond to the defense case; it would be a rehash of testimony already given.

At the end of the case, can the judge instruct the jury to find the defendant guilty?

No. As the representative of the community, the jury has the absolute power to find any defendant not guilty. The judge has no power to instruct the jury to return a guilty verdict. And if the jury comes back not guilty, the judge has no power to change its verdict or order a new trial.

Closing Argument

Attorneys take center stage during closing argument. This is the most free-wheeling phase of trial, but rules do exist.

During closing argument, can the defense mention evidence it forgot to offer when it was putting on its case?

No. Just as the opening statement is limited to evidence that will be offered, so closing argument is limited to evidence that has been offered. Referring to evidence that was not offered during testimony is improper argument outside the record.

If the defense realizes during closing argument that it forgot to offer important evidence, is there anything it can do?

A defense that rests its case having forgotten to offer important evidence can ask the judge for permission to reopen the case-in-chief. Even during closing argument, the judge has the power to allow the defendant to present additional evidence. The more important the evidence, and the better excuse the defendant can offer for not presenting the evidence earlier, the likelier the judge is to allow a defendant to reopen the defense case.

> **EXAMPLE:** Jezza Bell is on trial for child endangerment for leaving her infant son unattended while she went shopping. Jezza's defense was that she left the child in the care of a responsible babysitter who took off without Jezza's knowledge. Jezza testified that a neighbor, Jebediah, saw the babysitter with Jezza's son when Jezza left. However, Jezza's lawyer could not locate Jebediah and thus could not call him as a witness. Just before Jezza's lawyer finishes her closing argument, Jebediah rushes into court, apologizes for having been away and offers to testify as above. The defense lawyer should immediately ask the judge for permission to reopen her case-in-chief. The lawyer should explain what Jebediah will say and why she was unable to produce him as a witness earlier. Jebediah's testimony is important, and the judge should grant the request.

What should the defense talk about during closing argument?

Closing argument is an opportunity for the defense to explain why the evidence requires a not guilty verdict. Most defense closing arguments include these features:

- a reminder that the prosecution has the burden of proving its case beyond a reasonable doubt, and that the defendant is presumed innocent
- a summary of important evidence with a defense spin, especially if the trial has extended over a few days
- an attack on weaknesses in the prosecution's case. Typically, the defense tries to stress that prosecution witnesses were biased or had motives to lie (for instance, a prosecution witness had charges dismissed in return for testifying against the defendant), gave inconsistent testimony, did not have a sufficient opportunity to perceive events, or offered implausible testimony; and
- if the defendant presented evidence, support for the strength of that evidence. For example, the defense may stress that defense witnesses were unbiased, and that they testified in a consistent manner.

During closing argument, can the prosecutor play to jurors' emotions, as in movies and TV?

Dramas often misleadingly portray what prosecutors can say during closing argument. Prosecutors are supposed to appeal to jurors' reason, not their emotion and prejudice. Prosecution arguments that emphasize name-calling and community biases rather than evidence are improper. The defense should ask the judge to instruct jurors to ignore such comments. If the prosecutor's comments are very prejudicial, the defense can ask the judge to declare a mistrial.

> **EXAMPLE:** Abner Savage is charged with sexually molesting a young girl. During closing argument, the prosecutor calls Savage "a piece of vermin, a filthy beast who must be locked up like the wild animal that he is." The prosecutor also tells the jurors to "send a message to all other would-be child molesters in our community that this kind of behavior won't be tolerated." The first part of the argument improperly appeals to the jurors' passions and emotions instead of to their reason. The second part is improper because the message that a verdict sends is irrelevant. Jurors are supposed to base verdicts on the evidence at trial, not on community members' possible reactions to the verdicts.

Who argues first?

Most judges allow the prosecution to argue first, again on the theory that the prosecution carries the burden of proof. In fact, many judges also allow the prosecution a rebuttal argument following the defendant's argument. Judges who allow a prosecutor only one argument often allow the prosecutor to choose whether to argue first or second.

Dramas Often Overemphasize Closing Argument

Movies and TV dramas often portray closing argument as the most critical phase of trial. Through words as stirring as Marc Antony's over the fallen Caesar, movie attorneys always seem to sway jurors with last-minute dramatic appeals. (An excellent example is defense attorney Jake Brigance's final argument in *A Time to Kill*.) However, judges and jurors rarely decide a case according to which attorney has the better oratorical skills. Studies indicate that most of the time, judges and jurors have made up their minds before closing argument.

Instructing the Jury

Witnesses provide the evidence, and the judge provides the law the jury must apply to that evidence, in the form of jury instructions.

How do jurors find out about the rules they are to apply?

Judges instruct jurors as to the legal principles that apply to a defendant's case. Typically, the judge's instructions are the last words the jurors hear before they begin deliberating. However, some judges prefer to instruct jurors before closing arguments.

Where do jury instructions come from?

Prosecutors and defense attorneys submit proposed instructions to judges, who decide which instructions to give. In many cases, the instructions are routine and drawn from books of approved jury instructions. For example, *Federal Jury Practice and Instructions*, by Kevin F. O'Malley, et al., is widely used in federal court trials. The instructions themselves often are the products of committees formed for the purpose of updating a jurisdiction's jury instructions. Other times, instructions originate in appellate court opinions. In their written opinions, appellate court justices often define crimes or other legal principles (such as the meaning of reasonable doubt). These definitions find their way into jury instruction books, and trial judges in turn read the pertinent principles to juries.

Prosecutors and defense attorneys are not limited to proposing the instructions found in jury instruction books. They may formulate their own instructions because of shortcomings in the preapproved instructions. For example, an attorney may have to develop a new instruction when a case raises a legal issue for which no preapproved instruction exists. Or, an attorney may propose an alternative to a preapproved instruction. For example, in a particular appellate court jurisdiction, Cases A, B, and C (decided by different justices at different times) may each provide a somewhat different definition of reasonable doubt. A book of preapproved instructions may include only the definition in Case A. However, if a defense attorney considers the definitions in Case B or C to be more favorable to the defendant, the defense attorney may ask the judge to replace the book's preapproved definition with the more favorable one.

> **EXAMPLE:** Bea Leaver is on jury trial for violating a newly enacted consumer protection law. Bea is the first person to be prosecuted under the new law. It is unclear from the text of the law itself whether the prosecution has to prove that Bea intended to violate the law, and the local book of preapproved instructions does not cover the law. With no preapproved instructions available, the defense and prosecution attorneys will probably submit their own proposed instructions for the judge to give. In this case, the defense might propose an instruction telling the jurors that the prosecutor has to prove intent, while the prosecution may propose an instruction stating that intent isn't necessary. The judge will instruct the jury with the instruction that he or she believes is a correct interpretation of the new law.

Does it really matter whether the defense can convince a judge to give its desired instruction?

It can be hard for jurors to pay attention while a judge recites a lengthy list of complex jury instructions. However, appellate court justices often take the instructions quite seriously if and when they are asked to review a conviction. Defense attorneys trying to convince appellate courts to overturn guilty verdicts often have their greatest success when they can point to errors in jury instructions, including the wrongful refusal of the judge to give a jury instruction that the defense had proposed.

> **EXAMPLE:** Same case. Believing that the new consumer protection law does not require proof of Bea's intent to violate the law, the judge refuses to give the defense's proposed instruction to the jury. Bea is convicted and appeals. The appellate court disagrees with the trial judge, and concludes that the law does require proof of intent. The appellate court is likely to fasten on the trial judge's failure to give the correct instruction as a reason to reverse the conviction. It doesn't matter that the jury might have convicted Bea even if the trial judge had given the correct instruction.

What do jury instructions typically cover?

Jury instructions encompass a variety of legal principles. The principles that judges typically review when instructing a jury include:

- the elements of the crime(s) with which the defendant is charged (for instance, the elements of burglary)
- the definition of reasonable doubt, the requirement of a unanimous verdict (in most jurisdictions), and other legal principles that apply to all criminal cases

- factors the jurors may consider when evaluating the credibility of witnesses, and
- housekeeping rules, such as how to select a foreperson and how the jurors should conduct their deliberations.

Even in a short trial, the judge may take up to an hour to read all the necessary instructions to the jurors.

When instructing the jury, is it common for a judge to tell the jury what verdict the judge favors?

No. That is a frequent feature of English trials, but American judges rarely if ever express personal views as to what result they think juries ought to reach.

Can jurors look at the instructions while they deliberate?

Traditionally, judges read instructions aloud to jurors. If a juror wanted an instruction repeated, the jurors had to file back into the courtroom and ask the judge to reread it. Many judges now try to simplify the jury's task by handing out written copies of the instructions or allowing jurors to look at the instructions on computer monitors.

What can the defense do to help jurors understand the instructions critical to the defense?

Studies have repeatedly shown that jurors have great difficulty understanding the meaning of jury instructions. Some states

have tried to rewrite their instructions in plain English, but abstract legal terms like reasonable doubt cannot be precisely defined. When a defense rests on the jury's understanding of a legal principle, the defense can:

- stress the meaning of the principle in everyday language during closing argument, and
- draft a version of the principle that the defense thinks the jury can understand, submit the draft to the judge, and ask the judge to include it with the other jury instructions. Obviously, the draft must be legally accurate as well as understandable.

Jury Deliberations and Verdict

Ideally, jury deliberations are an iconic symbol of a democratic process in action. This section explains how the jury is supposed to deliberate and reach a verdict.

Can jurors discuss the case before the judge sends them off to deliberate?

No. Judges do not want jurors jumping to conclusions based on partial information. Thus, whenever a break occurs in a trial (for a recess, lunch, or the end of the day), judges admonish jurors "not to discuss the case among yourselves or with anyone else." Jurors who fail to obey the admonition may be removed from the jury, and may even cause a mistrial.

EXAMPLE: Sneezy and Doc are jurors in a felony trial. On the second day of trial, they decide to eat lunch together. During the lunch, Sneezy remarks, "I didn't think much of the witness who said she saw the defendant from across the street. She seemed pretty unsure of her testimony." Doc responds, "Well, remember, this was the only time she's ever been in a courtroom. Maybe she was just nervous." They discuss the witness's testimony for a minute or so, but come to no conclusions. Another juror sitting at a nearby table overhears the conversation. After lunch, the third juror reports Sneezy and Doc's conversation to the judge. The judge should talk to Sneezy and Doc in chambers to find out firsthand what they said about the case. The judge should then privately meet with the prosecution and defense to discuss what happened. Depending on the seriousness of the violation and the thoughts of the parties, the judge may (1) allow Sneezy and Doc to remain as jurors after giving them and the other jurors a sterner admonition against talking about the case; (2) remove Sneezy and Doc from the jury and replace them with alternates or (if the attorneys agree) continue with a smaller jury; or (3) declare a mistrial.

Besides premature case discussion, what other activities constitute juror misconduct during trial?

Jurors have committed a variety of no-nos over the years. These include:

- falling asleep during testimony

- coming into court under the influence of drugs or alcohol—particularly after a lunch recess (in one notorious case, jurors were engaging in drug transactions during testimony!)
- lying about their backgrounds during *voir dire* in order to get a spot on the jury
- conducting independent investigations, such as personally visiting the scene of the crime or looking up case-related information on the Internet
- discussing the case with the prosecutor or defense attorney, and
- listening to a friend carry on about the need to convict the defendant to protect society.

Judges and attorneys sometimes find out about such misdeeds either by observing them personally in the courtroom or from reports by other jurors or third parties. Again, depending on the severity of the misconduct, the judge may admonish a wayward juror to shape up, replace the juror with an alternate, continue with a smaller jury, or declare a mistrial.

Do jurors stay together until they reach a verdict?

No. In extraordinary cases with great publicity, jurors may be sequestered (required to remain together night and day). Otherwise, jurors generally deliberate during a normal workday and go home in the evening. However, jurors normally do eat lunch together while they deliberate.

Sequestering Jurors

Judges may take the extraordinary step of sequestering jurors when trials are subjected to intense TV and newspaper coverage. A famous example of this occurred in the 1995 internationally covered O.J. Simpson murder trial. Sequestered jurors can remain together throughout an entire trial or, more commonly, only during the time they are deliberating on a verdict. Sequestered jurors eat meals together and stay in the same hotel, and bailiffs closely monitor what they read and watch on TV.

The purpose of sequestration is to protect jurors from the opinions of reporters and to prevent jurors from hearing about information that is never entered into evidence. However, sequestration can seriously interfere with other aspects of a trial. For example, it's hard to imagine that jurors who are together constantly for weeks—or even nine months, as in the O.J. Simpson case—follow the admonition not to discuss the case before official deliberations begin. In addition, sequestration affects jury composition, because only people who can be separated from their daily lives for a long period of time can serve as jurors.

How long do jurors have to reach a verdict?

Jury deliberations are like baseball games—they aren't subject to fixed time limits. A judge will order jurors to continue deliberating as long as they are making progress toward a verdict. During this time, jurors may submit written questions to the judge or ask to have portions of a transcript read to them. Meanwhile, the judge will continue to hear other cases. When all of the jurors have agreed on a verdict (in those jurisdictions requiring unanimous verdicts), the foreperson tells the bailiff, the lawyers and defendant return to the courtroom, and the verdict is announced.

What happens if the jurors cannot agree on a verdict?

When a foreperson reports that jurors are unable to agree on a verdict (that is, unanimous for guilty or not guilty), a judge is likely to encourage jurors to keep trying. Judges try to achieve verdicts whenever possible, to avoid the time and expense of a retrial. But if encouragement fails and a jury is hopelessly deadlocked (called a hung jury), the judge has to dismiss the jurors and declare a mistrial. The prosecution can drop the case or retry the defendant before another jury. Most of the time, however, cases are settled through plea bargains after mistrials caused by deadlocked juries.

> **EXAMPLE:** Rosetta Stone is on trial for drunk driving. After the jury begins to deliberate, the foreperson announces that one of the 12 jurors has been taken ill and cannot continue. The judge orders the remaining 11 jurors to continue deliberating. The judge's order is improper. Stone is entitled to a 12-person jury, and a judge

cannot force her to accept an 11-person jury. Thus, Stone's lawyer could force the judge to declare a mistrial. In the alternative, Stone could agree to waive the 12-person requirement and continue with the remaining jurors. Stone might choose this option if she thinks her chances of winning are good.

EXAMPLE: Assume that Rosetta Stone's drunk driving case is being tried to Judge Schnell sitting without a jury. As soon as the attorneys finish their arguments, Judge Schnell pronounces Stone guilty. Judges sometimes take cases under submission, which means they'll delay making a decision. But as Judge Schnell did, judges often render immediate decisions.

Good Citizenship Rules for Jurors

The jury trial system relies on citizens' willingness to serve as jurors and apply legal rules in a rational and responsible manner. Citizens who are called for jury duty should be aware that:

- Ignoring a summons for jury duty is a crime in many jurisdictions. Willful failure to respond to a jury summons may result in a fine or even jail time. Even people who know they are exempt from jury service (say because of a medical infirmity) should respond to a summons.
- They may be allowed to bring magazines and books to court, but newspapers may be off limits. Cellphones may be banned or their use restricted. Jurors may be allowed to bring a laptop computer, and the courthouse may even offer free Wi-Fi. But jurors and their computers will probably have to pass through a security system similar to those in airports, so jurors should leave pocket knives, nail files, and scissors at home. And sorry, knitters—knitting needles may have to be left behind.
- The information in Chapter 9 on courtroom behavior, including how to

dress for court, applies to jurors. Casual dress is acceptable, but apparel should show respect for courts. For example, no shorts, tank tops, or T-shirts with words or logos that may be offensive or inappropriate.
- Most states still pay jurors for service— but not much (usually a few dollars per day).

A prosecutor does not secure justice when a defendant is wrongfully convicted by a jury that overlooks reasonable doubt, nor is justice promoted by jurors who acquit a guilty person because they don't like the victim. Citizens who serve on juries should keep these principles in mind:

- Potential jurors should honestly answer attorneys' *voir dire* questions. Both sides are entitled to an impartial jury, and justice is not served by jurors who try to hide their backgrounds and predispositions.
- Jurors act as minidemocracies when they deliberate. The foreperson should give all jurors a chance to speak, and jurors should consider each others' views before making up their minds.

Sample Subpoena/Subpoena Duces Tecum (Criminal and Juvenile)

CR-125/JV-525

ATTORNEY OR PARTY WITHOUT ATTORNEY *(Name, State Bar number, and address):*	FOR COURT USE ONLY

TELEPHONE NO.:   FAX NO. *(Optional):*

E-MAIL ADDRESS *(Optional):*

ATTORNEY FOR *(Name):*

SUPERIOR COURT OF CALIFORNIA, COUNTY OF

STREET ADDRESS:

MAILING ADDRESS:

CITY AND ZIP CODE:

BRANCH NAME:

CASE NAME:

ORDER TO ATTEND COURT OR PROVIDE DOCUMENTS: Subpoena/Subpoena Duces Tecum	CASE NUMBER:

You must attend court or provide to the court the documents listed below. Follow the orders checked in item 2 below. If you do not, the judge can fine you, send you to jail, or issue a warrant for your arrest.

1. To: *(name or business)* _____

2. You must follow the court order(s) checked below:

    a. ☐ Attend the hearing.

    b. ☐ Attend the hearing *and* bring all items checked in c. below.

    c. ☐ Provide a copy of these items to the court (Do not use this form to obtain Juvenile Court records):

        (1)_____

        (2)_____

        (3)_____

        ☐ *If this box is checked, provide all items listed on the attached sheet labeled "Provide These Items."*

    d. ☐ If someone else is responsible for maintaining the items checked in c. above, that person (the Custodian of Records) must also attend the hearing.

    e. ☐ If this box is checked and you deliver all items listed above to the court **within 5 days of service of this order,** you do not have to attend court if you follow the instructions in item 5.

3.   **Court Hearing Date:**   The court hearing will be at *(name and address of court):*

Date: _____   Time: _____   _____

Dept.: _____   Rm.: _____   _____

Call the person listed in item 4 below to make sure the hearing date has not changed. If you cannot go to court on this date, you must get permission from the person in item 4. You may be entitled to witness fees, mileage, or both, in the discretion of the court. Ask the person in item 4 after your appearance.

4. The person who has required you to attend court or provide documents is:

Name: _____   Phone No.: _____

Address: _____

    Number, Street, Apt. No.

_____

    City   State   Zip

FOR COURT USE ONLY

Date: _____   Signature ▶ _____

                               Name and Title

Form Adopted for Mandatory Use
Judicial Council of California
CR-125/JV-525 [Rev. July 1, 2007]

ORDER TO ATTEND COURT OR PROVIDE DOCUMENTS:
Subpoena/Subpoena Duces Tecum
(Criminal and Juvenile)

Page 1 of 2

Sample Subpoena/Subpoena Duces Tecum (Criminal and Juvenile) (continued)

CR-125/JV-525

CASE NAME:	CASE NUMBER:

5 a. Put all items checked in item 2c and your completed *Declaration of Custodian of Records* form in an envelope. (You can ask the person in item 4 where to get this form.) Attach a copy of page 1 of this order to the envelope.

   b. Put the envelope inside another envelope. Then, attach a copy of page 1 of this form to the outer envelope or write this information on the outer envelope:

      (1) Case name

      (2) Case number

      (3) Your name

      (4) Hearing date, time, and department

   c. Seal and mail the envelope to the Court Clerk at the address listed in ☐ item 3 or ☐ The court address in the caption on page 1 . You must mail these documents to the court within five days of service of this order.

   d. If you are the Custodian of Records, you must also mail the person in item 4 a copy of your completed *Declaration of Custodian of Records*. Do *not* include a copy of the documents.

—— *The server fills out the section below.* ——

Proof of Service of CR-125/JV-525

1. I personally served a copy of this subpoena on:

   Date: _____ Time: _____ ☐ a.m. ☐ p.m.

   Name of the person served: _____

   At this address: _____

   After I served this person, I mailed or delivered a copy of this Proof of Service to the person in item 4 on *(date):* _____

   Mailed from *(city):* _____

2. I received this order for service on *(date):* _____ and was not able to serve *(name of person)*

   _____ after *(number of attempts)* _____ attempts because:

   a. ☐ The person is not known at this address.

   b. ☐ The person moved and the forwarding address is not known.

   c. ☐ There is no such address.

   d. ☐ The address is in a different county.

   e. ☐ I was not able to serve by the hearing date.

   f. ☐ Other *(explain):* _____

3. Server's name: _____ Phone no. _____

4. The server *(check one)*

   a. ☐ is a registered process server.   d. ☐ works for a registered process server.

   b. ☐ is not a registered process server.   e. ☐ is exempt from registration under Business and Professional Code

   c. ☐ is a sheriff, marshal, or constable.   section 22350(b).

5. Server's address: _____

   If server is a registered process server:

   County of registration: _____ Registration no.: _____

I declare under penalty of perjury under the laws of the State of California that I am at least 18 years old and not involved in this case and the information above is true and correct.

Date: _____

▶ _____   ▶ _____

    TYPE OR PRINT NAME OF SERVER   *SIGNATURE OF SERVER*

CR-125/JV-525 [Rev. July 1, 2007]   **ORDER TO ATTEND COURT OR PROVIDE DOCUMENTS:**   Page 2 of 2
                    Subpoena/Subpoena Duces Tecum
                    (Criminal and Juvenile)

Can a judge set aside a jury's guilty verdict?

Yes. While this move is unusual, a judge has the power to set aside a jury's guilty verdict and find a defendant not guilty based on the weakness of the prosecution's evidence. If the judge takes this action, the prosecution can appeal it. A judge may also set aside a guilty verdict (and order a new trial) when jurors have been influenced by outside information or jurors' racist remarks.

> EXAMPLE: After a jury finds a defendant guilty, two jurors prepare affidavits stating that while a deputy was escorting the jurors to the jury deliberation room, the deputy mentioned the defendant's previous convictions. The judge had ruled that these convictions were not admissible as evidence. The judge may decide to set aside the guilty verdict and order a new trial.

> EXAMPLE: After a jury finds a defendant guilty of sexual assault, two jurors prepare affidavits stating that during the deliberations one of the jurors had made racist remarks, claiming that people who are part of the same ethnic minority as the defendant are probably illegal immigrants who have no respect for women. The racist remarks taint the jury process so badly that the judge has the power to set aside the verdict and order a new trial. (*Peña-Rodriguez v. Colorado*, U.S. Sup. Ct. 2017.)

Sentencing

entences are the punishments that result from guilty or no-contest pleas, or from guilty verdicts following trials. A judge's sentencing options used to be quite limited: A defendant could be incarcerated (put in jail or prison), ordered to pay a fine, or both. But in recent years, courts and legislatures faced with overcrowded jails and prisons have gotten as creative with sentences as stockbrokers have with investments. This chapter examines sentencing policies and procedures, and concludes with a discussion of the death penalty.

Overview of Sentencing

As the old saying goes, "If you do the crime, expect to do the time." Here's an overview of sentencing rules and processes.

Do judges or juries make sentencing decisions?

Judges almost always determine punishment, even following jury trials. In fact, a common jury instruction warns jurors not to consider the question of punishment when deciding a defendant's guilt or innocence.

Juries can play a role in sentencing decisions. When statutes identify circumstances that permit judges to hand down harsher sentences, such a sentence is possible only if the jury (in a jury trial) finds that the circumstance is true beyond a reasonable doubt. (*Apprendi v. New Jersey*, U.S. Sup. Ct. 2001.) For example,

if a statute authorizes harsher punishment of an offender who used a weapon when committing a crime, a judge can mete out the harsher punishment only if the jury finds specifically and beyond a reasonable doubt that the offender used a weapon.

EXAMPLE: Cunningham is convicted of child molestation following a jury trial. After dismissing the jury and conducting a posttrial sentencing hearing, the judge decides to increase Cunningham's sentence because the victim was particularly vulnerable and Cunningham carried out the crime in a violent manner. The sentence is improper. The judge could have increased Cunningham's sentence only if the jury had decided that the victim was particularly vulnerable and Cunningham carried out the molestation in a violent manner. (*Cunningham v. California,* U.S. Sup. Ct. 2007.)

Bad Prison Conditions Rarely Qualify as Cruel and Unusual

It is very tough for prisoners to challenge substandard prison conditions as "cruel and unusual." (*Farmer v. Brennan,* U.S. Sup. Ct. 1994). To prevail in a lawsuit based on a "cruel and unusual" claim, a prisoner must prove that: (1) prison officials actually knew about the conditions being challenged, and (2) despite the substantial risk to inmates caused by the conditions, the officials did nothing about them. You'll find more on prisoners' rights in Chapter 27.

How can people find the punishments for crimes?

Criminal laws identify crimes and their penalties. For example, a statute that defines shoplifting as a misdemeanor might go on to state, "A first offense is punishable by a fine of up to $1,000 or imprisonment for not more than six months, or both." Alternatively, a statute may identify a crime as a "Class A felony," with a separate statute identifying the punishment for Class A felonies.

Restorative Justice

Restorative justice is an alternative model of punishment in which victims of crime meet with perpetrators in the presence of other community representatives to work out mutually satisfactory responses to criminal acts. For example, an "RJ" response to a theft may include a payment of money from the thief to the victim and others harmed by the theft, along with an apology and other forms of amends. Proponents of RJ argue that it strengthens communities while diminishing recidivism. The RJ approach generally is limited to the mediation of minor and nonviolent offenses and requires that victims agree to participate.

Are there limits on the severity of punishment for the commission of a crime?

Yes. The Eighth Amendment to the U.S. Constitution provides that punishment may not be cruel and unusual. For example, a law saying that all convicted robbers must have their left hands cut off would no doubt violate the Eighth Amendment.

The Eighth Amendment also forbids sentences of life without possibility of parole for juvenile offenders who commit nonhomicide crimes before they are 18 years old. (*Graham v. Florida*, U.S. Sup. Ct. 2010.) In *Montgomery v. Louisiana* (U.S. Sup. Ct. 2016), the Court made *Graham* retroactive, meaning that prisoners whose cases were final could petition to have the "no possibility of parole" portion of their sentences removed.

Can a judge disregard a plea deal and give a different sentence?

Prosecutors and defense lawyers usually know judges' sentencing policies, and judges often "rubber-stamp" plea bargains that adhere to these policies. But to protect their right to go to trial when a judge disregards a plea bargain and gives a harsher-than-expected sentence, defendants should make it clear that the guilty plea is contingent on the judge going along with the agreed-upon sentence. (For more information about plea bargaining, see Chapter 20.)

> **EXAMPLE:** Mickey Finn is charged with drunk driving. Mickey agrees to plead guilty after the prosecutor promises to recommend that the judge not impose any jail time. The prosecutor also says, "I can't promise that Judge Seagram will follow my recommendation; the judge almost always gives first-timers like you 48 hours in jail."

After Mickey pleads guilty, Judge Seagram in fact sentences Mickey to 48 hours in jail. Mickey cannot withdraw the guilty plea. The deal was not contingent on the judge following the prosecutor's sentence recommendation.

EXAMPLE: Same case. Again, the prosecutor says, "I can't make any promises that Judge Seagram will go along with the deal." Mickey's attorney then says, "We'll plead guilty only if the judge agrees to no jail time. Let's get an indicated sentence from Judge Seagram." Judge Seagram informs the prosecutor and defense attorney that if Mickey pleads guilty, the sentence will be two days in jail. Because Mickey never entered a guilty plea, Mickey's attorney had the right to cancel the deal when the judge refused to go along with it. Of course, Mickey could end up with an even longer jail sentence if he takes the case to trial and is convicted.

Do mandatory sentencing laws mean that everyone convicted of the same crime receives the same punishment?

Some statutes specify a minimum sentence, often known as a "mandatory minimum." Mandatory sentencing laws usually reflect what the legislature sees as public sentiment that judges have been too lenient.

But criminal statutes usually carry a range of possible imprisonment and fines within which the judge can set the punishment. Judges can take a number of factors into account when deciding on an appropriate sentence. For instance, judges may usually consider:

- the defendant's past criminal record, age, and sophistication
- the circumstances under which the crime was committed, and
- whether the defendant expresses genuine remorse.

Understanding Statutory Sentencing Provisions

Criminal statutes must be carefully studied to understand whether or not they specify mandatory sentences. For example, a statute may say that an offense is punishable "by not more than six months in the county jail." This language is not mandatory. A judge could sentence an offender to three months, three weeks, three days, or no time at all. On the other hand, a statute might say that an offense is punishable "by no less than 15 years in the state penitentiary." A judge would then have to sentence an offender to at least 15 years. Many criminal laws provide for a range of punishment, such as "not less than one year nor more than three years," and leave it to the judge to decide the precise sentence.

In addition to a fine and/or incarceration, are there other consequences of a conviction?

A judge may make a "restitution order." Unlike fines (which offenders pay to the government), restitution orders require offenders to compensate victims for economic losses. For example, an offender convicted of robbery may be ordered to compensate the victim up to the value of the stolen property, as well as for wages the victim lost while recuperating from injuries incurred during the robbery. Like civil court judgments, restitution orders may be enforced in a variety of ways—for example, by garnishing an offender's wages.

Laws may also authorize judges to order an offender to forfeit personal property used to commit a crime. For example, a judge may order the forfeiture of the car that an offender used to transport illegal drugs.

In many states, a convicted felon may not vote or hold public office. Additionally, a conviction may trigger separate administrative proceedings that result in the loss of professional or business licenses. Convictions can have other "downstream" consequences, too—for example, having to register as a sex offender.

Perhaps one of the most serious consequences of having a criminal record is that a defendant will likely be punished much more severely if convicted of a future crime. Both prosecutors (in plea negotiations) and judges (handing down sentences following guilty verdicts) usually consider a defendant's rap sheet to be a key factor influencing the severity of a sentence. Judges almost always give repeat offenders stiffer sentences than they do to first-timers.

Even Acquittals May Have Later Effects

Judges can generally take into account defendants' prior crimes during sentencing, even if the defendants have been found not guilty of the prior crimes. The acquittal only means the defendant was not guilty beyond a reasonable doubt; the judge may still believe that a preponderance of the evidence shows the defendant committed the crime. (*U.S. v. Watts*, U.S. Sup. Ct. 1997.)

What are "ban-the-box" laws?

Employers are often reluctant to hire applicants with criminal pasts. Some states and cities have responded by passing "ban-the-box" laws, which prohibit employers from asking about criminal history during the early stages of the application process. Employers are generally not allowed to ask about criminal history on a job application; in some states, they can't inquire about the topic until the applicant is brought in for an interview or given a conditional offer of employment. The idea is that an employer who has already decided that an individual is qualified for a position will be less likely to deny employment solely based on the applicant's criminal past.

Can a conviction result in a noncitizen's deportation?

Yes. A noncitizen of the United States, whether an undocumented immigrant or a lawful permanent resident (a green card holder) needs to understand the immigration consequences of a conviction. Conviction can, in many cases, lead to deportation (removal) from the United States.

It's difficult to generalize about which crimes make a noncitizen deportable under federal immigration law. The analysis depends in many cases on whether the crime is viewed as one involving "moral turpitude" (a "CMT"). A conviction of one CMT within five years of admission to the country is a ground for deportation, as is conviction of two CMTs committed any time after entry.

Deportation and the 364-Day Year

Some states have made the maximum imprisonment for many or all misdemeanors 364 days rather than 365. That change is designed to avoid deportation consequences that would have been triggered if the misdemeanor in question carried the possibility of, or if the misdemeanor defendant actually received, a full one-year sentence.

The analysis also depends on whether the type of crime is specifically listed among the grounds for deportability, as are various drug crimes, domestic violence, child abuse, weapons trafficking, and others.

Yet another common way for noncitizens to become deportable is through conviction of an aggravated felony. This includes serious crimes like murder and rape. It can also include less dramatic-sounding crimes, however, such as theft with a sentence of at least one year. In some cases, crimes that are prosecuted as misdemeanors can constitute aggravated felonies under U.S. immigration law.

> **EXAMPLE:** Eight years after her lawful admission to the country, Mia Palabra is convicted of possession of more than 30 grams of marijuana for personal use, a misdemeanor. Mia is subject to deportation even though the crime is a misdemeanor, because it qualifies as a drug offense.

Many noncitizens serve their sentences and are then deported (removed). The noncitizen might not find out about the intended deportation until the last minute, when the immigration authorities file a "hold" or "detainer," then transfer him or her to a Department of Homeland Security detention facility for further proceedings.

How do three strikes laws work?

Three strikes laws generally allow judges to impose lengthy sentences on offenders who have at least two prior convictions for "serious" or "violent" crimes. In the many states that have three strikes laws, a conviction for a third offense would allow (and sometimes require) a judge to impose a lengthy sentence.

Sealing or Expunging Arrest and Conviction Records

When records of an arrest or conviction are sealed or expunged, defendants can, for some purposes, treat the arrests or convictions as though they had never happened. (Many states have enacted "second chance" laws, which generally make sealing or expunging criminal records easier.) For example, assume that a defendant's conviction for misdemeanor possession of an illegal drug is expunged. On applications for school, a job, or a professional license, the defendant may be able to answer that the defendant has no arrests or convictions (assuming no others exist). However, the rules about who is eligible for sealing or expungement and the effect of sealing or expungement vary from state to state, so interested people should consider seeking the advice of an experienced attorney. These general guidelines apply to many programs:

- People have to apply (in writing) for expungement. Arrest and conviction records are normally not automatically expunged or sealed just because a certain number of years have passed.
- Even though a conviction has been expunged, it can still be used to increase the severity of a sentence should a defendant again be convicted. For example, an expunged conviction may be considered a strike under a three strikes sentencing law.
- Convictions usually cannot be expunged until at least a year after they occur, and then only if the defendant is done serving the sentence and is facing no new charges.
- Not all convictions are eligible for expungement. For example, in some states defendants cannot expunge felony convictions or convictions involving sex offenses. (But it may be possible to have a felony conviction reduced to a misdemeanor, then expunged.) Juvenile and misdemeanor convictions are most often subject to expungement.
- A defendant acquitted of a criminal charge may be able to have the records of the arrest and charge sealed immediately. A defendant whose charges are dismissed, who is never charged, or who wins on appeal may be entitled to similar relief.

The most controversial aspect of three strikes laws is their use to punish offenders whose third conviction is for a nonviolent crime. In one case, an offender with two strikes already on his record was convicted of stealing about $150 worth of videotapes. Ordinarily, punishment for such a crime might be a few months in jail at most. However, under a three strikes law, the offender was deemed a "career criminal" and sentenced to 25 years to life. The U.S. Supreme Court upheld the validity of the sentence. (*Lockyer v. Andrade,* U.S. Sup. Ct. 2003.) At the same time, courts can invalidate three strikes sentences if they are unduly harsh. For example, a court determined that a life sentence constituted cruel and unusual punishment in violation of the Eighth Amendment when a defendant's third strike was a conviction for a short delay in reregistering as a sex offender. (*Gonzalez v. Duncan*, 9th Cir. Ct. of Appeals 2008.)

Some states have looked at reforming their three strikes laws. One type of reform requires that a conviction count as a third strike only if it is for a serious or violent felony. Some three strikes laws allow for resentencing of offenders whose convictions would not qualify as a third strike under a revamped three strikes law.

Can defendants avoid three strikes laws by having prior convictions stricken from their records?

Perhaps. Given the crucial impact of prior convictions on sentences, it's not surprising that pruning clients' past convictions is often the most important impact a defense attorney can have on the severity of a sentence—whether or not a three strikes law is at play. For example, attorneys might attempt to:

- seal or expunge juvenile convictions
- void prior convictions, perhaps because a guilty plea was taken improperly, or
- demonstrate that a conviction that appears as a felony on a client's record was only a misdemeanor.

What factors tend to result in lighter sentences?

The defense may bring to a judge's attention an infinite number of factual circumstances that may bring about a lighter sentence. The following are a few examples of such factors (called "mitigating" factors):

- The offender has little or no history of criminal conduct.
- The offender was an accessory (helped the main offender) to the crime, but was not the main actor.
- The offender committed the crime when under great personal stress; for example, the offender had lost a job, his rent was due, and he had just been in a car wreck.
- No one was hurt, and the crime was committed in a manner that was unlikely to have hurt anyone.

 RESOURCES
For more information on record sealing or expungement, go to the nonprofit Collateral Consequences Resource Center at http://ccresourcecenter.org and visit www.criminaldefenselawyer.com, a Nolo website.

What factors tend to result in harsher sentences?

Just as mitigating circumstances can sway a judge to lessen a sentence, "aggravating" circumstances can persuade a judge to throw the book at an offender. A previous record of the same type of offense is the most common aggravating factor. In other cases, aggravating circumstances grow out of the way a crime was committed, as when an offender is particularly cruel to a victim. However, except for prior convictions, judges in jury trials may not base harsher sentences on aggravating factors unless the jury has decided that those factors are accurate. (*Cunningham v. California*, U.S. Sup. Ct. 2007.) Sometimes laws themselves specify aggravating factors. Here are some examples:

- Use of a dangerous weapon when assaulting, intimidating, or interfering with a federal employee carrying out official duties increases the punishment from eight years to 20 years. (18 U.S.C. § 111.)
- Committing mail fraud against a financial institution (as opposed to an individual or some other type of institution) can add ten years to the punishment and/or trigger a fine of up to $1,000,000. (18 U.S.C. § 1341.)

EXAMPLE: Tommy Rotten robbed several teachers from the Kind 'R Garden Nursery School by pointing a loaded gun at the children and demanding that the teachers hand over their purses. Bob Bracci, brandishing a silver nail file, robbed a convenience store clerk at 4 a.m.; no customers were present. Rotten and Bracci probably will not receive the same sentences even if they are in the same jurisdiction, took the same amount of money, and were convicted of the same crime, robbery. The judge would likely take aggravating and mitigating factors into account, and these differ greatly in the two cases. Rotten used a clearly dangerous weapon (a loaded gun), and by doing so put many people, including children, at risk. Bracci used a makeshift weapon that is not inherently dangerous. He robbed the store in the middle of the night when few customers, and certainly no children, would likely be present. Because of these factors, Rotten would almost certainly get a much harsher sentence than Bracci.

How do judges find out about factors that can affect the severity of sentences?

Especially when jail time is a possibility, judges often ask a probation officer to prepare a presentence report. Both the prosecution and defense may also present witnesses in open court, the defendant may personally address the judge, and, increasingly, crime victims may also make statements.

Can judges modify sentences?

Yes, under certain circumstances. Like rules in many states, Rule 35 of the Federal Rules of Criminal Procedure authorizes judges to reduce the sentence of a defendant who provides information that leads to the investigation or prosecution of another person. Also, a general principle is that "the power to grant probation includes the power to modify it." In many states, judges can reward an offender's good conduct by terminating probation early, shortening the duration of probation, and even shortening a term of incarceration that was imposed as a condition of probation.

RESOURCES

Families Against Mandatory Minimums (FAMM) is a national group that advocates on behalf of prisoners in the sentencing process. For information, consult FAMM's website at www.famm.org.

Sentencing Procedures

Just as there's "often a slip twixt cup and lip," there's often a gap twixt a guilty verdict and pronouncement of sentence. This section explains how and when sentences are imposed.

Do judges hand down sentences immediately after defendants are convicted?

In minor misdemeanor cases, judges frequently hand down sentences immediately after defendants plead guilty or no contest, or are found guilty after trial. Where the possibility of significant incarceration exists, however, a judge might not impose a sentence until some days or weeks later, in a separately scheduled sentencing hearing. The sentencing hearing often follows an investigation by a probation officer, who prepares a presentence report for the judge to review.

Can judges delay the imposition of a jail sentence?

Defendants who are out on bail when they are sentenced to jail are sometimes hauled off immediately. Other times, the judge may agree to "stay" (delay) the start of the sentence for at least a few days, to allow a defendant time to handle important personal matters. Defense attorneys are usually well acquainted with the stay policies of local judges.

What is likely to happen during a sentencing hearing?

The sentencing portion of a criminal case often takes only moments, especially if the judge is rubber-stamping the sentence agreed to in plea negotiations. For example, the judge may sentence a defendant to "a fine of $250, ten days in jail suspended, and one year probation" while the echoes of the defendant's guilty plea still reverberate in the courtroom. Even felony cases can wrap up quickly when sentences are negotiated as part of a plea bargain. For example, in a felony drug possession case involving a three strikes law, a defendant who pleaded guilty was sentenced to seven years in prison after a hearing that lasted six minutes.

However, sentencing is not always so brief an affair, especially when the judge has legal authority to order a long period of imprisonment. Typically, the probation department will have prepared a presentence report, and the defense and prosecution will have a chance to argue against or in favor of the probation officer's recommendations and the factual findings on which those recommendations are based.

The judge also must allow the defendant an opportunity to make a personal statement (called the defendant's "allocution") before pronouncing sentence.

And, the defendant can call witnesses to testify to the defendant's good character and rehabilitative efforts. Victims also may make personal presentencing statements to the judge.

What is a presentence report?

Especially in felony and more serious misdemeanor cases, judges typically rely on presentence reports, prepared by probation officers, when making sentencing decisions. Probation officers usually prepare these reports during a several-week interval between a conviction and the date set for sentencing.

To prepare the report, a probation officer (or a social worker or psychologist working for the probation department) may interview the victim, the arresting officer, and the defendant.

In addition to the information gleaned from these sources, most probation presentence reports also provide:

- the circumstances of the offense
- the defendant's personal history, including the defendant's criminal record, and
- a statement by the victim as to what the victim lost or how the victim suffered, sometimes called a victim impact statement.

Probation reports typically include probation officers' sentencing recommendations. Probation officers can rely on information that would not have been admissible in evidence at trial, such as inadmissible hearsay and illegally obtained evidence, to justify their recommendations. Judges typically don't have time to investigate the circumstances of individual cases, and so usually rely heavily on—and often rubber-stamp—these sentencing recommendations.

A Judge's View of Presentence Reports

The contents of presentence reports and probation officers' sentence recommendations are often crucial, as judges may have little time to exercise independent judgment. As one judge put it:

"Most judges are so burdened with simply getting through the day and 'disposing' of the allotted quota of cases that they are usually too weary to undertake the painful examination of the justice, morality, or common sense of the sentences [that] they impose." (*Criminals and Victims: A Trial Judge Reflects on Crime and Punishment*, by Judge Lois G. Forer.)

How can defendants encourage favorable presentence reports?

Defense lawyers typically try to make sure that probation officers hear about all the good things their clients have done and are doing. For example, if a defendant has enrolled in an addiction treatment or counseling program or has an employer willing to say nice things about him or her, a defense attorney will transmit that information to the probation officer.

Defense lawyers often take a number of steps to try to ensure that a judge is aware of information favorable to the defendant. Defense lawyers can:

- Research possible alternative sentences —such as placing the defendant in a treatment center or under home detention rather than in prison, or requiring extensive community service and restitution—and prepare a concrete plan to implement the proposed sentence.
- Improve the defendant's personal profile by enrolling the defendant in a treatment or rehabilitation program and school, helping the defendant find an appropriate job, or getting the defendant set up to perform volunteer community service.
- Meet with the probation officer before the defendant does to present helpful information.
- Prepare a written statement in mitigation of the crime stating why the defendant should receive a lighter sentence.
- Seek a private presentence report. These are written by private parties— often retired probation officers— engaged in the business of writing presentence reports for a fee.

If a probation officer will interview a defendant, it's obviously important for the defendant to try to make a positive impression.

The defendant should be as prepared as possible before meeting with the probation officer, because the defendant may not be allowed to bring a lawyer into that interview. The defendant must be careful about what he or she says in the interview, because probation officers can use the defendant's statements in their reports.

Probation officers often question defendants very closely. An officer is likely to want to know a defendant's:

- version of the criminal act giving rise to the conviction
- reason or motive for committing the crime
- prior criminal record, including juvenile record
- personal and family history
- education
- employment history
- health
- past and present alcohol and drug use
- financial status, and
- military record (if any).

The defendant should rely on his or her attorney for guidance on the probation officer interview.

How should defendants behave when they meet with probation officers?

What defendants say and how they behave when they meet with a probation officer can be critical. Defendants should meet with their lawyer ahead of time to discuss exactly what they should say to a probation officer. In general, it is important for a defendant to:

- Show up on time and be dressed appropriately. Probation officers have busy schedules and deal with lots of defendants who don't seem to care about what happens. Simply showing up on time and being respectful may go a long way toward positively influencing a probation officer.
- Stress any mitigating factors when relating the facts surrounding the crime in question and when discussing any past criminal involvement.
- Stress any rehabilitative activities that have taken place between the time the crime occurred and sentencing, such as attending a 12-step program, getting a job, enrolling in or going back to school, voluntarily performing community service, or obtaining medical or psychological services. Defendants should substantiate their activities whenever possible by bringing written documents to a probation officer interview.
- Discuss family ties and, if applicable, job stability.

Counsel's Arguments to Reduce Pizza Sentence

Here are some snippets from arguments made by the prosecution and defense attorney during the January 1997 sentencing hearing in which a life sentence for stealing a pizza (under California's three strikes law) was reduced to six years.

The prosecution. The prosecutor told the judge about the defendant's past criminal record and showed the judge the lengthy rap sheet printout, "which extended from [the D.A.'s] outstretched arm to the floor." The assistant D.A. argued, "This case is not about stealing a single slice of pizza. It is about recidivism [the problem of repeat offenders] and how society deals with it." He further argued, "If the foremost purpose of [the justice system] is to protect society, then [the defendant] is a person we need protection

from. He is a repeat offender. He has not learned. He has not repented." And the D.A. went on to say that the defendant did not take the pizza because he was hungry, but, "He took the pizza out of meanness ... it was literally taking candy from babies."

The defense. The defense, on the other hand, argued essentially that the punishment was way too extreme for the crime. The public defender "described [the defendant] as a reformed criminal whose last crime was a dumb but hardly life-threatening offense." The P.D. told the judge, "No one is going to suggest to the court that [the defendant's] judgment was not faulty ... but [the circumstances of the crime] suggest a lesser sentence."

("Judge Slashes Life Sentence in Pizza Theft Case," *L.A. Times*, January 29, 1997 at A1.)

- Show remorse. One thing judges claim to take seriously in sentencing is the risk of recidivism (repeated criminal behavior). Apparently, many judges believe that defendants who try to rationalize (explain away) a crime are more likely to commit repeat crimes than offenders who admit responsibility and show remorse. It could therefore be of great benefit to the defendant if the probation officer's report notes that the defendant exhibits genuine remorse.

Showing Genuine Remorse

Though many of the regular players in the criminal justice system (judges, prosecutors, defense lawyers, probation officers) are hardened to the stories of criminal defendants, they may still be moved and influenced by a defendant who genuinely expresses remorse and feels bad for the victim hurt by the crime. The opposite is also true. Consider these words written by a probation officer in a 1996 murder case: "To have so violently and completely abused another human being is unthinkable by anyone of conscience…. To show or express no sincere remorse, or acknowledge culpability for his actions, as the defendant has done, discloses the full depth of his malevolent character." (Source: *L.A. Times*, December 17, 1996, A28.)

Can defendants review probation reports before sentencing hearings take place?

Defendants and their attorneys usually have access to the presentence report before the sentencing hearing. However, the sentence recommendations and information from confidential sources may be excluded from the copy given to the defense. The defense should review the report thoroughly for factual mistakes. Procedural rules typically give defendants and their attorneys the right to comment on the presentence report at the sentencing hearing and to introduce evidence to rebut any factual mistakes.

Can defendants address judges directly at sentencing hearings?

The people who most commonly speak at a sentencing hearing are the prosecutors, the defense attorney, the victims, and the defendant. Rule 32 (i)(4)(A) of the Federal Rules of Criminal Procedure grants both the defendant and defense counsel the right to speak to the court before a sentence is imposed.

As can be expected, the prosecutor's comments will tend to highlight aggravating factors in the crime and past criminal behavior on the part of the defendant. And defense counsel typically responds with arguments justifying a lighter penalty. Also, if defense counsel has not already pointed out factual mistakes in the presentence report, this would be the last appropriate opportunity to do so.

No one, not even defense counsel, may be able to speak in as persuasive a way as the person facing the sentence. Thus, defendants also have a right to speak on their own behalf before the judge imposes the sentence. This is known as the defendant's right of allocution. Defendants will likely want to work with their lawyers to prepare what, if anything, they will say to the judge.

What Not to Say in Allocution

In 1996, Richard Allen Davis was sentenced to death for the kidnapping, molestation, and murder of a young girl named Polly Klaas. The case had shaken the nation for many reasons, not least because the victim had been taken from her home in a nice neighborhood during a slumber party with girlfriends. Before being sentenced, Davis spoke on his own behalf. Instead of using the allocution to beg for mercy, show remorse, or at least apologize, legal analysts saw his comments as an obvious attempt to lash out and inflict one last painful blow to the victim's family. In front of a packed courtroom, Davis said that just before he killed Polly she said something like, "Just don't do me like my daddy." The suggestion that Polly's father had sexually abused his daughter, wholly unfounded by all accounts, threw flames into the courtroom, prompting angry retorts from the father, tears from other family members, and the wrath, rather than sympathy, of the judge.

What role does the victim play in sentencing?

It used to be that the victim played a minimal role in a criminal prosecution. The victim's only job, if any, was to testify at trial about the circumstances of the offense. Now victims participate more, from the beginning, when they are involved in prosecutors' pretrial investigations, to later, when they give statements in court to the judge during sentencing hearings. The victim may tell the judge about the impact the crime has had on the victim's life, pain the victim has suffered, and any other details to show why the defendant should receive a harsh sentence. The victim typically will also meet with the probation officer, who will include a victim impact statement in the presentence report. This statement may include the victim's version of the offense and detail any physical, psychological, or monetary damage the victim suffered as a result of the crime.

Rules in some jurisdictions provide victims with a right to address judges at sentencing proceedings. In these jurisdictions, judges cannot forbid victims from making statements before sentence is pronounced. (*Kenna v. District Court*, 9th Cir. 2006.)

Sentence Options

Among the many sentencing options a judge might consider are incarceration, fines, probation, and community service.

These components might be imposed separately or together. For example, a defendant might be sentenced pay a $1,000 fine, perform 40 hours of community service, and spend one year on probation.

Incarceration

This subsection examines why certain defendants are ordered to serve time in jail or prison.

What are some of the reasons judges order convicted defendants locked up?

Competing theories exist as to why some laws require, and some judges order, convicted criminals to be incarcerated:

- **Retribution.** Some people think that the primary goal of sentencing is retribution: to take out society's vengeance against a defendant.
- **Rehabilitation.** Others argue that the primary purpose of incarceration is rehabilitation. Under this theory, the sentence is supposed to help the defendant turn away from crime and adopt a lawful lifestyle. Rehabilitation is commendable in theory, but today's jails and prisons tend not to rehabilitate. Many defendants say that they come out better criminals than they went in, because they have learned the tricks of the trade from other prisoners.
- **Deterrence.** Some believe that because prison is so harsh, the threat of a prison sentence will deter people from

committing crimes. Like rehabilitation, deterrence doesn't seem to be effective, for several reasons. Often, crimes are committed on impulse or under the influence of a drug or alcohol, without thought of the possible consequences. Also, people who commit crimes have often spent major parts of their lives in institutions and do not fear incarceration the way people who have been free all their lives might. And finally, a sizable number of criminal defendants actually seek punishment because of various psychological pathologies.

Preparing Victim Impact Statements

With sentences increasingly reflecting the impact of crimes on victims' lives, a crime victim might seek assistance from a friend or counselor when writing an impact statement. Statements may touch on the physical, emotional, and/or financial effects of crimes. For example, how did a crime change the victim's daily life or general lifestyle? How did it affect relationships with family members and friends? What medical and/or psychological treatment has a crime necessitated?

Victims might also be eligible for restitution (from the perpetrator) or crime victim assistance funds (from the county or state), and if so might have to fill in a questionnaire. (For further information, see Chapter 24.)

- **Punishment and public safety.** Increasingly, people in the know admit that prison doesn't rehabilitate criminals or deter crime. They lock defendants up to punish them and get them off the streets for as long as possible.
- **Politics.** Finally, and unfortunately, an influential group of leaders emphasize incarceration as a way of getting votes. By building more prisons and locking more people up, politicians can cite statistics that make them look tough on crime, whether or not the actual crime rate is actually reduced or the underlying problems causing the crime are ever addressed.

Alex's Experience

As a young man named Alex was nearing the end of an approximately year-long jail sentence, the authors asked him to reflect on how he spent his time and what he would have liked to know before he started serving his sentence. Among Alex's responses were these:

- "I spent most of my time reading. I also meditated, did sit-ups and push-ups, and sometimes played cards and board games. Having a routine helped me stay busy and focused on my goals of getting out and bettering my life."
- "I learned to make delicious spreads that I put on the snacks that I bought from the jail commissary."
- "Before I learned to control my anger and sadness, I was disciplined for disrespecting a female deputy and making 'pruno,' a jailhouse alcoholic drink."
- "I learned to respect all different types of people whose beliefs are very different from mine."
- "I appreciated the health care, which may not be great, but is free. I could be seen by a nurse every day. I was given medications for my mental illness. I was also taken to a clinic every month for treatment of Hepatitis C."
- "The food was okay. I especially liked the hot dogs and fried chicken sandwiches."
- The biggest "don'ts": "Don't disrespect others or try to 'double up' on food."
- The biggest "do": "Stay calm and think out your activities in advance; this will keep you out of trouble."
- "The best thing was that family members visited me regularly, wrote to me frequently, and let me know how much they loved me."
- "Jail was depressing. I had been in Juvenile Hall before, and jail was much worse. The worst aspects were seeing the same grey walls every day and listening to other inmates scream and yell."
- "I missed my family. I wished I could have spent time with them instead of being locked up."

Height of Controversy?

In May 2006, Nebraska Judge Kristine Cecava created controversy by sentencing convicted sex offender Richard Thompson to ten years' probation rather than ten years in prison because she feared that he might not survive in prison because he was only 5'1" tall. The decision angered victims' rights advocates and puzzled Nebraska prison officials, who reported that many prisoners were shorter than Thompson and that they had never been harmed. The appellate court upheld the sentence as a legitimate exercise of judicial discretion, but Nebraska voters removed Judge Cecava from the bench in a 2008 election.

What is the difference between jail and prison?

Jails (sometimes called community correctional centers) are short-term lockups normally run by counties and staffed by county sheriffs. Defendants housed in jails include those awaiting trial and unable to make bail, those serving sentences for misdemeanor offenses, and those felons who have to do jail time as a condition of probation. Because jails are devoted to short-term incarceration, they typically lack many of the facilities and programs that are sometimes available in prisons, such as libraries and exercise areas.

Prisons (also called penitentiaries and, in slang, "the joint," "the pen," "the big house," or "up the river") are normally operated by the federal and state governments, and their purpose is long-term incarceration. Most prison inmates serve sentences well in excess of a year.

What's the difference between a determinate and indeterminate sentence?

A determinate sentence is a fixed-term sentence pronounced by a judge. For example, a defendant sentenced to "30 days in county jail" or "five years in state prison" has received a determinate sentence. Defendants who receive determinate sentences at least know the maximum period of incarceration as soon as they are sentenced, but they may get out earlier because of parole, because they have behaved well (good-time credits), or because the jail or prison is overcrowded and their bed is needed for a new inmate.

Indeterminate sentences are those in which a judge sets a minimum and/or maximum time of incarceration, but leaves the decision as to when to release an inmate to prison officials. For example, a defendant sentenced to "serve not less than two nor more than 20 years in the state penitentiary" has received an indeterminate sentence. As a general rule, indeterminate sentences are imposed only on people who are sentenced to state prison after being convicted of a felony.

What does it mean for sentences to run "concurrently" or "consecutively"?

Judges often have discretion to decide whether to give defendants who are convicted of separate crimes concurrent or consecutive sentences. (See *Oregon v. Ice*, U.S. Sup. Ct. 2009.) If a defendant is convicted of a number of crimes that carry lengthy prison terms, the difference between consecutive and concurrent sentences can be tremendous. When sentences run concurrently, defendants serve all the sentences at the same time. When sentences run consecutively, defendants have to finish serving the sentence for one offense before they start serving the sentence for any other offense. The same factors that judges tend to consider when deciding on the severity of a sentence (for example, a defendant's past record) also affect their decisions on whether to give concurrent or consecutive sentences.

EXAMPLE: Haydn Goseek was convicted of 20 counts of forgery for forging and cashing 20 separate checks. Each count carries a maximum possible prison term of five years. If the judge gives Haydn a maximum sentence on each count and runs the sentences consecutively, Haydn's total sentence would be 100 years in prison. If the judge runs the sentences concurrently, Haydn's total sentence would be five years in prison because he would serve all of the sentences at the same time. (Whether he receives consecutive or concurrent sentences, Haydn might be released early on parole.) If Haydn previously had a clean record and forged the checks when he had been temporarily laid off from work, the judge might well sentence Haydn to less than the statutory maximum of five years on each count, and run the sentences concurrently.

EXAMPLE: Same case. Haydn's forgery conviction was in Michigan. At the time of the Michigan conviction, Haydn was already serving a sentence in Indiana for forgeries committed in Indiana. (Indiana turned Haydn over to Michigan temporarily to stand trial.) When the Michigan judge sentences Haydn on the Michigan forgeries, Haydn's attorney can ask the Michigan court to allow Haydn to serve the Michigan sentence concurrently with the Indiana sentence. If the judge agrees, every day that Haydn serves in Indiana will count as though it were served in Michigan.

One Sentence for Separate Crimes?

Sometimes, a sentencing judge can legally give just a single sentence to a defendant who is convicted of separate crimes. The reason is that what the law regards as a single unlawful act may violate several statutes. For example, assume that a defendant sets a house on fire in an attempt to kill the occupants. The defendant may be convicted both of arson and attempted murder, but could probably be given only a single sentence. Typically, the sentence would be for the more serious crime, which in this instance would probably be attempted murder.

 CAUTION

Determining whether a defendant's illegal conduct will be considered a single unlawful act for sentencing purposes can be quite complex. Judges often have to consider a variety of uncertain factors, such as a defendant's purpose in committing a crime.

What is a "time served" sentence?

Defendants who are sentenced to the time they have spent in jail prior to conviction are sentenced to "time served."

While defendants who are told that they will be sentenced to time served may be very tempted to plead guilty and go home, there are serious consequences that a defendant should consider before doing so. For example,

- The offender will still have a criminal record; time served doesn't erase the conviction.
- Time served is given almost always in conjunction with probation and sometimes with a fine, community service, or both. Probation may have onerous conditions attached to it. Defendants who violate even one of the probation conditions may be returned immediately to jail.

What is a suspended sentence?

A sentence is suspended when a judge imposes a jail sentence but allows a defendant not to serve all or part of it. For example, a judge may impose a sentence of a "$750 fine and ten days in county jail, five days suspended." The catch is that the suspension is conditional on the defendant complying with the terms and conditions that a judge specifies. For example, a judge may condition suspension on a defendant's compliance with the conditions of probation or completion of a drug treatment program. If a defendant violates one of the conditions (for example, fails to complete a drug

treatment program), a judge can order the defendant to serve the suspended portion of the sentence.

Mistreatment in Prison

Most defendants facing imprisonment for the first time are scared, and often with good reason. Jails and prisons nationwide are overcrowded. Many inmates are subjected to harsh treatment both from guards and from fellow prisoners. One thing a defendant should do is to work closely with a lawyer, from arrest on, to develop an effective sentencing plan and present the best possible case for an alternative (nonincarceration) sentence to the probation officer and the judge. For more information about prisons and prisoners' rights, see Chapter 27.

Fines

Fines are a common component of criminal sentences. While a fine may be the exclusive punishment for minor offenses, fines often accompany other punishments, such as jail, prison, and restitution.

What is a "day fine"?

Fines have been subject to a great deal of criticism. One frequent complaint is that they impact rich and poor offenders very differently: "The rich pay the fine, the poor do the time." One recent trend to combat that critique has been the implementation of day fines. With day fines, employed defendants do not have to pay a fine all at once. Instead, they pay a percentage of their earnings on a weekly or monthly basis. The payment amounts depend on the offender's salary.

Is "restitution" a fancy word for a fine?

No. Fines go to the state (or federal or local government prosecuting the crime).

Restitution is money the defendant pays to the victim or to a state restitution fund. In some cases, the "victim" is society, such as in welfare and Medicare fraud schemes, in which case defendants may be sentenced to pay the state back the money that was fraudulently taken. More typically, in both state and federal jurisdictions, offenders may be required to return or replace stolen

---

More About Restitution

In some states, restitution orders are limited to the victim's out-of-pocket economic losses, such as medical expenses and lost pay for missing work. With few exceptions—such as when a child has been sexually assaulted by the defendant—a judge cannot order a defendant to compensate a victim for noneconomic damages such as pain and suffering and emotional distress. Victims who want compensation for noneconomic losses have to sue the defendant in a separate civil action.

When multiple offenders injure a single victim, a restitution order against any one offender must reflect only the damages caused by that offender. (*Paroline v. U.S.*, U.S. Sup. Ct. 2014.) So, if a defendant is convicted of downloading from the Internet two pornographic pictures of a child victim, the restitution order can be based only on counseling and other costs attributable to that defendant's possession of the photos. This is a difficult task for judges to carry out.

Courts typically enforce their restitution orders in two ways:

If probation is granted, the defendant is required to pay the restitution as a condition of remaining on probation. If the supervising probation officer believes that the defendant is willfully avoiding paying the restitution, the officer can seek to have the probation revoked and the defendant incarcerated.

- The restitution order is considered to be the equivalent of a civil judgment and can be enforced by the victim by attaching or garnishing a defendant's assets or wages. However, under this method of enforcing the restitution order, the defendant can't be put in jail for not paying up.

Of course, many perpetrators are unable to pay for even a portion of the economic harm that their crimes have caused. For this reason, many states have set up victim compensation funds that provide at least partial restitution to crime victims. State agencies that operate victim compensation programs may also provide counseling services to crime victims. (See Chapter 24 for more on restitution and victim compensation.)

or damaged property, to compensate victims for physical injuries and medical and psychological treatment costs, or to pay funeral and other costs if the victim dies.

Typically, the defendant will be ordered to pay restitution as just one part of the sentence, in addition to a fine, prison time, community service, probation, and/or some other punishment. Sometimes, plea bargains are struck by which criminal charges are dropped altogether if the defendant admits guilt and completely compensates the victim for stolen property or a vandalized car. This type of arrangement is called a "civil compromise."

Can the government confiscate an offender's property?

Yes. The government may institute civil forfeiture proceedings to take property (such as money and cars) that was used to commit a crime or came from the criminal activity. However, the Eighth Amendment's ban on excessive fines applies to state governments and forfeiture. The Supreme Court established this rule in *Timbs v. Indiana*, a case in which the government wanted to keep the defendant's $42,000 Land Rover even though the maximum fine for his conviction was $10,000.

Probation

Probation allows convicted people to serve all or a portion of a sentence in their communities rather than in jail or prison.

How does probation work?

Probation is a figurative leash that the criminal justice system attaches to offenders in addition to or instead of other forms of punishment. Offenders who are put on probation are typically required to adhere to a number of conditions. Common conditions of probation include:

- obeying all laws (breaking even petty laws like jaywalking have been known to land a probationer back in jail)
- abiding by any court orders, such as an order to pay a fine or restitution
- reporting regularly to the probation officer
- reporting any change of employment or address to the probation officer
- abstaining from the excessive use of alcohol or the use of any illegal drugs
- refraining from travel outside of the jurisdiction without prior permission of the probation officer, and
- avoiding certain people and places (for example, an offender convicted of assaulting his ex-wife may have as one condition of probation that he avoid any contact with his ex-wife or her family).

Probation officers also can check in on a probationer—at home or at work, announced or unannounced. Some probationers, such as those convicted on drug charges, are also subject to random searches and drug tests. Most courts have concluded that probationers do not have the same Fourth Amendment rights to be free from unreasonable searches and seizures as other people.

Can judges order probation along with other punishment?

A judge may put an offender on probation while also ordering other punishment—like having to pay a fine, make restitution, and serve time in jail or prison.

What is the difference between summary and supervised probation?

Summary probation is an invisible leash; offenders placed on summary probation do not need to check in with probation officers and may not need a probation officer's permission to go from one state to another.

Offenders placed on supervised probation have to contact a probation officer regularly, sometimes in person.

With either form of probation, offenders may be subject to conditions of probation such as submitting to random drug tests.

Can offenders seek to change conditions of probation?

Yes. Judges retain the power to modify conditions of probation or terminate probation early.

> **EXAMPLE:** Greta Victor was sentenced to 48 hours in jail, a large fine, community service, and probation on a second drunk driving offense. One condition of probation was that she not drive for one year. Six months later, Greta got a job that required her to drive. Greta contacted her probation officer, who agreed that she had complied with all of the probation conditions for the first six months. The officer told Greta

that he would not oppose her petition to the judge to lift the ban on driving for the remainder of the probation term. The judge has discretion to grant Greta's petition and likely would do so because she has fulfilled all of her probation conditions and has a valid basis for her request.

What happens to offenders who violate conditions of probation?

Offenders who violate one or more conditions of probation are subject to revocation of probation. The consequences of revocation can be severe. For example, violation of a condition of probation may result in an offender serving a suspended sentence. Because one typical condition of probation is to obey all laws, a probationer who is rearrested on even a minor charge may be punished for both the new violation and for the probation violation.

Are probationers entitled to a hearing before probation is revoked?

Yes. Before revoking probation, judges typically conduct a probation revocation hearing. If a new criminal charge is the basis of the proposed revocation, the revocation hearing may take place after the new offense has been disposed of. If the violation was not a new criminal offense but nevertheless broke a condition of probation (for instance, socializing with people the judge prohibited an offender from contacting), then the revocation hearing may take place as soon as practicable after the violation is reported. Offenders are entitled to written notification of the time, place, and reason for the probation revocation hearing.

What happens at a probation revocation hearing?

A probation revocation hearing is like a minitrial without a jury. Both the defense and prosecution may present evidence to show the judge why the offender should or should not be subjected to whatever penalty the judge originally imposed. The defendant is allowed counsel at this hearing, but the judge does not have to follow strict rules of evidence.

Additionally, the legal standard in a probation revocation hearing is lighter than the "beyond a reasonable doubt" standard in criminal trials. In the revocation hearing, typically, the prosecution will only have to prove by a preponderance of the evidence that the offender violated a condition of probation. (These legal standards are difficult to quantify, but essentially this means that it doesn't take as much evidence, or that the evidence doesn't have to be as compelling, to revoke probation as it does to prove guilt at trial. In essence, probation is a privilege that can be lost more easily than one's initial freedom.)

Is it possible to plea bargain a probation revocation charge?

Yes. When an offender arrested on new charges is found also to be in violation of an earlier probation order, the defense may negotiate a new plea bargain to cover both offenses in one package deal. This is especially common in busy, big-city courts where calendars are backlogged.

Community Service

Work in the community can be an alternative to spending time in jail.

Can judges order offenders to perform community service?

Yes. Judges can sentence defendants to perform unpaid community work called community service. A defendant may be required to perform community service in addition to receiving other forms of punishment, such as a jail sentence, probation, a fine, or paying restitution.

What kind of work does community service usually involve?

Typically, offenders are assigned to work for nonprofit groups or government agencies, such as parks, libraries, schools, cemeteries, religious institutions, and drug and alcohol treatment centers. They may be sentenced to do a wide range of work—from cleaning highways to lecturing students on the dangers of drunk driving. In one very effective community service program, gang member offenders work in a home for mentally and physically challenged children, helping them to dress, eat, and play.

Some offenders do community service work in group settings with other offenders; others work alone. They may be supervised directly by the nonprofit group or government agency they work for or by the probation department. And they may have to report to the court or probation officer at regularly scheduled times to prove that they are complying with the community service order.

Miscellaneous Alternative Sentences

The high costs of incarceration have led communities to develop alternative forms of punishment.

What is alternative sentencing?

Alternative sentencing is the buzzword for an increasingly visible movement in the criminal justice system. Largely inspired by overcrowded and nonrehabilitative prisons, some judges are beginning to work with prosecutors and defense lawyers to impose nontraditional sentences, especially in cases that don't involve violence.

To some, alternative sentencing means anything other than incarceration. And it is true that many alternative sentences are simply variations of probation—perhaps with a fine and community service thrown in. But alternative sentencing can also include fairly innovative punishments. Offenders have been required to:

- install breathalyzer ("ignition interlock") devices in their cars so that their cars will not start unless the offender blows into the device and has "clean" breath (after drunk driving convictions)
- drive around with signs on their cars notifying others they'd been convicted of a drunk driving offense (this may be a modern equivalent of the scarlet letter)
- give lectures or teach classes about the dangers of criminal behavior
- attend lectures given by crime victims (convicted drunk drivers may be required to listen to families of people who were killed or maimed in alcohol-related accidents)
- complete a drug or alcohol treatment program
- do weekend jail time
- stay at home under house arrest; a person under house arrest may be required to wear an electronic monitoring device, such as an ankle bracelet
- live in their own slummy building, and
- serve time in private jails. Private contractors provide jail services for a fee, which they charge both governments and inmates.

Another alternative approach to handling offenses, especially minor ones and those for which prosecutors have declined to press charges, is for the prosecutor to send the defendant and the victim to a neighborhood justice center to resolve their dispute through a process known as mediation. In mediation, a neutral third party helps the disputing parties arrive at a mutually satisfactory agreement.

"Megan's Law" (Sex Offender Registration)

A "Megan's Law," in effect in many jurisdictions, applies to offenders who have been convicted of certain types of sexual crimes, especially sexual crimes against children. (The law was named after Megan Kanka, a seven-year-old New Jersey girl who was raped and killed by a previously convicted child molester who lived across the street from Megan's family.)

A Megan's Law typically requires sex offenders to register with local law enforcement annually and upon release from prison, starting at a new job or school, or changing residences. Depending on the level of risk that an offender poses to the public (the assessment of risk is normally based on criminal history), a Megan's Law also requires police agencies to notify schools, other agencies, and the public as to a registered offender's whereabouts. The names of registered offenders become part of a national database of sex offenders.

Some types of sexual conduct that once were crimes have in recent years been decriminalized. For example, the U.S. Supreme Court invalidated laws prohibiting consensual sex between a same-sex couple. (*Lawrence v. Texas*, U.S. Sup. Ct. 2003.) People convicted under such laws who had to register may be able to apply to their state's justice department to have their names removed from its sex offender database.

What are drug courts?

Founded in the late 1980s, drug courts originally dealt with first-time drug offenders but now often handle cases involving repeat offenders. In drug courts, judges and lawyers often work together to encourage offenders with addiction problems to maintain enrollment in a drug treatment program for a minimum period of time and submit to regular drug testing. The treatment programs may include acupuncture, counseling, education, and job training, along with regular court appearances. The results of these programs have generally been positive. Among other achievements, studies show significantly less recidivism (fewer rearrests) in drug court graduates than among regularly sentenced defendants.

Some states have downgraded less serious drug offenses (such as simple possession of a small amount of illegal drugs) from felonies to misdemeanors. The advantages include reducing prison populations and sparing people who may not pose a threat to themselves or to society from being branded as felons. A big disadvantage is that without the threat of a conviction and imprisonment hanging over their heads, drug users may choose to serve a short term in jail rather than enroll in a drug treatment program. As a result, downgrading the punishment for so-called minor drug offenses may interfere with the goal of helping users learn how to stay sober.

How is parole different from probation?

Parole is early prison release granted by prison officials. Parole is similar to probation in that the offender is free from prison, with rights limited by the parole conditions. Conditions of parole tend to be similar to but more restrictive than probation conditions.

How is a pardon different from probation and parole?

A pardon (also sometimes called a "grant of clemency") is an order from a jurisdiction's chief executive (a state's governor or the president of the United States) relieving a convicted person of the penalties for having committed a crime. While a pardon does not necessarily erase a conviction, a pardon normally restores an offender's civil rights.

The Death Penalty

This section examines the rules, procedures, and controversies concerning the ultimate criminal sentence, the death penalty.

What is the current status of the death penalty in the United States?

As of 2019, 29 states as well as the federal government and the U.S. military retain the death penalty; 21 states as well as the District of Columbia have abolished the death penalty. The governors of four of the states that retain the death penalty (California, Oregon, Colorado, and Pennsylvania) have placed a moratorium on executions. The number of states that have the death penalty on their books has generally declined; in 2007, 38 states authorized capital punishment.

A number of states that authorize capital punishment have not carried out any executions since 1976, the year that the U.S. Supreme Court decided in *Gregg v. Georgia* that the death penalty was a constitutionally permissible form of punishment under a properly written statute.

The number of annual executions has gradually declined over the last two decades from a high of 98 in 1999 to 20 in 2016 to nine in 2019.

Federal criminal laws authorize capital punishment for those convicted of more than 40 different kinds of crimes, including treason, aggravated murder, and drug trafficking. Among the most notable people executed by the federal government are Ethel and Julius Rosenberg, executed in 1953 after being convicted of espionage for passing atomic secrets to the Soviet Union, and Timothy McVeigh, executed in 2001 for blowing up a federal office building in Oklahoma City and killing 168 people.

However, comparatively few cases involving the death penalty arise in federal court. As of 2019 there are 62 federal prisoners who have been sentenced to death. The federal government announced in 2019 its intention to resume executions, after a 16-year hiatus. (For additional statistical information related to the death penalty, visit the Death Penalty Information Center. (https://deathpenaltyinfo.org.)

Do some parts of the country carry out more executions?

Yes. Between 1976 and 2019, 1,499 state prisoners were executed. Southern states carried out 1,226 of these executions; the Midwest, with 184 executions, was a distant second. Texas had the most executions (561) in this span of time, followed by Virginia (113) and Oklahoma (112).

Have any prisoners sentenced to death been exonerated?

Yes. Since 1973, 165 former death row inmates have been exonerated of all charges and been set free. Almost all of these exonerations were based on DNA testing that revealed that the prisoners were factually innocent.

How is the death penalty carried out?

Lethal injection (depicted in graphic detail in the film *Dead Man Walking*) is generally considered to be the most humane form of execution and is currently the most common method of carrying out executions. Some states use a three-drug protocol intended to sedate, paralyze, and then kill. Others use a single-drug protocol, due in part to the unavailability of certain drugs. Though administration of the three-drug protocol can cause excruciating pain, it has been found not to constitute cruel and unusual punishment in violation of the Eighth Amendment. (*Baze v. Rees*, U.S. Sup. Ct. 2008.) While a one-drug protocol using midazolam has raised similar concerns, it too has been found constitutional.

(*Glossip v. Gross*, U.S. Sup. Ct. 2015.) Some states (such as Arkansas) have accelerated execution schedules as drug expiration dates approach.

A few states still authorize methods such as electrocution and the gas chamber, but they are rarely used. Hanging and firing squads are outmoded forms of execution that may remain "on the books" in a few states but are no longer used. Dissection and dismemberment, two favorite forms of execution in the 18th century, designed to make the idea of capital punishment as frightening as possible, are long gone.

What factors determine whether a death penalty law is valid under the U.S. Constitution?

The United States Supreme Court has established a variety of standards capital punishment laws must comply with to satisfy the federal Constitution.

Statutes authorizing judges and juries to impose the death penalty must set out specific sentencing guidelines that they must consider when determining whether to sentence a particular defendant to death. (*Gregg v. Georgia*, U.S. Sup. Ct. 1976.) These statutory guidelines consist of "aggravating factors" (factors suggesting a defendant merits a harsher sentence) and "mitigating factors" (factors suggesting a lesser degree of culpability). For example, a statute might instruct jurors who have convicted a defendant of a capital crime to take factors such as these into account when deciding on punishment:

- whether a defendant has a prior violent felony conviction
- whether the crime was "heinous, atrocious, or cruel" or "cold, calculated, and premeditated"
- whether a defendant was at the time a crime was committed under extreme duress or the domination of another person
- a defendant's character, background, history, and mental and physical condition, and
- evidence of innocence that the defendant had offered into evidence at trial. (*Oregon v. Guzek*, U.S. Sup. Ct. 2006.)

So important are such factors that a defense attorney's failure to investigate a defendant's personal background thoroughly can constitute "ineffective assistance of counsel" that requires a sentence of death to be reversed. (*Wiggins v. Smith,* U.S. Sup. Ct. 2003.)

Another principle established by the Supreme Court is that defendants tried by juries are entitled to have jurors rather than judges find aggravating circumstances that support imposition of the death penalty. (*Hurst v. Florida*, U.S. Sup. Ct. 2016.)

The trial must be "bifurcated," which means that a jury has to first decide whether a defendant is guilty of a capital crime. Then, in a separate proceeding, the jury considers evidence relating to aggravating and mitigating factors and decides whether to sentence a defendant to death or impose a lesser sentence. In many states, if a jury recommends death, the judge retains the power to decide on a lesser sentence, such as life without possibility of parole (LWOP). On the other hand, should a jury in one of these states recommend a life sentence, the judge has no power to impose the death penalty.

If a serious legal mistake occurs during the penalty phase of a bifurcated trial, a court can uphold the guilty verdict and order a new penalty phase hearing. For example, in *Buck v. Davis* (U.S. Sup. Ct. 2017), a Texas jury convicted an African American man of murder and sentenced him to death. During the penalty phase hearing, an expert witness told the jury that black men are more violence-prone than other people. The Supreme Court upheld the guilty verdict but ruled that the "noxious strain of racial prejudice" required a new sentencing hearing.

The Supreme court has also established that the Eighth Amendment's ban on "cruel and unusual punishment" limits the crimes for which the death penalty can be imposed. For example, a defendant convicted of rape of an adult cannot constitutionally be sentenced to death (*Coker v. Georgia*, U.S. Sup. Ct. 1977.) And a death sentence cannot be given to defendants who are convicted of raping children. (*Kennedy v. Louisiana*, U.S. Sup. Ct. 2008.)

Further, the death penalty cannot be carried out on prisoners who are intellectually disabled. (*Atkins v. Virginia,* U.S. Sup. Ct. 2002.) Judges must evaluate the severity of an individual's intellectual disability according to current mental health standards. When a defendant's IQ score is close to, but above, 70, courts must account for the test's standard error of measurement; when the lower range of a defendant's score is at or below 70, deficits in his or her adaptive functioning must be properly considered. (*Moore v. Texas*, U.S. Sup. Ct. 2017.) A state law preventing defendants who score more than 70 on an IQ test from offering evidence that they are too mentally disabled to be executed is invalid. (*Hall v. Florida*, U.S. Sup. Ct. 2014.)

And the death penalty cannot be imposed on offenders who were under age 18 at the time they committed a crime potentially punishable by death. (*Roper v. Simmons*, U.S. Sup. Ct. 2005.) Imposition of death in these circumstances violates both the Eighth ("cruel and unusual punishment") and Fourteenth ("due process of law") Amendments. (In *Graham v. Florida* (U.S. Sup. Ct. 2010), the Court extended the ruling in *Roper* by deciding that juvenile offenders cannot be given a mandatory sentence of life in prison without possibility of parole for nonhomicide crimes. Following *Graham*, the California Supreme Court ruled that a 110-year sentence for a juvenile is the functional equivalent of life without possibility of parole, and equally impermissible. (*People v. Caballero* (2012).)

What are "special circumstances"?

Among the states that authorize capital punishment, many limit its possible use to murder cases in which special circumstances exist. In these states, a prosecutor has to file a murder charge as a special circumstances case and prove beyond a reasonable doubt that one or more of the charged circumstances apply. Here are some special circumstances that might lead a prosecutor to seek the death penalty:

- A murder was committed for the purpose of financial gain.
- The defendant has a prior conviction for murder.
- The murder was committed for the purpose of escaping from custody.
- The victim was a police officer, firefighter, or government official.
- The murder was committed by means of poison or an explosive device.
- The murder was carried out in a particularly heinous and cruel manner.

EXAMPLE: Shemp is charged with first-degree murder for killing Moe "with malice aforethought." The jury convicts Shemp of murder and on the verdict form indicates that "we the jury conclude that Shemp carried out the murder in such a vicious and cruel manner that he ought to be put to death." The sentence isn't proper for two reasons. First, a death sentence may be handed down only if the prosecutor seeks the death penalty at the outset of a case and identifies in advance the "special circumstances" that allow the death penalty to be handed down; the jury must also be told that the special circumstances must be proved beyond a reasonable doubt. Second, the death penalty can be imposed only after a separate penalty hearing in which both sides have an opportunity to present evidence of aggravating and mitigating factors.

Do prosecutors use special procedures when deciding whether to seek the death penalty?

Yes. In the usual case in which capital punishment is not an option, charging decisions are made by a single prosecutor who reviews police reports and decides what charges to file. By contrast, a charging decision in a capital case is usually made by a team of a District Attorney's most experienced prosecutors, often including the head District Attorney personally. Before deciding to seek the death penalty, the prosecutorial team must of course be convinced that it can prove the defendant committed a capital crime, and that the crime is among the worst of the worst, for which death is a constitutional punishment. (*Gregg v. Georgia*, U.S. Sup. Ct. 1976.) Charging decisions may also be influenced by factors such as the following:

- **Costs.** Compared to cases in which LWOP is the ultimate sentence, capital cases normally add dramatically to a case's costs and complexity. For example, capital cases ordinarily take longer to try and may involve automatic appeals. Also, in some states, a defendant facing the death penalty is entitled to two government-paid lawyers rather than one. And appellate courts are more prone to overturn death sentences based on a defendant's "ineffective assistance of counsel" claim, often for counsel's failure to investigate thoroughly a defendant's personal background. When this happens, a new sentencing hearing usually takes place. Finally, racial bias in jury selection can require reversals of convictions. (*Foster v. Chatman*, U.S. Sup. Ct. 2016.)

- **Adverse jury reaction.** A prosecutor may fear that a jury will acquit a defendant for whom it may feel some sympathy rather than see the defendant face the possibility of execution. (This was apparently a major factor in the L.A. District Attorney's decision not to ask for the death penalty in the 1995 famous prosecution of O.J. Simpson. Of course, Simpson was acquitted anyway.)

- **Popular support.** A prosecutor may believe that continued popular support of the death penalty depends on seeking it only in the most egregious cases.

- **Excuse of defense-minded jurors.** A prosecutor who seeks the death penalty is entitled to remove potential jurors who have serious qualms about voting for capital punishment. Because the jurors removed by this process may be defense-oriented, prosecutors may seek capital punishment in order to select a jury that may be prosecution-minded.

- **Improper biases and prejudices.** Some commentators contend that prosecutors are more likely to seek the death penalty when defendants are poor or members of ethnic minorities, especially when their victims are Caucasian. On the other hand, if the jury recommends LWOP, the judge has no power to impose the death penalty.

What are the issues in the death penalty debate?

The debate over the morality and wisdom of the death penalty began to heat up in the latter half of the twentieth century. One factor was that many Western European and other countries, including Canada, Mexico, and New Zealand, abolished the death penalty in the period between 1950 and 1970, leaving the United States increasingly isolated as a country with both a modern and complex criminal justice system and capital punishment. Another factor was that the appeal process began to lengthen, making death row prisoners increasingly visible. Among the most famous of these was Caryl Chessman, the so-called "red light bandit," who was sentenced to death in California in 1948 for committing a number of "lovers lane" kidnappings (he killed nobody). A series of appeals kept Chessman alive until his execution in 1960. While in prison, he wrote four books that called international attention to the United States' use of the death penalty; some of his books were translated into other languages and became popular in other countries. (One of his books became a 1955 film, *Cell 2455, Death Row*.)

Recent public opinion surveys indicate that about 60% of Americans support alternatives to the death penalty such as life without possibility of parole (LWOP). However, the debate over the legitimacy of the death penalty is likely to continue for many years. At the center of the debate are conflicting beliefs about the morality of the death penalty, and attitudes based on what people view as moral imperatives are not easily changed.

Does the death penalty serve as a deterrent?

Proponents of the death penalty often argue that it deters at least some people who would otherwise commit murders from doing so, and that its deterrent effect would be even greater were unnecessary delays in carrying out death sentences eliminated.

Statistics do not support the argument for the deterrent effect of capital punishment. Through 2017, the per capita rate of murder in states with the death penalty was 5.4 per 100,000 people; the rate was 3.9 per 100,000 in states without the death penalty.

However, the answer to the question of whether the death penalty acts as a deterrent is uncertain. Many social science researchers have investigated the deterrence hypothesis; some studies have shown a deterrent effect while others have not. Whatever their conclusions, the weakness in all these studies is that consensus is lacking on how to "model" the murder rate. That is, deterrence can be measured only by comparing murder rates in different jurisdictions that have or don't have the death penalty using variables such as poverty rates, racial makeup, and the like. Because researchers don't agree on which variables to include and how much weight to give them, there exists "a raging methodological disagreement over how best to pick the variables, and a nagging suspicion that researchers' own attitudes toward capital punishment were subconsciously influencing the forms of equations." (*The Death Penalty: An American History*, by Stuart Banner.) The claim that the death penalty's deterrent effect would be greater were it carried out more quickly or frequently is also untestable because the federal Constitution prevents states from eliminating or severely cutting back on prisoners' access to the courts.

Does capital punishment involve racial disparities?

Many death penalty opponents argue that capital punishment has a disparate racial impact. The U.S. Supreme Court has ruled that racial disparities in the use of the death penalty, if any, do not render its use unconstitutional. (*McCleskey v. Kemp*, U.S. Sup. Ct. 1987.) Nevertheless, in an effort to convince states to abolish capital punishment, opponents argue that the disparity in the use of the death penalty concerns not the defendants but the victims of crimes. The death penalty is unfair, they argue, because research studies tend to show that it is imposed when victims are Caucasian much more often than when they are Black or members of other racial minorities. For example, statistics indicate that more than 75% of executions involve murders of Caucasian victims, though only about half of all murder victims are Caucasian. However, the merits of this argument are unclear. As Banner points out, "Most murders involved criminals and victims of the same race, so equalizing the treatment of victims would cause more black defendants to be sentenced to death. From the point of view of one concerned with race discrimination, was that a desirable outcome?" Banner concludes that the consequences of the racial disparity argument are unclear. (*The Death Penalty: An American History*, by Stuart Banner.)

 RESOURCES

More information on the death penalty is provided by the following references:

The Death Penalty: An American History, by Stuart Banner, is a thorough and largely neutral account of the history of the use of the death penalty.

Actual Innocence: Five Days to Execution, and Other Dispatches from the Wrongly Convicted, by Jim Dwyer, et al., explains the use of DNA evidence in murder trials and describes a number of fascinating cases of "getting the wrong guy."

The Cornell Death Penalty Project (www.lawschool.cornell.edu/research/death-penalty-project/index.cfm) is an anti-capital-punishment website administered by the Cornell Law School.

The American Civil Liberties Union provides anti-capital-punishment information at its website (www.aclu.org/issues/capital-punishment).

The Death Penalty Information Center (https://deathpenaltyinfo.org) sponsors an anti-death-penalty website.

Is capital punishment more costly than other forms of punishment?

Yes. Prosecutions become far more expensive when prosecutors seek the death penalty. The high costs are attributable to the legal system itself. For example, in many states defendants facing the death penalty who cannot afford to hire private attorneys (and that includes almost all defendants) are represented by two lawyers rather than one, both paid for by the government. Also, both the prosecution and the defense are likely to call on a variety of expert witnesses at both the guilt and sentencing phases of capital cases, adding significantly to their cost. Another reason for the high costs of capital punishment is that death penalty verdicts typically generate lengthy appeals and "collateral attacks" via habeas corpus and other procedures. Finally, "death rows" themselves entail higher costs, in part because states take extra precautions with prisoners sentenced to death. Successful opponents of capital punishment have pointed to the financial impact of the death penalty on state budgets and the alternative sentence of life in prison without possibility of parole.

Appeals and Writs

Defendants who think they've been wrongfully convicted have a number of options, including:

- making a motion asking the trial judge to overturn the jury's guilty verdict and enter a verdict of not guilty
- moving for a new trial—that is, asking the judge to set aside the jury's verdict, declare a mistrial, and start over, and
- appealing (asking a higher court to reverse the conviction based on legal errors during the trial).

This chapter focuses on the third option, appeals.

The Appeal Process

Convicted defendants are generally entitled to one appeal as a matter of right. This section explains how the appeal process works.

What is an appeal?

An appeal is a request to a higher (appellate) court to review and change the decision of a lower court. Because posttrial motions asking trial courts to change their own judgments or order new jury trials are seldom successful, a defendant who hopes to overturn a guilty verdict must usually appeal. The defendant may challenge the conviction itself or may appeal the trial court's sentencing decision without actually challenging the underlying conviction.

Can the prosecution appeal a "not guilty" verdict?

No. A judge or jury's not guilty verdict is final, even if the verdict seems wrong. But the prosecution can appeal if a judge sets aside a jury's guilty verdict and orders a new trial. (For example, a judge might do this if he or she thinks that evidence favoring the prosecution was improperly admitted or that a jury instruction was erroneous.) In this situation, the prosecution can ask a court of appeal to overturn the new-trial order and reinstate the guilty verdict.

Should a defendant who had a private lawyer at trial use the same lawyer for the appeal?

As a general rule, a convicted defendant should try to find a lawyer who is experienced in appeals. While this may be the same lawyer who tried the case, often attorneys who handle criminal appeals possess a special expertise regarding that process. Also, many appeals challenge the competency of the trial attorney as a reason why the conviction should be overturned.

Are bailed-out defendants allowed to remain free pending the outcome of an appeal?

Defendants who have been at liberty during a trial are usually allowed to remain at liberty pending an appeal. Provisions in some states, however, can require convicted defendants to convince a judge that the conviction hasn't made them a flight risk.

When can a defendant file an appeal?

The general rule is that cases may not be appealed until the trial court enters a final judgment. The entry of judgment is the official recording of the judge or jury's guilty verdict or the judge's order denying any post-trial motions. Not surprisingly, this is known as the "final judgment rule." The policies behind the final judgment rule are to prevent piecemeal and repetitive appellate review of trial judges' rulings, and to avoid appeals altogether in cases that end with not guilty verdicts.

> **EXAMPLE:** Eileen Johnson is on trial for assault with a deadly weapon. During the testimony of a prosecution witness, the judge admits evidence that Eileen's attorney thinks is improper hearsay. Under the final judgment rule, Eileen cannot appeal until the case is over. If Eileen is convicted, Eileen can ask the appellate court to set aside the judgment based on the erroneous admission of hearsay evidence and on any other grounds that may exist.

Are there time limits on the right to appeal?

Appeals are subject to strict time limits. A defendant may have to file a document called a notice of appeal very soon, often within seven to ten days after the entry of the final judgment.

A notice of appeal tells the prosecution and the court that the defendant intends to

---

Self-Representation on Appeal

As mentioned throughout this book, self-representation in a criminal case can be tremendously risky because:

- the rules are complex
- the stakes—liberty or life—can be higher than "just" losing money, as in civil cases, and
- court personnel, judges, and even jurors are often hostile toward self-represented defendants.

These factors are arguably even more evident in appeals, which tend to be more formal and to involve more written work and pickier rules. Appellate courts have requirements for every aspect of appellate practice; written briefs are no exception.

Rules for briefs often specify the number of pages, type and color of paper, binding, size of spacing, and even print type.

For these reasons, and particularly because the law is complex, drafting an appellate brief can be difficult even for an experienced attorney. Counsel may have to undertake extensive legal research to effectively understand and make appropriate references to necessary statutes, court cases, and administrative regulations, and sometimes even the state or federal constitution. Appellate courts also have their own sets of rules for oral arguments, which may differ from the rules in trial courts.

appeal. Defendants who later change their minds may withdraw notices of appeal without penalty, but if they don't first file their notices in time, they will likely have lost their right to appeal.

How long will the whole appeal process take?

The appeals process usually takes many months. A trial transcript must be prepared, and both the defense and prosecution prepare briefs setting forth legal arguments, and respond to each other's briefs. Also, some cases go through two or even three levels of appellate courts.

What does it mean to "make a good record" for appeal?

Appellate court judges do not consider new evidence. Their rulings are based only on the trial court "record." A record includes such materials as a transcript of testimony, documents or other exhibits that the trial judge admitted into evidence, pre- and posttrial motions, and the parties' arguments. A record can also include information that the parties unsuccessfully sought to introduce into evidence.

Thus, to make a good record is to put before the trial court judge all the information that a defendant wants an appellate court judge to have when deciding whether to reverse a guilty verdict or sentencing decision. In addition to offering all the testimony and documents supporting their claims, the actions that defense attorneys can take to produce a good trial court record include:

- **Make offers of proof.** An offer of proof typically consists of a summary of the testimony that a witness will give if the judge allows the witness to testify. If the trial court judge rules that the testimony is inadmissible, making an offer of proof provides an appellate court with a basis for determining the ruling was wrong.

- **Translate gestures into words.** If a court reporter can't transcribe testimony, an appellate court judge may be unable to determine its meaning or admissibility. For example, assume that a witness testifies, "I was standing this close to her," and holds up his hands to indicate the distance. The distance may be clear to everyone in the courtroom, but not to appellate court judges who are limited to what appears on the record. To make a good record, a lawyer should translate the gesture into words: "For the record, the witness is holding his hands about two feet apart."

- **Make all legitimate objections and arguments.** As a general rule, appellate court judges ignore objections and arguments that are made for the first time on appeal. The idea is that if the trial court judge doesn't have a chance to rule on the admissibility of the adversary's evidence, the defendant has given up the right to argue on appeal that the evidence should not have been allowed. (The "plain error rule" is an exception to this requirement. If the trial court judge makes an obvious mistake that affects a defendant's substantial rights and the integrity of the trial process, an appellate court may reverse a conviction even though the defendant failed to object during the trial. (See Federal Rule of Evidence 103(e).))

EXAMPLE: A prosecution witness, the alleged victim Suzie Fels, sneers at the defendant Andrew Williams while he is testifying. Suzie mouths in a whisper (so the court reporter can't hear) to the jury, "Evil man ... I hope he hangs." The defense attorney should recite what happened "for the record." The attorney may say something like, "Your Honor, let the record reflect that the witness is making faces at my client and whispering to the jury. Please instruct the witness to stop that prejudicial behavior and instruct the jury to disregard her actions and statements." Unless the witness's misconduct is a matter of record, an appellate court will not consider it.

What happens after the filing of a notice of appeal?

Once the defense files a notice of appeal, a transcript of the trial is prepared and sent to the appellate court and the parties. Then the appellate court schedules the dates for submission of legal briefs (written arguments). The appellate court may also schedule a date for oral argument, should the parties want to appear before the judges personally to supplement their written arguments and respond to questions the judges may have.

What do "appellant" and "appellee" mean?

When the appellate process starts, the defendant is usually called the "appellant" or "petitioner." And the government is called the "appellee" or "respondent."

What information do appellate courts consider when ruling on an appeal?

An appellate court will not look at new evidence or hear witnesses. Unlike trial courts that decide issues of fact (deciding who is telling the truth or what happened), appellate courts decide issues of law. Appellate judges consider a transcript, exhibits, and the parties' briefs and decide whether to affirm, overturn, or modify the trial court results.

What goes into a written appellate brief?

Briefs typically refer to:

- Specific parts of the trial transcript. (Appellate judges might look only at those portions of the record cited in the briefs.)
- Statutes and previous court opinions that the parties rely on as authority for the appellate court to uphold or overturn the trial judge's rulings. Lawyers develop the arguments in briefs by doing legal research into how other courts have decided similar legal problems and then applying the reasoning in these earlier decisions to the present case.

Typically there are three briefs in an appeal from a criminal case:

- The appellant files an opening brief.
- The respondent files a responding brief.
- The appellant files a reply brief.

What happens after the briefs are written and filed?

After briefs are filed, the lawyers may have the opportunity to appear before the appellate court to orally argue the appeal. It is an increasingly common practice, however, for courts to decide appeals on the briefs and trial record without hearing argument. If an oral argument does take place, it will likely be limited in time—from a few minutes in some state appellate courts to 30 minutes in some federal courts. Because both sides will have submitted their arguments in writing ahead of time, the appellate judges will know what the issues are and often limit the discussion to specific questions. An appellate court may take days, weeks, or even months to decide an appellate case.

If an appellate court decides that an error occurred during the trial, will a conviction be reversed?

Often, the answer is, "No." As appellate court judges sometimes say, "Defendants are entitled to fair trials, but not perfect ones." Appellate courts reverse guilty verdicts only if a trial court error affected a "substantial right" of a party. (See Federal Rule of Evidence 103.) An error that affects a party's substantial right is called a "reversible error." Appellate courts do not usually rule that errors are reversible, so only a very small percentage of convictions are reversed on appeal.

Appellate court judges deem most errors to be "harmless." A harmless error is one that does not affect a party's substantial right. For example, assume that despite the defendant's objection, a trial judge allows a prosecutor to offer improper hearsay evidence connecting a defendant to a crime. If the prosecution's properly admitted evidence leaves no doubt of the defendant's guilt, the appellate court will probably rule that the trial judge's error was harmless.

Appellate court judges apply a much stricter test when a trial court error affects one of a defendant's constitutional rights. In this situation, the rule is that an appellate court will reverse a conviction unless the prosecution can establish beyond a reasonable doubt that the error did not contribute to the guilty verdict. For example, assume that a trial judge admitted tangible evidence that the appellate court determines was seized from the defendant in violation of the Fourth Amendment. The appellate court will reverse the conviction unless the judges are convinced beyond a reasonable doubt that the jurors would have convicted the defendant in the absence of the unconstitutionally seized evidence.

Sentences are a different matter. When a trial judge has discretion over the type or length of sentence, an appellate court will rarely reverse the judge's sentencing decision, and then only if the judge committed an abuse of discretion. However, if a sentence is legally improper, the appellate court will either correct the error itself or send the case back to the trial court for resentencing. For example, a familiar rule provides that a defendant can be punished only once for engaging in a criminal act, even if that act results in convictions for separate crimes. If a trial court judge were to mistakenly punish a defendant separately for each conviction that was based on a single criminal act, an appellate court would rectify the mistake itself or order the trial court judge to do so.

Do appellate court decisions that change the law apply retroactively to cases that ended before the law was changed?

When the U.S. Supreme Court changes the law, defendants whose cases ended before the change went into effect may seek to reopen their cases so that they can benefit from the change. As a general rule, however, U.S. Supreme Court rulings do not apply retroactively. (*Teague v. Lane*, U.S. Sup. Ct. 1989.) The Constitution does not require retroactivity, and judges are worried about the huge disruptive impact on the criminal justice system that routine retroactive application of new rulings would cause.

For example, in *Miranda v. Arizona* (U.S. Sup. Ct. 1966), the U.S. Supreme Court established the rule that confessions are admissible in evidence at trial only if police officers advised suspects of their "*Miranda* rights" before questioning them. Thousands of criminal defendants had been convicted based in part on confessions in response to police questioning that did not comply with *Miranda*. The U.S. Supreme Court ruled that *Miranda* did not apply retroactively. (*Johnson v. New Jersey* (U.S. Sup. Ct. 1966).) Defendants whose cases were final before *Miranda* was decided could not challenge their convictions based on the failure of the police to advise them of their "*Miranda* rights."

Exceptions to the general policy against retroactivity exist. For example, the U.S. Supreme Court ruled in 2012 that mandatory life sentences with no possibility of parole were unconstitutional when imposed on defendants who were juveniles when they committed their crimes. In *Montgomery v. Louisiana* (U.S. Sup. Ct. 2016), the Court made this rule retroactive so that prisoners whose cases were final could petition to have the "no possibility of parole" portion of their sentences removed. And in *Welch v. United States* (U.S. Sup. Ct. 2016) the Court ruled that prisoners who had been given harsher sentences for committing what were considered "violent felonies" under a federal law could apply retroactively for sentence reductions. (The Court had decided in 2015's *Johnson v. U.S.* that the term "violent felony" was unconstitutionally vague.)

For more on "retroactivity," see the "Writs" section, below.

Writs

While appeals can be taken only from final judgments, writs are "extraordinary" requests that allow defendants to seek help from a higher court before a trial has concluded.

What is a writ?

The word "writ" traces its roots to English common law. In Merrie Olde England, a writ was a letter, often written by an attorney. The word "writ" came to describe types of legal court claims. There were different kinds of writs for different actions—writs to recover land or personal property, writs to enforce judgments, and writs to seek damages for broken contracts. Most of the common law writs have been abolished and replaced by the civil claims that exist today, such as tort and breach-of-contract claims.

For the purposes of this chapter, the word "writ" means an order. For example, an "original writ" in old England was a letter from the king to the local sheriff ordering someone who committed a wrong to either make repairs to the person wronged or appear in court to face formal accusations. In this context, the original writ is most like a "summons" ordering a party to appear in court.

In most modern American jurisdictions, a writ is an order from a higher court to a lower court or to a government official, such as a prison warden. Defendants may seek several types of writs from appellate judges directed at the trial court or at a lower appellate court. (Many states have two levels of appellate courts—an intermediate appellate court and the state supreme court.) This section provides an overview about common writs. Writs, like appeals, are complex and involve picky details. Defendants facing situations in which they may be entitled to take a writ should consult counsel.

What's the difference between a writ and an appeal?

Writs usually are considered to be extraordinary remedies, meaning they are permitted only when the defendant has no other adequate remedy, such as an appeal. In other words, a defendant may take a writ to contest a point that the defendant is not entitled to appeal. Any one of the following reasons, for example, may prohibit an appeal (and justify a writ):

- The defense did not lodge a timely objection at the time of the alleged injustice.
- The matter at issue concerns something that goes beyond the trial record.
- A final judgment has not yet been entered in the trial court, but the party seeking the writ needs relief at once to prevent injustice or unnecessary expense.
- The matter is urgent. Writs are heard more quickly than appeals, so defendants who feel wronged by actions of the trial judge may need to take a writ to obtain an early review by a higher court.

- The defendant has already lodged an unsuccessful appeal. (Defendants may file multiple writs, but have the right to appeal only once.)

Suspension of the Great Writ

During the Civil War, President Lincoln suspended the right of *habeas corpus*, pursuant to Article 1, Section 9 of the U.S. Constitution. Generals in the field thus had authority to arrest and keep people in custody whom they considered "threats to public safety"; those arrested no longer had the right they previously enjoyed to challenge the legality of their imprisonment in the court system.

In the aftermath of the September 11, 2001, terrorist attacks, the Bush administration also curtailed the right of *habeas corpus*. So-called terrorists who were classified as enemy combatants had no right to question their detention in court until a special "combatant status review tribunal" reviewed their status. In the case of *Boumediene v. Bush* (U.S. Sup. Ct. 2008), the Supreme Court declared this policy invalid and ruled that terrorism suspects had the right to file writs of *habeas corpus* in federal court to challenge the lawfulness of their detention. This ruling potentially affected the rights of some 270 people arrested for suspected terrorist activities, some of whom had been imprisoned as long as six years without a court hearing to review their imprisonment.

What is a writ of *habeas corpus*?

Defendants who want to challenge the legality of their imprisonment—or the conditions in which they are being imprisoned—may seek help from a court by filing what is known as a petition for "writ of *habeas corpus*."

A writ of *habeas corpus* (literally to "produce the body") is a court order to a person (such as a prison warden) or an agency (such as a prison) holding someone in custody to deliver the imprisoned individual to the court issuing the order. Many state constitutions provide for writs of *habeas corpus*, as does the United States Constitution, which specifically forbids the government from suspending writ proceedings except in extraordinary times—such as war. (U.S. Constitution, Article 1, § 9(2).)

Known as "the Great Writ," *habeas corpus* gives citizens the power to get help from courts to keep government and any other institutions that may imprison people in check. In many countries, police and military personnel, for example, may lock people up for months—even years—without charging them, and those imprisoned have no legal channel by which to protest or challenge the imprisonment. The writ of *habeas corpus* gives jailed suspects the right to ask an appellate judge to set them free or order an end to improper jail conditions, and thereby ensures that people in this country will not be held for long periods in prison in violation of their rights. Of course, the right to ask for relief is not the same as the right to get relief; courts are very stingy when it comes to granting writs.

 CAUTION

Rules governing writs are complex and changing. Defendants seeking review through writs, especially writs of *habeas corpus*, must be aware that the rules governing these proceedings are even more complex than the rules governing appeals, and the law in this area changes frequently. A defendant should consult an experienced attorney for an explanation of the applicable law.

EXAMPLE: Defendant Ed Ippus was convicted of murder. He contends that the only reason he was convicted was that his attorney, Johnny Baily, was incompetent. The basis for Ed's contentions is that his attorney came to court drunk every day during the trial, thus depriving Ed of his Sixth Amendment right to effective assistance of counsel. Ed can petition for a writ of *habeas corpus* to ask a court to consider this argument even if the trial court transcript does not reveal that counsel was intoxicated. In response to the petition, an appellate court has jurisdiction to consider this argument, and if appropriate, grant Ed a new trial.

What is the connection between the writ of *habeas corpus* and the exoneration of wrongfully convicted prisoners?

Writs of habeas corpus have resulted in the exoneration of numerous wrongly convicted prisoners. Often prepared by lawyers working on a pro bono basis on behalf of organizations known as Innocence Projects, the writs enable prisoners to put evidence before judges to prove that they are factually innocent and never should have been convicted. Often this evidence comes to light many years after a conviction occurs, such that the writ of *habeas corpus* is a prisoner's only way to ask a judge to consider the evidence.

Newly discovered evidence that proves a prisoner's factual innocence often consists of:

- DNA test results proving that a prisoner was not at a crime scene
- eyewitnesses admitting that their testimony was false
- evidence proving that eyewitnesses were mistaken or unreliable, or
- evidence that the prosecution concealed from the defense vital evidence that undermines the reliability of the conviction.

Many factually innocent and exonerated prisoners are released only after they have spent many years behind bars. They include:

- Michael Hanline, who was freed at age 69 after serving 36 years in prison for a murder that he did not commit. Hanline's DNA did not match the DNA found at the crime scene, and the prosecution's key witness was discredited.
- Ricky Jackson, who was freed after serving 39 years in prison for murder. The conviction was based on the testimony of a single 12-year-old eyewitness who later admitted he did not see the crime take place.

- Susan Mellen, who was freed after serving 17 years in prison for murder after the prosecution's principal witness was proven to be a habitual liar who had committed perjury in a number of cases.

Can *habeas corpus* be used for anything other than freeing prisoners from custody?

In recent decades, defendants have filed increasing numbers of *habeas corpus* petitions requesting new and unusual forms of relief. For example, defendants have filed writs (successfully or unsuccessfully) to:

- reduce or set bail
- speed up an arraignment
- contest denial of a jury trial
- challenge a conviction when not informed of the right to counsel at pretrial proceedings, and
- contest prison overcrowding, excessive solitary confinement, and other prison conditions.

Can a prisoner file a *habeas corpus* petition in federal court to challenge the validity of a state court conviction?

Federal law (28 U.S.C. § 2254) permits people convicted in state court to file a habeas corpus petition in federal court, claiming that the conviction or one of its legal consequences (such as the sentence or prison conditions) violates federal law or the U.S. Constitution. Federal judges, including the U.S. Supreme Court, tend to be reluctant to interfere with state court criminal proceedings. As a result, federal judges reject the vast majority of *habeas corpus*

challenges to state court convictions. Federal court judges generally act only when a lot is at stake and an error is extreme.

> **EXAMPLE:** A federal judge cannot grant a *habeas corpus* petitioner's request to set aside a state court conviction on the ground that the evidence was insufficient to support the conviction if any rational jury could have found the defendant guilty. (*Coleman v. Johnson*, U.S. Sup. Ct. 2012.)

> **EXAMPLE:** A state court prisoner on death row lost a chance to challenge the legality of his conviction in state court because the attorneys who had filed the petition for state court review abandoned the case without notifying either the prisoner or the court. (The attorneys' abandonment caused the prisoner to miss a critical filing deadline.) The prisoner filed a petition for *habeas corpus* in federal court, asking a federal court judge to order the state court to consider his claim on its merits. The U.S. Supreme Court allowed the prisoner to pursue his effort to overturn his conviction because he lost the right to seek state court review through no fault of his own. (*Maples v. Thomas*, U.S. Sup. Ct. 2012.)

Custody Doesn't Only Mean Jail

A person doesn't have to be in jail or prison to use the writ of *habeas corpus*. A defendant committed to a mental institution, for example, after pleading not guilty by reason of insanity, may also use the writ of *habeas corpus* to contest an illegal commitment or unlawful conditions.

Potential Post-Conviction Processes

As discussed in this chapter, convicted defendants can take a number of steps to challenge guilty verdicts and/or to correct violations of rights. The following nonexclusive list illustrates many of these steps, which can add up to years.

- **Motion for Acquittal.** Requests that the judge decide that there is not enough evidence to convict the defendant. Depending on the court's rules and whether the trial is before a judge or a jury, this motion may be made either after the prosecution presents its evidence or after all the evidence is presented.
- **Motion for a New Trial.** Requests that the trial judge declare a mistrial and grant a new trial.
- **Appeal to State Appellate Court.** Contends that the trial judge made reversible legal errors.
- **Petition for Rehearing to State Appeals Court.** Requests that appeals court judges change their own decision.
- **State Supreme Court Appeal.** Requests that the highest court in the state review and overturn the decision of the trial court or the midlevel appeals court.

- **U.S. Supreme Court Appeal.** Requests that the highest court in the nation intervene to correct an error on the part of the state courts that violates the U.S. Constitution.
- **State Court *Habeas Corpus* Petition.** Requests that the state appeals courts order the jail or prison holding the defendant to release the defendant upon a showing that he is being held in violation of some state law or constitutional right.
- **Federal *Habeas Corpus* Petition to District Court.** Requests the federal trial court to order the jail or prison holding the defendant to release him because he is being held in violation of the U.S. Constitution or federal law.
- **Appeal of Federal *Habeas Corpus* Petition to Circuit Court.** Requests the midlevel federal court to review the federal trial court's decision denying the writ.
- **Appeal of Federal *Habeas Corpus* Petition to U.S. Supreme Court.** Requests the highest court in the land to review the midlevel federal court's decision denying the writ.

What other writs might be relevant to a case?

The writ of prohibition and the writ of *mandamus* are also sometimes used in criminal cases. These writs, often used together and sometimes interchangeably, are complements of one another. The writ of prohibition is an order from an appellate court to the trial court to halt a particular action, such as a trial. A writ of *mandamus* (also known as a writ of mandate) orders a lower court to do something (such as move a trial to a different venue). The purpose of both writs is in essence to keep lower courts (and others affected) from exceeding their lawful jurisdiction.

Because of their similarity to appeals, writs are discussed in this chapter on post-conviction proceedings. But parties may take a writ (apply to an appellate court for relief through a writ proceeding) before, during, or after a trial.

> **EXAMPLE:** Rodney Prince, facing charges of resisting arrest, objects to the trial judge's ruling preventing him from gaining access to relevant portions of the arresting officer's personnel file. Prince submitted affidavits as his basis for believing that the file contained information about numerous incidents in which the arresting officer, Noah Kontrol, had been reprimanded for beating suspects. In order to effectively raise his defense that he was forced to resist Kontrol because he was scared for his life, Prince wants access to the personnel file. Prince may be able to overturn the trial judge's ruling by requesting a writ of *mandamus* from an appellate court. If the court grants the writ, Prince can gain access to the personnel file in time to identify evidence that will be admissible at trial.

Can a writ of *habeas corpus* be used to challenge the legality of a conviction based on a rule that came into effect after the defendant's conviction?

As U.S. Supreme Court decisions aren't always retroactive (*Teague v. Lane*, U.S. Sup. Ct. 1989), a prisoner cannot normally use the federal writ of *habeas corpus* to take advantage of a change in the law that occurred after a case became final.

For example, in *Danforth v. Minnesota* (U.S. Sup. Ct. 2008), the Court observed that the interpretation of the Sixth Amendment's Confrontation Clause that it adopted in *Crawford v. Washington* (U.S. Sup. Ct. 2004) was not retroactive. Therefore, the Court said, prisoners whose convictions were final before *Crawford* was decided could not obtain *habeas corpus* relief based on *Crawford* in federal court. But the Court noted in *Danforth* that the petitioner in that case could seek relief in state court.

For more on "retroactivity" and exceptions to it, see the "Appeals" section earlier in this chapter.

Victims and Their Rights

Though identifiable victims—rather than society at large—suffer the most serious effects of crime, the criminal justice process has traditionally left them on the outside looking in. For instance, various provisions of the Bill of Rights protect the rights of criminal defendants, but none mention the rights of crime victims. This chapter focuses on basic rights of crime victims and their role in the prosecution of criminal cases. (In addition to the information in this chapter, other parts of this book briefly discuss victims' rights and roles in the criminal justice process, and some of these parts list victim resources.)

Victims and the Criminal Justice System

This section reviews the general role of crime victims in the criminal justice system.

Were victims ever in charge of prosecuting offenders?

Yes. As late as the early 20th century, in parts of the United States, the prosecution of criminals was largely a private matter. The system reflected a now-bygone belief that crimes were wrongs against individuals rather than against society as a whole. When governments took over the prosecutorial duties, crime victims went from center stage to inconvenient bit players who created inefficiencies for the professionals: judges, district attorneys, and other prosecutors who controlled the criminal justice system. But the role of victims began to expand with the advent of the victims' rights movement in the 1970s.

EXAMPLE: An electronics store security guard watches as Red Handed leaves the store with stolen items concealed in his clothes. The guard detains Red and calls the police. At the guard's direction, an officer takes Red into custody. The guard's "citizen's arrest" of Red is a vestige of the earlier era when victims prosecuted offenders.

What is a Victims' Bill of Rights?

"Victims' Bill of Rights" laws legitimate and formalize the role of crime victims in the criminal justice process. "Marsy's Law" is one such law; its backers seek to have it included in the constitutions of all states and ultimately in the U.S. Constitution. Proponents of Marsy's Law argue that victims should have equivalent rights to those who have been accused or convicted of crimes. Critics of the law argue that many of the rights already exist and that constitutions are for broad policies—not the day-to-day minutiae of the criminal justice process. The specified rights for victims vary from one state to another and even among localities in the same state. For example, a state's victims' rights laws may apply only to felony cases, only to serious cases, or only to cases involving crimes of violence. And many of the rights are procedural—for example, they require notice to victims of the progress of cases and invite input from victims at various stages. Importantly, these laws generally don't require that judges and prosecutors defer to victims' views.

Among the rights commonly extended to victims are the right to:

- notice of a defendant's arrest
- notice of an arraignment/bail hearing
- notice of a defendant's release on bail
- consult with a prosecutor in connection with a negotiated plea (plea bargaining)
- notice of a plea agreement
- remain in the courtroom throughout a trial even if a judge orders the exclusion ("sequestration") of other witnesses
- address the judge concerning a prosecutor's or defendant's request to continue (delay) proceedings to a later date
- address the court as to the impact of a crime on the victim and the victim's family, and as to an appropriate sentence, and
- obtain an order of restitution from the perpetrator and seek compensation from the state.

Can crime victims compel prosecutors to file criminal charges?

No. Prosecutors have wide discretion when it comes to deciding which cases to prosecute. Procedures in a very few states hearken back to the Middle Ages by allowing some victims to proceed with criminal charges as "private prosecutors." Other than in these few states, victims generally have recourse only to the civil courts. In those courts, for example, victims can often sue, and some victims may also be able to obtain protective or restraining orders against perpetrators.

(Victims can seek these remedies even when the offenders who harmed them are prosecuted.)

Pretrial Processes

This section describes the role of crime victims during common pretrial phases of criminal proceedings.

What generally happens after a crime is reported to the police?

The events that take place after the police receive a crime report vary greatly depending on, among other factors, the severity of the crime. A police officer's first duty is to arrange for medical help for an injured victim, and often for a suspect as well. After ensuring victim safety, officers seek information and try to apprehend offenders. During an investigation, police officers may talk to victims, witnesses, and professionals like forensic experts. Victims must do their best to provide accurate information to the police, in part because the defense has a right of access to their statements after the filing of charges.

Following a quick arrest, a police officer might return with the suspect to the crime scene and ask the victim whether the apprehended person is the perpetrator.

This is called a "showup." Officers might otherwise ask victims to aid identification by looking at photos in "mug books" or viewing lineups.

In theft cases, the police often ask victims to identify recovered property. The property constitutes evidence of the crime, and the prosecutor might need it if the case goes to trial. As a result, the police might hang onto it until a case concludes.

Prosecutors take over from police officers following a suspect's arrest. Prosecutors, not police officers or crime victims, decide what, if any, criminal charges are warranted. (Where utilized, grand juries are part of the charging process.) Depending on the severity of a crime and a state's victims' rights laws, prosecutors might consult victims before filing or dropping charges. A victim's unwillingness to cooperate can affect the prosecution's charging decision.

> **EXAMPLE:** A police officer issues a misdemeanor citation to Hatfield based on a claim by nextdoor neighbor McCoy. McCoy asserts that Hatfield vandalized McCoy's newly built fence. McCoy later asks the prosecutor's office to drop the case because Hatfield apologized and paid to repair the fence. The private settlement (often called a "civil compromise") and the minor nature of the crime persuade the prosecution not to charge Hatfield.

> **EXAMPLE:** The police respond to Ophelia's cries for help and arrest her live-in boyfriend Brutus for domestic violence. The next day, Ophelia tells the prosecutor that Brutus didn't do anything wrong and that she doesn't want him prosecuted. As domestic violence is a priority crime and victims often try to protect their violent attackers, the prosecutor is very likely to ignore Ophelia's request and charge Brutus with domestic violence.

Are charging decisions solely for prosecutors to make?

In some states, prosecutors decide on their own whether to file charges. Other states require or allow prosecutors to secure indictments (documents that lay out criminal charges) from grand juries, at least in felony cases. Victims are typically subpoenaed to testify under oath if a prosecutor brings a case to a grand jury.

What involvement in a prosecution can crime victims expect after criminal charges are filed?

After the filing of charges, a victim may be notified of the time and place of the defendant's court appearances, such as for setting of bail, arraignment, and hearings on motions. But victims typically have no formalized role to play in pretrial court proceedings like these. The small percentage of victims who do attend simply do so as observers.

Defense lawyers or their investigators (though not defendants personally) often seek to interview crime victims. Victims can talk to defendants' representatives if they want to, but aren't legally obliged to do so. Prosecutors do not represent victims and cannot ethically instruct them not to cooperate with the defense.

Can defendants find out where victims live and work?

Virtually all Victims' Bill of Rights laws provide for the privacy of victims' personal contact information. Defense attorneys generally may not disclose this information to their clients. Crime victims may also obtain restraining orders that order defendants (and on a showing of good cause, other specified persons) not to contact or be in close proximity to victims and their family members.

What is a victim's role in a preliminary hearing?

Preliminary hearings typically take place in felony cases when prosecutors file charges without first presenting evidence to a grand jury. At "prelims," prosecutors have to present sufficient evidence for a judge (not a jury) to conclude that "probable cause" exists that the defendant committed a crime.

Traditionally, victims have testified under oath at preliminary hearings and been subject to cross-examination by the defense. However, in an effort to make pretrial proceedings less burdensome for victims, many states allow the prosecution to call a police officer rather than the victim as a witness. The officer then testifies to the circumstances of the crime based on the victim's statements. (Both the hearsay rule and the Sixth Amendment typically prevent prosecutors from offering evidence this way at trial.)

> **EXAMPLE:** A nine-year-old boy is the victim in a child abuse prosecution. The boy's mother doesn't want her son to testify at trial and asks the prosecutor to call a police officer instead to testify to her son's description of what happened. The police officer may be able to testify to the boy's statements during a preliminary hearing. But the Sixth Amendment to the federal Constitution, as interpreted by U.S. Supreme Court decisions, disallows this procedure at trial. But, though the boy has to testify, the judge may allow him to do so in a private room with the mother and lawyers present and the defendant watching the testimony via feed from another location.

What happens if a case ends with a plea bargain?

Only a small percentage of criminal cases go to trial. Most are resolved with pretrial plea bargains (or "plea agreements") in which defendants plead guilty (or *nolo contendere*) to reduced charges or in exchange for reduced punishments. State laws often require prosecutors to consult with victims before entering into plea agreements.

Before sentencing defendants who plead guilty, judges often ask probation officers to prepare presentence reports. This kind of report describes a defendant's background and the circumstances giving rise to the charges. State laws often require probation officers to contact victims and include information from them in presentence reports.

The Trial-and-Sentencing Process

This section reviews a victim's role at trial and during sentencing.

Do special rules apply to trial testimony by crime victims?

Generally, no. The same evidentiary rules and procedures that apply to other witnesses also apply to the testimony of crime victims. In especially sensitive cases (such as child abuse prosecutions), judges often allow victims to testify privately with only the judge and attorneys present, and the defendant observing electronically from a remote location.

Will a sequestration order prevent a victim from being inside the courtroom throughout a trial?

Generally, no. Sequestration orders typically include two components:

- Witnesses cannot be present inside the courtroom until after they have testified.
- Witnesses cannot discuss their testimony with other witnesses.

Sequestration orders typically instruct victims not to discuss testimony with other witnesses. However, the orders generally allow victims to be present in the courtroom at all stages of a trial.

Can victims' family members and friends attend court proceedings?

Yes. Except in unusual circumstances, courts and trials are open to the public. Victims' family members and friends can attend but cannot dress or act disruptively.

> **EXAMPLE:** Members of a victim's family attending the trial audibly gasp in sorrow while the victim testifies to his injuries. They wear big buttons showing a close-up of the injuries to the victim's face that allegedly resulted from the defendant's attack. A judge

will likely view the loud verbal reactions and the buttons as an improper attempt to influence the jury. The victim's family members wouldn't be allowed to wear the buttons inside the courtroom or anywhere else in and around the courthouse where jurors might see them. The judge could order the removal of the supporters who reacted loudly and noticeably to testimony. In extreme circumstances, the judge might even terminate the case by declaring a mistrial.

What is a victim impact statement?

For victims (or in a homicide case, a family member), victim impact statements are an opportunity for victims to tell judges about the effect of crimes on their lives. While victims may submit written statements, victim impact statements are typically made orally during a sentencing hearing, prior to the pronouncement of a sentence. Victims (and sometimes family members and friends) can talk freely about the physical, emotional, and financial impacts of a crime on their lives. Regardless of whether a statement affects a sentence, victims may feel a measure of closure and psychological healing by making a statement. (For more, see Chapter 22.)

Is a restitution order the same as a fine?

No. Convicted offenders pay fines to the government. The purpose of restitution orders is for a perpetrator to compensate a victim for financial losses directly attributable to the perpetrator's crime.

How do restitution orders help victims?

As part of a sentence, judges often order defendants to make victims financially "whole" for financial losses directly attributable to the crime for which the defendant was convicted. For example, a restitution order may order:

- a defendant convicted of embezzling funds from a former employer to repay the funds
- a defendant convicted of stealing a work of art to return it or its value to the owner, or
- a defendant convicted of assault and battery to pay the victim for lost wages and for the expenses of counseling and physical rehabilitation.

Restitution orders are enforceable in civil courts. But, as the old saying goes, it's impossible to "squeeze blood out of a turnip." A defendant who is broke ("judgment proof") cannot be jailed for inability to comply with a restitution order.

> **EXAMPLE:** Paroline was convicted of having two widely circulated pornographic pictures of a child sexual abuse victim on his computer. Paroline's responsibility to pay restitution to the now-young-adult victim is limited by the degree to which he alone contributed to her losses. (Here, those losses are expenses for treatment and counseling, lost income, and attorney expenses.) Paroline is liable only for his role—not the roles of all the other Internet users whose possession of the same photos harmed the victim. In

reaching this conclusion, the U.S. Supreme Court admitted that its approach was "not without difficulties" for trial judges trying to fashion an appropriate restitution order. (*Paroline v. United States*, U.S. Sup. Ct. 2014.)

Posttrial Processes

This section discusses some victims' rights after a case concludes.

How do victim compensation laws protect crime victims?

When criminal defendants are indigent, restitution orders are of no help to victims. But all states have enacted compensation laws that may—at least in part—restore some of a victim's financial losses. (Victims may be able to seek compensation before a case has concluded or if the police have been unable to make an arrest.) While these laws differ in scope from one state to another, most of them focus on victims of violent crimes like assault, rape, and domestic violence. Compensation is also typically available to families of homicide victims. For general information, visit the website of the National Association of Crime Victim Compensation Boards (www.nacvcb.org).

Can a victim seek compensation even if a perpetrator is never found?

Yes. Compensation does not depend on the arrest or successful prosecution of a perpetrator.

What are state compensation funds?

Most states have compensation funds from which victims can seek compensation for financial losses attributable to crimes.

Victims typically have to apply to the state agency that administers a victim compensation fund within a specified amount of time following the commission of a crime. Victims have to provide records supporting their claims, including the amount and type of out-of-pocket losses. Victims may have to meet other requirements, too, such as having cooperated in the crime's investigation. Depending on the state, either an administrative agency or a judicial officer determines the amount of compensation.

Victims are not entitled to compensation for expenses covered by outside sources, such as workers' compensation or private insurance.

Are victims notified of the time and place of parole hearings?

Generally, the answer is yes—and crime victims can typically participate in the hearings. They can talk about the continuing impact of a crime and the likely effect of parole on their lives. But parole boards aren't bound to accede to victims' opinions.

EXAMPLE: R served 27 years in prison for a drug-related murder. While in prison he turned his life around with the help of CGA (Criminals and Gangmembers Anonymous). The mother of R's victim attended R's parole hearing and told the hearing officers that though she felt the loss of her son during every waking moment, she had forgiven R and had no objection to his release on parole. Based on the mother's statements and R's prison record, R was granted parole. Over six years into his parole, R remains sober and steadily employed, and he remains in touch with the mother. R celebrates sober birthdays annually, and each year he dedicates his cake and his life to his victim and the mother who helped him obtain parole.

Are victims notified of prisoners' release from incarceration?

Generally, no—unless the crime was a serious felony and the victim filled out a form that may be called a "Request for Notification of Release."

VINELink (www.vinelink.com) is a national victim notification registry that provides registrants with information about the release of prisoners, prisoners' movement from one prison to another, and other related matters. Visitors to the VINELink website with confidentiality concerns should be aware that VINELink is a privately operated website.

The System at Work: DUI Laws and Processes

This chapter is a step-by-step description of two criminal cases. Both defendants are charged with "DUI," driving under the influence of alcohol or drugs. As so often happens in the justice system, the cases end with guilty pleas.

The preceding chapters have focused on distinct aspects of the criminal justice process, so this chapter is an opportunity to examine the system as a whole.

DUI (Driving Under the Influence)

Driving under the influence of alcohol or other substances is a common but often misunderstood crime.

Are there terms other than "DUI" for drunk driving?

States have different terms for DUI. Some of these are:

- DUIL (driving under the influence of liquor)
- DWI (driving while intoxicated)
- OMVI (operating a motor vehicle while intoxicated)
- OWI (operating while intoxicated), and
- OUI (operating under the influence).

What type of behavior describes a DUI offense?

In many states, a DUI offense consists of the following facts (elements):

- driving, operating, or being in physical control of a vehicle (sometimes even sitting behind the wheel will suffice)

- while under the influence of an intoxicating beverage or drug, or with a blood alcohol level that exceeds the legal limit.
- The motor vehicle is typically a car, but a motor vehicle can generally also be a truck, a motorcycle, a boat, a golf cart, a tractor, a bicycle, a horse, and possibly even a skateboard.
- Driving with a blood alcohol concentration of 0.08% or higher constitutes a DUI in all states; some jurisdictions use an even stricter mark of 0.05%. In many jurisdictions, the BAC mark for drivers under the age of 21 is 0.01%.

The Popular Term "Drunk Driving" Misses the Point

Notice the difference between the legal term "driving under the influence" and the more familiar term "drunk driving." The former does not have the word "drunk" in it. This difference can have tremendous legal importance in a criminal case. It means that the prosecution does not have to show the defendant was drunk, but simply that the defendant had consumed enough alcohol or drugs to be affected by it when in control of a motor vehicle. It may in some cases be enough, for example, for the arresting officer to testify that the defendant's breath smelled of alcohol and that the defendant's speech was slurred. Bottom line: What the typical DUI law defines as a crime can differ drastically from the image many people have in mind when they hear the word "drunk."

What are "illegal per se" laws?

With illegal per se laws, defendants whose blood alcohol levels meet or exceed the legal limit (usually, a blood alcohol content of 0.08%) are guilty of a DUI offense, regardless of whether the alcohol has in fact affected their driving or they are actually intoxicated. The only facts (elements) the prosecution has to prove are:

- The defendant was driving, operating, or in physical control of a vehicle (generally, a driver who pulls over to rest is considered still in control of a vehicle).
- At the time the defendant was driving, operating, or in physical control of the vehicle, the defendant's blood alcohol level was at or above the legal limit.

Separately, the prosecution may use the defendant's blood alcohol level as evidence of being "under the influence." But typically, to prove someone was actually under the influence, the prosecution will also provide further evidence either that the person suffered from symptoms of the influence of alcohol (for instance, slurred speech) or was driving poorly in some way (for example, weaving in and out of lanes or following the car in front too closely).

Prosecutors often bring charges under both general driving under the influence laws and per se laws. Then, if the defense pokes holes in one of the approaches (for instance, by showing the testing procedure was faulty or the officer's observations were not trustworthy), the prosecution can still rely on the other approach to secure a conviction.

When might prosecutors reduce a DUI charge to a less serious offense?

Prosecutors' willingness to plea bargain a DUI to a lesser crime, such as reckless driving, normally depends on factors such as:

- How far over the legal limit is a driver's BAC?
- Is the driver a first-time or a repeat offender?
- Was the driver involved in a traffic accident?

A driver who pleads guilty to a lesser offense may be punished less severely. And without a DUI conviction on the record, a driver who is arrested a second time for a DUI offense might be spared the mandatory jail time that a second DUI conviction often entails.

Use of Plea in a Later Civil Trial

Defendants who end up plea bargaining a DUI case in which injuries or property damage occurred usually hope to plead no contest rather than guilty. This is because, in most jurisdictions, a no-contest plea can't be admitted as evidence in a later civil case, whereas a guilty plea can (as an admission of guilt). (But see "The Effect of a No-Contest (*Nolo Contendere*) Plea" in Chapter 10.)

Will a DUI conviction affect driving privileges?

In most states, in addition to criminal proceedings, an accused drunk driver faces administrative proceedings in which the agency in charge of motor vehicles and licenses can take the defendant's driver's license away for a lengthy period of time (often six to 12 months). A state may allow a driver to apply for a restricted license for driving to and from places like work and school.

What is a field sobriety test?

Field sobriety tests, or FSTs, are tests given by police officers to drivers in order to determine if they are driving under the influence of alcohol or drugs. The word "field" means at the scene of the stop (usually the side of the road or highway), as opposed to the station house. The classic FSTs involve the police asking suspected DUI offenders to:

- follow an object such as a pen with their eyes (called the "horizontal gaze by stages" test)
- touch their nose
- stand on one foot
- walk a straight line, and
- recite the alphabet, forward or backward.

Also, the police may conduct blood alcohol tests in the field, using a portable machine that calculates blood alcohol content by analyzing a suspect's breath. Other blood alcohol tests, such as blood or urine tests, are typically done at the police station or a local hospital.

What are blood alcohol tests?

Three commonly used tests measure the amount of alcohol in a suspect's body:

blood, breath, and urine tests. Blood tests directly measure the amount of alcohol in a suspect's bloodstream. Breath and urine tests measure essentially the same thing but do so by using a mathematical formula to convert the percentage of alcohol in the breath or urine to the likely corresponding blood alcohol content. Some states no longer require breath and urine percentages to be converted to blood alcohol content, however. Instead, the laws of those states now define a legal urine alcohol or breath alcohol limit.

There are, of course, a number of variables that can affect the overall accuracy of these tests, including human factors, such as the rate at which different people absorb alcohol, and technical factors, such as the competence of the person performing the tests and the accuracy of the testing machines.

Does a police officer have to obtain a search warrant before administering an alcohol test?

The answer depends on the type of alcohol test. No warrant is necessary in order for an officer to demand that a suspect who's lawfully under arrest for DUI to take a breathalyzer test. The physical intrusion of having to blow air into a mouthpiece is so negligible that the government's interest in traffic safety justifies a warrantless test. But drawing blood requires piercing the skin and is so much more intrusive that ordinarily a police officer can't require a driver to submit to a blood test without first getting a warrant. (*Birchfield v. North*

Dakota, U.S. Sup. Ct. 2016.) But police officers generally don't need a warrant to have medical personnel draw blood from a drunk driving suspect who passes out. The need to run a test before alcohol disappears from the bloodstream is an "exigent circumstance" that normally justifies the warrantless intrusion. (*Mitchell v. Wisconsin*, U.S. Sup. Ct. 2019.)

Do blood alcohol tests violate the Fifth Amendment privilege against self-incrimination?

No. The privilege applies to information that is testimonial in nature, such as answering questions or providing documents. (*Schmerber v. California*, U.S. Sup. Ct. 1966.) Just as suspects don't provide testimonial information when they are fingerprinted or photographed, or when their cheek is swabbed for a DNA sample, they don't provide testimonial information when they undergo blood alcohol testing.

Independent Blood Tests

When police test a defendant's blood, they often take two samples. One is for the police laboratory to analyze, while the other is preserved for possible testing in an independent laboratory at the behest of the defendant. It is often a good idea for the defense to arrange for an independent test.

What are the consequences of refusing to take an alcohol test?

"Implied consent laws" mean that by obtaining a driver's license, a motorist agrees to submit to a police officer's request to take a blood alcohol test in appropriate circumstances. If a motorist refuses to take a test, the potential consequences can be severe even if DUI charges are dropped or the motorist is found not guilty of driving under the influence. For example:

- The state can suspend a motorist's driver's license for a period of time, often for six months to a year.
- In some states, suspects who refuse to take a breath test for blood alcohol can be charged with a crime, typically a misdemeanor.

Implied consent laws allow the government to suspend the licenses of motorists who refuse to take a blood test. However, motorists cannot be criminally punished for refusing to submit to a blood test where there is no warrant. (*Birchfield v. North Dakota*, U.S. Sup. Ct. 2016.)

> **EXAMPLE:** Drivers A and B are pulled over for suspected DUI. The officer doesn't have and doesn't get a warrant. Driver A refuses to take a breath test and Driver B refuses to take a blood test. Depending on state law, Drivers A and B can both have their driving privileges suspended. If state law allows it, Driver A can also be criminally convicted of refusing to take a breath alcohol test, but Driver B cannot be prosecuted for refusing a blood test.

Can people choose which blood alcohol test to take?

The implied consent laws of many states allow drivers to choose whether to take a blood, breath, or urine test. In many states, police officers must advise drivers that they have such a choice.

How can people protect their rights when officers ask them to take a field sobriety test (FST)?

Generally, people have the right to decline an officer's request to perform an FST. But people who do agree to take an FST should do their best to be aware of conditions that may invalidate the results. A driver asked to stand on one foot or walk a straight line should note any road conditions, such as a soft shoulder or incline, that make performing such tests particularly difficult. If any such conditions exist, a driver charged with DUI should report them as soon as possible to his or her lawyer.

And people wearing tight shoes or heels may want to ask the police for permission to remove their shoes before trying to stand on one foot or walk a straight line. Drivers suspected of DUI should never, though, reach down to remove their shoes—or make any other movements for that matter, especially with their hands—without first asking for permission. Such movements may be interpreted by police as an attempt to grab a weapon.

Defense Strategy on Taking the Alcohol Test

Often, if a driver has never before been convicted of DUI, it makes sense to take the test, even if the defendant has been drinking. This is because the penalty for refusal is usually as or more severe than for the DUI offense itself. However, for second or subsequent offenders, the decision is not quite so simple. Sometimes, and of course depending on the state's law, the penalty for a second offense may be so severe that it makes tactical sense to refuse the test and thereby possibly deprive police of the evidence they need to obtain a conviction. As one former public defender confessed, "When arrestees would call me up in the middle of the night to ask whether they should take the BAC test, I had pretty much of a standard routine. I'd first ask if they had in fact been drinking. They'd invariably answer, yeah, but just a couple. I'd then ask if they had ever been busted for DUI before. If not, I told them to take the test. But if they had a prior, I'd tell them to refuse the test. It was the best legal advice I could give under the circumstances."

What type of evidence is used in a typical DUI trial?

Typically, arresting police officers testify in DUI cases. They testify to symptoms they observed, such as a defendant's driving pattern, bloodshot eyes, and the smell of alcoholic beverages on the breath Prosecutors may also introduce documents to prove their case, such as photographs of the scene or people involved, and scientific evidence such as doctor's reports, lab analyses, and blood, breath, or urine test results. The police or arrest report and the officer's notes, while they may not be introduced as evidence in the case, may nonetheless be used to "refresh the officer's recollection" if the officer forgets something in the report.

What should people do if they are involved in a DUI-related accident?

Other than calling for emergency medical assistance (for anyone who is hurt) or filing a report on the accident (in conjunction with an attorney) as may be required by state law, suspects involved in DUI-related accidents should avoid making oral or written statements to:

- **Police officers.** Suspects do not have to and almost always should not talk to the police at length, at least before consulting a lawyer. They should say something along the lines of "I am exercising my right to remain silent."
- **Witnesses or victims.** Even statements like "I'm sorry" can come back to haunt a defendant, because in court they can sound like admissions of wrongdoing. (Laws in some states exclude expressions of regret from evidence. Judges may do so on their own in states that don't have such laws.)

As soon as possible after the accident, defendants should write down their version of what happened and note the date and time of the writing (perhaps also mailing a copy of the statement to themselves in order to retain a postmark with the date on it). At the top of any such statement, defendants should write "Privileged and Confidential Document—For My Attorney Only," and they should not show the document to anyone except their attorney.

What are the chances of defeating a DUI charge in court?

Defendants whose blood alcohol tested clearly above the legal limit seldom win at trial, especially if they also failed field sobriety tests. If there is no blood test, or the test results are at or below the limit, there is a much greater chance of successfully fighting the charges.

Though many prosecutors' offices are tough on DUI cases, skilled defense lawyers (sometimes aided by forensic experts) can sometimes get an acquittal by undermining the prosecutor's case. For instance, some defense lawyers routinely request maintenance and accuracy records for breathalyzer machines and may mount a successful defense if the machine has not been properly serviced or calibrated.

What sentences are typically handed down for violating DUI laws?

DUI sentences vary greatly depending on factors such as whether it's a first-time or repeat offense and whether or not anyone was injured. But, as with many crimes, the typical sentence includes a fine and perhaps a few days of jail time. Convicted defendants may also suffer other consequences. For instance, they may:

- lose their driver's license, at least temporarily
- have to participate in an alcohol- or drug-related treatment program
- see their car insurance rates climb astronomically, and
- have a breath test device (called a certified ignition interlock device) installed in their cars—at their own expense—which prevents the car from being started if alcohol is detected.

Does a previous DUI conviction affect the severity of the sentence in a new case?

Repeat DUI offenders are routinely sentenced more severely than first offenders, with jail time often mandatory. State law determines how long ago a prior DUI conviction must have happened to not count as a "prior" for sentencing purposes. For instance, a case that ended more than ten years ago might not count as a prior.

Are there defense lawyers who specialize in DUI cases?

Yes. A general criminal defense lawyer may not be as effective in representing a defendant's interests in a DUI charge as one who concentrates on this particular type of case. DUI defendants who seek to retain private counsel should be sure a lawyer has handled DUI cases in the past.

How can people find out about the DUI laws in their states?

In addition to consulting a lawyer, you can get information about DUI laws from:

- a state driving/automobile agency (for instance the Department of Motor Vehicles or DMV—in some states called the "Department of Public Safety"), and
- Nolo's online content (see https://dui. drivinglaws.org and www.nolo.com/ legal-encyclopedia/dui-traffic-tickets).

DUI Case Examples

The DUI case examples below follow defendants from arrest through conviction, in both cases by way of plea bargaining— which is how the overwhelming majority of these cases end. (The case examples don't cover the administrative proceedings, like a DMV license suspension, that also typically occur in DUI cases.)

CAUTION
These are examples only. We provide these sample cases to illustrate typical DUI scenarios, but you should understand that any particular DUI case may be handled differently depending on:

- the state
- the court
- the attorneys, and
- the facts.

Facts Leading to the Arrests of Julian Daniels and Shelly Rogers for DUI

On December 1, Shelly Rogers headed home after a party at Keith's Tavern. Officer Wood noticed her weaving in and out of her lane and following closely behind the car in front of her. Officer Wood put on the flashing red light, and Rogers pulled over.

That same evening, across town, as Julian Daniels drove home from Mick's Pub, he hit a tree in a residential neighborhood. A neighbor heard the crash and phoned the police. Officer Charles drove up a few minutes later, lights flashing. Daniels was standing in front of his car, surveying the damage when Officer Charles approached him.

About the same time as Daniels hit the tree, Rogers rolled down her window after pulling over. She put her hands on the steering wheel and waited for the police officer to approach. When the officer approached the car, the officer smelled the characteristic odor of an alcoholic beverage on Rogers's breath. The officer asked for Rogers's driver's license, then asked her to step out of the car. Rogers politely complied with both requests.

> **Question:** Does the officer have a legal basis to stop Rogers?
>
> **Answer:** Yes.

The officer asked Rogers where she'd come from and whether she'd been drinking. Rogers politely answered the questions.

The officer then told Rogers she would need to take a couple of tests. The officer asked Rogers to recite the alphabet, to stand on one leg, and to touch her finger to her nose. Rogers was successfully able to recite the alphabet but stumbled somewhat when she tried standing on one foot. The officer then shined a flashlight in Rogers's eyes and asked her to look left and right. The officer then gave Rogers a breath test with a PBA (portable breath analyzer). Rogers's BAC (blood alcohol content) measured 0.11% (beyond the legal limit of 0.08% for that state), so she was arrested for DUI, handcuffed, and put in the back of the squad car. Nothing further was said by either Rogers or the police officer.

> **Question:** Did the officer err in not giving Rogers her *Miranda* warnings after arresting her?
>
> **Answer:** No, the officer didn't ask Rogers any questions, so he wasn't required to warn her.

Meanwhile, across town, Daniels was given the same field sobriety tests. Though Daniels passed all three, the officer still suspected DUI because Daniels had red, watery eyes and had hit a tree. Consequently, the officer arrested Daniels and brought him to the station for the blood test that Daniels chose to take. Daniels's blood alcohol content measured 0.09% (just above the legal limit of 0.08%).

Booking

Both Daniels and Rogers were brought to the Main County Jail and booked. They were photographed, their possessions except for clothes and wristwatches were taken and inventoried, and they were put into jail cells.

> **Question:** Was it right for the police to take their possessions as part of the booking process?
>
> **Answer:** Yes.

Their respective booking records read in part as follows:

Suspect: Julian Daniels
Inventory: Brown leather wallet, containing identification, photos, and $25; 4-door white Toyota Corolla (license _____) impounded.

Suspect: Shelly Rogers
Inventory: Black leather purse containing wallet (with credit card and driver's license, hair brush, nail file, and $62); red Corvette (license _____) impounded.

Preparation of the Police Reports

Later that night, the arresting officers completed their paperwork documenting the arrests, including arrest and investigation reports, a statement for the Department of Motor Vehicles, and additional pages with notes and comments.

Preparation of the Criminal Complaint

The officers' reports were delivered to the district attorney's intake desk at the courthouse. Both defendants' reports ended up on the desk of D.A. Ira Davidson. Davidson glanced at the police reports and filled in the appropriate blanks on the criminal complaint forms as he had done with nearly 150 criminal complaints that day.

Phone Calls and Bail

A couple of hours later, after handling other matters and running computer checks to see if the suspects had criminal records, a police officer went to their respective cells, told Daniels that his bail had been set at $500, and told Rogers that hers had been set at $3,500 (Rogers, it turned out, had been convicted of a DUI the year before).

Both were allowed to make phone calls. Daniels reached his mother, who came to the jail and posted cash bail of $500. Before he walked out, Daniels was given a summons to appear in court for an arraignment the following week. Rogers wasn't as successful. She was too embarrassed to call her parents, and none of the friends she phoned were home, so she spent the night in jail.

The Arraignment of Rogers

The next morning, Rogers was taken to court for an arraignment.

> **Question:** Are people usually arraigned that quickly?
>
> **Answer:** If they are in custody, yes. They usually have to be arraigned within 48 hours after arrest.

Rogers spent two hours in the courthouse lockup waiting for Judge Diana Benjamin.

When the case was finally called, a bailiff led Rogers into the courtroom. Rogers stood before the judge and waited. Judge Benjamin was looking over some papers and talking with her clerk. Rogers heard the judge ask her clerk for another cup of coffee, then look down and say, "Rogers?"

"That's me."

> **Question:** Should Rogers have said, "That's me, Your Honor"?
>
> **Answer:** Adding "your Honor" would have made Rogers's reply more respectful and certainly couldn't have hurt.

"Do you have counsel?"

> **Question:** Does Rogers have the right to counsel at an arraignment?
>
> **Answer:** Yes.

"What?"

"Do you have a lawyer?"

"No, Your Honor."

"Do you want a lawyer?"

"Yeah. I guess so."

"Have you been given a chance to call a lawyer?"

"They let me make a phone call last night, but no one was home. But I don't think I have the money to hire a lawyer."

> **Question:** Will Rogers get a public defender if she can't afford a lawyer?
>
> **Answer:** Yes, or some other court-appointed attorney paid for by the government.

"Let's see. You can talk to the public defender if you want, and we'll see you back here this afternoon. Or you can plead now if you intend to plead guilty."

> **Question:** Should Rogers plead guilty?
>
> **Answer:** No. Rogers hasn't yet met with a lawyer, so she should certainly do that before even considering a plea bargain.

"Yes, I'd like a public defender."

The judge called to her clerk, "Get somebody from the P.D.'s office down here." And to Rogers the judge said, "Okay, we'll get you a lawyer and see you back here later."

Rogers Gets a Public Defender

The bailiff returned Rogers to the lockup. A few hours later, a young man approached her cell.

"Shelly Rogers?"

"Yes?"

"I'm Andrew Duncan. I'm from the public defender's office. How are you?"

"Tired, bored. Sick of this place."

"Well, unfortunately, I don't think I can get you out today. I talked to the D.A. The D.A. said for a second offense, you gotta do 48 hours—no way around it. But if you plead guilty this afternoon, then you can get out tomorrow with probation. You'll have to pay a fine and do another alcohol program. I see you did a three-month one last time you were arrested. But that's it."

Question: Would Rogers be sentenced to jail time if she went to trial and lost?

Answer: Yes. If that's the mandatory state law for a second DUI, she would get the time either way—and possibly even more time if she went to trial and lost.

"Yeah. Listen, what if I want to fight it?"

"Well. You could fight it, but it doesn't look good." He read from the reports, "Blood alcohol—0.11, failed field sobriety tests...."

"I did the alphabet, didn't I?" Shelly interrupted.

"Um. Yeah, but you couldn't stand on one foot, your eyes were bloodshot, they smelled some type of alcoholic beverage on your breath. Look, we can talk more in a little bit. I have to go back into court now to meet another client. Your case will be called after lunch. I'll come talk to you again before then. In the meantime, think it over. I'll tell you this much, if you go to trial and lose, on a second DUI a judge might give you a lot more than 48 hours in jail. You can get up to a year in jail, plus the probation, plus fines and an alcohol program. You might want to cut your losses."

Andrew Duncan left Shelly Rogers and ran back upstairs to court to meet with another client.

Rogers Considers a Plea Bargain

After lunch, Shelly Rogers was returned to the courtroom. Standing before the judge, Shelly wondered what was going on. Duncan hadn't been back to see her.

Duncan ran in, put his briefcase down, pulled out a file folder and leaned in to whisper to Shelly.

"I was in another courtroom on another case and couldn't come talk to you. Sorry. I want you to know, though, I spoke to the D.A. If you do the 18-month alcohol rehab program and plead guilty now, they'll let you out tomorrow—as soon as the 48 hours are done. You'll be on probation for three years. And you'll do some community service instead of the fines; they do that when people can't afford to pay them. Okay?"

"Yeah. I guess that's the best I can do."

"Well, you do risk a lot more if you fight and lose."

"Okay."

Rogers Pleads Guilty

"All right, just say yes to all the questions the judge asks you and we'll be out of here in three minutes," Andrew told his client.

"All right people, we're back on the record, let's go," the judge called as she sat down at the bench. "What's next?" she asked her clerk.

"Rogers is back—continued from this morning."

"Okay, Ms. Rogers. Let's see, you now have counsel," said the judge.

"Yes."

"And how do you now plead to the charges of second offense driving under the influence?"

"Say 'guilty,'" Andrew Duncan whispered to Rogers.

"Guilty," Rogers said.

"Counsel, have you reached a settlement?"

D.A.: "Yes, your Honor; 18-month program, three years probation, $500 fine, which we'll convert to community service hours, plus 48 hours in custody—if she pleads guilty now."

"Ms. Rogers, do you know that by pleading guilty you lose the right to a jury trial?"

"Yes."

"Do you give up that right?"

"Yes."

"Do you understand what giving up that right means?"

"Yes."

"Do you know that you are waiving the right to cross-examine your accusers?"

"Yes."

"Do you know that you are waiving your privilege against self-incrimination?"

"Yes."

"Did anyone force you into accepting this settlement?"

"No."

"Are you pleading guilty because you in fact were driving under the influence?"

"Yes."

> **Question:** If Shelly Rogers wants to plead guilty, why does the judge ask her so many questions?
>
> **Answer:** Because a judge is required by law to ensure that defendants understand the rights they are giving up by pleading guilty and that they are pleading guilty voluntarily.

The Judge Sentences Rogers

"Ms. Rogers, the court accepts your guilty plea. You are hereby sentenced to be incarcerated for a term of 48 hours. You shall enroll by no later than 14 days from today in a court-approved 18-month alcohol treatment program and file evidence of completion of the program with the court. You shall be on summary probation for a period of three years, and you'll have to do 50 hours of community service. Do you understand?"

> **Question:** Will Rogers have to report to a probation officer?
>
> **Answer:** No.

"Yes, Your Honor."

"Bailiff, take her back to lockup." To Shelly the judge said, "You may go home tomorrow. Counsel will explain the paperwork you have to complete. I don't want to see you back here, Ms. Rogers, or hear that you killed somebody because you got drunk and went for a drive. I hope you take the alcohol program more seriously this time around."

When Shelly was released the next day, she was given a packet of information from the public defender's office. It included a list of court-approved treatment programs.

Daniels Meets His Public Defender

Daniels, meanwhile, had been free on bail. A week after Shelly Rogers was sentenced, Andrew Duncan, the same public defender, met with Julian Daniels in the hallway outside the courtroom just before Daniels's arraignment.

"Hi. Daniels, right?"

"Yes."

"My name is Andrew Duncan, I'm your lawyer. I spoke with you on the phone a few days ago?"

"Yes. Yes, thank you."

"You've never been arrested before, right?"

"No, never."

"What happened? Says here you hit a tree?"

"Yeah. I was looking down for a second and next thing I knew I'd plowed into this tree."

"Okay, you were 0.09.... I think I can get you a decent deal, probably three years probation, three-month alcohol program, and some community service if you plead guilty today."

"Look. I don't need an alcohol program. I had a couple of beers with my girlfriend. That's it. I'm not an alcoholic. What's community service? Is that picking up trash like those guys in orange vests I see out on the roadway?"

"Well, that's one kind of community service, yes. But, we could arrange for you to work in a library or school, or some volunteer program like that."

"How many hours of community service are we talking?"

"They said 200 hours."

"I can't do that. I'm in school full time and I have a job. Man, I don't want this on my record; I'm applying to grad schools. You know that cop didn't even read me my rights."

"Did the cop question you?"

"Not really. I mean he asked if could say the alphabet and touch my nose, and told me to stand on one foot. Then he put me in the car."

"Well, technically, they don't have to read you your rights unless they question you."

"Oh?"

"Yup. Listen, your girlfriend was with you the whole time at the bar?"

"Yeah."

"She can testify that you only had, how many beers?"

"Two. Two beers. She was with me the whole time. That's all I had."

"And you're in college where?"

"State University. I'm graduating this spring."

"Okay, let me talk to the D.A. There's pretty much no way to get around doing an alcohol program on a DUI—even a first-timer. Our only chance is if she reduces the charge to reckless driving. Come into the courtroom with me, but you sit in the back and wait. Your case will be called in the next hour or two."

"Do your best, Mr. Duncan," Daniels called.

"Thanks."

"Sure."

Daniels's Lawyer Proposes a Plea Bargain to the Prosecutor

In the courtroom, Duncan found the assistant D.A. handling the case, Suzanne O'Larky, sitting toward the front in the audience section of the courtroom waiting for her next case. He slid in to the seat next to her.

"Larky," Duncan whispered.

"Yeah," she replied quietly, putting a folder in front of her mouth so the judge wouldn't see she was talking.

"I gotta talk to you about the Daniels case, set for this afternoon. Your case."

"I'm listening."

"Have you looked at it? 0.09—just over the limit, no priors, good kid—finishing college this spring, wants to go to grad school. What can we do here?"

"You know my boss. No forgiveness on DUIs. He spoke at a MADD (Mothers Against Drunk Driving) conference last week. My hands are tied."

"Look, make an exception here. He's a nice kid. He was just looking down and hit a tree. Dumb luck. No one was hurt. Knock it down to reckless. It's bad enough this is going to go on his record—he's clean. He passed all the FSTs, says right here on the police report."

Just then the judge called the next case. The D.A. jumped up and whispered,

"That's mine, Duncan. Hang on. I'll think about it and get back to you."

"I'm waiting right here," Duncan replied, and the D.A. went up before the judge to handle a different case. Ten minutes later she was back.

"All right, Duncan. But only for you. Reckless. $750 fine, two years probation, 150 hours community service—best offer. And he pleads today, or no deal."

"Thanks, Larky. I'll talk to him. Sounds good."

Andrew Duncan quietly slipped out and went to the back of the courtroom to find Daniels. He told Daniels the deal the prosecutor had offered, and Daniels agreed to plead.

Daniels Pleads No Contest

Daniels's case was called some time later. And after asking Daniels the same questions Judge Benjamin asked Shelly Rogers earlier (and getting all the same answers from Daniels), she accepted Daniels's plea of no contest.

Question: What is a no-contest plea?

Answer: In most respects the same as a guilty plea, but it likely cannot be used as an admission of guilt against Daniels in a later civil suit should the owner of the tree he hit decide to sue Daniels for property damage. (But see "The Effect of a No-Contest (*Nolo Contendere*) Plea" in Chapter 10.) Daniels was convicted of reckless driving and sentenced as agreed.

Juvenile Courts and Procedures

This chapter provides an overview of the juvenile justice process. Juvenile justice is an umbrella term for the special procedures set up by every state to deal with youthful offenders. This chapter focuses on the general policies and procedures of juvenile courts, and explains principal differences between juvenile and adult courts. For anyone who has to deal with them, we hope the chapter makes juvenile courts seem a little less foreign and intimidating.

A Brief History of U.S. Juvenile Courts

Juvenile courts were an early example of specialized courts that develop expertise in particular types of legal problems.

When were the first juvenile courts established in the United States?

The first juvenile court was established in 1899. However, it wasn't until 1945 that all states had juvenile courts.

How were children dealt with before juvenile courts were established?

In the mostly rural society of the early nineteenth century, parents, churches, and local community organizations punished children who committed crimes. Children were typically disciplined by force, sometimes brutally.

The urbanization that followed the industrial revolution in the last half of the nineteenth century posed particular problems for children. Many were subject to harsh conditions, including extensive poverty and labor. At that time, children who got into trouble (whether by committing a crime or by suffering abuse or neglect at the hands of others) were often put to work or sent away to relatives. So-called "reform schools," the precursors of modern juvenile halls, were also set up. The ostensible purpose of these schools was to change or reform children, in part by giving them skills and training. In fact, these facilities were often little more than warehouse-type jails, some with deplorable living conditions, where most of the learning was about how to become a better criminal.

Around the turn of the twentieth century, many social leaders came to believe that reform schools were not working. They also began to understand children not simply as mini-adults, but as people with special needs who should be treated differently than adults. Consequently, the movement for a separate juvenile justice system began.

Juvenile Court Paternalism

The roots of paternalism are deep in the juvenile justice system. In part, they stem from an English concept called *parens patriae* (Latin for "parent of the country"). Under this concept, minors really belong to the government; parents are only their temporary custodians. Juvenile and family courts, as an arm of the government, are therefore ultimately responsible for minors. Programs in the juvenile justice system often reflect a paternalistic attitude toward minors. For example, judges may follow "tough love" or "scared straight" programs out of the belief that juveniles benefit from a strict but caring approach.

Too Young to Punish?

Based on principles developed by English common law, most states consider children under the age of seven to be legally incapable of forming the *"mens rea"* (guilty state of mind) necessary to be morally blameworthy and therefore subject to criminal punishment. As a result, minors under age seven are usually excused because of their age if they commit acts that would be crimes if committed by adults. Instead, the parents of these children may have to pay restitution (compensation) to the victims. In addition, a court may determine that a child's parents are unfit, remove the child from the parents' custody, and place the child with a relative, foster family, or treatment facility.

Children between the ages of seven and 14 often occupy a middle ground. Using what legal rules often refer to as a "rebuttable presumption," minors in this age range are often presumed to be incapable of forming a guilty mind. However, if a prosecutor can show that a particular child in this age range is capable of forming and did form a guilty mind, the child can be criminally punished.

Once minors reach age 14, most states regard them as fully capable of forming a guilty mind. Therefore, minors older than 14 are usually held accountable for the crimes they commit, either in juvenile or adult court.

What are the goals of juvenile courts?

As with adult courts, juvenile court goals are a mix of rehabilitation, punishment, and community safety. Juvenile courts have traditionally considered children less dangerous and more amenable to rehabilitation than adults.

Juvenile Court Jurisdiction

Jurisdiction refers to a court's power to hear cases and make enforceable orders. This section covers the jurisdiction of juvenile courts.

How old is a "juvenile"?

In most states, juvenile courts handle cases involving kids who are 17 years of age or younger. However, depending on the severity of a criminal charge and a minor's age, a case that may start out in juvenile court may be transferred to end up in an adult court.

Is juvenile court jurisdiction limited to criminal cases?

No. In addition to having jurisdiction over cases involving crimes allegedly committed by minors (often called "juvenile delinquency" cases), juvenile courts in most states also have jurisdiction over:

- Cases involving minors who are allegedly abused or neglected by their parents or guardians. These are often called "juvenile dependency" cases. Abused or neglected minors may be removed from parental homes and placed with relatives or foster parents. At a minimum, parents are often ordered to undergo counseling as a condition of keeping or regaining custody. A juvenile court may also declare parents permanently unfit and approve a minor's adoption.

- Cases involving minors who commit status offenses. A status offense is a type of violation that only a juvenile can commit. For example, a 14-year-old who skips school (is truant) for no valid reason commits a status offense if the law requires all children under the age of 16 to attend school. An adult could not violate this law.

Do the same procedures apply to dependency, status offense, and juvenile delinquency cases?

No. Even though juvenile courts may have jurisdiction over all three types of cases, different procedures typically apply to each. This chapter focuses on juvenile delinquency cases, the juvenile court counterpart of adult criminal proceedings. However, keep in mind the following about status offenses:

- Juvenile court personnel may use the term "juvenile delinquency" as an umbrella term that covers both juvenile crimes and status offenses.
- Minors who commit status offenses may end up in juvenile hall. For

example, if a minor violates a judge's order to attend school, the judge may send the minor to juvenile hall for disobeying the court order.

- Minors charged with status offenses do not have a constitutional right to counsel. Some states do, however, provide attorneys to minors charged with status offenses.

EXAMPLE: Officer Steve Roberts sees Jack Aranda, who appears to be a teenage boy, shopping at the local mall on a Wednesday morning. When Officer Roberts stops Jack and asks him how old he is, Jack says, "I'm 15." Jack then tells Officer Roberts, "I wanted to shop before the mall gets crowded." Officer Roberts can arrest Jack because laws typically require minors to be in school on weekdays. Because Jack appeared to be of school age, the officer had a right to question him. When Jack's responses indicated that he was truant, the officer had a right to arrest him.

Deciding Whether to File Charges

Discretion characterizes virtually every phase of the juvenile justice system, including the decision to file charges.

How do most minors come to the attention of the police?

Unlike adults, juvenile offenders often come to police attention through complaints made by parents and school officials.

Juvenile Justice Lingo

Juvenile courts tend to have their own jargon, in part to portray a gentler image than adult criminal courts. Here are some of the unique terms that are common in juvenile court proceedings:

- **Adjudication:** A juvenile court trial, similar to an adult trial.
- **Admission of petition:** The juvenile court counterpart to a guilty plea.
- **Camp:** A locked facility for juvenile offenders. Camps often house minors who will be locked up for many weeks or months, while juvenile halls tend to be shorter-term holding facilities. States may have various types of camps differing in degrees of security, rigidity, and facilities. Many camps have school facilities.
- **Custody order:** An arrest warrant.
- **Dependency court:** A branch of the juvenile court that hears cases involving minors who have allegedly been neglected or abused by parents or guardians.
- **Detention order:** An order that a minor be placed in custody.
- **Disposition:** A juvenile court sentence or other final order, which juvenile court regulars often shorten to "dispo."
- **Dispositional hearing:** A sentencing hearing.
- **Fact-finding hearing:** Along with adjudication, a juvenile court term for a trial.
- **Infant:** A minor, in most states a person under the age of 18. (Few teenagers appreciate being referred to as infants!)
- **Involved:** The juvenile court equivalent of guilty.
- **Juvenile hall:** A jail (or temporary holding facility) for minors.
- **Petition:** The juvenile court equivalent of a criminal complaint, which charges a child with a violation.
- **Referee:** A judicial officer, usually a lawyer appointed by a court's presiding judge, who performs many of a judge's functions but has not been formally elected or appointed as a judge.
- **Respondent:** A juvenile court defendant.
- **Suitable placement:** A court order removing a juvenile from the juvenile's parental home and placing the juvenile into a foster home, group home, treatment facility, camp, or some other type of placement.
- **Sustained (or not sustained):** The equivalent of a verdict, a juvenile court finding that the charge in a petition is (or is not) true.
- **Ward of the court:** A minor who is under the jurisdiction of the juvenile court.

Does every minor who is taken into custody by the police end up in juvenile court?

No; a variety of scenarios are possible. A police officer who has reason to believe that a juvenile committed a crime may:

- detain and warn the minor against further violations, and then let him or her go free (in juvenile court and police lingo, the minor was "counseled and released")
- detain and warn the minor against further violations, but release the minor only into the custody of a parent or guardian, or
- place the minor in custody and refer the case to the juvenile court.

What happens once a case has been referred to juvenile court?

The following is an overview of how juvenile cases typically flow through the system:

- A prosecutor or a juvenile court intake officer (often a probation officer) decides whether to:
  - dismiss the case
  - handle the case informally, or
  - petition the case (file formal charges).
- In some localities, the probation officer makes only a preliminary assessment of whether to file formal charges, leaving the final decision to a prosecutor.
- A decision to proceed informally often results in the minor having to appear before a probation officer or a judge. The minor may receive a stern lecture and may also be required to attend counseling sessions or after-school classes, repay a victim for damaged property, pay a fine, perform community service work, or go on probation. If the intake officer suspects that a minor taken into custody has been abused or neglected, proceedings to remove the minor from the custody of parents or guardians may also be started.
- If the decision is to proceed formally, the intake officer or prosecutor files a petition and the case is placed on the juvenile court's calendar. (In large cities, a juvenile court may handle hundreds of cases a day.)
- The minor is arraigned (formally charged) before a juvenile court judge or referee. At this point, the juvenile court either takes jurisdiction of the case or waives (transfers) the case to adult criminal court.
- If the case remains in juvenile court, the minor either enters into a plea arrangement or faces trial (often called an adjudication).
- If, after trial, the juvenile court judge sustains the petition (concludes that the charges are true), the judge decides on an appropriate sentence (usually referred to as a disposition).
- Postdisposition hearings may occur. For example, a judge's disposition order may require a minor to appear in court periodically so that the judge can monitor the minor's behavior.

RESOURCES
For statistical information on juvenile justice, visit www.ojjdp.gov/ojstatbb. The Office of Juvenile Justice and Delinquency Prevention (OJJDP) prepares a Statistical Briefing Book that has extensive information on the juvenile justice system.

What factors do intake officers normally consider when deciding whether to file formal charges?

The factors that an intake officer is likely to consider include:

- **The severity of the offense.** A serious crime is more likely to result in the filing of a petition than a less serious crime.
- **The minor's age.** Petitions are more likely to be filed in cases involving older than younger children.
- **The minor's past record.** Formal charges are more likely when a minor has had previous juvenile court involvement.
- **The strength of the evidence that a minor committed a crime.**
- **The minor's gender.** Formal charges are more likely to be filed against boys than girls.
- **The minor's social history.** Petitions are more likely to be filed when children have a history of problems at home or at school.
- **The parent or guardian's apparent ability to control the minor.** The greater the lack of parental control over the minor, the more likely the intake officer is to file a petition.

In addition to these reasons, the filing decisions of many intake officers cannot help but be swayed—off the record—by a number of subjective factors. These may include:

- **The minor's attitude.** Formal proceedings are less likely when a child shows remorse for a bad deed.
- **The minor's manner of dress.** If the minor dresses well, is groomed neatly, and is polite, intake personnel are more likely to handle the case informally than if the minor dresses sloppily or in a way that shows obvious gang involvement or disrespect for the juvenile justice system.
- **Whether the minor has family or community support.**
- **Whether the minor has an attorney.** Disposing of a case informally may be less likely when a child has a lawyer. (See "Is It Helpful for Minors to Have Lawyers in Juvenile Cases?" later in this chapter.)
- **Ethnicity and socioeconomic status.** Statistics suggest (though few, if any, intake officers would admit, on or off the record) that the ethnicity and socioeconomic status of minors sometimes affects how aggressively cases are handled.

Does the filing of a formal petition mean that a case has to go to trial or end by plea bargain?

No. Juvenile court judges often informally divert cases. In other words, working with other community service agencies (schools, social services, and child welfare departments) a judge may retain jurisdiction over a case while the minor undergoes a recommended program. For example, the minor (and/or the minor's parents) may have to participate in counseling. Or, the minor may have to pay restitution, repair damaged property, perform community service work, or attend special classes. If the minor fails to complete the recommended program, formal charges may be reinstated. Juveniles in some cities may also be able to participate in another form of diversion, called "teen court."

The Right to Counsel and Other Constitutional Rights

While juvenile court procedures resemble those of adult criminal courts in many respects, important differences remain, as explained below.

Do minors have the same constitutional rights as adults?

Until the 1960s, juvenile courts offered few of the rights guaranteed to adult criminal defendants. Up until then, juvenile court judges dispensed justice pretty much as they saw fit. Outside criticism of their sometimes arbitrary approach was rare. Juvenile court proceedings were closed to the public. Parents could not and did not object. Defense lawyers were not often present, and minors had virtually no rights.

Since the 1960s, the U.S. Supreme Court has issued several rulings that have afforded minors at least some of the rights enjoyed by adults.

Do police officers have to give *Miranda* warnings to juvenile suspects?

Just as with adult suspects in custody, police officers have to warn in-custody juvenile suspects of their *Miranda* rights before interrogating them. If the officers don't, statements made by the suspect are not admissible in evidence. A juvenile suspect who chooses not to answer a police officer's questions should respond to the warning by telling the officer, "I want to remain silent. I want to talk to a lawyer as well as my parents."

Do the police need probable cause to search and arrest a minor?

Yes. However, public officers in quasi-parental relationships with minors (for example, public school officials) do not need probable cause to justify the temporary detention and search of a minor. A reasonable suspicion that a child has committed a crime is all that many public officials need to detain and search the minor or the minor's property, such as a school locker or backpack.

> **EXAMPLE:** School authorities get a report that 13-year-old Savana Redding is distributing over-the-counter pills to other students in violation of school policy. The authorities

search Savana's backpack and other personal belongings but find nothing. A school nurse then takes Savana into a private room and conducts a modified strip search. Savana has to remove and shake out her bra and loosen the elastic around her underwear. The initial search of Savana's belongings is legitimate because the school authorities reasonably suspected her of violating school rules. But the strip search is not. No immediate risk of harm exists, so the invasion of Savana's personal privacy is unjustified. (*Safford Unified School District v. Redding*, U.S. Sup. Ct. 2009.)

Do minors taken into custody have a right to bail?

No. Minors generally do not have the bail option that most arrested adults have. Minors who are taken into custody by the police are usually either released to the custody of a parent or guardian, or detained (locked up) until they can be taken before a juvenile court judge for arraignment. (This period may be called "preadjudication detention.")

Are minors ever locked up with adult offenders?

Yes, despite the fact that laws in most states require that minors be kept in separate juvenile halls or jail facilities. Studies all across the country routinely show that minors are often jailed with adults. The reasons for this vary. Police officers sometimes mistake older minors for adults, and some minors lie to the police about their age. In other instances, juvenile facilities don't exist, are overcrowded, or are located at an inconvenient distance.

Advantages and Risks of Preadjudication Release

Police officers and other intake officers are often willing to release arrested minors to their parents' custody pending a court date. Preadjudication release is usually good for both minor and family. It gives the minor a chance to get cleaned up and prepare for the hearing, and perhaps consult with an attorney. Also, some studies have shown that detained minors consistently receive harsher dispositions.

In some instances, parents may be justifiably reluctant to accept custody of their arrested children. Some state laws make parents liable in certain circumstances for their children's acts of juvenile delinquency. (For example, parents of a minor who steals may have to make restitution to the victim.) Parents who fear that their child may commit further crimes, especially if they fear that the child is violent and beyond their control, may be hesitant to agree to preadjudication release. Parents in such situations should try to determine the extent of their potential liability and inquire (perhaps of a public defender or a private defense lawyer, if resources permit) how they can keep their child safely detained with as little damage as possible to the child's chances for receiving rehabilitative treatment.

Do minors have the right to legal representation in juvenile delinquency cases?

Yes. In *In re Gault*, (U.S. Sup. Ct. 1967), the Supreme Court said, "The juvenile needs the assistance of counsel to cope with problems of law, to make skilled inquiry into the facts, to insist upon regularity of the proceedings, and to ascertain whether he has a defense and to prepare and submit it." The Court confirmed that juveniles who face delinquency proceedings that could lead to detention are entitled to counsel.

Does a minor who cannot afford a lawyer have the right to a court-appointed attorney?

Yes. Minors who can't afford a lawyer are entitled to have one provided by the state.

Can minors who are locked up make a phone call for help?

Often, yes. Minors who are not quickly released from custody can exercise their right to counsel by politely requesting permission to make a phone call to secure legal representation. If the family situation allows, the minor should probably call a parent or guardian, who can in turn contact a lawyer. Otherwise, the minor may contact a lawyer directly, or, if the minor and the minor's family can't afford a private lawyer, ask to speak with a public defender.

How and when are lawyers appointed for minors?

In some jurisdictions, public defenders are automatically appointed for minors. In other jurisdictions, minors have to formally request appointed counsel at arraignment.

Will a minor who comes from a wealthy family still be eligible for an appointed attorney?

Yes. The right to counsel attaches to the minor, not to the minor's family. While some counties may try to collect payment for legal services from the minor's family, it is doubtful that the family could be legally compelled to pay.

Are parents allowed to participate in meetings between their child and the child's lawyer?

Sometimes. Most defense lawyers will initially want to meet with a minor alone, because the minor is the client even if the parents are paying for the lawyer's services. In fact, in order to preserve lawyer-client confidentiality, it's important that minors speak privately with their lawyers. However, when the time comes to make important decisions, it is common for lawyers to include parents in the discussion, assuming the minor consents.

Parents may certainly—and should—tell lawyers to keep the parents informed about what is happening. Parents should also ask if they can be of any assistance. For example, parents may be able to provide relevant family history and contact people familiar with the child (for example, teachers, clergy, or employers) who might agree to testify or write letters on the child's behalf.

Other than the right to counsel, what other constitutional rights do juveniles have?

The *Gault* case (U.S. Sup. Ct. 1967) decided that, in addition to the right to counsel, juveniles charged with crimes have:

- the right to notice of the charges
- the right to confront and cross-examine witnesses, and
- the privilege against self-incrimination (they cannot be compelled to testify).

Is there a right to a jury trial in juvenile courts?

Generally, no. Only some states allow jury trials in juvenile delinquency cases. Even in those states, the right to a jury trial may be confined to specific types of cases, such as those involving minors who have prior records and are facing serious charges.

What is the burden of proof in juvenile cases?

To convict an adult of a crime, the government must prove guilt beyond a reasonable doubt. This standard generally applies to juvenile court cases, too.

Trying Juveniles as Adults

Juvenile courts may transfer more serious cases to adult criminal courts.

What does it mean to be tried as an adult?

Juveniles who are tried as adults are subject to the harsher punishment options of adult criminal courts. For example, juveniles who are tried as adults and convicted can receive sentences that juvenile court judges lack the power to impose (for example, life imprisonment) and will normally be locked up in adult jails and prisons rather than juvenile treatment facilities. On the other hand, adult criminal courts afford rights that some juvenile courts do not, such as the right to a jury trial.

Even if they are tried as adults and convicted of capital offenses, juvenile offenders may not be sentenced to death. (*Roper v. Simmons,* U.S. Sup. Ct. 2005.) Likewise, mandatory life imprisonment without parole for those who were younger than 18 at the time of their crimes is unconstitutional. (*Miller v. Alabama*, U.S. Sup. Ct. 2012.)

Why might a case be transferred from juvenile to adult court?

A juvenile court judge may transfer a case to adult court when, in the judge's opinion, the minor is not amenable to rehabilitation as a juvenile. Typically, juveniles are transferred to adult court when they are charged with serious and violent offenses and/or have a lengthy juvenile court record. Juvenile court judges usually also take into account the minor's age (older minors are more likely to be transferred to adult courts than younger minors) and mental and physical abilities.

Is It Helpful for Minors to Have Lawyers in Juvenile Cases?

Almost always, yes. And the attorney should normally be one who specializes in or is at least familiar with juvenile court procedures. Research indicates that effective assistance of counsel can greatly affect a case's outcome. For example, attorneys often can help by:

- getting cases diverted, or handled informally, so the juvenile is not incarcerated and has no juvenile court record
- arranging for a juvenile's release from preadjudication detention
- keeping juveniles from being tried as adults, and
- putting together, and convincing a judge to agree to, a creative and compassionate disposition.

Nevertheless, some juvenile court professionals say that a lawyer's involvement often prolongs cases, turning what a prosecutor might be willing to handle informally into a formal adversarial proceeding. Some probation officers, intake personnel, judges, and other juvenile court staff admit that they are hostile to defense attorneys because they think the attorneys slow down already overcrowded calendars. Some judges may even give harsher treatment to juveniles represented by lawyers.

Because the variables are so great, there are no meaningful guidelines regarding when a lawyer should be used. However, juvenile court regulars, such as a deputy public defender assigned to the court, may have an informed opinion on whether the minor is likely to benefit from legal representation. Also, the more serious the crime and the worse the minor's record, the more important it is to have legal representation. On the other hand, an "A" student with no prior record who is accused of putting graffiti on a school wall may decide that a quick, informal, and satisfactory disposition is more likely if no lawyer is involved.

At what age can a minor be tried as an adult in an adult court?

The age at which a minor may be tried as an adult varies from state to state. In many states, a minor can be tried as an adult only if the minor has reached a minimum age, often 16. In other states, 13-year-olds may be tried as adults. In still other states, a child of any age may be tried as an adult depending on the nature of the crime.

What procedure does a juvenile court judge follow when deciding whether to transfer a case to adult court?

While juvenile court judges can themselves begin transfer proceedings, these proceedings are normally initiated at the request of a prosecutor. Following the prosecutor's request, a juvenile court judge hears evidence relating to the minor's amenability—or lack thereof—to juvenile court services.

A juvenile's right to a hearing before a case can be transferred to adult court was established by *Kent v. U.S.* (U.S. Sup. Ct. 1966.) Minors are entitled to counsel at transfer hearings.

Other Names for Transfer Hearings

The hearing in which a judge considers whether to transfer a case to adult court has a variety of names. The hearing may be called a "waiver" hearing, because the juvenile court waives (gives up) jurisdiction by transferring the case to adult court. It may also be called a "fitness" hearing, because the judge decides whether a minor is fit to be tried as an adult. Another common name is a "certification" hearing, because a judge certifies that a minor is fit to be tried as an adult.

To convince a juvenile court judge to transfer a case to adult court, the prosecutor normally has to offer evidence showing probable cause to believe that the minor committed the charged offense. If the judge concludes that probable cause exists, the judge may then hear additional evidence concerning the minor's general background, prior juvenile court record, and amenability to treatment. Then, taking into account the seriousness of the offense, the judge will decide whether to transfer the case to adult court. After transfer to adult court, a case typically goes back to square one, with an adult court arraignment.

Help For Accused Minors

Family members, friends, employers, teachers, and others who want to help a minor can appear in court or write letters demonstrating their support. Supporters should be prepared to give concrete examples of the minor's behavior indicating that the minor is basically a good person who has potential and should be given an opportunity to turn things around. Supporters can submit school records showing that the minor has attended school regularly. Parents may want to have a psychological assessment of the minor done and submit it to the court. The fact that the minor has learning difficulties, for example, can be very relevant and persuasive evidence supporting treatment rather than punishment. Parents may be able to research and suggest possible alternative treatment programs (such as wilderness programs or military schools) instead of a detention camp or juvenile hall. Finally, parents or other supporters can examine the prosecution's file for inaccuracies, particularly concerning the minor's previous juvenile court records.

What are automatic transfer laws?

Some states have laws mandating that juveniles be tried as adults in certain types of cases. The typical automatic transfer law is activated when a minor has reached a certain age (often 16) and is charged with a serious and violent offense, such as robbery, rape, or murder.

What are reverse transfer hearings?

Juveniles have the right to request a juvenile court transfer hearing even when a case is subject to an automatic transfer law. In this situation, however, the law has already automatically transferred the case, so the minor is put in the position of trying to convince a juvenile court judge to take back jurisdiction. Thus, this type of hearing is commonly called a "reverse waiver" or "reverse transfer" hearing.

What arguments can a minor's lawyer use to try to persuade a judge not to transfer a juvenile case to adult court?

Arguments that children's lawyers commonly put forward at transfer or reverse transfer hearings include:

- Although an offense is serious, the minor is still a child who would benefit from the services available in the juvenile system. Factors indicating that a minor is likely to benefit from juvenile court services include:
  - The minor has close family attachments.
  - Older friends, teachers, counselors, employers, and so on, have submitted statements indicating their belief that a minor has good potential.
  - The minor was not thinking as an adult at the time of the offense.
  - The minor has good moral judgment and expressed remorse for the improper behavior.
  - Other minors in similar situations have benefitted from juvenile court services.

- It is realistic to expect that a minor's delinquent behavior will improve from services meeting the minor's needs.
- The minor has not in the past had sufficient opportunity to be rehabilitated.
- The minor is likely to suffer physical or emotional harm in the adult system.
- The juvenile court system provides sufficient safeguards so that the community can be protected while the minor undergoes treatment as a juvenile.

What are the advantages of being tried as a juvenile rather than as an adult?

Common advantages of being tried in juvenile rather than adult court include:

- Juvenile court records are easier to seal (keep private) than adult court records.
- A finding that a minor committed an offense usually carries less social stigma than an adult criminal record.
- Juvenile court dispositions are often less severe than adult criminal sentences, and are more likely to be tailored to the minor's personal situation. For example, rather than simply imposing a fine or a jail term, a juvenile court judge may impose a curfew and require a minor to attend school and regular counseling directed toward minors.
- Even when incarceration is ordered, a juvenile court judge is less likely to impose a lengthy sentence than an adult court judge. (Juvenile court

judges cannot impose the most severe punishments, such as life imprisonment.)

- Minors incarcerated by juvenile courts serve their sentences in juvenile facilities rather than adult prisons.

Is there ever an advantage to being tried as an adult rather than as a juvenile?

A potential benefit of being tried as an adult is having a right to a jury trial. Jury trials are not available in most juvenile courts. A jury could perhaps be more sympathetic in a given case than a judge would be.

Sentencing (Disposition) Options

A wide range of disposition options is often available to juvenile court judges.

Can juvenile court judges incarcerate minors?

Yes. After sustaining a petition (finding that a juvenile committed a crime), juvenile court judges can order juveniles confined in a variety of placements. From the least to the most restrictive alternatives, some common confinement options include:

- **Home confinement** (house arrest). The minor has to remain home at designated times, and is typically subject to a curfew during the week and on weekends.
- **Suitable placement.** A judge may order a juvenile to live with a relative or in a group or foster home.

- **Juvenile jails** (often called juvenile hall or juvenile detention facilities). Similar to adult jails, juvenile jails are designed for short-term incarceration.
- **"Shock probation"** (also called a "split" or "intermittent" sentence). The minor is incarcerated for three to six months before going on probation. The place of incarceration may be a "boot camp," in which minor offenders are subject to strict discipline and physical labor. The taste of jail hopefully shocks minors into improved behavior.
- **Secured facilities ranging from minimum to maximum security.** (A juvenile detention camp is a form of secure facility.) Juveniles may be detained in secured facilities for months or even years. Typically, juveniles have to work and attend school and counseling sessions while in a secured facility.
- **Adult jails.** Juvenile judges may have the authority to sentence certain offenders to serve their sentences in adult facilities.

You Owe Me a Day in Jail

One juvenile court proceeding is suggestive of how judges can tailor probation conditions to a minor offender's personal situation. Following the sustaining of a petition, a judge placed the offender on probation and told the young offender that he would serve one day in juvenile hall for every unexcused school absence and every unexcused tardy.

Other than confinement, what dispositions are common in juvenile court?

Juvenile judges can also impose a variety of nonincarceration dispositions, either alone or in combination with each other. The most common nonincarceration options are:

- a verbal warning or reprimand
- payment of a fine to the court, restitution to the victim, or both
- counseling, either individual or group therapy
- community service
- electronic monitoring, which uses wrist-anklet transmitters to verify a minor's location, and
- probation, which allows minors to remain free if they fulfill specified conditions. For example, regular attendance at counseling sessions is a typical condition of probation. A minor who violates a condition of probation may be incarcerated. The sample Informal Probation Agreement below suggests the wide variety of probation conditions that a juvenile court judge may impose.

What are blended sentences?

Judges in some jurisdictions have the power to sentence juveniles to serve time both in adult and juvenile facilities. For example, after a case has been transferred from juvenile to adult court, the adult court judge may sentence a minor to serve time in a juvenile facility until age 18 and then complete the sentence in an adult prison.

Similarly, a judge may have the authority to sentence a minor to serve time in an adult prison, but suspend that sentence while the minor serves time in a juvenile facility.

How do juvenile court judges make disposition decisions?

Like their adult court counterparts, juvenile court judges take a number of factors into account when deciding on an appropriate disposition. The seriousness of the offense and the offender's prior record are always of major importance. Juvenile court judges tend to rely heavily on the recommendations of probation officers. A juvenile court judge's particular philosophy concerning the proper role of the juvenile court may also influence the disposition. For example, a judge who views the court's primary function as rehabilitative may resist imposing incarceration despite a locality's get-tough-on-crime attitude.

As this last factor suggests, dispositions are often a product of a host of subjective and unpredictable factors. For example, a minor appearing in court at the end of a day after the judge has processed numerous cases, each more depressing than the last, may be treated more harshly than someone whose case happened to be first on the calendar. A disposition may depend on whether a probation officer or judge views the minor as rebellious, confrontational, or remorseful. Even a minor's demeanor and manner of dress may be critical. A minor whose clothes demonstrate respect for the court and who answers questions politely may be given a less harsh disposition than a minor who shows up in gang-type clothing and rudely mumbles responses. While some of these factors may be unfair, they are a necessary byproduct of a system in which human beings have to decide what is in the minor's and society's best interests.

"Scared Straight"

Scared Straight was a New Jersey program started in the late 1970s. The idea was to frighten juvenile offenders into reforming their behavior by confronting them with adult prison inmates who would curse at the minors and tell them of the horrors of prison life. The program was discontinued when research indicated that it had little effect on the rate at which minors committed crimes.

Can a minor's juvenile court record affect a later sentence in adult criminal court?

Yes—but it depends on state law and the circumstances of the offense. Statutes in some states provide for harsher sentences when the offender has a prior juvenile court disposition, especially where the disposition was for a serious offense. Some prior juvenile offenses may even count as strikes under a state's "three strikes" law.

EXAMPLE: As an adult, Anne Apolis is convicted of attempted murder. Six years earlier, Anne had been declared a ward of the court after a juvenile court adjudication of carjacking. A statute in Anne's state doubles the mandatory minimum sentence for convicted felons who have previously been convicted of specified crimes, including carjacking. Because Anne has a juvenile prior for carjacking, she will probably be sentenced to double the mandatory minimum.

Can a minor challenge or alter a juvenile court judge's disposition order?

Yes. Like adults, juvenile offenders have the right to file appeals and writs. They can also ask a juvenile court judge to modify a disposition based on changed circumstances. For example, a minor who was placed outside the family home in part because a stepparent was a bad influence may ask the judge to return her home when the stepparent moves away. Or, a relative whose home can serve as a suitable placement may be located after a disposition order has been made. A minor may also ask for a change if a placement is unsafe or the minor is not receiving the treatment the judge anticipated at the time of disposition. Juvenile court judges usually have broad power to change their orders, so postdisposition changes are always possible.

Sample Informal Probation Agreement

ATTORNEY OR PARTY WITHOUT ATTORNEY *(Name, State Bar number, and address):*	*FOR COURT USE ONLY*
TELEPHONE NO.: FAX NO. *(Optional):* E-MAIL ADDRESS *(Optional):* ATTORNEY FOR *(Name):*	

SUPERIOR COURT OF CALIFORNIA, COUNTY OF
STREET ADDRESS:
MAILING ADDRESS:
CITY AND ZIP CODE:
BRANCH NAME:
CHILD'S NAME:

INFORMAL PROBATION AGREEMENT	CASE NUMBER:

This agreement is a **CONTRACT** between the probation officer, the above named child, and his or her parent or parents or legal guardian.

The agreement is for up to six (6) months, and during that period and for up to 90 days after that, the probation officer has the right to request that the district attorney file a petition in juvenile court to have the child declared a ward of the court if the child does not successfully complete the terms of the program described below. If within the first 60 days after this agreement is signed, the child does not become involved in the program, the probation officer MUST take the necessary steps to bring the case before the juvenile court.

TERMS AND CONDITIONS OF THE PROGRAM

The child must *(check all that apply to this child):*

1. ☐ Report to the probation officer _____ times each month until or unless directed differently.
2. ☐ Obey all city, county, state, and federal laws and ordinances.
3. ☐ Obey his or her parent or parents or legal guardian.
4. ☐ Attend school regularly, obey school rules and regulations, and not leave the school campus during school hours without permission of school officials or the probation officer.
5. ☐ Not use, possess, or be under the influence of any alcoholic beverage or illegal or intoxicating substance, or possess any associated paraphernalia.
6. ☐ Not use, possess, or be under the influence of the following *(specify):* _____ .
7. ☐ Not possess, own, or handle any firearm, knife, weapon, fireworks, explosives, or chemicals that can produce explosives.
8. ☐ Not contact or associate with _____

   _____ .
9. ☐ Not be a member or associate with any known members of any criminal street gang.
10. ☐ Participate in individual, group, or family counseling, as directed by the probation officer.
11. ☐ Submit to chemical testing in the form of, but not limited to, blood, breath, urine, or saliva on the direction of the probation officer or a peace officer.
12. ☐ Consent to the search of his or her person, vehicle, or place of residence at any time, day or night, with or without a search warrant and without probable or reasonable cause, on the direction of the probation officer or a peace officer.
13. ☐ Perform _____ hours of community service and provide proof of completion by *(date):* _____ .
    Community service to be arranged
    a. ☐ by the child with the approval of the probation officer.
    b. ☐ through the probation officer.

Sample Informal Probation Agreement (continued)

JV-622

CHILD'S NAME:	CASE NUMBER:

14. ☐ Be at his or her place of residence between the hours of _____ p.m. and _____ a.m. unless with a parent or legal guardian or with the prior permission of the probation officer.

15. ☐ _____

16. ☐ _____

17. ☐ _____

18. ☐ _____

19. ☐ _____

20. ☐ _____

I have read and understand the terms and conditions. I consent to them and promise to follow them and to cooperate with the probation officer. I understand that if I do not follow the terms and conditions, I may have to go to juvenile court. I have received a copy of this agreement.

Date:

_____   ▶ _____
(TYPE OR PRINT CHILD'S NAME)   (SIGNATURE OF CHILD)

I am the ☐ parent ☐ legal guardian of the child, and he or she has agreed to the terms of this agreement. I agree to cooperate with the probation officer and to assist the child to follow the terms and conditions.

Date:

_____   ▶ _____
(TYPE OR PRINT NAME)   (SIGNATURE OF PARENT/LEGAL GUARDIAN)

Date:

_____   ▶ _____
(TYPE OR PRINT NAME)   (SIGNATURE OF PARENT/LEGAL GUARDIAN)

Date:

_____   ▶ _____
(TYPE OR PRINT NAME)   (SIGNATURE OF PARENT/LEGAL GUARDIAN)

A Sampling of Innovative Juvenile Justice Programs

Teen Courts. Teen courts are the product of collaborative efforts of schools, juvenile courts, and probation departments. In teen courts, first-time teenaged offenders agree to be "tried" by a jury of their peers: other teenagers. Usually, the minor gives up the right to be represented by counsel. The jurors hear evidence, often presented by a probation officer. The juvenile being tried may admit to the charges or present additional evidence. Though teen courts cannot fine or imprison offenders, their sentences can carry serious consequences. With the consent of a minor's parents, teen court sentences can impose community service, counseling, drug or alcohol rehab programs, curfews, and restrictions on whom the minor can associate with. Teen courts may also impose more creative sanctions, such as requiring a minor to scrub graffiti off a school wall, attend tutoring, write an essay about the minor's improper behavior, or write a letter apologizing to the victim. After a teen court trial, the offender may have to report to the probation department to verify compliance with the sanctions.

L.A.'s Juvenile Traffic Court. Despite its name, the Juvenile Traffic Court has jurisdiction over a variety of cases, including those in which minors are charged with status offenses (truancy and curfew violations) and minor drug or traffic offenses. The Juvenile Traffic Court follows a "fast track" process designed to dispose of cases within 45 days instead of the usual juvenile court average of nine months. Lawyers are not permitted, and judges have great leeway in tailoring dispositions to individual offenders. For example, a judge dismissed the case of one minor who brought to court a certificate showing that she attended school every day, and waived the fine for the student who completed summer school with at least a "C" average.

Denver's Project New Pride. This is a community-based program aimed at hard-core offenders. Minors get tutoring help for school assignments, job counseling, and training. For example, project staff help minors fill out job applications and even start small businesses (for example, providing lawn and garden services) to help defray program costs.

The Boston Offender Project. Targeting violent offenders, the project features decreasing levels of incarceration and case supervisors with low caseloads who provide intensive psychological and employment counseling.

The Allegheny Academy. Minor offenders in this program live at home but attend the academy after school and on weekends. At the academy, minors receive meals, job training, and individual and group counseling.

Sealing Juvenile Court Records

By sealing or expunging juvenile court records, former offenders can avoid being hampered in adulthood by their juvenile misbehavior.

RESOURCES
For more information on sealing or expunging juvenile records, visit the nonprofit Collateral Consequences Resource Center at http://ccresourcecenter.org and check out www. criminaldefenselawyer.com, a Nolo website.

What is a juvenile court record?

A juvenile court record consists of the documents relating to a juvenile court case. If a minor is arrested and the case is closed without charges being filed, the record will be short, perhaps no more than a record of the arrest. If a minor is adjudicated a ward of the court for violating the law and given an in-custody disposition, the record may be much longer.

What does it mean to seal a juvenile court record?

To seal or expunge a juvenile court record means to treat the juvenile court proceedings as though they never took place. Allowing juveniles to keep their records sealed helps people who've cleaned up their acts from forever being haunted by things they did when they were young.

EXAMPLE: Some years ago, Rick was adjudicated a ward of the juvenile court for committing a residential burglary. Rick later went to court and had the record sealed. Then, when Rick applied for a job, the employer asked, "As a minor or an adult, have you ever been convicted of a criminal offense?" Because his juvenile court record was sealed, Rick legally can and should answer "No."

Are juvenile court records sealed automatically when a person becomes an adult?

No. Normally, a person who meets a state's eligibility requirements for record sealing has to file a petition with the juvenile court clerk, often in the county where the juvenile adjudication occurred, formally asking the court to issue a written order sealing the record. However, some states do have limited automatic sealing provisions. One such law provides that unless a judge decides that a former juvenile court offender has continued to violate the law, juvenile court records are destroyed automatically on an offender's 38th birthday.

Is it necessary to hire an attorney to have a record sealed?

Often, no. An experienced attorney may be able to quickly complete the necessary paperwork, but will certainly charge a fee to do so. Many states have preprinted fill-in-the-blanks petition forms, available at a court clerk's office or online. These forms ordinarily contain instructions for completing and filing the petition. In some states, a county probation officer also has the authority to file paperwork on a petitioner's behalf. Public defender offices and court websites sometimes have information on record sealing. Free legal services, as from a legal clinic or even a public defender's office are occasionally available for record sealing.

When is a juvenile offender eligible to ask for the sealing of a juvenile court record?

Eligibility rules vary from state to state. Typically, eligibility for record sealing depends on such factors as:

- **Age.** Usually, a petitioner must be an adult (18 years or older) to be eligible for record sealing.
- **How much time has passed since an offense was committed or since the juvenile court proceedings ended.** Often, even if a juvenile offender has reached adulthood, the offender has to wait a specified period of time (perhaps five years) from the date of an offense or from the termination of juvenile court proceedings.
- **Seriousness of the juvenile court offense.** Misdemeanor records may be more readily sealed than felony records.
- **Conduct following the juvenile court proceedings.** A juvenile offender with adult criminal violations may be ineligible to have juvenile court records sealed.

Can sealed records ever come back to haunt a juvenile offender?

Yes. Sealing records rewrites history for many, but not all, purposes. For example:

- It may be that a sealed record of a juvenile court adjudication can be used to increase the severity of a sentence following a later conviction.
- An application for a job in law enforcement may give the police agency access to sealed records.
- An application for auto insurance may allow the insurance company to have access to sealed records pertaining to automobile-related offenses.

Further Reading on Juvenile Courts and Procedures

- *Trial Manual for Defense Attorneys in Juvenile Court,* by Randy Hertz, et al. (ALI/ABA), a treatise written for lawyers that provides comprehensive instruction on the lawyer's role in juvenile delinquency proceedings.
- *Representing the Child Client,* by Mark Soler, et al. (Matthew Bender), another lawyer's treatise that provides an in-depth analysis of the laws affecting accused children.
- *The Juvenile Justice System: Law and Process,* by Mary Clement (Butterworth-Heinemann), a textbook that gives a clear and detailed introduction to the civil and criminal aspects of the juvenile justice system.
- *No Matter How Loud I Shout,* by Edward Humes (Simon & Schuster), a compelling and personalized account of a year in the life of one California juvenile court judge.

Prison Rules

Prison inmates lose many of their civil rights. But the Eighth Amendment to the U.S. Constitution, which prohibits "cruel and unusual punishment," as well as many other federal and state laws, ensures that prisoners do not lose all of their rights just because they are incarcerated. This chapter discusses important prisoners' rights, focusing on federal rights that are common to prisoners nationwide. It includes a section on resources for prisoners and their families. The chapter also explains the basics of parole (early release from prison under supervision) and pardons (grants of executive clemency).

A System of Limited Rights

Prisoners retain rights to basic freedoms such as freedom of speech, religion, and equal protection of the laws (meaning a right not to be treated differently than other prisoners based on characteristics such as race, sex, or religion). Prisoners also have the right to basic—albeit minimum—living standards. However, these rights may be curtailed to some extent because courts must balance them against a prison's need for safety, order, and security. Courts tend to uphold prison rules that limit prisoners' exercise of constitutional rights as long as the prison rules are reasonably related to legitimate prison needs. This section examines the balance that courts have struck between prisoners' rights and prison regulations in a variety of common situations.

Is a prison the same thing as a jail?

A jail generally houses defendants who are awaiting trial and unable to make bail, or who have been convicted of and are serving sentences of a year or less for misdemeanors. A prison, also known as a penitentiary, houses inmates convicted of felonies and serving lengthy sentences. Jails are normally funded and run by local governments; prisons are administered by state or federal prison bureaus.

Supermax Prisons

Supermax prisons house a state's most dangerous inmates. Notorious supermax prisoners have included Theodore Kaczynski (the Unabomber), John Muhammed (the Beltway sniper), and Eric Rudolph (the Atlanta Olympic Games bomber). About 30 states currently operate supermax prisons.

By isolating the "worst of the worst" in separate, super-secure facilities, supermax prisons are designed to reduce the risk of harm that prison guards and the general prison population would otherwise face. Typically, supermax prisoners remain in their cells 23 hours a day and eat all their meals alone in their cells. States need comply only with relatively informal procedures when deciding which inmates to send to supermax facilities. (*Wilkinson v. Austin*, U.S. Sup. Ct. 2005.)

Do prisoners have the right to decent living conditions?

The Eighth Amendment requires that state and federal prison systems provide at least "the minimal civilized measure of life's necessities." (*Rhodes v. Chapman*, U.S. Sup. Ct. 1981.) Because this rule is so vague, prisons can be deficient in a variety of ways yet still meet minimum constitutional standards. (Depending on the jurisdiction, however, there may be laws that hold prison authorities to higher standards than those the federal Constitution imposes.)

To prove that prison conditions are cruel and unusual under the U.S. Constitution, prisoners must show that they were forced to live with seriously hazardous or oppressive conditions (an objective test that looks at the conditions themselves). They must also establish that prison officials were deliberately indifferent to the conditions (a subjective question that considers the state of mind of the officials responsible for them). (*Wilson v. Seiter*, U.S. Sup. Ct. 1991.)

What factors have judges considered when deciding whether prison conditions are adequate?

When determining the adequacy of prison conditions, judges consider both the conditions themselves and how prison officials have subjected inmates to them. Examples of inadequate prison conditions include:

- overcrowding
- lack of supplies necessary for personal hygiene, such as soap and water
- unsanitary food preparation
- nutritionally inadequate food
- lack of access to medical treatment and poor medical care
- failure to protect prisoners' physical safety
- substandard shelter, such as lack of adequate heating, cooling, clothing, and blankets
- unsafe building conditions, such as exposed wiring and vermin infestation
- inadequate facilities for prisoners put in solitary confinement
- lack of opportunities for prisoners to get physical exercise, and
- inadequate opportunities for prisoners to access the courts, such as a prison law library that has few books or is unavailable to prisoners in solitary confinement.

A condition may be improper even if it affects only a small group of prisoners. For example, prison officials may violate both the First (free exercise of religion) and the Eighth (freedom from cruel and unusual punishment) Amendments if they do not provide pork-free meals to prisoners whose religions forbid eating pork, even if the non-pork-eaters make up a minority of the population.

Does the right to equal protection of the laws require equal treatment of all prisoners?

No. Prison officials have wide discretion to manage prison life. For example, many prisons classify inmates as maximum, medium, or minimum security risks, and treat them accordingly. As a result, minimum security risk prisoners are usually housed in a section of a prison with fewer restrictions on their movement and greater work opportunities compared to maximum security risk prisoners. Factors that prison officials consider when assessing a prisoner's security classification include:

- the length and severity of a sentence
- previous behavior in other jails or prisons
- medical needs
- gang affiliations (or the existence of known enemies within the prison population)
- work skills
- proximity to outside family (especially if a relative is ill or aged)
- likelihood of rehabilitation, and
- whether a prisoner poses a threat to other inmates, guards, or him- or herself.

Prisoners who are unhappy with their confinement status may seek a review of this process, especially if the prisoner can show proof of specific factors that warrant a lower risk classification, such as work skills or medical needs. But it's most effective to present such documentation when a prisoner is first confined. Prison officials will be less inclined to change their minds once they make a designation, and courts often refuse to second-guess prison officials on a process they view as a prison management function.

Can prisoners observe religious holidays, meet with clergy, and wear ritual clothing?

Yes. The First Amendment guarantees free exercise of religion, and that right cannot be denied to prisoners absent valid, rational prison management concerns. For example, a prisoner cannot carry a knife on the ground that "carrying a knife is a practice of my religion." On the other hand, a prison rule that forbids observant Muslims to grow a short (half-inch) beard is invalid. It substantially interferes with a prisoner's exercise of his religious practice while doing nothing to enhance prison security. (It doesn't prevent prisoners from hiding weapons or contraband on their person or disguising their identity.) (*Holt v. Hobbs*, U.S. Sup. Ct. 2015.)

Do prisoners have the right to medical treatment?

Yes. To deliberately or intentionally withhold necessary medical treatment constitutes cruel and unusual punishment under the Eighth Amendment. (*Estelle v. Gamble*, U.S. Sup. Ct. 1976.) State and federal health and safety rules also set forth efforts that prisons must make to prevent and detect diseases.

> **EXAMPLE:** Joseph Dabney, a state prison inmate, complained to prison guards several times about chest pains and shortness of breath during outdoor exercise. Joseph saw several prison doctors, none of whom gave Joseph any treatment other than telling him

to take it easy. Joseph subsequently suffered a massive heart attack. Because prison officials (both guards and doctors) were aware of symptoms commonly associated with serious heart trouble yet failed to provide treatment, Joseph may be able to recover money damages because the prison was deliberately indifferent to his medical needs. A judge might also order "injunctive relief," requiring the prison to upgrade its medical procedures.

May prison officials withhold food to punish prisoners?

No. Prisons must provide inmates with basic sustenance and nourishment. However, food restrictions of various types may be a permissible form of punishment, especially if they are temporary. For example, a prison may withhold hot foods or provide a prisoner with only one meal a day. In an extreme case, even a temporary diet of bread and water may be permissible.

> **EXAMPLE:** Miller, a federal prisoner, found mouse parts in the chicken dinner he was served one night. Miller's claim for damages based on a violation of his Eighth Amendment rights will not succeed if the court finds this was an isolated incident or that prison officials had taken steps to fix the problem (such as hiring exterminators to rid the facility of mice). Miller might have a valid legal claim if the problem was ongoing, there were other incidents of unclean food, or the court determined that prison officials knew about the mice and had done nothing to get rid of them.

Can prison guards use physical force against inmates?

Prison staff violate the Eighth Amendment when they use force "maliciously and sadistically for the very purpose of causing harm," but they are permitted to use force in a good-faith effort to maintain or restore discipline. (*Hudson v. McMillan*, U.S. Sup. Ct. 1992.) Generally, this means an inmate must show that the force was not used for a legitimate disciplinary purpose or that the degree of force the officials used was completely out of proportion to the needs of the situation.

> **EXAMPLE:** Toby and Cervi, prison guards, fire tear gas and plastic bullets into the prison yard after a disturbance in which three inmates from one gang attacked an inmate from a rival gang. Toby and Cervi then forcibly herd all the prisoners on the yard into their cells. Alper, an older inmate who was not involved in the disturbance, slipped and fell while being herded back to his cell, suffering a painful sprained ankle. Alper's claim for damages against the guards and the prison would be unlikely to succeed. Under the circumstances, the guards' actions were reasonably necessary to quell a disturbance. Especially in such an emergency situation, Alper would have to prove that the guards acted maliciously (that is, spitefully or wickedly), an extremely difficult task.

Prison Assault and Rape

Widely acknowledged to be a serious problem for both men and women serving time in prison, prison rape has been condemned by many, including the U.S. Supreme Court: "The horrors experienced by many young inmates, particularly those who are convicted of nonviolent offenses, border on the unimaginable. Prison rape not only threatens the lives of those who fall prey to their aggressors, but it is potentially devastating to the human spirit. Shame, depression, and a shattering loss of self-esteem accompany the perpetual terror the victim thereafter must endure." (*Farmer v. Brennan*, U.S. Sup. Ct. 1994.)

Estimates are that thousands upon thousands of unwanted sexual acts take place behind bars in the United States every day. These include both inmate-on-inmate assaults and guard-on-inmate assaults.

The federal Prison Rape Enforcement Act establishes guidelines and policies for preventing sexual assaults in prisons. The Act has led to the development of standards for correctional officer training and for the detection, prevention, and punishment of prison rape.

Do prisons have to protect inmates from attacks by other prisoners?

Yes. But to have a valid legal claim against a prison for failing to provide adequate protection, the victimized prisoner generally has to prove that prison staff was aware that the prisoner had been threatened by a particular inmate and that the staff was deliberately indifferent to the prisoner's safety.

Do prisoners have the right to outdoor exercise?

Prisoners must be afforded reasonable opportunities for physical movement. A few lower courts have recognized access to outdoor exercise as a right that may not be taken away unless justified by other prison needs (such as when a prisoner is denied access because he assaulted another inmate on the prison yard). Other courts have upheld prison programs of indoor-only physical activities.

May prison officials search prisoners' cells?

Yes. Although a cell is a prisoner's "home" during incarceration, prisoners have no judicially recognized expectation of privacy in their cells. Therefore the Fourth Amendment right to be free from unreasonable searches and seizures is extremely limited for prisoners. Prison officials do not need warrants to search prisoners' cells, and searches may be random and unannounced. Typically, though, to be considered reasonable, officials must have legitimate reasons for conducting their searches, such as the prison's need to keep the facility free of drugs and weapons.

EXAMPLE: Victor Michaels, a prison inmate, filed a complaint against prison officials for failure to provide him with adequate access to the prison law library. After the complaint was filed, guards began waking Victor up twice nightly and searching his cell. The guards said they were looking for drugs and weapons, but Victor believes that the guards conducted the searches in retaliation for him complaining about the library. Other prisoners were not subjected to these "shakedown" searches after lights out. Even though prison officials do not need a warrant to search Victor's cell, cell searches must still be reasonable. A search made in order to intimidate and harass, rather than for a legitimate prison purpose, is not reasonable. Victor's claim for damages based on a violation of his Fourth Amendment rights might succeed, and a judge might issue an injunction against the abusive and retaliatory searches.

Are prison officials allowed to seize a prisoner's property during a "shakedown" search?

Prison officials can almost always justify seizures of prisoners' personal belongings, because they are permitted to take away property in order to maintain security and order.

Can prison officials conduct strip searches and body cavity searches of inmates?

Intrusive body searches can be legitimate if they are necessary to maintain prison safety and keep out contraband. However, invasive searches are not valid if they are performed to humiliate or harass a prisoner, or to retaliate against a prisoner for angering a member of prison staff.

Can family members and friends visit prisoners?

Visitation has never been declared to be a fundamental constitutional right. Most prisons do allow visits, but if prison officials have valid reasons for placing limits on visitation, judges almost always uphold those restrictions. It is typical for prisons to:

- limit visiting hours
- minimize physical contact, requiring prisoners to communicate with visitors through a barrier such as a wall (though lawyers can usually arrange full contact visits with their clients)
- restrict the numbers and types of visitors (for example, a prison may limit visits to only certain family members, or ban visits altogether from people who have violated prison rules on previous visits or are suspected of gang-related activity), and
- require both a visitor and a prisoner to be searched before and after the visit to ensure that contraband does not enter the prison.

The U.S. Supreme Court has ruled that prison regulations such as these are valid. (*Overton v. Bazzetta,* U.S. Sup. Ct. 2003.)

Do prisoners have a right to privacy during prison visits?

No. Prison officials may monitor most visits. But visits from lawyers must be private enough to allow for confidential communication.

Do prisoners have the right to make phone calls?

As a general rule, inmates have a right to make phone calls. However, prisons can severely restrict the right: A typical prison rule limits inmates to two short social calls per week. Prisoners may also be required to pay for long distance phone charges.

May prisoners be transferred from one prison facility to another?

Prisoners do not have a right to liberty, and therefore they have no right to be incarcerated in the prison of their choice. Prisons are often located in remote rural areas where family visits are difficult, so the distance from home is not enough to invalidate a transfer. If a prisoner wants to contest a scheduled transfer, prison officials must usually give the prisoner a hearing to object to the move. If the prisoner loses at the hearing and takes the case to court, a judge will typically approve the transfer so long as prison officials have a rational basis for their actions.

> **EXAMPLE:** Mohammed is incarcerated in a federal prison in New York. Mohammed's attorney is in New York and his family lives there. Mohammed is then transferred to a prison in New Mexico, though none of his family members can afford to visit him there. If Mohammed can show that he was transferred because the New York warden is prejudiced against people of Middle Eastern descent, the transfer would be invalid. A prisoner's ethnicity is not a rational reason for a transfer. Similarly, Mohammed might successfully challenge the transfer if he could show that he was transferred as punishment for having requested a pork-free diet, or if he were too weak to travel and the move would cause him serious pain or injury. On the other hand, the transfer would be valid if Mohammed was transferred in order to testify before a grand jury in Santa Fe, New Mexico. Mohammed's presence as a witness before the grand jury would certainly be a legitimate government reason to move him. (*Olim v. Wakinekona*, U.S. Sup. Ct. 1983.)

Do prisoners have the right to send and receive mail?

Yes, but prison officials may typically open and read the mail first. However, prison censorship must be related to rational prison concerns. For example, they can justify examining incoming mail more strictly than outgoing mail, because mail entering the facility must be more carefully screened for contraband.

May prison officials open and read mail to and from a prisoner's lawyer?

Prison officials have a limited right to open letters and packages from lawyers. Officials can open mail to be sure that it does not contain contraband. However, they typically must open it in front of the inmate. Moreover, officials may not read the contents of lawyer-client communications. Lawyers who send mail to prison inmates mark it as "privileged legal communication" or "confidential legal correspondence," and inmates should do the same when they write letters to their lawyers.

May prison officials place limits on inmates' mail privileges?

Yes. A prison may limit the people with whom a prisoner corresponds when necessary for prison order, safety, or security. Prisons may also limit the type of mail a prisoner receives. For example, prisons may forbid mail that contains nudity or sexually explicit material.

> **EXAMPLE:** Bruce, who is in a maximum security prison serving time for selling narcotics, has been corresponding with his girlfriend Rainy. A prison guard recently found photos and maps of the land around the prison as well as references in the girlfriend's letter that officials felt might help Bruce to plan an escape. The prison can forbid future correspondence between Bruce and Rainy. It has an adequate basis for believing that letters to and from Rainy pose a security threat.

Are prisoners who have disabilities protected under the Americans with Disabilities Act?

Yes. Prison officials at state and federal facilities must provide reasonable accommodations for prisoners with disabilities. (*Pennsylvania Dept. of Corrections v. Yeskey*, U.S. Sup. Ct. 1998.)

How Successful Are Prisons at Rehabilitating Inmates?

Judges often sentence offenders to prison in the hope that they will emerge as lawful, productive citizens. However, the unfortunate fact is that imprisonment generally fails to produce rehabilitation. For example, studies have found that 60% of ex-inmates remain unemployed a year after their release from prison. And the federal Bureau of Justice Statistics has found that two-thirds of parolees are rearrested within three years of their release.

Prisons' typical failure to achieve rehabilitation is due partly to lack of resources, which translates into a lack of prison programs. For example, estimates are that somewhere between 70% and 85% of inmates have substance abuse problems. However, less than 15% of inmates are treated for those problems while they are incarcerated. Similarly, though many inmates are functionally illiterate, prisons do little to enhance their literacy skills.

Compounding the inability of prisons to provide rehabilitative services are a variety of laws that can make life on the outside very difficult for many ex-felons. For example:

- Federal welfare rules bar those convicted of buying or selling drugs from ever receiving food stamps or cash assistance.
- Federal housing laws allow public housing agencies to exclude ex-felons and their families from public housing.
- Federal education laws bar ex-felons who have violated drug laws from receiving student loans.
- Ex-felons may be unable to vote or pursue a wide variety of professions.

For further information, see *Gates of Injustice: The Crisis in America's Prisons*, by Alan Eisner.

EXAMPLE: An informant reported that he had seen Kathi Andrews, a deaf inmate, with a sharpened kitchen knife in violation of prison rules. Kathi was given an informal prison hearing to review the charges but was not provided a sign language interpreter at the hearing. The prison may have violated Kathi's rights under the Americans with Disabilities Act (ADA). If the hearing officer spoke slowly and looked directly at Kathi so that she was able to understand everything by lip-reading, the prison may have done enough to reasonably accommodate her disability. If, however, the hearing was before a panel of officers and Kathi (who is only able to lip-read one person at a time) could not understand the proceedings without an interpreter, then the prison may have needed to provide one. In such a case, the prison may also have needed to remove any restraints on Kathi's hands so that she could respond through the interpreter.

May prisoners get married while in prison?

Yes, but prison officials may limit the type and length of any wedding ceremony.

Can prisoners be required to work while in prison, and, if so, are they paid?

Yes to both questions. The Thirteenth Amendment, which forbids slavery and other involuntary servitude, has a specific exception for people who have been convicted of a crime. According to the Federal Bureau of Prisons, "All Federal inmates have to work if they are medically able. Most inmates are assigned to an institution job such as food service worker,

orderly, plumber, painter, warehouse worker or groundskeeper. These jobs pay from twelve cents to forty cents per hour." Most states pay prisoners similarly low wages for prison work, and some allow for compensation in the form of "credits" toward a reduced sentence rather than money.

Money earned from prison work is placed in accounts that prisoners may draw on to buy personal items through the prison commissary (store), to make phone calls, pay court filing fees, or to satisfy court judgments such as victim restitution or child custody.

EXAMPLE: Lynn Felder is in jail awaiting trial on murder charges. Lynn cannot be forced to work in the jail's kitchen facility because she has not yet been convicted of a crime. The Thirteenth Amendment permits forced labor as punishment only for those convicted of a crime.

Can prisoners choose their work assignments?

Generally, no. But prison officials may not discriminate against prisoners in making work assignments. For example, officials cannot base work assignments on an inmate's race or religion.

Can prisoners lose professional or business licenses as a result of imprisonment?

Whether conviction and imprisonment will cause a prisoner to lose a business or professional license often depends on the rules of the agency that issued the license. In most states, for example, lawyers who are convicted of crimes involving fraud will almost certainly be disbarred. To determine how incarceration might affect a particular license, an inmate should consult both state licensing rules and the rules of the organization that issued the license. (See Chapter 22 for more on this topic.)

Can prisoners vote while in prison or after they are released?

Almost all states bar felons from voting while they are in prison. (Only a few states, such as Vermont, allow prisoners to vote by absentee ballot.) At least seven states permanently bar convicted felons from voting. An estimated four million United States citizens are currently prohibited from voting due to felony convictions. Because a disproportionate number of those convicted of felonies are members of minority groups, these bans have prevented a higher percentage of minorities from voting than nonminorities.

Even in states that do not permanently ban those with felony convictions from voting, the restoration of the right to vote is not necessarily automatic. In many states, the right to vote, along with the right to hold public office and serve on a jury, are part of a "package" of civil rights that may be restored upon the completion of a sentence (which includes any parole or probationary term in addition to any imprisonment associated with that conviction). In some states, these civil rights are restored automatically once a felon finishes the full sentence. In other states, corrections officials must notify the state's Office of Elections, or

the released felon must personally obtain a Certificate of Discharge and submit it to the governor's office, affirmatively requesting the restoration of civil rights.

 RESOURCES

The Collateral Consequences Resource Center (CCRC) is a nonprofit that has general and state-specific information and resources on getting relief from the collateral consequences of criminal convictions. ("Collateral consequences" generally refers to the effects of the criminal justice system former defendants can feel long after their cases have ended.) You can visit the CCRC at http://ccresourcecenter.org.

Do prisoners lose custody of their children when they are imprisoned?

Inmate parents do not automatically lose formal custody of their children just because they are sent to prison (although this may happen to parents convicted of crimes involving child abuse or neglect). Because an imprisoned parent is not available to care for children, however, either the parent or the state must make other custodial arrangements. In some cases, prisoners may even have their parental rights terminated, but the inmate parent must first be given notice and the opportunity for a hearing. There is no federal constitutional right to be provided with a lawyer during a termination of parental rights proceeding, but many states provide lawyers for prisoners facing this situation.

Must a parent who is paying child support continue to make payments while in prison?

Many states require inmates to pay up to 50% of what they earn in prison toward satisfying court judgments like child support or victim restitution. An inmate parent may also be required to make up any payments missed during the prison term once released and employed. In other states, however, an inmate parent's child support obligations are suspended and do not have to be paid while the inmate is incarcerated.

Legal Resources for Prisoners and Their Families

The following section focuses on how prisoners can enforce their legal rights.

Do prisoners have any recourse when prison officials seek to revoke their privileges for violating prison rules?

Prison officials must normally afford prisoners limited due process before revoking their privileges. This means that officials must provide prisoners with notice of the actions they intend to take and the reasons for them. Inmates can then have a hearing to contest the officials' punitive actions. These hearings are usually informal. Inmates have no right to a lawyer at these disciplinary hearings, and they may even be restricted from presenting witnesses if doing so would create security or safety problems.

EXAMPLE: Raphael Chipec was found with a sharpened nail file taped to his foot, in violation of prison regulations. Prison officials notified Raphael in writing that because of the violation, he would lose all the "good time credits" he had accumulated as a model prisoner (credits that would have gone toward an early release on parole). Raphael has a right to appear before the prison ombudsman to tell his side of the story, but he does not have the right to legal representation or to cross-examine witnesses. Because a nail file could be used as a weapon, prison officials had valid security reasons for revoking Raphael's good time credits. Also, the officials gave Raphael written notice and an opportunity to appear at a hearing. If Raphael wanted to call a witness to explain that he had a legitimate reason for carrying the nail file, then prison officials should allow the witness to appear at the hearing unless officials could show that the appearance threatened safety or security.

How can prisoners use the courts to enforce their legal rights?

Prisoners who believe that the conditions in which they are living are unlawful should normally begin by making a written complaint to the prison administration. The courts often will not consider prisoners' complaints unless the prisoners can prove that they first tried to resolve their problem within prison channels. Many facilities have complaint forms; if not, a letter will do. A prisoner may also want to send the complaint to the state or federal agency that is ultimately responsible for the facility's operation. If the complaint fails to remedy the problem, a prisoner may then seek help from the courts. A prisoner can also seek help from a nonprofit prisoners' rights group.

Prisoners' rights legal claims can take a variety of forms. A prisoner may file suit in state court under a state's Tort Claims Act to try to recover money damages for personal injuries, perhaps as a result of physical abuse by a guard or another prisoner. A prisoner may file a federal civil rights claim (also known as a "Section 1983" action) to recover money damages for physical injuries or to redress the violation of a federal civil right, such as interference with the right to practice one's religion. A prisoner's lawsuit may seek money damages or a court order (called "injunctive relief") requiring prison officials to take action, such as improving substandard conditions or transferring the prisoner to another facility.

The regulations that govern prison life vary among jurisdictions, but many of them have been the subject of lawsuits. Here are a few examples of claims about prison conditions that prisoners have brought to court:

- overcrowding
- segregating prisoners by race
- inadequacy of medical, dental, and mental health services
- unreasonable prohibitions on the use of the Internet by prisoners
- noncompliance with the Americans with Disabilities Act

- inhumane conditions of solitary confinement
- sexual abuse by inmates and prison personnel
- meal deprivation as punishment
- illegitimacy of disciplinary measures
- lack of protection of prisoners from abuse by other prisoners, and
- restrictions on religious practices by prisoners.

Resources for Prisoners' Lawsuits

Here are some publications for prisoners who are filing a prisoners' rights lawsuit without the help of a lawyer (and for their friends and family, if they are helping with the lawsuit):

- *Prisoner's Self-Help Litigation Manual*, by John Boston and Daniel E. Manville
- *Rights of Prisoners*, by Michael B. Mushlin, and
- *A Jailhouse Lawyer's Manual*.

The Prison Law Office is a nonprofit office that provides assistance to prisoners in California. The group's website (www. prisonlaw.com) includes self-help materials on *habeas corpus*, parole, personal injury claims, HIV in prison, prison staff misconduct, and problems with confinement conditions.

Does the right of access to the courts include the right to counsel?

The right to counsel (meaning the right to assistance from a lawyer, appointed free of charge for those who cannot pay) is guaranteed only through a defendant's first appeal. As a general rule, a prisoner has no right to counsel for the purpose of filing prisoners' rights claims. However, judges have the power to appoint lawyers to represent prisoners who challenge conditions of confinement. Generally, a judge will do so only when a prisoner's complaint raises serious issues that are likely to affect a sizable group of prisoners. One paradox of this approach is that judges may be least likely to find out about and appoint attorneys for the very prisoners who most need the assistance of counsel, such as those in solitary confinement or those who cannot read or write English.

Can prisoners be plaintiffs and defendants in civil lawsuits?

Yes. Prisoners may sue and be sued in civil courts. But prisoners do not have the right to representation by an attorney at government expense in a civil case. And incarceration combined with restricted access to legal materials means that most prisoners find it difficult to pursue and defend against civil claims themselves (*"in pro per"*). For example, a statute of limitations on a prisoner's civil claim might expire while the prisoner is incarcerated.

> **EXAMPLE:** Lauri Van Luven is convicted and sentenced to prison in Illinois. An appeals court overturns the conviction on the ground that the police illegally arrested Lauri. After the state decides not to prosecute again, Lauri files a civil lawsuit against Illinois seeking damages for being falsely arrested. Illinois' statute of limitation on civil rights claims was two years, and Lauri filed her complaint more than two years after the case started. Because Lauri did not file her complaint in time, the judge correctly dismissed her complaint. (*Wallace v. Kato,* U.S. Sup. Ct. 2007.)

Sources of Information on Prison Life

Here are some additional places for prisoners and their families to look for information on adjusting to life in prison:

- The ACLU's National Prison Project publishes *The Prisoners' Assistance Directory,* which refers prisoners and their families to helpful support organizations.
- The Federal Bureau of Prisons' website is located at www.bop.gov.
- The website of the National Institute of Corrections (www.nicic.gov) has an array of articles and other information about prison conditions.
- The National Resource Center on Children and Families of the Incarcerated provides information on prison conditions and publishes a *Directory of Programs Serving Children and Families of the Incarcerated.* For further information visit https://nrccfi.camden.rutgers.edu.

Criminals and Gang Members Anonymous (CGA)

Criminals and Gang Members Anonymous (CGA) was started by California prison inmate Richard Mejico in the mid-1990s. CGA adapts the 12-step principles of Alcoholics Anonymous to the needs of prisoners who may suffer from three addictions: substance abuse, criminal behavior, and a gang lifestyle. CGA's goal is to help all prisoners break away from their destructive pasts and lead decent lives. The 12 steps of CGA are as follows:

1. We reviewed our past admitting a lack of strength and control over our addictions to all forms of illegal activity and that our lifestyle was not decent nor manageable.

2. We became willing to believe that change is possible, by learning a different way of living through suggestions from those who trudged the path of recovery before us out of insanity.

3. We made a decision to let go of destructive self-will, in exchange for spiritual principles, becoming willing to seek God's care and protection, as we understood God.

4. We searched our past thoroughly, making inventory lists of the good we have done and our wrongs and resentments towards others.

5. We sought forgiveness from God, ourselves, and admitted to someone we trusted, the wrongs we have done.

6. We made a personal commitment to abandon "our" defects of character to practice decent or reasonable conduct through daily actions and behavior.

7. We honestly recognized our short-comings whenever bad habits surfaced, promptly correcting our thinking and actions.

8. We made a thorough list of all those we had harmed, realizing how our negative actions impacted their lives, and became willing to make amends to them all.

9. We made direct amends and restitution whenever possible to the persons we injured, except when doing so would cause further injury or harm.

10. We continued daily to take a personal inventory of ourselves, and whenever wrong, had the courage to honestly admit it.

11. We sought to improve our "spiritual awareness" through prayer and meditation with God, asking for guidance in being decent and responsible to ourselves and more caring towards others.

12. We, each experiencing a "spiritual awakening" by applying these steps, freely share our truth and experiences with others like us, and continue living in good orderly direction in all our affairs.

For certain cases, prisoners may also have to show they tried to resolve their problems informally within the prison system before going to court (a requirement called "exhausting administrative remedies"). Other rules specify that a prisoner must file with the court that has jurisdiction (power) to hear a case, or limit the length of documents and require certain papers to be officially witnessed ("notarized").

Because the rules governing these cases can be complex, prisoners who have funds available are usually best served by hiring lawyers to represent them. Most prisoners cannot afford to hire lawyers. To make matters worse, most public defender groups are not authorized to represent prisoners whose convictions are final. A limited number of lawyers or prison legal rights organizations provide free ("*pro bono*") legal representation to prisoners. Because these resources are scarce, many prisoners represent themselves. Self-representing inmates have to follow the same rules as lawyers, so they should plan on spending as much time as they are permitted in the prison law library researching the legal basis of their claim and the technical requirements for filing their case.

May prisoners have access to legal materials?

Yes. Judges have acknowledged that prisoners' legal rights may be meaningless unless prisoners have some ability to enforce them. Inmates therefore have a "right of access" to the courts. To comply with this, prisons must provide inmates with either an adequately stocked prison law library or help from legal assistants. Prisons must also provide supplies necessary to file court documents, such as paper, pens, postage stamps, and sometimes notaries.

Increased Restrictions on Prisoners' Litigation

Prisoners' lawsuits challenging the conditions of their confinement constitute about 10% of all civil cases filed in federal court. Judges and lawmakers increasingly view many prisoners' legal claims as "frivolous"—that is, unreasonable claims that waste judges' time. This has led to harsh limits on cases brought by prisoners.

For example, the United States Supreme Court has ruled that a state has no obligation to "enable [a] prisoner to discover grievances, and to litigate effectively." (*Lewis v. Casey*, U.S. Sup. Ct. 1996.) Moreover, a federal law known as the Prison Litigation Reform Act (PLRA) cut back on prisoners' rights to file legal claims *in forma pauperis* (without paying court filing fees). As a result, prisoners may be required to pay part of the fees when they file and to continue making payments during the remainder of their prison term (drawing on earnings from prison labor).

The PLRA also gives federal judges the power to dismiss prisoners' lawsuits immediately unless the prisoners have "exhausted their prison remedies." However, judges have to consider "exhausted" claims even if prisoners' lawsuits improperly add new ("unexhausted") claims. The judges rule on the merits of the "exhausted" claims but ignore the "unexhausted" ones. (*Jones v. Bock*, U.S. Sup. Ct. 2007.)

What is the First Step Act?

The First Step Act is a law enacted in 2018 that made a variety of federal prison reforms. The Act's passage reflected the government's interest in rehabilitating federal prisoners and thereby reducing recidivism. Included in the Act's reforms were:

- earlier release of prisoners through an increase in the number of good conduct time credits that prisoners can earn per year,
- increased pre-release job training and counseling for prisoners,
- restrictions on the use of restraints on pregnant women,
- expanded compassionate release for terminally ill prisoners,
- reduction of sentences for crack cocaine offenses (because of their disparate racial impact),
- making it easier for family members and friends to visit prisoners by incarcerating them closer to home, and
- greater training of correctional officers and employees.

What are second chance laws?

Second chance laws seek to ameliorate "collateral" consequences of criminal records that often prevent former prisoners from finding employment and otherwise leading normal lives. Many states have enacted second chance laws. Common provisions of second chance laws include rules that:

- make it more likely that people with criminal records will be able to regain or obtain professional licenses,
- allow speedier, or more chances for, sealing or expungement of criminal records, and
- restore voting privileges.

Parole

Parole is conditional release from prison before the end of a sentence. Parolees remain under supervision until the end of a fixed term, and they normally have significant and strict conditions with which they must comply to remain at liberty. Parolees are supervised by parole department officers; the parole department is usually an arm of the state's prison agency.

What are typical parole conditions?

Here is a list of requirements and rules that parolees typically must follow in order to remain at liberty:

- report regularly to a parole officer
- report their whereabouts (some parolees are required to wear electronic monitoring devices that track their location)
- obtain permission in advance for any travel out of the county
- submit to random searches of their homes, cars, and persons (including blood, urine, and saliva testing, for disease, drugs, or other contraband)
- obey all laws
- refrain from using, buying, or selling alcohol or illegal drugs

- avoid certain people, such as victims, witnesses, gang members, or persons with criminal records
- pay money for court-ordered restitution, and
- attend classes or counseling sessions, such as court-ordered drug or alcohol treatment classes or anger management classes.

If the parole board concludes that a parolee violated parole, parole can be revoked. If this happens, a parolee often has to return to prison to serve all or most of the remainder of the sentence. If the parolee violates his parole by committing another crime, the parolee can be forced to serve the remainder of the original sentence (as a parole violation) and then serve a sentence for the new conviction.

What is the difference between probation and parole?

Parole is early release from a partially served prison term, granted by a parole board. The parole board is an administrative agency that is part of the state corrections department. In contrast, probation is imposed by a judge at the time of sentencing, to be served as an alternative to or in addition to a jail term. There is no parole in the federal prison system; a federal prisoner earns "good time" credits for good behavior in prison but still has to serve at least 85% of his sentence. (Post-release supervision in the federal system is called "supervised release.")

How long can a person remain on parole?

Parole terms vary widely and are a function of the length of time left to serve on the original sentence. Parole may be as short as a year or as long as a lifetime. Upon evidence of good behavior, a parole board may terminate parole before its scheduled end.

Can a parolee relocate?

Parole conditions typically prevent a parolee from moving from one county to another within the same state without permission from a parole officer. Reasons that might incline a parole officer to grant a request for a move include:

- to protect the parolee
- to allow the parolee the opportunity to work or study
- to permit the parolee to live closer to family members who can aid in a parolee's rehabilitation, or
- to permit a parolee to obtain necessary medical or mental health treatment.

Do judges decide when to release prisoners on parole?

Not usually. Decisions to grant and revoke parole are made by a group of prison officials called a parole board. But in some cases, parolees have the right to appeal the decisions of the parole board to a court or to a Board of Appeals within the parole agency.

What factors do parole boards consider when deciding whether to parole a prisoner?

Although the decision to grant parole is ultimately a subjective one, parole boards are usually required to consider a prescribed set of factors in making a parole determination. These factors typically include:

- the severity of the original offense and any sentencing recommendations affecting parole
- the prisoner's behavior while incarcerated
- statements submitted by victims, and
- a prisoner's chance for successful reintegration into the community.

Can victims affect parole decisions?

In many states, victims or their surviving family members have a right to be notified that the prisoner who harmed them is eligible for parole and has an upcoming parole hearing. The victims can submit their views to the parole board either in writing or by making a personal appearance at the hearing.

> **EXAMPLE:** LW had served 21 years in prison for killing V. during a drug deal gone bad. V's mother attended LWs parole hearing and told the parole board that though she missed V terribly every day, she had forgiven LW for his youthful violence and supported his parole. LW was released on parole, went to school, and became a drug and alcohol counselor. Each year, LW dedicates his sober birthday cake to V.

What happens if a parolee violates a condition of parole?

The parole board may revoke parole and order the parolee returned to prison. Before this happens, however, due process entitles a parolee to:

- written notice of the alleged violation(s) and of the evidence against the parolee
- a hearing, usually conducted by a hearing officer or the parole board rather than a judge; at the hearing, a parolee may present witnesses and other evidence and cross-examine adverse witnesses unless the hearing officer or parole board has good cause not to allow witnesses to appear, and
- at the conclusion of the hearing, a written decision setting out the reasons for the parole revocation.

Parolees facing revocation of their parole often try to cut a deal (sometimes called a "screening deal") by which they give up the right to a hearing in exchange for receiving less prison time than would have been imposed following a complete hearing and revocation decision.

Do parolees have a right to appointed counsel at parole revocation hearings?

Generally, the answer is "No." Only a few states routinely provide parolees with attorneys at parole revocation hearings. Parolees may ask the court that sentenced them to appoint counsel for a parole revocation hearing. Judges have the discretion to appoint counsel in those circumstances, and they are more likely to do so when facts are seriously disputed or involve complex documentary evidence, or when a parolee is not capable of self-representation because of language or mental deficiencies.

What is temporary release?

Temporary release allows prisoners to leave prison for a short time to deal with important personal matters. For example, a prisoner might apply for temporary release in order to attend a parent's funeral. Another reason for temporary release is to allow prisoners to work outside of prison during the day and look for housing prior to being formally paroled. Typically, prisoners who are granted temporary release are considered nonviolent, have behaved well while in prison, do not have extensive histories of criminal behavior, and are virtually certain to return to prison in accordance with the terms of their leave.

What is compassionate release?

Compassionate release policies allow for the release of prisoners for whom death is imminent. Family members may contact a state's prison bureau to ask that a terminally ill prisoner can die surrounded by family and friends rather than in prison.

> **EXAMPLE:** California prison inmate Richard Mejico, the founder of Criminals and Gang Members Anonymous (CGA), was serving a life sentence for murder. When Mejico was terminally ill in 2010, his family successfully requested compassionate release. Mejico died at home about ten hours after he was released from prison.

Pardons

A pardon, also called a grant of clemency, is an order by the chief executive that releases the convicted person from prison and/or from further penalties that result from that conviction.

Who has the power to grant pardons?

Only a jurisdiction's chief executive has pardon power. A state's governor has the power to pardon those who have been convicted of state offenses, and the president of the United States can issue pardons for those convicted of federal crimes.

Can a pardon be challenged in court?

No. Chief executives are accountable only to the political process when making pardon decisions, and those decisions normally are final. Few established standards exist, though many cynics insist that a record of campaign contributions is often a way to influence a chief executive's decisions.

> **EXAMPLE:** On his last day as Governor of California in 2011, Arnold Schwarzenegger granted a partial pardon to Esteban Nuñez, reducing his prison term for manslaughter from 16 years to seven years. The partial pardon was hugely controversial, as Esteban Nuñez was the son of Schwarzenegger's political ally Fabian Nuñez, the former Speaker of the California Assembly. The parents of Luis Santos, the college student in whose murder Esteban Nuñez participated, filed a lawsuit seeking to block the pardon

under California's Victims Bill of Rights law, on the ground that Schwarzenegger failed to notify the family in advance so that they could formally oppose the partial pardon. The lawsuit was not successful, though the judge opined that the Governor's decision was "repugnant." (MercuryNews.com, September 10, 2012.)

Is sealing a criminal record the same as a pardon?

No. Sealing criminal records (often called "expunging" the records) is similar to a pardon in that convicted persons whose records are sealed generally may lawfully tell prospective employers that they were never convicted of a crime. Unlike pardons, however, decisions to seal criminal records are made by judges. And typically, someone seeking sealing must wait a period of time after completing a sentence for records to be sealed, whereas prisoners may be pardoned at any time. (For information on sealing juvenile court records, see Chapter 26; see Chapter 22 for similar information that's not limited to juveniles.)

Can DNA test results be the basis of a pardon?

Yes, though for defendants who are proven to be factually innocent by DNA tests, going through the court process for an official declaration of innocence might be the best option. A prisoner whose innocence is proven by a DNA test may be able to seek release through a petition for writ of *habeas corpus* in court. For more on *habeas corpus*, see Chapter 23. Virtually all states have laws and procedures that allow prisoners to demand DNA testing. However, prisoners do not have a right to DNA testing under the due process clause of the federal Constitution, even if they agree to pay for the testing themselves. (*District Attorney's Office for the Third Judicial District v. Osborne*, U.S. Sup. Ct. 2009.)

The Innocence Project

The Innocence Project (www.innocence project.org) was established in 1992 with the goal of exonerating the innocent through postconviction DNA testing. Since its inception, hundreds of innocent people, including some who were at one time sentenced to death, have been exonerated by postconviction DNA evidence. When DNA testing reaffirms a client's guilt, The Innocence Project closes the case, and the results of all testing may become a matter of public record. Through federal legislation that The Innocence Project helped bring about, defendants wrongfully convicted in the federal system are entitled to significant compensation. Having determined that mistaken eyewitness identification played a role in 75% of the convictions overturned through DNA testing, The Innocence Project has made strides in achieving eyewitness identification reform in a number of U.S. jurisdictions, thus improving identification procedures used by law enforcement and reducing the number of wrongful convictions.

Glossary

This glossary provides short definitions of many of the criminal law terms in this book. Many of the definitions include examples of how the terms are used.

Abuse excuse: A type of self-defense claim by which defendants seek to justify their actions by proving that they were subjected to years of prolonged child or spousal abuse.

Accessory after the fact: A person who takes an active role in concealing criminal activity that has already taken place. ("Jake was convicted of being an accessory after the fact because he destroyed evidence of Steve's failed kidnap attempt.")

Accessory before the fact: A person who aids criminal activity but is not present when the crime is committed. ("Jake was convicted of being an accessory before the fact for helping his friend Steve to plan a kidnapping.")

Accomplices: Partners in criminal activity.

Acquit: A judge or jury "acquits" a defendant by finding the defendant not guilty.

Acquittal: A final judgment that a defendant is not guilty.

Actus reus: An act that gives rise to criminal charges. People are punished for illegal acts, not for "bad thoughts."

Administrative agency: A government department charged with enforcing laws and developing regulations. For example, the Department of Homeland Security is a federal agency that enforces laws relating to public safety, and it has the power to develop regulations.

Admissible evidence: Evidence that a trial judge can consider or can allow a jury to consider when reaching a verdict.

Admission: A defendant's out-of-court statement offered into evidence against the defendant by the prosecution as an exception to the hearsay rule. An admission is also called an opposing party statement.

Adversary: Party on the opposite side of a legal case; opponent. Typically, in a criminal case, the prosecution and the defense are the adversaries.

Affidavit: A written statement of facts and assertions made under oath.

Affirmative defense: A type of defense that a defendant has to assert and support with evidence, such as self-defense.

Aggravated offense: A crime that is made more serious because of the way in which it was committed. For example, the use of a weapon could turn what otherwise would have been a simple assault into an aggravated assault.

Alibi: A defense that asserts that the defendant could not have committed the crime in question because the defendant was somewhere else at the time the crime was committed. ("Defendant Evelyn has a strong alibi. All the employees and numerous parents working at the Martinez day care center can testify that Evelyn was picking her kids up at that time, so could not have committed the robbery in a bank across town.")

Allegation: In a formal written criminal complaint, a prosecutor's claim that a defendant violated the law.

Allocution: A defendant's pre-sentencing remarks to a judge.

Anticipatory search warrants: Search warrants that police obtain before contraband arrives at the location to be searched.

Appeal: A request to a higher court to review the rulings or decision of a trial court judge. Appeals are often heard by panels of three judges, who do not reweigh the evidence but rather focus on claimed legal errors.

Appellant: The party who appeals to an appellate court.

Appellate court: A higher court that reviews the decision of a lower court.

("The appellate court reviewed and overturned the decision of the trial court to exclude the evidence of the officer's use of racial epithets.")

Appellee: The party who responds to an appeal brought by an appellant.

Appointed counsel: A lawyer who represents indigent defendants at government expense.

Argument: A rhetorical presentation to a judge or jury that supports a prosecutor's or defendant's legal claims.

Arraignment: Often an initial court hearing, during which a defendant formally enters a plea to criminal charges, counsel is appointed, and bail is set.

Arrest: An arrest occurs when the police (or a citizen making a citizen's arrest) detain a person in a manner that makes it clear the person is not free to leave.

Arrest report: A report prepared by an arresting officer summarizing the circumstances leading to the arrest. ("Julia Daniels went to the police station to obtain a copy of the arrest report so that she could compare her story to the police's account of her arrest.")

Arrest warrant: An order signed by a judicial officer authorizing the police to arrest the person named in the warrant.

Assault: A crime often defined as either an attempt to batter (unlawfully touch) someone, or intentionally placing a person in fear of an immediate battery.

Attempt: Starting but not completing an intended criminal act. Attempts to commit crimes are crimes themselves, though often punished less severely than completed crimes.

Attorney: Another name for a lawyer.

Attorney work product: Legal work, including the lawyer's research and development of theories and strategies, that is considered privileged or confidential and therefore need not be disclosed to an adversary.

Authenticate: To show that an exhibit at trial is genuine.

Bail: Money paid to the court to ensure that an arrested person makes all required court appearances. If not, the bail is forfeited.

Bail bond: A guarantee given to a court by a bail bond seller to pay a defendant's bail should the defendant fail to appear in court.

Bailiff: A uniformed peace officer who maintains order in the courtroom and performs other courtroom duties, such as escorting defendants in custody to and from a courtroom, attending to the needs of a jury, and handing exhibits to witnesses.

Bar: The partition that separates spectators from the "business section" of a courtroom.

Battery: The uninvited touching of another person. Battery is usually a misdemeanor, although it becomes a felony if the touching results in—or is intended to cause—serious injury. ("Lorne Cooper committed a battery by striking career counselor Chip Donalds in the face with a leather briefcase.")

Bench: The area a judge occupies in a courtroom. The term can by a synonym for a judge, so that to ask for a "bench trial" is to ask for trial by a judge without a jury.

Best evidence rule: An evidence rule that restricts a witness from orally testifying to the contents of a document unless the document is produced in court. This rule is also frequently used to require production of the original document rather than a copy.

Beyond a reasonable doubt: The burden of proof that the prosecution must carry in a criminal trial to obtain a guilty verdict. The burden does not require absolute certainty, as all human affairs are open to some level of doubt.

Bill of Rights: The first ten amendments to the U.S. Constitution—those primarily dealing with rights of individuals. For example, among those rights guaranteed by the Bill of Rights are the right to remain silent (to not incriminate oneself) and the right to a jury trial.

Blue card warnings: The name police use for Miranda warnings in some locations.

Booking: The procedure in which jailers record information about arrestees, often including a mug shot, fingerprints, and a DNA swab.

Bounty hunter: Person who hunts for defendants who skip bail.

Brief: A written argument submitted to support a party's legal position, often prepared as part of an appeal.

Burglary: A crime that generally consists of entering into a building with the intention to commit a felony such as theft or murder.

Business records exception: An exception to the hearsay rule that allows a business document to be admitted into evidence despite its being hearsay if it is shown to be trustworthy.

Calendar or court calendar: Cases a particular judge will hear on a given day. ("The defendant's arraignment is on calendar for July 12 at 9:00 a.m.")

Capital crime or offense: A crime that can be punished by death.

Caption: The portion of a pleading that indicates basic information such as the defendant's name, the court, and the case number.

Case citation: Information for locating an appellate court opinion. Example: The citation of *Miranda v. Arizona*, 384 U.S. 436 (1966), indicates that the Supreme Court opinion begins on page 436 of Volume 384 of United States Reports.

Certiorari: A petition for *certiorari* asks a higher court to exercise discretion and review a lower court's ruling.

Challenge: A prosecution or defense request for the judge to excuse (dismiss) a potential juror.

Challenge for cause: A claim made during jury *voir dire* that a potential juror is legally disqualified from jury service—usually because of factors that would prevent the juror from being fair to one side or the other.

Chambers (also called **judge's chambers**): A judge's private business office, often located adjacent to the courtroom. ("Judge Elias asked counsel to meet in chambers to discuss the possibility of a plea bargain before trial.")

Charge(s): Formal allegation or accusation of criminal activity. ("The defendant, Ira Benjamin Rogers, is hereby charged with murder in the first degree.")

Circumstantial evidence: Evidence that proves a fact by means of an inference. ("From the evidence that Victor Michaels was observed running away from the scene of a crime, a judge or jury may infer that Victor was the person who committed the crime.")

Citation: An order to appear in court issued by a police officer to an arrested person in lieu of taking the person to jail.

Citizen's arrest: An arrest made by a private individual rather than a police officer.

City attorney: A lawyer who prosecutes criminal cases on behalf of a municipality.

Civil: Noncriminal. Civil lawsuits are generally between two private parties, whereas criminal actions involve government enforcement of the criminal laws. The same action may give rise to both a criminal prosecution and a civil action. ("After Bob's car hit Steve, the state charged Bob with drunk driving, and Steve sued Bob for personal injuries.")

Clear and convincing evidence: The burden of proof placed on a party in certain types of civil cases, such as cases involving fraud. Also, in some jurisdictions, a defendant relying on an insanity defense must prove that defense by clear and convincing evidence. Clear and convincing is a higher standard than preponderance of the evidence, the standard typical in most civil cases, but not as high as beyond a reasonable doubt, the burden placed on the prosecution in criminal cases.

Closing argument (also called **final argument**): A persuasive presentation made by the prosecution and the defense to the judge or jury at the conclusion of a trial. ("In closing argument, the public defender argued that the eyewitness ID was too weak to prove the defendant's guilt beyond a reasonable doubt.")

Colloquy: A judge's questioning of a defendant prior to the judge's acceptance of a plea bargain.

Common law: Laws that originate in judicial opinions rather than legislatures. While judges have no power to create crimes, many aspects of criminal procedure emanate from U.S. Supreme Court decisions.

Community service: Unpaid work that benefits the community and may be required of a convicted defendant as an alternative or in addition to a jail sentence.

Compassionate release. Early release of a prisoner whose death is imminent.

Complaint: A pleading by which a prosecutor formally charges a defendant with a crime. This initial charging document may be called an information.

Concurrent sentences: Sentences for more than one conviction that defendants serve at the same time.

Confession: A defendant's oral or written admission of guilt. ("After being promised leniency by the police (who did not actually have authority to ensure a light sentence), Chris confessed to having embezzled funds from his employer.")

Consecutive sentences: Sentences for more than one conviction that defendants serve in sequence (that is, one after another).

Conspirators: Two or more people who join together to commit a crime.

Contempt of court: Behavior, punishable by fine or imprisonment that obstructs court administration or violates a court order.

Contingency fees: A method of compensating a lawyer for legal services in which the lawyer receives a percentage of the money the client is awarded at the close of a civil trial or by a settlement in a civil case. Contingency fee arrangements are not permitted in criminal cases.

Continuance: A delay in a scheduled court proceeding.

Contraband: Property that is illegal to possess or transport.

Conviction: A finding of guilty following a trial or plea bargain.

***Corpus delicti*:** "*Corpus*" is Latin for "body," so this phrase is often misunderstood as meaning that the prosecution must produce a body on a murder case—and a tasty one at that. In fact, the *corpus delicti* rule provides that a confession is not a sufficient basis for a conviction; a prosecutor must offer additional evidence of a defendant's guilt.

Costs (also, **court costs**): Expenses of trial other than attorneys' fees, such as fees and costs for filing legal documents, witness travel, court reporters, and expert witnesses.

Counselors: Attorneys or lawyers.

County attorney: Prosecuting lawyer for county government.

Court clerk: A court employee who assists a judge with the many administrative tasks of moving cases through the court system. For example, the court clerk may prepare and maintain the judge's calendar, retrieve case files from the main clerk's office, administer oaths to witnesses during trial, and prepare orders and verdict forms.

Court-martial: A military criminal trial.

Court reporter: The person who records every word that is said during official court proceedings (hearings and trials) and depositions, and who prepares a written transcript of those proceedings upon the request of the judge or a party. ("Judge Arietti ordered the witness to speak slower so that the court reporter could transcribe the testimony.")

Credibility: Believability. ("The credibility of witness Joe Pepsi was put in grave doubt when he testified that he only drank Coca-Cola.")

Crime: Illegal conduct. Crimes, and the punishments for committing them, are defined by Congress and state legislatures.

Cross-examination: Questioning of an adversary's witnesses. ("The prosecutor Kris Dawden cross-examined the maid who said she'd seen the defendant's car parked in his driveway at the same time the defendant's ex-wife was murdered.")

Culprit: A person who commits a crime.

Curfew: The time when people (often minors) are required to be off the streets.

Custodial interrogation: Police questioning of an arrestee.

Damages: Money that civil courts award to compensate those who have been injured or lost property through another's wrongdoing. (Many crimes can result both in criminal penalties and money damages.)

Defendant: A person who has been formally charged with a crime.

Defense lawyer: The appointed or privately retained lawyer who represents a defendant.

Deposition: More common in civil cases, a deposition is pretrial questioning of a witness under oath.

Determinate sentences: Sentences for fixed terms, such as for 36 months. Offenders may be released early for good behavior or on parole before they finish serving a determinate sentence.

Dicta: Language in appellate court decisions that indicates judges' attitudes but is unnecessary to case outcomes. ("The statement in the judge's written appellate court opinion that drug use is the country's biggest threat was *dicta*.")

Direct evidence: Evidence that proves a fact of consequence without the need of an inference. ("The witness's testimony that the defendant pointed a gun at the store clerk was direct evidence that the defendant committed an armed robbery.")

Direct examination: The questioning of a witness by the party who called the witness.

Discovery: Pretrial exchanges of information between the prosecution and defense.

Disqualifying a judge: A procedure for asking that a case be assigned to a different judge on the ground of an assigned judge's bias.

Dissenting opinion: An appellate court judge's written reasons for disagreeing with the outcome of a case. Judges may prepare dissenting opinions in the hope of influencing judges in higher courts or in future cases, or to encourage legislators to change laws.

District attorney: In many jurisdictions, the lawyer who prosecutes defendants on behalf of the government.

Diversion: An alternative sentencing procedure under which the defendant can typically escape conviction by staying out of trouble for a specific period of time and cooperating in particular rehabilitation activities.

Domestic violence: Violence against a family member or intimate partner.

Double jeopardy: A rule from the Fifth Amendment to the U.S. Constitution that prohibits a defendant from being twice put in jeopardy (typically, made to stand trial) for the same offense.

Due process: A constitutional requirement (from the Fifth and Fourteenth Amendments) guaranteeing procedural fairness when the government seeks to deprive people of property, liberty, or life.

DUI: Short for "driving under the influence," which is a crime.

Elements: Component parts of crimes. For example, "Robbery is defined as (1) the taking and carrying away (2) of property of another (3) by force or fear (4) with the intent to permanently deprive the owner of the property." A prosecutor has to prove each of these elements to convict a defendant of robbery.

Entrapment: A defense to a criminal charge claiming that actions by police officers or their agents induced a defendant to commit a crime.

Evidence: Information presented to a judge or jury, including the testimony of witnesses, documents, and exhibits that bear on the question of guilt or innocence.

Ex parte: One-sided. Contact with the judge by one party outside the presence of the other party is considered an "*ex parte* contact" and is generally forbidden unless it concerns a routine procedure.

Ex post facto law: A law that attempts to punish behavior that was not illegal when the behavior took place; such laws are generally unconstitutional.

Excited utterance: An exception to the hearsay rule that allows an out-of-court statement made in reaction to a startling event.

Exclusionary rule: A judge-created rule that excludes illegally seized evidence.

Exculpatory evidence: Evidence that points toward a defendant's innocence. ("The prosecutor disclosed the exculpatory evidence to the defense during discovery.")

Exhibit: A tangible object presented to the judge or jury during trial to help the prosecution or defense establish its case.

Expert witness: A person who, because of special knowledge or training, is permitted to draw conclusions based on information that the expert did not personally observe. Lay (non-expert) witnesses, by contrast, usually may only testify to firsthand observations.

False arrest: Holding a person against the person's will without legal justification. This crime is similar to kidnapping but doesn't involve the culprit moving the victim.

Felony: A more serious crime (contrasted with misdemeanors and infractions) that's usually punishable by a prison term of more than one year.

Fifth Amendment right against self-incrimination: The constitutional right of every person to remain silent when being questioned by the police and—as a criminal defendant—to decline to testify.

Forensic expert: A witness who applies knowledge of scientific principles to matters involved in legal disputes. These experts normally provide explanations about the significance of evidence.

Forfeiture: Government seizure of property connected to or coming from criminal activity. For instance, the government may seek to take away the boat a drug dealer used to transport heroin.

Forgery: Altering or falsifying a document with the intent to defraud. ("Chipeco committed forgery by altering her birth certificate in order to secure a fake ID.")

Foundation: Preliminary evidence demonstrating the admissibility of other evidence. ("The foundational evidence demonstrated that the letter was genuine.")

Frivolous motion: A motion that is made without legally valid grounds, such as a motion made solely to delay proceedings.

Fruit of the poisonous tree: Evidence that is inadmissible at trial because it resulted from an illegal search or seizure.

Grand jury: Jurors who issue an indictment if evidence establishes probable cause to believe that a defendant committed a crime.

Grand Theft: A felony that consists of stealing property worth more than a statutory amount, such as $1,000.

Habeas corpus: Literally, "you have the body." A *habeas corpus* petition challenges the legality of custody by a governmental authority (such as a prison warden).

Harmless error: A trial judge's mistake that an appellate court decides did not impact a trial's outcome.

Hate crime: A criminal act that manifests prejudice against a defined group of people. ("The robbery was a hate crime because the defendant chose a victim based on the victim's religious background.")

Hearing: A court proceeding before a judge, typically much shorter than a trial. ("Judge Marietti told the jury to report at 11 a.m. because she had four hearings set for 10 a.m.")

Hearsay: An out-of-court statement offered in court to prove the truth of what the statement asserts. As a general rule, hearsay cannot be used as evidence. However, there are so many exceptions to the hearsay rule that many cynical observers comment, "hearsay is admissible unless there is no exception to the general rule."

Holding: A rule of law established by an appellate court opinion.

Holding pens or holding cells (also called **lock-ups** and sometimes **bullpens**): Courthouse jail cells where defendants who are in custody remain before and after court hearings.

Hostile witness (sometimes called an **adverse witness**): A witness so hostile to the party who called him or her that cross-examination is permitted.

Immunity: Freedom from prosecution. ("The prosecutor granted the accomplice immunity in exchange for testimony against the defendant.")

Impanel (sometimes spelled **empanel**): The act of assembling a panel (group) of prospective jurors for jury selection.

Impeach: To discredit. ("The defense lawyer impeached the eyewitness with evidence that the witness had drunk four martinis in the hour before the robbery occurred.")

In camera: Court session that is closed to the public, not in open court; often conducted in the judge's chambers.

Inadmissible: Potential evidence that a judge disallows; it may not be considered in arriving at a verdict.

Incompetence to stand trial: Lacking the mental ability to understand or participate in legal proceedings. A defendant may be sane at the time a crime was committed yet incompetent to stand trial, or vice versa.

Indeterminate sentences: Sentences for an unfixed period of time, such as "five years to life." A parole board often decides how long an offender given an indeterminate sentence actually serves in prison.

Indictment: A formal criminal charge issued by a grand jury.

Indigent: A defendant's not having financial resources to pay for a lawyer and being entitled to legal representation at government expense.

Information: A document that formally charges a defendant with a crime.

Infraction: A low-level offense that typically results in a fine rather than incarceration.

Inquest: A hearing that seeks to uncover evidence about whether a crime occurred and, if so, who committed it. ("When a body was found floating in a river, the coroner convened an inquest to determine the cause of death.")

Insanity: A mental disease or defect that interferes with a defendant's ability to control his or her actions or distinguish right from wrong, meaning that he or she technically isn't guilty.

Irrelevant: Information that is inadmissible in evidence because it is not logically related to a charged crime or to the credibility of a witness.

Jail: The place where people convicted of minor crimes and defendants awaiting trial are held in custody.

Judge: A public official who presides over court hearings and trials.

Jurisdiction: A court's power and legal authority to hear a case. ("Nevada courts had jurisdiction to try a resident of Montana who was charged with committing a crime in Nevada.")

Juror: A person selected to serve on a jury.

Jury: A group of people who hear evidence and render a verdict, typically guilty or not guilty.

Jury instructions: Legal rules given by the judge to the jury. Jury instructions can originate in approved books or be hand-crafted by judges and lawyers according to the facts of a case.

Juvenile: A minor, typically a person under age 18.

Juvenile court: Rehabilitation-oriented courts that oversee charges involving juveniles.

Larceny: Theft; the taking of property belonging to another with the intent to permanently deprive the owner of the property of its possession.

Lawyer (also called **attorney**): The legal representative of a party. In a criminal case, the primary lawyers are the prosecutor and defense attorney.

Leading question: A question that suggests the answer the lawyer wants. It's often an assertion disguised as a question. ("That was your coat tangled in the bush when the murder was committed, wasn't it?'") Leading questions are normally allowed for cross-examination.

Lesser-included offense: A less-serious crime that includes some but not all of the elements of a more serious crime.

Lineup: A procedure in which the police place a suspect in a line with a group of other people and ask eyewitnesses if they recognize anyone as the culprit.

L.W.O.P.: A sentence of life in prison without possibility of parole.

Magistrate: A court official who acts as a judge in certain (often lower level) court proceedings. ("Officer Gregory Bran went before Magistrate Donna Gold to obtain an arrest warrant.")

Malice: A willful or intentional evil purpose, which is generally inferred from actions.

Manslaughter: An illegal killing of a person without the malice (evil intent) required to classify the killing as murder.

Marshal: A law officer who is empowered to carry out court rulings and enforce orders.

Mens rea: A "guilty mind"—the moral basis of criminal punishment.

Miranda warning: A warning that police officers are supposed to give prior to interrogation of in-custody suspects that advises them of their constitutional rights. ("Before interrogating Johnson, the police officer advised her that she had the right to remain silent, to have an attorney present during questioning, and to a free court-appointed attorney, and that any statements she made could be used against her at trial.").

Misdemeanors: Crimes generally punishable by no more than one year in jail. ("The D.A. reduced the crime from a felony to a misdemeanor as part of a plea bargaining agreement.")

Mistake of fact: Misapprehension of circumstances that is a potential defense to a criminal charge.

Mistake of law: Ignorance that an act is illegal; rarely a defense to a criminal charge.

Mistrial: A trial that ends before the full proceeding has been completed because of a prejudicial error. ("After finding out that several jurors had visited the crime scene on their own, the judge declared a mistrial and ordered a new trial.")

Motion: An oral or written request to the court for an order or ruling. Depending on the ruling sought, a motion can be made before, during, or after trial. ("The defense moved to suppress the witness's lineup identification because police's conduct was impermissibly suggestive.")

Motion in limine: A pretrial request for a court ruling, often made by a defendant seeking to exclude prosecution evidence.

Movant (moving party): The party making a motion.

Mug shot: Photo taken of a suspect, typically at a jail during the booking process.

Mugging: An informal term for a street robbery.

Murder: The unlawful killing of a person with malice aforethought.

Nolo contendere: A defendant's "no contest" plea—it's basically the equivalent of a guilty plea but usually isn't admissible in a related civil case.

Not guilty verdict: An acquittal following a trial.

Notice: Informing an adversary of a future court action. ("The defendant served a notice on the prosecutor that the defense would move for exclusion of the evidence at the preliminary hearing.")

Objection: A statement of a legal ground for the exclusion of evidence. ("The defense objected that the question called for hearsay.")

Offer of proof: A summary of a witness's expected testimony, often made by a lawyer at the bench before a judge rules on an objection.

Off-the-record remarks: Comments by judges or lawyers made in court or in other formal settings (such as depositions) that are intended to be private and therefore do not become part of a case's official record.

Opening statement: A summary of the expected evidence usually made before any witnesses testify.

Opinions: Appellate court judges' written explanations for their decisions.

Opposing party statement: A defendant's out-of-court statement offered into evidence by the prosecution as an exception to the hearsay rule.

O.R. (own recognizance) release: Pretrial release of a defendant from jail that doesn't require the posting of bail.

Order: A court's ruling or decision.

Overrule: Denial of an objection. ("The judge overruled the prosecutor's hearsay objection.")

Over-charge: A prosecutor's filing of a more serious criminal charge in order to induce a defendant to plead guilty to a less serious charge.

Panel attorney: A defense lawyer in private practice appointed by a judge to represent an indigent defendant.

Pardon: A chief executive's release of a prisoner from further punishment.

Partial defense: A defense that reduces the seriousness of a conviction.

Parties: Adversaries in court. The government and defendants are the parties to a criminal case.

Percipient (lay) witness: A witness who testifies to personally perceived case-related events.

Peremptory challenge: A request to excuse a potential juror for suspected but unproven bias. ("The defense used one of its three peremptory challenges to excuse Juror Number One on a hunch that the juror would be sympathetic to the police.")

Perjury: Lying under oath about a material fact.

Petitioner: A party who makes a formal written request to a higher court asking it to review the ruling of a lower court.

Petty theft: A misdemeanor that consists of the theft of property valued at less than an amount specified by statute (for example, $500).

Phishing: A form of Internet fraud in which a fake website or email is made to resemble a legitimate one, in order to steal valuable information.

Plain error: An obvious mistake that affects a defendant's substantial rights and the integrity of the trial process.

Plea: A defendant's formal response to criminal charges. ("The defendant entered a not-guilty plea during the arraignment.")

Plea bargaining: Negotiations aimed at resolving criminal charges on terms satisfactory to both parties. ("Defendant Charlie Keith got a lighter sentence when prosecutor Ronnie Mick agreed to plea bargain the assault charge to disturbing the peace in exchange for Keith's guilty plea.")

Prejudicial error: An erroneous legal ruling that deprived a convicted defendant of a fair trial and justifies a reversal of the case by an appellate court. ("Judge Pickholtz erred by allowing Officer Janus to testify to illegally seized evidence. The error was prejudicial and requires reversal of the guilty verdict.")

Preliminary hearing: A hearing in which a prosecutor seeks to offer evidence that con-stitutes probable cause of a defendant's guilt.

Preponderance of the evidence: The burden of proof in most civil court actions. By contrast, the prosecution's higher burden of proof in criminal cases is beyond a reasonable doubt.

Present sense impression: An exception to the hearsay rule that admits into evidence statements made contemporaneously with or immediately after case-related events.

("The judge overruled the defense objection to the officer's testimony that a witness said, while observing the robbery, that the robber had a scar on his right cheek.")

Presentence report: A written summary of an investigation prepared to help a judge determine a defendant's sentence. ("Based on the information in the presentence report, Judge Shelly sentenced the defendant to a term of months in jail rather than a term of years in prison.")

Presumption of innocence: A sacred principle of American criminal justice that defendants are presumed to be innocent until the government proves their guilt beyond a reasonable doubt.

Pretrial conference: A meeting between the parties and the judge, often held in an effort to settle a case or resolve pretrial evidentiary disputes.

Pretrial motion: A request to the court made in advance of trial for an order or ruling. An example is a motion to exclude evidence that was allegedly illegally seized.

Prior inconsistent statement: A witness's pretrial statement that contradicts the witness's trial testimony, admissible either to discredit the witness or to support an argument that the judge or jury should believe the contradictory statement. ("The defense lawyer impeached the witness at trial with a prior inconsistent statement from the preliminary hearing.")

Priors: Past convictions.

Privileges: Rules that exclude confidential communications between parties to certain special relationships, such as attorneys and clients and physicians and patients.

("Dr. Neil could not testify to the patient's statement because the statement was privileged.")

Pro bono: Legal services performed by lawyers on a no-fee or reduced-fee basis.

Pro per (also **pro se**): Self-represented; a term for defendants who represent themselves.

Probable cause: A standard that judges use to evaluate certain police actions, like searches and arrests. Probable cause is also normally the standard for a judge's decision at a preliminary hearing as to whether there's enough evidence that a defendant committed a crime. Probable cause is more than a mere hunch but less than beyond a reasonable doubt. ("David's presence at the crime scene and possession of a handgun of the same type as that used in the murder provided probable cause for issuance of a warrant to search his house.")

Probative value: The strength of the connection between evidence and the legal issue to which it relates. A judge may exclude relevant evidence if its probative value is substantially outweighed by the risk of unfair prejudice. ("The judge excluded the close-up autopsy photos because their emotional impact far outweighed their probative value.")

Prosecutors: Government lawyers whose duty is to seek justice by going forward with criminal charges only when they are convinced that the evidence proves a defendant's guilt beyond a reasonable doubt.

Public defenders: Government lawyers whose offices represent indigent defendants.

Quash: Nullify. ("The prosecutor moved to quash the defendant's subpoena of the arresting officer's personnel file, arguing that the defense was on a fishing expedition.")

Rap sheet: A defendant's criminal record.

Rebuttal evidence: Evidence offered to contest the accuracy of the opposing party's evidence.

Recess: A temporary break in a hearing or trial.

Reckless endangerment: Actions that put another person at risk of serious injury or death. ("Leaving the young child in a hot car for nearly an hour constituted reckless endangerment.")

Record: The compilation of everything that took place in a criminal case, including a judge's rulings and transcripts of proceedings.

Recross-examination: Additional cross-examination of witnesses called by an adversary, following redirect examination.

Recusal: A judge's self-removal from a case, usually due to a conflict of interest.

Redact: To delete or obscure portions of a document that are not admissible in evidence.

Redirect examination: Additional direct examination of a witness by the party who called the witness, following the adversary's cross-examination.

Regulations: Rules issued by administrative agencies.

Relevance: Relevant evidence is evidence that helps to prove or disprove some significant fact in connection with the case.

Relief: A party's desired legal remedy. ("The prisoner's desired relief was an order requiring the prison cafeteria to provide vegetarian meals.")

Respondent: In an appeal, the party seeking to uphold a decision by a lower court.

Restitution: Punishment consisting of money that a judge orders a convicted offender to pay to a victim as compensation for losses directly related to the crime.

Retainer agreement: A written contract for legal services between a private lawyer and a client.

Retroactivity: The applicability of a changed rule to previous cases that are final.

Reversible error: A trial court error that affects a substantial right and results in the reversal of a conviction.

Sanctions: Penalties (often fines) imposed by a judge on a party for improper conduct during a case.

Seal: A designation that makes a prior arrest or conviction inaccessible for most purposes. ("Donna Gregory enhanced her chance of becoming a licensed esthetician by successfully petitioning the court to seal the record of her juvenile conviction.")

Search warrant: An order signed by a judicial officer authorizing police officers to search the locations and seize the items identified in the warrant.

Self-defense: A defense usually based on a claim that an alleged victim was the aggressor.

Self-incrimination: Statements that provide evidence of a speaker's guilt.

Sentence: Post-conviction punishment, which can include a fine, imprisonment, probation, community service, and restitution.

Sequestration (of witnesses): Orders that witnesses not be present in court while other witnesses testify, and not discuss their expected testimony with other witnesses.

Sentencing guidelines: Laws that either recommend or require judges to issue sentences that adhere to legislatively set parameters.

Showup: A procedure in which the police return with a possible suspect to a crime scene to find out if witnesses can make an identification.

Specific intent: A purpose that a statute identifies as an element of a crime.

Standing: A right to seek a remedy in court based on having a sufficient stake in a legal dispute. ("The passengers in Rich Sim's car did not have standing to complain that Officer Randolph lacked probable cause to search Rich's pockets.")

Statutes of limitations: Time limits for charging people with crimes. ("The judge dismissed the assault charge because the statute of limitations had expired.")

Stipulation: An agreement between parties. ("Your Honor, the defense stipulates that Learned Hand is qualified to testify as a fingerprint expert.")

Stop and frisk: A police officer's brief and limited pat-down of a suspect's outer clothing; an intrusion that is less invasive than a full-scale search.

Strike: A judge ruling that testimony is improper and should not be considered as evidence, often in response to an attorney's Motion to Strike. Separately, "strike" refers to a prior conviction for a specified crime that leads to harsher punishment for a later conviction.

Subpoena: A court order compelling a person to appear in court at the date and time set forth in the subpoena.

Subpoena *duces tecum*: A court order compelling a person to appear in court with the tangible objects or documents listed in the subpoena.

Supermax prison: A federal prison that houses the most dangerous and violent offenders.

Suspended sentence: A sentence that the judge orders but does not require the defendant to serve right away or at all if certain conditions—such as successfully completing probation—are met.

Sustain: To uphold an objection to an adversary's offer of evidence. ("The judge sustained the defense lawyer's hearsay objection.")

Time served: The time a defendant spends in jail awaiting resolution of his or her case. If convicted, the time served may be credited toward the ultimate sentence.

Torts: Civil wrongs for which people generally may seek money. Many acts, such as assault and battery, are both crimes and torts.

Transcript: A written record of a court proceeding or deposition.

Trial: The adversarial court proceeding for determining whether a defendant is guilty beyond a reasonable doubt.("Most criminal cases don't go to trial because they are settled by plea bargains.")

U.S. Attorneys: Lawyers who prosecute criminal cases on behalf of the federal government.

Vacate: To overturn a lower court's decision. ("The state supreme court vacated the guilty verdict after deciding that the trial judge had not allowed the defendant a sufficient opportunity to cross-examine the police officer.")

Venue: The geographic area in which a court has authority to hear a case.

Verdict: A judge's or jury's guilty or not-guilty decision following a trial.

***Voir dire*:** Preliminary questioning, usually in the context of determining whether a potential juror should serve on a jury or a witness is qualified to testify as an expert.

Waive: Give up. ("The defendant waived her right to a jury trial and opted for a bench trial.")

Waive time: Agree to a delay in court proceedings.

Warrant: Order from a judge or magistrate authorizing the police to make an arrest or conduct a search.

White-collar crime: A nonviolent crime that typically involves money or property obtained through deception, including fraud, forgery, embezzlement, counterfeiting, and computer tampering.

Wobbler: A crime that can be charged or punished as either a misdemeanor or a felony.

Writ: A court order from a higher court to a lower court or governmental official.

Index

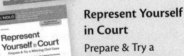

On Nolo.com you'll also find:

Books & Software

Nolo publishes hundreds of great books and software programs for consumers and business owners. Order a copy, or download an ebook version instantly, at Nolo.com.

Online Forms

You can quickly and easily make a will or living trust, form an LLC or corporation, apply for a provisional patent, or make hundreds of other forms—online.

Free Legal Information

Thousands of articles answer common questions about everyday legal issues, including wills, bankruptcy, small business formation, divorce, patents, employment, and much more.

Plain-English Legal Dictionary

Stumped by jargon? Look it up in America's most up-to-date source for definitions of legal terms, free at Nolo.com.

Lawyer Directory

Nolo's consumer-friendly lawyer directory provides in-depth profiles of lawyers all over America. You'll find information you need to choose the right lawyer.

KYR16